ASPEN
PUBLISHERS

Federal & State Taxation of Limited Liability Companies

2004 Edition

by David J. Cartano

The limited liability company is a relatively new form of business entity. It has become one of the most popular forms of business entity since the IRS issued the check-the-box regulations. *Federal & State Taxation of Limited Liability Companies* attempts to cover all of the tax laws applicable to limited liability companies. It analyzes every revenue ruling, private letter ruling, revenue procedure, tax advisory memorandum, IRS notice, treasury regulation, and federal court case dealing with limited liability companies.

Federal & State Taxation of Limited Liability Companies also discusses the tax laws for limited liability companies in all 50 states. It includes a summary table of taxes that must be paid in each state and state tax forms that must be filed for limited liability companies in each state.

Highlights of the 2004 Edition

The 2004 Edition of *Federal & State Taxation of Limited Liability Companies* brings you up to date on the latest developments including:

- Changes made by the Jobs and Growth Tax Relief Reconciliation Act of 2003.

- Section 2.03[D] discusses the rules applicable to professional LLCs in all 50 states.

- Section 2.08[B] discusses the liability of members in an LLC under the "piercing of the corporate veil" doctrine.

- Section 5.01[E] discusses the new classification election requirements for LLCs owned by a husband and wife as community property.

- Section 5.04[H] is revised to discuss the new requirements regarding late classification elections.

- Sections 6.01[A][6] and 10.03[E] set forth the rules that must be followed when a member contributes depreciable property to an LLC, or receives depreciable property in a distribution from an LLC, including basis and methods of depreciation following the contribution or distribution, and depreciation recapture rules.

- Sections 9.02[D] and 15.03 discuss the alternative methods of determining basis in an LLC, and the modified capital account method that is commonly used to determine gain or loss on sale of a membership interest.

- Chapter 11 updates tax laws regarding reorganizations of LLCs, including the temporary regulations issued in 2003 on mergers between LLCs and other entities.

- Section 11.06[A] discusses the permissible methods of incorporating an LLC, and the tax consequences of each method.

- Section 11.15 discusses the final IRS regulations on divisions of LLCs.

- Section 11.19 discusses the final IRS regulations on mergers between LLCs.

- Section 11.23 discusses the temporary IRS regulations issued in 2003 on corporate mergers and acquisitions, and the use of an LLC in such mergers. An LLC may now be used to facilitate tax-free corporate mergers and acquisitions, and to avoid the tax and non-tax problems associated with the five major types of tax-free corporate acquisitions (statutory merger, forward triangular merger, reverse triangular merger, B reorganization, and C reorganization).

- Chapter 12 is revised regarding the circumstances that cause a termination of an LLC, and the tax consequences for each type of termination.

- New § 13.06 examines the anti-abuse regulations that the IRS is now using to disallow losses in an LLC.

- Chapter 14 is revised regarding the six ways in which a payment from an LLC may be classified and taxed to the member. The fringe benefit rules under § 14.06 have also been updated.

- Chapter 15 discusses the final IRS regulations issued in June 2003 on transfers of membership interests, Section 754 basis adjustments, and LLC and member reporting requirements for transfers of membership interests.

- Chapter 16 discusses the new tax rules regarding employment taxes and self-employment taxes for members and non-member employees.

- Sections 21.03[A] and [B][1] set forth the valuation discounts that the IRS will permit for estate and gift tax purposes based on the different types of LLCs, including a table of valuation discounts permitted by the IRS.

- Section 21.03[B][4] discusses the new case law under IRC Section 2036(a), and how the IRS is now successfully challenging ''pocketbook'' LLCs and certain other types of LLCs.

- Chapter 21 sets forth the requirements that must be met in order to obtain valuation discounts and avoid challenges by the IRS.

- Chapter 23 has been revised to update the tax laws in all 50 states.

- New Chapter 24 deals with asset protection, creditors' rights and charging orders in all 50 states, and the tax consequences of charging orders and other creditor rights.

- The primary source materials are now available without charge on the Cartano Internet home page at: http://home.earthlink.net/~cartano/tax/. The web site includes state and federal tax law provisions, tax regulations, tax forms, state LLC laws and regulations, links to the home pages of the state taxing authorities and revenue departments, and links to the major free Internet tax web pages.

10/03

For questions concerning this shipment, billing, or other customer service matters, call our Customer Service Department at 1-800-234-1660.

For toll-free ordering, please call 1-800-638-8437.

A WoltersKluwer Company

Federal & State Taxation of Limited Liability Companies

2004 Edition

Federal & State Taxation of Limited Liability Companies

2004 Edition

David J. Cartano
Barton, Klugman & Oetting LLP

PUBLISHERS

1185 Avenue of the Americas, New York, NY 10036
www.aspenpublishers.com

This publication is designed to provide accurate and authoritative information in regard to the subject matter covered. It is sold with the understanding that the publisher is not engaged in rendering legal, accounting, or other professional services. If legal advice or other professional assistance is required, the services of a competent professional person should be sought.

© 2004 Aspen Publishers, Inc.
A Wolters Kluwer Company
www.aspenpublishers.com

Printed in the United States of America

ISBN: 0-7355-3900-6
ISSN: 1526-4793

1 2 3 4 5 6 7 8 9 0

About Aspen Publishers

Aspen Publishers, headquartered in New York City, is a leading information provider for attorneys, business professionals, and law students. Written by preeminent authorities, our products consist of analytical and practical information covering both U.S. and international topics. We publish in the full range of formats, including updated manuals, books, periodicals, CDs, and online products.

Our proprietary content is complemented by 2,500 legal databases, containing over 11 million documents, available through our Loislaw division. Aspen Publishers also offers a wide range of topical legal and business databases linked to Loislaw's primary material. Our mission is to provide accurate, timely, and authoritative content in easily accessible formats, supported by unmatched customer care.

To order any Aspen Publishers title, go to *www.aspenpublishers.com* or call 1-800-638-8437.

To reinstate your manual update service, call 1-800-638-8437.

For more information on Loislaw products, go to *www.loislaw.com* or call 1-800-364-2512.

For Customer Care issues, e-mail *CustomerCare@aspenpublishers.com*; call 1-800-234-1660; or fax 1-800-901-9075.

Aspen Publishers
A Wolters Kluwer Company

SUBSCRIPTION NOTICE

This Aspen Publishers product is updated on a periodic basis with supplements to reflect important changes in the subject matter. If you purchased this product directly from Aspen Publishers, we have already recorded your subscription for the update service.

If, however, you purchased this product from a bookstore and wish to receive future updates and revised or related volumes billed separately with a 30-day examination review, please contact our Customer Service Department at 1-800-234-1660, or send your name, company name (if applicable), address, and the title of the product to:

Aspen Publishers
7201 McKinney Circle
Frederick, MD 21704

About the Author

David J. Cartano was born in Seattle, Washington, on November 6, 1949. He was admitted to the bar in California in 1976. He graduated from the University of Washington in 1972, magna cum laude. He received a J.D. from Cornell University in 1976 and a Masters in Taxation from the University of Southern California in 1989, where he had the highest GPA in the history of the tax program.

Mr. Cartano is a partner in the Los Angeles law firm of Barton, Klugman & Oetting. He has been with the firm since his graduation in 1976. He works in all areas of domestic and international taxation.

Mr. Cartano is the author of *Taxation of Compensation and Benefits* and *Taxation of Individual Retirement Accounts*, both published by Aspen Publishers. He is a contributor to three other books, including *Limited Liability Partnerships, Formation, Operation and Taxation*, published by John Wiley and Sons, Inc. He was one of the first persons to publish a book on taxation on the Internet, published by Internet Publications, Ltd. He is the author of numerous articles, including "The Tax Benefit Rule in Corporate Liquidations," The Journal of Corporate Taxation, Autumn, 1983; "Incentive Stock Options — The Sequential Exercise Restriction," TAXES — The Tax Magazine, August, 1982; "ESOPs and Restricted Securities," Journal of Pension Planning and Compliance, November, 1977; "Meeting the New IRS Requirements," Financial Operations, Fall, 1987. He is a frequent speaker on taxation at bar association meetings and for the California Continuing Education of the Bar.

Summary of Contents

Contents

*A complete table of contents for each chapter is
included at the beginning of the chapter.*

4

Special Issues Regarding S Corporations and LLCs

5

Classification of LLCs

6

Contributions

7

Taxation of LLC Income

Contents

8

Allocations

9

Basis and Member's Share of Debt

10

Distributions

11

Reorganizations

12

Terminations

13

Loss Limitations

14

Payments and Benefits to Members

15

Transfer of Membership Interests

16

Self-Employment and Employment Taxes

17

Accounting Methods and Procedures

18

Foreign LLCs

19

Foreign-Owned Domestic LLCs

Contents

20

Investment LLCs

21

Estate and Gift Tax Planning

22

Federal and State Filing Requirements

23

State Tax Laws

24

Asset Protection, Charging Orders, and Creditors' Rights

Preface

This 2004 Edition of *Federal & State Taxation of Limited Liability Companies* attempts to cover all of the tax laws applicable to limited liability companies. It analyzes every revenue ruling, private letter ruling, revenue procedure, tax advisory memorandum, IRS notice, Treasury regulation, and federal court case dealing with the tax laws applicable to limited liability companies.

The tax laws for LLCs in all 50 states are discussed in detail in Chapter 23. There is a summary table of the taxes that must be paid in each of the 50 states at the beginning of Chapter 23. The tax forms that must be filed for an LLC in each of the 50 states are listed in Chapter 22.

The book is divided into 23 chapters by subject matter. There is a sample operating agreement in Appendix A that is intended to comply with the tax laws. All of the reported revenue procedures, revenue rulings, IRS notices, private letter rulings and tax advisory memoranda are summarized in Appendices B and C.

LLCs are now taxed under federal law as disregarded entities (branch, division or sole proprietorship), partnerships, or corporations. The tax laws for each of these three types of LLCs are analyzed in detail in this book. The most common type of LLC is classified as a partnership. As a result, there is a more detailed discussion in the book of the tax laws applicable to LLCs classified as partnerships.

The LLC is a relatively new form of business entity. It has become one of the most popular forms of business entity after the IRS issued the check-the-box regulations. Those regulations provided much greater tax certainty for LLCs. However, there are many new issues that the IRS is just starting to address. This book is updated and completely revised each year to incorporate all of the many tax law changes.

1

Introduction

---

§1.01   History of LLCs
§1.02   Terminology Used
§1.03   Applicability of Partnership Tax Rules

§1.01   HISTORY OF LLCs

There are seven principal forms of business organizations: sole proprietorship, C corporation, S corporation, general partnership, limited partnership, limited liability company (LLC), and registered limited liability partnership (LLP).

The LLC is a relatively new form of business organization. Wyoming was the first state to authorize LLCs in 1977. It wanted to provide an organization that had the tax benefits of a partnership and the limited liability benefits of a corporation. During the next 12 years, Florida was the only other state that enacted LLC laws. Other states were reluctant to enact LLC laws because there was too much uncertainty regarding the tax consequences of an LLC.

The Internal Revenue Service (IRS) at first proposed to tax LLCs as corporations because none of the owners had unlimited liability, as they do in a partnership. It issued proposed regulations to that effect in 1980.[1] The proposed regulations received little support and were later withdrawn in 1983.[2] After a six-year study of the limited liability issue, the IRS announced in 1988 that an entity could be taxed as a partnership even if none of the owners were personally liable.[3] Later that year it issued a ruling that a Wyoming LLC would be classified as a partnership for federal tax purposes.[4]

After the 1988 ruling, the other states enacted laws authorizing LLCs. Two states enacted LLC laws in 1990; four states enacted LLC laws in 1991; 10 states enacted LLC laws in 1992. All of the states and the District of Columbia now have LLC laws.

In 1996, the Treasury issued final regulations permitting almost all LLCs with two or more members to be classified as partnerships.[5] They were issued in response to the numerous state limited liability statutes that blurred the distinction

---

§1.01   [1] Prop. Reg. §301.7701-2, 45 Fed. Reg. 75709 (Nov. 17, 1980).
[2] IRS News Release IR-82-145 (Dec. 16, 1982).
[3] IRS Ann. 88-118, 1988-38 I.R.B. 26.
[4] Rev. Rul. 88-76, 1988-2 C.B. 360.
[5] T.D. 8697 (Dec. 18, 1996), enacting final regulations under Reg. §301.7701.

between corporations and partnerships. The regulations are referred to as the "check-the-box" regulations because they permit LLCs and most other unincorporated entities to select classification as a proprietorship, partnership, or corporation by checking the applicable box on an IRS form. The regulations removed much of the uncertainty regarding the tax consequences of forming an LLC.

In 1995, the National Conference of Commissioners on Uniform State Laws approved and recommended for enactment in all of the states the Uniform Limited Liability Company Act.[6]

LLPs are similar to LLCs with one major exception. In most states, partners in an LLP are personally liable for the contractual liabilities of the LLP. They are not liable for the tort liabilities of the LLP except to the extent caused by their own negligent acts. Conversely, members in an LLC are not liable for the tort or contractual liabilities of an LLC (except for the contractual liabilities that the members personally guarantee). State laws generally require an LLP to maintain a minimum amount of liability insurance to cover potential tort liability. A few states, such as New York, now provide that partners of an LLP are not liable for the contractual or tort liabilities of other partners, thus making the LLP similar to the LLC.

§1.02   TERMINOLOGY USED

The basic terminology for LLCs is as follows:

Articles of organization: The articles of organization are filed with the secretary of state in order to form the LLC. This document is analogous to the articles of incorporation for corporations and the certificate of limited partnership for limited partnerships.

Certificate of formation: Some states, such as Delaware, refer to the articles of organization as the certificate of formation.

Economic interest: An economic interest is the right of a member or nonmember to receive an allocable share of income, gain, loss, deductions, and credits in the LLC. An economic interest does not include the right to vote or participate in management. Normally, a member may transfer an economic interest in an LLC without the consent of the other member unless the organizational documents otherwise provide. However, transfer of the economic interest normally transfers only the member's right to share in distributions and profit and loss allocations. It does not transfer the member's voting and management rights without the consent of the other members (as specified in the operating agreement).

Governors: Three states refer to the managers of the LLC as governors.[7] The

---

[6] A free copy of the Act may be obtained from the following address: Uniform Law Commissioners, 211 East Ontario Street, Suite 1300, Chicago, Illinois 60611; or from the Website of the National Conference of Commissioners on Uniform State Laws: <http://www.law.upenn.edu/library/ulc/ulc.htm>.

[7] Minn. Stat. §§322B.03, 322B.606 to 322B.666; N.D. Cent. Code §10-32-69; Tenn. Code Ann. §§48-239-101 to 48-239-116.

governors serve on a board of governors. This is similar to a board of directors for a corporation. The business and affairs of the LLC are conducted under the direction and control of the board of governors. Officers are also appointed to carry out the day-to-day activities of the LLC.

Limited liability company agreement: Some states, such as Delaware, refer to the operating agreement as the limited liability company agreement.

Managers: Managers are the persons designated by the members to manage the LLC. Most state laws allow members to designate managers. If there are no designated managers, all members normally manage the LLC in accordance with their proportionate interests in the LLC. Managers are analogous to the officers and directors in a corporation and the general partners in a limited partnership.

Members: Members are the owners of an LLC.

Membership interest: A membership interest is all of a member's ownership rights in an LLC. A membership interest includes the member's right to vote and participate in management and the member's economic interest in the LLC. A membership interest is analogous to the shares of stock in a corporation and the partnership units in a limited partnership.

Operating agreement: The operating agreement sets forth the rules regarding the operation of the LLC and the rights and obligations of the members. It is similar to the bylaws in a corporation and the partnership agreement in a partnership.

Regulations: Texas[8] and Florida refer to the operating agreement as the regulations.

§1.03   APPLICABILITY OF PARTNERSHIP TAX RULES

The partnership tax laws apply to LLCs that are classified as partnerships for federal tax purposes. This causes a problem in many cases because the partnership laws were enacted prior to the time that LLCs existed as legal entities. Partnerships and LLCs are different types of organizations, and thus the partnership rules do not neatly fit the LLC organization in certain cases.

For example, the partnership tax laws provide for different tax treatment if the partner is a general partner or a limited partner for the following purposes:

- Self-employment taxes[1]
- Payments to retiring and deceased partners of a service partnership[2]

---

[8] Tex. Rev. Civ. Stat. Ann. art. 1528n, 2.09.

§1.03   [1] *See* §§16.01, 16.02[B] *infra*. In 1997, the IRS issued detailed regulations setting forth when a member in an LLC would be treated as a limited partner or general partner for self-employment tax purposes. Prop. Reg. §1.1402(a)-2. The proposed regulations drew immediate criticism from the tax community and small businesses. In the same year, Congress passed a law temporarily prohibiting the IRS from implementing the regulations. Pub. L. No. 105-34, §935, 105th Cong., 1st Sess. (Aug. 5, 1997).

[2] *See* §10.08[D], [E] *infra*.

- Cash method of accounting[3]
- Passive loss limitations[4]
- Tax matters partner[5]
- Pension and profit-sharing plans[6]

It is often unclear whether a member in an LLC should be classified as a general partner or a limited partner for those purposes. A member is similar to a general partner in some respects (e.g., voting and management rights) and similar to a limited partner in other respects (e.g., limited liability).

Since there is little specific statutory guidance applicable to LLCs, the major body of LLC tax law is based on revenue rulings and private letter rulings issued by the IRS applying the partnership tax rules to LLCs.

---

[3] *See* §17.01[E][3][b] *infra.*
[4] *See* §13.04[B] *infra.*
[5] *See* §17.07[B] *infra.*
[6] *See* §14.06[A][3] *infra.*

2

Summary of LLC Laws

---

§2.01   INTRODUCTION

LLC laws vary from state to state. The principal features of LLC laws concern the following issues:

- Formation
- Purposes for which LLCs may be formed
- Membership interests
- Duration of LLCs
- Management
- Rights of members
- Limited liability
- Restrictions on transfer
- Withdrawal of members

In 1995, the National Conference of Commissioners on Uniform State Law (NCCUSL) enacted a model statute for LLC state laws. The model statute is called the Uniform Limited Liability Company Act (ULLCA). South Carolina, West Virginia, Vermont, and Hawaii adopted the ULLCA. The ULLCA is likely to gain wider acceptance in future years.

The following chart sets forth the citations to the LLC laws in each state. These may be accessed without charge via the Internet:[1]

Citations to State LLC Laws

State	LLC Act
Alabama	Ala. Code §§10-12-1 to 10-12-61
Alaska	Alaska Stat. §§10.50.010 to 10.50.995
Arizona	Ariz. Rev. Stat. Ann. §§29-601 to 29-857
Arkansas	Ark. Code Ann. §§4-32-10 to 4-32-1401
California	Cal. Corp. Code §§17000 to 17705
Colorado	Colo. Rev. Stat. Ann. §§7-80-101 to 7-80-1101
Connecticut	Conn. Gen. Stat. Ann. §§34-100 to 34-299
Delaware	Del. Code Ann. tit. 6, §§18-101 to 18-1109
D.C.	D.C. Code Ann. §§29-1001 to 29-1075
Florida	Fla. Stat. Ann. §§608.401 to 608.703
Georgia	Ga. Code Ann. §§14-11-100 to 14-11-1109
Hawaii	Haw. Rev. Stat. §§428-101 to 428-1302
Idaho	Idaho Code §§53-601 to 53-672
Illinois	Ill. Ann. Stat. ch. 805, paras. 180/1-1 to 180/60-1
Indiana	Ind. Code Ann. §§23-18-1-1 to 23-18-13-1
Iowa	Iowa Code Ann. §§490A.100 to 490A.1601
Kansas	Kan. Stat. Ann. §§17-7601 to 17-7706
Kentucky	Ky. Rev. Stat. Ann. §§275.001 to 275.455
Louisiana	La. Rev. Stat. Ann. §§12:1301 to 12:1369
Maine	Me. Rev. Stat. Ann. tit. 31, §§601 to 762
Maryland	Md. Code Ann., Corps. & Assns. §§4A-101 to 4A-1103
Massachusetts	Mass. Gen. Laws Ann. ch. 156C, §§1-68
Michigan	Mich. Comp. Laws Ann. §§450.4101 to 450.5200
Minnesota	Minn. Stat. Ann. §§322B.01 to 322B.960

§2.01   [1] http://www.law.cornell.edu/states/index.html

Mississippi	Miss. Code Ann. §§79-29-101 to 79-29-1201
Missouri	Mo. Ann. Stat. §§347.010 to 347.740
Montana	Mont. Code Ann. §§35-8-101 to 35-8-1307
Nebraska	Neb. Rev. Stat. §§21-2601 to 21-2653
Nevada	Nev. Rev. Stat. Ann. §§86.010 to 86.590
New Hampshire	N.H. Rev. Stat. Ann. §§304-C:1 to 304-C:85
New Jersey	N.J. Stat. Ann. §§42:2B-1 to 42:2B-70
New Mexico	N.M. Stat. Ann. §§53-19-1 to 53-19-74
New York	N.Y. L.L.C. Law §§101 to 1403
North Carolina	N.C. Gen. Stat. §§57C-1-01 to 57C-10-07
North Dakota	N.D. Cent. Code §§10-32-01 to 10-32-156
Ohio	Ohio Rev. Code Ann. §§1705.01 to 1705.58
Oklahoma	Okla. Stat. Ann. tit. 18, §§2000 to 2060
Oregon	Or. Rev. Stat. §§63.001 to 63.990
Pennsylvania	15 Pa. Cons. Stat. Ann. §§8101 to 8998
Rhode Island	R.I. Gen. Laws §§7-16-1 to 7-16-75
South Carolina	S.C. Code Ann. §§33-44-101 to 33-44-1207
South Dakota	S.D. Codified Laws Ann. §§47-34A-101 to 47-34A-1207
Tennessee	Tenn. Code Ann. §§48-201-101 to 48-248-606
Texas	Tex. Rev. Civ. Stat. Ann. art. 1528n, 1.01-11.07
Utah	Utah Code Ann. §§48-2c-101 to 48-2c-1902
Vermont	Vt. Stat. Ann. tit. 11, §§3001-3162
Virginia	Va. Code Ann. §§13.1-1000 to 13.1-1123
Washington	Wash. Rev. Code Ann. §§25.15.005 to 25.15.902
West Virginia	W. Va. Code §§31B-1-101 to 31B-13-1306
Wisconsin	Wis. Stat. Ann. §§183.0102 to 183.1305
Wyoming	Wyo. Stat. §§17-15-101 to 17-15-147

§2.02   FORMATION OF LLCs

The LLC is an organization separate and apart from its owners. It can sue and be sued, sign contracts, buy property, and take other action in its own name.

The founders must file articles of organization with the secretary of state or other designated government agency. The articles of organization contain information similar to articles of incorporation for corporations. Most states require the articles of organization to include the name of the LLC, the period of duration, the purpose of the LLC, and the name and address of the registered agent. Other states also require provisions dealing with the following issues:

- Membership interests
- The right to admit additional members[1]
- The name and address of the members or designated managers[2]

---

§2.02   [1] *See* Fla. Stat. Ann. §608.407; Kan. Stat. Ann. §17-7607; Nev. Rev. Stat. Ann. §86.161.
[2] *See* Kan. Stat. Ann. §17-7607; Utah Code Ann. §48-2b-116; Wyo. Stat. §17-15-107.

In addition to the articles of organization, there is usually an operating agreement. The operating agreement governs the rights, duties, and obligations of members and managers except as otherwise stated in the articles of organization or required by state law. The operating agreement is similar to corporate bylaws or a partnership agreement. The operating agreement may be verbal or in writing.[3]

LLCs must have at least two members in some states, although most states permit LLCs to have only one member.[4]

The members of an LLC may be individuals, corporations, partnerships, other LLCs, trusts, estates, and associations. There are no restrictions on membership except as provided in the organization documents.

The company name must ordinarily contain "limited liability company," "limited company," or "LLC" at the end of the name. The name may not conflict with other registered names.

§2.03 PURPOSES FOR WHICH LLCs CAN BE FORMED

[A]   *Generally*

An LLC can be formed for any lawful purpose,[1] subject to certain restrictions in some states. For example, some states provide that an LLC may not engage in the following activities:

- Operating a homestead or building and loan association[2]
- Engaging in the banking, insurance, or trust company business[3]
- Engaging in a profession[4]

---

[3] *E.g.*, Cal. Corp. Code §§17000(ab), 17050(a).

[4] For a listing of states that permit single-member LLCs, *see* §5.02[A] *infra*.

§2.03   [1] Ala. Code §10-12-3; Alaska Stat. §10.50.075(2); Ark. Code Ann. §4-32-106; Colo. Rev. Stat. Ann. §7-80-103; D.C. Code Ann. §29-1003; Ga. Code Ann. §14-11-201(a); Idaho Code §53-605(1); Ind. Code Ann. §23-18-2-1(a); Iowa Code §490A.201.1; Kan. Stat. Ann. §17-7668(a); Ky. Rev. Stat. Ann. §275-005; La. Rev. Stat. Ann. §12:1303; M.G.L.A. ch. 156C, §6(a); Me. Rev. Stat. Ann. tit. 31, §611; Mich. Comp. Laws Ann. §450.4203(1)(b); Miss. Code Ann. §79-29-108(1); Mo. Rev. Stat. §347.039.1(2); Neb. Rev. Stat. §21-2602(1); Nev. Rev. Stat. Ann. §86.141; N.H. Rev. Stat. Ann. §304-C:7.I; N.J. Stat. Ann. §42:2B-8.a; N.Y. LLC §201; N.C. Gen. Stat. §57C-2-01(a); N.D. Cent. Code §10-32-04; Ohio Rev. Code Ann. §1705.02; Or. Rev. Stat. §63.074(1); 15 Pa. Cons. Stat. §8922(a); R.I. Gen. Laws §7-16-3; S.C. Code Ann. §33-44-112; S.D. Codified Laws Ann. §47-34A-112(a); Tenn. Code Ann. §48-203-101; Tex. Rev. Civ. Stat. Ann. art. 1528n, 2.01.A; Utah Code Ann. §48-2c-105; Vt. Stat. Ann. tit. 11, §3012(a); Va. Code Ann. §13.1-1008; Wash. Rev. Code §25.15.030(1); W. Va. Code §31B-1-112(a); Wis. Stat. §183.0107; Wyo. Stat. §17-15-103(a).

[2] *See, e.g.*, La. Rev. Stat. Ann. §12:1302.

[3] *See, e.g.*, Ariz. Rev. Stat. Ann. §29-609; Cal. Corp. Code §17002; Conn. Gen. Stat. Ann. §34-119; Del. Code Ann. tit. 6, §18-106; 805 ILCS §180/1-25; Kan. Stat. Ann. §17-7668(a); La. Rev. Stat. Ann. §12:1302; Md. Corps. & Ass'ns Code Ann. §4A-201; Mont. Code Ann. §35-8-106(2); Neb. Rev. Stat. §21-2602(1); Nev. Rev. Stat. Ann. §86.141; N.H. Rev. Stat. Ann. §304-C:7.I; Okla. Stat. Ann. tit. 18, §2002; 15 Pa. Cons. Stat. §8911(a); Vt. Stat. Ann. tit. 11, §3012(b); Wash. Rev. Code §25.15.030(1); Wyo. Stat. §17-15-103(a).

[4] Cal. Corp. Code §17375. See §2.03[D] *infra* regarding professional LLCs.

- Engaging in any other business or activities to the extent limited by the articles of organization[5]

[B]   Tax-Exempt Organizations

[1]   Qualification as Exempt Organization

An LLC may qualify as a tax-exempt organization.[6] However, qualification as and participation in an LLC are subject to special scrutiny.[7] An LLC that wants to qualify as a tax-exempt organization must have a compelling reason why it should be organized as an LLC.[8]

[2]   Unrelated Business Income

Payments received by a tax-exempt organization from an LLC as a distributive share of income, or for goods, property, services, or personnel in connection with the business of the LLC, are not subject to the tax on unrelated business taxable income if the income is from a trade or business that is substantially related to the organization's tax-exempt purposes.[9]

A charity's share of income from an LLC's disposition of timber contracts is not subject to the tax on unrelated business income.[10]

[3]   Participation as Members, Managers, or Joint Venturers

Tax-exempt organizations may participate as members or managers in an LLC.[11] If a nonprofit organization participates as a manager in an LLC, the exempt organization must demonstrate that it is in control of the operation and that all of the LLC's business transactions and operations further its exempt purposes.[12] The exempt organization must also show that assets are not being siphoned off in a manner that constitutes use for nonexempt purposes.[13]

---

[5] D.C. Code Ann. §29-1003; Ga. Code Ann. §14-11-201(b); Haw. Rev. Stat. Ann. §428-111; Ind. Code Ann. §23-18-2-1(a); Iowa Code §490A.201.1; Utah Code Ann. §48-2c-105.

[6] *See, e.g.,* Ltr. Rul. 9736043, in which exempt organizations formed an LLC to provide financing for prepaid group general services to subscribers of the nonprofit organization; Ltr. Rul. 9840054, in which exempt organization used an LLC as an exempt title-holding company under IRC §501(c)(25); Ltr. Ruls. 9839016-017, in which nonprofit organizations formed an LLC to promote a regional network of hospitals and other health care entities that agreed to common supervision and oversight by the LLC; Ltr. Rul. 200118054, in which a nonprofit health system participated in an ambulatory surgery center.

[7] BNA Daily Tax Rep., G-3, G-4 (May 23, 1995).

[8] *Id.*

[9] Ltr. Ruls. 200044040, 199913051, 199913035, 9739036-039. *See also* Ltr. Rul. 9736043 in BNA Daily Tax Rep., G-3, G-4 (May 23, 1995); Ltr. Rul. 200118054.

[10] Ltr. Rul. 200151046.

[11] *See, e.g.,* Ltr. Ruls. 200044040, 9851054.

[12] BNA Daily Tax Rep., G-3, G-4 (May 23, 1995); Ltr. Rul. 200118054.

[13] *Id.*

For example, a public charity may form an LLC to obtain loans and financing for minority and disadvantaged businesses in the community. The tax-exempt status of the public charity will not be adversely affected even though the public charity acts as the manager of the LLC, receives interest and loan fees, issues membership interests in the LLC to for-profit investors, and pays a profit participation interest to the investors. The public charity must own a controlling interest in the LLC and operate the LLC primarily for charitable purposes. Income earned by the public charity from the LLC is not considered income from an unrelated business under IRC Section 513.[14]

A tax-exempt hospital may form an LLC with a for-profit corporation and contribute its hospital and other operating assets to the LLC. The tax-exempt organization will continue to maintain its tax-exempt status if (a) the governing instruments of the LLC require that the LLC give charitable purposes priority over maximizing profits for the owners of the LLC, (b) the tax-exempt organization appoints a majority of the board of directors of the LLC, (c) the LLC designates an independent management company to run the hospital, (d) the terms of the management contract are reasonable, and (e) distributions by the LLC to the tax-exempt organization are used for charitable purposes.[15] The tax-exempt organization will not be a private foundation and will not have unrelated business income even though its only source of revenue is distributions from the LLC.[16] However, the hospital may lose its tax-exempt status if (a) the LLC can deny services to certain segments of the community such as indigents, (b) the for-profit owner of the LLC can appoint one-half or more of the directors of the LLC, (c) the governing documents for the LLC do not require the LLC to give priority to the charitable purposes instead of profits, or (d) the for-profit owner controls the management company.[17]

Two or more public charities may combine their operations by forming a limited liability company and contributing their assets to the limited liability company. Placing the charitable activities under the control of the LLC will not change the exempt status of the charities or the nonprivate foundation status of the exempt entities involved in the reorganization. There will be no unrelated business taxable income as a result of the reorganization. The public charities may remain in control of the LLC after the reorganization, with the LLC serving the interests only of the charities.[18]

[4] Subsidiary LLC

A tax-exempt organization may form a single-member LLC to receive and hold contributions of real estate and other high liability assets. The LLC is used to protect the tax-exempt parent organization from liability.[19]

---

[14] Ltr. Rul. 199909056.
[15] Rev. Rul. 98-15, 1998-12 IRB 6; Ltr. Ruls. 9739036-039.
[16] Id.
[17] Rev. Rul. 98-15; 1998-12 IRB 6; Ltr. Ruls. 9739036-039.
[18] Ltr. Ruls. 199913035, 199913051.
[19] Ltr. Ruls. 200150027, 200134025.

The contribution of property to the LLC is deductible as a charitable contribution under IRC Section 170(a), subject to the same percentage limitations and other restrictions that apply to deductible contributions made directly to the exempt entity.[20] However, the IRS will not rule on the deductibility of a charitable contribution of real property to an LLC.[21]

The assets owned or transferred to the LLC are treated as owned or transferred to the charitable organization.[22] The LLC is treated as part of the charitable organization unless it elects classification as a separate corporation.[23] Thus, the charitable organization is not required to file separate returns or make separate public disclosures for the LLC.[24]

A single-member LLC is not required to file an application for exemption on Form 1023.[25] The acceptance of the charitable contribution by the LLC will not adversely affect the tax-exempt status of the charitable organization that owns the LLC.[26] If the LLC acquires property encumbered by debt, it may obtain an exemption from the unrelated business income tax for its debt-financed income.[27]

A tax-exempt charitable organization may form a wholly owned LLC to perform charitable activities that are related to the parent organization's exempt purposes. If the LLC is a disregarded entity, the charitable activities performed by the LLC will be attributable to the parent organization. The use of the LLC as a separate charitable entity will not jeopardize the tax-exempt status of the parent organization.[28] The LLC's ownership and operation of a functionally related business will not constitute a business enterprise or result in the excess business holdings excise tax to the charitable organization that owns the LLC.[29]

[5] Charitable Lead and Remainder Trusts

An LLC may be the grantor of a charitable remainder unitrust. An LLC that is classified as a partnership for federal tax purposes is a permissible recipient of the unitrust amount.[30]

A charitable lead annuity trust may form an LLC and sell an interest in the

---

[20] Ltr. Rul. 200134025.

[21] Ltr. Rul. 200150027, *citing* Rev. Proc. 2000-1, 2000-1 I.R.B. 4, §5.14(3).

[22] Ltr. Rul. 200150027.

[23] Ltr. Rul. 200150027, *citing* Ann. 99-102, 1999-43 IRB 545.

[24] Ltr. Rul. 200150027.

[25] Ltr. Ruls. 200150027, 200134025.

[26] Ltr. Rul. 200150027.

[27] Ltr. Rul. 200134025, *citing* IRC §514(c)(9).

[28] Ltr. Rul. 200124022, in which a tax-exempt parent organization formed a wholly owned LLC, classified as a disregarded entity, to purchase, renovate, and operate a parking lot that was related to the exempt functions of the parent organization; Ltr. Rul. 200202077, in which a private foundation formed an LLC to build, own, operate, and lease a racetrack and campground facility that was related to the exempt function of the private foundation.

[29] Ltr. Rul. 200202077.

[30] Ltr. Rul. 199952071 (*citing* Reg. §1.664-3(a)(3)).

LLC to the remainder beneficiaries in exchange for a promissory note. The sale does not constitute an act of self-dealing under Section 4941 of the Code.[31]

[C] Cooperative Housing Corporations

A tenant-stockholder in a cooperative housing corporation may deduct interest and taxes paid or accrued by a cooperative housing corporation during the tax year. The amount of the deduction is equal to the tenant-stockholder's proportionate share of the taxes and interest. In order to qualify for this favorable tax treatment, the cooperative housing corporation must meet various requirements. One of the requirements is that 80 percent or more of the gross income of the cooperative housing corporation for the tax year must be received from tenant-stockholders.[32]

The tenant-stockholders may contribute some of their shares to an LLC. Income that the cooperative housing corporation receives from the LLC in its capacity as a tenant-shareholder qualifies as income derived from the tenant-shareholders for purposes of the 80 percent rule.[33] The LLC must be classified as a partnership for federal income tax purposes. All of the stock in the LLC must be freely transferable and not stapled to any stock in the cooperative housing corporation.

[D] Professional Organizations

Most states permit an LLC to engage in a profession, subject to certain conditions.[34] For example, some states provide that an LLC does not protect members from professional malpractice.[35] Other states permit professional LLCs if the LLC

---

[31] Ltr. Rul. 200124029.

[32] IRC §216(b)(1)(D).

[33] Ltr. Ruls. 200125013, 9802047. *See also* Ltr. Rul. 200244013 regarding a partnership of two LLCs.

[34] Ala. Code §10-12-45; Alaska Stat. §10.50.015; Ariz. Rev. Stat. Ann. §§29-841 to 29-847; Ark. Code Ann. §§4-32-102(13), 4-32-106, 4-32-1401; Colo. Rev. Stat. Ann. §7-80-103; Conn. Gen. Stat. Ann. §§34-119(b), 34-133; D.C. Code Ann. §§29-101(25), 29-1014(c) 29-1075; Fla. Stat. Ann. §608.403; Idaho Code §§53-605(2), 53-615; Ind. Code Ann. §23-18-2-1(b); Iowa Code §§490A.1501 to 490A.1519; Kan. Stat. Ann. §17-7668; Ky. Rev. Stat. §275.005; M.G.L.A. ch. 156C, §6(b), (c); Me. Rev. Stat. Ann. tit. 31, §611; Md. Corps. & Ass'ns Code Ann. §§4-101(p), 4A-203.1, 4A-301.1; Mich. Comp. Laws Ann. §§450.4901 to 450.4910; Miss. Code Ann. §§79-29-901 to 79-29-933; Mont. Code Ann. §§35-8-1301 to 35-8-1307; Neb. Rev. Stat. §§21-2426, 21-2632; Nev. Rev. Stat. Ann. §86.555; N.Y. LLC §§1201-1216, 1301-1309; N.D. Cent. Code §§10-31-01.7, 10-31-07.1, 10-31-02.2; Ohio Rev. Code Ann. §§1705.01(L), 1705.04(C); Or. Rev. Stat. §63.074(2); 15 Pa. Cons. Stat. §§8908, 8922(b), 8995-8998; R.I. Gen. Laws §7-16-3.1; S.D. Codified Laws Ann. §47-34A-112(a); Tenn. Code Ann. §§48-248-101 to 48-248-606; Tex. Rev. Civ. Stat. Ann. art. 1528n, 11.01 to 11.07; Utah Code Ann. §§48-2c-602(5)(a), (b), 1501 to 1513; Va. Code Ann. §§13.1-1100 to 1123; Vt. Stat. Ann. tit. 11, §3012(C); Wash. Rev. Code §25.15.045; W. Va. Code §§31B-13-1301 to 31B-13-1306; Wyo. Stat. §17-15-103(b).

[35] Ala. Code §10-12-45(a); Conn. Gen. Stat. Ann. §34-133; D.C. Code Ann. §29-1014(c); Idaho Code §53-615(3); Iowa Code §490A.1507; Md. Corps. & Ass'ns Code Ann. §4A-301.1; Mont. Code Ann. §35-8-1306(1); Tenn. Code Ann. §48-218-406; Tex. Rev. Civ. Stat. Ann. art. 1528n, 11.05.A; Utah Code Ann. §48-2c-602(5); Wyo. Stat. §17-15-103(b).

obtains malpractice insurance,[36] complies with additional provisions governing professional LLCs,[37] or complies with the separate laws regulating the profession.[38]

California prohibits an LLC from engaging in any profession, including any of the 67 professions listed in the California Business and Professions Code.[39]

[E]   State and Governmental Organizations

A state or other governmental organization may form an investment LLC. Memberships must be limited to a state, a political subdivision of a state, or another entity that may exclude its income under IRC Section 115(1). The gross income from the LLC allocable to the members qualifies for the exclusion under IRC Section 115(1).[40]

§2.04   MEMBERSHIP INTERESTS

Members may contribute property, services, or almost anything else of value to the LLC in exchange for membership interests. Some states prohibit issuance of membership interests in exchange for services[1] or promissory notes. A member may not be required to make additional contributions unless otherwise provided in the articles of organization or operating agreement.[2]

Membership interests may be treated as securities subject to state registration or notification requirements, particularly if members are passive investors. Most states permit division of membership interests into different classes or groups.

§2.05   DURATION OF LLCs

Unlike corporations, LLCs are, in most states, of limited duration. Upon termination and dissolution, the LLC must pay its creditors, distribute its remaining assets

---

[36] R.I. Gen. Laws §7-16-3.3.

[37] Ariz. Rev. Stat. Ann. §§29-841 to 29-847; Iowa Code §§490A.1501 to 490A.1519; Kan. Stat. Ann. §17-7668; Mich. Comp. Laws Ann. §§450.4901 to 450.4910; Miss. Code Ann. §§79-29-901 to 79-29-933; Mont. Code Ann. §§35-8-1301 to 35-8-1307; N.Y. LLC §§1201-1216 (New York LLCs), 1301-1309 (LLCs from other states); Tenn. Code Ann. §§48-248-101 to 48-248-606; Tex. Rev. Civ. Stat. Ann. art. 1528n, 11.01 to 11.07; Va. Code Ann. §§13.1-1100 to 1123; Vt. Stat. Ann. tit. 11, §3012(C); Wash. Rev. Code §25.15.045.

[38] Alaska Stat. §10.50.015; Ark. Code Ann. §4-32-1401 (medical and dental LLCs); Colo. Rev. Stat. Ann. §7-80-103; Conn. Gen. Stat. Ann. §34-119(b); Fla. Stat. Ann. §608.403; Idaho Code §53-615; 805 ILCS §180/1-25(3), (4) (medical and dental LLCs); Ind. Code Ann. §23-18-2-1(b); M.G.L.A. ch. 156C, §6(b), (c); Neb. Rev. Stat. §21-2646 (law LLCs); N.H. Rev. Stat. Ann. §304-D:1; N.C. Gen. Stat. §57C-2-01(c); S.D. Codified Laws Ann. §47-34A-112(a); Vt. Stat. Ann. tit. 11, §3012(C); Wyo. Stat. §17-15-103(b).

[39] Cal. Corp. Code §17375.

[40] Ltr. Rul. 200243023.

§2.04   [1] See, e.g., Fla. Stat. Ann. §608.4211; Wyo. Stat. §17-15-115.

[2] Cal. Corp. Code §17200(b).

to members, and make a filing with the secretary of state or other designated government agency.

An LLC typically terminates and dissolves after a fixed period, by the consent of the members, upon withdrawal of one or more members, or by involuntary dissolution.

[A] Fixed Period

An LLC may terminate after the expiration of the period fixed in the articles of organization or by statute. An LLC may also be terminated in most states upon the happening of other events specified in the articles of organization or operating agreement.[1]

[B] Consent

An LLC may dissolve by the consent of the members. In some states, the consent must be unanimous.[2] In other states, the consent must be by a majority in interest.

[C] Withdrawal of Member

An LLC normally dissolves at the death, retirement, resignation, expulsion, or bankruptcy of a member unless the remaining members agree to continue the LLC. The consent to continue the LLC is made by a majority in interest, by unanimous consent,[3] or as otherwise provided in the LLC agreements.

Some states also permit members to pre-approve continuation at the loss of a member. Such a statute typically provides that the LLC may be continued at the loss of a member by unanimous consent of the members or under a right to continue stated in the articles of organization of the LLC.

[D] Involuntary Dissolution

An LLC may be terminated involuntarily in most states. There are different grounds for involuntary dissolution. These include the following:

- Failing to pay minimum franchise taxes imposed on LLCs
- Failing to maintain a registered agent[4]

---

§2.05 [1] *See, e.g.,* Del. Code Ann. tit. 6, §18-801; Iowa Code Ann. §490A.1301; Okla. Stat. Ann. tit. 18, §2037.

[2] *See, e.g.,* Ariz. Rev. Stat. Ann. §29-781; Okla. Stat. Ann. tit. 18, §2037; W. Va. Code §31-1A-35.

[3] Iowa Code Ann. §490A.1301; Md. Code Ann., Corps. & Assns. §4A-904; Okla. Stat. Ann. tit. 18, §2037; Va. Code Ann. §13.1-1046.

[4] Colo. Rev. Stat. Ann. §7-80-808; Fla. Stat. Ann. §608.448; Nev. Rev. Stat. Ann. §86.271; R.I. Gen. Laws §7-16-41; Wyo. Stat. §17-15-112.

- Obtaining a certificate of organization through fraud[5]
- Abusing its authority or powers[6]
- Carrying on illegal activities[7]
- Undergoing judicial dissolution where it is no longer practical for the LLC to carry on its business in accordance with its operating agreement

§2.06 MANAGEMENT OF LLCs

The members of an LLC may participate in management without personal liability. Typically, the members designate one or more managers to handle day-to-day operations. The manager is not liable for LLC debts or obligations by virtue of that position. The manager's functions are similar to those of a general partner or president of a corporation.

Management may be vested in designated managers, in all of the members, or as otherwise provided in the LLC agreements. Some states require LLCs to designate managers.[1]

Three states provide for management by governors and a board of governors, rather than managers.[2]

§2.07 RIGHTS OF MEMBERS

LLC statutes give members various rights. These rights typically include the right to inspect certain LLC records, such as the articles of organization, operating agreement, names and addresses of other members, tax returns, and other relevant records.[1]

§2.08 LIMITED LIABILITY

[A] General

Members of an LLC have limited liability similar to that of shareholders in a corporation. They are not liable for the tort liabilities, debts, and other obligations

---

[5] Colo. Rev. Stat. Ann. §7-80-808; Fla. Stat. Ann. §608.448; Kan. Stat. Ann. §17-7629; Minn. Stat. Ann. §322B.843; R.I. Gen. Laws §7-16-41; Utah Code Ann. §48-2b-142.

[6] Colo. Rev. Stat. Ann. §7-80-808; Fla. Stat. Ann. §608.448; Kan. Stat. Ann. §17-7629; Minn. Stat. Ann. §322B.843; R.I. Gen. Laws §7-16-41; Utah Code Ann. §48-2b-142.

[7] Colo. Rev. Stat. Ann. §7-80-808; Fla. Stat. Ann. §608.448; Kan. Stat. Ann. §17-7629; Minn. Stat. Ann. §322B.843; R.I. Gen. Laws §7-16-41; Utah Code Ann. §48-2b-142.

§2.06 [1] *See, e.g.,* Colo. Rev. Stat. Ann. §7-80-401 (LLC must be managed by one or more managers). [2] Minn. Stat. §§322B.03, 322B.606 to 322B.666; N.D. Cent. Code §10-32-69; Tenn. Code Ann. §§48-239-101 to 48-239-116.

§2.07 [1] Cal. Corp. Code §§17106(a), 17058; Del. Code Ann. tit. 6, §18-305(a), (e); Nev. Rev. Stat. Ann. §86.271; R.I. Gen. Laws §7-16-41; Wyo. Stat. §17-15-112.

of the LLC.[1] Agents and managers of an LLC are also not personally liable for LLC debts and obligations. However, certain states provide that members may be liable for the following:

- Debts personally guaranteed by the member. All states permit members to guarantee or to agree to be personally liable for the LLC's debts.[2]
- Wrongful acts committed by the member.[3]
- Amounts that the member promised to contribute to the LLC.[4] A member may be relieved of an obligation to contribute if all other members consent. However, the member may still be liable to creditors. For example, a member in certain states is liable to creditors who relied on the promised contribution in extending credit to the LLC.[5] In Nevada and Wyoming, members are liable to creditors who extend credit after the articles of organization are filed[6]
- Amounts treated as wrongful distributions under state law.[7] These distributions include distributions while the LLC is insolvent. Members are liable for a specified number of years after the wrongful distribution.[8]

§2.08   [1] Alaska Stat. §10.50.265; Ariz. Rev. Stat. Ann. §29-651; Ark. Code Ann. §4-32-304; Colo. Rev. Stat. Ann. §7-80-705; Ind. Code Ann. §23-18-3-3; Idaho Code §53-619; 805 ILCS §180/10-10(a); Iowa Code §§490A.601, 490A.603; Ky. Rev. Stat. Ann. §275-150; Kan. Stat. Ann. §17-7688(a); M.G.L.A. ch. 156C, §22; Md. Corps. & Ass'ns Code Ann. §4A-301; Mich. Comp. Laws Ann. §450.4501(2); Miss. Code Ann. §79-29-305(3); Mont. Code Ann. §35-8-304(1); Neb. Rev. Stat. §21-2612(1); Nev. Rev. Stat. Ann. §86.371; N.H. Rev. Stat. Ann. §304-C:25; N.J. Stat. Ann. §42:2B-23; N.M. Stat. Ann. §§53-19-13, 53-19-16; N.C. Gen. Stat. §57C-3-30; N.Y. LLC §609(a); N.D. Cent. Code §10-32-29.1; Or. Rev. Stat. §63.165(1); Okla. Stat. Ann. tit. 18, §2022; R.I. Gen. Laws §7-16-23; S.C. Code Ann. §33-44-303(a); S.D. Codified Laws Ann. §§47-34A-201, 47-34A-303(a); Tenn. Code Ann. §48-217-101(a)(1), (2); Tex. Rev. Civ. Stat. Ann. art. 1528n, 4.03.A; Utah Code Ann. §48-2c-601; Vt. Stat. Ann. tit. 11, §3043(a); Va. Code Ann. §13.1-1019; Wash. Rev. Code §25.15.155(1); W. Va. Code §31B-3-303; Wis. Stat. §183.0304(1); Wyo. Stat. §17-15-113.

[2] Cal. Corp. Code §§17101(c)(2), 17101(e); Ga. Code Ann. §14-11-303(b); Haw. Rev. Stat. Ann. §428-303(c); 805 ILCS §180/10-10(d); Kan. Stat. Ann. §17-7688(b); Ky. Rev. Stat. Ann. §275-150(2); Me. Rev. Stat. Ann. tit. 31, §645.4; Miss. Code Ann. §79-29-305(3); Mont. Code Ann. §35-8-304(3); N.Y. LLC §609(b); 15 Pa. Cons. Stat. §8922(e); S.C. Code Ann. §33-44-303(c); S.D. Codified Laws Ann. §47-34A-303(c); Tex. Rev. Civ. Stat. Ann. art. 1528n, 4.03.A; Utah Code Ann. §48-2c-603; Vt. Stat. Ann. tit. 11, §3043(b); W. Va. Code §31B-3-303(c).

[3] Ala. Code §10-12-20(C); Cal. Corp. Code §17101(c); Fla. Stat. Ann. §608.4228(1)(b)(5); Ind. Code Ann. §23-18-3-3(a); Iowa Code §490A.603.3; N.M. Stat. Ann. §53-19-13; Tenn. Code Ann. §48-217-101(a)(3); Vt. Stat. Ann. tit. 11, §3043(a); Wash. Rev. Code §25.15.155(1); Wis. Stat. §183.0304(1).

[4] Ala. Code §10-12-20(b); Alaska Stat. §10.50.280; Colo. Rev. Stat. Ann. §7-80-502; Haw. Rev. Stat. Ann. §428-402(b); La. Rev. Stat. Ann. §12:1322.C; R.I. Gen. Laws §7-16-25(d)(2); Vt. Stat. Ann. tit. 11, §3052(b).

[5] Colo. Rev. Stat. Ann. §7-80-502; R.I. Gen. Laws §7-16-25(d)(2).

[6] Nev. Rev. Stat. Ann. §86.391; Wyo. Stat. §17-15-121.

[7] Cal. Corp. Code §§17254(e), 17353; Del. Code Ann. tit. 6, §18-804(c); D.C. Code Ann. §§29-1029, 29-1030; Fla. Stat. Ann. §608.428; Iowa Code §490A.808; M.G.L.A. ch. 156C, §35; Minn. Stat. §322B.56; N.M. Stat. Ann. §53-19-27; N.D. Cent. Code §10-32-65; Ohio Rev. Code Ann. §1705.23; R.I. Gen. Laws §7-16-32; S.C. Code Ann. §33-44-407; Tenn. Code Ann. §48-237-101; Utah Code Ann. §§48-2c-602(b), 1006; Vt. Stat. Ann. tit. 11, §3057; W. Va. Code §31B-4-407.

[8] Cal. Corp. Code §§17254(f), 17255(c) (four years); Iowa Code Ann. §490A.808 (five years); Va. Code Ann. §13.1-1036 (six years); W. Va. Code §31-1A-30 (four years).

- Sales taxes not remitted,[9] the trust fund portion of employment taxes not paid,[10] or any other tax liabilities of the LLC.[11]
- Transactions under which the member received an improper personal benefit.[12]
- Violations of criminal laws.[13]
- Malpractice claims in states that permit professional LLCs, including negligence and misconduct by another person under the professional's direct supervision and control.[14]
- Any other liabilities to the extent provided in the articles of organization.[15]

[B]   Applicability of Piercing the Corporate Veil Doctrine to LLCs

Several states provide that members of an LLC may be personally liable for the debts, judgments, and other liabilities of an LLC to the same extent the shareholders may be liable to corporate creditors under the "piercing the corporate veil" doctrine.[16] For example, the members of an LLC may be liable to creditors in those states if the LLC is undercapitalized or fails to obtain sufficient insurance to cover the risks of the business.[17]

A number of states provide that the failure to hold meetings of members or to comply with other formalities does not result in personal liability of the member.[18]

[C]   Differences Between Partnerships and LLCs

There are several differences between the liability of members in an LLC and that of partners in a partnership. In a general partnership, all partners are liable. In a limited partnership, the general partner is liable. In an LLC, none of the members are liable. The Treasury Department at one time believed that an LLC

---

[9] Cal. Rev. & Tax. Code §6829; Tenn. Code Ann. §48-217-101(d).

[10] Any person who is a "responsible person" is potentially liable if employment taxes are not paid.

[11] Ga. Code Ann. §14-11-303(a); Neb. Rev. Stat. §21-2612(2).

[12] Fla. Stat. Ann. §608.4228(1)(b)(2); Wash. Rev. Code §25.15.155(2); Wyo. Stat. §17-15-103(b).

[13] Fla. Stat. Ann. §608.4228(1)(b)(1).

[14] Ala. Code §10-12-45(a); Conn. Gen. Stat. Ann. §34-133; D.C. Code Ann. §29-1014(c); Idaho Code §53-615(3); Iowa Code §490A.1507; Md. Corps. & Ass'ns Code Ann. §4A-301.1; Mont. Code Ann. §35-8-1306(1); Tenn. Code Ann. §48-218-406; Wyo. Stat. §17-15-103(b).

[15] Fla. Stat. Ann. §608.4227; Haw. Rev. Stat. Ann. §428-303(c); 805 ILCS §180/10-10(d).

[16] Cal. Corp. Code §17101(b); Colo. Rev. Stat. Ann. §7-80-107(1); Fla. Stat. Ann. §608.701; Me. Rev. Stat. Ann. tit. 31, §645.3; Minn. Stat. §322B.303, subd. 2; N.D. Cent. Code §10-32-29.3; Wash. Rev. Code §25.15.060; Wis. Stat. §183.0304(2).

[17] See, e.g., Cal. Corp. Code §17101(d) regarding insurance.

[18] Cal. Corp. Code §17101(b); Colo. Rev. Stat. Ann. §7-80-107(2); Haw. Rev. Stat. Ann. §428-303(b); 805 ILCS §180/10-10(c); Iowa Code §490A.603.2; Me. Rev. Stat. Ann. tit. 31, §645.2; Mont. Code Ann. §35-8-304(2); Or. Rev. Stat. §63.1165(2); S.C. Code Ann. §33-44-303(c); S.D. Codified Laws Ann. §47-34A-303(b); Tenn. Code Ann. §48-217-101(f); Utah Code Ann. §48-2c-602(5); Wash. Rev. Code §25.15.060; W. Va. Code §31B-3-303(b).

could not be taxed as a partnership unless at least one member was personally liable, as in a limited partnership. The Treasury Department later determined that an LLC could be taxed as a partnership even though no member was personally liable. The current IRS classification regulations do not consider the liability of members in determining classification except for foreign LLCs.[19]

Another difference between LLCs and partnerships concerns participation in management. Limited partners are liable if they participate in the management of the partnership, subject to certain exceptions under state law. LLC members are not liable if they participate in management or become designated managers.

§2.09   RESTRICTIONS ON TRANSFER

An LLC membership involves two basic rights. The first is a right to receive a share of profits, gain, and other compensation from the LLC. This is referred to as the member's "economic interest." Generally, this right is freely transferable unless otherwise provided in the LLC agreements.

The second membership right is a right to vote and participate in management. This right is not freely transferable. State law provides that this right may not be transferred without the consent of a majority[1] or all[2] of the other members or as otherwise provided in the LLC agreements. The state laws were adopted at a time when the IRS regulations required restrictions on transfer in order for the LLC to be classified as a partnership. The current IRS regulations on entity classification no longer require restrictions on transfer.[3]

§2.10   WITHDRAWAL OF MEMBERS

The articles of organization or operating agreement may specify the terms and conditions for a member's withdrawal.[1] In some states, a member has a right to

---

[19] *See* Chapter 5 *infra.*

§2.09 [1] Cal. Corp. Code §17303(a); Conn. Gen. Stat. Ann. §34-172(a); Ky. Rev. Stat. Ann. §275-265(1); Neb. Rev. Stat. §21-2621; Nev. Rev. Stat. Ann. §86.351.1; N.Y. LLC §604; Okla. Stat. Ann. tit. 18, §2035.A.2; Or. Rev. Stat. §63.245(2)(a), (b); Utah Code Ann. §48-2b-131; Va. Code Ann. §13.1-1040.

[2] Ala. Code §10-13-33(a)(1); Alaska Stat. §10.50.165(a); Ariz. Rev. Stat. Ann. §29-731.B.2; Ark. Code Ann. §4-32-706; Colo. Rev. Stat. Ann. §7-80-701; Del. Code Ann. tit. 6, §18-702; D.C. Code Ann. §29-1032(b); Fla. Stat. Ann. §608.432; Ga. Code Ann. §14-11-505(b); Haw. Rev. Stat. Ann. §428-503(a); 805 ILCS §180/30-10(a); Ind. Code Ann. §§23-18-6-1(a)(1), 23-18-6-4.1(b); Idaho Code §53-640; Iowa Code §490A.903.1; Kan. Stat. Ann. §17-76,114; La. Rev. Stat. Ann. §12:1332.A(1); Me. Rev. Stat. Ann. tit. 31, §687.1.B; Md. Corps. & Ass'ns Code Ann. §4A-601(b)(1); M.G.L.A. ch. 156C, §§39(a)(1), 41(a)(1); Mich. Comp. Laws Ann. §450.4506(1); Minn. Stat. §322B.313, subd. 2; Miss. Code Ann. §79-29-301(2)(a); Mo. Rev. Stat. §347.113.2; Mont. Code Ann. §35-8-707(2); N.H. Rev. Stat. Ann. §§304-C:23.II(a), 304-C:46.I(a), 304-C:48.I(a); N.J. Stat. Ann. §42:2B-46.a(1); N.M. Stat. Ann. §§53-19-33.A, 53-19-36.A(1); N.C. Gen. Stat. §§57C-3-01(b)(1), 57C-5-04(a); N.D. Cent. Code §10-32-32.2; Ohio Rev. Code Ann. §1705.20(a)(2); 15 Pa. Cons. Stat. §8924(a); R.I. Gen. Laws §7-16-36; S.C. Code Ann. §33-44-503(a); S.D. Codified Laws Ann. §47-34-21; Tenn. Code Ann. §48-218-102(b); Tex. Rev. Civ. Stat. Ann. art. 1528n, 4.07, 4.07A; Utah Code Ann. §§48-2c-703(1), 1104; Vt. Stat. Ann. tit. 11, §3073(a); Va. Code Ann. §13.1-1040; Wash. Rev. Code §25.15.260(1)(a); W. Va. Code §31B-5-503; Wis. Stat. §183.0706(1); Wyo. Stat. §17-15-122.

[3] *See* Chapter 5 *infra.*

§2.10 [1] *See, e.g.,* Del. Code Ann. tit. 6, §§18-306, 18-603.

withdraw from the LLC and receive the fair market value of his membership interest unless otherwise provided in the LLC agreements. Other states require at least six months' notice of withdrawal.[2] A member is ordinarily entitled to receive only cash upon withdrawal even though he has contributed property to the LLC.[3] No member can be compelled to accept a distribution of any asset in kind in lieu of a proportionate distribution of money made to other members.[4]

[2] *See, e.g.,* Cal. Corp. Code §17252; Kan. Stat. Ann. §17-7616; Md. Code Ann., Corps. & Assns. §4A-606.
[3] Cal. Corp. Code §17253(a).
[4] Cal. Corp. Code §17253(b).

3

Advantages and Disadvantages of LLCs

§3.01   OVERVIEW

An LLC is designed to incorporate the most favorable aspects of corporations, general partnerships, limited partnerships, and other entities. It provides a single tax at the shareholder level. Losses may pass through to the owners. The LLC may make special allocations of income, gain, loss, credit, and deductions to members. A member may increase his basis in the membership interest by the amount of LLC debt. The members, owners, and managers of the LLC receive the same limited liability protection as shareholders, officers, and directors of a corporation. Overall, the LLC is the most flexible vehicle for a business.

Nevertheless, there are some serious drawbacks to the LLC. In certain instances, LLCs are not permitted. Some states prohibit single-member LLCs. Many states prohibit professional LLCs or place restrictions on professional LLCs.

Venture capitalists normally prefer a corporation rather than an LLC. Venture capitalists know that 51 percent ownership in a corporation gives them control of the business, whereas it may not in an LLC. Venture capitalists normally provide funding on the hope that they can take the business public. The membership interests in an LLC may not be publicly traded.

Corporations give more certainty. There is a large body of case law that has developed over many years for corporations. Most businesses, lenders, and investors are comfortable with a corporation. On the other hand, many owners, lenders, and investors may not know what a manager is or how an LLC operates. Banks, title companies, lenders, and third parties may impose greater due diligence requirements on LLCs because of their lack of familiarity.

Many states impose a franchise or entity-level tax on LLCs.[1] For example, California imposes an $800 minimum tax and a gross receipts tax up to $11,790. The tax applies even if the LLC has no income.

At one time, the Treasury Department proposed regulations making all managers of LLCs liable for self-employment taxes on their distributive shares of LLC income. Congress then passed legislation temporarily preventing the Treasury Department from implementing regulations on self-employment taxes for LLCs. The ability to reduce or eliminate self-employment taxes for employees of an S

---

§3.01   [1] *See* §23.01 *infra* for a listing of the entity level taxes for each state.

corporation is often the principal reason that a business will choose to operate as an S corporation rather than an LLC.[2]

The use of a limited partnership may in some cases be more favorable from a negotiating standpoint to promoters of a new business venture. For example, the promoters can advise limited partner investors that they cannot have voting or management rights in the business (except in limited cases permitted by state law), since voting and management rights would make them personally liable as general partners. If an LLC were used instead, the promoters could not use this argument. The passive investors could demand full voting rights and management authority without subjecting themselves to unlimited liability.

It may also be easier for the promoters to keep the profits in a corporation than an LLC. A corporation may accumulate profits at a lower graduated tax rate. There is no double taxation if the corporation never distributes its profits as dividends. An LLC, on the other hand, has more pressure to distribute profits to investors, who are taxed on those profits each year whether or not distributed.

§3.02 ADVANTAGES OVER C CORPORATIONS

[A] Single Level of Tax

There is no corporate-level tax for an LLC. There is a single tax at the member level. This is similar to the tax treatment of partnerships and S corporations. A C corporation, conversely, is subject to double taxation. The corporation is first taxed on its earnings and profits. The shareholders are then taxed when the corporation distributes the earnings and profits to the shareholders as a nondeductible dividend.

A C corporation may be able to avoid double taxation by reducing its income to zero through payments to shareholders of deductible salary, interest, and rents. The corporation may also avoid double taxation by not distributing the income in the corporation. Most corporations need some permanent level of working capital. Thus, some of the corporate income that is taxed at the low graduated rates can be kept in the corporation permanently. Finally, the combined corporate tax and the capital gains tax when the shareholder sells the shares may be lower than the individual tax rate on dividend or personal service income.

The problem of double taxation for a corporation usually applies only when the corporation sells its assets, or liquidates. The corporation is taxed on the appreciation in the assets and the shareholders are taxed at the capital gains rate on distribution. There is no double taxation when an LLC sells its assets or distributes the assets to the members.

Practice Note: Most accountants advise their clients never to put real estate into a C corporation because it is difficult to get the property out of the corporation without double taxation on the appreciation. Instead, the owner of the real estate

---

[2] *See* §4.04 *infra* for a more detailed discussion.

should lease the property to the corporation or contribute the property to an LLC, general partnership, or limited partnership.

[B] Pass-Through of Losses

LLCs may pass through losses to investors.[1] These losses may offset other taxable income earned by the members. Conversely, shareholders in a C corporation may not deduct corporate losses or excess deductions on their personal income tax returns. The losses may be used only to offset corporate profits, if any.

[C] Capital Contributions

Members in an LLC that is classified as a partnership for tax purposes do not recognize gain or loss on property contributed to the LLC in exchange for membership interests.[2]

Shareholders may contribute appreciated property to a corporation on a tax-free basis only when the transferee-shareholders possess at least 80 percent of the total combined voting power of all classes of stock entitled to vote and at least 80 percent of the outstanding shares of all classes of stock. Thus, a new shareholder is taxed on contributions of appreciated stock unless the 80 percent requirement is met. This rule often limits contributions by new shareholders to cash or other unappreciated property.

The LLC is more flexible because it can add members who contribute capital at any time on a tax-free basis for any percentage ownership interest in the LLC. No gain or loss is recognized to the LLC or its members upon the contribution of capital.

[D] Special Allocations

An LLC may make special allocations of income, gain, deductions, credits, and loss.[3] The special allocations may be made at any time prior to the due date of the return (not including extensions).[4] A corporation may not make special allocations to shareholders.

[E] No Personal Holding Company Tax

There is no personal holding company tax on an LLC that is classified as a partnership for federal tax purposes. An LLC may be used as an investment

---

§3.02 [1] There are limits on the deductibility of LLC losses. *See* Chapter 7 *infra*.
[2] IRC §721.
[3] *See* Chapter 8.
[4] IRC §761(c).

vehicle.[5] For example, an LLC may be used in place of a family limited partnership to hold family investments, to facilitate gifts from parents to children, and to help protect assets from creditors. There is no personal holding company tax even if all of the passive income is retained in the LLC.[6] C corporations that have investment and passive income exceeding 60 percent of adjusted gross income are potentially liable for the 39.6 percent penalty tax on undistributed personal holding company income.[7] The penalty tax is in addition to the regular corporate income tax and the dividend tax on shareholders.

[F]   Debt Increases Members' Bases

One of the advantages of an LLC is that liabilities incurred by the LLC increase a member's basis in the LLC.[8] In an S corporation[9] and a C corporation, liabilities incurred by the corporation do not increase a shareholder's basis.

Basis is important for three main reasons. First, a member's basis in a membership interest determines the amount of gain or loss upon the sale of the membership interest. Second, losses may be deducted only to the extent of a member's basis in the membership interest.[10] Finally, distributions of money in excess of basis result in taxable gain.

[G]   Election to Step Up Basis of Assets under Section 754

An LLC may step up the basis of its assets upon the death of a member or the sale of membership units if the LLC makes an election under Section 754 of the Internal Revenue Code (IRC).[11] There is no step-up in basis of assets in a corporation upon the death of a shareholder or the sale of stock.

The LLC must make an election under Section 754. Normally, there is a tax advantage to making the election if the underlying assets have a fair market value in excess of their basis (e.g., because of tax depreciation). However, many LLCs do not want to make this election because of the resulting accounting problems. Once the election is made, the LLC must make the basis adjustment any time a member sells membership units, a member dies, or distributions are made to members that result in taxable gain or loss. If the LLC has many members, then each asset could have many different bases. There is an adjustment of basis only with respect to the interest of the purchasing member or the estate of the deceased member in the underlying assets.

In the case of a purchase, the total basis adjustment by the LLC is the difference

[5] *See* Chapter 8.
[6] Ltr. Rul. 9330009.
[7] IRC §§541-547.
[8] IRC §752.
[9] IRC §1367.
[10] However, nondeductible losses may be carried over to years in which the member has basis in the LLC. IRC §704(d).
[11] *See* §15.08 *infra*.

between the price the member pays for the membership units and the member's share of the adjusted basis of LLC property at the time of purchase. There is an upward adjustment in basis if the purchase price is greater than the member's share of the adjusted basis of LLC property. There is a downward adjustment in basis if the purchase price is less than the member's share of the adjusted basis of LLC property. The adjustment results in the member's basis in the LLC being equal to the adjusted basis of the member's share of the underlying LLC assets.

[H] Receipt of Membership Interests by Employees

An LLC may issue membership interests to employees as options or otherwise. There are no withholding taxes upon receipt of the membership interests unless any of the following apply:

- The member receives a capital interest in the LLC or a profits interest that relates to a substantially certain and predictable stream of income from LLC assets;
- Within two years of receipt, the member disposes of the profits interest; or
- The profits interest is characterized as a limited partnership interest in a publicly traded partnership.[12]

An employee who receives stock in a corporation in exchange for services is subject to income and employment taxes under IRC Section 83 unless the stock is subject to a substantial risk of forfeiture or subject to the claims of the employer's creditors.[13]

[I] Distributions and Liquidations

There are ordinarily no adverse tax consequences to an LLC or its members when the LLC distributes appreciated assets to members.[14] The distribution of appreciated property to a member is not a taxable event.

It is very difficult to get appreciated property out of a C corporation without double taxation. The corporation recognizes gain on the appreciation.[15] The shareholders recognize dividend income to the extent of the corporation's current or accumulated earnings and profits. Upon liquidation, the shareholders recognize

---

[12] Rev. Proc. 93-27, 1993-2 C.B. 343.

[13] Reg. §§1.61-2(d)(4), 31.3401(a)-1(a)(4). *See also* Weaver v. Commissioner, 25 T.C. 1067 (1956). The value of stock, when made available without restrictions, is wages subject to withholding. Rev. Rul. 79-305, 1979-2 C.B. 350. Stock transferred by a major shareholder to employees for services rendered is also compensation. It is treated as a contribution of stock to the capital of the corporation followed immediately by a transfer of the stock from the corporation to the shareholder. The value of the stock is taxable compensation to the employee and is deductible by the corporation. Reg. §1.83-6(d)(1); Ltr. Rul. 9004003.

[14] IRC §731.

[15] IRC §311.

capital gain to the extent the value of property distributed exceeds their basis in the stock.[16]

[J]   Other Benefits

Corporations are subject to the accumulated earnings tax in addition to income and other taxes.[17] LLCs, conversely, are not subject to the accumulated earnings tax. An LLC is a pass-through entity that does not have accumulated earnings and profits.

A C corporation may be denied a tax deduction for unreasonable compensation paid to officers and shareholders. The excess compensation may be taxed as a dividend. Members of an LLC are not exposed to the unreasonable compensation problem, since a member's share of income is taxed as salary, a guaranteed payment, or a distributive share of income.

The favorable tax accounting methods available to LLCs may not be available to corporations. For example, C corporations may not use the cash receipts and disbursement method of accounting, subject to certain exceptions.[18]

The average or marginal tax rate for individual shareholders may be lower than for corporations. The highest corporate marginal tax rate is 35 percent. The corporate tax base also includes items not applicable to individuals, such as items included in the corporate alternative minimum tax. The pass-through of income and losses to members of an LLC may therefore provide a tax benefit over corporations under certain circumstances.

§3.03   ADVANTAGES OVER S CORPORATIONS

There are a number of advantages to operating a business as an LLC rather than as an S corporation; these advantages are discussed below. However, the principal advantage of an S corporation over an LLC is that shareholders of an S corporation can reduce or eliminate the self-employment tax on their distributive share of income of the S corporation. This is a significant advantage and often the principal reason that a business chooses to operate as an S corporation rather than an LLC.[1]

[A]   Number of Owners

An S corporation may have only 75 shareholders.[2] An LLC may have an unlimited number of members. However, an S corporation may be preferable for one-

---

[16] IRC §§311(b), 336(a).
[17] IRC §§531-537.
[18] IRC §448.
§3.03   [1] See §4.04 infra for a discussion of the advantages of an S corporation over an LLC.
[2] IRC §1361(b)(1)(A).

person companies. Some states require that an LLC have at least two members. Other states, such as Texas, New Mexico, New Hampshire, and New York, permit one-member LLCs.[3]

[B]   Types of Owners

An S corporation may not have shareholders other than individuals, estates, certain trusts, financial institutions, tax-exempt qualified retirement trusts, and tax-exempt charitable organizations.[4] Nonresident aliens may not be shareholders.[5] Generally, there are no restrictions on eligibility for LLC membership.

[C]   Special Allocations

An LLC may make special allocations of income, deductions, gain and loss items if the allocations have substantial economic effect.[6] An S corporation may not make special allocations to shareholders. Because of the one-class-of-stock rule for S corporations,[7] the items of income, gain, loss, deduction, and credit of an S corporation cannot be separately allocated to a particular shareholder. Instead, they are taken into account by all of the shareholders on a per-share, per-day basis.

[D]   Ownership Interests

LLCs may issue different ownership interests. An S corporation may issue only one class of stock.[8] Advances by shareholders to the corporation[9] or buy-sell agreements among shareholders[10] may create a second class of stock that disqualifies an S corporation election. No such restrictions apply to LLCs.

[E]   Borrowings Increase Basis

S corporation shareholders and LLC members may deduct company losses on their individual tax returns to the extent of basis and the amount at-risk. In addition, LLC members may increase the basis of their membership interests for loss deduction purposes when the LLC borrows money, even when the debt is

---

[3] See §5.02[A] infra for a listing of states that permit single-member LLCs.
[4] IRC §1361(b)(1)(B).
[5] IRC §1361(b)(1)(C).
[6] IRC §704(a), (b).
[7] IRC §1361(b)(1)(D).
[8] IRC §§1361(b)(1)(D), 1361(c)(4).
[9] Reg. §1.1361-1(e)(4)(ii)(B)(1).
[10] Reg. §1.1361-1(e)(2)(iii)(A).

nonrecourse. S corporation shareholders may not increase the basis of their stock when the corporation borrows money from third parties or when the shareholders guarantee a corporate loan. An S corporation shareholder may increase the basis of stock only by the direct loans made by that shareholder to the corporation.[11]

[F]   Distribution of Refinancing Proceeds

It is easier to distribute the proceeds of refinanced property in an LLC than in an S corporation. In both cases, distributions are normally taxable to the extent that the cash distributed exceeds the owner's basis in the LLC or S corporation. In an LLC, loans increase a member's basis in the LLC. [12] The proceeds from cash borrowings against LLC property can usually be distributed to members without tax because of the basis increase when the money is borrowed against LLC property. In an S corporation, the cash proceeds from refinanced loans are more likely to result in tax to shareholders, since the corporate loan does not increase a shareholder's basis.

[G]   Distributions of Appreciated Property

The distribution of appreciated property by an S corporation to a shareholder is treated as a taxable sale of the property.[13] The rule applies to dividends, redemption of shares, and liquidations.[14] The gain equals the difference between the fair market value of the property and the LLC's adjusted basis in the property. The gain passes through and is taxable to the shareholders on a per-share, per-day basis[15] and increases a shareholder's adjusted basis in his shares. The shareholder who receives the distribution then reduces his basis by the fair market value of the distributed property and receives a fair market value basis in the property.[16]

By contrast, an LLC's distribution of appreciated property to a member is generally not treated as a taxable sale of the property.[17] There is no tax unless the money distributed exceeds the member's basis in the LLC interest or the LLC makes a disproportionate distribution of unrealized receivables or substantially appreciated inventory.[18]

---

[11] IRC §1366(d)(1)(B).

[12] See §3.03[E] supra.

[13] IRC §§311, 336, 1371(a)(1).

[14] IRC §§302, 331, 1371(a)(1). See also Joint Committee on Taxation Staff Review of Selected Entity Classification and Partnership Tax Issues (JCS-6-97), at 23 (Apr. 8, 1997).

[15] IRC §1366.

[16] See Joint Committee on Taxation Staff Review of Selected Entity Classification and Partnership Tax Issues (JCS-6-97), at 23 (Apr. 8, 1997).

[17] IRC §731.

[18] IRC §§731, 752(b).

[H] Other Tax Benefits

LLCs are not subject to certain penalty taxes that apply to S corporations that were formerly C corporations, such as the built-in gains tax[19] and the excess passive income tax.[20]

An S corporation may not adjust the basis of its assets upon the death of a shareholder or the sale of stock by a shareholder. An LLC may elect to step up the basis of its assets upon the death of a member or the sale of a membership interest.[21] Therefore, if a shareholder in an S corporation dies, the heirs will receive a step-up in basis for the stock.[22] If the corporation thereafter sells appreciated assets, the gain will flow through and be taxed to the inheriting shareholders even though the appreciation occurred before the shareholder's death. The same problem arises for a person who purchases stock in an S corporation that has appreciated assets.

The S corporation has advantages over the LLC in certain cases. A C corporation may obtain pass-through tax treatment by converting to an S corporation. The conversion does not result in taxation of appreciated assets or other adverse tax consequences, subject to four main exceptions.[23] A C corporation may also obtain pass-through treatment by converting to an LLC. However, the conversion is usually taxable. It is treated as a liquidation of the corporation, taxable both to the corporation and to its shareholders.[24]

A second advantage of the S corporation is that the tax-free rules for mergers and other reorganizations apply to S corporations. For example, an S corporation may merge into a C corporation on a tax-free basis. Similar rules do not apply to combinations of LLCs and corporations.[25]

§3.04 ADVANTAGES OVER PARTNERSHIPS

[A] Limited Liability

There is limited liability for all members of an LLC. In a limited partnership, the general partner is personally liable. In a general partnership, all partners are

---

[19] IRC §1374.

[20] IRC §1375.

[21] IRC §754. *See* §15.08 *infra*.

[22] IRC §1014.

[23] Upon conversion, there is a corporate-level tax on (1) the recapture of LIFO benefits under IRC §1363(d) (the amount by which the FIFO value of inventory exceeds the LIFO value) and the adjustment of basis of inventory to account for the recapture, (2) certain built-in gain recognized within 10 years after the conversion under IRC §1374, and (3) certain passive investment income earned while the corporation retains its former C corporate earnings and profits under IRC §1375. There is also a loss of carryforwards except to reduce built-in gain.

[24] *See* Chapter 12 *infra*.

[25] *See* Joint Committee on Taxation Staff Review of Selected Entity Classification and Partnership Tax Issues (JCS-6-97), at 24-25 (Apr. 8, 1997).

personally liable. The problem of personal liability can be overcome to some extent in a limited partnership by using a corporate general partner.

[B]   Participation in Management

Limited partners in a limited partnership may not participate in management without becoming personally liable. Members in an LLC may participate in management of the LLC without becoming personally liable. For tax purposes, LLC members must "materially participate" in the business of the LLC in order to avoid the passive loss rules.[1]

§3.05   DISADVANTAGES OF LLCs

[A]   State Taxes and Fees

Some states impose significant taxes and fees on LLCs in addition to the tax on a member's shares of distributable income.[1] The states with the highest taxes and fees are:

- *California.* There is an $800 annual franchise tax on LLCs,[2] and an additional gross receipts tax of up to $11,790 for LLCs with gross receipts over $250,000.[3]
- *Texas.* There is a franchise tax of .25 percent of an LLC's net taxable capital or 4.5 percent of its net taxable earned surplus.[4]
- *New York.* There are significant publications costs and filing fees. The annual filing fee is $50 per member up to $10,000.[5]

[B]   Restrictions on Transfer of Interests

There may be restrictions on transfers of LLC membership interests under state law. The state laws were adopted at a time when the IRS regulations required restrictions on transfer in order for the LLC to be classified as a partnership. The IRS regulations on entity classification no longer require restrictions on transfer.[6]

---

§3.04   [1] The material participation and passive loss rules are discussed in §13.04 *infra.*
§3.05   [1] *See* §23.01 *infra* for a listing of states that impose taxes and the amount of these taxes.
[2] Cal. Rev. & Tax. Code §23091.
[3] Cal. Rev. & Tax. Code §23092. The tax ranges from $500 to $4,500 for LLCs with gross receipts in excess of $5 million.
[4] Tex. Tax Code Ann. §171.002.
[5] N.Y. Tax Law §658(c)(3).
[6] *See* Chapter 5 *infra.*

[C]   Public Trading

Generally, membership interests in an LLC may not be publicly traded. The LLC may be taxed as a corporation if its interests are publicly traded unless at least 90 percent of its income is specified passive income and certain other requirements are met.[7]

[D]   Formalities

A general partnership may be formed in any state by an agreement between the parties. No charter from the state is required. An LLC, on the other hand, must generally file articles of organization with the state and pay the filing fees.

[E]   Fiscal Year

An LLC may not ordinarily have a fiscal year. It must use the tax year of members having a majority interest in the LLC or the tax year of all principal members if there is no majority interest. The LLC must use a calendar year if all of the members of the LLC are individuals.

[F]   Members' Withdrawal Rights

Some states allow members to withdraw from the LLC and receive the fair market value of their membership interests unless the operating agreement otherwise provides. Other states provide different protections for withdrawing members.[8]

[G]   Automatic Dissolution

An LLC may dissolve upon the loss of a member unless a majority or all of the remaining members agree to continue the business of the LLC. This makes LLCs unattractive for large organizations with many investors. Many states permit the operating agreement to provide for automatic continuation upon the loss of a member.

[H]   Self-Employment Taxes

Managers may be subject to self-employment taxes on their distributive shares of income, whether or not distributed.[9] Conversely, limited partners are not subject

---

[7] IRC §7704. *See* Chapter 20 *infra*.
[8] *See* §2.10 *supra*.
[9] *See* Chapter 16 *infra*; Prop. Reg. §1.1402(a)-2; IRC §1402(a)(13).

to self-employment taxes except for guaranteed payments for services to the LLC. In addition, S corporation shareholders do not pay self-employment taxes on dividends. They pay the self-employment tax only on salary payments, provided they receive reasonable compensation for their services.

The extent to which LLC members must pay self-employment taxes is sometimes unclear. However, it is generally believed that an S corporation can save a substantial amount of self-employment taxes in many cases.

[I] Complicated and Expensive Setup and Operation

LLCs are often more complicated and expensive to set up. The partnership tax rules that apply to LLCs are intricate and arcane. The LLC operating agreements are more complicated than the standard boilerplate bylaws for a corporation. Moreover, LLCs typically have more complicated management structures, restrictions on sales of membership interests, and special allocation provisions.

The LLC offers more flexibility than a corporation. However, owners of an LLC that take advantage of this flexibility may incur additional accounting and attorney fees in establishing and operating the LLC.

[J] Fringe Benefits

Members of an LLC are *ineligible* for certain fringe benefits available to employees in a corporation. The types of eligible and ineligible fringe benefits are discussed in Chapter 14.[10]

[K] Tax-Free Reorganizations

Shareholders in a corporation may sell the stock or assets in the corporation in a tax-free reorganization under Section 368 of the Internal Revenue Code. Members of an LLC may not sell the LLC in a tax-free reorganization. Consequently, a business that plans to grow quickly and then be acquired by another company should probably be organized in corporate form.

An LLC, however, may use the tax-free reorganization provisions by electing to be taxed as a corporation.[11] A corporation may also merge into a disregarded LLC owned by an acquiring corporation in a tax-free merger if certain requirements are met.[12] The merger of a corporation into an LLC that is classified as an S corporation will not adversely affect the LLC's status as an S corporation.[13]

---

[10] See §14.06 infra.

[11] See e.g., Ltr. Rul. 200005016 (acquisition of membership units in an LLC that has elected to be classified as a corporation qualifies as a tax-free C reorganization).

[12] See §11.23 infra.

[13] Ltr. Rul. 200248023.

[L]   Single-Member LLCs

An LLC must have at least two members in some states. Most states now permit LLCs to have one member. However, single-member LLCs are not classified as partnerships for federal tax purposes.[14] An individual owner of a single-member LLC must report all income and other items on Schedule C of IRS Form 1040, rather than as a pass-through from Schedule K-1 of the partnership return. This increases the audit risk. C corporations and S corporations may have one shareholder.

[M]   Stock Sales

Owners of certain C corporations may exclude 50 percent of their gain upon the sale of original issue stock. The exclusion applies mainly to manufacturing and sales companies. The shareholder must own the stock for at least five years.[15] This tax advantage is not available to members of an LLC.

[N]   Reinvesting Profits

Some C corporations may save taxes by keeping earnings in the corporation rather than distributing the earnings to shareholders as deductible salary, rent, or interest. The graduated tax rates on corporate income up to $75,000 are low. This may be a significant benefit to small businesses that need to keep earnings in the corporation to meet expansion and working capital needs. The overall tax burden is reduced because the corporate tax rate is often lower than the shareholders' personal tax rates. The corporation and the shareholders also avoid paying FICA and FUTA taxes on salary to shareholders by keeping the money in the corporation. The shareholders are subject to the lower capital gains rate when they sell the stock or liquidate the corporation.

The difference in tax rates is not significant for professional corporations, which are taxed at a flat 35 percent rate and do not receive the benefits of the graduated rate brackets up to $75,000.[16]

Members of an LLC do not have this flexibility. Members must pay taxes on income that is retained by the LLC to meet working capital, expansion, or other business needs. They are taxed at their individual tax rates on their allocable share of income, whether or not distributed.

[O]   Stock Options

A corporation may compensate an employee with stock options. There is no tax on the grant of the option, and there is no tax on the exercise of the option if

[14] *See* §5.02 *infra.*
[15] IRC §1202.
[16] IRC §11(b)(2).

the option qualifies as an incentive stock option under Section 422 of the Internal Revenue Code. An LLC, however, cannot use stock options. A member of an LLC recognizes compensation income upon the receipt of a membership interest in exchange for services. This may be a significant disadvantage, especially for small start-up companies that need stock options to hire and retain qualified employees.

[P] Uncertainty in the Law

There is some uncertainty regarding how various laws will be applied to LLCs, since the LLC is a new form of legal entity. For example, there is uncertainty regarding special allocations for tax purposes and the liability of members under CERCLA for environmental liabilities. In some states, it is uncertain when the LLC "veil" can be pierced, thus imposing liability on the individual members. Members may not always have the same limited liability as corporate shareholders, especially in single-member LLCs.

§3.06   COMPARING BUSINESS ENTITIES

The following table summarizes the main differences among LLCs, C corporations, S corporations, and partnerships.

Entity Comparison Chart

Item	Entity	Comparison
Tax rate	LLC	There is no tax to the LLC on LLC income. All items of income, gain, and loss pass through and are taxed to the members.
	C corporation	Graduated tax rates of up to 35% apply to taxable income over $10 million. Personal service corporations are taxed at the 35% rate on all income.
	S corporation	There is no tax to the S corporation except in two limited circumstances (recognized built-in gains and excess passive net income).
	Partnership	There is no tax to the partnership on partnership income. All items of income, gain, and loss pass through and are taxed to the partners.

Item	Entity	Comparison
Eligible owners	LLC	There are no restrictions on eligible owners.
	C corporation	There are no restrictions on eligible owners.
	S corporation	An S corporation may not have more than 75 shareholders. It may not have nonindividual shareholders, subject to certain exceptions.
	Partnership	There are no restrictions on eligible owners.
Types of owner-ship interests	LLC	Membership interests. There may be different classes of membership interests.
	C corporation	Stock. There may be different classes of stock.
	S corporation	Stock. There may be only one class of stock. However, there may be voting and nonvoting common stock.
	Partnership	General and limited partnership units. There may be different classes of ownership interests.
Special allocations	LLC	Special allocations are permitted if the allocations have substantial economic effect.
	C corporation	Special allocations are not permitted. Dividends must be paid based on stock ownership.
	S corporation	Special allocations are not permitted. Income, gain, and loss pass through to the shareholders based on stock ownership.
	Partnership	Special allocations are permitted if the allocations have substantial economic effect.

Item	Entity	Comparison
Liability of owners	LLC	There is limited liability for owners and managers.
	C corporation	There is limited liability for shareholders, officers, and directors.
	S corporation	There is limited liability for shareholders, officers, and directors.
	Partnership	All partners in a general partnership are personally liable. The general partner in a limited partnership is personally liable. There is limited liability for the limited partners in a limited partnership.
Transferability of ownership interests	LLC C corporation	There may be restrictions on transfer under state law. Shares may be freely transferred.
	S corporation	Shares may be freely transferred only to eligible S corporation shareholders.
	Partnership	Partnership interests may be transferred in accordance with the terms of the partnership agreement. Ordinarily, a general partnership interest may not be transferred without the consent of the other partners.
Duration	LLC	An LLC dissolves at the time specified in the operating agreement or upon the loss of a member unless the other members agree to continue the LLC.
	C corporation	A C corporation continues indefinitely.
	S corporation	An S corporation continues indefinitely.
	Partnership	A partnership terminates at the time specified in the partnership agreement or when there is more than a 50 percent change in partnership interests during any 12-month period.
Management	LLC	Managed by all members or designated managers. Members who participate in management are not personally liable.

Item	Entity	Comparison
Management *(continued)*	C corporation	Managed by directors and officers.
	S corporation	Managed by directors and officers.
	Partnership	Managed by general partners. Limited partners who participate in management are personally liable.
Liabilities and basis	LLC	Liabilities incurred by the LLC increase a member's basis in his membership interest.
	C corporation	Liabilities incurred by the corporation do not increase a shareholder's basis in her stock.
	S corporation	Liabilities incurred by the corporation do not increase a shareholder's basis in his stock.
	Partnership	Liabilities incurred by the partnership increase a partner's basis in her partnership interests.
Pass-through of losses	LLC	Losses of an LLC may be passed through to and deducted by members, subject to certain restrictions (basis, at-risk, and passive loss limitations).
	C corporation	Losses of a C corporation may not be passed through to and deducted by shareholders.
	S corporation	Losses of an S corporation may be passed through to and deducted by shareholders, subject to certain restrictions (basis, at-risk, and passive loss limitations).
	Partnership	Losses of a partnership may be passed through to and deducted by partners, subject to certain restrictions (basis, at-risk, and passive loss limitations).
Fringe benefits	LLC	Members are ineligible for certain fringe benefits.

Item	Entity	Comparison
Fringe benefits *(continued)*	C corporation	Shareholder-employees are eligible for most fringe benefits.
	S corporation	Two percent shareholders are ineligible for certain fringe benefits.
	Partnership	Partners are ineligible for certain fringe benefits.
Fiscal year	LLC	Must use the tax year of members having a majority interest in the LLC or the tax year of all principal members if there is no majority interest.
	C corporation	May use any fiscal year. Personal service corporations must use a calendar year, subject to certain exceptions.
	S corporation	Must use the calendar year, subject to certain exceptions.
	Partnership	Must use the tax year of partners having a majority interest in the LLC or the tax year of all principal partners if there is no majority interest.
Tax upon sale or distribution of appreciated assets	LLC	There is a single tax at the member level upon the sale of appreciated assets. Generally, there is no tax upon the distribution of appreciated assets.
	C corporation	There is potential double taxation. There is a corporate-level tax upon the sale or distribution of appreciated assets. There is a potential dividend or capital gains tax upon the distribution of sale proceeds to shareholders.
	S corporation	There is a single tax at the shareholder level upon the sale of appreciated assets. There is also a potential built-in gains tax at the corporate level if the corporation had appreciated property at the time of conversion from a C corporation to an S corporation.

Item	Entity	Comparison
	Partnership	There is a single tax at the member level upon the sale of appreciated assets. Generally, there is no tax upon the distribution of appreciated assets.
Tax to entity upon liquidation	LLC	There is no tax to the LLC upon the sale or distribution of assets.
	C corporation	The corporation is taxed on appreciation in assets upon the sale or distribution of assets.
	S corporation	There is no tax to the corporation except for a potential built-in gains tax if a C corporation was converted to an S corporation in the prior 10 years.
	Partnership	There is no tax to the partnership upon the sale or distribution of assets. Gain upon the sale of assets passes through to the partners.
Tax to owners upon liquidation	LLC	Gain upon a liquidating sale of appreciated assets by the LLC passes through to the members. No gain is recognized upon a distribution except to the extent that the money distributed exceeds the member's basis in his membership interest.
	C corporation	Gain is recognized to extent that the fair market value of property distributed exceeds the shareholder's basis in her stock.
	S corporation	Gain is recognized to the extent that the property distributed exceeds the shareholder's basis in his stock.
	Partnership	Gain upon a liquidating sale of appreciated assets by the partnership passes through to the partners. No gain is recognized upon a distribution of appreciated or other assets except to the extent that the money distributed exceeds the partner's basis in her partnership interest.

4

Special Issues Regarding
S Corporations and LLCs

§4.01   PASSIVE INCOME RECEIVED BY S CORPORATION FROM LLCs

[A]   Subchapter S Rules

A corporation's election as an S corporation is terminated if the corporation has subchapter C earnings and profits at the close of each of three consecutive taxable years and if more than 25 percent of the gross receipts for each such year is passive investment income.[1] There is also a tax on the income of an S corporation if the corporation has subchapter C earnings and profits at the close of the year and if more than 25 percent of the gross receipts is passive investment income.[2]

Whether income is active or passive is determined at the LLC level rather than the S corporation level. For example, an S corporation's distributive share of LLC gross receipts attributable to an active trade or business is not passive income, even if the LLC is a passive investor in the S corporation.[3]

The receipt by an S corporation of a distributive share of rental income from an LLC is not passive income for these purposes if the LLC provides significant services or incurs substantial costs in the rental business.[4]

---

§4.01   [1] IRC §1362(d)(3)(A)(i).
[2] IRC §1375(a).
[3] Ltr. Rul. 200102024, ruling under IRC §1375.
[4] Ltr. Ruls. 9536008, 9536007, 9615025.

The distributive share of income is normally passive income if the LLC rents the property on a triple net lease basis.[5] However, the rents received by the S corporation from the LLC under a triple net lease may be characterized as active trade or business income in exceptional cases. For example, the rental income will be trade or business income if the LLC rents property used in a franchise in which it is a limited partner and performs significant services or incurs significant costs in monitoring the franchise operations.[6]

[B] Section 469 Rules

The receipt by an S corporation of a distributive share of rental income from an LLC is passive income under the passive activity loss limitation rules,[7] unless an exception applies, even when it is not passive income under the rules that provide for termination of an S corporation election when passive investment income exceeds 25 percent of the gross receipts for three consecutive tax years and the corporation has accumulated earnings and profits.[8]

§4.02   S CORPORATION OWNERSHIP OF LLC

Before 1997, an S corporation was prohibited from owning 80 percent of an LLC that was classified as a corporation.[1] If an LLC owned by an S corporation was classified by the IRS as a corporation, the S corporation's election as an S corporation was terminated unless it obtained a ruling from the IRS that the termination was inadvertent.[2] The IRS issued favorable rulings involving reclassifications of LLCs owned by S corporations if all of the following applied:[3]

- The S corporation's election was terminated as a result of the reclassification of the LLC;
- The IRS determined that the termination was inadvertent;
- Steps were taken to make the corporation an S corporation within a reasonable period of time after discovery that the LLC could not be classified as a partnership; and
- No tax avoidance resulted from the continued treatment of the corporation as an S corporation.

Before 1997, an S corporation was also prohibited from owning 80 percent of the stock in another corporation. However, it could own the stock indirectly

---

[5] Ltr. Ruls. 9536008, 9536007.
[6] Ltr. Ruls. 9536008, 9536007.
[7] IRC §469.
[8] IRC §1362(d)(3).
   §4.02 [1] Ltr. Ruls. 9532008, 9433008; IRC §1361(b)(2)(A), prior to amendment by Pub. L. No. 104-188, §1301, 104th Cong., 2d Sess. (Aug. 20, 1996).
[2] Ltr. Rul. 9433008 (*citing* IRC §1362(f)).
[3] Ltr. Rul. 9433008.

through an LLC that was classified as a partnership for federal tax purposes.[4] For example, an S corporation could own all of the membership interests in an LLC that owned all of the stock in a corporation.[5] The IRS issued favorable rulings on an S corporation's indirect ownership of stock through an LLC if all of the following applied:[6]

- The LLC was classified as a partnership for federal tax purposes;
- The LLC was the owner of the stock for federal tax purposes and was not acting as the nominee for another person; and
- No other person, including the S corporation that owned the LLC, was the beneficial owner of the stock in the corporation owned by the LLC.

Under the law before and after 1997, an S corporation may own the membership interests in an LLC that is classified as a partnership for federal tax purposes.[7]

An S corporation may also own the membership interests in a single-member LLC that is classified as a disregarded entity.[8]

EXAMPLE

An S corporation owns all of the stock in another S corporation that is a qualified Subchapter S subsidiary. The qualified Subchapter S subsidiary is the sole owner of an LLC that is classified as a disregarded entity. The LLC owns a general partnership interest in a limited partnership. The parent S corporation is treated as the general partner in the limited partnership since both the qualified Subchapter S subsidiary and the LLC are disregarded entities.[9]

§4.03   LLC OWNERSHIP OF S CORPORATIONS

[A]   Permissible Stock Ownership

An S corporation may not have shareholders other than individuals, estates, and certain trusts, financial institutions, tax-exempt qualified retirement trusts, and tax-exempt charitable organizations.[1] Nonresident aliens may not be shareholders.[2]

---

[4] *See* Ltr. Ruls. 9640010, 9626031 (*citing* IRC §§1361(b)(1), 1504(a)(1), (2)).
[5] Ltr. Ruls. 9716007, 9640010, 9626031.
[6] Ltr. Ruls. 9716007, 9640010, 9626031.
[7] Ltr. Rul. 9637033.
[8] Ltr. Rul. 200143012.
[9] Ltr. Rul. 200143012.
§4.03   [1] IRC §1361(b)(1)(B).
[2] IRC §1361(b)(1)(C).

An LLC may own stock in an S corporation if all of the following conditions apply:[3]

- The LLC is a single-member LLC;
- The LLC is disregarded as an entity separate from its owner (rather than classified as a corporation) under the federal check-the-box regulations; and
- The owner of the LLC is a permitted S corporation shareholder.

For example, an LLC owned by an individual or a qualified trust may own stock in an S corporation.[4]

An S corporation may own stock in another S corporation only if it owns 100 percent of the stock in the S corporation subsidiary and files an election with the IRS.[5] The parent S corporation may transfer some or all of the stock in the S corporation subsidiary to an LLC if the parent corporation owns the LLC, and if the LLC is classified as a disregarded entity for federal tax purposes. The transfer of the stock to the subsidiary will not cause the termination of the parent corporation's qualified Subchapter S subsidiary election.[6]

[B] Impermissible Stock Ownership

An LLC that is classified as a partnership for federal tax purposes may not own stock in an S corporation.[7] Such an LLC's acquisition of stock in an S corporation will terminate the S corporation election.

The IRS may grant relief from inadvertent termination as a result of an LLC's acquisition of stock in an S corporation if all of the following apply:[8]

- The S corporation's election was terminated because the corporation ceased to be a small business corporation or had excessive passive investment income;[9]
- The IRS determines that the termination was inadvertent;
- The parties take steps to make the corporation a qualifying S corporation no later than a reasonable period of time after discovery of the events resulting in the termination; and
- The corporation and each person who was a shareholder of the corporation at any time after termination and prior to corrective steps agree to make adjustments required by the IRS consistent with the treatment of the corporation as an S corporation (in those cases, the corporation is treated as continuing to be an S corporation during the period specified by the IRS).

---

[3] Ltr. Ruls. 200008015, 9745017, 9739014.

[4] Ltr. Ruls. 9745017, 9739014.

[5] IRC §1361(b)(3).

[6] Ltr. Rul. 200107018.

[7] Ltr. Ruls. 200250008, 200250007, 199904008, 9750004-9750008.

[8] Ltr. Ruls. 200250008, 200250007, 199904008, 9750004-9750008.

[9] IRC §1362(d)(2), (3).

In the normal case, the LLC would take corrective steps by distributing the stock in the S corporation to its members immediately after it determines that the LLC may not own stock in the S corporation. The S corporation must then apply to the IRS for a ruling that the termination was inadvertent and that the S corporation should be treated as an S corporation throughout the period notwithstanding the disqualified shareholder.

In granting relief, the IRS normally requires that the LLC be treated as the owner of the stock during the period of ownership and that it include in income its pro rata share of the S corporation's separately and nonseparately computed items,[10] make adjustments to stock basis,[11] and take into account any distributions made by the S corporation to the LLC,[12] as provided in IRC §1368.

§4.04   ADVANTAGES OF S CORPORATIONS OVER LLCs

The main advantage of an S corporation over an LLC is that a shareholder's distributive share of income from the S corporation is not subject to self-employment taxes.[1] Generally, all of a member's share of trade or business income from an LLC is subject to self-employment taxes unless the member is classified as a "limited partner" and the payments are not guaranteed payments for services rendered.

The self-employment taxes are significant. For 2003, the self-employment taxes are imposed at the rate of 15.30 percent on earned income up to the taxable wage base of $87,000 and 2.90 percent on earned income above $87,000. An S corporation shareholder may avoid the self-employment taxes by recharacterizing earned income as pass-through income from the S corporation rather than wages for services rendered.

The IRS sometimes determines that a shareholder's distributive share of S corporation income should be recharacterized as earned income subject to the self-employment taxes if the amount of wages paid to the shareholder for services rendered is unreasonably low.[2]

To avoid IRS audit problems, the shareholders of the S corporation should normally pay themselves at least some wages or salary each year. The IRS is more likely to audit a shareholder's return if the S corporation pays the shareholder only a nominal salary or no salary at all. The S corporation can also minimize

---

[10] *See* IRC §1366.

[11] *See* IRC §1367.

[12] *See* IRC §1368.

§4.04   [1] See §3.02 *supra*.

[2] Rev. Rul. 74-44, 1974-1 C.B. 287 (S corporation distributions can be reclassified as wages where uncompensated services are performed by the shareholders); Joseph M. Grey Public Accountant, P.C. v. Commissioner, 119 T.C. No. 5 (2002); Spicer Accounting Inc. v. United States, 918 F.2d 90 (9th Cir. 1990); Esser v. United States, 750 F. Supp. 421 (D. Ariz. 1990); Radtke v. United States, 712 F. Supp. 143 (E.D. Wis. 1989); C.D. Ulrich, Ltd. v. United States, 692 F. Supp. 1053 (D. Minn. 1988); Paula Constr. Co. v. Commissioner, 58 T.C. 1055 (1972); D. Spradling, *Are S. Corp Distribution Wages Subject to Withholding?*, 71 J. Taxn. 104 (Aug. 1989); Ltr. Rul. 7949022.

audit problems by not making distributions of cash to a shareholder in excess of the amount declared as wages or salary by the shareholder during the taxable year.

The ability to reduce or eliminate self-employment taxes for an S corporation is often the principal reason that a business will choose to operate as an S corporation rather than an LLC.

§4.05   COMPARISON OF LLC TO QUALIFIED SUBCHAPTER S SUBSIDIARIES

The Small Business Job Protection Act of 1996 made several changes regarding stock ownership in an S corporation. First, the S corporation's parent may now own any percentage of stock in a C corporation. The dividends paid by the C corporation to the parent S corporation are excluded from passive income if they are attributable to the active conduct of business in the C corporation.[1] Before 1997, an S corporation could not own more than 80 percent of the voting stock or value in a C corporation.[2]

Second, the law has generally not changed regarding corporate shareholders of S corporations. Corporations are not allowed as shareholders of an S corporation.[3] However, an S corporation parent may now own 100 percent of the stock in another electing S corporation subsidiary if the subsidiary is a qualified subchapter S subsidiary. A corporate parent may elect S corporation status for a subsidiary if the following four requirements are met:[4]

1. The subsidiary is a domestic corporation;
2. The subsidiary is not an ineligible corporation, such as a financial institution or an insurance company;
3. One hundred percent of the stock in the subsidiary S corporation is owned by a parent corporation that is also an S corporation; and
4. The parent S corporation elects to treat the subsidiary as a "qualified subchapter S subsidiary."

After the parent makes the election, the subsidiary is not treated as a separate corporation for federal income tax purposes. The parent is treated as owning all of the assets, liabilities, income, and expenses of the subsidiary. The subsidiary's debts are treated as debts of the parent corporation.

The qualified subchapter S subsidiary provides similar tax treatment to an S corporation's ownership of a single-member LLC. There is flow-through tax treatment for both structures. Both subsidiaries are disregarded for federal tax purposes. However, the single-member LLC is more flexible than the qualified

---

§4.05   [1] IRC §1361(b).

[2] IRC §1361, prior to amendment by Pub. L. No. 104-188, §1308, 104th Cong., 2d Sess. (Aug. 20, 1996).

[3] IRC §1361(b)(1)(B).

[4] IRC §1361(b)(3).

subchapter S subsidiary. The parent S corporation must own 100 percent of the stock in the S corporation subsidiary. The S corporation parent may own any percentage of stock or membership units in the single-member LLC. The parent corporation does not lose the flow-through treatment when other members or owners are added to the subsidiary. The LLC retains its pass-through entity tax treatment regardless of the number of owners.

§4.06   OTHER SUBCHAPTER S ISSUES

Other special issues concerning S corporations and LLCs include the following:

- Advantages of an LLC over an S corporation.[1]
- Conversion of an S corporation into an LLC.[2]
- Ruling requests as a result of the inadvertent termination of S corporation status after an LLC's acquisition of stock in the S corporation.[3]
- Election by an LLC to be classified as an S corporation. An LLC may be an S corporation if it first makes an election to be classified as a corporation, and then makes an election to be classified as an S corporation.[4]
- Foreign members and shareholders.[5]
- Election to be an S corporation for the calendar year in which an LLC is incorporated.[6]

---

§4.06   [1] *See* §3.03 *supra.*

[2] *See* §11.08 *infra.*

[3] *See* §17.06 *infra.*

[4] Ltr. Ruls. 200321004, 200240048, 9853045. In Ltr. Rul. 200248023, the IRS determined that the merger of a corporation into an LLC that was classified as an S corporation pursuant to a Section 368(a)(1)(F) reorganization would not adversely affect the LLC's status as an S corporation.

[5] *See* §19.06 *infra.*

[6] *See* §11.06[A][7] *infra.*

5

Classification of LLCs

§5.01   CLASSIFICATION RULES

[A]   Overview

On December 17, 1996, the IRS issued final regulations on the classification of LLCs and other entities for federal tax purposes.[1] The regulations are referred to as the "check-the-box" regulations because they permit most unincorporated entities to select classification as a proprietorship, partnership, or corporation by checking the applicable box on an IRS form.

Almost all single-member LLCs are classified as disregarded entities without the need for filing any form or elections. Almost all LLCs with more than one member are classified as partnerships without the need for filing any form or elections. These are the desired classifications in most cases.

[B]   Automatic Classification as Corporation

The regulations automatically classify the following eight types of business entities as corporations for federal tax purposes:[2]

1. A business entity organized under federal or state law if the statute describes or refers to the entity as incorporated, a corporation, body corporate, or a body politic;
2. An association;
3. A business entity organized under state law if the statute describes or refers to the entity as a joint-stock company or a joint-stock association;
4. An insurance company;
5. A federally insured state-chartered bank;
6. A business entity wholly owned by a state or any political subdivision of a state;
7. A publicly traded business entity taxable as a corporation under IRC Section 7704; and
8. Certain foreign business entities.

These entities are always classified as corporations except for associations. Associations and other entities, referred to as "eligible entities" or "foreign eligible entities," may elect classification for federal tax purposes. Most LLCs are eligible entities or foreign eligible entities that may elect classification.

---

§5.01   [1] T.D. 8697 (Dec. 18, 1996), enacting final regulations under Reg. §301.7701.
[2] Reg. §301.7701-2(b).

[C]   *Default Classification for LLCs*

A single-member LLC is by default classified as a disregarded entity. It is treated as a pass-through entity (e.g., proprietorship).[3] A single-member LLC may instead elect to be classified as a corporation.[4] It may also change its classification back to a proprietorship after a 60-month waiting period.[5]

An LLC with two or more members is by default classified as a partnership (subject to certain exceptions discussed below).[6] It may instead elect to be classified as a corporation.[7] It may also change its classification back to a partnership after a 60-month waiting period.[8]

An LLC organized in a foreign country is classified under separate default rules.[9]

For tax purposes, it is usually advisable for an LLC to be classified as a partnership. It will be classified as a partnership unless any of the following conditions apply:

- The LLC is a single-member LLC.[10]
- The LLC is a foreign LLC that does not meet the requirements for classification as a partnership.[11]
- The LLC elects to be classified as a corporation.[12]
- The LLC was classified as a corporation on the effective date of the IRS regulations and did not elect to be classified as a partnership.[13]
- The LLC is a publicly-traded LLC.[14]

The new regulations eliminate the four-factor test that was previously used to determine whether an LLC was a corporation or a partnership for tax purposes.[15]

An LLC in existence before January 1, 1997, will by default have the same classification that the LLC claimed before that date unless it otherwise elects. This default rule applies only to LLCs that are "eligible entities," which are those entities that are not required to be taxed as corporations.[16]

---

[3] Reg. §301.7701-2(a).
[4] Reg. §301.7701-3(a).
[5] Reg. §301.7701-3(c)(1)(iv).
[6] Reg. §301.7701-3(a).
[7] *Id.*
[8] Reg. §301.7701-3(c)(1)(ii).
[9] *See* §5.03 *infra.*
[10] *See* §5.02 *infra.*
[11] *See* §5.03 *infra.*
[12] *See* §5.04 *infra.*
[13] Reg. §301.7701-3(b)(3)(i).
[14] *See* §5.05 *infra.*
[15] The four-factor test is discussed at §5.10 *infra.*
[16] Reg. §301.7701-3(b)(3)(i). *See* §5.02[B] *infra* for discussion of the default classification rules for single-member LLCs existing before January 1, 1997. *See* §5.03[B] *infra* for discussion of the default classification rules for foreign corporations existing before January 1, 1997.

[D] Reasons for Electing Classification as a Corporation

An LLC may want to elect classification as a corporation, rather than accept the default classification as a partnership or disregarded entity, for one of the following reasons:

- A corporation that owns an LLC in a foreign state may be treated as doing business in and subject to tax in that foreign state if the LLC is a disregarded entity.[17] The parent corporation may avoid paying taxes in the foreign state if it elects to classify the LLC as a corporation. In that case, the taxes payable by the LLC in the foreign state are separately determined based on the LLC's income, deductions, and credits, rather than under the allocation and apportionment formulas of the foreign state's tax laws.
- If the LLC has foreign members, the LLC may want to avoid withholding taxes on undistributed income. Foreign members are subject to a withholding tax on their allocable share of trade or business income earned by the LLC, whether or not the income is distributed.[18]
- The classification of an LLC as a corporation may be necessary in order to obtain financing in a public offering.[19] An LLC must be classified as a corporation if its membership units are publicly traded.[20]
- The classification of an LLC as a corporation will permit the LLC to engage in tax-free corporate reorganizations, such as mergers, reincorporations, and liquidations of subsidiary LLCs into parent corporations or parent LLCs.[21]
- If a corporation owns the LLC, the corporate owner may want to file a consolidated tax return that includes the LLC as a separate entity rather than a disregarded entity. The tax consequences are similar. An LLC that is owned by a member of a control group and that is classified as a disregarded entity is treated as part of the control group for consolidated tax purposes.[22]

---

[17] See, e.g., Massachusetts Department of Revenue Ltr. Rul. LR 00-9 (June 9, 2000), which determined that a Georgia corporation was subject to Massachusetts taxation when it acquired a Massachusetts LLC that was classified as a disregarded entity. The Georgia corporation was treated as doing business in Massachusetts based on its ownership of the membership units in the LLC. The Georgia corporation was entitled to apportion its income in accordance with the provisions of Georgia law in determining the taxable income allocable to Massachusetts. See also Corporation Tax Opinion: Pennsylvania S Corporation Filing Responsibilities, Pennsylvania Department of Revenue (Feb. 2, 2000), in which the Department of Revenue determined that the Ohio corporate owners of an Ohio LLC that was doing business as an LLC were subject to the Pennsylvania corporate net income tax because the income and activity of the LLC doing business in Pennsylvania flowed through to the corporate members. The corporate members were not, however, subject to the Pennsylvania capital stock and franchise tax.

[18] IRC §1446. See §19.02 infra.

[19] Ltr. Rul. 200151039.

[20] See §20.03 infra.

[21] Ltr. Ruls. 200248023, 200204004, 200119016.

[22] Ltr. Rul. 200111053.

- The LLC may want to keep its profits inside the business and take advantage of the lower corporate tax rates for corporations that are not personal service corporations (e.g., 15 percent on the first $50,000 of income).
- An LLC that is taxed as a corporation may adopt certain employee benefits that are not available to partnerships.[23]
- A corporation may want to convert to an LLC that is classified as a corporation in order to obtain the non-tax benefits available to an LLC under state law. For example, a corporation may not under the laws of some states repurchase stock or make distributions to shareholders unless it has sufficient retained earnings or legally available funds. An LLC is not normally subject to such restrictions. A corporation may be able to avoid the restrictions on stock repurchases and distributions to shareholders by converting to an LLC that is classified as a corporation.[24]
- An LLC may be an S corporation if it first makes an election to be classified as a corporation and then makes an election to be classified as an S corporation.[25] Normally, an LLC that is classified as a partnership is more flexible than an LLC that is classified as an S corporation. However, some LLCs file an election to be classified as a corporation in order to obtain the tax benefits of an S corporation.[26]

[E]   Community Property Ownership

An LLC that is owned by a husband and wife may elect to be classified either as a partnership or disregarded entity if:[27]

- The LLC is wholly-owned by a husband and wife as community property under the laws of a state, a foreign country, or a U.S. possession.
- No person other than one or both of the spouses is an owner for tax purposes.
- The LLC is not classified as a corporation for federal tax purposes.

Normally, a husband and wife will want to treat the LLC as a partnership rather than a disregarded entity. An LLC that is classified as a partnership must report each member's allocable share of income and expense on Schedule K-1. The owners of an LLC that is classified as a disregarded entity must report income and expenses on Schedule C. There is a higher audit risk for tax returns with Schedule C items.

---

[23] See §14.06 infra.
[24] Ltr. Rul. 200119016.
[25] Ltr. Ruls. 200248023, 200240048, 9583045.
[26] Ltr. Rul. 9853045.
[27] Rev. Proc. 2002-69, 2002-45 I.R.B. 831.

§5.02 SINGLE-MEMBER LLCs

[A] State Laws

Many states permit single-member LLCs. Several states prohibit single-member LLCs. Prior to the issuance of the check-the-box regulations, it was generally believed that an LLC should have at least two members in order to be classified as a partnership. Most states now permit single-member LLCs, since the federal regulations permit single-member LLCs to achieve pass-through tax treatment.

The following chart sets forth the states in which single-member LLCs are and are not permitted.

States Permitting Single-Member LLCs

State	Permitted	Not Permitted	Comments
Alabama	x		
Alaska	x		
Arizona	x		
Arkansas	x		
California	x		
Colorado	x		
Connecticut	x		
Delaware	x		
D.C.	x		
Florida	x		
Georgia	x		
Hawaii	x		
Idaho	x		Does not have a two-member requirement, thus implying that a single-member LLC is allowed.
Illinois	x		
Indiana	x		
Iowa	x		
Kansas		x	
Kentucky	x		
Louisiana	x		

State	Permitted	Not Permitted	Comments
Maine	x		
Maryland	x		
Massachusetts	x		Not permitted for tax years before 2003
Michigan	x		
Minnesota	x		
Mississippi	x		Does not have a two-member requirement, thus implying that a single-member LLC is allowed.
Missouri	x		
Montana	x		Does not have a two-member requirement, thus implying that a single-member LLC is allowed.
Nebraska	x		Does not have a two-member requirement, thus implying that a single-member LLC is allowed.
Nevada	x		Does not have a two-member requirement, thus implying that a single-member LLC is allowed.
New Hampshire	x		
New Jersey	x		
New Mexico	x		
New York	x		
North Carolina	x		
North Dakota	x		
Ohio	x		
Oklahoma	x		
Oregon	x		
Pennsylvania	x		
Rhode Island	x		

State	Permitted	Not Permitted	Comments
South Carolina	x		
South Dakota		x	
Tennessee		x	
Texas	x		
Utah	x		
Vermont	x		
Virginia	x		
Washington	x		
West Virginia	x		
Wisconsin	x		
Wyoming	x		

[B] Classification of Single-Member LLC

A single-member LLC is disregarded as an entity separate from its owner[1] unless it makes an election to be classified as a corporation.[2] If a single-member LLC does not elect to be classified as a corporation, it is taxed as follows:

- A single-member LLC owned by an individual is taxed as a sole proprietorship.[3] The owner of the LLC must file a Schedule C to IRS Form 1040 to report the income and expenses of the LLC.[4]
- A single-member LLC owned by a U.S. corporation is taxed as a division.[5] The consolidation rules, such as deferred intercompany gain and excess loss accounts, do not apply. All intercompany transactions are disregarded for federal tax purposes.
- A single-member LLC owned by a foreign corporation is taxed as a branch for U.S. tax purposes.[6] The LLC is subject to the branch profits tax.[7]

A bank may not treat a wholly owned non-bank LLC as a disregarded entity for purposes of applying the special rules of the Code applicable to banks.[8]

§5.02   [1] Reg. §301.7701-3(b)(1)(ii). *See also* Reg. §301.7701-2(a), (c)(2).
[2] Reg. §301.7701-3(a).
[3] Reg. §301.7701-2(a).
[4] IRS Publication 334, Tax Guide for Small Businesses; Reg. §301.7701-2(a).
[5] Reg. §301.7701-(2)(a); Ltr. Rul. 200111053.
[6] Reg §301.7701-2(a).
[7] *See* §19.02[B] *infra.*
[8] Reg. §301.7701-2(c)(2)(ii).

[C]   Related Members

An LLC may be treated as owned by two or more members even if the members are related. The determination of whether an organization has more than one owner is based on all the facts and circumstances. The fact that some or all of the owners of an LLC are under common control does not require the common parent to be treated as the sole owner.[9] For example, an LLC may be classified as a partnership if the membership interests are owned by any of the following:

- Two corporations that are wholly owned subsidiaries of the same parent corporation.[10]
- A parent and a wholly owned subsidiary corporation.[11]
- An individual and a corporation wholly owned by the same individual.[12]

An LLC may also be treated as a single-member LLC and classified as a disregarded entity if an individual and a grantor trust owned by the same individual own the LLC.[13]

[D]   Multiple-Member LLCs Treated as Single-Member LLCs

An LLC with more than one member may be treated as a single-member LLC and classified as a disregarded entity for federal tax purposes if the second member has no interest in profits and losses, does not manage the LLC, and has only limited voting rights.[14] The LLC cannot be classified as a partnership if the members have not entered into an agreement to share profits and losses from the operation of a business.[15] The controlling member of the LLC will be treated as owning directly the property owned by the LLC for most tax purposes, including the following:

- Qualification to make a like-kind exchange;[16]
- Nontaxability of contributions of appreciated property to the LLC;[17] and

---

[9] T.D. 8697, Part B, Discussion of Comments on the General Approach and Scope of the Regulations (Dec. 18, 1996) (*citing* Rev. Rul. 93-4, 1993-1 C.B. 225).

[10] Ltr. Rul. 9520036 (Texas LLC owed by two foreign subsidiaries of a foreign parent corporation); Ltr. Ruls. 9510037, 9520036 (Texas LLC owed by two subsidiaries of a parent corporation); Rev. Rul. 93-4, 1993-1 C.B. 225 (German GmbH owned by two wholly owned U.S. subsidiaries of a common parent).

[11] Ltr. Rul. 9507004.

[12] Ltr. Rul. 9321070.

[13] Ltr. Rul. 200102037.

[14] Ltr. Ruls. 200201024, 199914006, 199911033.

[15] Ltr. Ruls. 199914006, 199911033.

[16] Ltr. Rul. 199911033.

[17] Ltr. Rul. 199914006.

- Exemption from tax under IRC Section 707 when the LLC reimburses the member for capital expenditures in excess of 20 percent of the fair market value of the property.[18]

[E] Tax Consequences

[1] LLC Disregarded for Tax Purposes

The single member of an LLC that is classified as a disregarded entity is treated as the owner of the underlying assets of the LLC. This means that:

- There is no gain or loss on the transfer of assets and liabilities by a corporation or other entity to the LLC.[19]
- A charitable contribution to an LLC owned by a tax-exempt organization is treated as a tax-deductible contribution to the charitable organization. The tax-exempt organization is not required to file an application for exemption for the LLC owned by it.[20]
- The LLC may own stock in an S corporation if the member of the LLC is a qualified S corporation shareholder.[21]
- The owner may use the LLC to engage in a like-kind exchange or involuntary conversion of property.[22]
- The member's sale of membership units is treated as a sale of the underlying assets subject to state sales taxes.[23]
- The owner and the LLC must file federal tax returns as a sole proprietor.[24]
- The merger of an LLC into a corporation is treated as if the owner of the LLC transferred all of the assets to the corporation. The merger of a corporation into an LLC is treated as if the owner of the LLC acquired all of the assets of the corporation. Neither merger qualifies as a tax-free merger under IRC Section 368(a)(1)(A).[25]
- The merger of a subsidiary corporation into an LLC owned by the parent corporation is treated as a tax-free liquidation of the subsidiary into the parent.[26]
- The employees of the LLC may participate in an employee stock ownership plan of the corporate owner of the LLC. The stock in the corporate owner or another member of the controlled group of corporations constitutes

---

[18] *Id.*

[19] Ltr. Rul. 200132014.

[20] Ltr. Rul. 200134025.

[21] *See* §4.03 *supra.*

[22] *See* §15.06 *infra.*

[23] *See* §15.01 *infra.*

[24] IRS Publ. No. 334, Tax Guide for Small Businesses.

[25] Prop. Reg. §1.368-2(b)(1). *See also* Ltr. Rul. 200102038, involving the merger of a subsidiary corporation into an LLC that was wholly owned by the parent corporation.

[26] Ltr. Rul. 200129024.

qualifying employer securities for the employee stock ownership plan adopted by the LLC.[27]

- The employees of the LLC may participate in a Section 423 employee stock purchase plan of the corporate owner of the LLC.[28] If the corporate owner of the LLC is a subsidiary of a parent corporation, the employees of the LLC may receive stock of the parent corporation under a Section 423 stock purchase plan or an incentive stock option plan.[29]
- The owner of the LLC may not deduct rent paid to the LLC to lease real property owned by the LLC, and the LLC is nontaxable on the rental income received.[30]
- The owner of the LLC is entitled to any Section 29 synthetic fuel credit attributable to the single-member LLC.[31]

[2] LLC as Separate Entity for Tax Purposes

A single-member disregarded entity is treated as a separate entity for tax purposes in the following cases:

- *Employment taxes.* Under temporary regulations, employment tax obligations of a single owner of an LLC that is classified as a disregarded entity may be met by reporting and payment by the disregarded entity. However, the owner remains ultimately responsible for the employment tax obligations.[32]
- *Tax collection and tax liens.* A single-member LLC is treated as a separate entity for IRS tax collection and tax lien purposes if the LLC is a legal entity separate from its member, and if the member has no transferable interest in property of the LLC, under state law. The IRS may only collect from the property of a taxpayer to satisfy the taxpayer's liability. It may not proceed against the taxpayer's limited liability company even though the LLC is disregarded for federal tax purposes.[33] The IRS has various other collection options, including (a) collecting from the taxpayer's distributive share of income, and (b) collecting from the assets of the LLC on the ground that it is the alter ego of the taxpayer. Whether any of these options is available is determined on a case-by-case basis.[34] If the IRS makes an assessment against a disregarded LLC, and provides a collection due process notice to the LLC, the IRS must also issue a separate collection due process notice

---

[27] Ltr. Rul. 200116051.
[28] Ltr. Rul. 200046013.
[29] Ltr. Rul. 200112021.
[30] Ltr. Rul. 200102037.
[31] Ltr. Rul. 200316003.
[32] Notice 96-6, 1999-3 IRB 12; C.C.A. 200235023.
[33] Ltr. Rul. 199930013; C.C.A. 200235023.
[34] *Id.*

to the single-member owner if the IRS adds the owner's name to the assessment.[35]

- *Sales taxes.* An LLC that is a disregarded entity for income tax purposes is not a disregarded entity for sales tax purposes in some states. In New York, for example, the lease or sale of tangible personal property by the owner of an LLC to the LLC constitutes a retail sale subject to sales tax even though the LLC is a disregarded entity.[36] Other states have reached the opposite conclusion.[37]

[F]   *Default Classification of Single-Member LLCs Existing Before January 1, 1997*

A single-member LLC in existence before January 1, 1997, will be disregarded as an entity separate from its owner under the default rules. The partnership classification of a single-member LLC may be respected for periods before January 1, 1997, under transition rules, but not for periods after that date.[38] Thus, a single-member LLC that claimed partnership status for periods before January 1, 1997, will be classified as a proprietorship, branch, or division on January 1, 1997, unless it elects to be classified as a corporation.

§5.03   FOREIGN LLCs

[A]   *General Rules*

The classification of a foreign LLC depends on the number of members and whether the members have limited liability under local law. If the foreign LLC does not make an election, it will be classified as follows:[1]

- The LLC will be classified by default as a partnership if it has two or more members and if at least one member has unlimited liability.[2] A member has unlimited liability if he is personally liable for any or all of the debts of or claims against the LLC, by reason of being a member, based solely on the statute or law pursuant to which the entity is organized.[3] A member has personal liability if creditors of the entity may seek satisfaction of debts of or claims against the LLC from the member as such.[4] If a taxpayer is

---

[35] C.C.A. 200235023, 200216028.

[36] Advisory Opinion, Department of Revenue, TBS-A-99(7)S (Jan. 28, 1999).

[37] *See, e.g.,* Rev. Rul. 98-005, Ala. Dept. of Rev. (June 18, 1998). In that ruling, the Alabama Department of Revenue determined that because a single-member LLC was a disregarded entity for federal income tax purposes, it should also be treated as a disregarded entity for sales tax purposes.

[38] Reg. §301.7701-3(b)(3).

§5.03   [1] Reg. §301.7701-3(b)(2)(i).

[2] Reg. §301.7701-3(b)(2)(i)(A).

[3] Reg. §301.7701-3(b)(2)(ii).

[4] *Id.*

uncertain whether there is limited liability in a particular case, it may file an election to secure the desired classification. A foreign LLC with two or more members may elect classification as a corporation instead of a partnership under the default rules.

- The LLC will be classified by default as a corporation if no member has unlimited liability.[5] The presence of any member with personal liability for any of the debts of or claims against the LLC will cause the LLC to be classified by default as a partnership. The LLC may instead elect classification either as a proprietorship if the LLC has a single member or as a partnership if the LLC has two or more members and is otherwise eligible for partnership classification.[6]
- The LLC will by default be classified as a proprietorship or entity separate from its owners if it has a single owner with unlimited liability.[7] The LLC may instead elect classification as a corporation.[8]

If a foreign LLC's classification is determined under the default rule, changes in any member's liability will not affect the tax classification of the LLC.[9] Therefore, if a foreign LLC is classified as a partnership when the LLC's classification first becomes relevant because one of the members has personal liability, the subsequent elimination of the member's personal liability will not cause the LLC to be classified as a corporation.

For tax purposes, it is usually advisable for a foreign LLC to be classified as a partnership.[10] It will be classified as a partnership unless:

- The LLC is one of the foreign entities designated on a list in the regulations. This is referred to as the "(b)(8) list" or the "per se list." The IRS has designated over 80 foreign limited liability entities on this list that are always classified as corporations.[11] For example, a U.K. Public Limited Company and a French *Societe Anonyme* are always classified as corporations. Other foreign entities listed in the regulations are corporations that are not closely held and whose shares can be traded on a securities exchange. The IRS will update the list in notices of proposed rulemaking on a prospective basis only.[12]
- The LLC elects classification as a corporation.[13] An LLC with one or more members may elect classification as a corporation.[14]

---

[5] Reg. §301.7701-3(b)(2)(i)(B).
[6] Reg. §301.7701-3(a).
[7] Reg. §301.7701-3(b)(2)(i)(C).
[8] Reg. §301.7701-3(a).
[9] *Id.*
[10] *See* Chapter 18 *infra*.
[11] Reg. §§301.7701-2(b)(8), 301.7701-3(a) (first sentence).
[12] T.D. 8697, Part B, Discussion of Comments on the General Approach and Scope of the Regulations (Dec. 18, 1996).
[13] Reg. §§301.7701-3(b)(2)(i), 301.7701-3(c).
[14] Reg. §301.7701-3(a).

- The LLC is a single-member LLC, and the member has unlimited liability.[15] The LLC is by default classified as a proprietorship, branch, or division unless it elects classification as a corporation.[16]
- The LLC has one or more members, and no member has unlimited liability.[17] The LLC is by default classified as a corporation unless it elects classification as a proprietorship (LLC with a single member) or as a partnership (LLC with two or more members that is otherwise eligible for the election).[18]
- The LLC was classified as a corporation before the effective date of the IRS classification regulations (January 1, 1997).[19] A foreign LLC that is classified as a corporation may nevertheless elect classification as a partnership if certain requirements are met.[20]

[B] Default Classification of Foreign LLCs Existing Before January 1, 1997

A foreign LLC existing before January 1, 1997, may keep its same classification under the default rules only if it is a "foreign eligible entity" and the claimed classification affected the liability of any person for U.S. tax or information purposes at any time during the five years before January 1, 1997.[21]

Foreign LLCs on the per se list[22] are not foreign eligible entities and may not elect partnership classification. However, under grandfather rules, foreign LLCs that claimed classification as a partnership, branch, or division before January 1, 1997, may continue to be classified as a partnership, branch, or division after January 1, 1997, if six requirements are met.[23]

- The LLC was in existence on May 8, 1996 (or formed thereafter under a written binding contract in effect on that date).
- The LLC's claimed classification was relevant[24] to any person for U.S. tax purposes on May 8, 1996.
- Neither the LLC nor any member for whom U.S. classification was relevant treated the LLC as a corporation for purposes of filing U.S. tax returns, information returns, and withholding documents for the tax year that included May 8, 1996.
- Any change in the LLC's claimed classification during the 60 months before May 8, 1996, occurred solely as a result of a change in the organizational documents of the LLC, and the LLC and all of its members recognized the

---

[15] Reg. §301.7701-3(b)(2)(i)(C).
[16] Reg. §§301.7701-3(a), 301.7701-3(b)(2)(i)(C).
[17] Reg. §301.7701-3(b)(2)(i)(B).
[18] Reg. §§301.7701-3(a), 301.7701-3(b)(2)(i)(B).
[19] Reg. §301.7701-3(b)(3).
[20] Reg. §301.7701-3(b)(3)(ii).
[21] Id.
[22] Reg. §301.7701-2(b)(8). See §5.03[A] supra.
[23] Reg. §301.7701-2(d).
[24] Reg. §301.7701-3(d)(1).

federal tax consequences of any change in the LLC's classification during the 60 months before May 8, 1996.
- There was a reasonable basis for treating the LLC as other than a corporation.
- The LLC was not under tax audit with respect to the classification on May 8, 1996.

A foreign LLC on the per se list that qualifies under these transition rules may instead elect to be classified as a corporation. However, after making that election, it may not later elect classification as a partnership or branch. The grandfather status of an entity on the per se list will end upon a termination of the LLC caused by either the sale or exchange of 50 percent or more of the interests in the LLC's capital or profits within a 12-month period,[25] a division of the LLC into two or more LLCs,[26] or when one or more persons were not owners of the LLC as of November 29, 1999, become owners of 50 percent or more of the equity interests in the LLC.[27] The successor entity will thereafter be permanently treated as a corporation.

§5.04   CLASSIFICATION ELECTION

[A]   Generally

An LLC may file an election regarding its classification for federal tax purposes. However, LLCs normally do not need to file an election.[1] The default classification rules are designed to provide most LLCs with the classification that they would likely choose without requiring them to file an election.

Absent an election, an LLC with a single member is classified as a proprietorship or entity separate from its owner.[2] A domestic LLC with two or more members is classified as a partnership.[3] Partnership classification is usually the preferred classification.

An election should be filed in the following three cases:

1. The LLC wants initially to be classified differently than under the default rules.
2. The LLC wishes to change its previous classification.

---

[25] IRC §708(b)(1)(B). However, the LLC's grandfather status will not end in the case of a termination caused by the sale or exchange of membership interests in an LLC described in Reg. §301.7701-2(d)(2) if the sale or exchange is to a related person within the meaning of IRC §§267(b) and 707(b) and occurs no later than 12 months after the date the LLC is formed. Reg. §301.7701-2(d)(3)(ii).

[26] IRC §708(b)(2)(B).

[27] Reg. §301.7701-2(d)(3)(i)(D).

§5.04   [1] Reg. §301.7701-3(a).

[2] Reg. §301.7701-3(b)(1)(ii).

[3] Reg. §301.7701-3(a).

3. There is doubt about the proper classification. The uncertainty is more likely to arise for foreign LLCs where the rules are more complex.[4]

[B] Manner of Election

An LLC must file an election on IRS Form 8832, Election Classification. The election must specify the name, address, and taxpayer identification number of the LLC; the chosen classification; whether the election results in a change in classification; and whether the LLC is a domestic or foreign LLC.[5] An election will not be accepted unless all information on the form is completed.

The election must be signed by all members of the LLC or by any officer, manager, or member who is authorized to make the election. Any such authorized officer, manager, or member must represent under penalty of perjury that he is authorized to sign on behalf of the LLC.[6]

[C] Effective Date of Election

The election is effective on the date specified on the election or on the date filed if no date is specified.[7] The effective date specified may not be more than 75 days prior to or 12 months after the date on which the election is filed. Thus, an election may be retroactive to a date up to 75 days before the date of the election. If an election is effective for any period before the filing date, each person who was an owner between the effective date and the filing date and who is not an owner at the time the election is filed must also sign the election.[8]

If an election specifies an effective date more than 75 days before the date on which it is filed, it will be effective 75 days before the filing date. If an election specifies an effective date more than 12 months after the date on which the election is filed, it will be effective 12 months after the filing date.[9]

No election may be effective for a period before January 1, 1997.

[D] Filing Requirements

There are two filing requirements for Form 8832. First, Form 8832 must be filed with the IRS Service Center in Philadelphia. Second, a copy of the form must be attached to the LLC's federal tax return for the year in which the election is

---

[4] For example, there may be uncertainty concerning the member's liability under the law of a foreign jurisdiction, which may affect the default classification. The preamble to the check-the-box regulations states that protective elections are not prohibited. In those cases, Form 8832 should state that the election is protective.

[5] Reg. §301.7701-3(c)(1)(i).

[6] Reg. §301.7701-3(c)(2).

[7] Reg. §301.7701-3(c)(1)(iii).

[8] Reg. §301.7701-3(c)(2).

[9] Reg. §301.7701-3(c)(1)(iii).

made.[10] If the LLC is not required to file a return for that year, a copy of Form 8832 must be attached to the federal income tax or information return of each direct and indirect owner of the LLC for the tax year of the owner that includes the date on which the election was effective. An otherwise valid election will not be invalidated if the LLC or its owners fail to attach a copy of Form 8832 to the federal tax return as required. However, the nonfiling party may be subject to penalties.[11]

[E] Limitations on Change in Classification

If an LLC changes its classification, it may not elect to change its classification again during the 60-month period after the effective date of the election. An LLC may change its classification during the 60-month period in the following cases:

- More than 50 percent of the ownership interests in the LLC as of the effective date of the subsequent election are owned by persons who did not own any interest in the LLC on the filing date or on the effective date of the LLC's prior election. The Commissioner must consent to the change in classification.[12] The 60-month limitation does not apply if an LLC transfers its business to another entity.[13] The transferee may make a new election at any time consistent with the regulations.
- The LLC makes no election on the date of organization and is therefore classified under the default rules. The 60-month limitation applies only to changes in elections.
- The LLC makes an election effective on the date of formation to be classified other than under the default rules. This is not considered a change in classification.[14]
- The classification of the LLC changes as a result of a change in the number of members. A change in the number of members does not result in a new entity for purposes of the 60-month limitation on elections.[15] However, a classification election that is made at the time that the classification of the LLC would automatically change because of a change in the number of members is treated as an election classification for purposes of the 60-month rule.

EXAMPLE 1

Member A forms an LLC in which she is the sole member. The LLC is classified as a disregarded entity under the default classification rules.

---

[10] Reg. §301.7701-3(c)(1)(ii).
[11] Id.
[12] Reg. §301.7701-3(c)(1)(iv).
[13] T.D. 8697, Part C, Discussion of Comments Relating to the Elective Regime (Dec. 18, 1996).
[14] Reg. §301.7701-3(c)(1)(iv).
[15] Reg. §301.7701-3(f)(3).

However, Member A wants the LLC to be classified as a corporation. She makes an election to be classified as a corporation when the LLC is formed. Member A may make an election to change the classification at any time. She is not restricted in making an election classification change for 60 months because the initial election was effective on the date of formation. An initial election is not considered a change in classification even though it changes the classification that would otherwise apply under the default classification rules.[16]

EXAMPLE 2

Member A is the sole owner of an LLC that is classified as a disregarded entity. On January 1, 2000, Member B acquires a 50 percent interest in the LLC. Under the regulations, the LLC is automatically classified as a partnership when the number of members of an LLC that is classified as a disregarded entity is increased from one to two. However, the members want to be classified as a corporation rather than a partnership. They make an election on January 1, 2000, to be classified as a corporation. The election is a change in classification. Therefore, the LLC may not change its classification by election during the next 60 months.[17]

EXAMPLE 3

Member A and Member B form a foreign LLC on April 1, 2000. The LLC is treated as the corporation under the default classification rules. The LLC does not make an election to be classified as a partnership. Member A subsequently purchases all of the membership interests of Member B. Under the regulations, the LLC continues to be classified as a corporation. However, the LLC may elect at any time to be a disregarded entity. The 60-month limitation on new classification elections does not prevent the LLC for making an election because it has not made a prior election.[18]

EXAMPLE 4

Member A and Member B form an LLC on January 1, 1998. The LLC is a foreign LLC that is classified as a corporation under the default classification rules for foreign LLCs. On January 1, 1999, the LLC elects to be classified

---

[16] Reg. §301.7701-3(c)(1)(iv).
[17] Reg. §301.7701-3(f)(4), example 1.
[18] Reg. §301.7701-3(f)(4), example 2.

as a partnership for federal tax purposes. On June 1, 2000, Member A purchases the entire membership interest of Member B. After the purchase, the LLC can no longer be classified as a partnership since there is only one member. The LLC is automatically classified as a disregarded entity when Member A becomes the only member of the LLC. The LLC may not elect at that time to be classified as a corporation because it made a classification election within the prior 60 months. The LLC is not treated as a new entity for purposes of the 60-month rule as a result of a change in the number of members. As a result, the 60-month limitation period continues to apply to the LLC until January 1, 2004 (60 months after January 1, 1999, the effective date of the election by the LLC to be classified as a partnership). Thus, the LLC may elect to be classified as a corporation on or after January 1, 2004.[19]

[F] Change in Classification

[1] Types of Elective Changes

The following four elective changes in classification are permitted under the final check-the-box regulations:[20]

1. *A partnership elects to be taxed as a corporation.* If a partnership elects to be taxed as a corporation, the partnership is deemed to contribute all of its assets and liabilities to the corporation in return for stock in the corporation. The partnership is then deemed to have liquidated by distributing the stock in the corporation to its partners.[21]

2. *A corporation elects to be taxed as a partnership.* If a corporation elects to be taxed as a partnership, the corporation is deemed to liquidate by distributing its assets and liabilities to its shareholders. The shareholders are then treated as having contributed all of the assets and liabilities to the partnership.[22]

3. *A corporation with a single member elects to be disregarded as an entity for tax purposes.* If a corporation with a single member elects to be disregarded as an entity separate from its owner, the corporation is deemed to liquidate by distributing its assets and liabilities to its sole shareholder.

4. *A disregarded entity elects to be taxed as a corporation.* If a disregarded entity with a single member elects to be classified as a corporation, the owner of the entity is deemed to contribute all of the assets and liabilities of the

---

[19] Reg. §301.7701-3(f)(4), example 3(ii).

[20] Reg. §301.7701-3(g).

[21] The Treasury Department stated in the preamble to the proposed regulations that the regulations would not affect Rev. Rul. 84-111, 1984-2 C.B. 88, in which the IRS ruled that it would respect the particular form undertaken by the taxpayer when a partnership converts to a corporation.

[22] The Treasury Department pointed out that this characterization is consistent with Rev. Rul. 63-107, 1963-1 C.B. 71. *See* T.D. 8697, Part A, Summary of the Regulations (Dec. 18, 1996) regarding conversions from corporations to partnerships.

disregarded entity to the corporation in exchange for stock in the corporation.

[2]   Timing of Elections

The election to change the tax classification occurs at the start of the day for which the election is effective. Any transactions that are deemed to occur because of a change in classification are treated as occurring immediately before the close of the day before the effective date of the election.[23]

EXAMPLE

An LLC is classified as a corporation. It elects to be classified as a partnership on January 1, 2000. The LLC is treated as having distributed all of its assets and liabilities to its shareholders in liquidation of the LLC immediately before the close of the day on December 31, 1999. The shareholders are treated as having contributed all of the distributed assets and liabilities to a newly formed LLC that is classified as a partnership immediately before the close of the day on December 31, 1999. The members must report both transactions on December 31. Thus, the last day of the corporate LLC's tax year is December 31, and the first date of the partnership LLC's tax year is January 1.[24]

The owners of the LLC when the election is effective may be different from the owners of the LLC when the conversion transactions are deemed to occur. The election must be signed by every owner on the date of the deemed conversion transactions, even though the persons are not owners on the effective date of the change in classification.[25] The rules are designed to insure that the taxpayers who recognize the tax consequences of a conversion election approved the election. Therefore, purchasers who wish to make a classification election effective as of their first day of ownership must obtain the consent of the previous owners.

[3]   Changes in Number of Members

A change in the number of members of an LLC has the following effects on the classification of the LLC:[26]

---

[23] Reg. §301.7701-3(g)(3).
[24] Reg. §301.7701-3(g)(3).
[25] Reg. §301.7701-3(c)(2)(iii).
[26] Reg. §301.7701-3(f).

- The change in the number of members of an LLC classified as a corporation does not affect the classification of the LLC as a corporation.
- If an LLC classified as a partnership subsequently has only one member and is still treated as an entity under local law, the LLC will be disregarded as an entity separate from its owner.
- If a single-member LLC that is disregarded as an entity separate from its owner subsequently has more than one member, the LLC is classified as a partnership as of that date.

The tax consequences of a change in the number of members are discussed in Chapter 11.[27]

[4]   Tax Consequences of Elective Change

The tax treatment of an elective change in classification is based on all the relevant provisions of the Internal Revenue Code and general principles of tax law, including the step transaction doctrine.[28] The tax consequences of an elective change are identical to the tax results that would have occurred if the taxpayer had actually taken the deemed steps specified by the regulations.

For example, an LLC that changes its classification from a partnership to a corporation is subject to IRC Section 351, which deals with transfers to a corporation controlled by the transferor. Normally, there are no adverse tax consequences unless the liabilities exceed the basis of the assets at the time of conversion.[29] The tax consequences of the election to be classified as a corporation are discussed in Chapter 11.[30]

The change in classification of an LLC from a corporation to a partnership is a deemed liquidation resulting in gain or loss to the corporate LLC and the members.[31] Gain or loss is not generally recognized on the deemed transfer back to the partnership LLC.[32] There is no gain or loss recognized if a subsidiary corporation makes an elective classification change to a partnership or disregarded entity.[33]

The basis of property in a deemed contribution by a partnership electing to be taxed as a corporation includes the special basis adjustment under IRC Section 743. However, the amount of gain, if any, recognized upon the deemed contribution is determined without reference to the special basis adjustment.[34]

---

[27] See §§11.17, 11.18 infra.
[28] Reg. §301.7701-3(g)(2).
[29] IRC §357(d).
[30] See §11.06[A][5] infra.
[31] IRC §§336, 331.
[32] IRC §721.
[33] Reg. §301.7701-3(g)(2)(ii); REG-110659-00, IRS Proposed Regulations on Amending Check-the-Box Regulations for Subsidiary Corporations. The change in classification by the subsidiary corporation is treated as a tax-free liquidation under IRC §332 even though the parent corporation does not adopt a formal plan of liquidation.
[34] Reg. §1.743-2.

EXAMPLE

An LLC owns property with a common basis of $1,000. The LLC makes an election to step up the basis of the property under Section 754. A member has a special basis adjustment of $5 under Section 743(b). The LLC elects to be classified as a corporation. The LLC is deemed to contribute all of its assets and liabilities to the corporation in exchange for stock in the corporation. The LLC is then deemed to have distributed the stock to its members. If the transfer qualifies under IRC Section 351 as a transfer to a corporation controlled by the transferor, then the LLC's basis in the property includes the member's special $5 basis adjustment. The LLC, which is now classified as a corporation, has a basis in the property of $1,005. The member's basis in the membership units of the LLC, which is now classified as a corporation, will be increased by the $5 special basis adjustment.

[G] Employer Identification Number

An LLC that does not have a taxpayer identification number at the time of election must apply for one on Form SS-4 at the time of classification.[35] An LLC whose classification changes as a result of an elective change or a change in the number of members retains the same employer identification number.[36] There are the following exceptions:

- An LLC classified as a partnership that becomes a single-member LLC must use its owner's Social Security number or taxpayer identifying number.[37]
- A single-member LLC disregarded as an entity separate from its owner that is later classified as a corporation or partnership must use the employer identification number of the LLC prior to the change in classification. However, if the LLC did not have a separate employer identification number apart from the Social Security number or taxpayer identification number of the single member, then it must obtain a new employer identification number.[38]

The regulations do not prevent a single-member LLC that is classified as a disregarded entity from applying for and receiving its own taxpayer identification number. The regulations merely state that, except as otherwise provided in regulations or other guidance, the single-member LLC that is a disregarded entity must

---

[35] Reg. §301.7701-3(c)(1)(i).
[36] Reg. §301.6109-1(h).
[37] Reg. §301.6109-1(h)(2)(i).
[38] Reg. §301.6109-1(h)(2)(ii).

use the owner's taxpayer identification number for federal tax purposes, and may not use the identification number of the disregarded entity.[39]

[H]   Late Elections

An LLC that fails to file a timely classification election on Form 8832 may request the IRS to approve the late election classification. The LLC may obtain IRS approval in one of the following ways:

- *Initial classification election prior to unextended due date of first return.* The LLC may request relief from the IRS for a late initial classification election by complying with Revenue Procedure 2002-59. The LLC must apply to the IRS prior to the unextended due date for the first tax return. It must file an application on Form 8832. The form must state at the top of the document that it is "FILED PURSUANT TO REV. PROC. 2002-59." The LLC must attach a statement to the form explaining the reason for failure to file a classification election on a timely basis. The LLC is eligible to apply for relief under this revenue procedure if (a) the LLC failed to obtain the desired classification solely because of failure to file Form 8832 on a timely basis, (b) the due date for the LLC's tax return (excluding extensions) for the tax year beginning with the date of formation has not yet passed, and (c) the LLC has reasonable cause for failure to make the classification election on a timely basis.[40] There is no filing fee for requesting the late classification.
- *Initial classification election after unextended due date for the first tax return.* An LLC that is not eligible for relief under Revenue Procedure 2002-15, or that is denied relief by the IRS, may apply to the IRS for a private letter ruling. The LLC must comply with the regular procedures for obtaining a private letter ruling in such case.[41] The IRS will grant extensions for LLCs that want to elect classification as a partnership,[42] corporation,[43] or disregarded entity.[44]
- *Change in classification election.* The LLC may apply to the IRS for a private letter ruling to change a classification election after the deadline for making the initial classification election has passed. The IRS may grant an extension

---

[39] T.D. 8844, Preamble to IRS Final Regulations on Treatment of Changes in Elective Entity, 64 Fed. Reg. 66580, Nov. 29, 1999. The Preamble pointed out that Notice 99-6, 1999-3 IRB 1 provides guidance on the limited circumstances under which a disregarded entity may use its own employer identification number.

[40] Rev. Proc. 2002-59.

[41] Rev. Proc. 2002-59, I.R.B. 2002-6, §3.

[42] Ltr. Ruls. 200229035, 200115023, 200115024, 200215022, 200211025, 200209009, 200139016, 200122035, 200045015, 200045024, 200045022, 9859009.

[43] Ltr. Ruls. 200320014, 200320003, 200313025, 200310010, 200303047, 200240023, 200247016, 200247015, 200241047, 200239019, 200234051, 200225012, 200222010, 200219024, 220217020, 200211024, 200209048, 200209041, 200209040, 200205005, 200151039, 200147018-020, 200114017, 200110016, 200046031, 200024024, 199920023, 199904020-022, 199904018, 199908057.

[44] Ltr. Ruls. 200316029, 20304019, 200304018, 200251006, 200215029, 200207019, 200202052, 200202003-020, 200133038, 200133018, 200131016, 200112004, 200109033, 200109032, 200052005, 200001016, 199952068, 199901051, 9845008.

of time to make a new election, even though the LLC previously filed an election to be classified in a different manner.[45] Revenue Procedure 2002-59 does not apply to a subsequent election to change the classification of an LLC.[46]

§5.05 PUBLICLY TRADED LLCs

A publicly traded LLC is normally classified as a corporation for federal tax purposes.[1] There are the following exceptions:

- The LLC has fewer than 100 investors.
- The LLC has more than 100 investors, and at least 90 percent of its income is passive-type income.[2] Qualifying passive income includes interest; dividends; capital gains; income from investments in stocks, securities, or currencies; and certain other income. Most common investments of private investment LLCs are permissible and constitute qualifying passive income. However, it is unclear whether income from notional contracts and from derivative instruments and payments with respect to securities loans are permissible investments.[3]
- The membership units are issued in a transaction that is not registered under the Securities Act of 1933, and the LLC has fewer than 500 members or had an initial offering price of less than $20,000.[4]
- The sum of capital and profits interests sold or disposed of during the year is less than 5 percent of the total capital or profits of the LLC.[5]

§5.06 TERMINATION OF LLC

An LLC that is classified as a partnership terminates if there is a sale or exchange of 50 percent or more of the total interests in the LLC's capital and profits within a 12-month period.[1] The LLC is treated as transferring its assets to a new LLC. The new entity is classified as a partnership, but may elect to change its classification thereafter.[2]

---

[45] Ltr. Ruls. 200133038, 9740011.
[46] Rev. Proc. 2002-15, I.R.B. 2002-6, §3 (last sentence).
§5.05 [1] IRC §7704; Reg. §301.7701-2(b)(7).
[2] IRC §7704(c).
[3] *See* BNA Daily Tax Rep. at G-1 (June 14, 1996).
[4] IRS Notice 88-75, 1988-2 C.B. 386.
[5] *Id.*
§5.06 [1] IRC §708(b)(1)(B).
[2] Reg. §301.7701-3(e).

§5.07   TRANSITION RULES FOR PRIOR PERIODS

An LLC's claimed classification for periods before January 1, 1997, will be respected, notwithstanding provisions in the new regulations prohibiting that classification, if all of the following requirements are met:[1]

1. The LLC is not one of the business entities described in regulations that are per se corporations;[2]
2. The LLC had a reasonable basis[3] for its claimed classification (for example, if the LLC claimed classification as a partnership, it should have a reasonable argument that it lacked at least two of the four corporate characteristics under the four-factor test of the prior regulations);
3. The LLC and all members of the LLC recognized the federal tax consequences of any change in the LLC's classification during the 60 months before January 1, 1997; and
4. The LLC's classification was not under audit on May 8, 1996, the date the regulations were proposed.

There are special transition rules for foreign LLCs.[4]

§5.08   RULING REQUESTS

The LLC must comply with Revenue Procedure 95-10[1] in order to obtain an IRS ruling on the classification of an LLC. The IRS issued the check-the-box regulations on the classification of LLCs so that ruling requests will generally not be necessary. However, it will still issue classification rulings under the check-the-box regulations.[2]

§5.09   STATE TAX CLASSIFICATION

The following chart summarizes the state tax classification of limited liability companies.[1]

---

§5.07   [1] Reg. §301.7701-3(f)(2).
[2] Reg. §301.7701-2(b)(1), (3), (4), (5), (6), (7).
[3] Reasonable basis is determined under IRC §6662.
[4] *See* §5.03 *supra*.
§5.08   [1] 1995-1 C.B. 501. This revenue procedure lists the documents and information that must be submitted to the IRS in order to obtain a classification ruling. The revenue procedure was issued prior to the check-the-box regulations. The references in the revenue procedure to the four-factor classification test under the old regulations and the requirements for meeting those tests are now outdated.
[2] Ltr. Rul. 200214016.
§5.09   [1] *See* Chapter 23 *infra* for discussion of state tax classification.

Summary of State Tax Classification of LLCs

State	Follows Federal	Always Taxed as Corporation	Always Taxed as Partnership	Determination Based on State Law
Alabama	x			
Alaska				$100/year tax
Arizona	x			
Arkansas	x			
California	x			
Colorado	x			
Connecticut	x			
Delaware	x			
D.C.	x			
Florida	x			Taxed as a corporation prior to July 1, 1998
Georgia	x			
Hawaii	x			
Idaho	x			
Illinois	x			
Indiana	x			
Iowa	x			
Kansas	x			
Kentucky	x			
Louisiana	x			
Maine	x			
Maryland	x			
Massachusetts	x			
Michigan	x			LLC subject to the single business tax
Minnesota	x			
Mississippi	x			
Missouri	x			
Montana	x			
Nebraska	x			

State	Follows Federal	Always Taxed as Corporation	Always Taxed as Partnership	Determination Based on State Law
Nevada				No state income tax
New Hampshire				An LLC is taxed as a separate legal entity regardless of its classification for federal tax purposes. If the LLC has foreign members, then there is an apportionment formula. Members of the LLC are not taxed on their distributive shares of income.
New Jersey	x			
New Mexico	x			
New York	x			
North Carolina	x			
North Dakota	x			
Ohio	x			
Oklahoma	x			
Oregon	x			
Pennsylvania		x		Always classified as a corporation for franchise and excise tax purposes; state follows federal classification for corporate net income and personal tax purposes
Rhode Island	x			
South Carolina	x			
South Dakota				No state income tax
Tennessee				LLC subject to franchise tax

State	Follows Federal	Always Taxed as Corporation	Always Taxed as Partnership	Determination Based on State Law
Texas		x		LLC subject to franchise tax
Utah	x			
Vermont	x			
Virginia	x			
Washington				No state income tax
West Virginia	x			
Wisconsin	x			
Wyoming				No state income tax

§5.10   LAW BEFORE 1997

Before 1997, LLCs received the favorable tax status of partnerships[1] and were not taxed as corporations unless they possessed more corporate characteristics than noncorporate characteristics.[2] A corporation had the following characteristics:[3]

- Associates
- Objective to carry on business and to divide the gains from the business
- Continuity of life
- Centralization of management
- Limited liability
- Free transferability of interests

The corporate characteristics of associates and an objective to carry on business and divide the gains were disregarded because they were also characteristics of a partnership.[4] The four other characteristics were common to corporations, but not to partnerships.

Therefore, the determination of whether an LLC was taxed as a corporation or a partnership depended on whether there was continuity of life, centralized management, limited liability, and free transferability of interests. The LLC was taxed as a partnership if it possessed only one or two of these characteristics. It was taxed as a corporation if it possessed three or four of these characteristics.[5]

Almost all LLCs had the corporate characteristic of limited liability, since LLC

---

§5.10   [1] The main tax benefit is that income, gain, and losses pass through to the members. There is a single tax at the member level. There is no corporate or LLC tax.

[2] Reg. §301.7701-2(a)(3).

[3] *Id.*

[4] Reg. §301.7701-2(a)(2).

[5] Rev. Rul. 93-38, 1993-1 C.B. 233.

members were not personally liable for the debts and obligations of the LLC.[6] Therefore, the LLC had to lack two of the remaining three corporate characteristics to be taxed as a partnership.

The Treasury Department proposed regulations regarding the classification of LLCs in 1980.[7] These proposed regulations were later withdrawn.[8] The Service issued a revenue procedure in 1995 regarding the classification of an LLC for ruling purposes.[9] The revenue procedure based its analysis on the traditional four-factor tests.

Before 1997, there were two main types of statutes relating to the classification of LLCs. These were commonly referred to as "bulletproof" and "flexible" statutes. In a state with a bulletproof statute, an LLC was always classified as a partnership for federal tax purposes regardless of the optional provisions chosen by the LLC in the articles of organization or operating agreement. In a state with a flexible statute, the organizers could draft the organizational documents so that the LLC was classified as a corporation for federal tax purposes.

Some states had flexible bulletproof or default bulletproof statutes. The laws in such states contained default provisions that could be varied by agreement among the members. The LLC was automatically classified as a partnership if the default provisions were chosen. The LLC was classified as a corporation if the default provisions were modified by the members.

The IRS issued the following revenue rulings and private letter rulings on the classification of LLCs under the old law before issuance of the check-the-box regulations.

IRS Rulings on LLC Classification

State	Rev. Rul.	Pvt. Ltr. Rul.	IRS Tax Classification
Alabama	94-5		Partnership or corporation depending on tax attributes
Alaska	None	None	
Arizona	93-93		Partnership or corporation depending on tax attributes
		9321047	Partnership
California	None	None	
Colorado	93-6		Partnership
Connecticut	94-79		Partnership or corporation depending on tax attributes
		9611041	Partnership

---

[6] See §5.10[C] infra. A few states allow an LLC to waive limited liability.

[7] Prop. Reg. §301.7701-2, 45 Fed. Reg. 75,709 (Nov. 17, 1980).

[8] IRS News Release IR-82-145 (Dec. 16, 1982).

[9] Rev. Proc. 95-10, 1995-1 C.B. 501.

State	Rev. Rul.	Pvt. Ltr. Rul.	IRS Tax Classification
Delaware	93-38		Partnership or corporation depending on tax attributes
		9308027 9335032 9415005 9416025 9416026 9507004 9602012 9609029	Partnership
District of Columbia	None	None	
Florida	93-53		Partnership or corporation depending on tax attributes
		8937010 9010027 9029019 9030013 9119029 9443018	Partnership
Georgia	None	None	
Hawaii	None	None	
Idaho	None	None	
Illinois	93-49		Partnership or corporation depending on tax attributes
		9325039 9333032	Partnership
Indiana		9422034 9647028 9647029 9647030 9647031	Partnership
Iowa		9644059	Partnership

State	Rev. Rul.	Pvt. Ltr. Rul.	IRS Tax Classification
Kansas	94-30		Partnership or corporation depending on tax attributes
		9625013 9625014 9625015 9625016 9625017 9625018 9625023 9625024	Partnership
Kentucky	None	None	
Louisiana	94-5		Partnership or corporation depending on tax attributes
		9404021 9409014 9412030 9419016 9606006 9622007	Partnership
Maine	None	None	
Maryland		9501033	Partnership
Massachusetts	None	None	
Michigan	None	None	
Minnesota	None	None	
Mississippi	None	None	
Missouri	None	None	
Montana	None	None	
Nebraska	None	None	
Nevada	93-30		Partnership or corporation depending on tax attributes
		9227033	Partnership
New Hampshire	None	None	

State	Rev. Rul.	Pvt. Ltr. Rul.	IRS Tax Classification
New Jersey	94-51		Partnership or corporation depending on tax attributes
New Mexico	None	None	
New York	None	None	Partnership or corporation depending on tax attributes
North Carolina	None	None	
North Dakota		9425013	Partnership
Ohio	None	None	
Oklahoma	93-92		Partnership or corporation depending on tax attributes
Oregon	None	None	
Pennsylvania	None	None	
Rhode Island	93-81		Partnership or corporation depending on tax attributes
South Carolina	None	None	
South Dakota	95-9		Partnership
Tennessee	None	None	
Texas		9210019 9218078 9242025 9510037 9520036 9520046	Partnership
Utah	93-91		Partnership or corporation depending on tax attributes
		9210019 9218078 9219022 9226035 9242025 9313009	Partnership

State	Rev. Rul.	Pvt. Ltr. Rul.	IRS Tax Classification
Utah (continued)		9320019 9320045 9321070 9325048 9443024	
Vermont	None	None	
Virginia	93-5		Partnership
Washington	None	None	
West Virginia	93-50	9308039	Partnership
Wisconsin	None	None	
Wyoming	88-76	8106082	Partnership
Jurisdiction Not Identified		8304138 8828022 9215009	Corporation
		39798 6707214880A 7817129 7935051 8003072 8004010 8012080 8104129 8304138 9001018 9010028 9029019 9035041 9038027 9052039 9119029 9147017 9210039 9216004	Partnership
Brazilian Limitada		7817129 8003072 8019112 8401001 9526029	Partnership

State	Rev. Rul.	Pvt. Ltr. Rul.	IRS Tax Classification
Brazilian *Limitada* (continued)		7814012 7828063 7831021 7928063 7941054 8019112	Corporation
Chilean *Limitada*		7936050	Corporation
Columbian SRL		35294	Corporation
French SAS		9524022	Partnership
German GmbH	77-214	8221136 8309062 9010028 9341018	Partnership
	93-4	7908004 7937054 7952027 8114095	Corporation
		7747089	Proprietorship
		8436030	No opinion expressed
Greek LLC		7843006	Corporation
Hong Kong LLC		7935046	No opinion expressed
Italian SRL		7841008	Corporation
Mexican *Limitada*		7108110470A	Partnership
Portuguese LLC		7826023	Corporation
Saudi Arabian LLC		7921079 8006068 8007029	Partnership
		7926034	Corporation
Spanish *Limitada*		8106082	Partnership
U.K. LLC		9002056 9152009 9306008	Partnership

As a result of the check-the-box regulations, the IRS determined that 37 revenue rulings and 1 revenue procedure issued prior to 1995, a majority of which dealt with the entity classification of LLCs, are now obsolete.[81]

---

[81] Rev. Rul. 98-37, 1998-32 IRB 5.

6

Contributions

§6.01   CONTRIBUTIONS TO LLC

[A]   *LLC Classified as Partnership*

There a number of tax consequences of forming an LLC that is classified as a partnership and contributing property to the LLC. These consequences are discussed below.

[1]   Gain or Loss Recognition

An LLC and its members do not recognize gain or loss when the members contribute property to the LLC in exchange for membership interests[1] unless any of the following apply:

- The LLC is an investment company.[2] The investment company rules are discussed in Chapter 20.
- There is a net decrease in liabilities of a member exceeding that member's basis in the assets transferred.[3]
- There is a disguised sale.[4]
- The member contributes services to the LLC in exchange for a capital interest[5] or a profits interest that does not meet IRS guidelines.[6]
- The LLC acquires stock of a corporate member in exchange for property.[7]
- The member receives property other than a membership interest (boot) in exchange for the contribution.[8]

---

§6.01   [1] Ltr. Ruls. 200125013, 200123035, 9713007, 9701032, 9409016, 9409014, 9404021, 9331010, 9321047, 9313009, 8106082 (*citing* IRC §721(a)).

[2] Ltr. Ruls. 9751048, 9331010 (*citing* IRC §721(b)).

[3] Ltr. Ruls. 9604014, 9313009 (*citing* IRC §752 and Reg. §1.752-1(f)). *See* §6.01[A][2] *infra*.

[4] IRC §707(a)(2)(B). This is likely to result if a member contributes appreciated property to an LLC and within two years thereafter receives cash or other non-like-kind property from the LLC. *See* §6.05 *infra*.

[5] Reg. §1.721-1(b)(1). *See* §6.04[A] *infra*.

[6] Rev. Proc. 93-27, 1993-1 C.B. 343. *See* §6.04[B] *infra*.

[7] Notice 89-37, 1989-1 C.B. 679.

[8] The receipt of property other than a membership interest is treated as a distribution under IRC §731, or as consideration received in a disguised sale under IRC §707(a)(2)(B).

The contribution of a long-term leasehold interest to an LLC in exchange for a membership interest is nontaxable.[9] No gain or loss is recognized if a member contributes only cash to the LLC in exchange for a membership interest.[10]

[2]   Contribution of Property Subject to Liabilities

A member recognizes gain on the contribution of property to an LLC subject to liabilities in excess of basis if the net liability shift to the other members exceeds the contributing member's basis in the property.[11]

The basic rules are set forth in Section 752 of the Code. IRC Section 752(a) treats an increase in a member's share of LLC liabilities as a contribution of money by the member to the LLC. The deemed money contribution increases the member's basis in membership interest.[12] IRC Section 752(b) treats a decrease in a member's share of LLC liabilities as a distribution of money to the member. The deemed distribution decreases the member's basis in the membership interest.[13] A money distribution in excess of basis results in taxable gain.[14]

The same rules apply when a member contributes property to an LLC that is subject to a liability, or for which the member is personally liable.[15] The amount of liabilities assumed by the LLC, and the amount of other liabilities encumbering property contributed to the LLC,[16] is treated as a money distribution to the member. The amount of liabilities that the LLC allocates to the member after the contribution under the recourse and nonrecourse debt rules is treated as a money contribution.[17] However, there is a netting process. Only the net amount of liability increase or decrease for each member is treated as a money contribution or distribution. There is no gain to the contributing member unless the net decrease in liabilities as a result of the contribution exceeds the contributing member's basis in membership units.[18]

EXAMPLE

Member B contributes a building to an LLC with an adjusted basis of $1 million. The property is subject to recourse debt of $10 million. The LLC agrees to pay the debt in full. However, the member remains personally

---

[9] Ltr. Rul. 199915040.

[10] Ltr. Ruls. 201123035 (Ruling 2), 9713007 (*citing* IRC §721).

[11] Reg. §1.752-1(f), (g) Example 1; Ltr. Rul. 9751048.

[12] IRC §722.

[13] IRC §733(1).

[14] IRC §731(a)(1).

[15] eg. §1.752-1(f), (g) Example 1.

[16] Reg. §1.752-1(e).

[17] The LLC must allocate the recourse liabilities to the members who are liable on the recourse debt. *See* §9.03[B] *infra*. Generally, the LLC must allocate the nonrecourse liabilities to the members based on each member's percentage interest in the LLC. *See* §9.03[C] *infra*.

[18] Reg. §1.752-1(f), (g) Example 1.

liable for repayment to the bank if the LLC defaults. Member B receives an initial basis in the LLC of $1 million equal to the adjusted basis of property contributed to the LLC. Member B's individual liabilities decrease by $10 million. This is treated as a money distribution. At the same time, however, Member B's share of LLC liabilities increases by $10 million. The LLC must allocate the entire recourse liability to Member B for basis purposes since Member B is personally liable to the bank. This is treated as a money contribution. The net amount of the money contribution and distribution is zero. Therefore, Member B's initial basis in the LLC is equal to the $1 million basis for the contributed property.[19] There is no taxable gain as result of the contribution since there is no net money distribution to Member B in excess of his basis in the membership units.

[3]   Member's Basis in Membership Interest

A member's basis in the membership interest is determined under one the following methods:

- general rule;
- alternative asset method; or
- alternative capital account method.

These basis rules are discussed in detail in Chapter 9.

[4]   LLC Basis in Contributed Assets

The LLC's basis in the contributed assets equals the members' adjusted bases in the assets immediately prior to the contribution.[20] The LLC takes a transferred basis in the contributed assets. The liabilities assumed by the LLC have no effect on the basis as a result of the Tax Reform Act of 1984 which repealed the last part of IRC Section 723, and provided the basis would only be increased by the amount of gain recognized by the member under IRC Section 721(b) on contribution of assets to the LLC. This creates a potential for double taxation if a member contributes appreciated property to the LLC. First, the member is taxed on the sale of the membership interest. The membership interest is likely to have a fair market value higher than the adjusted basis of the membership interest if the member contributes appreciated property to the LLC. Second, the LLC is taxed on the gain (which flows through to the members) if the LLC later sells the property. The

---

[19] Reg. §1.752-1(g) Example 1.
[20] Ltr. Ruls. 200125013, 9720008013, 9719015, 9719019029, 9331919, 9331010, 8106082 (*citing* IRC §723).

LLC may avoid double taxation by making an election under Section 754 of the Code.[21]

The LLC's basis in its assets is generally referred to as the "inside basis." The member's basis in the membership interest is generally referred to as the "outside basis." Upon formation of the LLC, the inside basis is generally equal to the outside basis, since the LLC receives a carryover basis for the assets and the member receives a basis in the membership interest equal to the cash and adjusted basis of assets contributed. The inside basis and outside basis may become different under a number of circumstances.[22]

[5]   Holding Period

There is a tacking of the holding period for certain property contributed to the LLC.[23] The LLC's holding period for capital assets and Section 1231 assets contributed to the LLC includes a member's holding period for those assets prior to contribution.[24]

A member's holding period for the membership interest includes the holding period of capital assets and Section 1231 assets that the member contributes to the LLC in exchange for a membership interest.[25] There is no tacking of the holding period for contributions of property other than capital assets or Section 1231 assets. The member's holding period for a membership interest received in exchange for the contribution of such other assets commences on the day after the contribution. The member will have a fragmented holding period for the membership interest when the member contributes a combination of assets. Thus, if a member contributed long-term capital gain assets to an LLC in exchange for 50 percent of his membership units, and sold all his membership units less than one year thereafter, then 50 percent of the gain on sale would be long-term capital gain. The balance of the gain would be short-term capital gain.[26]

The holding period of a membership interest acquired by purchase commences on the date of purchase.[27]

---

[21] See §15.08 infra.

[22] See §9.01[B] infra. The LLC and the members may eliminate the disparity between inside and outside basis in such cases by making an election to adjust the basis of LLC assets under IRC §754.

[23] Ltr. Rul. 9701032 (citing Rev. Rul. 84-52, 1984-1 C.B. 157).

[24] IRC §§1223(2), 723; Reg. §1.723-1.

[25] IRC §1223(1).

[26] Reg. §1.1(h)-1(f), Example 5(iv). In such case, the long-term capital gain is determined by (a) computing the total gain that the member realized on sale of the membership interest (amount realized less adjusted basis in membership interest), (b) reducing that gain by the portion of gain treated as ordinary income (e.g., the member's share of gain under IRC §751 from unrealized receivables and inventory items that would be allocated to the member if the LLC sold those items in a taxable transaction), and (c) multiplying such amount by the percentage of the member's capital contribution attributable to capital gain assets or Section 1231 assets that have a one-year holding period (combined holding period of member and LLC) at the time of sale of the membership interest.

[27] Rev. Rul. 67-65, 1967-1 C.B. 168.

[6] Depreciation and Depreciation Recapture

The LLC is required to use the same method and period of depreciation for contributed property as used by the contributing member.[28]

There is no depreciation recapture income when a member contributes property to an LLC.[29] The member's adjusted basis in the property carries over to the LLC.[30] The property is subject to depreciation recapture when the LLC sells or disposes of the property at a later date.[31]

The member's share of depreciation recapture on sale of the property is equal to the lesser of (a) the member's share of total gain from the disposition of the property under the normal provisions of the operating agreement, or (b) the member's share of depreciation that was previously allocated to the member, including any depreciation allowed or allowable to the member before the property was contributed to the LLC. The LLC must allocate to the other members any depreciation recapture that cannot be allocated to a member because his share of gain from the disposition of the property is less than his share of depreciation recapture. This additional depreciation recapture is allocated among such other members in proportion to their relative shares of total gain from the disposition of the property.[32]

[7] Investment Tax Credit Recapture

There is no recapture of investment tax credits on a contribution to an LLC of property for which an investment credit was taken (currently the rehabilitation credit, the energy credit, and the reforestation credit) if the following conditions are met:[33]

- the LLC retains the property as investment credit property in its trade or business; and
- the contributing member retains a substantial interest in the LLC.

[8] Accounts Receivable

A member is not taxed on the transfer of accounts receivable to an LLC.[34] The LLC will recognize taxable income when it collects the receivables. The taxable income is equal to the amount collected, less the basis for the receivables (which

---

[28] IRC §168(i)(7).

[29] IRC §§1245(b)(3), 1250(d)(3); Reg. 1.1245-4(c)(1), (4), Examples (2)-(3), 1.1250-3(c)(1), (2)(vi).

[30] IRC §723.

[31] Reg. §§1.1245-2(c)(2), 1.1250-3(c)(3).

[32] Reg. §1.1245-2(e)(2)(i)-(iii). *See also* Reg. §1.1245-2(e)(2)(iii), Example (3) regarding allocation of depreciation recapture on sale of property in which there was both pre-contribution and post-contribution depreciation.

[33] IRC §50(a)(4) (flush paragraph).

[34] Rev. Rul. 80-198, 1980-2 C.B. 133.

is zero in the case of a contributing member using the cash method of accounting). The LLC must allocate all of the taxable income to the contributing member to the extent that the value of the receivables on the date of contribution exceeds the member's basis in the receivables.[35] The value of the receivables is likely to be far less than their face value, especially if there is a long period of time between the billing and collection dates or if there are collection problems associated with the receivables.

The LLC receives a basis in the receivables equal to the contributing member's basis at the time of the contribution.

[9]   Personal Use Property

A member's contribution of personal use property to an LLC is nontaxable. The LLC receives a basis in the property equal to the lower of the property's fair market value at the time of contribution or the contributing member's adjusted basis.[36]

[10]   Patent Rights

The holder of a patent may transfer patent rights to an LLC that is classified as a partnership.   The LLC is treated as any other partnership for purposes of IRC Section 1235 and regulations thereunder.[37] After the transfer, the holder of the patent rights retains his status as a "holder" for purposes of IRC Section 1235. Thus, assuming the other requirements of IRC Section 1235 are met, the member's share of gain recognized by the LLC on disposition of an interest in the patent qualifies as long-term capital gain.[38]

[11]   Installment Obligations

The contribution of an installment obligation to an LLC is not a disposition resulting in taxable gain to the member.[39] The LLC must continue to report the gross profits on the installment method as payments are received.[40] The LLC must allocate the gross profit to the contributing member to the extent that the value of the installment note exceeded its basis at the time of contribution.[41] Any additional gross profit may be allocated to all the members in accordance with the operating agreement.

---

[35] IRC §704(c).
[36] Au v. Commissioner, 40 T.C. 264 (1964), *aff'd per curiam*, 330 F.2d 1008 (9th Cir. 1964).
[37] Ltr. Rul. 200135015, *citing* Reg. §1.1235-2(d)(2).
[38] Ltr. Rul. 200135015.
[39] Reg. §1.453-9(c)(2).
[40] Reg. §§1.721-1(a), 1.453-9(c)(2).
[41] IRC §704(c).

[B]   LLC Classified as Corporation

A number of tax consequences flow from forming an LLC that is classified as a corporation and contributing property to the LLC. They are discussed below.

[1]   Member's Recognition of Gain or Loss

Members do not recognize gain or loss upon the contribution of property to the LLC, whether or not additional shares are issued.[42] The contributing members must have 80 percent control of the LLC and otherwise comply with the requirements of IRC Section 351. The same rule applies to foreign LLCs, subject to certain requirements and restrictions.[43] The shareholders do not recognize gain or loss when the corporation assumes liabilities if the liabilities do not exceed the basis of assets contributed.[44] Gain is recognized if the shareholders receive cash or other nonstock property in the exchange.[45]

[2]   Member's Basis in Membership Interest

A member's basis in his membership interest is the same as the basis of the assets transferred to the LLC in exchange, decreased by the amount of liabilities assumed by the LLC[46] and the liabilities to which the transferred assets are subject,[47] and increased by the amount of any gain recognized if the shareholder receives cash or other nonstock property in the exchange.[48] If an LLC shareholder already owns stock and makes an additional capital contribution, the basis in the stock is increased by the basis of property contributed to the capital of the LLC.[49]

[3]   Member's Holding Period

A member's holding period in the stock includes the period during which the shareholders held the assets prior to the transfer, provided the assets were held as capital assets or Section 1231 assets on the date of the exchange.[50]

---

[42] Ltr. Ruls. 8029031, 8011038, 7937054, 7821084 (*citing* IRC §351(a)). If no shares are issued, the capital contribution to the LLC is treated as a contribution in constructive exchange for additional shares under IRC §351.

[43] Ltr. Ruls. 8029031, 8023029, 7935046, 7843099, 7833112 (*citing* IRC §367(a)); Ltr. Ruls. 8029031, 8011038 (*citing* IRC §367(c)(2) and Rev. Rul 77-449, 1977-2 C.B. 110).

[44] Ltr. Rul. 7937054 (*citing* IRC §357).

[45] Ltr. Rul. 7935046 (*citing* IRC §351(b)).

[46] Ltr. Ruls. 7937054, 7843099 (*citing* IRC §358(a), (d)).

[47] Ltr. Rul. 7833112 (*citing* IRC §358(a)(1)).

[48] Ltr. Rul. 7935046 (*citing* IRC §358(a)(1)).

[49] Ltr. Ruls. 8029031, 80111038 (*citing* IRC §358(a)).

[50] Ltr. Ruls. 7937054, 7935046 (*citing* IRC §1223(1)).

[4]   LLC Gain Recognition

The LLC does not recognize gain upon the contribution to capital in exchange for the issuance of stock, or if no stock is issued.[51]

[5]   LLC Basis in Contributed Property

The LLC's basis in the contributed property is the same basis that the LLC shareholders had in the property immediately prior to the capital contribution.[52]

[6]   LLC Holding Period for Contributed Property

The LLC's holding period for the property received includes the period during which it was held by the shareholders.[53]

§6.02   CONVERSION FROM OTHER ENTITIES TO LLC

An LLC may be formed by the transfer of assets from a general partnership, limited partnership, corporation, or other entity.[1] These conversions are discussed in Chapter 11.

§6.03   CONTRIBUTION OF APPRECIATED AND DEPRECIATED PROPERTY

Generally, an LLC must make special allocations if a member contributes property to the LLC that has a book value that is different from its tax basis.[1] This property is referred to as "Section 704(c) property."[2] The special allocations must also be made if the LLC revalues its own property when a new member contributes other property to the LLC.[3] These allocations are referred to as "reverse Section 704(c)

---

[51] Ltr. Ruls. 8029031, 8011038, 7937054, 7843099 (*citing* IRC §1032(a)).
[52] Ltr. Ruls. 8029031, 8011038, 7937054, 7843099 (*citing* IRC §362(a)).
[53] Ltr. Rul. 7937054 (*citing* IRC §1223(2)).
§6.02   [1] *See* Chapter 11 *infra* for discussion of the tax consequences of a conversion.
§6.03   [1] *See* §8.03 *infra* for discussion of LLC allocations related to contributed property.
[2] IRC §704(c).
[3] Ltr. Rul. 199909045.

allocations," since they apply to noncontributed property.[4] There are three principal special allocations.

1. The built-in gain or loss must be allocated to the contributing member when the property is sold. The special allocation must be made for tax purposes, not book or accounting purposes.

EXAMPLE

An LLC has two members, who share equally in profits and losses. Member A contributes $10,000 cash to the LLC. Member B contributes nondepreciable property with a tax basis of $2,000 and a fair market value/capital account value of $10,000. The built-in gain is $8,000 (the difference between the capital account value and the tax basis when the property is contributed). The property is sold 10 years later for $12,000. The LLC must allocate the built-in gain of $8,000 to Member B for tax purposes. The LLC must allocate the remaining $2,000 of gain equally between members A and B.

2. The LLC must allocate tax depreciation to the noncontributing members in an amount that is at least equal to their book depreciation allocations (up to the amount of actual depreciation). This rule gives the noncontributing members the same depreciation deductions they would have received if the contributing members had contributed property with a tax basis equal to the assigned capital account value.

EXAMPLE

An LLC has two members, who share equally in profits and losses. Member A contributed $10,000 cash to the LLC. Member B contributed property with a tax basis of $2,000 and a fair market value/capital account value of $10,000. The property has a remaining depreciation life of 10 years. For book purposes, the LLC takes a depreciation deduction of $1,000 per year (10 percent of the book value). The LLC allocates $500 of book depreciation to each member. For tax purposes, the LLC takes a depreciation deduction of $200 per year (10 percent of the $2,000 tax basis). The LLC must allocate $500 of tax depreciation to Member A, which is equal to her book depreciation. However, since the LLC has only $200 of tax depreciation for the year, the

---

[4] Reg. §1.704-3(a)(6).

LLC may allocate only $200 of tax depreciation to Member A. No depreciation is allocated to Member B.

3. The LLC must comply with the anti-abuse provisions applicable to contributed property. These anti-abuse provisions are referred to as the "mixing bowl problem." They apply when one member contributes appreciated or depreciated property to the LLC and the LLC distributes property to members within a certain period of time thereafter.[5]

The special allocations for contributed property are discussed in greater detail in Chapter 8.[6]

§6.04 CONTRIBUTION OF SERVICES

A member may recognize compensation income upon the contribution of services to an LLC in exchange for an LLC interest. IRC Section 721 provides that a member does not recognize gain or loss upon the contribution of property to an LLC. However, this nonrecognition provision does not apply, since a contribution of services is not considered a contribution of "property."

The tax consequences are different depending on whether a member receives a capital interest or a profits interest in exchange for the contribution of services.

[A] Contribution of Services for a Capital Interest

A member recognizes compensation income upon receipt of an interest in the capital of an LLC in exchange for services if the other members in the LLC give up any part of their interest in capital.[1] The amount of income recognized is the fair market value of the capital interest received.

The date of recognition is the date that the property is substantially vested (i.e., the membership interest is transferable or is no longer subject to a substantial risk of forfeiture).[2] The capital interest is subject to a substantial risk of forfeiture and is not taxable when issued if the member is required to perform substantial additional services in order to receive the capital interest.[3]

A service member is not considered a partner or member of the LLC for tax purposes until the membership interest vests.[4] Presumably, payments to the

---

[5] See §6.05 *infra* for discussion of the three principal anti-abuse provisions.

[6] See §8.03 *infra*.

§6.04 [1] Reg. §1.721-1(b)(1); Mark IV Pictures, Inc. v. Commissioner, 969 F.2d 669 (8th Cir. 1992); ZuHone v. Commissioner, 55 T.C.M. 533 (1988); Larson v. Commissioner, 55 T.C.M. 1637 (1988); Hensel Phelps Constr. Co., 74 T.C. 939 (1980), *aff'd*, 703 F.2d 485 (10th Cir. 1983); Schneider & O'Conner, LLC *Capital Shifts: Avoiding Problems When Applying Corporate Principles*, 92 J. Tax. 1, 13 (Jan. 2000).

[2] Schulman v. Commissioner, 93 T.C. 623 (1989).

[3] IRC §83(c).

[4] Reg. §1.83-1(a)(1).

member are treated as personal service income rather than a distributive share of income. However, many LLCs ignore the regulations and treat the forfeitable membership interest as any other membership interest.

A member who receives a capital interest that is subject to a substantial risk of forfeiture may make an election under Section 83(b) of the Internal Revenue Code to be taxed immediately. The compensation income recognized is equal to the value of the membership interest received, without reduction in value for the risk of forfeiture or other restrictions on transfer except those that never lapse. The election must be made within 30 days after receipt of the interest. It may be made only if the membership interest has a readily ascertainable fair market value.

[B] Contribution of Services for a Profits Interest

Some courts have determined that a contribution of services for a profits interest is taxable.[5] Other courts have reached the opposite conclusion.[6] The IRS no longer treats the contribution of services for a profits interest as a taxable event unless one of the following is true:

- The profits interest relates to a substantially certain and predictable stream of income from LLC assets; (e.g., the LLC owns only triple net lease property);
- The member disposes of the profits interest within two years of receipt; or
- The profits interest is a limited partnership interest in a publicly traded LLC.[7]

A member who receives an interest in profits in exchange for services is not required to make an election under Section 83(b), even if the profits interest is substantially nonvested.[8] Neither the grant of the interest nor the event that causes the interest to become substantially vested is a taxable event if:[9]

- The LLC and the service provider treat the service provider as the owner of the membership interest from the date of grant.
- The service provider takes into account the distributive share of membership income, gain, loss, deduction, and credit associated with the membership interest for the entire period during which the member has the interest.
- On grant of the interest and when the interest becomes substantially vested, neither the LLC nor the members deduct any amount as wages, compensation, or otherwise for the fair market value of the interest.

---

[5] Diamond v. Commissioner 492 F.2d 286 (7th Cir. 1972).

[6] Campbell v. Commissioner, 943 F.2d 815 (8th Cir. 1991); Kabor v. Commissioner, 88-2 U.S.T.C. ¶9477 (C.D. Cal. 1987); Hale v. Commissioner, 24 T.C.M. 1497 (1965). *See also* St. John v. United States, 84-1 U.S.T.C. ¶9158, 53 A.F.T.R.2d 84-718 (C.D. Ill. 1983); S. Frost, *Receipt of Capital and Profits Interests Continues to Have Uncertain Tax Consequences,* 75 J. Taxn. 38 (July 1991).

[7] Rev. Proc. 93-27, 1993-2 C.B. 343.

[8] Rev. Proc. 2001-43, I.R.B. 2001-34, Sec. 3.

[9] Rev. Proc. 2001-43, I.R.B. 2001-34, Sec. 4.

- All other conditions of Revenue Procedure 93-27 discussed above are satisfied.

However, it may still be advisable to make a Section 83(b) election on the date of grant, showing the value of the profit interest as zero consistent with Revenue Procedure 93-27. If there is a disposition of the interest within two years after the date of grant, the taxpayer would presumably recognize ordinary income rather than capital gain. However, if the member made a Section 83(b) election on the date of grant, then the gain on disposition would be capital gain.[10]

[C]   *Consequences of Income Recognition*

There are the following tax consequences if a member recognizes income upon receipt of a capital or profits interest in exchange for services:

- The service member receiving the membership interest recognizes compensation income.[11]
- The service member who is taxed is treated as having contributed the compensation back to the LLC in exchange for the membership interest.
- The service member receives a basis in the membership interest equal to the compensation income recognized.[12]
- The LLC, as it existed before the admission of the new member, recognizes gain to the extent it gives the new member an interest in appreciated property. The gain is equal to the appreciation in the property that is used to satisfy the obligation of the LLC.[13]
- The LLC, as it existed before the admission of the new member, receives a deduction under IRC §83(h) when the contributing member recognizes ordinary income. However, the LLC is not entitled to a deduction if the services are capital in nature, nondeductible capital expenditures under IRC §263, or syndication expenses.
- The basis to the LLC in its assets is increased by the amount of appreciation in the capital interest transferred to the new member and decreased by the amount of depreciation in the capital interest transferred. The LLC is treated as having transferred an undivided interest in its assets to the service member who receives a basis equal to its fair market value. The LLC receives a transferred basis for the undivided interest in the property when the member transfers the interest in assets back to the LLC in exchange for the membership interest. The LLC's basis is then the sum of its basis in the

---

[10] *See* Blake Rubin and Shane Orr, "Recent Developments in Partnership Taxation From Congress, Treasury, and Courts," BNA Daily Tax Report No. 82, p. J-1, pt. II.B.4 (Apr. 29, 2002) for a detailed discussion of the advantages and disadvantages of making a Section 83(b) election.

[11] Hensel Phelps Constr. Co., 74 T.C. 939 (1980), *aff'd,* 703 F.2d 485 (10th Cir. 1983), *citing* IRC §83.

[12] Reg. §1.722.

[13] McDougal v. Commissioner, 62 T.C. 720 (1974).

retained property and the fair market value of the capital interest distributed to the service member and contributed back to the LLC.

- The tax consequences are less certain in the case of a taxable profits interest. The service member is taxed when the profits interest becomes substantially vested. The LLC should be able to deduct the value of the profits interest transferred. The member should not be taxed a second time when the profits interest is realized, at least to the extent of the income initially recognized.[14]

§6.05 CONTRIBUTIONS TREATED AS DISGUISED SALES

Under traditional partnership tax rules, taxpayers could sell appreciated property without recognizing taxable gain by making a disguised sale through an LLC. The three principal types of disguised sales are (a) a contribution of money, property, or services to an LLC followed by a related distribution of money or property to the contributing member within two years after the contribution, (b) a contribution of appreciated property to an LLC by one member followed by a distribution of that property to another member within seven years after the contribution, and (c) a contribution of appreciated property to an LLC followed by a distribution of other property to the contributing member within seven years after the contribution.

Congress enacted Sections 707(a)(2)(B), 704(c)(1)(B), and 737 of the Internal Revenue Code to prevent these disguised sales. Section 707(a)(2)(B) is referred to as the disguised sale rule. Sections 704(c)(1)(B) and 737 are referred to as the "anti-mixing bowl rules."

[A] Distributions that Are Related to a Contribution—Section 707(a)(2)(B)

[1] Taxable Disguised Sales

The first type of disguised sale is a contribution of money, property, or services to an LLC followed (or preceded) by a related distribution of money or property to the contributing member within two years after the contribution.[1] The most common disguised sale is a contribution of appreciated property to an LLC followed by a distribution of money from the LLC to the contributing member. Under traditional partnership tax laws, the distribution to the member was treated as a nontaxable return of capital rather than a taxable payment of the purchase price.

---

[14] But see T. Cuff, *New Partner in Professional Service Partnership Faces Unforeseen Tax Problems,* 64 J. Taxn. 302 (1986).

§6.05   [1] IRC §707(a)(2)(A), (B).

EXAMPLE

Mary owned a condominium in Aspen. Her basis in the condominium is $400,000. The fair market value is $800,000. Mary needs to sell a one-half interest in the condominium to pay for her retirement expenses. A management company is willing to pay her $400,000 cash for a one-half interest in the condominium. However, the sale would result in taxable gain of $200,000 ($400,000 cash payment, less $200,000 basis in the one-half interest). To avoid taxation, the parties form an LLC. Mary contributes her property to the LLC. The management company contributes $400,000 in cash. The LLC distributes the $400,000 cash to Mary one week later. The $400,000 cash payment reduces Mary's basis in her membership interest from $400,000 to zero. Under traditional partnership tax rules, there is no taxable gain, since distributions are taxable only if the cash distribution exceeds the member's basis in the membership interest.

IRC Section 707(a)(2) now provides that a distribution to a member that is related to the member's contribution of appreciated property to the LLC is a taxable disguised sale. A contribution to an LLC is presumed to be a disguised sale of the property if the LLC distributes money or other property to the member within two years after the member contributes the property to the LLC. There is a presumption that a disguised sale did not take place if the LLC distributes property or money to the contributing member more than two years after the contribution. Both presumptions are rebuttable.[2]

The regulations list the following ten facts and circumstances to determine whether a disguised sale has occurred:[3]

(i) That the timing and amount of a subsequent transfer are determinable with reasonable certainty at the time of an earlier transfer;

(ii) That the transferor has a legally enforceable right to the subsequent transfer;

(iii) That the partner's right to receive the transfer of money or other consideration is secured in any manner, taking into account the period during which it is secured;

(iv) That any person has made or is legally obligated to make contributions to the partnership in order to permit the partnership to make the transfer of money or other consideration;

(v) That any person has loaned or has agreed to loan the partnership the money or other consideration required to enable the partnership to make the transfer, taking into account whether any such lending obligation is subject to contingencies related to the results of partnership operations;

(vi) That the partnership has incurred or is obligated to incur debt to acquire the money or other consideration necessary to permit it to make the transfer, taking into account the likelihood that the partnership will be able to incur that debt (considering

---

[2] Reg. §1.707-3(c), (d); F.S.A. 199936011.
[3] Reg. §1.707-3(b)(2).

such factors as whether any person has agreed to guarantee or otherwise assume personal liability for that debt);

(vii) That the partnership holds money or other liquid assets, beyond the reasonable needs of the business, that are expected to be available to make the transfer (taking into account the income that will be earned from those assets);

(viii) That partnership distributions, allocations or control of partnership operations is designed to effect an exchange of the burdens and benefits of ownership of property;

(ix) That the transfer of money or other consideration by the partnership to the partner is disproportionately large in relationship to the partner's general and continuing interest in partnership profits; and

(x) That the partner has no obligation to return or repay the money or other consideration to the partnership, or has such an obligation but it is likely to become due at such a distant point in the future that the present value of that obligation is small in relation to the amount of money or other consideration transferred by the partnership to the partner.

The member is taxed at the time of the property distribution if the member cannot satisfy the presumptions under the facts and circumstances test. The portion of the contribution that is treated as a disguised sale and the basis of the contributed property is based on the ratio of the property received to the fair market value of the property contributed.[4]

EXAMPLE

Mary contributes property to an LLC with a basis of $400,000 and fair market value of $800,000. Immediately thereafter, the LLC distributes $400,000 to Mary. Under the disguised sales rules, Mary recognizes gain as if she had sold 50 percent of the property to the LLC (since she receives a distribution equal to 50 percent of the fair market value of the property).

Sales proceeds	$400,000
Less basis in contributed property treated as a disguised sale (1/2 × $400,000)	200,000
Taxable gain	$200,000

Mary is treated as contributing the balance of the property (with the basis of $200,000 and a fair market value $400,000) to the LLC in her capacity as a member. The transfer qualifies for nonrecognition under IRC Section 721.

---

[4] *See* Reg. §1.707-3(f), Example (1).

[2]   Cost Basis of Assets to LLC

The LLC obtains a cost basis in the assets that it is deemed to have purchased in the disguised sale.[5]

EXAMPLE

Two persons form an LLC. Member A contributes cash in exchange for a 50 percent interest. Member B contributes assets in exchange for a 50 percent interest. Since the assets have a slightly greater value than the cash contribution, the LLC makes an adjusting payment of cash to Member B in order to equalize the members' contribution values. The LLC has a cost basis in the assets that it is deemed to have purchased with the payment to Member B.[6]

---

[3]   Exceptions

The regulations set forth numerous types of cash and property distributions that may be made to a contributing member within two years after the date of the contribution without triggering the disguised sales rules. The basic rule is that a property distribution that is a return *on* capital does not cause a disguised sale, whereas a property distribution that is a return *of* capital (i.e., results in a withdrawal of the member's capital) does result in a disguised sale. Distributions that are treated as bona fide distributions (returns on capital) and that do not result in a disguised sale include the following:

- Guaranteed payments that are reasonable in amount and determined without regard to the LLC's income.[7]
- A preferred return or a preferential distribution of LLC cash flow matched to the extent available by an allocation of LLC income.[8]
- Operating cash flow distributions to the member that correspond to the member's percentage interest in the LLC's overall profits.[9]
- Cash reimbursements to the member for capital expenditures with respect to contributed property, or for organization and syndication expenses. The capital expenditures must have been incurred during the two years before the contribution to the LLC. Reimbursements may not exceed 20 percent

---

[5] FSA 199936011.

[6] *Id.*

[7] Reg. §1.707-4(a)(1). See, for example, Ltr. Rul. 199915010, in which an LLC contributed cash to a partnership to be used for renovations and the other partner contributed property and received a guaranteed payment. The IRS determined that there was no disguised sale, since the guaranteed payment was reasonable in amount.

[8] Reg. §1.707-4(a)(2).

[9] Reg. §1.707-4(b)(2)(i).

of the value of contributed property at the time of contribution, unless the value of the contributed property does not exceed 120 percent of the contributing member's adjusted basis in the property at the time of contribution.[10]

- Loan repayments from the LLC to the member and guaranteed payments for services.[11]

The parties must disclose on the tax return the amount of property distributions to a contributing member within two years after the date of the contribution.[12] The disclosure is made on IRS Form 8275, Disclosure Statement, or on an attachment to the member's Form 1040. The LLC may also file Form 8594 (the asset acquisition statement under IRC §1060).[13]

[4] Services

Prior to the enactment of IRC Section 707(a)(2), an LLC could convert certain nondeductible payments for services to a contractor into deductible payments by making the contractor a member. For example, an LLC must capitalize payments for services on a construction project. It may not deduct such payments to the extent they constitute capital expenditures. In order to obtain the deduction, the LLC would make the contractor a member and give that member a distributive share of income rather than a nondeductible payment for services. The distributive share of income would be similar to a deduction for the LLC since it would reduce the taxable income of the other members. The contractor would not care how the payments were characterized since a distributive share of income and a payment for services are both taxable as ordinary income.

IRC Section 707(a)(2) now allows the IRS to recharacterize the transaction as taxable compensation if the performance of services, and the payments to the member or contractor for those services, are related to each other.

[5] Purchases of Property from Outsiders

IRC Section 707(a)(2) prevents an LLC from obtaining a deduction for payments to a nonmember for property purchased by the LLC. Prior to the enactment of

---

[10] Reg. §1.707-4(d); Ltr. Rul. 9829027. See also Ltr. Rul. 9914006, in which the IRS determined that reimbursement of capital expenditures by an LLC to a member in excess of 20 percent of the fair market value at the time of the contribution did not cause the contribution of property to the LLC to be treated as a sale under IRC §707. Even though the LLC had two members, it was treated as owned by a single member, since the second member had no interest in profits and losses, did not manage the LLC, and had only limited voting rights. The LLC was not classified as a partnership, since the members did not enter into an agreement to share profits and losses from the operation of a business.

[11] *See* T.D. 8439 (Sept. 15, 1992).

[12] Reg. §§1.707-3(c)(2), 1.707-8.

[13] Ltr. Rul. 199936011.

IRC Section 707(a)(2), a person who was not a member would sell land or other property to an LLC. The LLC would not receive a deduction for the payment of the sales price, since it would be a capital expenditure. Certain capital expenditures could be amortized. However, if raw land was purchased, the LLC would not be entitled to depreciation or amortization. To obtain a deduction, the LLC would make the selling party a temporary member, and allocate income to that member up to the sales price. The distributive share of income would be similar to a deduction for the LLC, since it would reduce the taxable income of the other members. The selling party would receive ordinary income rather than capital gain. However, the selling party would not care if the selling party were a dealer in property, in which case all proceeds from the sale of the property would be taxable as ordinary income.

Section 707(a)(2) now allows the IRS to recharacterize the transaction as a sale if the sale of property, and the payment to the member, are related to each other.

[6]   Distribution of Loan Proceeds

IRC Section 707(a)(2) prevents an LLC from distributing loan proceeds on a tax-free basis to a member who contributes appreciated property to an LLC. This is referred to as an *Otey* transaction. Prior to enactment of IRC Section 707(a)(2), a member would contribute appreciated property to an LLC. The LLC would borrow money secured by the property. The borrowings would increase the member's basis in the LLC. The LLC would then distribute the loans proceeds to the contributing member in reduction of the member's basis. The LLC would receive a carryover basis in the property. All gain on a subsequent sale would be allocated to the contributing member under IRC Section 704(c). However, the contributing member could defer taxation until the date of subsequent sale of the property by receiving a distribution of basis from the LLC rather than receiving consideration from the sale of property.

IRC Section 707(a)(2) now allows the IRS to recharacterize such transactions as a sale in this case if the contribution of property, and the distribution of loan proceeds to the member, are related to each other.

[B]   Distributions of Contributed Property to Another Member—Section 704(c)(1)(B)

The second type of disguised sale occurs when one member contributes appreciated or depreciated property to an LLC and the property is later distributed to another member. Under traditional partnership tax laws, the contributing member (seller) could receive cash for the full purchase price of the property without recognizing gain. The distributee member (buyer) received a step-up in basis for the acquired property equal to the purchase price.

EXAMPLE

John owns property with a basis of $200,000 and a fair market value of $1 million. John wants to sell the property and invest the $1 million in proceeds in the stock market. However, he does not want to recognize taxable gain on the sale of the appreciated property. He finds a buyer, Mary, who is willing to pay him $1 million cash for the property. John contributes the property to an LLC. His friend contributes $100 to the LLC in exchange for a .01 percent interest in the LLC. Mary contributes $1 million cash to the LLC in exchange for a 50 percent interest in the LLC. Three weeks later the LLC distributes the property to Mary in a complete liquidation of her interest in the LLC. Mary receives a step-up in basis for the property from $200,000 to $1 million. In a liquidating distribution, distributed property receives a basis equal to the member's adjusted basis in the membership interest ($1 million basis for Mary as a result of her $1 million cash contribution). The LLC is left with $1,000,100 in cash. John does not recognize gain, since there has been no distribution of cash or property from the LLC to him. John can then invest the $1,000,100 cash in the stock market without any taxation on the precontribution appreciation in the property. John is left with the only other member in the LLC being his friend, who has a nominal .01 percent interest and can be outvoted on any investment matters. There is no decrease in the basis for the remaining LLC assets after distribution to Mary, assuming the LLC had not made an election to adjust the basis of its assets under Section 754.[14]

IRC Section 704(c)(1)(B) now prevents members from escaping taxation on such disguised sales. The member who contributes appreciated or depreciated property to the LLC recognizes gain or loss if the LLC distributes the property to another member within seven years[15] after the date of the contribution.

The amount of gain is the gain that would have been allocated to the contributing member under Section 704(c)(1)(A) if the LLC had sold the property to the distributee member at its fair market value on the date of distribution.[16] This is equal to the built-in gain or built-in loss on the date of contribution if the property is nondepreciable property.[17]

The amount of loss is the loss that would have been allocated to the contributing

---

[14] If the LLC had made an election under IRC §754 to adjust the basis of its assets upon sales of membership interests and distributions to members, the LLC must decrease the basis of its assets under IRC §734(b) when it distributes property to a member upon a liquidation that results in a step-up in basis for the property to the member. However, even if the LLC made an election under IRC §754, the LLC would not be required to have a step-down in the basis of its assets if it retained only cash or other assets that had not declined in value below the LCC's adjusted basis in the assets. Reg. §1.755-1(b)(3).

[15] The time period is five years rather than seven for property contributed by the member to the LLC before June 9, 1997.

[16] IRC §704(c)(1)(B)(i), (ii).

[17] See §8.03 *infra* for computations involving depreciable property.

member under Section 704(c)(1)(A) if the LLC had sold the property to the distributee member at its fair market value on the date of distribution.[18] This is equal to the built-in loss on the date of contribution if the property is nondepreciable property.[19] However, loss may be disallowed under the related party rules.[20]

The contributing member receives a basis increase in the membership interest for the amount of gain recognized.[21] The LLC may also increase the basis of its assets by the gain recognized. The basis adjustment is made immediately prior to the distribution to the noncontributing member.

Section 704(c)(1)(B) does not apply if:

- The LLC distributes the contributed property back to the contributing member or the member's successor in interest.[22]
- The distribution of the contributed property to another member occurs more than seven years after the date of its contribution.
- There is a distribution of like-kind property under Section 1031 to the contributing member not later than the earlier of the 180th day after the date of distribution of the contributed property to another member or the due date for the contributing member's tax return for the year in which the distribution was made.[23]

[C] Distributions of Other Property to the Contributing Member—Section 737

The third type of disguised sale is when one member of an LLC contributes appreciated property to the LLC and the LLC distributes other property to the member. Under traditional partnership tax laws, a taxpayer could use an LLC or a partnership to transfer appreciated property in exchange for other property and avoid taxable gain.

EXAMPLE

A taxpayer owns land with a basis of $20,000 and a fair market value of $60,000. The taxpayer wants to sell the land and purchase a Lincoln Continental automobile. However, the taxpayer will not have enough money to buy the car if he has to pay taxes on the sale of the land. The exchange would not qualify as a nontaxable like-kind exchange under Section 1031. A developer and several investors want to buy the land. They form an LLC and contribute $200,000 cash to the LLC. The taxpayer contributes his property

---

[18] IRC §704(c)(1)(B)(i), (ii).
[19] *See* §8.03 *infra* for computations involving depreciable property.
[20] IRC §707(b)(1); Reg. §1.704-4(b)(1).
[21] Reg. §1.704-4(e)(1).
[22] IRC §704(c)(1)(B); Reg. §1.704-4(c)(6).
[23] IRC §704(c)(2).

to the LLC in exchange for a 25 percent interest in the LLC. The taxpayer receives an adjusted basis in his membership interest of $20,000, equal to the adjusted basis of the land contributed to the LLC. The LLC purchases the Lincoln Continental for $60,000 cash. The LLC distributes the Lincoln Continental to the taxpayer one week later in complete liquidation of his interest. The taxpayer receives a basis in the Lincoln Continental of $20,000, equal to his basis in the membership interest immediately prior to the distribution.[24] The LLC makes a Section 754 election to adjust the basis of its assets. Therefore, the LLC increases the basis of its remaining assets by $40,000, which is the amount of the basis decrease in the Lincoln Continental upon distribution to the member.[25]

IRC Section 737 now provides that a member recognizes gain (but not loss) if the member contributes appreciated property to an LLC and the LLC distributes other property (other than money) to the member within seven years after the date of the contribution. This rule is similar to and sometimes overlaps with the rule under IRC Section 707(a)(2)(B). However, there are a number of differences. IRC Section 737 applies if there is a distribution of property to the member at any time within seven years after the contribution of appreciated property rather than during the two-year period under Section 707(c)(1)(B).

The amount of gain to the contributing member is also different under Section 737. The taxable gain is equal to the lesser of:

- The excess of the fair market value of the property received in the distribution over the member's adjusted basis in her membership interest immediately prior to the distribution (reduced by the amount of money received in the distribution); or
- The amount of the member's precontribution gain. This is the amount of remaining built-in gain on property contributed by the member to the LLC within seven years prior to the distribution.[26] Built-in losses for contributed property are netted against built-in gains in determining the net precontribution gain.

EXAMPLE 1

Same facts as in the prior example. The excess of the fair market value of the distributed property other than money (the $60,000 Lincoln Continental) over the member's adjusted tax basis in his membership interest ($20,000, equal to the basis of the contributed land) is $40,000. The amount of precontribution gain on all property contributed by the member to the LLC during

[24] IRC §732(b).
[25] IRC §734(b)(1)(B).
[26] IRC §737(b)(1); Reg. §1.737-1(c)(1).

the seven years prior to the distribution is also $40,000. Therefore, the member has taxable gain of $40,000.

EXAMPLE 2

Same facts as in the prior example, except that the member contributes $40,000 in cash to the LLC immediately prior to the distribution in exchange for an additional membership interest. The member's adjusted basis in his membership interest immediately prior to the distribution is $60,000. As a result of this basis stuffing prior to the distribution, there is no taxable gain to the member under Section 737. The $60,000 fair market value of the Lincoln Continental distributed to the member does not exceed the member's adjusted basis in his membership interest. However, the member may still be taxable under the disguised sales rules of Section 707(a)(2)(B) if the distribution is made within two years after the date of the land contribution.

EXAMPLE 3

Same facts as in the prior example, except that the member does not have any additional cash to contribute to the LLC. However, the member owns other land with a basis of $40,000 and a fair market value of zero as a result of a toxic waste dump discovered on the premises. The member contributes that land to the LLC. The member's adjusted basis in the LLC is $60,000, equal to the basis of the properties contributed to the LLC ($20,000 for the first parcel and $40,000 for the second parcel). During the first five years of operation, the LLC incurs substantial losses, $60,000 of which are allocated to the member, reducing his basis from $60,000 to zero. The LLC then purchases the Lincoln Continental for $60,000 and distributes it to the member in complete liquidation of the member's interest in the LLC. There is no tax under Section 737, since the amount of net precontribution gain is zero. The $40,000 of precontribution gain on the first parcel of contributed property may be offset by the $40,000 of precontribution loss on the second parcel of property contributed to the LLC.

A member's adjusted basis in his membership interest is increased by the amount of gain recognized under Section 737. The basis increase is treated as occurring immediately prior to the distribution of property.[27]

The LLC may increase the basis of the contributed appreciated property by gain that the member recognizes under Section 737.[28]

[27] IRC §737(c)(1).
[28] IRC §737(c)(2).

§6.06   ORGANIZATION, SYNDICATION, AND START-UP EXPENSES

[A]   Start-Up Expenses

An LLC may not currently deduct start-up costs for employee salaries, rents, and other expenses incurred before the LLC carries on a trade or business. Instead, such expenses may be amortized over a period of 60 months beginning with the month in which the LLC commences business.[1] The LLC must elect to amortize the start-up expenses no later than the due date of the tax return, plus extensions, for the year in which the trade or business begins.[2]

Start-up expenses include any amount paid or incurred in connection with (a) investigating the creation or acquisition of an active trade or business, (b) creating an active trade or business, or (c) any activity engaged in for-profit and for the production of income before the trade or business begins, in anticipation of the activity becoming an active trade or business. In addition, the start-up expense must be allowable as a deduction if incurred in connection with the operation of an existing active trade or business in the same field.[3]

[B]   Syndication Expenses

An LLC may not deduct syndication expenses.[4] The expenses must be capitalized, and may not be amortized over any period. The LLC may not deduct syndication expenses even if the syndication is unsuccessful.

Syndication expenses are expenses to sell or to promote the sale of membership interests in an LLC.[5] Syndication expenses include brokerage fees, underwriting commissions, registration fees, printing costs connected with issuing and marketing membership interests in an LLC, legal fees of the underwriter and issuer for securities and tax advice relating to the adequacy of tax disclosures in the prospectus or private placement memorandum, accounting fees for preparation of materials included in the prospectus or private placement memorandum, and other selling and promotional material.[6]

[C]   Organization Expenses

An LLC may not currently deduct organization expenses.[7] The expenses must be capitalized. The LLC may elect to amortize the organization expenses over a period of 60 months or more.[8]

§6.06   [1] IRC §195(b)(1).
[2] IRC §195(d)(1).
[3] IRC §195(c).
[4] IRC §709(a); Reg. §1.709-1(b)(2).
[5] IRC §709(a).
[6] IRC §709(a); Reg. §1.709-2(b); Rev. Rul. 85-32, 1985-1 C.B. 186.
[7] IRC §709(a).
[8] IRC §709(b)(1).

Organization expenses are expenses that are (a) incurred incident to the creation of the LLC, (b) chargeable to the capital accounts of the LLC, and (c) of a character that, if expended incident to the creation of an LLC having an ascertainable life, could be amortized over such life.[9] Expenses incurred more than 3½ months after the end of the LLC's initial tax return are not organization expenses.[10] Expenses incurred more than a reasonable period of time before the LLC commences business are not amortizable organization expenses.[11]

The LLC may make the election to amortize expenses by attaching a statement to the LLC's return for the tax year in which the LLC begins its business. The statement must describe the following:

- Each organization expense incurred, whether or not paid
- The amount of each expense.
- The date each expense was incurred.
- The month the LLC began its business.
- The number of months, not less than 60, over which the expenses will be amortized.

A cash basis LLC must also indicate the amount paid before the end of the year for each expense. A cash basis LLC may not deduct organization expenses that have not been paid prior to the end of the tax year.

---

[9] IRC §709(b)(2); Reg. §1.709-2(a).
[10] Reg. §1.709-2(a).
[11] Reg. §§1.709-1(b)(1), 1.709-2(a).

7

Taxation of LLC Income

§7.01   TAXABLE INCOME

An LLC that is classified as a partnership for federal tax purposes is subject to the partnership tax rules under subchapter K of the Internal Revenue Code.[1] The LLC does not pay taxes at the entity level.[2] It is a pass-through entity. All items of income, gain, credit, loss, and deduction pass through to the members.[3] The members report their distributive shares on their personal tax returns, whether or not the income or other amounts are distributed.[4]

An LLC must compute its taxable income for reporting purposes even though it is not a taxpaying entity.[5] The LLC reports its taxable income on IRS Form 1065, which is an annual information return. It reports each member's distributive share

---

§7.01   [1] IRC §§701-761.
[2] IRC §701.
[3] IRC §702(a).
[4] IRC §706(a).
[5] IRC §703.

on Schedule K-1. Schedule K-1 is filed as part of Form 1065 and sent to each member. The LLC must file the return for each year that it receives income or incurs expenditures allowable as deductions.[6]

The taxable income, loss, credit, and deductions of an LLC are determined on the last day of its tax year. Each member must report such items on his return for the tax year coinciding with the LLC's tax year, or for the tax year immediately following such year if the member has a different tax year.[7] Thus, if an LLC has a tax year ending on April 30, 2003, an individual member must report the distributive share of income and other items on the member's tax return for the year ending December 31, 2003.

The taxable income is computed in the same manner as for an individual, subject to certain exceptions.[8] However, the LLC must present its taxable income in a format that is very different than for an individual. The LLC must separately report or account for the following four types of income, gain, credit, loss, and deduction:

1. Items that must be separately stated.[9]
2. Nondeductible amounts.[10]
3. All other items of income and expense that are grouped together as "ordinary income (loss) from trade or business activities." The net amount of such items is the "bottom line" taxable income or loss of the LLC.[11] These are the items of income from operations, expenses, depreciation, and other items that are not separately stated because they do not affect each member differently.
4. Special allocations and each member's distributive share of income. A member's distributive share of income, gain, loss, credit, and deduction is determined in accordance with the operating agreement.[12] However, special allocations to members are not respected unless the allocations have substantial economic effect.[13]

---

[6] Reg. §1.6031(a)-1(a)(1).

[7] IRC §706(a).

[8] IRC §703. Section 703(a) provides:

> The taxable income of a partnership shall be computed in the same manner as in the case of an individual except that (1) the items described in section 702(a) shall be separately stated, and (2) the following deductions shall not be allowed to the partnership: (A) the deductions for personal exemptions provided in section 151, (B) the deduction for taxes provided in section 164(a) with respect to taxes, described in section 901, paid or accrued to foreign countries and to possessions of the United States, (C) the deduction for charitable contributions provided in section 170, (D) the net operating loss deduction provided in section 170, (E) the additional itemized deductions for individuals provided in part VII of subchapter B (sec. 211 and following), and (F) the deduction for depletion under section 611 with respect to oil and gas wells.

[9] IRC §702(a). *See* §7.03 *infra.*

[10] IRC §703(a)(2). *See* §7.04 *infra.*

[11] IRC §702(a)(8); Reg. §1.704-1(b)(1)(vii).

[12] IRC §704(a).

[13] *See* Chapter 8 *infra.*

Each member takes into account his or her distributive share of taxable income, the separately stated items, and the disallowed amounts.[14]

§7.02 CHARACTER OF GAIN OR LOSS

The character of any item of income, gain, loss, deduction, or credit is normally determined at the LLC level rather than at the member level.[15] The pass-through items retain the same character after the allocation and distribution to the members.[16] For example, if the LLC sells a depreciable business asset at a gain, the gain is a Section 1231 gain or depreciation recapture even though the member is not engaged in a trade or business.

The character of gain or loss is determined at the member level for the following three types of contributed assets:[17]

1. *Unrealized receivables.* Gain or loss on receivables contributed by a member to an LLC is ordinary income or loss to the LLC.[18] This would normally be the rule in the absence of a specific Code section.
2. *Inventory items.* Inventory that a member contributes to an LLC will result in ordinary income if the LLC sells the property within five years after the contribution, even if the property is investment property in the hands of the LLC.[19] This is the reverse of IRC Section 735(a)(2), which provides that inventory coming out of an LLC will result in ordinary income if sold by the member within five years after the date of distribution. The rule is designed to prevent a member from converting ordinary income items into capital gains by contributing the property to an LLC.
3. *Capital loss property.*[20] Loss recognized by the LLC on a sale or disposition of the property for a period of five years after the contribution is treated as a capital loss (up to the amount of built-in loss on the date of contribution) even though the property is inventory in the hands of the LLC. Any loss attributable to post-contribution depreciation may be characterized as ordinary loss by the LLC if the property is inventory in the hands of the LLC or is otherwise entitled to ordinary loss.

If the LLC has losses, the members may deduct the losses on their individual tax returns, subject to the passive loss rules. The LLC may not carry back or carry forward the losses to other years as a net operating loss. However, the members may use those losses as net operating loss carrybacks and carryovers on their individual returns.

---

[14] Reg. §1.702-1(a)(9).
[15] IRC §702(b); Reg. §1.702-1(b).
[16] IRC §702(b).
[17] IRC §724.
[18] IRC §724(a).
[19] IRC §724(b).
[20] IRC §724(c).

§7.03   SEPARATELY STATED ITEMS

The LLC must separately state certain items of income, gain, loss, deduction, and credit rather than aggregating these amounts into the taxable income figure. The separately stated items are items that could have potentially varying tax consequences to particular members.[1] The LLC must also separately state each member's share of nontaxable income and nondeductible expenditures. These items are necessary for basis computation purposes. The separately stated items include the following:[2]

[A]   Capital Gains and Losses

Capital gains and losses and Section 1231 gains and losses must be separately stated.[3] Short-term capital gains and losses and long-term capital gains and losses are separately netted and stated as two net amounts. The determination of whether gain is capital or ordinary (e.g., whether a person is a dealer or investor) is made at the LLC level.[4] However, the character of gain or loss on contributed unrealized receivables, inventory items, and capital loss property is made at the member level, subject to exceptions.[5] The LLC may not carry over unused capital losses.[6]

[B]   Nonbusiness Expenses

Nonbusiness expenses must be separately stated.[7] These are expenses incurred in connection with investments, and the production and conservation of income and capital, but which do not rise to the level of a trade or business. These expenses are not deductible by the LLC.[8] However, they must be separately stated, and are deductible by members. The only possible exception would be for corporate members, since the heading of IRC Section 212 states that such nonbusiness expenses are deductible only by an individual. To avoid this problem, the Section 212 expenses should be listed as Section 162 expenses for a corporate member.

[C]   Charitable Contributions

The LLC must separately state charitable contributions.[9] The LLC may not deduct charitable contributions.[10] However, the members may deduct charitable

---

§7.03   [1] IRC §§702(a), 703(a)(1).
[2] Reg. §1.702-1(a)(1) to (9).
[3] IRC §§703(a)(1), 702(a)(1)-(3); Reg. §1.702(a)(1)-(3).
[4] IRC §702(b).
[5] IRC §724. *See* §7.02 *supra.*
[6] Reg. §1.703-1(a)(2)(viii).
[7] Reg. §1.702-1(a)(8).
[8] IRC §703(a)(2)(E).
[9] IRC §§703(a)(1), 702(a)(4); Reg. §§1.702-1(a)(4), 1.703-1(a)(2)(iv).
[10] IRC §702(a)(3)(E).

contributions on their individual tax returns. Each member is treated as having paid his distributive share of a charitable contribution paid by the LLC within its tax year ending within or with the member's tax year.[11] Members must add their individual charitable contributions to their distributive shares of LLC contributions, and apply the percentage limitations[12] to the total amount.[13]

The LLC must attach a statement to Schedules K and K-1, indicating by amount the charitable contributions that are subject to the 20, 30, and 50 percent limitations.

Charitable contributions decrease a member's basis in the LLC since nondeductible expenses by the LLC reduce the member's basis.[14]

A member may not deduct charitable contributions passed through from an LLC for contributions in excess of $250, unless the LLC obtains a written acknowledgement from the charitable organization. The written acknowledgement must show the amount of cash contributed, describe the property contributed, and give an estimate of the value of any goods or services provided in return for the contribution. The LLC must obtain the acknowledgement by the due date, including extensions, for the LLC return or any earlier date that the LLC files its return. The LLC is not required to attach a copy of the acknowledgement to its return.[15]

The LLC must complete Form 8283 if it makes noncash charitable contributions in excess of $500. The LLC must give a copy of the form to every member if the charitable deduction for an item or group of contributed property exceeds $5,000. If it is less than $5000, the LLC must still give the form to each member, and each member must complete his or her own Form 8283.[16]

[D] Miscellaneous Itemized Deductions

The LLC must separately state miscellaneous itemized deductions. It may not offset deductions against other income. The 2-percent limitation on deductibility of miscellaneous itemized deductions does not apply at the LLC level, but instead applies to each member.[17] For example, investment expenses incurred by the LLC must be separately stated on Schedule K-1, and reported by the member as a miscellaneous itemized deduction on Schedule A of Form 1040.[18]

[E] Dividends

An LLC must separately state dividends received from domestic corporations with respect to which a member is entitled to a dividends-received credit, an exclusion from income, or a deduction from income.[19] A corporate member of an

---

[11] Reg. §1.703-1(a)(2)(iv).
[12] IRC §170(b).
[13] Reg. §1.702-1(a)(4).
[14] IRC §705(a)(2)(B).
[15] Instructions to Form 1065.
[16] Id.
[17] IRC §67(c).
[18] See instructions to Schedule K-1 of Form 1065.
[19] IRC §§703(a)(1), 702(a)(5); Reg. §1.702-1(a)(5).

LLC is entitled to a dividends-received deduction for the member's allocable share of dividends received by the LLC, including a 100-percent deduction for dividends received by the LLC from a foreign sales corporation.[20]

[F] Section 179 Expenses

An LLC must separately state Section 179 expenses. The maximum amount of Section 179 depreciation expense is $100,000 during 2003, indexed for inflation during 2004 and 2005. The limit is $25,000 during 2006 and thereafter.[21] The limitation applies at both the LLC and member level.[22] The member's own Section 179 expense and distributive share of LLC Section 179 expense cannot exceed the annual limit.[23]

The maximum deduction is reduced if the member or the LLC purchases more than $200,000 of Section 179 property during the year.[24] The $200,000 amount is $400,000 in 2003, indexed for inflation in 2004 and 2005. A member does not include the cost of any Section 179 property purchased by the LLC during the year in determining whether the $200,000 investment limit has been exceeded.[25]

The member must reduce his basis in the LLC by his distributive share of Section 179 expense even if the member cannot currently deduct the expense. The member's basis for determining gain or loss on sale of the membership interest is increased by any outstanding carryover Section 179 expense allocated from the LLC.

The LLC must reduce the basis of its Section 179 property by the amount of the deduction even if the member cannot deduct his allocable share because of the limits on deduction at the member level.[26]

An LLC may not allocate Section 179 expense deductions to its members in excess of the LLC's taxable income for the year.[27] The Section 179 expense deduction may not create a net trade or business loss at either the LLC or member level.[28] The LLC may carry over disallowed amounts to future tax years.[29] However, it may not carry over amounts in excess of the $100,000 annual limit.[30]

[G] Depreciation

Depreciation expenses are not separately stated unless there is a special allocation of depreciation. In such event, it is separately stated only to the extent of the special allocation. Depreciation does not otherwise affect the members differently.

---

[20] Ltr. Ruls. 200137038, 200009025.
[21] IRC §179(b)(1).
[22] IRC §179(d)(8); Reg. §1.179.
[23] *See* IRC §179(d)(8).
[24] IRC §179(b)(2).
[25] Reg. §1.179-2(b)(3)(i).
[26] Reg. §1.179-1(f)(2).
[27] Reg. §1.179-2(c)(2).
[28] IRC §179(b)(3); Reg. §1.179-3(g)(1).
[29] IRC §179(b)(3)(B); Reg. §1.179-2(c)(2).
[30] Reg. §1.179-3(b)(1).

[H]   Investment Interest Expense

Investment interest expense must be separately stated if there are individual members as opposed to corporate members. The reason is that there are limits on the deductibility of investment interest expenses for individuals.[31] Prior to 1982, the limits on investment interest expense were determined at the LLC level. This provision was repealed. The limits of deductibility of investment interest are now applied to each member separately based on his or her allocable share of LLC interest expense deduction.[32]

[I]   Cancellation of Indebtedness Income

An LLC must separately state cancellation of indebtedness income.[33] A member is taxable on his or her distributive share of cancellation of indebtedness income.[34] There are exceptions if the taxpayer is insolvent, the discharge occurs in a federal bankruptcy reorganization, the debt is qualified farm indebtedness, or the debt is qualified real property business indebtedness in the case of a taxpayer other than a C corporation.[35] These exceptions apply at the member level rather than at the LLC level.

The cancellation of indebtedness income increases basis. The relief of debt decreases basis by a corresponding amount (assuming no special allocations).[36]

EXAMPLE

An LLC has two equal members. The LLC owns an office building with a fair market value of $7,000. The office building was acquired with a recourse debt of $10,000. The lender agrees to reduce the debt by $3,000 in a workout arrangement. Each member has a basis of $4,000 in her membership interest (which includes each member's $5,000 share of nonrecourse liabilities). The

---

[31] IRC §163(d).

[32] Instructions to Form 1065.

[33] Rev. Rul. 92-97, 1992-2 C.B. 124.

[34] Id.

[35] IRC §108(a).

[36] See Rev. Rul. 92-97, 1992-2 C.B. 124, which states, "When the COD income is properly allocated, the outside bases of A and B are increased under section 705(a)(1)(A) of the Code by $90x and $810x, respectively, for their distributive shares of the partnership's COD income. Under section 108(d)(6), A and B individually determine if any portion of their distributive shares is excluded from gross income. Under section 705(a)(2), the outside bases of A and B are decreased by $90x and $810x, respectively, for their distributions of money under section 752(b) resulting from the cancellation of the debt. A and B recognize no gain under section 731 in year 6 because the distributive shares of COD income provide an outside basis increase for each partner sufficient to cover the distribution of money to that partner. Because of the integral relationship between the COD income and the section 752(b) distribution of money from the cancelled debt, section 1.731- 1(a)(1)(ii) of the regulations treats the distribution of money to each partner from the cancellation of the debt as occurring at the end of AB's taxable year as an advance or drawing against that partner's distributive share of COD income." See also Rev. Rul. 72-205, 1972-1 C.B. 37.

debt reduction is cancellation of indebtedness income to the LLC. The income is allocated to each member equally and is taxable at the member level. The income allocation increases each member's basis by $1,500 from $4,000 to $5,500. The $3,000 debt reduction also decreases each member's share of liabilities for basis purposes, thus reducing the $5,500 basis for each member back down to $4,000.[37]

The insolvency and bankruptcy exceptions apply at the member level if the LLC is classified as a partnership.[38] The insolvent or bankrupt member may exclude the debt discharge from taxable income only if the member reduces net operating loss carryforwards and other tax attributes.[39] A member may elect to reduce the basis in depreciable property owned by the member instead of reducing tax attributes.[40] A member may also reduce the basis in the membership interest instead of reducing tax attributes, if the LLC makes a corresponding basis reduction in LLC depreciable property with respect to that member. There are detailed regulations regarding this election.[41] A solvent member who has not filed for bankruptcy must include the allocable share of debt discharge in gross income.

The rules are different for an S corporation. The insolvency and bankruptcy exceptions to income recognition apply at the corporate level (rather than at the shareholder level). The shareholder is not taxed if the corporation is insolvent or bankrupt after the debt cancellation. After October 11, 2001, the excluded cancellation of indebtedness income does not increase the basis of the shareholder's stock in the S corporation.[42]

The cancellation of indebtedness income rules are partially or wholly inapplicable if the debt is secured by LLC property and the LLC transfers the property to the lender in a foreclosure proceeding, voluntary transfer, abandonment, or otherwise. The rules in such case are as follows:

- *Nonrecourse debt.* If the debt is nonrecourse debt, the entire amount of the debt is treated as an amount realized on disposition of the property. There is no cancellation of indebtedness income.[43] However, there is cancellation of indebtedness income when a creditor (who is not the seller of the underlying property) reduces the principal amount of an unsecured nonrecourse loan to an LLC without repossessing the property.[44]
- *Recourse debt.* If the debt is recourse debt, then gain is recognized to the extent that the fair market value of the property exceeds the LLC's adjusted basis in the property. There is cancellation of indebtedness income to the extent that the debt discharged exceeds the fair market value of the prop-

---

[37] Rev. Rul. 92-97, 1992-2 C.B. 124; Rev. Rul. 94-4, 1994-1 C.B. 195.
[38] TAM 9739002; IRC §108(d)(6); Rev. Rul. 99-43, 1999-42 I.R.B. 506; Rev. Rul. 92-97, 1992-2 C.B. 124.
[39] IRC §108(b).
[40] IRC §§108(b)(5), 1017.
[41] Reg. §1.1017-1(g).
[42] IRC §108(d)(7).
[43] Rev. Rul. 76-111, 1976-1 C.B. 214.
[44] Rev. Rul. 91-31, 1991-1 C.B. 19; Rev. Rul. 99-43, 1999-4 C.B. 506.

erty.[45] The entire debt canceled is cancellation of indebtedness income if the lender cancels the debt without repossessing the property.[46]

[J]   Other Items

An LLC must separately state any other items of income, gain, loss, deduction, or credit to the extent provided in IRS regulations.[47] The IRS has specified numerous additional items that must be separately stated. These items include the following general classes:

- Items that the LLC specially allocates to members under the operating agreement.[48]
- Items that an LLC must separately state in all cases, such as medical expenses and insurance premiums for members and employees, dependent care expenses for members and employees, taxes and interest paid to cooperative housing corporations, intangible drilling and development costs, exploration expenditures, and certain mining expenditures.[49]
- Items that an LLC must separately state only if the allocation would result in income tax liability for a member that is different from that which would result if the member did not take the item into account separately.[50] These items include earned income for a member who is a *bona fide* resident of a foreign country; pensions annuities, interest, rents, dividends, and earned income for a member who qualifies for the retirement income credit; and all losses for a member if the business of the LLC constitutes a hobby loss for the member.

§7.04   NONDEDUCTIBLE ITEMS

An LLC may not deduct the following items in determining LLC income:[1]

- taxes paid or accrued to foreign countries and to possessions of the United States;[2]

---

[45] Rev. Rul. 90-16, 1990-1 C.B. 12; Reg. §1.1001-2(c), Example (8).

[46] Rev. Rul. 92-97,1992-2 C.B. 124.

[47] IRC §§703(a)(1), 702(a)(7).

[48] Reg. §1.702-1(a)(8)(i) (last clause).

[49] Reg. §1.702-1(a)(8)(i).

[50] Reg. §1.702-1(a)(8)(ii).

§7.04   [1] IRC §703(a)(2).

[2] This item must be separately stated and is deductible by the members. IRC §§703(a)(1), 702(a)(6); Reg. §1.703-1(a)(2)(iii). Each member must add his distributive share of taxes paid by the LLC to foreign countries or possessions of the United States to any such paid or accrued by him. The member may then elect to use the total amount either as a credit against taxes owed or as a deduction from income. Reg. §1.703-1(b)(2)(i).

- charitable contributions;[3]
- capital expenditures, including expenses incurred in connection with property acquisitions and real estate development;[4]
- standard deduction;[5]
- personal exemptions;[6]
- net operating loss deduction carrybacks and carryforwards;[7]
- capital loss carryovers;[8]
- depletion with respect to oil and gas wells;[9] and
- additional itemized deductions for an individual set forth in IRC Section 211 *et seq.* For example, the LLC may not deduct medical expenses under IRC Section 213, alimony under IRC Section 215, moving expenses under IRC Section 217, and IRA deductions under IRC Section 219.[10]

The LLC must separately state the nondeductible items. In most cases, the member is treated as if the member paid the nondeductible amounts directly. For example, the member may deduct charitable contributions if the aggregate charitable contributions by the member and the member's allocable share of LLC contributions do not exceed the percentage limitations under IRC Section 170(b).[11]

The member's basis in the membership interest is reduced by the member's share of nondeductible items.[12]

§7.05   AGGREGATION RULE

Unless otherwise provided in the Code, a member must aggregate the amount of separately stated deductions and exclusions passed through to the member from the LLC with the member's own deductions and exclusions in determining the amount of allowable deductions and exclusions for which a limitation is imposed.[1] For example, the member must aggregate the following items in applying limitation amounts and the elections under the Code for those items:

---

[3] This item must be separately stated and is deductible by the members. IRC §§703(a)(1), 702(a)(4); Reg. §1.703-1(a)(2)(iv).

[4] FRGC Investment, LLC v. Comm'r, 84 TCM 508 (2002).

[5] Reg. §1.703-1(a)(2)(i).

[6] Reg. §1.703-1(a)(2)(ii).

[7] Reg. §1.703-1(a)(2)(v).

[8] Reg. §1.703-1(a)(2)(viii).

[9] Reg. §1.703-1(a)(2)(vii).

[10] Reg. §1.703-1(a)(2)(vi).

[11] *See* §7.03[C] *supra.*

[12] IRC §705(a)(2)(B).

§7.05   [1] Reg. §1.702-1(a)(8)(iii).

- mining exploration expenditures;[2]
- income received by a nonresident alien from the LLC related to real property located in the United States;[3]
- charitable contributions;[4]
- taxes paid or accrued by the LLC to foreign countries or possessions of the United States;[5]
- miscellaneous itemized deductions; and
- Section 179 expenses.[6]

§7.06 ELECTIONS REGARDING INCOME, DEDUCTIONS, AND CREDITS

[A] Elections by LLC

The LLC must make most elections regarding its income, deductions, and credits.[1] For example, it must elect the following:[2]

- Accounting methods.[3]
- Depreciation and cost recovery methods.[4]
- Nonrecognition of gain on an involuntary conversion.[5]
- Expensing the cost of certain depreciable property.[6]
- Amortization of organization and start-up costs.[7]
- Adjustments to basis.[8]
- Reporting of gain on the installment basis.[9]
- Amortization of cost of pollution control facilities.
- Choice of inventory method. The contribution by members of LIFO inventory to an LLC that is classified as a partnership does not trigger recapture of the LIFO reserve. However, the LLC must file IRS Form 970 and comply with IRC Section 472 in order to adopt the dollar-value LIFO inventory method.[10] Any LIFO inventory contributed to the LLC is IRC Section 704(c) property. Thus, any built-in gain or loss attributable to the inventory must

---

[2] Reg. §1.703-1(b)(2)(ii).
[3] Reg. §1.703-1(b)(2)(iii).
[4] Reg. §1.702-1(a)(4).
[5] Reg. §1.703-1(b)(2)(i).
[6] IRC §179(d)(8).
§7.06 [1] IRC §703(b); Reg. §1.703-1(b)(1).
[2] Reg. §1.703-1(b)(1).
[3] *Id.*
[4] Reg. §1.703-1(b)(1); Prop. Reg. §1.168-5(e)(7); Rev. Rul. 81-261, 1981-2 C.B. 60.
[5] *Fuchs v. Comm'r*, 80 T.C. 506 (1983).
[6] *See* IRC §179.
[7] IRC §709(b).
[8] *See* IRC §754.
[9] Reg. §15A.453-1(d)(3)(i).
[10] Ltr. Rul. 200124030.

be allocated to the contributing member for tax purposes when the inventory is sold[11] On approval by the IRS, the LLC may treat the items included in its opening inventory as having been acquired at the same time, and determine their cost by the average cost method as provided under IRC Section 472(b)(3).[12]

- Reinvestment of involuntary conversion proceeds. If gain is realized, the LLC must reinvest in similar or related property.[13]
- Election not to use the installment method of reporting.[14]
- Election to adjust the basis of LLC assets under IRC Sections 734 and 743 on the transfer of membership interests or on distributions from the LLC.[15]
- Treatment of income from discharge of indebtedness.[16]
- Expensing of assets under IRC Section 179.[17]
- Treatment of soil and water conservation expenditures.[18]

[B] Elections by Members

The members rather than the LLC must make certain elections regarding LLC income, deductions, and credits. These elections include the following:

- Basis reduction related to discharge of debt.[19]
- Deduction and recapture of certain mining exploration expenditures.[20]
- Optional 10-year write-off of certain tax preferences.[21]
- Use of the foreign tax credit, rather than deduction, for taxes paid to foreign countries in United States possessions.[22]
- Election by nonresident alien individuals and foreign corporations to treat gross income from real property that is not trade or business income as if it were trade or business income.

---

[11] Id.

[12] Id.

[13] T.K. McManus v. Comm'r, 65 T.C. 197 (1975), aff'd, 575 F.2d 1177 (6th Cir. 1978); M. Demirjian v. Comm'r, 457 F.2d 1 (3d Cir. 1972).

[14] Reg. §15a.453-1(d)(1), (d)(3)(i); Rev. Rul. 79-92,1979-1 C.B. 180. However, an LLC that is required to use the accrual method of accounting may not use the installment method of reporting.

[15] Atlantic Veneer Corp., 85 T.C. 1075, aff'd, 812 F.2d 158 (4th Cir. 1987).

[16] IRC §703(b)(1).

[17] IRC §179(c), (d)(8); Reg. §1.179-1(h).

[18] Reg. §1.703-1(b)(1).

[19] See IRC §703(b)(1).

[20] See IRC §703(b)(2).

[21] See IRC §59(e).

[22] See IRC §703(b)(3).

8

Allocations

§8.01   GENERAL RULES

An LLC that is classified as a partnership does not pay taxes except in limited cases.[1] The income and losses of the LLC pass through to and are allocated to the members.[2] A member must take into account separately the member's distributive share of each class or item of LLC income, gain, loss, deduction, or credit, whether or not distributed.[3]

The members can decide what amount of income, gain, loss, deduction or credit will be allocated to each of the members. The LLC is not required to make the allocations in proportion to each member's percentage ownership interest in the LLC. For example, the LLC may provide that all depreciation will be allocated to one of the members, or that certain members will receive all the cash distributions until they have recovered their initial capital contributions. The ability to make special allocations to members is one of the principal benefits of an LLC.

A member's distributive share of income and other tax items is normally determined by the operating agreement.[4] The allocations provided in the operating agreement are usually respected, subject to certain exceptions. The principal exceptions are the following:

- *Special allocations.* Special allocations are allocations of one or more items of income, gain, loss, or deduction to a member that differ from the member's percentage interest in capital, or percentage interest in profits and losses. The general rule is that tax allocations must follow book allocations,[5] and

---

§8.01   [1] For example, the LLC is subject to state and local taxes in some jurisdictions.
[2] IRC §701.
[3] Ltr. Rul. 8003072 (*citing* Reg. §1.702-1).
[4] IRC §704(a).
[5] IRC §704(b). That section is designed to ensure that LLC tax allocations reflect the actual economic arrangements (book allocations) of the members.

book allocations must have "substantial economic effect."[6] Special allocations must comply with several requirements in order to have substantial economic effect. Otherwise, the allocations will be made in accordance with each member's interest in the LLC.[7]

- *Contributed property.* Built-in gain or loss must be allocated to the member who contributed the property to the LLC when the property is sold. There are special rules for allocation of depreciation on contributed property.[8] The allocation must be made for tax purposes only. The book allocation may be made as determined by the operating agreement. Unlike the rule for special allocations, the tax allocations in this case do not follow the book allocations.
- *Retroactive allocations.* The LLC cannot allocate items to new members that are attributable to periods prior to the time that such persons became members in the LLC.[9]
- *Gifts and sales to family members.* If a member donates or sells a membership interest to a family member, there are special rules on allocation of LLC income between the donor and the donee.[10]

§8.02   SPECIAL ALLOCATIONS

[A]   *Overview*

An LLC may make special allocations to members if the allocations have "substantial economic effect."[1] Allocations that do not have substantial economic effect are allocated according to each member's economic interest in the item of income or deduction.[2] The determination of a member's economic interest in the item of income or deduction is based on all the facts and circumstances.[3] Because of the uncertainty in the facts and circumstances analysis, LLC special allocations should have substantial economic effect.

The Treasury Department issued safe-harbor regulations setting forth when the substantial economic effect test will be met. Under the regulations, allocations have substantial economic effect if:[4]

---

[6] IRC §704(b)(2).

[7] *See* §8.02 *infra.*

[8] *See* §8.03 *infra.*

[9] *See* §8.04 *infra.*

[10] *See* §8.05 *infra.*

§8.02   [1] IRC §704(b)(2).

[2] Reg. §1.704-1(b)(1)(i).

[3] Reg. §1.704-1(b)(1)(i). The facts and circumstances include the members' respective interests in (a) capital contributions, (b) economic profits and losses, if different from their interests in taxable income and losses, (c) cash flow, (d) nonliquidating distributions, and (e) liquidating distributions of capital. Reg. §1.704-1(b)(3)(ii).

[4] Reg. §1.704-1(b)(2)(ii)(b).

- The LLC maintains capital accounts.
- The LLC makes liquidating distributions in accordance with the members' positive capital account balances.
- Each member or transferree is unconditionally obligated to restore any deficit in his capital account on liquidation of the membership interest. However, members are not obligated to restore deficit capital account balances if the operating agreement contains a loss limitation and "qualified income offset" provision.
- The economic effect of such allocations is substantial.
- Allocations that are attributable to property secured by nonrecourse debt comply with additional requirements, including a "minimum gain chargeback" provision.

[B] Capital Accounts

The first requirement under the safe-harbor regulations is that the LLC maintain capital accounts.[5] The capital accounting under the regulations is not based on generally accepted accounting principles, tax accounting, or other normal methods of accounting. Instead, there is a completely separate type of accounting invented by the drafters of the regulations. The capital accounts are sometimes referred to as Section 704(b) capital accounts. The accounting method is sometimes referred to as Section 704(b) accounting. The basic principles of the regulations are as follows.

[1] Contributed Property

The capital accounts must reflect the fair market value of the property contributed to the LLC rather than the tax basis of the property or other valuation.[6]

EXAMPLE

An LLC has three equal members. Each of the members has a capital account of $10,000 and an adjusted basis in the membership interest of $10,000. The LLC has an adjusted basis in its assets of $30,000. The LLC admits Member D to the LLC as a 25 percent equal member in exchange for a contribution of land with a basis of $2,000 and a fair market value of $10,000. Member D has an adjusted basis in his membership interest of $2,000, which is the basis of property contributed to the LLC. The LLC receives a carryover basis in the property and has a total adjusted basis in all of its property of $32,000. However, the LLC must credit Member D's

---

[5] Reg. §1.704-1(b)(2)(ii)(b)(1).
[6] Reg. §1.704-1(b)(2)(iv)(d).

capital account with $10,000, which is the fair market value of the contributed property.

[2]   Distributed Property

Distributed assets must be revalued for book purposes to fair market value whenever there is a distribution. The capital account of the member receiving the distribution must be reduced by the fair market value of the property distributed. The LLC must pretend that it sold the asset for fair market value. The gain or loss is allocated to the members' capital accounts. However, there is no gain or loss for tax purposes, since the distribution of property to a member is not a taxable event.[7]

EXAMPLE

An LLC has four equal members. Member A has a 25 percent interest in the LLC. Her capital account is $10,000. The adjusted basis of her membership interest is $8,000. One of the assets of the LLC is a building that the LLC purchased for $100,000. There is $90,000 of depreciation on the building. The LLC's tax basis and adjusted book value in the property are $10,000. The property has a fair market value of $30,000. The LLC distributes the property to Member A, who retains her 25 percent interest in the LLC after the distribution. The distribution has the following consequences:

- The distribution is treated as a sale of the property to Member A at its fair market value of $30,000. The LLC has book gain of $20,000, equal to the fair market value, less its $10,000 book value for the property. There is no tax gain, since a distribution of property to a member is not a taxable event.
- The $20,000 book gain is allocated to the four members equally for capital account purposes. Therefore, $5,000 of book gain is allocated to Member A.
- Member A's capital account is a negative $15,000, computed as follows:

Initial capital account prior to distribution	$ 10,000
Plus book gain upon distribution	5,000
Less distribution of property at fair market value	(30,000)
Ending capital account	$(15,000)

- Member A's tax basis in the property is $8,000. Normally, a member receives a carryover basis in property in a nonliquidating distribution.[8]

[7] Reg §1.704-1(b)(2)(iv)(e).
[8] IRC §732(a)(1).

However, the basis of the distributed property cannot exceed the member's adjusted basis in her membership interest immediately before the distribution.[9] Therefore, Member A receives a step-down in basis for the property from $10,000 to $8,000.

- Member A's $8,000 adjusted basis in her membership interest is reduced to zero. The basis is reduced by the $8,000 basis that the member receives in the distributed property.[10]
- The LLC may increase the basis of its remaining assets by $2,000, the amount of step-down in the basis of the asset to the member, if the LLC makes an election to adjust the basis of its assets under Section 754 of the Internal Revenue Code.[11]
- If the LLC sells its remaining property and liquidates, the proceeds must be distributed to the members according to the ending positive capital account balances after the above adjustments are made.

[3] Contributions of Encumbered Property

If a member contributes encumbered property to the LLC, the LLC must credit the member's capital account with the fair market value of the property less liabilities encumbering the property that the LLC assumes or takes subject to.[12]

EXAMPLE 1

John purchases a building for $100,000. He pays no cash down and gives the seller a promissory note. The promissory note provides for interest only for 10 years with a balloon payment after 10 years. John receives $80,000 of depreciation on the building, which reduces his tax basis from $100,000 to $20,000. The fair market value of the property increases to $125,000. John contributes the property to the LLC in exchange for a 25 percent interest in the LLC. The LLC assumes the $100,000 debt on the property. The following capital account and basis adjustments must be made:

- The LLC must credit John's capital account with $25,000. This is the fair market value of the property, less the debt encumbering the property.
- The LLC's book value for the property is equal to the $125,000 fair market value. Its basis in the property is $20,000, which is John's basis in the property prior to the contribution.
- John has net debt relief of $75,000. Prior to the contribution, he owed the lender $100,000. After the contribution, his share of the liability

---

[9] IRC §732(a)(2).
[10] IRC §733(2).
[11] IRC §734(b)(1)(B).
[12] Reg. §1.704-1(b)(2)(iv)(b).

assumed by the LLC is $25,000 (25 percent of the $100,000 debt). The net debt relief is treated as a money distribution to John.[13]

- The deemed money distribution of $75,000 to John first reduces his basis in the LLC. John's initial basis in the LLC is $20,000, which is the basis of the property contributed to the LLC. The deemed money distribution reduces this basis to zero. The $55,000 money distribution in excess of John's basis is taxable gain to John.[14]
- If the LLC makes an election under Section 754, it may increase the tax basis of the contributed property by $55,000, which is the gain that John recognizes upon the contribution to the LLC.[15]
- If John sells his membership interest for $25,000 cash, equal to his capital account of $25,000 (fair market value of equity contributed to the LLC), then John recognizes an additional taxable gain of $50,000. This is equal to the amount realized of $50,000 upon the sale ($25,000 cash, plus $25,000 debt relief), less his zero basis in his membership interest.
- John's total gain after the sale is $105,000. This is equal to the $55,000 gain upon the contribution of the property to the LLC and the $50,000 gain upon the sale of the membership interest for $25,000 in cash. This $105,000 of gain is the same gain that John would have recognized if he had sold the property himself for the fair market value of $125,000 rather than contributing it to the LLC. His gain would have been the amount realized of $125,000 ($25,000 cash, plus $100,000 debt relief), less his $20,000 basis in the property.

EXAMPLE 2

Same facts as in Example 1, except that John does not sell his membership interest or the land. After John contributes the land to the LLC, the LLC sells the land for its fair market value of $125,000. The purchase price consists of $25,000 cash and assumption of the $100,000 debt by the buyer. The capital account and tax consequences are as follows:

- There is no book gain that is allocated to the members' capital accounts. The LLC's book value prior to the sale is the $125,000 fair market value on the date of contribution. The amount realized from the sale is also $125,000, resulting in zero book gain.
- The LLC realizes $105,000 of gain for tax purposes. This is equal to the amount realized of $125,000, less the $20,000 carryover basis for the property when John contributed the property to the LLC. The $105,000 of tax gain must be allocated entirely to John. When contrib-

[13] IRC §752.
[14] IRC §731(a)(1).
[15] IRC §734(b)(1)(A).

uted property is sold, the built-in gain or loss must be allocated entirely to the contributing member.[16] John now has a total taxable gain of $160,000. This is equal to the $55,000 of gain upon the contribution of the property to the LLC, plus the $105,000 of gain that must be allocated to him under Section 704(c) when the LLC sells the property.

- If the LLC makes an election under Section 754, then it may step up the basis in the contributed property by $55,000, equal to the gain recognized by John upon the contribution of the property to the LLC.[17] In that case, the LLC would step up the basis of the contributed property from $20,000 to $75,000. The amount of gain upon the sale would be only $50,000 ($125,000 amount realized, less $75,000 basis). Again, the entire $50,000 of built-in gain would be allocated to John.

- The total gain recognized by John in this case would be $105,000. This would be equal to the $55,000 gain recognized upon the contribution of the property to the LLC, plus the $50,000 of gain allocated to him under Section 704(c) when the property is sold. This gain would be exactly the same as if John had sold the property directly to the buyer without first contributing it to the LLC ($125,000 purchase price, less $20,000 basis in the property).

- John increases the basis in his membership interest by $25,000 after the sale by the LLC, assuming that it has made an election under Section 754. The $50,000 gain allocated to John increases his basis by that amount. The $25,000 debt relief (25% × $100,000 of debt assumed by the buyer) decreases John's basis. The net basis increase of $25,000 increases his basis in the LLC from $20,000 to $45,000.

[4] Depreciation

The amount of depreciation taken for book purposes must be based on tax depreciation multiplied by a fraction. The numerator is the book value of the assets on the date of contribution, and the denominator is the tax basis.[18]

EXAMPLE

A member contributes a 15-year depreciable asset to the LLC. The fair value of the asset is $100. The tax basis is $50. The book value is twice as much as the tax basis. Therefore, the amount of depreciation for book purposes is twice the amount of depreciation for tax purposes.

---

[16] IRC §704(c).
[17] IRC §734(b)(1)(A).
[18] Reg. §1.704-1(b)(2)(iv)(g)(3).

[5]   Other Gains and Losses

The LLC must increase each member's capital account by the amount of income and gain allocated to the member, including tax-exempt income. The LLC must decrease each member's capital account by the amount of losses and deductions allocated to the member, including nondeductible expenses.[19]

The income and deductions that are allocated to the members' capital accounts are accounting income and deductions. This is normally different from taxable income and deductions. However, many LLCs keep their capital accounts on a tax basis rather than on an accounting or book basis. In such case, the LLC would allocate taxable income, gain, loss, and deduction to the members' capital accounts.

[6]   Distributions of Encumbered Property

If the LLC distributes encumbered property to a member, the LLC must reduce the member's capital account by the fair market value of the property, less the debt encumbering the property that the member assumes or takes subject to.[20] The LLC must also treat the distribution as a sale resulting in book gain or loss that is allocated to all of the members.

EXAMPLE

An LLC has four equal members. The LLC distributes a building to Member A in a nonliquidating distribution. The financial statements of the LLC show the following:

Fair market value of building distributed	$100,000
Book value of building (original purchase price, less book depreciation)	$ 80,000
Liabilities encumbering the building assumed by Member A in the distribution	$ 70,000
LLC's tax basis in the property	$ 40,000
Member A's tax basis in LLC	$ 20,000
Member A's capital account determined under IRC §704(b)	$ 20,000

The nonliquidating distribution of the building to Member A has the following capital account and tax consequences:

- The LLC must treat the distribution as a sale. The sale results in book gain of $20,000. This is equal to the fair market value of $100,000, less

---

[19] Reg. §1.704-1(b)(2)(iv)(b).
[20] *Id.*

the book value of $80,000. There is no taxable gain on the distribution, since a distribution of property to a member is not a taxable event.

- The $20,000 of book gain must be allocated to the four members for capital account purposes. Therefore, the LLC allocates $5,000 of the book gain to Member A.
- Member A is treated as receiving a capital account distribution of $30,000. This is equal to the $100,000 fair market value of the property, less the $70,000 in liabilities assumed by Member A.
- The distribution results in a negative capital account for Member A of $5,000, determined as follows:

Beginning capital account	$ 20,000
Plus 1/4 share of book gain upon the sale of the property	5,000
Less capital account distribution (fair market value of property, less liabilities)	(30,000)
Ending capital account balance	$(5,000)

- Member A has an ending adjusted tax basis in his membership interest in the LLC after the distribution of $2,250, determined as follows:

Beginning basis	$ 20,000
Plus net increase in Member A's share of liabilities as a result of the distribution. The net increase is treated as a contribution of money by Member A to the LLC. The net increase is equal to $30,000 of liabilities assumed by Member A, less Member A's $7,500 relief from LLC liabilities (1/4 share of the $30,000 of LLC liabilities prior to the distribution).	22,500
Less basis in property distributed to Member A	(40,000)
Ending tax basis	$ 2,250

- The property distributed to Member A has a tax basis of $40,000, which is equal to the tax basis that the LLC had in the property prior to the distribution.

[7] Optional Revaluation of Capital Accounts and Property

An LLC is required to revalue only contributed property and distributed property for capital account purposes on the date of a contribution or distribution. The LLC is not required to revalue any other property for capital account purposes. However, the LLC may elect to revalue all of its property on the date of contribution, distribution, or liquidation.[21] The revaluation of noncontributed or nondistributed property must be for substantial nontax business purposes. There must

---

[21] Reg. §1.704-1(b)(2)(iv)(f).

be a corresponding revaluation of all of the members' capital accounts. The LLC must use the following procedures in making the revaluation:

1.   The LLC must adjust the value of its properties to fair market value on the date of contribution or distribution.
2.   The LLC is treated as having sold the property and recognizing gain or loss for capital account purposes. The amount of gain or loss is the difference between the fair market value of the property and the LLC's capital account value for the property immediately prior to the revaluation. There is no tax gain, since the revaluation of the property is not a taxable event.
3.   The LLC must allocate the book gain or loss to the members' capital accounts. The book gain or loss is normally allocated based on the members' share of profits and losses in the LLC.
4.   The LLC must allocate book depreciation, amortization, depletion, and book gain or loss for the revalued property in accordance with the safe-harbor regulations. For example, the amount of depreciation taken for book purposes must be based on tax depreciation multiplied by a fraction, the numerator of which is the book value of the assets on the date of contribution and the denominator of which is the tax basis.
5.   The LLC must allocate tax depreciation, amortization, depletion, and tax gain or loss based on the rules contained in Section 704(c) of the Internal Revenue Code.[22] For example, if the property contributed by one member is revalued for capital account purposes, the other members must be allocated tax depreciation attributable to the property equal to what they would have received if the revalued property had a tax basis equal to its capital account value.

EXAMPLE 1

Three equal members each contribute $50 to an LLC to buy land for $150. After three years, the land increases in value to $300. The members have a basis and capital account in the LLC as follows:

Member	Basis in Membership Interest	Capital Account	Fair Market Value of Membership Interest
A	$50	$50	$100
B	$50	$50	$100
C	$50	$50	$100

If Member D contributes $100 to the LLC in exchange for a one-fourth interest in the LLC, then the LLC has several alternatives. If the LLC does not revalue its assets, Member D will receive one-fourth of the book gain on sale of property, and one-fourth of the tax gain (since tax gain must

---

[22] Reg. §1.704-1(b)(4)(i).

ordinarily be allocated in the same manner as book gain). This allocation is not fair since $150 of any gain on sale of the property is attributable to the precontribution gain for the land when held by Members A, B, and C.

Alternatively, the LLC could make a special allocation of the first $150 of book gain to Members A, B, and C. It would also allocate the first $150 of tax gain to those members since tax gain must ordinarily follow book gain.[23] All the members would share equally in book and tax gain to the extent that the property sold for more than $300.

The LLC could also elect to revalue all of its assets for book purposes when Member D makes the initial capital contribution to the LLC. The LLC would treat the revaluation as a sale of the asset for fair market value, resulting in book gain (but not tax gain) of $150. All of the book gain would be allocated to the capital accounts of Members A, B, and C since they were the only members who owned an interest in the LLC immediately prior to the contribution. Under IRC Section 704(c), the LLC must allocate the built-in tax gain of $150 (difference between capital account value and tax basis) to Members A, B, and C for tax purposes when the property is sold. In this case, the tax gain is not allocated in the same manner as book gain. For example, if the LLC sold property for $300, there would be $150 of tax gain, but no book gain since the LLC previously revalued the land for book purposes from $150 to $300. By rebooking its assets to fair market value on the date of Member D's contribution, the LLC has avoided different ratios for allocating book income. It may then allocate all book income on a sale of the assets equally to the four members in accordance with their one-fourth interest in the LLC, since there is no book gain unless the property sells for over $300.

EXAMPLE 2

An LLC has two equal members, Members A and B. The LLC owns depreciable equipment. The financial statements for the LLC show the following:

Fair market value of equipment	$30,000
LLC's tax basis for equipment	$10,000
LLC's capital account value for equipment (original purchase price, less book depreciation)	$10,000
Member A's capital account	$10,000
Member B's capital account	$10,000
Remaining annual tax depreciation on equipment at 10% a year for 10 years	$ 1,000

---

[23] IRC §704(b).

Members C and D contribute land to the LLC in exchange for a 50 percent interest in the LLC (25 percent each). The land has a tax basis and a fair market value of $30,000. The LLC is not required to revalue any of its assets on the date of contribution, since the contributed property's fair market value is equal to its tax basis. The LLC elects not to revalue its remaining property. Therefore, the capital accounts for the four equal members in the LLC are as follows after the contribution:

Member A	$10,000
Member B	$10,000
Member C	$15,000
Member D	$15,000

EXAMPLE 3

Same facts as in Example 2, except that the LLC makes the election to adjust the basis of its remaining assets for capital account purposes. The rebooking of the assets to fair market value has the following capital account and tax consequences:

- The LLC is treated as having sold the equipment at a $10,000 gain. This is the difference between the fair market value of the property and the book value of the asset to the LLC. The gain is recognized for book purposes only. There is no tax gain, since the revaluation of the property is not a taxable event.
- The $10,000 of book gain is allocated $5,000 to Member A and $5,000 to Member B in accordance with their profit-sharing ratio immediately prior to the contribution. No part of the gain is allocated to Members C and D, since they had no interest in the property prior to the date of contribution.
- Each member has a capital account of $15,000 after the revaluation. This is equal to one-fourth of the $60,000 fair market value of the property. The LLC increases the book value of its property from $50,000 to $60,000 as a result of the revaluation.
- Since the tax depreciation is $1,000 per year, the book depreciation must be $3,000 per year. The $30,000 fair market value of the equipment is three times as high as the $10,000 tax basis of the equipment. Therefore, there must be three times as much depreciation for book purposes as there is for tax purposes. The book depreciation must be allocated equally to all of the members ($750 each) in accordance with their equal shares of profits and losses, as set forth in the operating agreement.
- The tax depreciation of $1,000 must be allocated entirely to Members C and D ($500 each). They did not contribute any property to the LLC that was revalued. The equipment would have generated $3,000 of tax depreciation if it had a tax basis of $30,000, equal to its fair market

value. Members C and D would have received $750 of depreciation (1/4 × $3,000) if Members A and B had contributed equipment with a fair market value equal to its tax basis. Therefore, Members C and D must each be allocated $750 of tax depreciation each year, equal to their book depreciation. Since the LLC has only $1,000 of tax depreciation, it allocates only $500 of tax depreciation each to Members C and D.

EXAMPLE 4

Same facts as in Example 2, except that the LLC sells the equipment for $28,000 before taking any additional depreciation. There is $2,000 of book loss, equal to the difference between the $30,000 book value and the $28,000 sale price. The $2,000 of loss is allocated equally to the members for book purposes ($500 each) in accordance with their percentage interests in profits and losses. For tax purposes, there is an $18,000 gain. This is equal to the difference between the $28,000 sale price and the $10,000 tax basis in the equipment. The entire $18,000 gain must be allocated to Members A and B ($9,000 each). Under Section 704(c), the built-in gain or loss must be allocated to the members who contributed the property to the LLC or who were members in the LLC at the time of revaluation. The $18,000 allocation of tax gain to Members A and B has no effect on the members' capital accounts. Each member has a capital account value of $14,500 after the sale (original capital account value of $15,000, less book depreciation of $500).

[C] Liquidating Distributions

The second requirement under the safe-harbor regulations is that liquidating distributions (after payment to creditors) be made in accordance with positive capital account balances.[24] The capital account balances are determined after taking into account the revaluations and adjustments referred to above. For example, the LLC must book up the gain on the appreciated assets prior to liquidation, and allocate that gain to the members' capital accounts.

Practice Note: Liquidating distributions are not always equal to the members' positive capital account balances. There are certain circumstances under the safe-harbor regulations in which distributions may exceed positive capital account balances. The operating agreement should provide that distributions will be made in accordance with the members' positive capital account balances, and that distributions in excess of positive capital account balances will be made in accordance

---

[24] Reg. §1.704-1(b)(2)(ii)(b)(2).

with each member's percentage interest in the LLC (or based on the number of membership units owned by each member compared to the number of membership units owned by all members).

The LLC must make the liquidating distributions by the later of (a) the end of the LLC tax year in which the LLC is liquidated, or (b) within 90 days after the date of the liquidation.[25]

[D]   Restoration of Deficits

The third requirement under the safe-harbor regulations is that a member be unconditionally obligated to restore any deficit capital account balance following the liquidation of his interest. The deficit account must be restored by the later of the end of the tax year or 90 days following the liquidation.[26] Any member who has a negative capital account balance on liquidation must contribute sufficient cash to the LLC to restore the capital account to zero.

Members may satisfy an alternative test so that they are not obligated to restore negative capital account balances on liquidation of the LLC. Under the alternative test, the operating agreement must contain a loss limitation. The LLC may not allocate losses to members that cause a negative capital account balance. The operating agreement must also contain a qualified income offset. If a member has an unexpected negative capital account balance, the LLC must allocate additional income or gain to the member as quickly as possible in order to bring that member's capital account balance back up to zero. These requirements are discussed below.

This alternative test applies only to recourse debt. There are separate rules that apply to nonrecourse debt.[27]

[1]   Loss Limitation

The first additional provision that an LLC operating agreement must contain under the alternative deficit restoration test is a loss limitation provision. The LLC may not allocate losses to a member to the extent that such losses create a deficit capital account balance for that member[28] in excess of the member's share of LLC minimum gain that would be recognized on a foreclosure of the LLC's property.[29] The LLC minimum gain for such purposes is the amount by which nonrecourse liabilities encumbering LLC property exceed the book value of the property. Any loss not allocated to a member as result of this restriction must be

---

[25] *Id.*

[26] Reg. §1.704-1(b)(2)(ii)(b)(3).

[27] *See* §8.02[F] *infra.*

[28] *See* Reg. §1.704-1(b)(2)(ii)(d)(3).

[29] *See* Reg. §1.704-1(b)(2)(ii)(d)(6).

allocated to the other members (to the extent such other members are not also limited with respect to loss allocations).

Any loss reallocated to another member as a result of this restriction may be taken into account in computing subsequent allocations of income and losses so that the net amount of any item so allocated, and income and losses allocated to each member, is, to the extent possible, equal to the amount that would otherwise have been allocated to each member if there had been no loss reallocation.

In determining whether an allocation creates a negative capital account balance, the LLC must first reduce each member's capital account by the following amounts:[30]

- All reasonably expected future depletion allowances for oil and gas depletion.
- All reasonably expected future allocations of loss or deduction mandated by certain Code provisions that may override Section 704(b). These include the required allocations under the family partnership rules,[31] the varying interest rules,[32] and the gain and loss rules.[33]
- All reasonably expected future distributions that, as of the end of the year, exceed reasonably expected increases in the member's capital account,[34] other than expected gain from the sale of LLC assets.[35] This is the most important adjustment and the only adjustment that will apply for most LLCs. The purpose of this rule is to prevent the LLC from delaying a promised distribution until the year following a loss year so that the member will have a sufficient capital account to cover the current-year loss allocation. Under the safe-harbor regulations, the LLC may make distributions that cause a negative capital account. The LLC may not make loss allocations that cause a negative capital account.

EXAMPLE 1

An LLC has 10 equal members. All members share equally in profits and losses except that the LLC allocates all depreciation to Member A. The capital account of each member during 1999 is $1,000. The LLC earns $20,000 of income, which it allocates equally to all of the members ($2,000 each). It has $1,500 of depreciation, which it allocates entirely to Member A. It also has $30,000 of cash flow available for distribution and sends a $3,000 check to each of the members on December 31. The $1,500 special allocation of depreciation to Member A may not be made because it causes a negative capital account for Member A as follows:

---

[30] Reg. §1.704-1(b)(2)(iv)(k).
[31] IRC §704(e)(2).
[32] IRC §706(d).
[33] IRC §751.
[34] Reg. §1.704-1(b)(2)(ii)(d)(6).
[35] Reg. §1.704-1(b)(2)(ii)(d).

Initial capital account	$ 1,000
Plus income allocation	2,000
Less distribution	(3,000)
Less special allocation of depreciation	(1,500)
Ending capital account balance	$(1,500)

EXAMPLE 2

Same facts as in Example 1. In order to prevent the special allocation from causing a negative capital account at the end of the year, Member A asks the LLC to delay his distribution from December 31 to January 1 of the following year. As a result, Member A's ending capital account balance for 1999 is $1,500, determined as follows:

Initial capital account	$ 1,000
Plus income allocation	2,000
Less special allocation of depreciation	(1,500)
Ending account balance	$ 1,500

The $3,000 distribution on January 1 of the following year reduces Member A's positive capital account balance of $1,500 to a negative capital account balance of $1,500. The special allocation safe-harbor rules do not prevent distributions that cause negative capital accounts. They only prevent special allocations that create negative capital accounts. Unfortunately, Member A is still not entitled to receive the $1,500 special allocation in 1999. His 1999 capital account balance must be reduced by the $3,000 distribution that is reasonably expected on January 1 of the following year. The $1,500 special allocation of depreciation may not be made for 1999, since it causes a negative capital account balance after taking into account the reasonably expected distribution in 2000. The special allocation for 1999 may be made only if Member A is required to restore any negative capital account balance upon liquidation of the LLC.

EXAMPLE 3

Members A and B each contribute $1,000 to the capital of the LLC at the beginning of 2003. The operating agreement provides that each member will share equally in profits and that all the net losses will be allocated to Member B. The LLC incurs $1,400 of net losses in 2003, which it allocates to Member B. The capital accounts are as follows:

	A	B
Capital account at beginning of year	$1,000	$1,000
Loss allocation		($1,400)
Capital account at end of year	$1,000	($ 400)

The allocation of the first $1,000 in losses to Member B has economic effect because it reduces the amount that she will receive on liquidation of the LLC. The allocation of the remaining $400 has no economic effect because it does not reduce the amount that Member B will receive on liquidation. If the LLC liquidated, Member A would receive $600 and Member B would receive nothing. The only effect of the $400 allocation is to reduce Member B's taxable income.

The LLC may do one of two things in order to comply with the safe-harbor regulations. First, it may include a deficit restoration provision in the operating agreement. Under the deficit restoration provision, each member would be required to restore any deficit capital account balance on liquidation of the LLC by contributing cash to the LLC equal to the deficit amount. Thus, if the LLC liquidated at the end of 2003, Member B would be required to contribute $400 to the LLC. In such case, Member A would receive a liquidating distribution of $1,000 and Member B would receive nothing. The special loss allocation of $1,400 in 2003 would have economic effect because it would affect the amount that Member B would be entitled to receive on liquidation of the LLC.

Alternatively, the LLC operating agreement may provide that a special allocation may not cause or increase a deficit balance in a member's capital account as of the end of the year in which the allocation is made. Under this provision, the LLC could only allocate $1,000 of losses to Member B in 2003. It would allocate the remaining $400 of losses to Member A. This is the more common provision in an operating agreement. A member is not required to restore negative capital accounts on liquidation of the LLC if this alternative provision (and the qualified income offset provision discussed below) are included in the operating agreement.

[2] Qualified Income Offset

The second additional provision that an LLC operating agreement must contain under the alternative deficit restoration test is a qualified income offset. The special allocation rules restrict the LLC from allocating losses to a member that create a deficit capital account balance, but do not restrict the LLC from making distributions to a member that cause, or increase, a deficit account balance. For example, if a member's capital account has been reduced to zero as a result of loss allocations, the LLC may make distributions to that member. The distributions in such case would create a negative capital account balance.

However, if a member unexpectedly receives any adjustment, allocation, or distribution described Regulations Section 1.704-1(b)(2)(ii)(d)(4), (5), or (6) that causes a deficit capital account balance, the LLC must allocate to that member items of income and gain (consisting of a *pro rata* portion of each item of LLC income and gain for the year) in an amount sufficient to eliminate such deficit balance as quickly as possible.[36] This is called a "qualified income offset provision."

Any special allocations of income and gain under the qualified income offset provision may be taken into account in computing subsequent allocations of income and losses so that the net amount of any item so allocated, and income and losses allocated to each member, is to the extent possible equal to the amount that would have been allocated to each member if the LLC had not made the special allocation.

EXAMPLE

Member A has a $100,000 capital account balance at the beginning of 2002. Member A receives a loss deduction of $100,000 in 2002, which reduces her capital account balance down to $0. Member A receives a distribution of $10,000 during 2002 even though the LLC had no income or loss during the year. The distribution creates a $10,000 negative capital account balance. The distribution is an "unexpected" distribution, since it was not a projected or scheduled distribution as of the last day of the prior year. Under the qualified income offset rule, Member A must receive a special allocation of $10,000 during 2003 (or as soon as practical thereafter) in order to eliminate the negative capital account balance. The LLC operating agreement should provide that this special allocation will reduce the amount of any other income allocated to Member A during 2003 under the regular 50 percent–50 percent profit allocation provisions.

[E]   *Substantiality of Economic Effect*

The fourth requirement under the safe-harbor regulations is that the economic effect of such allocations be "substantial." The economic effect of an allocation is substantial if there is a reasonable possibility that it will affect the dollar amount that the members receive from the LLC, independent of tax consequences.[37] The economic effect of an allocation is usually not substantial if:

- The allocation enhances one member's after-tax economic position, but is not likely to substantially diminish another member's after-tax economic position;[38]

---

[36] *See* Reg. §1.704-1(b)(2)(ii)(d) (last flush paragraph).

[37] Reg. §1.704-1(b)(2)(iii).

[38] Reg. §1.704-1(b)(2)(iii)(a).

- The allocation shifts tax consequences among the members without substantially altering economic consequences;[39] or
- The allocation is temporary due to the likelihood of a subsequent offsetting allocation.[40]

EXAMPLE 1

An LLC has two equal members. During 2001, the LLC earns $100,000 of operating income and $100,000 of capital gains. Member A has $100,000 of net operating losses that will expire at the end of the year. Member B has $100,000 of capital losses. At the end of the year, the LLC decides to allocate all of the operating income to Member A and all of the capital gain to Member B. During the following year, it changes its allocation back to the normal allocation method, with each member sharing equally in all items of profit and loss. The economic effect of the allocation is not substantial because it is a temporary allocation that is designed to shift the after-tax benefits to the members without any other economic effect.

EXAMPLE 2

An LLC has two equal members, an individual and a tax-exempt organization. The LLC earns $500 of taxable income and $500 of tax-exempt income. It allocates all the tax-exempt income to the individual and all the taxable income to the tax-exempt organization. The allocation has economic effect because the LLC keeps capital accounts, allocates income and losses to the members' capital accounts, and provides for liquidating distributions in accordance with positive capital accounts. However, the economic effect of the allocation is not substantial because the allocation of the tax-exempt income to one member and the taxable income to the other member has no economic effect other than to reduce taxes.

[F] Nonrecourse Debt

[1] Overview

The fifth requirement under the safe-harbor regulations concerns nonrecourse debt allocations. The regulations assume that special allocations of nonrecourse deductions cannot have economic effect, after the outstanding loan balance exceeds the members' capital accounts, since it is the lender who bears the economic

---

[39] Reg. §1.704-1(b)(2)(iii)(b).
[40] Reg. §1.704-1(b)(2)(iii)(c).

risk of loss.[41] However, allocations of nonrecourse deductions will be respected under the safe-harbor regulations if:[42]

- All of the safe-harbor requirements discussed above for recourse debt are met. The LLC must maintain capital accounts, liquidating distributions must be made in accordance with capital account balances, and there must be an unconditional promise to restore deficit account balances upon liquidation (or compliance with the alternative test).[43]
- Nonrecourse deductions are allocated in a manner that is reasonably consistent with allocations that have substantial economic effect of other significant LLC items attributable to the property securing the nonrecourse liabilities.[44] Generally, this means that the LLC must allocate deductions to the members in the same way that it allocated deductions prior to the time that the outstanding loan balance exceeded the book value of the property. This rule is discussed below.[45]
- The LLC operating agreement contains a minimum gain chargeback. There are two types of minimum gain chargebacks, LLC minimum gain chargebacks and member minimum gain chargebacks. These are discussed below.[46]
- All other material allocations and capital account adjustments under the operating agreement must have substantial economic effect.[47]

[2] Determination of Nonrecourse Debt Deductions and Minimum Gain

The first step in applying the special allocation rules to nonrecourse debt deductions is determining the amount of deductions that are treated as nonrecourse deductions. Nonrecourse debt is debt for which no member of the LLC is personally liable in the event of default. Usually, the nonrecourse debt is secured by a mortgage or deed of trust on the property purchased with the debt proceeds.

An LLC is not required to comply with the allocation rules for nonrecourse debt deductions if the book value of the property exceeds the outstanding loan balance encumbering the property. When the book value exceeds the loan balance, the members bear the risk of loss if the property declines in value. The depreciation and other deductions attributable to the property reduce their equity in the property. The lender is not at risk since the book value exceeds the loan balance.

The regulations achieve this result by creating a concept called "minimum gain."[48] The LLC must comply with the special allocation rules for nonrecourse

---

[41] Reg. §1.704-2(b)(1).
[42] Reg. §1.704-2(e).
[43] Reg. §1.704-2(e)(1).
[44] Reg. §1.704-2(e)(2).
[45] *See* §8.02[F][3] *infra.*
[46] Reg. §1.704-2(e)(3).
[47] Reg. §1.704-2(e)(4).
[48] Reg. §1.704-2(d).

debt only if the depreciation or other deduction attributable to property securing the nonrecourse debt creates minimum gain. Minimum gain is the gain that the LLC would realize if the LLC abandoned the property or gave a deed to the lender in lieu of foreclosure. It is the amount by which the nonrecourse liability exceeds the tax basis (or book value, if different) of the encumbered property.[49]

EXAMPLE 1

LLC property has an adjusted tax basis of $300,000 and is encumbered by a mortgage of $400,000 for which the members are not personally liable. The minimum gain that would be recognized on transfer of the property back to the lender for no consideration is $100,000 (amount realized equal to the $400,000 debt relief, less tax basis of $300,000).

In computing minimum gain, book value is used instead of tax basis if the book value is different from tax basis.[50]

EXAMPLE 2

LLC property has a tax basis of $200,000 and a book value of $300,000. The property is encumbered by a mortgage of $400,000. The minimum gain that would be recognized on transfer of the property back to the lender for no consideration is $100,000 (amount realized equal to the debt relief of $400,000, less book value of $300,000).

These rules mean that an LLC must comply with the special allocation rules for nonrecourse debt deductions only if a deduction attributable to nonrecourse property causes the book value of the property to decline below the outstanding loan balance, or increases the amount of the deficit between book value and loan value.

Nonrecourse debt deductions normally arise from depreciation or amortization of LLC property. For example, if the nonrecourse debt encumbering the property remains constant, the depreciation or amortization deductions will eventually lower the book value of the property below the outstanding debt and result in minimum gain (i.e., excess of liabilities over the book value of property).

[3] Reasonable Consistency Requirement

Special allocations of nonrecourse debt under the safe-harbor regulations must satisfy the reasonable consistency test. The nonrecourse deduction allocations

---

[49] Reg. §1.704-2(d)(1), (3).
[50] Reg. §1.704-2(d)(3).

must be reasonably consistent with allocations of deductions attributable to the property securing the nonrecourse liabilities.

EXAMPLE

An LLC has two equal members, who each contribute $50,000 to the LLC. The LLC borrows $200,000 and purchases equipment for $300,000. Members A and B share equally in profits and losses except that all depreciation is allocated to Member A. The LLC operating agreement provides that liquidating distributions will be made in accordance with each member's positive capital account balance. It also provides that a member with a negative capital account must restore the deficit in the capital account upon liquidation only to the extent that other members have positive capital account balances after distribution of all liquidation proceeds. The LLC takes $50,000 of book and tax depreciation per year on the equipment. Its income and expenses are equal each year except for the depreciation, which is allocated to Member A. The loan is an interest-only loan for the first 10 years. The reasonable consistency test for special allocations is applied as follows:

- After the first year, the $50,000 of depreciation reduces the value of the equipment to $250,000 for book purposes. The regulations assume that the value of the property declines by the amount of book depreciation. At this point, the members of the LLC bear the economic risk of loss from the decline in value, since the $250,000 value for the equipment is still higher than the $200,000 nonrecourse loan encumbering the equipment.
- Member A's capital account is reduced from $50,000 to zero as a result of the $50,000 special allocation of depreciation. Member B's capital account stays at $50,000, since Member B does not receive distributions, loss allocations, or depreciation. If the LLC sold the equipment for its presumed value of $250,000, the lender would receive the first $200,000 of liquidation proceeds, and Member B would receive the remaining $50,000, equal to his positive capital account balance. The special allocations of depreciation during the first year are not subject to the special allocation rules for nonrecourse debt, since the members of the LLC rather than the lender bear the risk of loss for the decline in value due to the depreciation deduction.
- The same principles apply during the second year. The special allocation rules for nonrecourse deductions do not apply, since the members of the LLC rather than the lender bear the economic risk of loss attributable to the depreciation deduction. The regulations assume that the value of the property will decline to $200,000 after the second year as a result of the additional $50,000 of book depreciation. If the LLC sold the property for its $200,000 in value, the lender would receive the full proceeds of the sale in payment of the $200,000 debt. The members of the LLC would not receive any proceeds of the sale.

Member A would be required to restore his $50,000 deficit account balance, which would be distributed entirely to Member B, who has a $50,000 positive capital account balance.

- The special allocation rules for nonrecourse debt deductions would apply during the third year, since the next $50,000 of depreciation reduces the book value of the property to $150,000. This is less than the $200,000 outstanding debt encumbering the property. At this point, it is the lender who bears the economic risk of loss. If the property were sold for its book value of $150,000, the lender would receive only $150,000 and would incur a $50,000 loss. The allocation of the nonrecourse depreciation deduction must now be reasonably consistent with the allocation of deductions from the same source that had substantial economic effect. Therefore, the LLC may continue to allocate all of the depreciation deductions to Member A, since Member A received all the depreciation deductions on the same property when such allocations had substantial economic effect. The depreciation allocations to Member A during the third and subsequent years satisfy the reasonably consistent requirement.

[4] LLC Minimum Gain Chargeback

If there is a decrease in LLC minimum gain during the year, the LLC must allocate to each member items of income and gain for the year equal to that member's share of the decrease in minimum gain. Minimum gain is the amount by which the nonrecourse liability exceeds the tax basis (or book value, if different) of the encumbered property.[51] For example, there is $10,000 of minimum gain if the book value of the property is $20,000 and the nonrecourse debt encumbering the property is $30,000. The chargeback is made for both tax and book purposes.

Minimum gain increases when the LLC incurs additional liability with respect to encumbered property or when the book value of the property decreases (e.g., through depreciation deductions). Minimum gain decreases when there is a decrease in the amount by which nonrecourse liabilities exceed the book value of the encumbered property. For example, there is reduction in minimum gain when the LLC makes capital improvements to encumbered property, repays principal on the nonrecourse debt, or sells the property.

A member's share of minimum gain and the decrease in minimum gain is based on the amount of nonrecourse deductions and distributions of the proceeds of nonrecourse financing to the member that caused the minimum gain.

---

[51] Reg. §1.704-2(d)(1). Reg. §1.704-2(d)(3) states that book value must be used in making the computations if there is a disparity between book value and the adjusted tax basis of the property.

EXAMPLE 1

An LLC has three members, who share profits and losses equally. The members currently have the following capital account balances:

Member A	$20,000
Member B	$40,000
Member C	$30,000

The LLC owns property that was purchased with a nonrecourse loan. The property has been depreciated down to $0. The book value and tax basis of the property are $0. All of the depreciation deductions were allocated to Member C. The outstanding amount of the loan was $10,000 as of the end of the prior year. The LLC has no income or loss for the year. It uses $10,000 of cash to pay off the loan during the year. The minimum gain chargeback is determined as follows:

Step 1: Determine the amount of minimum gain as of the end of the prior year. This is $10,000, the amount by which the outstanding nonrecourse loan on the property exceeds its book value. The LLC would recognize $10,000 of book income if it gave the property back to the lender for no consideration (amount realized equal to the $10,000 debt relief, less book value of $0).

Step 2: Determine the net decrease in the minimum gain during the year. The net decrease is $10,000. After the loan is repaid during the year, there is no book gain that the LLC would recognize if it transferred the property back to the lender for no consideration.

Step 3: Determine each member's share of the decrease in minimum gain. All of the minimum gain and decrease in minimum gain must be allocated to Member C, since he received all of the nonrecourse depreciation deductions that caused the minimum gain (i.e., that caused the book value of the property to decline below the outstanding nonrecourse debt on the property).

Step 4: Allocate items of income and gain to Member C equal to the net decrease in minimum gain before the regular income allocations are made. Member C must be allocated $10,000 of income. Since the LLC has no income during the year, the minimum gain chargeback carries over to the next year. Member C must be allocated $10,000 of income during the next year as the minimum gain chargeback.

EXAMPLE 2

An LLC purchases depreciable equipment in 1999 for $100,000, subject to a $100,000 interest-only nonrecourse debt. There is $25,000 of depreciation during the first year. All of the depreciation deductions are allocated to Member A. The nonrecourse debt encumbering the equipment exceeds the book value of the equipment by $25,000 as a result of the depreciation allocated to Member A. Therefore, there is $25,000 of minimum gain at the end of 1999. The LLC then decides to make a $5,000 repayment on the loan. The debt repayment has no effect on the members' capital accounts. However, it reduces the minimum gain to $20,000, since the nonrecourse debt now exceeds the book value of the property by only $20,000. The LLC must allocate to Member A $5,000 of future LLC income, equal to the $5,000 reduction in the minimum taxable gain.[52]

The minimum gain chargeback rules do not apply to the extent a member contributes money to the LLC that is used to repay the nonrecourse liability, or that is used for capital improvements that increase the book value of the property encumbered by a nonrecourse debt.[53]

[5] Member Minimum Gain Chargeback

An LLC must comply with the member minimum gain rules when an LLC incurs debt that is nonrecourse as to the LLC, but recourse as to a member. The following rules apply in such case:

- LLC losses and deductions attributable to the nonrecourse liability must be allocated to the members who bear the economic risk of loss.[54] All of the members bear the economic risk of loss to the extent that the book value of the property exceeds the outstanding loan balance encumbering the property. The LLC may allocate the depreciation and other deductions to all the members in accordance with the operating agreement if the book value of the property exceeds the outstanding loan balance.
- The member against whom the liability is recourse bears the economic risk of loss when the book value of the property is less than the liabilities encumbering the property. The LLC must allocate all of the deductions attributable to the property to that member to the extent that the deductions reduce the book value of the property below the outstanding loan balance. For example, if a member makes a nonrecourse loan to an LLC that is used to purchase a building, the lending member bears the economic risk of loss if the LLC fails to repay the loan. The LLC must allocate all of the depreciation to the lending member when the book value of the property is less than the outstanding loan balance.
- The LLC must keep track of increases in member minimum gain. Member minimum gain is the book gain that the LLC would recognize if the LLC

---

[52] Reg. §1.704-2(f).
[53] Reg. §1.704-2(f)(3).
[54] Reg. §1.704-2(i)(1).

gave the property back to the lender for no consideration.[55] This is the amount by which the outstanding liabilities encumbering the property exceed the book value of the property.[56] Member minimum gain normally arises when the LLC takes deductions that cause the book value of the property to decline below the liabilities encumbering the property. As discussed above, the LLC must make a special allocation of these deduction items to the member who bears the risk of loss. During any year in which there is a net increase in member minimum gain, the LLC must simply note in its records that the member minimum gain arose as a result of deductions allocated to a particular member.

- During any year in which there is a net decrease in member minimum gain, there must be a member minimum gain chargeback. Under the member minimum gain chargeback rules, the LLC must make a special allocation of income or gain to the member who received the deductions in prior years that gave rise to the member minimum gain. The amount of the special allocation is equal to the net decrease in member minimum gain during the year.[57]

EXAMPLE 1

An LLC borrows $100,000 from Member B in 2002 (interest-only loan for 10 years) to buy property for $120,000. The loan is nonrecourse to the LLC. The first $20,000 of depreciation may be allocated to all of the members in accordance with the LLC operating agreement. The remaining depreciation that causes the book value of the property to decline below the debt encumbering the property must be allocated to Member B, who is then the only member who bears the risk of loss if the loan is not repaid.

EXAMPLE 2

Same facts as in Example 1. In 2005, the property has an adjusted basis and book value of $40,000. The outstanding loan balance is $60,000. Therefore, the member minimum gain is $20,000 (the amount of book gain that would be recognized if the LLC gave the property back to the lender for no consideration). The LLC must note in its records that this $20,000 increase in member minimum gain is attributable to depreciation and other deductions allocated to Member B that caused the book value of the property to decline below the outstanding loan balance of $60,000.

---

[55] Reg. §1.704-2(i)(3).

[56] The book gain in such case would be the amount realized (the debt canceled by the lender) less the book value of the property.

[57] Reg. §1.704-2(i)(4).

EXAMPLE 3

Same facts as in Examples 1 and 2. During 2006, the LLC repays the loan in full. There is a decrease in member minimum gain of $20,000, since the amount of liabilities in excess of book value has been reduced from $20,000 to $0. Therefore, the LLC must make a special allocation of income or gain to Member B during 2006 under the member minimum gain chargeback rules before any other allocations.

§8.03 ALLOCATIONS RELATED TO CONTRIBUTED PROPERTY

[A] Overview

An LLC must allocate income, gain, loss, and deductions with respect to contributed property among the members so as to take account of the variation between the tax basis and the fair market value of the property at the time of contribution.[1] Generally, this means that the LLC must allocate built-in gains and losses to the members who contributed the property to the LLC. If the LLC revalues its property when a new member contributes property to the LLC in exchange for a membership interest, the LLC must allocate the built-in gains and losses of the revalued LLC assets to the existing members of the LLC. The allocations must be made for tax purposes, not book (accounting) purposes.

On December 21, 1993, the IRS issued final regulations on contributed property.[2] Under the regulations, the LLC may use one of the following four methods for making allocations for contributed property:

1. The traditional method.
2. The traditional method with curative allocations.
3. The remedial allocation method.
4. Any other reasonable method that takes into account the built-in gains and losses so that the contributing member receives the tax burdens and benefits of any built-in gain or loss.

An LLC is not required to make the special allocations for contributed property if there is only a small difference between the book value (fair market value) and the contributing member's basis for the property. The difference is considered small if (1) the difference between the book value and the basis of all properties that a member contributes to the LLC during the same tax year is not more than

---

§8.03   [1] IRC §704(c)(1)(A).
[2] Reg. §1.704-3; T.D. 8500 (Dec. 21, 1993).

15 percent of the basis for such properties, and (2) the total gross difference between book value and basis does not exceed $20,000.[3]

[B]   Traditional Method

The first method of allocation for contributed property is the traditional method. The basic rules under the traditional method are as follows:

- The built-in gains or losses on contributed property must be allocated to the contributing member for tax purposes when the property is sold. There is no built-in gain or loss allocation for book purposes, since the value of the property is adjusted to fair market value in the contributing member's capital account on the date of contribution.
- The tax depreciation and other tax deductions allocated to the noncontributing members must equal the deductions they would have received if the contributed property had a tax basis equal to its fair market value on the date of contribution.
- If the contributed property is depreciable, the built-in gains and losses are reduced as the difference between the book value and basis of the contributed property decreases. The amount of the reduction is the difference between the book depreciation and the tax depreciation. When the property is sold, only the adjusted built-in gain or loss must be allocated to the contributing member.

[1]   Built-In Gains and Losses

The first rule under the traditional method is that built-in gains and losses for contributed property must be allocated to the contributing member when the property is sold.[4] The initial built-in gain is the amount by which the fair market value of the property as reflected on the books of the LLC exceeds its adjusted tax basis on the date of contribution. The built-in loss is the amount by which the member's adjusted tax basis for the property exceeds its fair market value as reflected on the books of the LLC on the date of contribution.[5] The built-in gains and losses are determined on a property-by-property basis rather than on an aggregate net basis.[6]

LLC operating agreements sometimes provide that the contributing member has a right to veto the sale of appreciated property for a period of time after the

---

[3] Reg. §1.704-3(e)(1).
[4] Reg. §1.704-3(b)(1).
[5] Reg. §1.704-3(a)(3)(ii).
[6] Reg. §1.704-3(a)(2). However, an LLC may aggregate built-in gains and losses from contributed property and from revaluations of property if certain requirements are met. Ltr. Ruls. 200123035 (regarding inventory), 200124030, 9909045; Reg. §1.704-3(e)(2), (3).

contribution, so that the contributing member will not immediately be taxed on the appreciation.

EXAMPLE 1

One of the members of an LLC contributes LIFO inventory to the LLC. The LIFO inventory constitutes Section 704(c) property. Any built-in gain or loss attributable to the inventory must be allocated back to the contributing member when the LLC recognizes gain or loss on the sale of the inventory. The built-in gain or loss is equal to the difference between the book value of the inventory (fair market value on date of contribution) over the contributing member's tax basis in the inventory.[7]

EXAMPLE 2

An LLC has two equal members. Member A contributes land to the LLC. The land has an adjusted basis of $10,000. The parties decide that the land has a fair market value of $17,000. The LLC credits Member A's capital account with $17,000. Member B contributes $17,000 in cash to the LLC. The LLC sells the property two years later for $19,000. The LLC recognizes $2,000 of book gain, equal to the difference between the $19,000 sale price of the property and the $17,000 book value of the property. The $2,000 of book gain is allocated equally to each member in accordance with the operating agreement and increases each member's capital account from $17,000 to $18,000. There is $9,000 of tax gain, equal to the difference between the $19,000 sale price and the LLC's $10,000 adjusted basis in the property. The first $7,000 of tax gain must be allocated to Member A, since there was $7,000 of built-in gains on the date of contribution to the LLC. The remaining $2,000 of tax gain is allocated equally between the members based on their equal profits interest in the LLC. The allocation of tax gain does not affect the members' capital accounts.

Under the ceiling rule, the total amount of tax gain or loss allocated to a member for a tax year cannot exceed the total LLC gain or loss with respect to the property for the tax year.[8]

EXAMPLE 3

Same facts as in Example 2, except that the LLC sells the land for $15,000. The LLC has a book loss of $2,000, equal to the difference between the

---

[7] Ltr. Rul. 200123035, *citing* Reg. 1.704-3(a)(3)(i).
[8] Reg. §1.704-3(b)(1).

$15,000 sale price and the $17,000 book value of the property. The book loss is allocated equally between the members in accordance with the operating agreement and decreases each of their capital accounts by $1,000, from $17,000 to $16,000. The LLC has a tax gain of $5,000, equal to the difference between the $15,000 sale price and the LLC's $10,000 adjusted tax basis in the property. Ordinarily, the $7,000 of built-in gains would be allocated to Member A, who contributed the property to the LLC. However, only $5,000 of tax gain is allocated to Member A, since the LLC has only $5,000 of tax gain on the sale of the property.

EXAMPLE 4

Two members formed an LLC that is classified as a partnership. A member contributes LIFO inventory to the LLC. The LIFO inventory is IRC Section 704(c) property. Thus, any built-in gain or loss attributable to the inventory must be allocated to the contributing member for tax purposes when the inventory is sold. On approval by the IRS, the LLC may treat the items included in opening inventory as having been acquired at the same time, and determine their cost by the average cost method as provided under IRC Section 472(b)(3).[9]

[2]   Allocations of Tax Deductions

The second rule under the traditional method is that tax depreciation and other tax deductions for contributed property must be allocated to the noncontributing members equal to what they would have received if the contributed property had a tax basis equal to its fair market value on the date of contribution. This means that depreciation and other tax deductions must first be allocated to the noncontributing members equal to their allocable share of such items as determined for book purposes.[10] The contributing members are then allocated any remaining amount of such tax deductions. The LLC may not allocate additional income to the noncontributing members to make up for the deficiency.

EXAMPLE 1

An LLC has two equal members. Member A contributed depreciable property to the LLC with an adjusted tax basis of $80,000 and a fair market value of $100,000. Member B contributed $100,000 of cash to the LLC. The LLC depreciates the property for book and tax purposes over a remaining

---

[9] Rev. Rul. 92-97, 1992-2 C.B. 124; Rev. Rul. 94-4, 1994-1 C.B. 195.
[10] Reg. §§1.704-3(b); 1.1245-1(e)(2)(iii), Example 3(ii).

period of 10 years on a straight-line basis. For book purposes, the LLC has $10,000 of depreciation (one-tenth of the $100,000 book value). It allocates $5,000 of book depreciation to Member A and $5,000 of book depreciation to Member B. The LLC has $8,000 of tax depreciation (one-tenth of the $80,000 adjusted basis). In the absence of Section 704(c) of the Internal Revenue Code, it would allocate $4,000 of tax depreciation to Member A and $4,000 to Member B. However, since there was built-in gain on the date of contribution, the LLC must allocate $5,000 of tax depreciation to Member B (the noncontributing member), equal to the depreciation that he would have received if the contributed property had a tax basis equal to its fair market value on the date of contribution. Member B would have received $5,000 of depreciation if the property had a $100,000 adjusted basis on the date of contribution. Therefore, the LLC must allocate $5,000 of tax depreciation to Member B, equal to his $5,000 of book depreciation. Member A, the contributing member, receives the remaining $3,000 of tax depreciation. The different allocations of tax depreciation do not affect the members' capital accounts. Both members' capital accounts are reduced from $100,000 to $95,000 as a result of the $5,000 of book depreciation for each member.

Under the ceiling rule, the tax deductions allocated to a member for a tax year with respect to contributed property cannot exceed the total LLC deductions with respect to the property.[11]

EXAMPLE 2

Same facts as in Example 1, except that the adjusted basis for the contributed property is $40,000 instead of $80,000. Since the LLC depreciates the property for book and tax purposes on a straight-line basis over 10 years, it has $10,000 of book depreciation and $4,000 of tax depreciation. Ordinarily, the LLC would be required to allocate to Member B, the noncontributing member, $5,000 of tax depreciation, equal to Member B's book depreciation. However, there is only $4,000 of allowable tax depreciation. Therefore, only $4,000 of tax depreciation is allocated to Member B, and no tax depreciation is allocated to Member A.

[3]   Reductions in Built-In Gains and Losses

The third rule under the traditional method is that the built-in tax gains and losses are reduced as the difference between the book value and basis of the contributed property decreases.[12] The reduction is equal to the difference between

---

[11] Reg. §§1.704-3(b)(1); 1.1245-1(e)(2)(iii), Example 3(ii).
[12] Reg. §1.704-3(a)(3)(ii).

book depreciation and tax depreciation. When the property is sold the LLC must allocate to the contributing member for tax purposes only the reduced amount of built-in gain or loss.

EXAMPLE

An LLC has two equal members. Member A contributes property to the LLC with an adjusted basis of $80,000 and a fair market value of $100,000. Member B contributes $100,000 cash. The LLC depreciates the property for book and tax purposes on a straight-line basis over a remaining period of 10 years. The LLC therefore has $10,000 of book depreciation and $8,000 of tax depreciation. It allocates the book depreciation equally between the members ($5,000 to each member). It is required to allocate $5,000 of tax depreciation to Member B, the noncontributing member, since that is the amount of tax depreciation that Member B would have received if Member A had contributed property to the LLC with a $100,000 tax basis, equal to its fair market value. The remaining $3,000 of tax depreciation is allocated to Member A. Since the book depreciation exceeds the tax depreciation by $2,000, the built-in gains are reduced by $2,000. The initial $20,000 of built-in gains is reduced to $18,000. The recomputed built-in gains are also equal to the difference between the LLC's book value for the property of $90,000 ($100,000 book value, less $10,000 of book depreciation) and the $72,000 adjusted tax basis for the property ($80,000 initial tax basis, less $8,000 of tax depreciation). If the LLC sold the property at a gain, the first $18,000 of tax gain would be allocated to Member A as the contributing member, and the remaining tax gain would be allocated equally between the members in accordance with their profits interests in the LLC.

[C]   Traditional Method with Curative Allocations

The second method of allocation for contributed property is the traditional method with curative allocations.[13] This method is the same as the traditional method, except that the LLC allocates additional items of income or loss to the members to make up for the limits on allocations required by the ceiling rule under the traditional method. The curative allocations reduce or eliminate the differences between book allocations and tax allocations for the noncontributing members. Curative allocations are tax allocations only. They have no effect on book allocations.

Curative allocations for built-in gain property may be made in one of the following two ways:[14]

---

[13] Reg. §1.704-3(c).
[14] Reg. §1.704-3(c)(3)(iii); Reg. §1.704-3(c)(4), examples 1 and 2.

- Allocate additional items of tax deduction or loss to the noncontributing member to substitute for a deduction or loss that is not available to the member as a result of the ceiling rule; or
- Allocate additional amounts of taxable income or gain to the contributing member equal to the deduction or loss that is not available to the noncontributing member as a result of the ceiling rule.

Similar rules apply for built-in loss property.

The allocation of additional items of tax deduction or loss to the noncontributing member, and the allocation of additional items of income or gain to the contributing member, come from the other member's share of those items. For example, if a noncontributing member is allocated less tax depreciation than book depreciation for built-in gain property as a result of the ceiling rule, the LLC must allocate more tax depreciation to that member from another item of LLC property to make up the difference.[15] Alternatively, the LLC may allocate more taxable income to the contributing member.

EXAMPLE 1

An LLC has two equal members. Member A contributes $2,800 cash to the LLC. Member B contributes Building 1 to the LLC. The property has a tax basis of $800 and a fair market value of $2,800. The LLC depreciates the property over a period of four years. Thus, there is $700 of book depreciation each year (1/4 × $2,800) and $200 of tax depreciation (1/4 × $800). The LLC must allocate $350 of book depreciation on the property to each member in accordance with the operating agreement. This allocation reduces each member's capital account by $350. Under the traditional method, the LLC would be required to allocate $350 of tax depreciation to Member A. This is equal to the book depreciation that Member A, as the noncontributing member, receives from the property. However, the LLC may allocate only $200 of tax depreciation to Member A under the ceiling rule because there is only $200 of tax depreciation.

EXAMPLE 2

Same facts as in Example 1, except that the LLC elects to make curative allocations under Regulations Section 1.704-3(c), using depreciation on other property owned by the LLC. The LLC also owns Building 2 that generates $400 of book and tax depreciation each year that is allocated equally to the members ($200 each). Thus, $150 of the $200 tax depreciation that would otherwise be allocated to Member B under the traditional method must

---

[15] Reg. §§1.704-3(c)(1); 1.1245-1(e)(2)(iii), Example 3(iii).

> be reallocated to Member A under the traditional method with curative allocations.[16] The book depreciation is not affected by the curative allocations and is allocated equally between the members.

The curative allocation must be made within a reasonable period of time. The LLC operating agreement must provide for the curative allocation for the year of contribution or revaluation. It may be made only to the extent necessary to avoid the distortion created by the ceiling rule. The items used for the curative allocations must have the same character (e.g., capital or ordinary) as the items affected by the ceiling rule.[17] If the LLC does not have a sufficient amount of like character items to make the curative allocation in a particular year, the LLC may not make catch-up curative allocations in succeeding years,[18] subject to two exceptions.[19]

[D] Remedial Allocation Method

The third method of allocation for contributed property is the remedial allocation method.[20] The LLC may correct distortions caused by the ceiling rule by making remedial allocations. The remedial allocations reduce or eliminate the differences between book allocations and tax allocations for the noncontributing members. Remedial allocations are tax allocations only. They have no effect on book allocations.

The LLC makes remedial allocations by creating pairs of tax items: an income or gain item to the contributing member, and an offsetting deduction or loss item for the noncontributing member. These items do not really exist. They are made up by the LLC. The aggregate taxable income or loss of the LLC remains the same because the income or gain item created by the LLC always equals the offsetting deduction or loss item created by the LLC.

The LLC creates the remedial allocation items only to the extent necessary to eliminate the disparity between book and tax allocations for the noncontributing member caused by the ceiling rule. The LLC makes a remedial allocation of tax items to the noncontributing member equal to the full amount of the disparity between book and tax allocations for the noncontributing member caused by the

---

[16] Reg. §1.1245-1(e)(2)(iii), Example 3(iii).

[17] Reg. §1.704-3(c)(3)(iii)(A).

[18] Reg. §1.704-3(c)(3)(i).

[19] Under the first exception, catch-up curative allocations are permitted on disposal of the property. Reg. §1.704-3(c)(3)(iii)(B). Under the second exception, catch-up curative allocations are permitted if they are made in subsequent years over a reasonable period of time, such as the property's economic life, and the membership agreement in effect for the year of contribution provides for the catch-up curative allocations. Reg. §1.704-3(c)(3)(ii). See also Reg. §1.704-3(c)(4), example 3(ii)(C), in which there were sufficient curative items in a subsequent year, but use of the full catch-up amount in such year would have been an unreasonable use of the curative method. The curative allocations would have been reasonable if made over the property's economic life of 10 years rather than over the property's remaining depreciation recovery period of one year.

[20] Reg. §1.704-3(d).

ceiling rule. The LLC then allocates the offsetting remedial item to the contributing member.

The remedial allocation method requires the contributing member to amortize its built-in book gain into taxable income, and enables the non-contributing member to amortize for tax purposes its share of the fair market value book basis in the contributed assets.

EXAMPLE 1

An LLC has two equal members. Member A contributes nondepreciable land to the LLC with a tax basis of $60,000 and a fair market value of $100,000. Member B contributes $100,000 in cash to the LLC. The LLC sells the land one year later for $80,000. There is $20,000 of tax gain ($80,000 sale price minus $60,000 tax basis). All of the $40,000 of built-in tax gain on the date of contribution must be allocated to Member A when the property is sold. However, since there is only $20,000 of tax gain, only $20,000 of tax gain is allocated to Member A under the ceiling rule. There is also a $20,000 book loss ($100,000 capital account value of property on date of contribution less $80,000 sale price). The $20,000 book loss is allocated equally to the two members, since the members share equally in profits and losses under the operating agreement for the LLC. The ceiling rule causes a discrepancy between the book and tax values for the members. If the remedial allocation method is not used, the book and tax values for each member are as follows (assuming no other items of income, gain, or loss).

Date of contribution

	Basis in LLC	Capital Account Value
Member A	$ 60,000	$100,000
Member B	$100,000	$100,000

Date of sale (using traditional method with ceiling rule)

	Basis in LLC	Capital Account Value
Member A	$ 80,000	$90,000
Member B	$100,000	$90,000

In order to eliminate the $10,000 discrepancy between book and tax values for each member, the LLC may elect to use the remedial allocation method. The LLC does this by creating $10,000 in tax capital gains that it allocates to Member A (which increases Member A's tax basis). The LLC also creates $10,000 in tax capital losses that it allocates to Member B (which decreases Member B's tax basis). This straightens out the imbalance between the tax basis and capital account for each member as follows.

Date of sale (using remedial allocation method)

	Basis in LLC	Capital Account Value
Member A	$90,000	$90,000
Member B	$90,000	$90,000

The effect of the remedial allocation method in this case is to increase the tax basis of the member contributing the appreciated asset to the LLC by the built-in gain prior to the date of contribution, less the member's share of postcontribution loss. Thus, Member A's original tax basis of $60,000 in the membership interest is increased by the $40,000 of precontribution built-in gain, reduced by the member's $10,000 share of postcontribution loss.

EXAMPLE 2

An LLC has two equal members. Member A contributed depreciable property to the LLC with a tax basis of $60,000 and a fair market value of $100,000. Member B contributed $100,000 of cash to the LLC. The LLC has no items of income, gain, loss, deduction, or credit other than depreciation. It has $20,000 of book depreciation, which it allocates equally between Member A and Member B in accordance with the operating agreement. It has $6,000 of tax depreciation. Normally, the LLC would be required to allocate $10,000 of tax depreciation to Member B as a noncontributing member, since that is the amount of book depreciation that was allocated to Member B for capital account purposes. However, because of the ceiling rule, the LLC can allocate only $6,000 of tax depreciation to Member B and no tax depreciation to Member A. The LLC cannot use the traditional method with curative allocations, since it has no other items of tax depreciation from other property to allocate to Member B. Under the remedial allocation method, the LLC creates $4,000 of additional tax depreciation, which it allocates to Member B. It also creates an additional $4,000 of ordinary income, which it allocates to Member A as the contributing member. The result is that Member B receives $10,000 of tax depreciation, equal to the $10,000 of book depreciation (even though the LLC has only $6,000 of tax depreciation). Member A recognizes $4,000 of taxable ordinary income (even though the LLC has no taxable income).

The amount of remedial allocation that must be made each year is the difference between the book allocation and the tax allocation of the income or deduction item for the noncontributing member. For example, if the noncontributing member receives $10,000 of book depreciation and $8,000 of tax depreciation for the year, then the remedial allocation amount is $2,000 of tax depreciation allocated to the noncontributing member and $2,000 of offsetting ordinary income allocated to the contributing members.

There is a special rule for depreciation under the remedial allocation method. Generally, the LLC must compute depreciation for book purposes over a longer period than under the curative method. There are two components to book depreciation.[21] First, the LLC has book depreciation on the tax basis of the contributed property. Second, the LLC has book depreciation on the built-in gain portion of the contributed property in excess of the tax basis. Under the remedial allocation method, the LLC may continue to compute book depreciation on the tax basis of the contributed property over the remaining tax depreciation period. However, it must compute book depreciation on the book value of the property in excess of the tax basis over the longer period that applies to newly acquired property of the same type. The result is that there will be less of a difference between book and tax depreciation each year, but the disparity between book and tax depreciation will continue for a longer period of time. Thus, the remedial allocations to each member are less each year, but continue for a longer period of time (i.e., over the longer depreciation period that applies to newly acquired property of the same type).[22] This rule differs from the curative allocation method, which allows the LLC to take book depreciation over the contributed property's remaining tax recovery period.

EXAMPLE 1

An LLC has two equal members. Member A contributes depreciable property to the LLC with an adjusted basis of $20,000 and a fair market value of $100,000. Member B contributes $100,000 of cash. The property is depreciable on a straight-line basis over 10 years for book and tax purposes. The property has two years remaining for tax depreciation. Consequently, the LLC has $10,000 of tax depreciation ($20,000 adjusted basis divided by the remaining two years). The LLC has $50,000 of book depreciation ($100,000 book value divided by the remaining two years). The LLC allocates $25,000 of book depreciation to Member A and $25,000 to Member B. Under the traditional method with curative allocations, the LLC allocates all of the $2,000 tax depreciation to Member B. It also makes a curative allocation of $23,000 of other tax deductions of the same type and character to Member B that would otherwise go to Member A. Member B, as the noncontributing member, thus receives $25,000 of ordinary tax deductions, equal to the $25,000 of book deductions allocated to him. The entire book/tax deferential is taken into account over the remaining two-year tax life of the property.

EXAMPLE 2

Same facts as in Example 1, except that the LLC uses the remedial allocation method rather than the traditional method with curative allocations.

---

[21] Reg. §1.704-3(d)(2).
[22] Reg. §1.704-3(c)(4), Example 1; Reg. §1.1245-1(e)(2)(iii), Example 3(iv).

Therefore, the LLC must use the special rule for calculating book depreciation. The portion of the book depreciation up to the $20,000 tax basis is recovered in the same manner as the tax basis over the remaining depreciation period. This results in book depreciation of $10,000 during each of the first two years. The remainder of the $80,000 book basis in excess of tax basis is recovered using any available tax method and period for newly purchased property of the type that Member A contributed to the LLC. In this case, the contributed property is 10-year straight-line depreciable property. This results in additional book depreciation of $8,000 per year ($80,000 remaining depreciation divided by 10 years). The total book depreciation during the first two years is $18,000 ($10,000, plus $8,000). This book depreciation is allocated $9,000 to each member. Since Member B, as a noncontributing member, received only $2,000 of tax depreciation ($7,000 less than his book depreciation), the LLC must create $7,000 of additional tax depreciation for allocation to Member B and $7,000 of ordinary income for allocation to Member A.

EXAMPLE 3

Same facts as in Example 1. After the second year, the LLC has no further tax depreciation. The book value of the depreciable asset has been reduced to $64,000 as a result of the $36,000 of book depreciation. The LLC must now depreciate the property for book purposes at the rate of $8,000 a year for the remaining eight years. It allocates $4,000 of book depreciation to each member in accordance with the operating agreement. Since Member B, as a noncontributing member, receives no tax depreciation, the LLC must make a remedial allocation to Member B of $4,000 of tax depreciation in years 3 through 10, equal to his book depreciation. The LLC must make a simultaneous remedial allocation of $4,000 of taxable income to Member A.

[E] Other Reasonable Methods

The LLC may use any other reasonable method of allocation for contributed property that takes into account the built-in gains and losses so that the contributing member receives the tax benefits and burdens of the built-in gains and losses.

[F] Disguised Sales

An LLC must allocate the built-in gain on appreciated property to the contributing member if there is a disguised sale. The three principal types of disguised sales are (a) a contribution of appreciated property to an LLC followed by a related distribution of money to the contributing member within two years after the contribution, (b) a contribution of appreciated property to an LLC by one member followed by a distribution of that property to another member within seven years after the contribution, and (c) a contribution of appreciated property to an LLC followed by a distribution of other property to the contributing member within seven years after the contribution.[23]

§8.04 RETROACTIVE ALLOCATIONS AND VARYING INTEREST RULE

[A] Overview

An LLC may make retroactive allocations after the close of its tax year by amending the operating agreement. The amendment may be made at any time prior to the due date (not including extensions) for filing of its tax return for the prior year.[1] Therefore, an LLC can decide after the end of the tax year how to allocate income, gains, losses, deductions, and credits to the members for the prior year.

However, there are various limitations on retroactive allocations, including the following:

- The allocation of cash items, such as interest, taxes, and payments for services or property, must be based on the number of days during the year that the taxpayer was a member in the LLC.
- The allocation of other items must take into account the varying interests of the members in the LLC during the tax year and cannot be allocated to new members to the extent attributable to periods prior to the time they became members.[2]
- Special allocations must have substantial economic effect.

[B] Varying Interest Rule

Under the varying interest rule, an LLC must take into account the varying interests of the members in the LLC during the tax year.[3] An LLC may not make retroactive allocations to a member of income, gain, loss, deduction, or credit that was received or incurred before that member joined the LLC. The LLC must take account of other changes in a member's interest in the LLC in making allocations, including increases or decreases in the membership interest during the year. The rule does not prevent an LLC from changing the shares of existing members where the changes are not attributable to additional capital contributions.[4]

There are two methods for allocating LLC items among members when their

---

[23] See §6.05 supra.
§8.04 [1] IRC §761(c).
[2] IRC §706(d).
[3] IRC §706(d)(1); Reg. §1.706-1(c)(4).
[4] Lipke v. Commissioner, 81 T.C. 689 (1983).

interests change during the year: the interim closing of the books method and the proration method. There is also a required proration rule for allocable cash-basis items.

[C] Interim Closing of the Books Method

Under the interim closing of the books method, the LLC closes its tax year on the date that membership interests are altered. The LLC allocates items of income, gain, credit, and deduction incurred before the change to the members based on their interests in the LLC prior to the change. The LLC allocates income, gain, credit, and deduction incurred after the change to members based on their interests in the LLC after the change.

An LLC that uses the interim closing of the books method may use a semi-monthly convention. Members entering the LLC during the first 15 days of the month are treated as entering on the first day of the month. Members entering the LLC after the fifteenth day of the month, but before the end of the month, are treated as entering on the sixteenth day of the month.

[D] Proration Method

To avoid an interim closing of the LLC's books, the LLC may use the proration method of accounting. Under the proration method, the members may use any reasonable proration method to determine the distributive shares of the withdrawing member and any successor member for the LLC year that closes early with respect to that member. Normally, this means that the LLC allocates each item of income, deduction, credit, and loss among the members in proportion to the number of days each was a member during the year. The IRS may require the proration method unless the LLC establishes that the interim closing of the books method would have produced a different result.[5] The proration method may be used only if there is an agreement among the members.[6]

Items may be prorated based on daily apportionment or any other method provided by regulations.[7] Legislative history indicates that IRS regulations should provide for use of a monthly convention to determine allocations.[8] Under the monthly convention, members entering the LLC after the fifteenth day of the month are treated as entering on the first day of the following month. Members entering the LLC during the first 15 days of the month are treated as entering on the first day of the month.

---

[5] Johnson v. Commissioner, 84 T.C. 344 (1985); Adams v. Commissioner, 82 T.C. 563 (1984).
[6] Reg. §1.706-1(c)(2)(ii).
[7] IRC §706(d)(1).
[8] Conference Committee Report to the Tax Reform Act of 1986, P.L. 99-514.

EXAMPLE

A member sells her membership interest on June 30. At the end of the tax year on December 31, the LLC determines that the member's distributive share of income would have been $30,000 if the member had remained a member for the entire tax year. Therefore, the members may agree to allocate $15,000 of income to the selling member (1/2 × $30,000) and $15,000 to the purchasing member. If the LLC had instead used the interim closing of the books method, it would have allocated income to the buying and selling members based on when the income was earned. Therefore, if $20,000 of the income had been earned during the first half of the year, it would have allocated $20,000 to the selling member and $10,000 to the buying member.

[E] *Allocable Cash-Basis Items*

[1] Definition

There is a special rule for cash-basis items. An LLC that uses the cash method of accounting must allocate the following "allocable cash basis items" to members on a daily apportionment basis:[9]

- Interest
- Taxes
- Payment for services or for use of property
- Any other item specified in IRS regulations[10]

Prior to the Tax Reform Act of 1976, there were certain abuses in the allocation of income and deductions. Since all losses of an LLC are deemed to occur on the last day of the fiscal year, persons would buy into an LLC on the final day of the fiscal year and receive an allocable share of losses for the entire year. In addition, it was very easy for an LLC that used the cash method of accounting to pay cash basis items after the period during which such items accrued, thus giving the benefits of tax deductions to persons who became members after the expenses accrued. These abuses were eliminated by the proration rule for cash-basis items.

[2] Allocation Rules

There is a two-step process for allocating cash-basis items. First, the cash-basis items are assigned to each day during the tax year in which the items accrued.[11]

---

[9] IRC §706(d)(2).
[10] IRC §706(d)(2)(B).
[11] IRC §706(d)(2)(A)(i).

Second, the cash-basis items are assigned to each member in proportion to his membership interest at the close of each day.[12]

EXAMPLE 1

An LLC has four equal members. The LLC earns interest income during the calendar year of $4,000. The interest income was attributable to a bank deposit on December 1 of the year. Member A became a member of the LLC on December 1. The $4,000 of interest must be assigned to the month of December, when it was earned. Since Member A was a 25 percent member of the LLC during the entire calendar month of December, the LLC must allocate to Member A $1,000 (25% × $4,000) of the interest income.

EXAMPLE 2

Same facts as in Example 1, except that the $4,000 of interest income received in December was interest on a promissory note that was outstanding for the entire calendar year. The LLC must allocate to Member A $83.33 of interest income (1/12 × 25% × $4,000).

The LLC may use a monthly convention for cash-basis items that is similar to the monthly convention for the regular proration method.

The LLC must allocate cash-basis items attributable to periods before the current tax year to the first day of the year.[13] These items are then allocated to the persons who were members during the prior period to which the cash-basis items were attributable based on their varying interests in the LLC during that period. The LLC must capitalize that portion of the cash-basis items that is allocated to persons who are no longer members in the LLC on the first day of the tax year in which the items are taken into account.[14] Capitalized expenses are allocated to the basis of LLC assets under Section 755 of the Internal Revenue Code.[15]

Any allocable cash-basis items attributable to periods after the current tax year must be allocated to the last day of the tax year.[16]

The purpose of the rules is to prohibit an LLC from retroactively allocating cash-basis deductions to a member that were generated prior to the admission of the member to the LLC. An LLC can often avoid the consequences

---

[12] IRC §706(d)(2)(A)(ii).
[13] IRC §706(d)(2)(C).
[14] IRC §706(d)(2)(D)(ii).
[15] IRC §706(d)(2)(D)(i).
[16] IRC §706(d)(2)(C).

of the rule by allocating a disproportionate share of other deductions to the new member if the deductions were generated after the member's admission.

[3] Expenses Allocated to Prior Years

If an LLC pays cash-basis expenses after the close of the fiscal year to which such expenses are attributable, then such expenses are treated as paid on the first day of the fiscal year.[17] The amounts are then allocated among persons who were members in the LLC during the period in the prior fiscal year to which the expenses are allocable in accordance with each member's varying interest in the LLP during such period.

If an amount is allocated to a person who is no longer a member in the LLC on the first day of the fiscal year, then such amount must be capitalized and allocated to the remaining assets under IRC Section 755. This will give the remaining members a deduction or reduced share of income to the extent it is allocable to depreciable items, inventory or other items that offset the gain.

[4] Prepaid Items

If there are prepaid items of interest, taxes, rent, or payment for services, then such items are assigned to the last day of the tax year.[18]

§8.05 FAMILY ALLOCATIONS

[A] In General

The family partnership rules restrict the ability of an LLC to shift income among family members through gifts and sales of membership interests.[1] A family member is a spouse, ancestor, lineal descendant, or trust established for the primary benefit of such person.[2] If the LLC does not comply with the family partnership rules, the donee will not be recognized as a member for tax purposes, and the IRS may reallocate the donee's distributive share of income and other items to the donor.[3]

---

[17] IRC §706(d)(2)(C)(i).
[18] IRC §706(d)(2)(C)(ii).
§8.05 [1] IRC §704(e).
[2] Reg. §1.704-1(e)(3).
[3] Reg. §1.704-1(e)(3)(i)(b).

[B]   Requirements

A donee who acquires a membership interest in an LLC by gift, or who purchases a membership interest from another family member, will be recognized as a member for tax purposes if the five requirements discussed below are met.

[1]   Capital Is Material Income-Producing Factor

The first requirement is that capital must be a material income-producing factor.[4] If capital is not a material income-producing factor, then all of the service income will be allocated to the members who perform the services under the assignment of income doctrine, rather than to the donee member who does not perform services (or only to the extent that the donee member performs bona fide services).

The determination of whether capital is a material income-producing factor is based on all the facts and circumstances. Generally, capital will be a material income-producing factor if a substantial portion of the LLC's gross income is attributable to capital. For example, capital will be a material income-producing factor if the LLC's operation requires substantial inventories or a substantial investment in plant, machinery, or other equipment. Capital is not a material income-producing factor if the LLC's income consists principally of fees, commissions, or other compensation for personal services performed by members and employees of the LLC.[5]

[2]   Donee Must Own Capital Interest

The second requirement is that the donee must own a capital interest in the LLC.[6] The donee may acquire the capital interest by purchase or gift from any other person. A capital interest is an interest in the assets of the LLC that is distributable to the member on withdrawal from the LLC or on liquidation of the LLC. The mere right to participate in earnings and profits of the LLC is not a capital interest.[7]

[3]   Reasonable Compensation

The third requirement is that the LLC must reasonably compensate the donor member for services rendered to the LLC.[8] Thus, the donor cannot assign income

---

[4] Reg. §1.704-1(e)(1)(ii).
[5] Reg. §1.704-1(e)(1)(iv).
[6] Reg. §1.704-1(e)(1)(ii).
[7] Reg. §1.704-1(e)(1)(v).
[8] Regs. §1.704-1(e)(1)(ii), (e)(3)(i)(a).

attributable to his services by making a gift to a family member who does not perform services.

If the LLC does not reasonably compensate the donor member for services, the IRS may make a reasonable allocation for the services of the donor, and then attribute the balance of any income to the LLC capital of the donor and donee. The portion of income allocated to LLC capital for the tax year must be allocated between the donor and donee in accordance with their respective interests in LLC capital.[9]

[4]   Donee's Share of Income

The fourth requirement is that the donee's distributive share of income relative to his or her capital interest may not be greater than the donor member's share of LLC income relative to his or her capital interest.[10]

If the LLC does not comply with this requirement, then the IRS may make a reasonable allocation for the services of the donor, and then attribute the balance of any income to the LLC capital of the donor and donee. The portion of income allocated to LLC capital for the tax year must be allocated between the donor and donee in accordance with their respective interests in LLC capital.[11]

[5]   Tax Avoidance Purposes

The fifth requirement is that the donor member's transfer of an LLC interest to the donee may not be a mere sham for tax avoidance purposes. The donee or purchaser must be the real owner of the membership interest. The transfer must vest dominion and control of the membership interest in the donee member. The determination of whether the donee is the real owner of the membership interest, and whether the donee has dominion and control over such interest, is based on all the facts and circumstances. Isolated facts are not determinative.[12] Transfers between family members are closely scrutinized.[13]

The following factors indicate that the donor has retained too much control:

- The donor has a right to withhold distributions of income, other than amounts retained by the LLC annually for the reasonable needs of the business.[14]
- There are restrictions on the donee's right to liquidate or sell his membership interest without financial detriment.[15]

---

[9] Reg. §1.704-1(e)(3)(i)(b).
[10] Regs. §1.704-1(e)(1)(ii), (e)(3)(i)(a).
[11] Reg. §1.704-1(e)(3)(i)(b).
[12] Reg. §1.704-1(e)(2)(i).
[13] Reg. §1.704-1(e)(1)(iii).
[14] Reg. §1.704-1(e)(2)(ii)(a).
[15] Reg. §1.704-1(e)(2)(ii)(b).

- The donor retains control of assets essential to the business, such as assets that the donor leases to the LLC.[16]
- The donor retains management powers inconsistent with normal relations among members.[17]
- The donee is a minor.[18]

The following factors indicate that the donee member exercises sufficient dominion and control:

- The donor signs legally sufficient and irrevocable deeds or other instruments under state law transferring the property to the donee.[19]
- The donee substantially participates in the control and management of the LLC, including participation in major policy decisions affecting the business.[20]
- The LLC makes actual distributions to the donee member of the entire amount or major portion of his distributive share of income for the sole benefit and use by the donee.[21]
- The donee is actually treated as a member in the operation of the business, and in relations with customers and creditors.[22] Some of the factors in this connection include (a) compliance with local LLC, fictitious names, and business registration statutes, (b) control of business bank accounts, (c) recognition of the donee's rights in distributions of LLC property and profits, (d) recognition of the donee's interest in insurance policies, leases, and other business contracts, and in litigation affecting the business, and (e) the existence of an operating agreement, records for memoranda that establish the LLC, and set forth the rights and liabilities of the members.[23]

EXAMPLE

John sells a 50 percent interest in his LLC to his daughter, Judy. Capital is a material income-producing factor. John performs services for the LLC that have a reasonable compensation value of $10,000. Judy does not perform any services for the LLC. The LLC has $50,000 of profits at the end of the year. The maximum profits that the LLCs may allocate to Judy for the year is $20,000 ($50,000 − $10,000 reasonable value of services by John × 50%).

---

[16] Reg. §1.704-1(e)(2)(ii)(c).
[17] Reg. §1.704-1(e)(2)(ii)(d).
[18] Reg. §1.704-1(e)(2)(viii).
[19] Reg. §1.704-1(e)(2)(i).
[20] Reg. §1.704-1(e)(2)(iv).
[21] Reg. §1.704-1(e)(2)(v).
[22] Reg. §1.704-1(e)(2)(vi).
[23] Id.

9

Basis and Member's Share of Debt

§9.01 GENERAL

[A] Importance of Basis

Basis is important for the following reasons:

- A member's basis in a membership interest determines the amount of gain or loss on sale,[1] liquidation,[2] or other disposition of the membership interest.
- Losses may be deducted only to the extent of a member's basis in the membership interest.[3] Losses in excess of basis are suspended and may be carried over to years in which the member has basis in the LLC.[4]

---

§9.01   [1] *See* §§15.02 and 15.03 *infra* for discussion of basis and gain computation on sale of a membership interest.

[2] *See* §10.03[B] *infra*.

[3] IRC §704(d). *See* §13.02 *infra* for discussion of basis limitations on loss pass-through to members.

[4] IRC §704(d); Reg. §1.704-1(d)(2).

- Distributions of money in excess of basis result in taxable gain.[5]
- The basis of property distributed in liquidation of a membership interest is equal to the member's basis in the membership interest, reduced by any money distributed.[6] The basis of property in a nonliquidating distribution cannot exceed the member's basis in the membership interest, reduced by any money distributed in the same transaction.[7]

[B] *Inside and Outside Basis*

A member's basis in the membership interest is referred to as the "outside basis." An LLC's basis in its assets is referred to as the "inside basis." The inside basis and outside basis are initially the same. There is a carryover basis for assets that a member contributes to an LLC. The inside and outside basis are initially the same when the members contribute property on formation of an LLC, subject to certain exceptions.[8] The inside and outside basis may become different under the following circumstances:

- The member sells a membership interest at a price that is different from the basis in the membership interest. The purchasing member's basis in the membership interest is the purchase price, rather than the selling member's basis.
- The member dies. The estate of the member receives a step up or step down in basis of the membership interest to fair market value as of the date of death or six months after the date of death.
- The LLC makes a nonliquidating money distribution to the member in excess of the member's basis in the membership interest. The member's outside basis is reduced to zero, and the money distribution in excess of basis is taxable gain.
- The LLC makes a nonliquidating property distribution to a member, in excess of the member's basis in the membership interest. The basis of distributed assets in a nonliquidating distribution cannot exceed the member's basis in his membership interest prior to the distribution, reduced by any money received in the same distribution.[9]
- The LLC makes a liquidating distribution to a member. The basis of property (other than money) distributed to the member is equal to the member's interest in the LLC prior to the distribution, reduced by any money distributed.[10] The inside and outside basis for the remaining members in the LLC will be different to the extent that the money and the adjusted basis of the

---

[5] IRC §731(a)(1).

[6] IRC §732(b).

[7] IRC §732(a)(2).

[8] For example, a member may incur legal, accounting, tax, and other expenses in connection with the acquisition of a membership interest that must be capitalized and added to the basis of the membership interest. These capitalized expenses do not give rise to inside basis.

[9] IRC §732(a)(2).

[10] IRC §732(b).

property distributed by the LLC are different from the distributee member's adjusted basis in the membership interest immediately prior to the distribution.

- The LLC receives money for the grant of an option. The grant of the option is not taxable income to the LLC, but will increase the inside basis, since the LLC has received money. The members' outside basis will not increase, since the option money is not taxable income and is not income exempt from tax. It is merely deferred income.

The LLC may normally keep the inside and outside basis the same in each of these cases by making an election under Section 754 of the Code.[11] Section 754 elections are discussed below.[12]

[C] Differences Between Capital Account and Basis

A member's basis is not the same as the member's capital account. There are the following differences:

- Basis includes a member's share of LLC liabilities. The capital account does not include LLC liabilities.[13]
- When a member contributes property to an LLC, the basis of the membership interest is increased by the adjusted basis of the property contributed. The capital account is increased by the fair market value of property contributed.[14]
- The capital account and basis for individual members will differ as a result of depreciation allocations if a member contributes appreciated property to the LLC. Under IRC Section 704(c), the LLC may allocate the book depreciation to the members in accordance with their percentage interest in the LLC, but must allocate all of the tax depreciation to the noncontributing members up to the amount of depreciation they would have received if the property had been contributed with a basis equal to fair market value. On sale of property, the LLC may allocate the book gain to the members in accordance with their percentage interest in the LLC, but must allocate all of the pre-contribution tax gain to the contributing member.[15]
- When a member sells a membership interest, the new member receives a basis equal to the purchase price of the membership interest. The new member receives a capital account equal to the capital account of the selling member.[16]

---

[11] See §10.06 *infra* regarding the Section 754 election in connection with distributions, and §15.08 regarding the Section 754 election in connection with transfers.

[12] See §10.06 *infra* with respect to distributions and §15.08 *infra* with respect to transfers of membership interests.

[13] Reg. §1.704-1(b)(2)(iv)(c).

[14] Reg. §1.704-1(b)(2)(iv)(b).

[15] See §8.03 *supra*.

[16] Reg. §1.704-1(b)(2)(iv)(l).

- The basis and capital account can each fluctuate in amount independently. For example, an LLC may revalue its property to fair market value for capital account purposes when members contribute additional property to the LLC.[17] The revaluation does not change the members' bases in their membership interests. Likewise, the death of a member results in a step up or step down in basis of the membership interest to fair market value. The adjustment to basis on death does not result in an adjustment to the capital account for the estate of the deceased member.
- The LLC depreciates its assets for book purposes based on the fair market value and useful lives of the assets. The LLC must depreciate assets for tax purposes under one of the methods permitted by the Code.

Many LLCs keep capital accounts on a tax basis. In such case, the only difference between capital accounts and basis is that basis includes a member's share of LLC liabilities, and capital accounts do not.

§9.02 BASIS DETERMINATIONS

[A] Initial Basis

A member's initial basis in a membership interest depends on how the member acquired the membership interest, as follows:

- *Contribution.* The initial basis of a member who acquires a membership interest in exchange for contributions to the capital of an LLC is the sum of (1) the cash contributed, (2) the adjusted basis of property contributed, and (3) any gain recognized on contribution of the property to the LLC.[1] A member may recognize gain on contributions of property to an LLC only in very limited circumstances.[2]
- *Promissory note.* The initial basis of a member who acquires a membership interest in exchange for a promissory note is zero since a promissory note has a zero basis. The member acquires basis, and is treated as contributing capital to the LLC, when the member makes payments on the promissory note to the LLC.[3]
- *Purchase.* The initial basis of a member who acquires a membership interest by purchase from another member is the purchase price.[4]
- *Gift.* The initial basis of a member who acquires a membership interest by gift is the sum of (a) the donor's adjusted basis for the membership interest,

---

[17] Reg. §1.704-1(b)(2)(iv)(f).

§9.02 [1] IRC §722.

[2] *See* §6.01[A][1] *supra.*

[3] Rev. Rul. 80-235, 1980-2 C.B. 229; Levy v. Commissioner, 732 F.2d 1435 (9th Cir. 1984); Irvin J. Bussing v. Commissioner, 88 T.C. 49 (1987).

[4] IRC §§742, 1012.

and (b) any gift taxes paid in connection with the gift.[5] However, if the basis exceeds the fair market value at the time of the gift and the property is subsequently sold at a loss, then the basis for determining loss is the fair market value on the date of the gift.[6] The basis may be increased by the amount of any gift taxes paid, up to the fair market value of the property on the date of the gift.[7]

*   *Inheritance.* The initial basis of a member who acquires a membership interest by inheritance is the fair market value of the membership interest as reported for estate tax purposes.[8] Fair market value is normally determined as of the date of death. However, if the estate of the decedent is obligated to pay estate taxes, the estate may elect the alternate valuation date that is six months after the decedent's death.[9]

[B]   Increases in Basis

A member's initial basis in a membership interest is increased by the following items:

*   Additional cash that the member contributes to the LLC;[10]
*   The member's adjusted basis in additional property contributed to the LLC;[11]
*   The member's distributive share of taxable income from the LLC, whether or not distributed;[12]
*   The member's distributive share of tax-exempt income from the LLC, whether or not distributed;[13]
*   The member's distributive share of deductions for depletion to the extent the deductions exceed the basis of LLC property subject to depletion;[14]
*   Any increase in the member's share of LLC liabilities.[15]

[C]   Decreases in Basis

A member's initial basis in a membership interest is decreased by the following items:

[5] IRC §§742, 1015.
[6] IRC §1015(a).
[7] IRC §1015(d).
[8] IRC §§742, 1014(a).
[9] IRC §§2031, 2032.
[10] Reg. §1.705-1(a)(2).
[11] Reg. §1.705-1(a)(2).
[12] IRC §705(a)(1)(A).
[13] IRC §705(a)(1)(B).
[14] IRC §705(a)(1)(C).
[15] IRC §752(a) provides that an increase in a member's share of LLC liabilities is treated as a contribution of money by the member to the LLC. IRC §722 provides a member's basis in an LLC is increased by the amount of money contributed to the LLC.

- The amount of cash that the LLC distributes to the member.[16]
- The LLC's adjusted basis of property distributed to the member.[17]
- The member's distributive share of taxable losses from the LLC.[18] Losses reduce basis even though the losses are not deductible by the member under the at-risk rules.[19]
- The member's distributive share of nondeductible LLC expenses that are not capitalized.[20] For example, charitable contributions,[21] life insurance premiums, and 50 percent of meals and entertainment are nondeductible and reduce basis.
- The member's distributive share of depletion deductions for oil and gas property owned by the LLC to the extent such share does not exceed the proportionate share of the adjusted basis of such property allocated to the member;[22]
- Any decrease in the member's share of LLC liabilities.[23]

EXAMPLE

An LLC has two equal members. Member A contributes $5,000 cash to the LLC, and property with a basis of $10,000 and a fair market value of $7,000. The LLC borrows $10,000 to purchase depreciable equipment. During the first year of operations, the LLC earns $4,000 of income. It distributes $1,000 to Member A at the end of the year. Member A's adjusted basis in her membership interest at the end of the year is $18,000, computed as follows:

Cash contributed to LLC:	$ 5,000
Adjusted basis of property contributed to LLC:	$ 7,000
One-half share of $10,000 LLC liabilities (treated as cash contributed to LLC):	$ 5,000
One-half share of LLC income:	$ 2,000
Distribution:	($ 1,000)
Ending adjusted basis:	$18,000

---

[16] IRC §733(1); Reg. §1.705-1(a)(3).
[17] IRC §733(2); Reg. §1.705-1(a)(3).
[18] IRC §705(a)(2)(A).
[19] Prop. Reg. §1.465-1(e).
[20] IRC §705(a)(2)(B).
[21] IRC §703(a)(2)(C) provides than an LLC may not deduct charitable contributions. IRC §702(a)(4) provides that charitable contributions must be separately stated. IRC §705(a)(2)(B) provides that basis is decreased by nondeductible LLC expenditures.
[22] IRC §705(a)(3).
[23] IRC §752(b) provides that a decrease in a member's share of LLC liabilities is treated as a distribution of money by the LLC to the member. IRC§773(1) provides that a distribution by an LLC to a member reduces the member's adjusted basis in the membership interest (but not below zero) by the amount of money distributed.

[D]   *Alternative Methods of Determining Basis*

There are two alternative methods of determining a member's adjusted basis.[24] The alternative methods may be used if it is impractical or impossible to determine basis under the normal rules, and if the IRS determines that the alternative methods will not produce a substantially different result.

[1]   Share of Basis in LLC Assets

Under the first alternative method, a member's basis is the member's share of the LLC's basis in its assets.[25] This is the basis of LLC property that would be distributed to the member on termination of the LLC. Generally, it is equal to the LLC's inside basis in its assets multiplied by the member's percentage interest in the LLC. Liabilities are ignored since they are taken into account in determining basis when an asset is purchased.

EXAMPLE

An LLC has three equal members. The members and the LLC do not keep track of the basis of the membership interests. The LLC has assets with a basis of $300,000 and a fair market value of $400,000. The LLC has liabilities of $150,000. Under the alternative rule for determining basis, Member A's basis in her membership interest is $100,000 (1/3 × $300,000).[26]

There are several problems with the alternative method of determining basis. First, the member must have access to the books and records of the LLC showing the tax basis in each of the LLC's assets. It is not always possible for the member to obtain access to the current books and records of the LLC.

Second, the member must make various adjustments in determining basis. For example, the member must make an adjustment if one or more of the members contribute property to the LLC with a tax basis different than its fair market value. The basis adjustment in this case is the difference between the member's percentage share of basis in LLC assets and the member's actual basis in the membership interest at the time of contribution.

EXAMPLE

There are three equal members in an LLC. Two of the members contribute $30,000 in cash to the LLC. The other member contributes property with an

---

[24] IRC §705(b); Reg. §1.705-1(b).
[25] *Id.*
[26] Reg. §1.705-1(b), Example (1).

adjusted basis of $10,000 and a fair market value of $30,000. Each member has a 33 1/3 percent interest in the total adjusted basis of LLC assets ($70,000). However, one-third of the adjusted basis for each member would be $23,333. This would be $6,667 too low for the members contributing cash and $13,333 too high for the member contributing the appreciated property. Thus, the basis of the member's interest in the LLC under the alternative method is determined each year by multiplying the member's percentage interest by the adjusted basis of LLC property, and then increasing that amount by $6,667 for the members contributing cash and decreasing that amount by $13,333 for the member contributing appreciated property.

A member who acquires a membership interest by purchase must make an adjustment to basis under the alternative method. The amount of the adjustment is the difference between the purchase price and the member's percentage share of basis in LLC assets at the time of purchase.[27]

EXAMPLE

There are three equal members in an LLC. Each member contributes $100 in cash. Each member has a basis of $100 in his membership interest. The LLC buys property for $300, which appreciates in value to $600. Member A sells his membership interest to Member D for $200. Member D has a basis of $200 in his membership interest equal to the purchase price. However, his one-third share of basis in LLC assets is only $100. That understates his basis by $100. Therefore, Member D must increase his basis by $100 under the alternative method of determining basis.

After 10 years of operations, the LLC has a basis in its assets of $6,000. Member D's basis is $2,100 (his one-third percentage share of basis in LLC assets plus the $100 adjustment).

[2] Capital Account Method

Under the second alternative method (which is more commonly used), a member's basis is equal to the member's capital account plus his share of LLC liabilities. This method may be used if the LLC maintains its books and records on a tax basis rather than an accounting basis.[28]

This method is normally easier to apply than the first alternative method. The member does not need access to the LLC books and records. The member can obtain the necessary information from the Schedule K-1 that the member receives

---

[27] Reg. §1.705-1(b), Example (2).
[28] IRC §705(b); Reg. §1.705-1(b), Example (3).

from the LLC each year. The member's capital account is set forth in Item J, column (e). The member's share of debt is set forth in Item F.

There are also fewer adjustments that must be made in applying the second alternative method. The member does not need to make an adjustment for the difference between the basis and fair market value of contributed assets since the actual tax basis of contributed assets is reflected in the member's capital account.

The second alternative method is different from the first alternative method in one other respect. The first alternative method disregards debt in determining basis. The second alternative method adds a member's share of LLC debt to the member's capital account in determining basis.

EXAMPLE

There are three equal members in an LLC. Member C wants to sell her membership interest in the LLC to Member D. Member C will be taxed on the difference between the sales price and her basis in the membership interest. The LLC has been in existence for many years. It is impossible for Member C to determine her tax basis under the general rule for determining basis. The LLC maintains its books and records on a tax basis. Thus, Member C may use the capital account method for determining basis. The balance sheet of the LLC is as follows:

Assets	Tax basis per books	Fair market value
Cash	$3,000	$3,000
Receivables	4,000	4,000
Depreciable property	5,000	5,000
Land held for investment	18,000	30,000
Total	30,000	42,000

Liabilities and capital accounts

Liabilities	6,000	
Capital accounts		
Member A	4,500	
Members B	4,500	
Member C	15,000	
Total liabilities and capital	30,000	

Members C's basis in the membership interest determined under the capital account method is $17,000. This is equal to her tax-basis capital account of $15,000 plus her one-third share of LLC liabilities.[29]

---

[29] Reg. §1.705-1(b), Example (3).

When a member sells a membership interest, the capital account of the seller carries over to the purchaser. If the purchaser uses the capital account method in determining basis, the purchaser must make a permanent adjustment. The adjustment is equal to the difference between the purchase price and the purchaser's original capital account plus his or her share of liabilities.

EXAMPLE

Member D pays $17,500 for the membership interest in the prior example. Member D's capital account is $15,000 and her one-third share of liabilities is $2,000 at the time of purchase. Member D paid $500 more for the membership interest than her original capital account and share of liabilities. Thus, if Member D uses the capital account method for determining basis in future years, Member D must increase her basis determined under the capital account method by $500.[30]

[E] Negative Capital Accounts and Basis

A member may not have a negative basis in a membership interest.[31] Therefore, a member with a zero basis who receives a distribution may not reduce the basis in the member's membership interest. Instead, the member is taxed on any cash distributions in excess of basis, and takes a zero basis in any non-cash property distributed to the member.

A member may have a negative capital account. On sale or disposition of the membership interest, the gain recognized is generally equal to the negative capital account plus any cash received.

§9.03 EFFECT OF LIABILITIES ON BASIS

[A] General

One of the advantages of an LLC is that liabilities incurred by the LLC increase a member's basis in the LLC.[1] Losses decrease basis, but not below zero.[2] In an S corporation[3] and a C corporation, liabilities incurred by the corporation do not increase a shareholder's basis.

---

[30] Id.
[31] IRC §705(a)(2), (3).
§9.03 [1] IRC §752.
[2] IRC §§705(a)(2)(A), 704(d).
[3] IRC §1367.

EXAMPLE

Two equal members of an LLC each contribute $10,000 cash to the LLC. The LLC borrows $80,000 to purchase land for $100,000. Each member has a capital account of $10,000, which is the amount of the member's contribution to the LLC. Each member has a basis in his membership interest of $50,000, consisting of the $10,000 cash contribution, plus the one-half share of LLC liabilities allocated to the member.

IRC Section 752(a) treats an increase in a member's share of LLC liabilities as a contribution of money by the member to the LLC. The deemed money contribution increases the member's basis in his membership interest.[4] This allows the member to take tax deductions passed through from the LLC in excess of the cash and property that the member contributes to the LLC.[5] Section 752(b) treats a decrease in a member's share of LLC liabilities as a distribution of money to the member. The deemed money distribution decreases the member's basis in his membership interest.[6] A money distribution in excess of basis results in taxable gain, but does not result in negative basis. A member's basis cannot be reduced below zero.[7]

The deemed money contributions and distributions can arise in a number of different circumstances, including contributions of encumbered property to an LLC, distributions of encumbered property by an LLC, assumption of debt by an LLC, and refinancing or payment of debt. In each case, any increase or decrease in the member's share of LLC liabilities results in a basis adjustment.

EXAMPLE

An LLC has two equal members, Member A and Member B. Each member contributes $500 in cash to the LLC. Each member has a basis in her membership interest and a capital account of $500. The LLC admits Member C to the LLC as an equal one-third member. Member C contributes property worth $800, subject to a nonrecourse debt of $300 (net equity of $500 in the property) in exchange for the one-third interest in the LLC. The LLC assumes the $300 debt on the property. Member A's and Member B's bases in their membership interests increase by $100, to $600, as a result of the contribution. Each has a one-third share of the $300 in liabilities assumed by the LLC. Their allocations of $100 in additional LLC liabilities are treated as cash contributions by them, which increase their bases in their LLC membership interests from $500 to $600. Member C's basis in her membership interest

---

[4] IRC §722.

[5] The tax deductions are also limited by the at-risk rules, the passive loss rules, and related parties rules discussed in Chapter 13.

[6] IRC §733(1).

[7] IRC §§733(1), 731(a)(1).

is also $600. Her initial basis was $800, which is the adjusted basis of the property contributed to the LLC. The basis in her membership interest had to be reduced by $200, which is her net debt relief as a result of the property contribution. Before the contribution, Member C was liable for $300 in debt. After the contribution, she was liable for only $100 (one-third share of $300 in liabilities assumed by the LLC).

[B] Allocation of Recourse Liabilities

The amount of liabilities that are allocated to each member for basis purposes depends on the type of liability. There are two types of liabilities, recourse debt and nonrecourse debt. Recourse debt is allocated to the members who bear the economic risk of loss for that liability.[8]

Recourse debt is debt for which one or more LLC members bear the economic risk of loss. A member bears the economic risk of loss if the member or a person related to the member would be obligated to make a payment to the LLC's creditor or a contribution to the LLC with respect to the liability if the LLC liquidated at that time on a zero asset value basis.[9] The zero asset value liquidation test is based on the following five assumptions:[10]

1. All of the liabilities of the LLC become payable in full.
2. All of the LLC's assets, including cash, have a zero value (with the exception of property contributed to the LLC to secure an LLC liability).
3. The LLC disposes of all of its assets in a fully taxable transaction for no consideration (except for relief from nonrecourse debt).
4. All items of income, gain, loss, and deduction are allocated among the members in accordance with the operating agreement.
5. The LLC liquidates.

EXAMPLE

An LLC has two members, Member A and Member B, who share equally in profits and losses. Member A contributes $300 to the LLC, and Member B contributes $500 to the LLC. The LLC borrows $1,000 and purchases property for $1,800. The $1,000 promissory note is a general obligation of the LLC. No member is relieved from personal liability on the note. The LLC operating agreement provides that all LLC debts will be paid with LLC assets and that members will be personally liable for the debts to the extent of their negative capital accounts if LLC assets are insufficient to repay the LLC debts. Consequently, $600 of the LLC liability is recourse liability

[8] Reg. §1.752-2(a).
[9] Reg. §1.752-2(b)(1).
[10] Id.

allocated to Member A, and $400 of the LLC liability is recourse liability allocated to Member B. Under the five-step zero asset value liquidation method, this computation is made as follows:

1. The $1,000 debt is treated as payable in full.
2. The $1,800 of LLC assets have a zero value.
3. The LLC is treated as selling all of its property in a fully taxable transaction for no consideration. Therefore, the LLC has a tax loss of $1,800 (zero consideration, less $1,800 adjusted basis in the property).
4. The $1,800 of tax losses are allocated among the members in accordance with the operating agreement. Therefore, $900 of tax losses are allocated to Member A, and $900 of tax losses are allocated to Member B.
5. The LLC liquidates. Upon liquidation, Member A has a negative $600 capital account (initial capital contribution of $300, less $900 in tax losses). Member B has a negative $400 capital account (initial capital contribution of $500, less $900 of tax losses). Since all the LLC assets have a zero value and were deemed sold in a taxable transaction for no consideration, the members of the LLC are personally liable for repayment of the $1,000 debt. In accordance with the terms of the operating agreement, Member A is liable for repayment of $600 of the debt, and Member B is liable for repayment of $400 of the debt based on their negative capital accounts as of the date of the hypothetical liquidation. Therefore, $600 of the recourse liability are allocated to Member A, and $400 of the recourse liability are allocated to Member B.

If a member makes a nonrecourse loan to the LLC, the loan will normally be treated as recourse for tax purposes.[11]

[C] Allocation of Nonrecourse Liabilities

Nonrecourse debt is debt for which no member bears an economic risk of loss. Only the general assets of the LLC secure the debt. Nonrecourse debt is allocated to the members[12] under a three-tier allocation approach.[13]

Under the first tier, liabilities are allocated to members in an amount equal to each member's share of LLC minimum gain. LLC minimum gain is the amount by which nonrecourse debt exceeds the book value of assets subject to nonrecourse liability.[14] This is the gain that the LLC would recognize for accounting purposes (not tax purposes) if it transferred the property back to the lender for no consider-

---

[11] Reg. §1.752-2(c)(1).
[12] Ltr. Ruls. 9720008013, 9719015, 9719019029 (*citing* IRC §752 and Reg. §§1.752-1(a)(2), 1.752-1(f)).
[13] Reg. §1.752-3(a); Rev. Rul. 95-41, 1995-1 C.B. 132.
[14] Rev. Rul. 95-41, 1995-1 C.B. 132; Reg. §1.704-2(d)(3).

ation other than cancellation of the debt. Generally, this minimum gain is allocated to the members in the same proportion as the nonrecourse deductions giving rise to the minimum gain were allocated to the members up to that time.[15]

Under the second tier, liabilities are allocated to members in an amount equal to the tax gain that would be allocated to the members under IRC Section 704(c) if the LLC sold all of its property subject to nonrecourse liabilities in a taxable transaction in full satisfaction of those liabilities and for no other consideration.[16] The tax gain is the amount by which the nonrecourse debt on the property exceeds the adjusted basis of the property. The Section 704(c) gain is normally allocated to the member who contributed the property to the LLC. The allocation under the second tier applies if a member contributes appreciated property to an LLC that is secured by nonrecourse liabilities in excess of the property's basis.

Under the third tier, any additional nonrecourse liabilities are allocated to the members in accordance with the members' shares of profits or with another permissible allocation method.[17]

EXAMPLE 1

Two equal members form an LLC. Member A contributes $20,000 in cash. Member B contributes services. The LLC uses the money to purchase a building for $100,000. The LLC obtains an interest-only nonrecourse loan for $80,000 that is secured by the property. The members decide to allocate all of the depreciation deductions to Member A, since she is the wealthy investor who needs the tax deductions. After five years, the LLC's basis in the property has been reduced to $70,000 as a result of $30,000 of depreciation deductions allocated to Member A. During the five years, Member A received no allocations of income or losses other than the depreciation, and received no distributions. Member A must compute her basis in the LLC as follows:

Initial contribution	$ 20,000
Plus income allocations	0
Plus additional contributions	0
Less deductions and loss allocations (depreciation)	(30,000)
Less distributions	0
Plus share of the LLC's $80,000 nonrecourse debt:	

---

[15] See Reg. §1.704-2(b)(2).

[16] Reg. §1.704-3(a)(2).

[17] Rev. Rul. 95-41, 1995-1 C.B. 132. The most common method of allocation under the third tier is based on each member's share of LLC profits. The LLC may specify in the operating agreement each member's share of LLC profits for purposes of allocating liabilities in the third tier provided the specified profit interests are reasonably consistent with allocations of some other significant item of LLC income or gain. The LLC may also allocate liabilities in the third tier in the manner in which it reasonably expects that the deductions attributable to those nonrecourse liabilities will be allocated. The LLC may allocate a portion of the nonrecourse liabilities in the third tier to the members based on each member's share of minimum gain for book purposes in excess of the minimum gain for tax purposes that was allocated to the member under the second tier. Reg. §1.752-3(a)(3). An example is set forth below. The LLC may change the allocation method from year to year. Reg. §1.752-3.

First Tier—Minimum Gain. The minimum gain is $10,000. This is the amount by which the outstanding loan balance of $80,000 exceeds the $70,000 book value of the property securing the nonrecourse debt. Liabilities equal to all of the minimum gain must be allocated to Member A, since she received all of the depreciation deductions that caused the book value of the property to decline below the outstanding loan balance.   10,000

Second Tier—Section 704(c) Gain. There is no Section 704(c) gain, since neither member contributed appreciated property to the LLC.   0

Third Tier—Profit Sharing Ratio. There is $70,000 of nonrecourse debt remaining after allocating $10,000 of the nonrecourse debt to Member A in the first tier. Under the third tier, the liabilities must be divided equally between the members, since they share equally in profits of the LLC.[18]   35,000

TOTAL BASIS IN LLC $35,000

EXAMPLE 2

Two persons form an LLC. Each member receives an equal allocation of profits and losses. Member A contributes depreciable property to the LLC. The property has a fair market value of $10,000, has an adjusted basis of $4,000, and is subject to a nonrecourse liability of $6,000. Member B contributes $4,000 cash. The $6,000 in nonrecourse liabilities are allocated $4,000 to Member A and $2,000 to Member B. Member A has an $2,000 adjusted basis in her membership interest, and Member B has a $6,000 adjusted basis in her membership interest. The computations are as follows:[18]

	Member A	Member B
Cash and adjusted basis of property contributed by each member	$ 4,000	$4,000
Less debt assumed by LLC, treated as cash distribution to member who incurred the liability prior to the contribution	$(6,000)	—
Plus nonrecourse liabilities allocated to members:		
First-tier minimum gain allocation	—	—
Second-tier built-in gain allocation	2,000	—
Third-tier profit-sharing allocation	2,000	2,000
Basis in membership interest	$2,000	$6,000

Under the first tier, none of the $6,000 in liabilities is allocated to the members because there is no LLC minimum gain for accounting purposes.

---

[18] This example was set forth in Rev. Rul. 95-41, 1995-1 C.B. 132.

For tax purposes, the LLC will realize a minimum gain of $2,000 if it transfers the property back to the lender in exchange for the cancellation of the debt (amount realized of $6,000 in debt relief, less $4,000 adjusted basis in the property). However, there is no minimum gain for accounting purposes because the $10,000 book value of the property at the time of contribution exceeds the $6,000 nonrecourse liability. The LLC will realize a $4,000 book loss if it transfers the property to the lender in consideration for the cancellation of the debt (amount realized of $6,000 in debt relief, less $10,000 book value of the property). Since there is no minimum gain for accounting purposes, no amount of the $6,000 in nonrecourse liabilities is allocated to either member under the first tier.

Under the second tier, the Section 704(c) "minimum tax gain" must be allocated to the member who contributed the property to the LLC. There is $6,000 of Section 704(c) built-in gain. This is the excess of the $10,000 book value of the property over its $4,000 adjusted basis. All of this gain must be allocated to Member A for tax purposes (but not book purposes) under Section 704(c) if the property is later sold for $10,000 or more. However, under the second-tier allocation rules, only the $2,000 of Section 704(c) minimum tax gain is allocated to Member A, who contributed the property. This is the amount of tax gain that the LLC would realize if it sold the property solely in exchange for cancellation of the nonrecourse debt (amount realized of $6,000 in debt relief, less adjusted basis of property of $4,000).

Under the third-tier allocation, the remaining $4,000 of nonrecourse liabilities may be allocated equally to Member A and Member B based on their equal 50 percent profit-sharing ratio. Alternatively, the LLC may allocate third-tier liabilities to the members who contributed appreciated property in an amount equal to the built-in gain that was not allocated to the members under the second tier (with any remaining third-tier liabilities allocated to the members based on their profit-sharing ratio). There was $2,000 of gain allocated to Member A under the second tier. The remaining $4,000 of built-in gains was not allocated to the members under the second tier. Therefore, the LLC may allocate the $4,000 of third-tier liabilities to Member A who contributed the property with the built-in gain.[19]

EXAMPLE 3

Members A, B, C, and D form an LLC. Each has a 25 percent interest in profits and losses. Member A contributes property with a basis of $500 and a fair market value of $5,000. The property is subject to a nonrecourse liability of $4,000. Members B, C, and D each contribute $1,000 to the LLC.

There is no allocation of liabilities under the first tier because there is no minimum gain attributable to the property securing the liability. There is no

[19] Prop. Reg. §1.752-3(a)(3). *See* explanation of this rule and the three tiers of allocation in IRS Proposed Rules and Hearing Notice on Allocation of Partnership Debt, REG-103831-99, Fed. Reg. (Jan. 13, 2000).

minimum gain on the date of contribution because the $4,000 liability does not exceed the $5,000 book value of property.

Under the second tier, $3,500 of liabilities must be allocated to Member A. This is the amount by which the $4,000 of liabilities encumbering the property exceeds Member A's $500 tax basis in the property.

The remaining $500 of liabilities must be allocated to all members equally under the third tier ($125 each) because each member shares equally in profits and losses.

Member A has potential income recognition of $3,500 on contribution of the property. Member A is relieved of $4,000 of liabilities on contribution of the property to the LLC. The debt relief is treated as a distribution of money. Member A has an initial basis of $500 in the membership interest (adjusted basis of contributed property) before considering the effect of liabilities on basis. The money distribution of $4,000 in excess of Member A's $500 basis in the membership interest is potentially taxable gain. However, $3,500 of liabilities is allocated to Member A under the second tier. This is exactly the amount of liabilities that Member A needs to avoid income recognition. The liabilities assumed under the second tier offset the liabilities that Member A is relieved of on contribution of the property, thus resulting in no income recognition.

EXAMPLE 4

An LLC has two members. Member A is the manager and contributes no cash or property to the LLC. Member B contributes $4,000 cash to the LLC. The LLC borrows $6,000 on a nonrecourse basis. The LLC uses the cash contribution and loan to purchase $10,000 of property. The property is depreciable over five years at the rate of $2,000 per year. The income and expenses on the LLC are exactly equal, except for the $2,000 of depreciation per year. The LLC operating agreement provides that 10 percent of profits are allocated to Member A, and 90 percent of the profits are allocated to Member B. The operating agreement also provides that each member shares in losses equally. Thus, each member is allocated $1,000 of the tax losses attributable to the depreciation each year for the first five years.

However, Member A may only deduct $600 of the $5,000 in tax losses allocated to Member A. All the liabilities are allocated under the third tier based on the profit sharing allocation for each member. There is no minimum gain or Section 704(c) gain that is allocated under the first two tiers. Thus, Member A has an initial basis of $600 (10% × $6,000 of nonrecourse liabilities). Tax losses allocated to Member A may not be deducted in excess of basis.

Alternatively, the LLC may specially allocate liabilities under the third tier based on the manner in which it expects that deductions attributable to the liability will be allocated.[20] In this case, the LLC allocates the depreciation

---

[20] Reg. §1.704-2(c).

deductions attributable to the liability equally to both members. Thus, the LLC could elect to allocate the $6,000 of nonrecourse liabilities equally to both members for basis purposes. This will partially solve Member A's basis problem. Member A could now deduct $3,000 of the $5,000 in tax losses allocated to Member A during the first five years.

EXAMPLE 5

An LLC has two members who share equally in profits and losses. All depreciation is allocated to Member A. Each member contributes $5,000 to the LLC. The LLC borrows $90,000 (interest-only loan). The LLC purchases property for $100,000. The property is depreciable at the rate of $20,000 per year for five years. Each member has an initial capital account of $5,000, consisting of the $5,000 contribution. Each member has an initial basis in her membership interest of $50,000, consisting of the $5,000 contribution plus the one-half share of LLC liabilities (1/2 × $90,000).

At the end of the first year, the LLC's income is exactly equal to its expenses, except for the $20,000 of depreciation that is allocated to Member A. There is now minimum gain of $10,000 because the $90,000 of LLC liabilities exceed the $80,000 book value of the property ($100,000 purchase price reduced by $20,000 of depreciation). All of this $10,000 of minimum gain must be allocated to Member A, since Member A received all of the depreciation deductions that gave rise to the minimum gain. Thus, $10,000 of nonrecourse liabilities are allocated to Member A under the first tier.

There are no second-tier allocations, since neither of the members contributed property to the LLC that had built-in gain.

Under the third tier, the remaining $80,000 of LLC liabilities are allocated equally between the members based on their equal profit-sharing ratio. As a result, Member A has an adjusted basis in her membership interest of $35,000 at the end of the first year. This consists of her $5,000 capital contribution, less the $20,000 of depreciation deductions, plus the $10,000 of nonrecourse liabilities allocated under the first-tier minimum gain allocations, plus the $40,000 of nonrecourse liabilities allocated under the third tier. Member B has an adjusted basis in her membership interest of $45,000, consisting of her $5,000 capital contribution, plus her $40,000 share of nonrecourse liabilities allocated to her under the third tier.

§9.04   CONVERSION FROM PARTNERSHIP TO LLC

When a partnership is converted to an LLC, some of the recourse debt may be assumed by the LLC. This will result in possible gain recognition under Section 752(b) of the Internal Revenue Code. The reason is that the recourse debt is reclassified as nonrecourse if no member is personally liable.

Before the conversion, the recourse debt is allocated entirely to the general partners (or other partners who are personally liable). After the conversion, the nonrecourse debt is allocated to all of the members. The net debt relief[1] to the general partner is treated as a cash distribution. The deemed distribution reduces the general partner's basis and results in taxable gain to the extent the debt relief exceeds the general partner's basis.[2]

§9.05 CONVERSION FROM LLC TO PARTNERSHIP

The conversion of an LLC to a limited partnership may result in taxable gain if the transfer of liabilities from the LLC to the partnership results in a net decrease in an LLC member's share of liabilities.[1] The transfer of nonrecourse liabilities from the LLC to the partnership may result in a net decrease in a member's share of liabilities.

A liability is nonrecourse as to the members of an LLC if no member currently bears the economic risk of loss for the liability. These liabilities are allocated to all the members in the LLC based on their shares of profits.[2] Thus, a member's basis is increased by the amount of nonrecourse liabilities multiplied by the member's percentage interest in profits. The nonrecourse liabilities normally become recourse liabilities when they are transferred to a limited partnership in a merger because a general partner is personally liable for all partnership liabilities.

Recourse liabilities are allocated to the partners who are personally liable. All of the recourse liabilities are allocated to the general partner if no limited partner is currently liable for those debts after the merger.

A member/limited partner is treated as receiving a distribution of money from the limited partnership to the extent of the decrease in his allocable share of liabilities.[3] The deemed distribution of money reduces the limited partner's basis in the partnership interest. The limited partner recognizes gain to the extent the deemed distribution of money exceeds the limited partner's basis in the partnership.[4]

The transfer of recourse liabilities from the LLC to the partnership does not result in a deemed distribution of money or taxation to members if the members who were personally responsible for the liabilities prior to the merger continue to be personally liable after the merger.[5]

---

§9.04 [1] Recourse debt that the general partner is relieved of, less the nonrecourse debt that is subsequently allocated to the general partner as a member of the LLC.

[2] IRC §752(a), (b); Reg. §§1.752-1(b), (c), (f), 1.752-4(a).

§9.05 [1] Ltr. Ruls. 9720008013, 9719015, 9719019029 (*citing* IRC §752 and Reg. §§1.752-1(a)(2), 1.752-1(f)).

[2] Reg. §1.752-1(e).

[3] Ltr. Ruls. 9720008013, 9719015, 9719019029 (*citing* IRC §752 and Reg. §§1.752-1(a)(2), 1.752-1(f)).

[4] Ltr. Ruls. 9720008013, 9719015, 9719019029 (*citing* IRC §§731(a), 752(b)).

[5] Ltr. Ruls. 9720008013, 9719015, 9719019029 (*citing* IRC §752 and Reg. §§1.752-1(a)(2), 1.752-1(f)).

10

Distributions

§10.01   GENERALLY

The tax consequences of a distribution to a member in an LLC that is classified as a partnership depend on numerous factors. The principal factors are:

- The type of assets distributed, such as money, property, marketable securities, unrealized receivables, and inventory;
- Whether the distribution is a liquidating or nonliquidating distribution;
- Whether the LLC has filed an election to adjust the basis of its assets under Section 754 of the Internal Revenue Code;
- Whether the distribution causes a disproportionate distribution of unrealized receivables and inventory property;
- Whether the distribution is a liquidating distribution to a retiring member of a service corporation; and
- How the LLC characterizes the distribution, such as a guaranteed payment, distributive share of income, draw, advance, loan, or distribution in payment of the member's interest in the LLC.

§10.02   MONEY DISTRIBUTIONS

The most common type of distribution is a cash distribution. A cash distribution first reduces a member's adjusted basis in her membership interest. The member recognizes gain only if the distribution exceeds his or her basis in the membership interest immediately before the distribution.[1]

There are four types of money distributions:

1. Cash.
2. Relief of debt. A member is treated as having received money when the member is relieved of his share of LLC debt as a result of either the sale of a membership interest or a liquidating distribution.[2] This is referred to as a "deemed money distribution."
3. Marketable securities, subject to an adjustment.[3]
4. The member's share of ordinary income assets when the member receives a disproportionate distribution.[4]

EXAMPLE

There are four equal members in a LLC. Member A has a basis in his membership interest of $1,000. The LLC incurred $1,000 of nonrecourse debt. The LLC makes a liquidating distribution of $1,000 cash to Member A. Member A recognizes $250 of gain. This is equal to the money distribution of $1,250 ($1,000 cash, plus relief of a one-fourth share of the LLC's nonrecourse debt), less the member's basis of $1,000.

A member recognizes capital gains to the extent the money distribution exceeds the member's basis in the LLC.[5] However, a portion of the gain is ordinary income if the distribution results in a disproportionate distribution of the member's share of LLC unrealized receivables and inventory.[6]

A member does not recognize a loss on a nonliquidating cash distribution.[7] The cash distribution merely reduces the member's adjusted basis in his membership interest. A member may recognize a loss on a liquidating cash distribution.[8] Loss is recognized to the extent of the member's adjusted basis in the membership interest over the money distributed (including debt relief).[9]

---

§10.02   [1] IRC §731(a).

[2] IRC §752(b); Reg. §1.752-(c).

[3] See §10.04 infra.

[4] See §10.05 infra.

[5] IRC §731(a)(1).

[6] See §10.05 infra.

[7] IRC §731(a)(2).

[8] A member may not recognize a loss upon a liquidating distribution if property other than cash, receivables or inventory is distributed in the liquidation. IRC §731(a)(2).

[9] Id.

§10.03   PROPERTY DISTRIBUTIONS

Different rules apply when property other than cash is distributed. The tax consequences depend on whether there is a liquidating or nonliquidating distribution, whether the LLC has elected to adjust the basis of distributed assets, and
whether the member is required to adjust the basis of distributed assets.

[A]   Nonliquidating Distributions

[1]   General Rule

Distributions of property to members are generally tax-free.[1] Distributions are
treated as made in the following order:

- *Money.* The member first reduces his outside basis by the amount of any
  money received in the distribution.[2] A member is taxed on any distribution
  of money in excess of outside basis.[3] The gain recognized is capital gain,[4]
  except as provided under IRC Section 751.[5]
- *Accounts receivable and inventory items.* The member next reduces his outside
  basis by the LLC's pre-distribution basis in unrealized receivables and
  inventory distributed to the member.[6] The member receives a carryover
  basis in such property,[7] up to the member's remaining outside basis.[8]
- *Other distributed property.* The member next reduces his outside basis by the
  LLC's pre-distribution basis in other property distributed to the member.[9]
  The member receives a carryover basis in such property,[10] up to the member's remaining outside basis.[11] Once the basis is reduced to zero, the member may not receive any more basis in the distributed property. There is no
  tax to the member even if the LLC's basis in the distributed property exceeds
  the member's remaining outside basis.[12]

---

§10.03   [1] IRC §731(a). The one major exception is IRC §751(b). Under that section, a member
recognizes ordinary income to the extent of his share of unrealized appreciation and inventory items
retained by the LLC. *See* §10.05 *infra.*

[2] IRC §733(1).

[3] IRC §731(a).

[4] IRC §§741, 731(a) (last sentence).

[5] *See* §10.05 *infra.*

[6] IRC §732(c)(1)(A)(i).

[7] IRC §732(a)(1).

[8] IRC §732(a)(2).

[9] IRC §732(a)(1). The property's basis includes any Section 743(b) basis adjustment related to the
member who receives the distribution. Reg. §1.743-1(b)(2)(ii). The LLC must reallocate Section 743(b)
basis adjustments to the distributed property to other members of the LLC if the basis adjustments
were related to other members of the LLC who did not receive a distribution. Treas. Reg. §1.743-
1(b)(2)(ii). The Section 743(b) basis adjustment is discussed in §10.06 *infra.*

[10] IRC §732(a)(1).

[11] IRC §732(a)(2).

[12] IRC §731(a).

Therefore, if the member has an outside basis in the membership interest that exceeds the LLC's basis in the distributed assets, the member receives a carryover basis in all distributed assets, and retains the excess amount as the new adjusted basis in the membership interest.

EXAMPLE

A member has a basis of $2,000 in her membership interest in an LLC. The LLC distributes property to the member having a basis of $1,000. The member receives a carryover basis of $1,000 in the property and must reduce her basis in the membership interest by $1,000.

If the member has an outside basis in the membership interest that is less than the LLC's adjusted basis in the distributed property, then the property receives a step-down in basis.

EXAMPLE

A member has a basis of $2,000 in her membership interest in an LLC. The LLC distributes property to the member with an adjusted basis of $2,500 in a nonliquidating distribution. The member's basis in the distributed property is $2,000, since the carryover basis cannot exceed the member's basis in her membership interest. The member must reduce her basis in the membership interest from $2,000 to zero as a result of the distribution.

---

[2] Distributions of Multiple Properties

If the LLC distributes two or more properties at the same time that have an adjusted basis in excess of the member's outside basis in the membership interest, then an allocation must be made. The aggregate basis allocated to the distributed properties may not exceed the member's basis in membership interest immediately prior to the distribution. The basis decrease is allocated among properties with unrealized depreciation in proportion to their respective amounts of unrealized depreciation (to the extent of each property's depreciation), and then in proportion to their respective adjusted bases (taking into account the adjustments already made).[13]

---

[13] IRC §732(c)(3).

EXAMPLE

The balance sheet of an LLC shows the following assets:

Asset	Adjusted Basis	Fair Market Value
Cash	$10,000	$10,000
Inventory	$ 5,000	$ 8,000
Desert land	$ 2,000	$ 2,500
Beach land	$ 3,000	$ 2,000

The LLC makes a distribution to a member of $1,000 cash, all of the inventory, the beach land, and the desert land. The total adjusted basis of those assets to the LLC is $11,000. The member's basis in her membership interest is $10,000. The $11,000 carryover basis of assets distributed by the LLC must be reduced to $10,000, since the member's basis in the assets cannot exceed her basis in the LLC. The member's $10,000 basis in her membership interest is allocated to the distributed assets as follows:

- The $1,000 cash distribution is treated as distributed first, reducing the member's basis in her membership interest from $10,000 to $9,000.
- The next $5,000 of the member's interest in the LLC is allocated to the inventory, reducing the member's remaining basis from $9,000 to $4,000.
- The remaining basis is allocated to the desert land and beach land, with a carryover basis of $2,000 and $3,000, respectively. However, since the LLC's $5,000 adjusted basis in those assets exceeds the member's $4,000 remaining basis in her membership interest, there must be a $1,000 downward adjustment in basis. The entire $1,000 downward adjustment is allocated to the beach land because it is the only property that has unrealized depreciation ($1,000 of unrealized depreciation). Therefore, the member receives a carryover basis of $2,000 in the desert land and a reduced basis of $2,000 in the beach land. The effect of the basis adjustment is to minimize the difference between the distributed properties' fair market values and adjusted bases.
- The member's ending basis in her membership interest in the LLC after the nonliquidating distribution is zero.

[B] Liquidating Distributions

[1] Generally

Liquidating distributions of property to members are subject to the following rules:

- *Gain recognition.* A member does not recognize gain except to the extent that money distributed exceeds the member's basis in his membership interest immediately prior to the distribution.[14]
- *Loss recognition.* A member does not recognize loss on a distribution unless three conditions are met. First, the member must receive only cash, unrealized receivables, or inventory. Second, the member must receive a liquidating distribution of his entire membership interest. Third, the adjusted basis of LLC assets distributed to the member must be less than the member's basis in his membership interest. The loss recognized is the amount by which the basis in the membership interest exceeds the money and the LLC's basis in unrealized receivables and inventory items distributed to the member.[15]
- *Character of gain or loss.* The gain or loss recognized is capital gain or loss,[16] except as provided under IRC Section 751.[17]
- *Substituted basis.* The member receives a substituted basis in the distributed property. The basis in the property is the same as a member's basis in the membership interest immediately prior to the distribution, reduced by any money received.[18] This differs from the basis rule for a nonliquidating distribution in which the member receives a carryover basis rather than a substituted basis.

EXAMPLE 1

An LLC distributes land with a basis and fair market value of $100,000 to Member A in a liquidating distribution. Member A has a basis of $2,000 in her membership interest. Member A receives a basis of $2,000 in the land, equal to her basis in the membership interest prior to the distribution.

EXAMPLE 2

Same facts as in Example 1, except that the LLC distributes property to the member with a basis and fair market value of $500. The member receives a basis of $2,000 in the distributed property.

---

[14] IRC §731(a)(1).
[15] IRC §731(a)(2).
[16] IRC §§741, 731(a) (last sentence).
[17] *See* §10.05 *infra.*
[18] IRC §732(b).

[2] Allocation of Basis to Multiple Properties

If the member receives more than one property in a liquidating distribution, the member must allocate his basis in the membership interest to the distributed assets as follows:[19]

- The member first reduces his outside basis by the amount of any money received in the distribution.[20] A member is taxed on any distribution of money in excess of outside basis.
- The member must then allocate his outside basis to the inventory and unrealized receivables in an amount equal to the LLC's basis in such property,[21] or the member's remaining outside basis if less.[22]
- The member must allocate any remaining outside basis to other property received in the distribution.[23] The member receives a zero basis in such property if the member has no remaining outside basis.
- The basis of property must be increased on distribution to the member if the member's basis in the membership interest is greater than the LLC's basis in the distributed property. The formula for increasing the basis of the distributed property is discussed below.[24]
- The basis of property must be decreased on distribution to the member if the member's basis in the membership interest is less than the LLC's basis in the distributed property. The formula for decreasing the basis of the distributed property is discussed below.[25]

[3] Basis Increase Formula

The basis of assets distributed in a liquidating distribution to a member is increased if the member's basis in the membership interest is greater than the LLC's basis in the distributed assets. In that case, the member's basis is allocated to all of the distributed assets to the full extent of the LLC's basis in those assets. The remaining basis in the membership interest is then allocated among the distributed properties with unrealized appreciation to the full extent of the properties' unrealized appreciation. If the remaining basis in the membership interest is less than the unrealized appreciation, then the remaining basis is allocated in proportion to the respective amounts of unrealized appreciation for each property.

---

[19] IRC §732(c).
[20] IRC §732(b).
[21] IRC §732(c)(1)(A)(i).
[22] IRC §732(c)(1)(A)(ii).
[23] IRC §732(c)(1)(B).
[24] See §10.03[B][3] infra.
[25] See §10.03[B][4] infra.

If the member's remaining basis is not fully allocated at this point, then it is allocated to all of the properties based on their respective fair market values.[26]

EXAMPLE

The balance sheet of the LLC shows that it has the following assets:

Asset	LLC's Adjusted Basis	Fair Market Value
Cash	$10,000	$10,000
Inventory	$ 5,000	$ 8,000
Desert land	$ 2,000	$ 4,000
Beach land	$ 3,000	$ 3,000

A member has a basis in her membership interest of $7,700. The LLC makes a liquidating distribution to the member. The LLC distributes the desert land and the beach land to the member in full liquidation of her interest in the LLC. The distributed assets must be increased in basis, since the member's basis in her membership interest exceeds by $2,700 the basis that the LLC has in the distributed assets. The allocation is as follows:

Step 1: Reduce the member's basis in her membership interest by the amount of cash distributed. Since no cash is distributed, the member's basis in her membership interest after step 1 is $7,700.

Step 2: Allocate the member's basis in her membership interest to distributed inventory and unrealized receivables in an amount equal to the LLC's basis in each such item. If the member's basis in the membership interest is less than the LLC's aggregate basis in those items, the amount of shortfall must be allocated among the distributed inventory and unrealized receivables in the following manner: (i) first to the distributed inventory or unrealized receivables with unrealized depreciation in proportion to and to the extent of each property's unrealized depreciation, and (ii) the balance, if any, to the distributed inventory and unrealized receivables in proportion to their adjusted bases (taking into account the adjustments already made). No inventory or unrealized receivables were distributed to the member. Therefore, the member's remaining basis in her membership interest is $7,700 after step 2.

Step 3: Allocate any remaining basis in the membership interest to each distributed property to the extent of each property's adjusted basis to the LLC. Therefore, $2,000 is allocated to the desert land and $3,000 to the beach land, equal to the LLC's adjusted bases in those assets. The member's basis in her membership interest is reduced to $2,700 after step 3.

---

[26] IRC §732(c)(2).

Step 4: Allocate any remaining basis in the membership interest to the distributed properties (other than inventory and unrealized receivables) with unrealized appreciation in proportion to and to the extent of each property's unrealized appreciation. Therefore, $2,000 of the member's basis is allocated to the desert land, since the desert land has $2,000 of unrealized appreciation. No amount is allocated to the beach land under step 4, since there is no unrealized appreciation in the beach land. The member's basis is reduced from $2,700 to $700 as a result of step 4. The desert land has a basis of $4,000 and the beach land has a basis of $3,000 after step 4.

Step 5: Allocate any remaining basis in the membership interest to the distributed properties (other than inventory and unrealized receivables) in proportion to their fair market values. Therefore, $400 is allocated to the desert land, and $300 is allocated to the beach land. The desert land has a basis of $4,400 and the beach land has a basis of $3,300 after all five steps.

EXAMPLE

On January 1, 2000, Ruth has a basis of $55,000 in her membership interest. The LLC distributes to her in complete liquidation an apartment and an office building. The apartment has an adjusted basis to the LLC of $5,000 and a fair market value of $40,000. The office building has an adjusted basis to the LLC of $10,000 and a fair market value of $10,000. After the liquidation, Ruth has a basis of $44,000 in the apartment and $11,000 in the office building.[27]

Before the Taxpayer Relief Act of 1997, an LLC was required to apportion a member's basis in its membership interest among the assets received in a liquidating distribution based on the relative proportion of adjusted basis to the LLC of each asset. After the Taxpayer Relief Act of 1997, the member's basis in the membership interest is allocated to the distributed assets up to the amount of the LLC's adjusted basis in those assets, with the remaining amount allocated based on fair market value.[28]

[4]   Basis Decrease Formula

A member may receive a liquidating distribution of property with an adjusted basis to the LLC that is greater than the member's basis in his membership interest. In that case, the basis of the distributed assets must be decreased by the difference between the LLC's adjusted basis in the distributed property and the member's

---

[27] 1999 IRS Special Enrollment Examination Questions and Official Answers, Part 2, Q&A-77.
[28] Pub. L. No. 105-34, §1061, 105th Cong., 1st Sess. (Aug. 5, 1997), *amending* IRC §732(c)(2).

basis in his membership interest. The formula used is almost the same as when a member receives a nonliquidating distribution of property with an adjusted basis to the LLC that is greater than the member's remaining basis in his membership interest. The member's basis in his membership interest is first reduced by the amount of money received. The member's basis is then allocated to unrealized receivables and inventory up to the amount of the LLC's adjusted basis in those assets.[29] Any remaining basis in the membership interest is then allocated among other distributed properties to the extent of each such property's adjusted basis to the LLC. The assets receive a step-down in basis to the extent the member has insufficient basis in his membership interest to allocate to the distributed assets. The basis decrease is allocated among properties with unrealized depreciation in proportion to their respective amounts of unrealized depreciation (to the extent of each property's depreciation) and then in proportion to their respective adjusted bases (taking into account the adjustments already made).[30] Before the Taxpayer Relief Act of 1997, the entire basis decrease was allocated to the distributed assets according to their relative bases.

EXAMPLE

The balance sheet of an LLC shows the following assets:

Asset	Adjusted Basis	Fair Market Value
Cash	$10,000	$10,000
Inventory	$ 5,000	$ 8,000
Desert land	$ 2,000	$ 4,000
Beach land	$ 3,000	$ 2,000

The LLC makes a liquidating distribution to a member of $1,000 cash, all of the inventory, the beach land, and the desert land. The LLC has a total basis in those assets of $11,000. The member's basis in her membership interest is $9,600. The LLC's $11,000 basis in the distributed assets must be reduced to $9,600, since the member's basis in the assets cannot exceed her basis in the LLC. The member's $9,600 basis in her membership interest is allocated to the distributed assets as follows:

Step 1: Reduce the member's basis in her membership interest by the amount of cash distributed. The $1,000 cash distribution reduces the member's basis in her membership interest from $9,600 to $8,600.

Step 2: Allocate any remaining basis in the membership interest to distributed inventory and unrealized receivables in an amount up to the LLC's basis in those assets. Therefore, $5,000 of the member's basis in her membership interest is allocated to the inventory, reducing her remaining basis from $8,600 to $3,600.

---

[29] IRC §732(c)(1)(A).
[30] IRC §732(c)(3).

Step 3: Allocate any remaining basis to each distributed property (other than inventory and unrealized receivables) to the extent of the LLC's adjusted basis in the property. Therefore, $2,000 is allocated to the desert land, and $3,000 is allocated to the beach land. However, since the LLC's $5,000 adjusted basis in those assets exceeds the member's $3,600 remaining basis in her membership interest, there must be a $1,400 downward adjustment in basis under the next two steps.

Step 4: Allocate the $1,400 basis decrease to the distributed properties (other than inventory and unrealized receivables) with unrealized depreciation in proportion to and to the extent of each property's unrealized depreciation. Therefore, there must be a $1,000 downward adjustment in basis allocated to the beach land because it is the only property that has unrealized depreciation ($1,000 of unrealized depreciation). The basis in the beach land is therefore reduced from $3,000 to $2,000. The basis in the desert land is not reduced under step 4 and stays at $2,000. The member's remaining basis in her membership interest is reduced from $1,400 to $400 under step 4.

Step 5: Allocate any remaining basis decrease to the distributed properties (other than inventory and unrealized receivables) in proportion to their adjusted bases (taking into account the adjustments already made). Therefore, the remaining $400 basis decrease is allocated $200 to the beach land and $200 to the desert land. As a result of all of the adjustments, the member receives a basis of $5,000 in the inventory, $1,800 in the beach land, and $1,800 in the desert land (total basis in assets of $8,600 and $1,000 cash, equal to the $9,600 basis in the membership interest).

[C] *Holding Period*

A member may tack the LLC's holding period to the member's holding period of distributed property,[31] unless the property is inventory or unrealized receivables.

[D] *Gain or Loss upon Subsequent Sale*

A member who receives a distribution of property from an LLC recognizes gain or loss upon a subsequent sale of the property. The amount of gain or loss is the difference between the amount realized upon sale and the member's basis in the property. The character of the gain or loss is capital or ordinary depending on the member's use of the property. The gain or loss is capital if the asset is a capital gain asset in the hands of the member and ordinary income or loss if the asset is an ordinary income asset in the hands of the member.

---

[31] IRC §735(b); Ltr. Rul. 200204005.

A member's sale or other disposition of an asset received from an LLC results in ordinary gain or loss to the member without regard to his personal use of the property in the following cases:

1. The property is an unrealized receivable.[32]
2. The property is inventory and is sold by the member within five years after the distribution from the LLC.[33] Sales of distributed LLC inventory more than five years after the date of distribution result in capital gain or loss if the property is a capital asset in the hands of the member.
3. The property is Section 1245 property. The member will recognize ordinary depreciation recapture income on sale of the property up to the lesser of the gain recognized or the recomputed basis adjustment. The recomputed basis adjustment includes the amount of depreciation recapture that the LLC would have recognized if the LLC had sold the property for fair market value immediately prior to the distribution.[34] Similar rules will apply to Section 1250 property to the extent the LLC took depreciation in excess of straight-line depreciation prior to 1987.

[E] Depreciation

[1] Depreciation Basis and Method

A member who receives depreciable property in a distribution is bound by the LLC's period and method of depreciation or amortization with respect to the LLC's basis in the property prior to the distribution.[35] A member may receive a basis in the property that is higher than the LLC's basis in the property if the member's outside basis in the membership interests exceeds the LLC's basis in the property.[36] The property will be treated as newly acquired property for depreciation purposes to the extent of the excess basis. Thus, the member will have a bifurcated basis for depreciation purposes.

[2] Depreciation Recapture

An LLC's distribution of depreciable property to a member does not trigger depreciation recapture.[37] The potential depreciation recapture inherent in the prop-

---

[32] IRC §735(a)(1).

[33] IRC §735(a)(2).

[34] *See* 10.03[E][2] *infra*. The recomputed basis adjustment will also include any depreciation that the member took on the property after the date of distribution.

[35] IRC §168(i)(7).

[36] *See* 10.03[B][3] *supra*.

[37] IRC §1245(b)(3) and §1250(d)(3) state that there will be no depreciation recapture in a distribution by an LLC under IRC §731 if the member's basis in the property is the same as the LLC's basis in the property on the date of distribution. IRC §1245(b)(6)(A) and §1250(d)(6)(A) provide that a member's basis in property distributed by LLC is the same as the LLC's basis in the property immediately prior to the distribution (even though the basis may actually be different under the substituted basis rules).

erty carries over to the member. The member recognizes ordinary income for the recapture amount on resale of the property. The Code accomplishes this result by defining two additional terms: "recomputed basis" for Section 1245 property; and "additional depreciation" for Section 1250 real property.

Generally, the member's initial basis in Section 1245 property distributed from the LLC is the member's outside basis in the membership interest, reduced by any cash received in the distribution.[38] The member's recomputed basis is the member's basis on distribution, increased by the amount of depreciation recapture that the LLC would have recognized if it had sold the Section 1245 property for fair market value immediately prior to distribution.[39] In subsequent years, the member's recomputed basis is the member's adjusted basis, increased by the amount of depreciation on the property taken by the member, plus the amount of depreciation recapture that the LLC would have recognized if it had sold the Section 1245 property for fair market value immediately prior to distribution.

When the member sells the property, the member recognizes ordinary income recapture up to the lesser of the gain realized or the amount by which the recomputed basis exceeds the member's adjusted basis.[40]

EXAMPLE

Member A has a basis of $75,000 in her membership interest. The LLC distributes Section 1245 property to the member in complete liquidation of her membership interest. The LLC originally purchased the property for $110,000 and took $25,000 of depreciation, resulting in an adjusted basis of $85,000. The property has a fair market value of $100,000 at the time of distribution. Member A receives a basis of $75,000 in the property on distribution equal to her outside basis in the membership interest. Member A's recomputed basis is $90,000. This is the basis of $75,000 on distribution plus the $15,000 of depreciation recapture that the LLC would have recognized if it sold the property for fair market value immediately prior to the distribution ($100,000 fair market value less the LLC's $85,000 adjusted basis).

If Member A sells the asset one month later for $103,000 prior to taking any additional depreciation deductions, then Member A would recognize $15,000 of depreciation recapture income (equal to the recomputed basis adjustment amount). The remaining $13,000 of gain would be Section 1231

---

[38] *See* §10.03[A][1] *supra*.

[39] IRC §1245(b)(6)(B)(i); Reg. §1.1245-4(f)(2). The recomputed basis is reduced to the extent that the LLC recognizes depreciation recapture income on distribution of the property. IRC §1245(b)(6)(B)(ii). This would apply if the LLC made a disproportionate distribution of depreciable assets and other hot assets to the member. The LLC in such case would be treated as making a proportionate distribution of other assets (cold assets), and then selling the excess depreciable assets to the member for the additional cold assets that the member would have received in a proportionate distribution. The LLC would recognize depreciation recapture income on the deemed distribution and sale. Tax practitioners largely ignore this provision.

[40] IRC §1245(a)(1).

gain, assuming that the aggregate holding period of the property for the LLC and Member A was more than one year.

If Member A instead sells the asset one month later for $80,000, then Member A would recognize $5,000 of depreciation recapture income. The amount of depreciation recapture cannot exceed the gain realized by Member A on sale of property (amount realized of $80,000 less adjusted basis of $75,000).[41]

[F]   *Investment Tax Credit Recapture*

An LLC's distribution of investment credit property to a member before the close of its estimated useful life used in computing the investment credit triggers recapture for all members, including any nondistributee members.[42]

§10.04   MARKETABLE SECURITIES DISTRIBUTIONS

[A]   *Generally*

A member recognizes gain to the extent that a money distribution exceeds the member's basis in the LLC. The term money includes marketable securities.[1] The amount treated as a money distribution is the fair market value of the securities distributed to the member,[2] reduced (but not below zero) by the excess of (a) the member's share of unrealized gains in the marketable securities held by the LLC immediately prior to the distribution, over (b) the member's share of unrealized gains in the marketable securities held by the LLC immediately after the distribution.[3]

EXAMPLE

An LLC has four equal members. Each member has a basis of $5,000 in her membership units. The LLC owns 20,000 shares of publicly traded stock with a basis of $80,000 and a fair market value of $100,000. The LLC makes a liquidating distribution to one of the members of 5,000 shares of stock with a basis of $20,000 and a fair market value of $25,000. The amount treated as a money distribution is $20,000. This is the $25,000 fair market value of the shares distributed to the member, less $5,000 determined as follows:

---

[41] Example from S. Rep. No. 1881, 87th Cong., 2d Sess. (1962), reprinted in 1962-3 C.B. 94.
[42] Reg. §1.47-6(a)(2).
§10.04   [1] IRC §731(c).
[2] IRC §731(c)(1)(B).
[3] IRC §731(c)(3)(B); Reg. §1.731-2(b)(2); Ltr. Ruls. 200223036-045.

Member's share of unrealized appreciation in the securities owned by the LLC before the distribution (1/4 of $20,000 total unrealized appreciation)	$5,000
Less member's share of unrealized appreciation in securities owned by the LLC after the liquidating distribution	0
Reduction amount	$5,000

Consequently, the member recognizes gain of $15,000, which is the amount of securities treated as money distributed ($25,000 − $5,000 = $20,000), less the member's $5,000 basis in her membership interest immediately prior to the distribution.

[B] Definition of Marketable Securities

The term "marketable securities" is defined broadly. It includes the following type of financial instruments:[4]

- Stocks
- Equity interests
- Debt
- Options
- Forward and futures contracts
- Notional principal contracts
- Derivatives
- Interests in actively traded precious metals and other financial instruments
- Other financial instruments and foreign currency that are actively traded within the meaning of the straddle provisions of Section 1092(d)(1) of the Internal Revenue Code
- A membership interest in an LLC if more than 90 percent of the value of the LLC is attributable to marketable securities.[5]

[C] Excluded Transactions

The following distributions of marketable securities do not result in gain recognition:[6]

- The member who received the distribution of the security contributed the security to the LLC.[7]

---

[4] IRC §731(c)(2).
[5] Ltr. Ruls. 200223036-045.
[6] IRC §731(c)(3)(A), (C).
[7] Reg. §1.731-2(d)(1)(i).

- The LLC acquired the security in a nonrecognition transaction. The value of the marketable securities and money exchanged by the LLC in the nonrecognition transaction must be less than 20 percent of a value of all assets exchanged by the LLC in the nonrecognition transaction. The LLC must distribute the security within five years after either the date of acquisition, or, if later, the date on which the security became marketable.[8]
- The security was not a marketable security on the date of acquisition. The entity that issued the security must not have marketable securities at the time of acquisition by the LLC. The security must be held by the LLC for at least six months before the security becomes marketable. The LLC must distribute the security within five years after the date that the security becomes marketable.[9]
- The LLC is an investment partnership, and the member is an eligible partner. An investment partnership includes an LLC that has never engaged in a trade or business if substantially all of its assets are investment assets as specified in the Internal Revenue Code and regulations. An LLC is not engaged in a trade or business for such purposes as a result of its activities as an investor, trader, or dealer in investment assets. An eligible partner includes any member of the LLC who before the date of distribution did not contribute any property other than specified investment assets.[10]

[D]   Basis in Distributed Securities

The basis in the distributed securities is the LLC's adjusted basis in the securities immediately prior to the distribution, increased by the amount of gain recognized by the member upon the distribution.[11] The gain is allocated to the securities in proportion to the amount of unrealized appreciation in the securities.

[E]   Basis in Membership Interest

The member's basis in his membership interest is the basis immediately prior to the distribution, decreased by the LLC's adjusted basis in the securities. The basis in the membership interest is not decreased by the fair market value of the securities distributed or the deemed money distribution under IRC Section 731(c). Thus, the gain recognized under that section does not affect the member's basis in his membership interest.

---

[8] Reg. §1.731-2(d)(1)(ii).
[9] Reg. §1.731-2(d)(1)(iii).
[10] Reg. §1.731-2(e)(1).
[11] IRC §731(c)(4); Reg. §1.731-2(f)(1)(i).

[F]   LLC's Basis in Its Assets

The LLC's adjusted basis in its remaining assets is not affected by the distribution of the marketable securities. There is no basis adjustment for the distributed securities under IRC Sections 754 and 734(b). The LLC may not adjust the basis of its assets as a result of the gain recognized by the member upon the distribution.

EXAMPLE

An LLC owns various assets, including 20,000 shares of common stock with a basis of $4 per share and a fair market value of $5 per share ($1 appreciation per share). The LLC files an election under Section 754 to adjust the basis of its assets upon transfers of membership interest and distributions to members. Member A has a basis in her membership interest of $5,000. The LLC makes a nonliquidating distribution to the member of 2,000 shares of the common stock with an aggregate basis of $8,000 and a fair market value of $10,000. Member A is a 25 percent owner of the LLC before and after the distribution. The distribution of the common stock is treated as a money distribution to the member. The initial amount of the money distribution is the fair market value of the securities of $10,000. However, the deemed money distribution is reduced by $500, from $10,000 to $9,500, as follows:

Member A's share of unrealized appreciation in the common stock immediately prior to the distribution (1/4 × 20,000 shares × $1 appreciation per share)	$ 5,000
Less member A's share of unrealized appreciation in the marketable securities immediately after the distribution (1/4 × 18,000 shares × $1 per share)	(4,500)
Reduction in the fair market value of securities that is treated as a money distribution	$ 500

Consequently, Member A's gain on the nonliquidating distribution is $4,500. This is the amount by which the deemed money distribution of $9,500 exceeds Member A's basis in her membership interest. Member A's basis in her membership interest is reduced to zero. Her basis in the common stock is $24,500. This is the LLC's adjusted basis of $20,000 in the distributed stock (5,000 shares × $4 per share), plus the member's $4,000 gain upon the distribution of the securities. Even though the LLC has made an election under Section 754, it may not adjust the basis of its remaining assets as a result of the gain recognized by the member. Therefore, the adjusted basis of its remaining assets stays the same, and the overall basis for its assets is reduced by the $20,000 basis in the distributed stock.

§10.05 DISPROPORTIONATE DISTRIBUTIONS

[A] Characterization of Gain

A member ordinarily recognizes capital gain when the member receives a liquidating distribution from an LLC of money in excess of the member's basis in his membership interest. The capital gain is equal to the amount of money in excess of the member's basis in his membership interest. A member recognizes capital loss if the member receives a liquidating distribution consisting only of cash, inventory, and/or unrealized receivables, and the basis to the LLC of the distributed property is less than the member's basis in the LLC interest.

However, a portion of the gain or loss is recharacterized as ordinary income or loss if the member receives a disproportionate distribution of "hot assets" or "cold assets." The "hot assets" are the unrealized receivables and inventory. These are assets that give rise to ordinary income for the LLC. The various types of hot assets are discussed in Chapter 15.[1]

The "cold assets" are the other assets that do not give rise to ordinary income, such as capital assets and Section 1231 assets.

For distributions, inventory is a "hot asset" only if it is substantially appreciated inventory. Substantially appreciated inventory is inventory with a fair market value in excess of 120 percent of its adjusted basis.[2] This rule differs from the rule for transfers of membership interests. After 1997, a member who sells or exchanges a membership interest may recognize ordinary income rather than capital gain if the LLC owns any inventory, whether or not substantially appreciated.[3]

There are two types of disproportionate distributions. The first type is when a member receives more than his share of the ordinary income assets.[4] The second type is when the member receives less than his share of the ordinary income assets.[5] In both cases, the member is treated as first receiving a proportionate share of both types of assets in the distribution and then selling back to the LLC the assets he would have received in a proportionate distribution for the assets actually received in excess of his proportionate share.[6]

EXAMPLE

An LLC has only cash and accounts receivable. One of the members of the LLC receives a liquidating distribution of only cash. That member is treated as having received a distribution of his pro rata share of receivables. He is then treated as having sold those receivables back to the LLC in a

---

§10.05   [1] *See* §15.07[A] *infra.*

[2] IRC §751(b)(1)(A), (b)(3).

[3] *See* IRC §751(a), as amended by the Taxpayer Relief Act of 1997, Pub. L. No. 105-34, §1062, 105th Cong., 1st Sess. (Aug. 5, 1997).

[4] IRC §751(b)(1)(A).

[5] IRC §751(b)(1)(B).

[6] Reg. §1.732-1(e).

taxable transaction in exchange for the cash received in excess of the cash he would have received in a pro rata distribution.

[B] Member Receives Less Than Member's Share of Ordinary Income Assets

The most common type of disproportionate distribution is when a member receives less than his proportionate share of ordinary income assets.[7] This type of disproportionate distribution occurs when an LLC owns inventory and/or unrealized receivables and makes a cash distribution to the member in exchange for the member's interest in LLC property. The purpose of this rule is to make sure that the distributee member pays tax on that member's share of the LLC's ordinary income property.

There is a short-cut method of determining the ordinary income on disproportionate distributions. The short-cut method works in the normal case if there is a liquidating cash distribution and if there are no special allocations, no special bases adjustments, and no differences in members' interests in profits and losses. The amount of ordinary income is the member's profit percentage multiplied by the total potential ordinary income to the LLC. The LLC's basis in the ordinary income assets immediately after the liquidating distribution is its adjusted basis in the assets before the distribution, plus the ordinary income recognized by the member.

EXAMPLE

An LLC has four equal members. The financial statements for the LLC show the following:

Asset	Adjusted Basis	Fair Market Value
Cash	$ 6,000	$ 6,000
Accounts receivable	$ 6,000	$ 8,000
Land	$10,000	$14,000
	$22,000	$28,000
Liabilities		$ 6,000
Capital account of Member A		$ 4,000
Adjusted basis in membership interest for Member A		$ 5,500

The LLC makes a liquidating cash distribution to Member A of $5,500. Consequently, the total amount of money deemed distributed to Member A is $7,000, consisting of the $5,500 cash payment and the $1,500 debt relief

---

[7] Reg. §1.751-1(b)(3).

(1/4 × $6,000). Member A's gain upon the liquidating distribution is $1,500. This is the portion of the $7,000 distributed in excess of Member A's adjusted basis in her membership interest of $5,500.

The LLC has only one ordinary income asset, the accounts receivable. There is unrecognized ordinary income potential of $2,000 (fair market value of $8,000, less $6,000 adjusted basis). Member A received a disproportionate distribution, since she received only cash and not her proportionate share of the ordinary income asset. Therefore, a portion of Member A's $1,500 of gain upon the distribution is recharacterized as ordinary income. Under the short-cut method, the amount of ordinary income is determined by multiplying Member A's profit percentage interest in the LLC (25 percent) times the total potential ordinary income of $2,000, which is $500. Therefore, Member A recognizes $1,000 of capital gain upon the distribution and $500 of ordinary income. The LLC may increase the basis of its ordinary income asset by the ordinary income recognized by Member A. Therefore, the basis of the accounts receivable to the LLC is increased from $6,000 to $6,500.

A member may need to compute the amount of ordinary income under the longer method prescribed by the regulations if there are special allocations, the LLC makes a nonliquidating distribution, or if a member has a different percentage interest in profits and losses. There are the following 10 steps in determining the tax consequences under the longer method:

Step 1: Determine the member's predistribution interest in the fair market value of each asset of the LLC. In the prior example, the predistribution interest of Member A would be as follows:

$$
\begin{array}{lll}
\text{Cash} & = 1/4 \times \$\ 6,000 & = \$1,500 \\
\text{Inventory} & = 1/4 \times \$\ 8,000 & = \$2,000 \\
\text{Land} & = 1/4 \times \$14,000 & = \$3,500
\end{array}
$$

Step 2: Determine the member's postdistribution interest in each asset retained by the LLC. In the case of a liquidating distribution, the member's postdistribution interest in each asset of the LLC is zero.

Step 3: Determine the actual property distributed to the member and whether that asset is an ordinary income asset (unrealized receivable or inventory). Member A has received only cash, which is not an ordinary income asset. Therefore, the member has received a disproportionate distribution.

Step 4: Allocate the amount of the distribution to each of the assets that the member should have received in the distribution. This is based on the fair market value of the assets immediately prior to the distribution (see step 1). Member A received a total money distribution of $7,000 in exchange for her one-fourth interest in LLC assets that had a fair market value of $7,000 ($1,500 cash, $2,000 accounts receivable, $3,500 land).

Step 5: Determine the member's predistribution interest in the adjusted basis of each asset of the LLC immediately prior to the distribution. Member A's predistribution interest in the adjusted basis of the assets is as follows:

$$
\begin{array}{llll}
\text{Cash} & = 1/4 \times \$\ 6{,}000 & = \$1{,}500 \\
\text{Inventory} & = 1/4 \times \$\ 6{,}000 & = \$1{,}500 \\
\text{Land} & = 1/4 \times \$10{,}000 & = \$2{,}500
\end{array}
$$

Step 6: Determine the total amount of gain realized by the member upon the distribution. This is the difference between Member A's money distribution of $7,000 and her adjusted basis in her membership interest of $5,500.

Step 7: Determine the gain realized upon the distribution of cash or other property for the member's interest in ordinary income assets. This is $500, determined as follows:

Money distribution received in exchange for the accounts receivable	$2,000
Less member's 1/4 share of the LLC's adjusted basis in its ordinary income asset (inventory) immediately prior to the distribution	1,500
Member A's ordinary income gain on the Section 751(b) deemed exchange	$ 500

Step 8: Determine the gain recognized by the LLC. The LLC has no gain because it is treated as having purchased Member A's interest in the ordinary income assets (with an adjusted basis of $1,500) with cash in the amount of $2,000.

Step 9: Determine the amount of capital gain recognized by the member. This is the total gain of $1,500, less the ordinary income of $500, or $1,000.

Step 10: Determine the basis of the ordinary income assets to the LLC. This is $6,500, which is the LLC's $6,000 adjusted basis in the accounts receivable prior to the distribution, plus the $500 of gain recognized as ordinary income by the member under Section 751(b). This is the same as its $6,000 adjusted basis in the receivables prior to the distribution, less the $1,500 of receivables deemed distributed to Member A, plus the $2,000 deemed cash purchase price for Member A's share of the receivables.

[C] *Member Receives More Than Member's Share of Ordinary Income Assets*

The second type of disproportionate distribution is when a member receives more than his share of ordinary income assets.

The member is treated as receiving a proportionate share of all assets and then using the share of "cold asset" property he should have received to purchase the extra share of ordinary income property actually received.[8] The member recognizes capital gain to the extent of the appreciation in the capital asset (or other cold asset) that was deemed distributed to the member (but that was not actually received). The member receives a basis in the ordinary income assets received equal to the LLC's adjusted basis in those assets prior to the distribution, increased by the capital gain recognized by the member. The LLC recognizes gain or loss on the deemed distribution and buyback. The LLC increases the basis of its assets by the ordinary income recognized by it upon the deemed sale of the ordinary income property to the member. It decreases the basis of its assets by the amount of loss recognized by the LLC.

The purpose of this rule is to make sure that the remaining members in the LLC pay their share of tax on the ordinary income property. The rule prevents the LLC from shifting ordinary income to the distributee member. The effect of the rule is that all members recognize approximately the same amount of ordinary income that they would have recognized if there had been no disproportionate distribution.

The Section 751(b) rules are not activated if a member receives a cash distribution and the member's share of profits in the LLC remains the same. The statute requires that a member must also receive a reduced share of ordinary income property in exchange for the cash or other "cold asset" property actually received. Consequently, most nonliquidating cash distributions to members are not covered by the disproportionate distribution rules.

EXAMPLE

An LLC has four equal members. The financial statements of the LLC show the following:

Asset	Adjusted Basis to LLC	Fair Market Value
Cash	$ 6,000	$ 6,000
Inventory	5,000	10,000
Land	13,000	16,000
	$24,000	$32,000
Member A's capital account		$ 6,000
Member A's adjusted basis in membership interest		$ 6,000

The LLC makes a liquidating distribution to Member A of a portion of the inventory with a basis of $4,000 and a fair market value of $8,000, representing one-fourth of the value of LLC assets. Prior to distribution, the total ordinary income potential is $5,000 ($10,000 fair market value of inventory, less $5,000 adjusted basis of the inventory). The land is a capital asset. Each member's proportionate share of the $5,000 inventory ordinary income

---

[8] Reg. §1.751-1(b)(2).

potential is $1,250. The disproportionate distribution rules are designed to ensure that each member recognizes $1,250 of ordinary income even though there is a disproportionate distribution of the ordinary income items to one of the members. This is accomplished through the following steps:

Step 1: Determine Member A's predisposition interest in the fair market value of LLC assets. These are the assets that are deemed distributed to the member. The deemed distribution values are based on the fair market values of the assets rather than their adjusted bases. Member A's predisposition interest in the LLC's assets is as follows:

$$
\begin{array}{lll}
\text{Cash} & = \$\ 6{,}000 \times 1/4 = \$1{,}500 \\
\text{Inventory} & = \$10{,}000 \times 1/4 = \$2{,}500 \\
\text{Land} & = \$16{,}000 \times 1/4 = \$4{,}000
\end{array}
$$

Step 2: Determine Member A's postdistribution interest in the fair market value of LLC assets. The difference between the predisposition interest and the postdistribution interest is the value of assets deemed distributed to Member A. In this case, the postdistribution interest is zero, since Member A received a liquidating distribution.

Step 3: Determine the adjusted basis of the LLC assets deemed distributed to Member A. The adjusted basis of the assets is as follows:

$$
\begin{array}{lll}
\text{Cash} & = \$\ 6{,}000 \times 1/4 = \$1{,}500 \\
\text{Inventory} & = \$\ 5{,}000 \times 1/4 = \$1{,}250 \\
\text{Land} & = \$13{,}000 \times 1/4 = \$3{,}250
\end{array}
$$

The value of the assets deemed distributed to Member A less the adjusted basis of those assets to the LLC represents the income that Member A will recognize upon the subsequent sale of the assets.

Step 4: Determine the excess amount of ordinary income assets that the member received in the disproportionate distribution. The member received $8,000 worth of inventory. Step 1 shows that the member should have received $2,500 of inventory in a proportionate distribution. Therefore, the member received excess inventory with a fair market value of $5,500 and an adjusted basis of $2,250 (one-half of $5,500). These excess assets have an ordinary income potential of $2,250.

Step 5: Determine the assets that the member gave up in the disproportionate distribution. Steps 1 and 2 show that Member A should have received land worth $4,000 and cash of $1,500 in a proportionate distribution. These were the assets that Member A was deemed to have received. Member A gave up the cash and land worth $5,500 in exchange for additional inventory worth $5,500.

Step 6: Determine the capital gain that the member recognizes in the disproportionate distribution. The member received additional inventory worth $5,500 in exchange for her $4,000 interest in the land and cash worth $1,500. The member is treated as selling the cash and land to the LLC in exchange for the additional inventory. Steps 1 and 3 show that the land that the member gave up in the exchange had a fair market value of $4,000 and an adjusted basis of $3,250. Therefore, the member recognizes $750 of capital gain on the deemed sale of the land to the LLC in exchange for the inventory.

Step 7: Determine the basis that the member has in the ordinary income assets received. This consists of two items. First, a member receives a basis equal to the purchase price of the excess inventory that the member is deemed to have purchased from the LLC in the disproportionate distribution. Since the member purchased the excess inventory for $1,500 cash and $4,000 in land, the member has a basis in the excess inventory of $5,500. Second, the member receives a carryover basis in the inventory received from the LLC that she would have received in a proportionate distribution of assets. Steps 1 and 3 show that the member would have received inventory with a fair market value of $2,500 and an adjusted basis of $1,250 in a proportionate distribution. Therefore, the member has a total adjusted basis in the inventory of $6,750 ($5,500 + $1,250). The total value of the inventory distributed is $8,000 ($2,500 that was distributed from the LLC in the proportionate distribution and $5,500 that Member A is deemed to have purchased from the LLC for the land and cash under the disproportionate distribution rules).

Step 8: Determine the amount of ordinary income recognized by the LLC in the disproportionate distribution. The LLC is treated as selling $5,500 of inventory to Member A for cash of $1,500 and land worth $4,000. The inventory has an adjusted basis to the LLC of $2,750 (one-half of $5,500). Therefore, the LLC recognizes ordinary income of $2,750 in the disproportionate distribution. The LLC adds that taxable income to the basis of the land that it is deemed to have purchased from Member A in the disproportionate distribution. This basis increase benefits the three remaining members.

Step 9: The LLC has $2,000 of additional inventory with an adjusted basis of $1,000. Therefore, the remaining members in the LLC have $1,000 more of ordinary income potential that will be passed through to the three remaining members.

Step 10: The ordinary income to the three remaining members includes the $2,750 recognized by the LLC as a result of the disproportionate distribution and the $1,000 that will be recognized from the sale of the LLCs remaining inventory in the future. The total ordinary income that the LLC will recognize is $3,750, or $1,250 per member.

Step 11: The total ordinary income for the distributee member is also $1,250, which is the $8,000 fair market value of the inventory received, less the $6,750 adjusted basis. Therefore, each of the four equal members in the LLC recognizes $1,250 of ordinary income even though the LLC made a disproportionate distribution of the ordinary income items to Member A.

Planning Note: An LLC can still shift gain among members by making disproportionate distributions of appreciated assets in the same class. For example, it can give appreciated inventory to one member and depreciated inventory to another member with no adverse tax consequences under Section 751(b) if the assets have equal values.

§10.06   SECTION 754 ELECTION

[A]   *Overview*

An LLC may make an election under IRC Section 754 to adjust the basis of its assets upon distributions to members. This is similar to the basis adjustment when members in an LLC sell their membership interests or transfer their interests upon death. If the LLC makes a Section 754 election, then it must adjust the basis of its assets upon transfers of membership interests under Section 743 and distributions to members under Section 734.

The purposes of the basis adjustment are to prevent double taxation and to keep the members' adjusted bases in their membership interests (the outside bases) in line with the LLC's adjusted bases for its assets (the inside bases).

An LLC that makes an election under Section 754 must make the following basis adjustments on distributions to members:

- *Money distributions in excess of basis.* A member recognizes gain on distribution of money in excess of the member's basis in the membership interest. The LLC must increase the basis of its assets by the amount of gain recognized by the member.
- *Money distributions that are less than basis.* A member recognizes loss on a distribution if (a) the distribution is in complete liquidation of the membership interest, (b) the member receives only cash and/or receivables and inventory items, and (c) the cash and the LLC's basis of any receivables and inventory items distributed to the member are less than the member's basis in the membership interest. The LLC must decrease the basis of its assets by the amount of loss recognized by the member.
- *Substituted basis decrease.* A member may in certain cases receive a basis in distributed assets that is less than the LLC's basis in the assets immediately prior to the distribution. The LLC must increase the basis of its assets by the amount of basis decrease to the member.
- *Substituted basis increase.* A member may receive a basis in distributed assets that is greater than the LLC's basis in the assets immediately prior to the distribution. This will occur only on a complete liquidation of the member's interest in the LLC. The LLC must decrease the basis of its assets by the amount of basis increase to the member.

[B]   Types of Basis Adjustments

[1]   Money Distributions that Are in Excess of Member's Adjusted Basis

A member recognizes gain if the member receives a distribution of money (cash plus debt relief) in excess of the member's adjusted basis in his membership interest.[1] The gain equals the amount by which the money distribution exceeds the adjusted basis.[2] The gain is normally capital gain. An LLC that makes a Section 754 election must increase the adjusted basis of its remaining assets by the amount of gain recognized to the distributee member.[3] The basis increase is allocated only to the capital assets,[4] and Section 1231(b) assets.[5] The basis increase must be allocated first to capital gain properties with unrealized appreciation (up to the total amount of unrealized appreciation) in proportion to their respective amounts of unrealized appreciation. Any remaining basis increase must be allocated among the capital gain properties in proportion to their fair market values.[6]

EXAMPLE

An LLC makes an election under Section 754 to adjust the basis of its assets upon transfers of membership interests and distributions to members. The financial statements of the LLC show the following:

Asset	Adjusted Basis to LLC	Fair Market Value
Cash	$100,000	$ 100,000
Beach land	80,000	200,000
Desert land	120,000	100,000
	$300,000	$ 400,000
Liabilities		(100,000)
Net equity of LLC		$ 300,000

Member A has a one-tenth interest in the LLC. The adjusted basis of her membership interest is $30,000. The LLC makes a liquidating cash distribution to the member of $30,000. Member A recognizes capital gain of $10,000. The money distribruted to the member is $40,000, consisting of the $30,000 cash and the $10,000 of debt relief. The money distribution exceeds the member's adjusted basis of $30,000 by $10,000 and is thus taxed as capital gain under Section 731(a)(1). The LLC must increase the basis of its remaining assets by the $10,000 of gain to the member upon distribution. All of this

---

§10.06   [1] IRC §731(a)(1).
[2] IRC §731(a)(1).
[3] IRC §734(b)(1)(A).
[4] Reg. §1.755-1(b)(1)(ii).
[5] Reg. §1.755-1(a).
[6] Reg. §1.755-1(c)(2)(i).

gain must be allocated to its remaining capital gain assets, which are the beach land and desert land. The basis adjustment must first be allocated to the capital gain property with unrealized appreciation. The beach land is the only capital gain assets that has a value in excess of its adjusted basis. The amount of the unrealized appreciation is more than the basis adjustment. Therefore, the entire $10,000 of basis adjustment must be added to the basis of the beach land. The LLC thus has an adjusted basis in the beach land of $90,000 and retains an adjusted basis in the desert land of $120,000.

[2]   Money Distributions that Are Less Than Member's Adjusted Basis

A member recognizes loss in a distribution if all of the following occur:[7]

- There is a liquidating distribution;
- The member receives solely money, unrealized receivables, and/or inventory in the complete liquidation; and
- The cash and adjusted bases of such properties received in the liquidation are less than the member's adjusted basis in his membership interest.[8]

In this case, the LLC must decrease the basis of its remaining assets by the amount of the loss recognized by the member.[9] The basis decrease is allocated only to capital gain assets,[10] including Section 1231(b) assets.[11] The basis decrease must first be allocated to capital gain properties with unrealized depreciation (up to the total amount of unrealized depreciation) in proportion to their respective amounts of unrealized depreciation. Any remaining basis decrease must be allocated among the capital gain properties in proportion to their adjusted bases (after making the prior basis adjustment).[12]

EXAMPLE

An LLC makes an election under Section 754 to adjust the basis of its assets upon transfers of membership interests and distributions to members. The financial statements of the LLC show the following:

---

[7] IRC §731(a)(2).
[8] IRC §731(a)(2).
[9] IRC §734(b)(2)(A).
[10] Reg. §1.755-1(c)(1)(ii).
[11] Reg. §1.755-1(a).
[12] Reg. §1.755-1(c)(2)(ii).

Asset	Adjusted Basis to LLC	Fair Market Value
Cash	$100,000	$ 100,000
Beach land	80,000	200,000
Desert land	120,000	100,000
	$300,000	$ 400,000
Liabilities		(100,000)
Net equity of LLC		$ 300,000

Member A has a one-tenth interest in the LLC. The adjusted basis of his membership interest is $30,000. The LLC makes a liquidating cash distribution to Member A of $10,000 in complete liquidation of the member's interest in the LLC. The amount of money distributed to the member is $20,000, consisting of the $10,000 cash distribution and the $10,000 of debt relief. The member recognizes a $10,000 capital loss, since the member received a money distribution in complete liquidation that was $10,000 less than the $30,000 adjusted basis in her membership interest immediately prior to the distribution. The basis adjustment must first be allocated to the capital gain property with unrealized depreciation. The desert land is the only capital gain asset that has a value below its adjusted basis. The amount of the unrealized depreciation is more than the basis adjustment. Therefore, the entire $10,000 of basis decrease must be allocated to the desert land. Thus, the LLC has an adjusted basis of $110,000 in the desert land, and retains an $80,000 basis in the beach land.

[3]   Substituted Basis Decrease

An LLC must make a third basis adjustment when a member receives a distribution from the LLC with an adjusted basis to the LLC that is greater than the member's basis in his membership interest. In this case, the member receives a substituted basis for the property equal to his lower basis in the membership interest rather than a carryover of the LLC's higher basis for the property. The LLC increases the basis of its remaining assets by the amount of the decrease in basis for the member.[13] The following two types of distributions result in a substituted basis decrease:

1.   *Nonliquidating distribution.* Normally, a member who receives property from an LLC in a nonliquidating distribution receives a carryover basis for the property equal to the LLC's adjusted basis for the property immediately prior to the distribution. However, the carryover basis cannot exceed the member's adjusted basis in his membership interest, reduced by any money received in the distribution. If the LLC's adjusted basis for the distributed assets exceeds the member's basis in his membership interest, then the basis for the assets is reduced to the member's basis in his membership

---

[13] IRC §734(b)(1)(B).

interest.[14] The member then has a zero basis in his membership interest after the distribution.

2. *Liquidating distribution.* Again, a member receives a substituted basis for property in a liquidating distribution. The cash and money part of the distribution first reduces the member's basis in his membership interest. The member's remaining basis is then allocated to inventory and unrealized receivables and then to capital gain property. If the LLC's adjusted basis for the distributed assets exceeds the member's basis in his membership interest, then the basis for the distributed assets is reduced to the member's basis in his membership interest.[15]

The LLC must allocate the basis increase to property of the same class that caused the basis decrease to the member upon distribution.[16] This is a two-step process. First, the LLC allocates the basis increase either to capital gain property or ordinary income property, depending on the class of property received by the member whose basis was adjusted. Thus, when the LLC's adjusted basis of distributed capital gain property immediately prior to the distribution exceeds the basis of such property to the distributee member, the basis of undistributed capital gain property remaining in the LLC is increased by an amount equal to the excess. Similarly, when the LLC's adjusted basis of distributed ordinary income property (inventory and unrealized receivables) immediately prior to the distribution exceeds the basis of such property to the distributee member, the basis of undistributed ordinary income property in the LLC is increased by an amount equal to the excess.[17]

Second, the LLC must allocate the basis increase within each class first to properties with unrealized appreciation (up to the total amount of unrealized appreciation) in proportion to their respective amounts of unrealized appreciation. Any remaining basis increase must be allocated among the LLC properties within the class in proportion to their fair market values.[18]

EXAMPLE 1

An LLC has four equal members. The financial statements of the LLC show the following:

Asset	Adjusted Basis to LLC	Fair Market Value
Cash	$ 60,000	$ 60,000
Beach land	40,000	30,000
Desert land	20,000	30,000
	$120,000	$120,000
Liabilities		$ 0
Member A's adjusted basis in LLC		$ 30,000

---

[14] IRC §732(a)(2).
[15] IRC §732(b).
[16] Reg. §1.755-1(c)(1)(i).
[17] *Id.*
[18] Reg. §1.755-1(c)(2)(i).

The LLC distributes the beach land to Member A in complete liquidation of the member's interest in the LLC. Although the beach land has an adjusted basis of $40,000 to the LLC, Member A takes a substituted basis in the property of $30,000. The basis of distributed property in a liquidating or nonliquidating distribution cannot exceed the member's remaining basis in her membership interest. Since no cash was received in the liquidation, Member A's basis in the distributed property is equal to her basis in the membership interest immediately prior to the distribution. If the LLC makes an election under Section 754 to adjust the basis of its assets, it must increase the basis of its remaining property by the amount of basis decrease to Member A. The $10,000 basis increase must be allocated to property that is similar to the distributed property. In this case, the desert land retained by the LLC is a Section 1221 capital asset, which is the same class of asset as the beach land. The fair market value of the desert land is $10,000 above the adjusted basis of the desert land. Therefore, the entire $10,000 basis increase must be allocated to the desert land. The LLC has a $30,000 adjusted basis in the desert land as a result of the Section 754 election.

EXAMPLE 2

An LLC makes an election under Section 754. The financial statements of the LLC are as follows:[19]

Asset	Adjusted Basis	Fair Market Value
Capital Gain Property:		
Asset 1	$ 25,000	$ 75,000
Asset 2	100,000	117,500
Asset 3	50,000	60,000
Ordinary Income Property:		
Asset 4	$ 40,000	$ 45,000
Asset 5	50,000	60,000
Asset 6	10,000	2,500
Total	$275,000	$360,000

The LLC distributes Assets 3 and 5 to Member A in complete liquidation of Member A's membership interest. Member A had a basis in the membership interest of $75,000. The basis adjustment to the LLC is determined as follows:

Step 1: Determine the amount of basis increase to the LLC. Member A receives a basis for the property on liquidation equal to his $75,000 basis in the membership interest. Since the LLC had a $100,000 basis in the property prior to distribution, there is a $25,000 decrease in basis for the member. The LLC must therefore increase the basis of its assets by $25,000.

---

[19] This example is from Reg. §1.755-1(c)(5).

Step 2: Determine the class of asset that caused the basis decrease to the member on distribution. Member A's basis in the membership interest is first reduced by cash distributions. There are no cash distributions. Member A's basis in the membership interest is next allocated to ordinary income property (inventory and unrealized receivables) up to the LLC's adjusted basis in the assets under IRC §732(c)(1)(A). Thus, Member A receives a $50,000 basis in Asset 5. Finally, Member A's remaining basis in the membership interest of $25,000 is allocated to the capital gain property under IRC §732(c)(1)(B). Thus, Member A receives a $25,000 basis in Asset 3. The LLC had a $50,000 basis in the asset immediately prior to distribution. Therefore, the class of asset that caused the $25,000 basis decrease to the member on distribution was a capital gain asset.

Step 3: Allocate the basis increase between classes of LLC assets. Since the class of asset that caused the basis decrease to the member on distribution was a capital gain asset, the entire $25,000 basis increase for the LLC must be allocated to its remaining capital gain assets (Assets 1 and 2).

Step 4: Allocate the basis increase within the class of assets. The basis increase is first allocated among the LLC's remaining capital gain assets with unrealized appreciation (up to the total amount of unrealized appreciation) in proportion to their respective amounts of unrealized appreciation. Asset 1 has appreciated by $50,000. Asset 2 has appreciated by $17,500. The proportion of increase attributable to Asset 1 is approximately 74 percent ($50,000/$67,500). The proportion of increase attributable to Asset 2 is approximately 26 percent ($17,500/67,500). Therefore, the LLC must increase the basis of Asset 1 by $18,519 ($25,000 basis increase × 74%) and increase the basis of Asset 2 by $6,481 ($25,000 basis increase × 26%).

[4] Substituted Basis Increase

A member of an LLC may receive a substituted basis increase for distributed property if the member receives a higher basis in the property than the LLC's basis in the property immediately prior to the distribution. The substituted basis increase can occur only upon a complete liquidation of a member's interest in the LLC. It cannot occur in a partial liquidation. In a complete liquidation, a member must first reduce the basis in his membership interest by the amount of money received in the liquidation. The member must then allocate outside basis to the inventory and unrealized receivables received in the distribution in an amount equal to the LLC's basis in such property, or the member's remaining outside basis if less.[20] The remaining part of the member's adjusted basis is allocated to the other property distributed in the complete liquidation. The member

---

[20] *See* §10.03[B][2] *supra.*

receives a higher basis in the distributed property if the member's remaining adjusted basis in his membership interest exceeds the LLC's adjusted basis in the distributed property immediately prior to the distribution.[21] In this event, the LLC must reduce the basis of its remaining assets by the amount of basis increase for the member.[22]

The LLC must allocate the basis decrease to property of the same class that caused the basis increase to the member on distribution. This is a two-step process. First, the LLC allocates the basis decrease either to capital gain property or ordinary income property, depending on the class of property received by the member whose basis was adjusted. Thus, when the LLC's adjusted basis of distributed capital gain property immediately prior to the distribution is less than the basis of such property to the distributee member, the basis of undistributed capital gain property remaining in the LLC is reduced by the decrease in basis. Similarly, when the LLC's adjusted basis of distributed ordinary income property immediately prior to the distribution is less than the basis of such property to the distributee member, the basis of undistributed ordinary income property in the LLC is reduced by the decrease in basis.[23]

Second, the LLC must allocate the basis decrease within each class first to properties with unrealized depreciation (up to the total amount of unrealized depreciation) in proportion to their respective amounts of unrealized depreciation. Any remaining basis decrease must be allocated among the LLC properties within the class in proportion to their adjusted bases (after making the basis adjustment above).[24]

EXAMPLE 1

An LLC has four equal members. The financial statements of the LLC show the following:

Asset	Adjusted Basis to LLC	Fair Market Value
Cash	$ 60,000	$ 60,000
Beach land	40,000	30,000
Desert land	20,000	30,000
	$120,000	$120,000
Liabilities		$ 0
Member A's adjusted basis in LLC		$ 30,000

The LLC distributes the desert land to Member A in complete liquidation of the member's interest in the LLC. Since there is a complete liquidation

---

[21] IRC §732(b).
[22] IRC §734(b)(2)(B).
[23] Reg. §1.755-1(c)(1)(i).
[24] Reg. §1.755-1(c)(2)(ii).

and no cash distribution, Member A receives a basis in the desert land equal to her $30,000 adjusted basis in her membership interest rather than the LLC's $20,000 adjusted basis in the property immediately prior to the distribution. Since there is a $10,000 basis increase to the member, the LLC must decrease the remaining basis of its assets. The basis decrease must be allocated to its assets that are similar in character to the distributed asset. Since the fair market value of the beach property is $10,000 less than the LLC's adjusted basis in the property, the entire $10,000 downward adjustment must be allocated to the beach land. The LLC therefore has a $30,000 adjusted basis in the beach land, with a fair market value of $30,000.

EXAMPLE 2

An LLC makes an election under Section 754. The financial statements of the LLC are as follows:[25]

Asset	Adjusted Basis to LLC	Fair Market Value
Capital Gain Property:		
Asset 1	$ 25,000	$ 75,000
Asset 2	100,000	90,000
Asset 3	50,000	60,000
Asset	Adjusted Basis to LLC	Fair Market Value
Ordinary Income Property:		
Asset 4	$ 40,000	$ 45,000
Asset 5	50,000	60,000
Asset 6	10,000	2,500
Total	$275,000	$332,500

The LLC distributes Assets 3 and 5 to Member A in complete liquidation of Member A's membership interest. Member A had a basis in the membership interest of $215,000. The basis adjustment to the LLC is determined as follows:

Step 1: Determine the amount of basis increase to the LLC. Member A receives a basis for the property on liquidation equal to his $215,000 basis in the membership interest. Since the LLC had a $100,000 basis in the property prior to distribution, there is a $115,000 increase in basis for the member. The LLC must therefore decrease the basis of its assets by $115,000.

Step 2: Determine the class of asset that caused the basis increase to the member on distribution. Member A's basis in the membership interest is first reduced by cash distributions. There are no cash distributions. Member A's basis in the membership interest is next allocated to ordinary

---

[25] This example is from Reg. §1.755-1(c)(5).

income property (inventory and unrealized receivables) up to the LLC's adjusted basis in the assets under IRC §732(c)(1)(A). Thus, Member A receives a $50,000 basis in Asset 5. Finally, Member A's remaining basis in the membership interest of $165,000 is allocated to the capital gain property under IRC §732(c)(1)(B). Thus, Member A receives a $165,000 basis in Asset 3. The LLC had a $50,000 basis in the asset immediately prior to distribution. Therefore, the class of asset that caused the $115,000 basis increase to the Member A on distribution was a capital gain asset.

Step 3: Allocate the basis decrease between classes of LLC assets. Since the class of asset that caused the basis increase to the member on distribution was a capital gain asset, the entire $115,000 basis decrease for the LLC must be allocated to its remaining capital gain assets (Assets 1 and 2).

Step 4: Allocate the basis decrease within the class of assets. The $115,000 basis decrease is first allocated among the LLC's remaining capital gain assets with unrealized depreciation (up to the total amount of unrealized depreciation) in proportion to their respective amounts of unrealized depreciation. Asset 1 has appreciated by $50,000. Asset 2 has depreciated by $10,000. Thus, the first $10,000 of basis decrease is allocated to Asset 2 since it is the only capital gain asset that has unrealized appreciation. The basis of Asset 2 is reduced to $90,000 after this reduction. The remaining $105,000 of basis decrease is allocated to the capital gain assets in proportion to their adjusted bases, after taking into account the prior basis adjustment. The percentage of total basis attributable to Asset 1 is approximately 22 percent ($25,000/$115,000). The percentage of total basis attributable to Asset 2 is approximately 78 percent ($90,000/115,000). Therefore, the LLC must decrease the basis of Asset 1 by $23,100 ($105,000 basis decrease × 22%) and decrease the basis of Asset 2 by an additional $81,900 ($105,000 basis decrease × 78%). Asset 1 ends up with a basis of $1,900 ($25,000–$23,100). Assets 2 ends up with the basis of $8,100 ($100,000–$10,000–$81,900).

[C]   Two-Year Optional Basis Adjustment

A member may elect to add to the basis of distributed assets any extra basis that the member would have had if an election under IRC Section 754 had been in effect if:[26]

- The member acquirers a membership interest by transfer from another member or on the death of a member.

---

[26] IRC §732(d); Reg. §1.732-1(d)(1).

- The LLC did not have an election in effect under IRC Section 754 at the time of the transfer.
- The member receives a liquidating or nonliquidating distribution of property within two years after acquiring the membership interest.
- The member files an appropriate election. The member must make the election with the return for the year of the distribution if the distributed property includes any depreciation, depletion, or amortization.[27] Otherwise, the member must make the election with the return for any taxable year no later than the first year in which the basis of any of the distributed property is relevant in determining taxable income.[28] The member must submit various items of information with the election. The member must state that he is electing to adjust the basis of property received in a distribution pursuant to IRC Section 732(d). The member must also show the computation of the basis adjustment and the properties to which the adjustment has been allocated.[29]
- If the member inherited the membership interest, the transferring member will receive a basis for the distributed assets equal to their fair market value if the distribution is made within two years after the death of the member, even though the LLC does not make a Section 754 election.

EXAMPLE

A member acquires her membership interest in an LLC in 1999. Her basis in the membership is $50,000. In 2000, the member receives a nonliquidating distribution of property that has an adjusted basis to the LLC of $25,000. The property would have had an adjusted basis of $30,000 if the LLC had made an election under Section 754 to adjust the basis of its assets upon transfers and distributions. The member may make the election under Section 732(d), since the member received a distribution of property within two years after acquiring her membership interest and since the LLC had not made an election under Section 754. The basis of the distributed assets is increased from $25,000 to $30,000 for the member. The member's basis in her membership interest is reduced by $30,000 (from $50,000 to $20,000) rather than by the LLC's $25,000 adjusted basis in the distributed assets. The LLC reduces the basis of its assets by $25,000.

[D] Section 732(d) Required Basis Adjustment

The IRS may require a transferee to adjust the basis of distributed property if all of the following apply:[30]

---

[27] Reg. §1.732-1(d)(2)(i).
[28] Reg. §1.732-1(d)(2)(ii).
[29] Reg. §1.732-1(d)(3)(i).
[30] IRC §732(d); Reg. §1.732-1(d)(4).

- The member acquires the membership interest in a transfer at a time when the LLC has not made an election to adjust the basis of its assets under IRC Section 754.
- The fair market value of all LLC property, other than money, exceeds 110 percent of the LLC's adjusted basis of its assets at the time of the transfer.
- If the LLC had made an IRC Section 754 election, there would have been a basis adjustment for the transferee member at the time of the transfer.
- There would have been a shift in basis from property not subject to an allowance for depreciation, depletion, or amortization, to property subject to such allowance, if the LLC made a liquidating distribution to the member immediately after the transfer.
- The property that would have received a basis adjustment at the time the transfer is later distributed to the member, including distributions more than two years after the transfer.

When this special rule applies, the basis is adjusted immediately before the distribution to reflect the basis that the property would have had if the LLC had had a Section 754 election in effect at the time the transferee acquired the membership interest. As a result, the basis of the distributed property in the hands of the LLC immediately before the distribution more closely approximates its fair market value.

The purpose of this rule is to prevent distortions that might inflate the basis of depreciable, depletable, or amortizable property above its fair market value. Changes in the tax laws in 1997 make such distortions less likely to occur. As a result, the IRS has requested comments on the proper scope of IRC Section 732(d) and under what circumstances, if any, the IRS should exercise its authority to mandate application of IRC Section 732(d) to transferees.

§10.07   CORPORATE DISTRIBUTIONS OF LLC UNITS TO SHAREHOLDERS

A corporation that is a member in an LLC may recognize gain upon the distribution of membership interests in the LLC to its shareholders. The corporation recognizes gain upon the distriburtion as if it sold the membership units to its shareholders at fair market value.[1] The amount of gain is equal to the difference between the fair market value of the LLC membership units and the corporation's adjusted basis in the membership units. If the membership units have depreciated in value, the corporation does not recognize loss on the distribution.[2]

The corporation's distribution of the membership units to its shareholders constitutes a transfer under IRC Section 743. Therefore, if the LLC has filed an election under IRC Section 754, then it must adjust the basis of its assets under IRC Sections 742 and 755 as a result of the distribution.

§10.07   [1] Ltr. Rul. 9751048 (*citing* IRC §311(b)(1)).
[2] Ltr. 9751048 (*citing* IRC §311(a)(2)).

The corporation's distribution of the membership units to its shareholders also causes the termination of the LLC if the distributed membership units constitute more than 50 percent of the LLC's outstanding membership interests.[3]

§10.08   DISTRIBUTIONS TO RETIRING AND DECEASED MEMBERS

[A]   *Generally*

IRC Section 736 governs the classification of payments to retiring members and successors in interest of deceased members. Section 736 deals only with the classification of those payments. Once the payments are classified, other LLC tax rules govern the income recognition, basis, timing, and other tax aspects of the distribution.

Section 736 governs liquidating payments to a member if all the following apply:[1]

- The payment is to a retiring member or to the successor in interest of a deceased member. Section 736 does not apply if the member is retiring, but continues to work on part-time basis.
- The payment is made in complete liquidation of the member's interest in the LLC. Section 736 does not apply if the member sells his membership interest to another member.
- The LLC continues to exist after the liquidating payment. Section 736 does not apply if the LLC completely liquidates. However, Section 736 may apply if the LLC liquidates the interest of one member in a two-member LLC.[2] The LLC continues for federal tax purposes as long as the Section 736 payments are made to the withdrawing member.
- The LLC is a service LLC, and the retiring or deceased member is a "general partner" of the LLC. Payments to retiring or deceased members of an LLC who are classified as "limited partners," and payments to all members of an LLC that is not a service LLC, are taxed under the regular Code provisions applicable to property distributions.[3]

If Section 736 applies, then liquidating distributions are taxed under either Section 736(a) or 736(b), depending on the character of the payment.

---

[3] Ltr. 9751048 (*citing* IRC §708(b)(1)(B)).
§10.08   [1] Reg. §1.736-1(a).
[2] IRC §1.736-1(a)(6).
[3] *See* §§10.08[C], [D] *infra*.

[B]   Types of Section 736 Payments

The first step in determining the taxation of distributions to a retiring or deceased member is to classify the payment. There are several different types of payments that a retiring or deceased member may receive from an LLC.

The first type of payment is a distributive share of income for the year and any guaranteed payments under the operating agreement. These payments are taxed under the normal rules applicable to distributive shares of income and guaranteed payments.[4] Distributive shares of income are ordinary income to the retiring member and reductions in taxable income to the remaining members. Guaranteed payments are ordinary income to the retiring member and deductible payments by the LLC.[5] Section 736 does not apply to these distributions.[6]

The second type of payment that a retiring member may receive from an LLC is a payment in exchange for his interest in property of the LLC, including capital account, inventory, goodwill, and unrealized receivables. These payments are taxed under Section 736(a) or 736(b).

A payment that is classified as a Section 736(a) payment is taxed as a guaranteed payment or distributive share of income. This classification is more favorable to the LLC. The LLC may deduct the guaranteed payment, or reduce the taxable income to the remaining members by the distributive share of income paid to the retiring member. The retiring member is taxed on the receipt of the payment.

A payment that is classified as a Section 736(b) payment is treated as a distribution of property to the member. This classification is more favorable to the member. The LLC may not deduct the payment. The retiring member is not taxed on the payment, with the exceptions noted below.[7]

The basic rule is that Section 736 applies only to distributions if (a) the retiring or deceased member was classified as a "general partner" of the LLC, and (b) the LLC is a service LLC in which capital is not a material income-producing factor. Section 736 does not apply to other distributions, which are taxed under the regular Code provisions governing liquidating distributions. These rules are discussed below.

[C]   LLCs in Which Capital Is Material
Income-Producing Factor

An LLC in which capital is a material income-producing factor has almost no flexibility in characterizing payments to retiring and deceased members. All of

---

[4] *See* Chapter 14 *infra*.

[5] Reg. §1.736-1(a)(4).

[6] C.J. Sherlock, 294 F.2d 836 (5th Cir. 1961), *cert. denied*, 82 U.S. 802 (1962); Ayrton Metal Co., Inc., 299 F.2d 741 (2nd Cir. 1962).

[7] The two major exceptions are for (a) money distributions in excess of the member's basis in the membership interest, and (b) the member's share of unrealized receivables, substantially appreciated inventory items, and depreciation recapture.

the payments in exchange for the member's interest in property of the LLC are classified as Section 736(b) property distributions rather than Section 736(a) income payments.[8] Once the payment is classified as a Section 736(b) payment, it is taxed under the regular Code provisions governing liquidating distributions. The main Code provisions are as follows:

- *IRC Section 731(b)*—The LLC does not receive a deduction for the payment to the member.[9]
- *IRC Section 731(a)(1)*—The member recognizes gain to the extent that a money distribution exceeds the basis of the member's interest in the LLC. The member is taxed in the year the payments are made.[10] The member recovers his or her entire basis before incurring any capital gain. However, if the total distribution amount is fixed, the retiring member may elect to recover basis and recognize capital gain on a pro rata basis. The member must attach a statement of the election to his or her return for the first year in which the payment is received.[11] There is no gain recognition as a result of a property distribution.
- *IRC Section 731(a)(2)*—The member recognizes loss if three conditions are met. First, the member must receive only cash, unrealized receivables, or inventory. Second, the member must receive a liquidating distribution of his entire membership interest. Third, the adjusted basis of LLC assets distributed to the member must be less than the member's basis in his membership interest. The loss recognized is the amount by which the basis in the membership interest exceeds the money and the LLC's basis in unrealized receivables and inventory items distributed to the member. This differs from the rule for nonliquidating distributions in which no loss is recognized.
- *IRC Sections 741 and 731(a)*—The gain or loss recognized is capital gain or loss,[12] except as provided under IRC Section 751(b).[13]
- *IRC Section 751(b)*—A portion of the member's gain is recharacterized as ordinary income to the extent of the member's share of unrealized receivables, depreciation recapture, and substantially appreciated inventory items[14] retained by the LLC.[15] A member does not recognize ordinary income

[8] IRC §736(b)(1), (b)(3)(A); Reg. §1.736-1(b)(1).

[9] Reg. §1.736-1(a)(2).

[10] Reg. §1.736-1(a)(5).

[11] Reg. §1.736-1(b)(6). If the election is made, the member recognizes capital loss if he or she does not recover the full amount of basis in the membership interest (e.g., because the expected payments were not received in full).

[12] IRC §§731(a) (last sentence), 741.

[13] *See* §10.05 *infra*.

[14] Reg. §1.736-1(b)(4). Inventory is substantially appreciated if its fair market value exceeds the adjusted basis by more than 120 percent. IRC §751(b)(3)(A).

[15] Under IRC §751(b), a member will recognize ordinary income or loss, or capital gain or loss, if the member does not receive his proportionate share of unrealized receivables, substantially appreciated inventory items, and other property in a distribution. In that case, the member is treated as having received a proportionate distribution of all assets, and as selling back to the LLC the excess assets retained by the LLC in exchange for the excess assets retained by the member. Reg. §1.732-1(e). Gain

if the member receives a distribution that is exactly equal to the member's share of unrealized receivables and substantially appreciated inventory items.[16] The LLC may step up the basis of its assets by the amount of ordinary income realized by the member.[17]

- *IRC Section 732(b)*—The member receives a basis in the distributed property equal to his or her basis in the membership interest, reduced by any money distributed. The basis is first allocated to the unrealized receivables and inventory items in an amount equal to the LLC's basis in those assets. Any remaining basis in the membership interest is allocated to the other properties received in the distribution.[18] This is a substituted basis.

- *IRC Section 735(b)*—The member's holding period for the distributed property includes the LLC's holding period for the property,[19] except for the amount attributable to unrealized receivables and substantially appreciated inventory items.

- *IRC Sections 1245, 1250*—There is no depreciation recapture with respect to the assets distributed to the member.[20]

- *IRC Section 754*—If the LLC makes an election under IRC Section 754, it must adjust the basis of its assets under IRC Section 734. It must increase the basis of its assets by the amount of gain recognized by the member on distribution, and by the amount of any basis decrease in assets to the member as a result of the substituted basis rules for distributed property. It must decrease the basis of its assets by any loss recognized by the member, and by the amount of any basis increase in assets to the member as a result of the substituted basis rules for distributed property.

---

on the deemed sale back to the LLC will be ordinary income if the member retains a disproportionate share of capital assets, and the LLC retains a disproportionate share of unrealized receivables and substantially appreciated inventory items. In that case, the member will be treated as having received his proportionate share of the unrealized receivables and inventory items, and as having sold them back to the LLC. Ordinary income is the difference between the fair market value of the capital assets being purchased from the LLC less the adjusted basis of unrealized receivables and inventory items deemed distributed to the member in excess of his proportionate share sold back to the LLC. Gain on the deemed sale back to the LLC will be treated as capital gain if a member receives a disproportionately large share of unrealized receivables and inventory items. In that case, the member will be treated as having received his proportionate share of capital assets and as having sold back to the LLC such capital assets in exchange for the unrealized receivables and inventory items retained by him in excess of his proportionate share.

[16] Reg. §§1.751-1(b)(2)(ii)-(iii), (3)(ii)-(iii).

[17] *See* §10.05[B] *supra*.

[18] IRC §732(c)(1).

[19] Ltr. Rul. 200204005.

[20] IRC §1245(b)(3) provides that if the basis in the hands of the transferee is determined by the basis in the hands of the transferor, then there is no depreciation recapture. The distributee member receives a substituted basis, rather than a carryover basis, for Section 1245 property. However, IRC §1245(b)(6)(A) provides that the basis of Section 1245 property distributed by an LLC is deemed to have a basis determined by reference to the basis of assets in hands of the LLC. Thus, there is no depreciation recapture. Similar rules apply to Section 1250 real property. IRC §1250(b)(3), (b)(6)(A).

[D]   Service LLC in Which Member Treated as Limited Partner

The second type of LLC is a service LLC in which the retiring or deceased member is treated as a limited partner. A service LLC must classify all payments as Section 736(b) property distributions (including distributions of capital account, inventory, accounts receivable, and goodwill) if the retiring or deceased member is a limited partner.[21] The same Code provisions that apply to the taxation of distributions from an LLC in which capital is a material income-producing factor apply in this case.[22] The LLC has no discretion in allocating payments between IRC Section 736(a) and (b). The payments do not give rise to a deduction or its equivalent for the LLC.

A service LLC is an LLC in which capital is not a material income-producing factor. Substantially all of the income of the LLC must consist of fees, commissions, or other compensation for personal services by individuals. The practice of a profession by a doctor, dentist, lawyer, architect, or accountant is treated as a service LLC, even though the service provider may have a substantial capital investment in professional equipment or in the premises.[23]

The IRS has not yet issued regulations addressing when a member in an LLC is a general or limited partner for Section 736 purposes. Members who do not actively participate in a service LLC are clearly limited partners. Regulations under other sections of the Code indicate that all members of an LLC are limited partners.[24] If this were the case, then liquidating distributions to retiring or deceased members of an LLC would always be nondeductible Section 736(b) property distributions, regardless of the classification of the LLC as a service or nonservice LLC, the type of payment to the member, or the degree to which the member actively participated in the business of the LLC.

[E]   Service LLC in Which Member Treated as General Partner

The third type of LLC is a service LLC in which the retiring or deceased member is treated as a general partner. In this case, the LLC must classify the payments for the member's interest in accounts receivable as Section 736(a) income payments. It may elect to classify payments for the member's interest in goodwill as either Section 736(a) income payments or Section 736(b) property distributions. It must classify payments for the member's interest in all other property as Section 736(b) property distributions.

Distributions from the LLC are made in the following order:

---

[21] IRC §736(b)(1), (b)(3)(B); Reg. §1.736-1(b)(1).

[22] See §10.08[C] supra.

[23] H. Rept. No. 103-111, Pub. L. 103-66. pp. 782-783.

[24] See, for example, §13.04[B] infra regarding LLC members as limied partners under the passive loss rules.

[1]   Accounts Receivable

The retiring member must first report the distribution as a distribution of the member's share of unrealized receivables of the LLC. After the Tax Reconciliation Act of 1993, unrealized receivables are generally limited to cash basis accounts receivable and unbilled work in process.[25] Payments for unrealized receivables in excess of the LLC's basis in the receivables[26] must be characterized under Section 736(a) as a distributive share of income or a guaranteed payment deductable by the LLC.[27] The member reports taxable income on this amount. The taxable income is based on the fair market value of the member's share of the unrealized receivables. This may be only 30 to 40 percent of the face amount of the receivables, since that is usually the maximum amount that an outside third party would pay for unsecured receivables.

In practice, retiring members often do not report their share of unrealized receivables even though the law requires them to do so. The reason is that it is too difficult for them to determine their share of unrealized receivables of the LLC and to value those receivables on a fair market value basis. In addition, the parties normally take the position that no amount should be allocated to receivables unless there is a specific allocation to receivables in the termination agreement.

[2]   Capital Account, Inventory, and Other Assets

The member next reports the payments as a distribution of the member's interest in other LLC property. This property includes cash, inventory, capital assets, tangible property, and all other assets except for goodwill. The payments often correspond to the member's capital account balance. These payments are classified as Section 736(b) payments.

Section 736(b) payments are taxed under the same Code provisions that apply to the taxation of distributions from an LLC in which capital is a material income-producing factor apply in this case.[28] For example, distributions of a member's

---

[25] IRC §§736(b)(2)(A), 751(c) (last paragraph). Depreciation recapture and other ordinary income items defined in IRC §751(c) are not treated as unrealized receivables for purposes of Section 736 but are instead treated as Section 736(b) payments. However, a liquidating cash distribution to the member attributable to depreciation recapture and the other ordinary income items may trigger ordinary income to the member and a step-up in basis to the LLC under IRC §751(b).

[26] Reg. §1.736-1(b)(2).

[27] Reg. §1.736-1(a)(3), (4). A fixed payment for the member's share of unrealized receivables is a guaranteed payment. A payment that is contingent on future income of the LLC is a distributive share of income.

[28] These tax consequences are discussed in §10.08[C] *supra*. However, the Section 751(b) provisions that apply to taxation of distributions from an LLC in which capital is a material income-producing factor do not apply to service LLCs in which the member is treated as a general partner. The member's share of accounts receivable in a service LLC is taxed as a Section 736(a) payment rather than a Section 736(b) distribution (assuming the member is classified as a general partner). The result is that the LLC receives a deduction for the Section 736(a) payment. An LLC that is not a service LLC is not entitled to a deduction for distributions in exchange for a member's share of accounts receivable, since such payments are taxed as Section 736(b) property distributions.

tax basis capital account are normally nontaxable (since cash distributions up to a member's basis in the LLC are nontaxable).

[3]   Goodwill

The member must report any remaining distribution as a payment in exchange for the member's interest in goodwill. The LLC may classify the goodwill payments as either Section 736(a) income payments or Section 736(b) property distributions. The rules are as follows:

- If there is no provision in the operating agreement providing for the payment of goodwill, payments by a service LLC to the retiring or deceased member in exchange for the member's interest in goodwill in excess of the LLC's basis in the goodwill are Section 736(a) income payments.[29] The payments give rise to deduction or its equivalent for the LLC.[30] An LLC that wants to classify goodwill payments under Section 736(a) should have no collateral agreements among the members referring to goodwill. The agreements should provide that the payments will be taxed under Section 736(a). If the LLC has a basis in the goodwill as a result of an acquisition or Section 743(b) basis adjustment, the payment is a Section 736(b) property distribution to the extent of basis.[31]
- The parties may instead classify all goodwill payments as Section 736(b) property distributions. The parties may make this "election" simply by including a provision in the operating agreement that provides for a payment to the retiring or deceased member for goodwill.[32] The parties may amend the operating agreement to provide for goodwill payments at any time prior to the due date for the tax return, not including extensions, for the year in which the member dies or withdraws from the LLC.[33] A collateral agreement among the members specifying that a payment is for goodwill is also effective to qualify the payment as a Section 736(a) payment.[34] The amount allocated to goodwill must be reasonable.[35]
- The LLC may make a Section 754 election. If the LLC makes this election, the LLC may step up the basis of its assets under Section 734(b) by the amount of goodwill payments received by the member in excess of the member's basis in the LLC. The basis step-up is equal to the capital gain recognized by the member. The LLC can amortize the step-up in basis over

---

[29] IRC §736(b)(2)(B); Reg. §1.736-1(b)(3).

[30] Reg. §1.736-1(a)(4).

[31] Reg. §1.736-1(b)(3).

[32] IRC §736(b)(2)(B); reg. §1.736-1(b)(3).

[33] IRC §761(c).

[34] Jackson Inv. Co. v. Comm'r, 346 F.2d 187 (9th Cir. 1965), *nonacq.*, 1967-2 C.B. 4.

[35] Reg. §1.736-1(b)(3). An arm's-length agreement between the parties regarding the value of goodwill will generally be respected.

a period of 15 years.[36] The Section 754 election applies only to goodwill payments that are classified as Section 736(b) property distributions.

EXAMPLE

An LLC is engaged in the telecommunications business. Member A retires at the end of 1999. The LLC pays Member A her distributive share of income for the year in accordance with the operating agreement. In addition, the LLC pays Member A $30,000 for her interest in the LLC. The LLC allocates $10,000 of the liquidating distribution for Member A's share of unrealized accounts receivable, $10,000 for Member A's share of inventory, and $10,000 for goodwill. Since capital is a material income-producing factor for the LLC, all payments are treated as Section 736(b) distributions rather than guaranteed payments or a distributive share of income. As a result, the $30,000 payment is not deductible by the LLC. The payment is not taxable to Member A to the extent of her adjusted basis in her membership interest. Member A recognizes capital gain only to the extent the cash payments exceed her adjusted basis in the LLC immediately before the distribution. A portion of the gain is recharacterized as ordinary income if Member A receives a disproportionate distribution of "hot assets" and "cold assets."[37]

If the LLC were a service LLC, and if Member A were classified as a general partner in the LLC, then the $10,000 payment for Member A's share of accounts receivable would be classified as a guaranteed payment under Section 736(a). The payment would be deductible by the LLC and taxable as ordinary income to Member A. The $10,000 payment for inventory would

---

[36] IRC §197(b)(9)(E); Reg. §§1.197-2(c)(1), (g)(3). The complex provisions of the Code and regulations are summarized by the Committee Report on Pub. L. No. 103-66, Omnibus Budget Reconciliation Act of 1993, as follows:

> As discussed more fully below, the bill also changes the treatment of payments made on liquidation of the interest of a deceased or retired partner in exchange for goodwill. Except in the case of payments made on retirement or death of a general partner of a partnership for which capital is not a material income-producing factor, such payments will not be treated as a distribution of partnership income. Under the bill, however, if the partnership makes an election under section 754, section 734 will generally provide the partnership the benefit of a stepped-up basis for the retiring or deceased partner's share of partnership goodwill and an amortization deduction for the increase in basis under section 197.

The Committee Report also makes clear that the anti-churning rules will not disallow the step-up in basis and amortization of goodwill, stating, "In addition, in determining whether the anti-churning rules apply with respect to any increase in the basis of partnership property under section 732, 734, or 743 of the Code, the determinations are to be made at the partner level and each partner is to be treated as having owned or used the partner's proportionate share of partnership property. Thus, for example, the anti-churning rules do not apply to any increase in the basis of partnership property that occurs upon the acquisition of an interest in the partnership that has made a section 754 election if the person acquiring the partnership interest is not related to the person selling the partnership interest."

[37] See §10.05 supra.

be classified as a nondeductible Section 736(b) distribution. The $10,000 payment for goodwill could be classified by the parties as either a deductible guaranteed payment under Section 736(a) or a nondeductible distribution under Section 736(b).

§10.09   LOSS RECOGNITION TO MEMBER

A member does not recognize loss upon a distribution unless the following three requirements are met:[1]

1. The member receives a liquidating distribution.
2. The member receives only cash, inventory, and/or unrealized receivables in the distribution. A member who receives any other type of asset in a liquidating distribution must add the potential loss to the property's basis regardless of its value.
3. The basis to the LLC of the distributed property is less than the member's basis in his LLC interest.

Any loss recognized is a capital loss.[2]

§10.10   TAX CONSEQUENCES TO LLC

An LLC does not recognize gain or loss upon the distribution of property or money to a member.[1] This differs from the tax treatment applicable to corporations, which recognize gain upon the distribution of appreciated property to shareholders.

There is a possible exception to the nonrecognition provisions if an LLC makes a disproportionate distribution of "hot assets" and "cold assets" to members. The LLC is treated as having made a proportionate distribution of assets to the member and selling the excess assets actually received by the member in exchange for the proportionate share of assets that the member did not receive. The LLC may recognize gain or loss on the deemed distribution and sale.

There is no effect on the basis of the LLC's remaining assets unless the LLC has made an election under IRC Section 754 or has made a disproportionate distribution of "hot assets" and "cold assets."[2]

---

§10.09   [1] IRC §731(a).
[2] *Id.* (last sentence).
§10.10   [1] IRC §731(b).
[2] IRC §734(a).

§10.11   DRAWS, ADVANCES, AND LOANS

An LLC does not have profits or income until the last day of its tax year. Therefore, "draws" against profits during the year are treated as advances during the year and as distributions on the last day of the year.[1] The LLC enters the amount of the draw or advance on its books and records, but not as a reduction of capital accounts.

A member cannot avoid taxable income by classifying a payment as a draw or advance, since the entire amount is taxable at the end of the year. However, a member is not currently taxed on distributions that are bona fide loans. A loan from an LLC is treated as a disguised distribution unless there is an unconditional and legally enforceable obligation to repay the loan at a determinable date.[2] The loan is considered a distribution at the time that the LLC cancels the loan rather than cancellation of indebtedness income.

---

§10.11   [1] Reg. §1.731-1(a)(1)(ii).
[2] Rev. Rul. 73-301, 1973-2 C.B. 216.

11

Reorganizations

§11.01 CONVERSION FROM GENERAL PARTNERSHIP TO LLC

[A] Methods of Converting to LLC

There are five principal methods of converting from a general partnership to an LLC. These methods are discussed below.

[1] Direct Contribution of Assets

The partnership may transfer its assets and liabilities to an LLC in exchange for all of the LLC membership interests. The partnership then dissolves and distributes the membership interests to the partners in liquidation of the partnership.[1] The partnership may also transfer its assets and liabilities to an LLC that is already owned by the partners.

[2] Contribution of Ownership Interests

The partners may contribute their partnership interests to an LLC in exchange for capital accounts and membership interests, followed by the dissolution of the partnership, the transfer of partnership assets to the LLC, and the assumption of all partnership liabilities by the LLC.[2]

[3] Liquidation Followed by Contribution of Assets

The partnership may dissolve and distribute all of its assets to the partners in complete liquidation. The partners then contribute some or all of those assets to the LLC as a capital contribution in exchange for membership interests.

---

§11.01 [1] Ltr. Ruls. 199916010, 9633021, 9538022, 9525065, 9434027, 9421025, 9321047.
[2] Ltr. Ruls. 9623016, 9538022, 9535036, 9511033, 9452024, 9432018, 9422034, 9407030, 9226035. *See also* Ltr. Ruls. 9416028029, 9119029 (contribution of limited partnership interests to LLC).

[4] Statutory Merger

The partnership may merge into an LLC under the laws of most states.[3] As part of the merger, the LLC assumes all of the assets and liabilities of the partnership. New membership interests are issued to the partners in the old partnership. Normally, the parties must file a certificate of merger with the secretary of state.

[5] Statutory Conversion

Several states permit a partnership to convert to an LLC by entering into a conversion agreement and filing a certificate of conversion with the secretary of state.[4] California permits a partnership or other business entity,[5] including a corporation,[6] to convert into an LLC.

---

[3] Ltr. Ruls. 9452024, 9412030, 9210019; Ala. Code §§10-12-54 to 58; Alaska Stat. §§10.50.500 to 590; Ariz. Rev. Stat. Ann. §§29-751 to 757; Cal. Corp. Code §§17550-17556; Colo. Rev. Stat. Ann. §§7-80-1003 to 7-80-1005; Conn. Gen. Stat. Ann. §§34-193 to 34-198; Del. Code Ann. tit 6, §18-209; D.C. Code Ann. §§29-1039 to 29-1042; Fla. Stat. Ann. §608.438; Ga. Code Ann. §§14-11-901 to 14-11-901; Haw. Rev. Stat. Ann. §§428-904 to 428-907; Idaho Code §§53-661 to 664; 805 ILCS §§180/37-20 to 180/37-35; Ind. Code Ann. §§23-18-7-1 to 23-18-7-8; Iowa Code §§490A.1201 to 490A.1206, 490A.1515; Kan. Stat. Ann. §§17-7701 to 17-7706; Ky. Rev. Stat. §§275.355 to 275.365; Me. Rev. Stat. Ann. tit. 31, §§741-745; Md. Corps. & Ass'ns Code Ann. §§4A-701, 4A-702; M.G.L.A. ch. 156C, §§59 to 62; Mich. Comp. Laws Ann. §§450.4701 to 4707a, 450.4910; 507; Minn. Stat. §§322B.70 to 322B76; Miss. Code Ann. §§79-29-209 to 79-29-219, 79-29-921; Mo. Rev. Stat. §§347.127 to 347.135; Mont. Code Ann. §§35-8-1201 to 35-8-1205; Neb. Rev. Stat. §§21-2647 to 21-2652; Nev. Rev. Stat. Ann. §§92A.030, 92A.150; N.H. Rev. Stat. Ann. §§304-C:18, 304-C:19; N.J. Stat. Ann. §42:2B-20; N.M. Stat. Ann. §§53-19-59 to 53-19-62.2; N.Y. LLC §§1001-1005; N.C. Gen. Stat. §§57C-9A-20 to 57C-9A-29; N.D. Cent. Code §§10-32-100 to 10-32-107; Ohio Rev. Code Ann. §§1705.36 to 1705.42; Okla. Stat. Ann. tit. 18, §2054; 15 Pa. Cons. Stat. §§8956-8959; R.I. Gen. Laws §§7-16-59 to 7-16-64; S.C. Code Ann. §§33-44-904 to 33-44-906; S.D. Codified Laws Ann. §§47-34A-904 to 47-34A-906; Tenn. Code Ann. §§48-244-101 to 48-244-104; Tex. Rev. Civ. Stat. Ann. art 1528n, 10.01-10.07; Utah Code Ann. §§48-2c-14.01 to 14.10; Va. Code Ann. §§13.1-1070-1073; Vt. Stat. Ann. tit. 11, §3124-6; Wash. Rev. Code §§25.15.395 to 25.15.415; W. Va. Code §§31B-9-904 to 31B-9-906; Wis. Stat. §§183.1201 to 183.1206; Wyo. Stat. §17-15-142.

[4] Ltr. Rul. 200252055; Alaska Stat. §10.50.570; Colo. Rev. Stat. Ann. §7-80-1001.5; Conn. Gen. Stat. Ann. §§34-198, 34-199; Del. Code Ann. tit. 6, §18-214; D.C. Code Ann. §29-1013; Fla. Stat. Ann. §608.439; Haw. Rev. Stat. Ann. §§428-902.5 to 428-903; 805 ILCS §§180/37-10 to 180/37-15; Iowa Code §490A.304; Kan. Stat. Ann. §§17-7684 to 17-7685; Ky. Rev. Stat. §§275.370 to 275.375; La. Rev. Stat. Ann. §§12:1357 to 12:1362; Md. Corps. & Ass'ns Code Ann. §§4A-211 to 4A-213; Me. Rev. Stat. Ann. tit. 31, §§746, 747; Mich. Comp. Laws Ann. §450.4707; Mo. Ann. Stat. §347.125; Mont. Code Ann. §§35-8-1210 to 35-8-1211; Nev. Rev. Stat. Ann. §§92A.030, 92A.150; N.H. Rev. Stat. Ann. §§304-C:17-a, 304-C:17-b; N.M. Stat. Ann. §§53-19-59 to 53-19-62.2; N.Y. LLC Law §§1006-1007; N.C. Gen. Stat. §§57C-9A-01 to 57C-9A-19; Okla. Stat. Ann. tit. 18, §§2054.1, 2054.2; R.I. Gen. Laws §7-16-5.3; S.C. Code Ann. §§33-44-902 to 33-44-903; S.D. Codified Laws Ann. §§47-34A-902 to 47-34A-903; Tex. Rev. Civ. Stat. Ann. art 1528n, 10.08-10.11; Utah Code Ann. §§48-2c-14.01 to 14.06; Va. Code Ann. §13.1-1010.1; Vt. Stat. Ann. tit. 11, §3122-3; W. Va. Code §§31B-9-901, 31B-9-902; Wis. Stat. §183.1207.

[5] Cal. Corp. Code §§15677.6, 16906, 17540.6.

[6] See Instructions to Cal. Form LLC-9; Cal. Corp. Code §§17540.8, 17001(ac).

[B]   Tax Consequences

For federal tax purposes, the conversion from a general partnership to an LLC is taxed as follows:

- No gain or loss is recognized to the partnership, LLC, partners, or members as a result of the transfer of assets from the partnership to the LLC, the assumption of liabilities by the LLC, or other steps in the conversion unless there is a change in the partners' share of liabilities.[7] No gain or loss is recognized to the partnership, LLC, partners, or members upon the transfer of partnership interests to the LLC in exchange for LLC membership interests, followed by the liquidation of the general partnership,[8] except as provided under the Internal Revenue Code sections governing recognition of gain or loss upon distributions[9] or the treatment of liabilities.[10] No gain or loss is recognized to the partners under the rules governing unrealized receivables and inventory,[11] since those rules are superseded by the provisions on nonrecognition of gain or loss upon the contribution of property to a partnership.[12]
- There is no termination of the partnership under the IRC provisions governing continuation of a partnership[13] if the LLC continues the business of the partnership.[14] The LLC is treated as the continuation of the general partnership.[15]

[7] Rev. Rul. 95-37, 1995-1 C.B. 130; Ltr. Ruls. 200022016, 9637030, 9525065, 9525058, 9421025, 9407030, 9321047, 9226035 (*citing* Rev. Rul. 84-52, 1984-1 C.B. 157, and IRC §721). The conversion is treated as a nontaxable exchange under IRC §721 (contribution of property to a partnership in exchange for an interest in the partnership). The tax consequences if there is a change in the partners' share of liabilities are discussed below.

[8] Rev. Rul. 95-37, 1995-1 C.B. 130; Ltr. Ruls. 9841030, 9834040, 9834039, 9809003, 9741021, 9741018, 9623016, 9602018, 9538022, 9511033, 9432018, 9226035.

[9] *See* IRC §731; Ltr. Ruls. 9511033, 9452024 (gain is recognized under IRC §731 to the extent provided under IRC §752).

[10] *See* IRC §752; Ltr. Ruls. 9834040, 9834039, 9623016, 9618021-023, 9602018, 9538022, 9525065, 9525058, 9511033, 9452024, 9434027, 9432018, 9422034, 9421025, 9407030, 9350013. Under IRC §752(b), the reduction in liabilities for a partner is treated as a distribution of money. The distribution first reduces basis. Distributions of money in excess of basis are taxable. Ordinarily, IRC §752 will not apply unless there is a refinancing of the debt in connection with the conversion. Recourse debt prior to a conversion remains recourse after the conversion.

[11] IRC §751.

[12] Ltr. Rul. 9421025; *see* IRC §721.

[13] IRC §708.

[14] Rev. Rul. 95-55, 1995-2 C.B. 313; Rev. Rul. 95-37, 1995-1 C.B. 130; Ltr. Ruls. 200022016, 9841030, 9834040, 9834039, 9809003, 9637030, 9623016, 9618021023, 9602018, 9538022, 9525065, 9525058, 9511033, 9501033, 9452024, 9417009, 9407030, 9343027, 9432018, 9426037, 9432040, 9432037, 9422034, 9421025, 9420028, 9407030, 9350013, 9321047, 9226035, 9029019, 9010027 (*citing* Rev. Rul 84-52, 1984-1 C.B. 157; IRC §708(b); and Reg. §1.708-1(b)(1)(ii) (transaction under IRC §721 is not treated as sale or exchange under IRC §708)).

[15] Rev. Rul. 95-55, 1995-2 C.B. 313; Rev. Rul. 95-37, 1995-1 C.B. 130; Ltr. Ruls. 9841030, 9834040, 9834039, 9637030, 9623016, 9618021023, 9602018, 9538022, 9525065, 9525058, 9511033, 9501033, 9452023, 9432018, 9426037, 9432040, 9432037, 9422034, 9421025, 9420028, 9407030, 9350013, 9321047, 9226035, 9029019, 9010027 (*citing* Rev. Rul. 84-52, 1984-1 C.B. 157; IRC §708(b); and Reg. §1.708-1(b)(1)(ii) (transaction under IRC §721 is not treated as sale or exchange under IRC §708)).

- The tax year does not close with respect to any partner[16] or for the partnership/LLC.[17] The LLC must continue to use the same tax year as the partnership.[18] A change in the tax year requires the consent of the Service.[19]
- A member's basis in the LLC membership interest is equal to the member's adjusted basis in the general partnership interest[20] if the member's share of liabilities does not change after the conversion.[21]
- The holding period for the LLC membership interests includes the holding period for the partnership interests.[22]
- The LLC's basis in the assets is the same as the basis of those assets in the partnership immediately prior to the conversion.[23]
- If there is an increase in a partner's share of liabilities as a result of the conversion, the increase is treated as a contribution of money by the member to the LLC. The basis of the member's interest in the LLC is increased by the amount of the deemed contribution.[24] No gain or loss is recognized.[25]
- If there is a decrease in a partner's share of liabilities as a result of the conversion, the decrease is treated as a distribution of money by the LLC to the member.[26] The basis of the member's interest in the LLC is reduced (but not below zero) by the amount of the deemed distribution.[27] Gain is recognized to the extent the deemed distribution exceeds the adjusted basis of the member's interest in the partnership.[28]
- The LLC must continue to use the same method of accounting as the general partnership until it receives permission to change its accounting method or until the IRS challenges the method upon examination.[29] For example, an LLC must continue to use the cash method of accounting if the general partnership used the cash method of accounting.[30] However, the cash

---

[16] Rev. Rul. 95-37, 1995-1 C.B. 130; Ltr. Ruls. 9841030, 9834040, 9834039, 9637030, 9501033.

[17] Ltr. Rul. 9501033.

[18] Ltr. Rul. 9525065.

[19] Ltr. Rul. 9525065 (*citing* Temp. Reg. §1.441-1T(b)(4)).

[20] Rev. Rul. 95-37, 1995-1 C.B. 130; Ltr. Rul. 9602018 (*citing* Rev. Rul. 95-37, 1995-1 C.B. 130); Ltr. Ruls. 9841030, 9538022, 9525065, 9452024, 9417009, 9321047 (*citing* Rev. Rul. 84-52, 1984-1 C.B. 157).

[21] Rev. Rul. 95-37, 1995-1 C.B. 130; Ltr. Ruls. 9618021-023, 9452024. The tax consequences if there is a change in the partners' share of liabilities are discussed below.

[22] Rev. Rul. 95-37, 1995-1 C.B. 130; Ltr. Ruls. 200022016, 9841030, 9417009, 9321047 (*citing* Rev. Rul. 84-52, 1984-1 C.B. 157, and IRC §1223(1)).

[23] Ltr. Ruls. 200022016, 9538022, 9417009 (*citing* IRC §723).

[24] Rev. Rul. 95-37, 1995-1 C.B. 130.

[25] Ltr. Ruls. 9421025, 9321047 (*citing* Rev. Rul. 84-52, 1984-1 C.B. 157, and IRC §§731, 752(a)). *See also* Reg. §1.752-1(e). The basis is increased under IRC §722.

[26] IRC §752(b).

[27] Rev. Rul. 95-37, 1995-1 C.B. 130.

[28] *Id.*; Ltr. Rul. 9321047 (*citing* Rev. Rul. 84-52, 1984-1 C.B. 157, and IRC §§731, 752(b)). Under IRC §733, the basis is first reduced by the amount of money distributed (including the demmed distribution under IRC §752(b)). Under IRC §731, gain is recognized to the extent the distribution of money (including the deemed distribution under IRC §752(b)) exceeds the partner's basis in the partnership units.

[29] Rev. Rul. 95-55, 1995-2 C.B. 313; Ltr. Rul. 9423040.

[30] Ltr. Ruls. 9623016, 9538022, 9525065.

method of accounting may not be used if the LLC is classified as a tax shelter after the conversion.[31]

- The LLC is not required to obtain a new employer identification number.[32]
- The members of the LLC are treated as partners for self-employment tax purposes. The members' distributive shares are not excepted from net earnings from self-employment under IRC Section 1402(a)(13).[33]
- The LLC remains the same employer for withholding tax purposes. The LLC is not required to withhold FICA and FUTA taxes with a new contribution base after the conversion. The same rule applies even if the LLC obtains a new employer identification number after the conversion.
- Because the LLC is a continuation of the partnership, the LLC will not be part of a tiered partnership with the general partnership as the lower-tier partnership.[34]
- There is no depreciation recapture under IRC Section 1245.[35]
- If two or more general partnerships with identical ownership interests convert or merge into an LLC, the LLC is treated as the continuation of the largest partnership.[36] The LLC retains the employer identification number of the largest partnership.[37] None of the partners, partnerships, or LLC recognizes gain or loss on the exchanges of their partnership interests for interests in the LLC or upon the transfer of assets from the partnership to the LLC.[38]
- The transfer of appreciated assets to the LLC will not result in a contribution or distribution of partnership property under IRC Sections 704(c)(1)(B) and 737 with respect to the partnership or the LLC.[39]
- The members' capital accounts in the LLC are the same as their capital accounts in the partnership prior to conversion.[40]

The federal income tax consequences are the same whether the resulting LLC is formed in the same state or in a different state than the converting partnership.[41] The tax consequences are the same regardless of the manner of conversion under

[31] See Chapter 20 infra.

[32] Rev. Rul. 95-37, 1995-1 C.B. 130; Ltr. Ruls. 200022016, 9841030, 9834040, 9834039, 9809003, 9618021-023, 9525065.

[33] Ltr. Rul. 9525065. See Chapter 16 infra for a complete discussion of the rules applicable to self-employment taxes.

[34] Ltr. Ruls. 9834040, 9834039, 9809003, 9618021-023. See §15.05 infra for a discussion of tiered partnerships and LLCs.

[35] Ltr. Rul. 9421025 (citing IRC §1245(b)(3), which provides that there is no depreciation recapture if the transferee receives a carryover basis and if no gain or loss is recognized upon the transfer).

[36] Ltr. Ruls. 9741021, 9741018.

[37] Id.

[38] Id.

[39] Ltr. Ruls. 9834040, 9834039, 9809003. The reason is that the conversion is not treated as a sale or exchange under IRC §708(b)(1)(B). See IRC §505 for a discussion of §§704(c)(1)(B) and 737.

[40] Ltr. Rul. 200022016.

[41] Rev. Rul. 95-37, 1995-1 C.B. 313.

state law.[42] The conversion of an interest in a partnership into an interest in an LLC is treated the same as a partnership-to-LLC conversion.[43]

§11.02 CONVERSION FROM LIMITED PARTNERSHIP TO LLC

A limited partnership may convert to an LLC. The conversion may take place in one of the five ways that a general partnership converts to an LLC.[1] The tax consequences of converting from a limited partnership to an LLC are basically the same as those of converting from a general partnership to an LLC.[2] These tax consequences include the following:

- No gain or loss is recognized to the LLC, the partnership, the members, or the partners upon the transfer of assets or partnership interests to the LLC in exchange for membership interests or upon the liquidation of the limited partnership[3] except as provided under the rules providing for treatment of liabilities.[4]
- There is no termination of the partnership under the continuation of partnership rules[5] if the LLC continues the business of the partnership. The LLC is treated as the continuation of the limited partnership.[6]
- The tax year does not close with respect to the partnership[7] or any partner.[8]
- A member's basis in the LLC membership interest is equal to the member's adjusted basis in the limited partnership,[9] assuming the member's share of liabilities does not change after the conversion.[10]
- The holding period for the LLC membership interests includes the holding period for the partnership interests.[11]
- The basis of the LLC assets is the same as the basis of those assets in the partnership immediately prior to the conversion.[12]
- If there is an increase in a partner's share of liabilities as a result of the conversion, the increase is treated as a contribution of money by the member

---

[42] *Id.*

[43] *Id.*

§11.02   [1] *See* §6.02 *supra.*

[2] Ltr. Ruls. 94156028-029, 9210019, 9119029, 9010027. *See also* Rev. Rul. 84-52, 1984-1 C.B. 157 (last sentence).

[3] Ltr. Ruls. 9741021, 9741018, 9738013, 9633021.

[4] IRC §752; Ltr. Ruls. 9607006, 9443024, 9417009, 9416028-029.

[5] IRC §708.

[6] Rev. Rul. 95-37, 1995-1 C.B. 130; Ltr. Ruls. 9633012, 9607006, 9443024, 9417009, 9416028-029 (*citing* IRC §708).

[7] Ltr. Rul. 9633021.

[8] Rev. Rul. 95-37, 1995-1 C.B. 130.

[9] *Id.*; Ltr. Rul. 9607006 (*citing* Rev. Rul. 95-37, 1995-1 C.B. 130); Ltr. Ruls. 9417009, 9416029, 9416028 (*citing* Rev. Rul. 84-52, 1984-1 C.B. 157).

[10] Rev. Rul. 95-37, 1995-1 C.B. 130; Ltr. Rul. 9607006.

[11] *Id.*; Ltr. Ruls. 9417009, 9416029, 9416028.

[12] Ltr. Ruls. 9417009, 9416029, 9416028.

to the LLC. The basis of the member's interest in the LLC is increased by the amount of the deemed contribution.[13] No gain or loss is recognized.[14]

- If there is a decrease in a partner's share of liabilities as a result of the conversion, the decrease is treated as a distribution of money by the LLC to the member.[15] The basis of the member's interest in the LLC is reduced (but not below zero) by the amount of the deemed distribution.[16] Gain is recognized to the extent the deemed distribution exceeds the adjusted basis of the member's interest in the partnership.[17]

- There may be adverse tax consequences if recourse debt is changed to nonrecourse debt during the conversion. A member's basis in a partnership or LLC is increased by an allocable share of recourse and nonrecourse debt. Recourse debt is allocated to the partners or members who bear the risk of loss. Nonrecourse debt is allocated to all the LLC members. If the limited partnership has recourse debt prior to the conversion, the debt is allocated entirely to the general partners who are personally liable. After the conversion to an LLC, the LLC rather than the general partner may be liable for the recourse debt. If only the LLC is liable, then the debt is recharacterized as nonrecourse debt and allocated to all the members for basis purposes. The general partners are treated as receiving a distribution of money to the extent of debt relief (i.e., the amount by which their share of recourse and nonrecourse debt in the partnership prior to the conversion exceeds their share of debt in the LLC after the conversion).[18] The deemed distribution first reduces the general partner's basis in the LLC. Gain or loss is recognized to the extent the deemed distribution exceeds the general partner's basis.

- The LLC must continue to use the same method of accounting as the limited partnership until it receives permission to change its accounting method or until the IRS challenges the method upon examination.[19]

- The LLC is not required to obtain a new employer identification number.[20]

- If two limited partnerships with identical ownership interests convert or merge into an LLC, the LLC is treated as the continuation of the largest limited partnership.[21] The LLC retains the employer identification number of the largest limited partnership.[22] None of the limited partners, limited partnerships, or LLC recognizes gain or loss upon the exchanges of their

---

[13] Rev. Rul. 95-37, 1995-1 C.B. 130.

[14] Rev. Rul. 95-37, 1995-1 C.B. 130 (*citing* Rev. Rul. 84-52, 1984-1 C.B. 157, and IRC §§731, 752(a)). *See also* Reg. §1.752-1(e). The basis is increased under IRC §722.

[15] Rev. Rul. 95-37, 1995-1 C.B. 130; IRC §752(b).

[16] Rev. Rul. 95-37, 1995-1 C.B. 130.

[17] Rev. Rul. 95-37, 1995-1 C.B. 130 (*citing* Rev. Rul. 84-52, 1984-1 C.B. 157, and IRC §§731, 752(b)). Under IRC §733, the basis is first reduced by the amount of the money distributed (including the deemed distribution under IRC §752(b)). Under IRC §731, gain is recognized to the extent the distribution of money (including the deemed distribution under IRC §752(b)) exceeds the partner's basis in the partnership units.

[18] IRC §752(b).

[19] Ltr. Rul. 9423040.

[20] Ltr. Rul. 9633021.

[21] Ltr. Ruls. 9741021, 9741018, 9738013.

[22] *Id.*

partnership interests for interests in the LLC or upon the transfer of assets from the limited partnerships to the LLC.[23]

The federal income tax consequences are the same whether the resulting LLC is formed in the same state or in a different state than the converting partnership.[24] The tax consequences are the same regardless of the manner of conversion under state law.[25] The conversion of an interest in a limited partnership to an interest in an LLC is treated the same as a partnership-to-LLC conversion.[26]

§11.03   CONVERSION OF GENERAL PARTNERS OF LIMITED PARTNERSHIP TO LLC

The general partners of a limited partnership may convert to an LLC.[1] The purpose of the conversion is normally to reduce liability for the individual general partners.

The conversion may take place by having the general partners contribute their general partnership interests to the LLC in exchange for proportional membership interests in the LLC. After the conversion, the LLC is the sole general partner of the limited partnership.[2]

The tax consequences of the conversion are the same as for conversions of general partnerships to LLCs.[3] The limited partnership may continue to use the cash method of accounting after the conversion if it is not a tax shelter.[4]

§11.04   TRANSFER OF SELECTED PARTNERSHIP ASSETS TO LLC

In some cases, a partnership may transfer only some of its assets to the LLC. The partnership continues in business after the transfer. The transfer is treated as a distribution by the partnership to its partners and a contribution of those assets to the LLC.[1]

A partnership may transfer some of its lines of business to an LLC in order to limit the liability of the partners with respect to that business. Generally, no gain

---

[23] Id.
[24] Rev. Rul. 95-37, 1995-1 C.B. 130.
[25] Id.
[26] Id.
§11.03   [1] Ltr. Rul. 9535036.
[2] Id.
[3] Id.
[4] Id.
§11.04   [1] Ltr. Rul. 9321070.

or loss is recognized to the LLC or the members upon the transfer of business or contribution of assets to the LLC.[2]

§11.05   CONVERSION FROM LLP TO LLC

The tax consequences of converting a registered limited liability partnership (LLP) to an LLC are basically the same as those of converting from a general partnership to an LLC.[1] The conversion may take place by merging the LLP[2] or by contributing partnership interests to the LLC in exchange for LLC interests. For federal tax purposes, the transactions are characterized as follows:

- No gain or loss is recognized to the LLP, LLC, or members of the LLP and LLC as a result of the conversion.[3]
- There is no termination of the LLP. The LLC is treated as the continuation of the LLP.[4]
- The LLC must continue to use the same taxable year as the LLP.[5]

§11.06   CONVERSION FROM LLC TO CORPORATION (INCORPORATION OF LLC)

[A]   LLC Classified as Partnership

[1]   Overview

The principal methods of incorporating an LLC that is classified as a partnership for federal tax purposes are as follows:

- *Method 1.* The LLC transfers its assets and liabilities to a newly formed corporation in exchange for stock. The LLC then distributes the stock to the members of the LLC.
- *Method 2.* The LLC distributes all of its assets and liabilities to its members. The members then transfer the assets and liabilities to the new corporation in exchange for stock.
- *Method 3.* The members transfer their membership interests in the LLC to the new corporation in exchange for stock. The new corporation then

---

[2] Ltr. Rul. 9713007 (*citing* IRC §721).

§11.05   [1] Ltr. Rul. 9412030.

[2] *Id.*

[3] Ltr. Ruls. 9407030, 9321047, 9226035 (*citing* Rev. Rul. 84-52, 1984-1 C.B. 157, and IRC §721). The conversion is treated as a nontaxable exchange under IRC §721 (contribution of property to a partnership in exchange for an interest in the partnership). The tax consequences if there is a change in the partners' share of liabilities are discussed below.

[4] Ltr. Rul. 9412030.

[5] *Id.*

liquidates the LLC and becomes the owner of all assets and liabilities of the LLC.

- *Method 4.* The members transfer their membership interests in the LLC to the new corporation in exchange for stock. This method is similar to Method 3. However, the LLC continues in existence. It does not transfer the assets and liabilities to the corporation. The LLC is classified as a disregarded entity wholly owned by the corporation.[1]
- *Method 5.* The LLC elects to be classified as a corporation by filing IRS Form 8832.
- *Method 6.* The members of the LLC form a corporation, and then merge the LLC into the corporation, or convert the LLC into a corporation.

Prior to 1984, the IRS took the position that the tax consequences of incorporating an LLC were the same regardless of the method of incorporation.[2] In 1984, the IRS determined that there were different tax consequences depending on the method of incorporation.[3] The basis and holding periods of assets received by the corporation, and the basis and holding periods of the stock received by the members of the LLC, will now vary depending on the method of incorporation.

[2] Method 1—Transfer of Assets to Corporation

Under the first method, the LLC transfers its assets and liabilities to a newly formed corporation in return for stock. The LLC then distributes the stock to the members of the LLC in proportion to their membership interests. The LLC terminates after the distribution.

There are the following tax consequences of incorporating an LLC under the first method:

- The LLC does not recognize gain or loss on the transfer of its assets to the corporation in exchange for stock.[4]
- The corporation receives a basis in the assets equal to the LLC's basis in the assets immediately prior to the transfer.[5]
- The LLC receives a basis in the stock equal to the corporation's basis in the transferred assets.[6]
- The corporation's assumption of the LLC's liabilities decreases each member's outside basis in the membership interest. The relief of debt is treated as a money distribution to the members.[7]

---

§11.06 [1] Ltr. Rul. 200139002.
[2] Rev. Rul. 70-239, 1970-1 C.B. 74.
[3] Rev. Rul. 84-111, 1984-2 C.B. 88.
[4] Rev. Rul. 84-111, 1984-2 C.B. 88 (*citing* IRC §351).
[5] Rev. Rul. 84-111, 1984-2 C.B. 88 (*citing* IRC §362(a)).
[6] Rev. Rul. 84-111, 1984-2 C.B. 88 (*citing* IRC §358(a)).
[7] Rev. Rul. 84-111, 1984-2 C.B. 88 (*citing* IRC §§752, 733).

- The LLC's distribution of the corporate stock to the members of the LLC results in a termination of the LLC.[8]
- The members of the LLC receive a basis in the stock of the corporation equal to their basis in the membership interests in the LLC, reduced by any cash received in the liquidation.[9]
- The LLC's holding period for the stock received in the exchange includes the corporation's holding period in capital assets and Section 1231 assets (to the extent that the stock was received in exchange for such assets).[10] The LLC's holding period for stock received in exchange for other assets begins on the date following the date of the exchange.[11] The members' holding periods for the stock received on liquidation of the LLC include the LLC's holding period for the stock.[12]
- The corporation's holding period for the assets received in the exchange includes the LLC's holding period.

[3]   Method 2—Distribution of Assets to Members

Under the second method, the LLC distributes all of its assets and liabilities to the members. The members then transfer the assets and liabilities to the new corporation in exchange for stock.

There are the following tax consequences of incorporating an LLC under the second method:

- The LLC terminates on transfer of its assets to its members.[13]
- The basis of assets distributed to each member on liquidation of the membership interest is equal to the member's outside basis in the membership interest, reduced by any money received in the distribution.[14]
- The transfer of liabilities to the members has no effect on the members' basis in the assets. The decrease in their share of LLC liabilities is exactly equal to their corresponding assumption of the liabilities.[15]
- The members do not recognize gain or loss on the transfer to the corporation of assets and liabilities in exchange for stock.[16]
- The members of the LLC receive a basis in the stock that is equal to the basis of the assets distributed to them on the liquidation of the LLC, reduced by liabilities assumed by the corporation.[17] The corporation's assumption of liabilities is treated as a payment of money to the members.[18]

---

[8] Rev. Rul. 84-111, 1984-2 C.B. 88 (*citing* IRC §708(b)(1)(A)).
[9] Rev. Rul. 84-111, 1984-2 C.B. 88 (*citing* IRC §732(b)).
[10] Rev. Rul. 84-111, 1984-2 C.B. 88 (*citing* IRC §1223(1)).
[11] Rev. Rul. 84-111, 1984-2 C.B. 88 (*citing* Rev. Rul. 70-59, 1970-2 C.B. 168).
[12] Rev. Rul. 84-111, 1984-2 C.B. 88 (*citing* IRC §§735(b) and 1223).
[13] Rev. Rul. 84-111, 1984-2 C.B. 88 (*citing* IRC §708(b)(1)(A)).
[14] Rev. Rul. 84-111, 1984-2 C.B. 88 (*citing* IRC §732(b)).
[15] Rev. Rul. 84-111, 1984-2 C.B. 88 (*citing* IRC §752).
[16] Rev. Rul. 84-111, 1984-2 C.B. 88 (*citing* IRC §351).
[17] Rev. Rul. 84-111, 1984-2 C.B. 88 (*citing* IRC §358(a)).
[18] Rev. Rul. 84-111, 1984-2 C.B. 88 (*citing* IRC §358(d)).

- The corporation's basis in the assets received from the members of the LLC is the same as the members' basis in such assets immediately prior to the transfer.[19]
- The members' holding period for the assets distributed to them includes the LLC's holding period for such assets.[20]
- The members' holding period for stock received includes their holding periods in the capital assets and Section 1231 assets transferred to the corporation (to the extent stock was received in exchange for such assets).[21] The members' holding period for stock received in exchange for other assets begins on the date following the date of the exchange.
- The corporation's holding period for the assets received includes the members' holding periods for such assets.[22]

[4] Method 3—Transfer of Membership Interests to Corporation; LLC Terminates

Under the third method, the members transfer their membership interests in the LLC to the new corporation in exchange for stock. The LLC then terminates. The corporation becomes the owner of all assets and liabilities of the LLC.

There are the following tax consequences of incorporating an LLC under the third method:

- The members of the LLC do not recognize gain or loss on the transfer of the membership interests to the new corporation in exchange for stock.[23]
- The LLC terminates immediately after the transfer of the membership interests to the new corporation.[24]
- The members of the LLC receive a basis in the stock equal to their basis in the membership interests,[25] reduced by each member's share of liabilities assumed by the corporation plus any liabilities to which the transferred assets are subject.[26]
- The corporation's assumption of the LLC's liabilities is treated as a payment of money to the members.[27]
- The corporation receives a basis in the assets equal to the members' outside basis in their membership interests. The corporation must allocate this outside basis to the assets under Section 732(c) of the Code.[28]

---

[19] Rev. Rul. 84-111, 1984-2 C.B. 88 (*citing* IRC §362(a)).
[20] Rev. Rul. 84-111, 1984-2 C.B. 88 (*citing* IRC §735(b)).
[21] Rev. Rul. 84-111, 1984-2 C.B. 88 (*citing* IRC §1223(1)).
[22] Rev. Rul. 84-111, 1984-2 C.B. 88 (*citing* IRC §1223(2)).
[23] Rev. Rul. 84-111, 1984-2 C.B. 88 (*citing* IRC §351); Ltr. Rul. 200139002, Ruling No. (3).
[24] Rev. Rul. 84-111, 1984-2 C.B. 88 (*citing* IRC §708(b)(1)(A)).
[25] Rev. Rul. 84-111, 1984-2 C.B. 88 (*citing* IRC §358(a)); Ltr. Rul. 200139002, Ruling No. (2).
[26] Ltr. Rul. 200139002, Ruling No. (3) (*citing* IRC §§752(d), 358(d)).
[27] Rev. Rul. 84-111, 1984-2 C.B. 88 (*citing* IRC §§752(d), 358(d)).
[28] Rev. Rul. 84-111, 1984-2 C.B. 88 (*citing* IRC §362(a)).

- The corporation's holding period for the assets received includes the LLC's holding period in the assets.[29]
- Each member's holding period for the stock received includes his or her holding period for the membership interest transferred. However, the holding period of the stock received by the members in exchange for Section 751 assets (hot assets) that are neither capital assets nor Section 1231 assets begins on the date following the date of the exchange.[30]

[5]   Method 4—Transfer of Membership Interests to Corporation; LLC Continues

Under the fourth method, the members transfer their membership interests in the LLC to the new corporation in exchange for stock. However, the LLC continues in existence. It does not transfer the assets and liabilities to the corporation as under Method 3. The LLC is classified as a disregarded entity wholly owned by the corporation,[31] unless it elects to be classified as a corporation.

The tax consequences under Method 4 are similar to the tax consequences under Method 3, with slight differences in basis in holding period computations. The tax consequences under Method 4 are as follows:

- The LLC (which was previously classified as a partnership) is treated as liquidating into the new corporation since it will become a disregarded entity wholly owned by the corporation.[32]
- The members of the LLC do not recognize gain or loss on the transfer of the membership interests to the new corporation in exchange for stock.[33]
- The members of the LLC receive a basis in the stock equal to their basis in the membership interests,[34] reduced by each member's share of liabilities assumed by the corporation plus any liabilities to which the transferred assets are subject.[35]
- The corporation's assumption of the LLC's liabilities is treated as a payment of money to the members.[36]
- Each member's holding period for the stock received includes his or her holding period for the membership interest transferred. However, the holding period of the stock received by the members in exchange for Section 751 assets (hot assets) that are neither capital assets nor Section 1231 assets begins on the date following the date of the exchange.[37]

---

[29] Rev. Rul. 84-111, 1984-2 C.B. 88.
[30] Rev. Rul. 84-111, 1984-2 C.B. 88 (*citing* IRC §1223(1)).
[31] Ltr. Rul. 200139002.
[32] Ltr. Rul. 200139002 (under Summary of Facts).
[33] Ltr. Rul. 200139002, Ruling No. (3).
[34] Ltr. Rul. 200139002, Ruling No. (2).
[35] Ltr. Rul. 200139002, Ruling No. (3) (*citing* IRC §§752(d), 358(d)).
[36] Rev. Rul. 84-111, 1984-2 C.B. 88 (*citing* IRC §§752(d), 358(d)).
[37] Ltr. Rul. 200139002, Ruling No. (4) (*citing* IRC §1223(1)); Rev. Rul. 84-111, 1984-2 C.B. 88.

- The corporation does not recognize gain or loss on receipt of the membership interests in exchange for stock.[38]
- The corporation's basis in the membership interest transferred equals the members' basis in such interests immediately before the transfer, increased by the amount of any gain recognized by a corporate member on the transfer.[39]
- The corporation's holding period for each membership interest includes the member's holding period immediately before the transfer.[40]
- The corporation does not recognize gain or loss on the deemed liquidation of the LLC into the corporation when the LLC becomes a wholly owned disregarded entity. However, the LLC recognizes gain to the extent that the deemed distribution of money from the LLC to the corporation exceeds the corporation's basis in the membership interest in the LLC immediately before the distribution.[41]
- The LLC does not recognize gain or loss on its deemed liquidation into the corporation.[42]
- The corporation's basis in the assets that it holds in the LLC as a disregarded entity is equal to the corporation's basis in the membership interest, reduced by any deemed distribution of money.[43]
- The LLC's holding period for the assets received in the deemed liquidation includes the period that such assets were held by the LLC.[44]

[6]   Method 5—Filing Election Classification

Under the fifth method, the LLC elects to be classified as a corporation by filing IRS Form 8832.

The tax consequences of electing to be classified as a corporation are the same as under Method 1. The LLC is treated as having contributed all of its assets and liabilities to the corporation in exchange for stock in the corporation. The LLC is then treated as having liquidated by distributing the stock in the corporation to its members.[45]

[7]   Method 6—Merger or Conversion

Under the sixth method, the members of the LLC form a corporation, and then merge or convert the LLC into the corporation. Some states permit an LLC to

---

[38] Ltr. Rul. 200139002, Ruling No. (6) (*citing* IRC §1032(a)).
[39] Ltr. Rul. 200139002, Ruling No. (7) (*citing* IRC §362(a)).
[40] Ltr. Rul. 200139002, Ruling No. (8) (*citing* IRC §1223(2)).
[41] Ltr. Rul. 200139002, Ruling No. (9) (*citing* IRC §731(a)).
[42] Ltr. Rul. 200139002, Ruling No. (10) (*citing* IRC §731(b)).
[43] Ltr. Rul. 200139002, Ruling No. (11) (*citing* IRC §732(b)).
[44] Ltr. Rul. 200139002, Ruling No. (12) (*citing* IRC §§735(b), 1223(2)).
[45] Reg. §1.301.7701-3(g)(1)(i).

merge into a corporation by filing a certificate of merger with the Secretary of State.[46] Other states permit an LLC to convert into a corporation.[47]

The merger or conversion of the LLC into the corporation is treated as an asset-over form of incorporation. The tax consequences are the same as under Method 1.

[8]   Which Method to Choose

Methods 2 and 3 are preferable to Method 1 if the members of the LLC have an aggregate basis in their membership interests that is higher than the LLC's basis in its assets. In such case, the LLC will receive the higher carryover basis for the assets under Methods 2 and 3. Under Method 1, the corporation receives a basis in the assets equal to the members' lower basis in their membership interests.

Method 3 may be preferable to Method 2 if the LLC transfers a substantial amount of cash to the new corporation. Under Method 2, the members' holding period for stock received in exchange for cash begins on the day after the incorporation. Under Method 3, the holding period for stock includes the holding period for the membership interests even if LLC assets include cash.

The LLC may be required to recapture investment tax credits under Methods 2 and 3. The corporation's basis in the assets received from the LLC is determined by reference to the members' bases in their membership interests rather than by reference to the LLC's basis in the assets transferred to the corporation.

The corporation may apparently not elect to be an S corporation under Method 1 for the first calendar year of incorporation. The stock in the corporation is issued momentarily to the LLC that is classified as a partnership. A corporation may not elect to be an S corporation if any of the shareholders are partners at any time during the tax year. This problem does not arise under Methods 2 and 3 if the members of the LLC are individuals since the stock in the corporation is issued directly to the members of the LLC.

The corporation may apparently not elect the benefits under Section 1244 of the Code (ordinary loss stock) under Method 1 for the same reason. Section 1244 is not available if stock is originally issued to non-individual shareholders except in limited circumstances. This problem does not arise under Methods 2 and 3 if the members of the LLC are individuals since the stock in the corporation is issued directly to the members of the LLC.

---

[46] For example, California permits a merger of a limited liability company into a corporation by filing with the California Secretary of State (a) Form LLC-9, Limited Liability Company Certificate Merger, (b) an Agreement of Merger signed by all managers of the LLC (or by the members in a members-managed LLC), by the Chairman of the Board, President, or Vice President, and by the Secretary or Assisting Secretary of the corporation, and (c) an Officers' Certificate for the corporation. Cal. Corp. Code §§1113(g)(1), 17550-17556, 17001(e), (ac).

[47] See, e.g., Wy. Stat. §17-15-146.

[B] LLC Classified as Corporation

An LLC that is classified as a corporation for federal tax purposes may convert to a regular corporation or an unlimited liability company. The following tax consequences apply if the conversion is made by an amendment to or a restatement of the LLC's charter documents:[48]

- The change in form is an F reorganization. The LLC and the corporation are each treated as a party to the reorganization.[49]
- The conversion is first treated as a constructive transfer of LLC assets and liabilities to the corporation in exchange for stock. No gain or loss is recognized by the LLC upon the constructive exchange of assets for the stock in the corporation and the assumption by the corporation of the LLC's liabilities.[50]
- No gain or loss is recognized by the corporation upon the constructive receipt of assets from the LLC in exchange for stock.[51]
- The LLC is then treated as having transferred the stock to its members in exchange for membership interests. No gain or loss is recognized to the members upon the exchange of membership interests solely for shares in the corporation.[52] Gain (but not loss) may be recognized to the extent boot is received.[53]
- The basis in the stock held by the members is the same basis that the members had in their membership interests prior to the conversion.[54]
- The holding period of the stock is the same as the holding period for the membership interests surrendered.[55]
- The LLC's basis and holding period in the transferred assets carry over to the corporation.[56]
- The corporation succeeds to the LLC's tax attributes.[57] The tax year of the LLC does not end on the date of the conversion. The corporation may carry back a net operating loss or a net capital loss to a pre-conversion tax year of the LLC.[58]

---

[48] Ltr. Ruls. 8908035, 7741040, 7729058. *See also* Ltr. Rul. 8809073, which treated the conversion as a nontaxable exchange of shares in the LLC for shares in the unlimited liability company, with a carryover in basis and holding period for the acquired shares.

[49] Ltr. Ruls. 8908035, 7741040 (*citing* IRC §§368(a)(1)(F), 368(b)).

[50] Ltr. Ruls. 8908035, 7741040 (*citing* IRC §§361(a), 357(a)).

[51] Ltr. Ruls. 8908035, 7741040 (*citing* IRC §1032(a)).

[52] Ltr. Ruls. 8908035, 7741040 (*citing* IRC §354(a)(1)).

[53] Ltr. Rul. 8908035 (*citing* IRC §356(a)(1)).

[54] Ltr. Ruls. 8908035, 7741040 (*citing* IRC §358(a)).

[55] Ltr. Ruls. 8908035, 7741040 (*citing* IRC §1223(1)).

[56] Ltr. Ruls. 8908035, 7741040 (*citing* IRC §§362(b), 1223(2)).

[57] Ltr. Rul. 8908035 (*citing* IRC §381(a)(2) and Reg. §1.381(b)-1(a)(2)). These tax attributes are listed in IRC §381(c).

[58] Ltr. Rul. 8908035 (*citing* IRC §381(b)(3)).

[C] LLC Classified as Disregarded Entity

An LLC that is classified as a disregarded entity may convert to a corporation on a tax-free basis. The owner of the LLC may make the conversion by merging the LLC into a corporation, or by contributing all the assets and liabilities of the LLC to a corporation.[59] The transfer of the assets and liabilities from the LLC to the corporation qualifies as a tax-free exchange under IRC Section 351.[60]

A disregarded LLC may also elect to be classified as a corporation by filing IRS Form 8832.

§11.07 CONVERSION FROM C CORPORATION TO LLC

[A] LLC Classified as Partnership

A corporation may convert to an LLC that is classified as a partnership for federal tax purposes.[1] The corporation is treated as liquidating and distributing its assets to the shareholders, followed by the shareholders' contribution of assets to the new LLC in exchange for interests in the LLC.[2] This type of reorganization is rare because of the adverse tax consequences.

If the corporation is a C corporation, there is potential double taxation. The first tax is on the corporation for the deemed sale of assets to shareholders.[3] The amount of gain or loss is the difference between the fair market value and adjusted basis in the assets. The shareholders recognize gain or loss to the extent that the fair market value of the assets distributed exceeds their basis in the stock.[4] The gain increases the basis of the shareholders' stock in the new corporation. No gain or loss is recognized upon the deemed contribution of property to the LLC.

Some states permit a statutory merger of a corporation into an LLC. The tax consequences are similar. The merger of a corporation into an LLC is treated as a nontaxable contribution of assets by the corporation to the LLC in exchange for membership interests, followed by a taxable distribution of the membership interests to the shareholders of the corporation in redemption of their stock. The corporation recognizes gain to the same extent as if it sold the membership interests to the shareholders for fair market value. The shareholders of the corporation also recognize capital gain or loss on distribution of the membership interests. The gain is equal to the difference between the fair market value of the membership interests less the members' basis in the stock. There is a technical termination of the LLC as a result of the merger. However, no gain or loss is recognized as a result of the deemed termination.[5]

---

[59] Ltr. Rul. 200204005.
[60] Ltr. Rul. 200204005 (LLC 2 merged into a newly-form corporation).
§11.07 [1] *See, e.g.,* Wy. Stat. §17-16-1115.
[2] Reg. §301.7701-3(g)(1). Ltr. Ruls. 9401014, 9252033.
[3] IRC §336(a).
[4] IRC §331(a).
[5] Ltr. Rul. 200214016. *See also* §11.20[A] *infra.*

Because of the adverse tax consequences of converting a corporation to an LLC, LLCs are used mainly for new businesses rather than for conversions of existing corporations. However, a corporation may be able to convert to an LLC without adverse tax consequences in the following cases:

- A parent corporation converts a subsidiary corporation into an LLC.[6]
- An S or C corporation has little or no built-in gain or appreciated assets.
- The shareholders of an S corporation have tax bases in their stock that exceed the value of the assets distributed. The capital loss on distribution may be sufficient to offset any gain from the deemed distribution of the assets.[7] An S corporation may convert to an LLC, and retain its status as an S corporation, even though the LLC is not a corporation under local law.[8]
- A C corporation has sufficient net operating losses to offset corporate gain recognized on the deemed distribution of appreciated assets. However, the shareholders will recognize gain on the deemed distribution unless the fair market value of the assets does not exceed the shareholders' tax bases in the shares, or the shareholders have sufficient capital losses to offset the gain on the deemed distribution.

[B] LLC Classified as Corporation

A corporation may convert to an LLC that is classified as a corporation for federal tax purposes.[9] The reorganization normally takes place through a merger, through an exchange of shares for membership interests, or in another way permitted by state law.

The Service treats the conversion either as a nontaxable exchange under IRC Section 1036[10] or as an F reorganization.[11]

[1] Section 1036 Exchange

The following tax consequences apply if the transaction is treated as an exchange under Section 1036:

---

[6] Ltr. Rul. 9409016. *See* §11.09 *infra*. The merger of the subsidiary into the LLC must comply with the requirements of IRC §332(b).

[7] Under IRC §1371, the distribution of appreciated property by an S corporation in liquidation results in taxable gain to the corporation equal to the difference between the fair market value of the corporate assets over the corporation's tax basis in the property. The gain is not subject to tax at the corporate level assuming that the corporation has been an S corporation since the date of its incorporation. The gain is passed through to the shareholders. Thus, there is a single tax at the shareholder level.

[8] Ltr. Rul. 9636007.

[9] Ltr. Ruls. 200205005, 200109011.

[10] Ltr. Ruls. 7911065, 7836019, 7831021.

[11] Ltr. Ruls. 7810072, 7729058, 7111100730A.

- No gain or loss is recognized to the shareholders upon the exchange of shares for membership interests.[12]
- The basis of the membership interests received by the shareholders is the same as the basis of the stock surrendered in the exchange.[13]
- The holding period of the membership interests includes the holding period of the stock surrendered in the exchange if the stock was held as a capital asset on the date of the exchange.[14]

[2] F Reorganization

The following tax consequences apply if the transaction is treated as an F reorganization:

- The corporation is treated as having transferred all its assets and liabilities to the LLC in exchange for LLC membership interests. This is followed by a deemed distribution of the LLC membership interests to the corporation's shareholders in exchange for their shares.
- No gain or loss is recognized to the corporation upon the transfer of its assets to the LLC in exchange for membership interests in the LLC and the assumption of the corporation's liabilities by the LLC.[15]
- The basis of the corporation's assets in the LLC's hands is the same as the basis of the assets in the corporation's hands immediately before the transfer.[16]
- The holding period of the corporation's assets in the LLC's hands includes the period during which those assets were held by the corporation.[17]
- No gain or loss is recognized to the LLC upon receipt of the corporation's assets in exchange for membership interests in the LLC.[18]
- No gain or loss is recognized by the shareholders upon receipt of membership interests in the LLC in exchange for stock in the corporation.[19]
- The basis of the LLC membership interests received by the shareholders of the corporation in exchange for stock in the corporation is the same as the basis of the stock in the corporation.[20]
- The holding period of the LLC membership interests received by the corporation's shareholders in exchange for stock in the corporation includes the holding period of the stock in the corporation.[21]

---

[12] Ltr. Ruls. 7911065, 7836019, 7831021 (*citing* IRC §1036).

[13] Ltr. Ruls. 7911065, 7836019, 7831021 (*citing* IRC §1031(d)). The basis would be increased by the amount of gain recognized and decreased by the loss recognized or money received.

[14] Ltr. Ruls. 7911065, 7836019, 7831021 (*citing* IRC §1223(1)).

[15] Ltr. Rul. 7729058; IRC §§361(a), 357(a).

[16] Ltr. Rul. 7810072 (*citing* IRC §362(b)).

[17] Ltr. Rul. 7810072 (*citing* IRC §1223(2)).

[18] Ltr. Rul. 7810072 (*citing* IRC §1032(a)).

[19] Ltr. Ruls. 7810072, 7729058, 7111100730A (*citing* IRC §354(a)(1)).

[20] Ltr. Ruls. 7810072, 7729058, 7111100730A (*citing* IRC §358(a)).

[21] Ltr. Ruls. 7810072, 7729058 (*citing* IRC §1223(1)).

- The new LLC is treated as if there had been no reincorporation for purposes of the Internal Revenue Code provision governing carryovers in corporate acquisitions.[22] The tax year does not end on the date of the reincorporation. The other tax attributes of the old LLC carry over to the new LLC.[23]

The reorganization of a C corporation as an LLC that is classified as a corporation is an F reorganization where (a) the membership units have identical rights, preferences, and restrictions as the corporate stocks surrendered in the exchange, and (b) the exchanging family members hold substantially the same interest before and after the transaction.[24]

[C]   LLC Classified as Disregarded Entity

A corporation may convert to an LLC that is classified as a disregarded entity. The conversion is treated as a distribution by the corporation of its assets and liabilities to the single owner of the LLC in liquidation of the corporation.[25] The regular taxes that apply to a corporate liquidation apply to the conversion.

A parent corporation may convert a subsidiary corporation into an LLC that is classified as a disregarded entity. The conversion is treated as a tax-free liquidation of the subsidiary into the parent.[26] However, the IRS will not rule on the tax consequences of the conversion.[27]

§11.08   CONVERSION FROM S CORPORATION TO LLC

[A]   Generally

There is typically one level of tax when an S corporation converts to an LLC. This differs from the conversion of a C corporation, where there are typically two levels of tax.

The S corporation is treated as liquidating and distributing its assets to the shareholders, followed by the shareholders' contribution of assets to the new LLC in exchange for LLC membership interests. If the S corporation has appreciated assets, the S corporation is treated as having sold the assets to the shareholders for fair market value.[1] The corporation recognizes gain equal to the difference

---

[22] IRC §381.

[23] Ltr. Rul. 8002076 (*citing* Reg. §1.381(b)-1(a)(2)). These tax attributes are listed in IRC §381(c).

[24] *See* Ltr. Rul. 199947034 in which the taxpayer represented that the transaction constituted an F reorganization.

[25] Reg. §301.7701-3(g)(1).

[26] *See* §11.09 *infra*.

[27] Ltr. Rul. 200214014, *citing* Rev. Proc. 2001-3, 2001-1 I.R.B. 111, §3.01(29).

§11.08   [1] IRC §§336(a), 1371(a)(1).

between the assets' fair market value and their adjusted bases. The gain passes through and is taxable to the shareholders.[2]

Typically, there is no second tax on the shareholders. The gain recognized by the corporation increases the shareholders' basis in their stock. Distributions to the shareholders are normally treated as a nontaxable return of basis.

No gain or loss is recognized upon the deemed contribution of property to the LLC.

[B]   Merger of S Corporation into LLC

The merger of an S corporation into an LLC has the following tax consequences:

- The merger is treated as a transfer by the S corporation to the LLC in exchange for the assumption of liabilities by the LLC and the S corporation's receipt of LLC membership interests (interests in the items of income, gain, deduction, or loss of the LLC), followed by the distribution of the membership interests in the LLC to the shareholders of the corporation in a complete liquidation of the corporation under Section 331.[3]
- The S corporation's basis in the membership interests upon the initial contribution to the LLC is the adjusted basis of the S corporation's assets,[4] increased by gain recognized to the S corporation upon the transfer of assets to the LLC.[5]
- The S corporation and the LLC do not recognize gain or loss upon the contribution of assets by the S corporation to the LLC in exchange for membership interests[6] unless the S corporation realizes a net decrease in liabilities exceeding its basis in the assets transferred to the LLC[7] and provided the LLC is not treated as an investment company.[8]
- The merger results in the liquidation of the S corporation. The S corporation recognizes gain or loss upon the distribution of the membership interests and other property (but not cash) to its shareholders in a complete liquidation of the S corporation.[9] Gain or loss is computed as if the corporation had sold the property to its shareholders for fair market value at the time of the distribution. The amount and character of the gain or loss are determined under Sections 741 and 751.[10] Under Section 741, the S corporation recognizes gain upon the transfer of an LLC membership interest. The gain or loss is capital gain or loss except as provided in Section 751, which deals with unrealized receivables and inventory items. The S corporation is not

---

[2] IRC §1366.
[3] Ltr. Rul. 9543017 (*citing* Rev. Rul. 69-6, 1969-1 C.B. 104).
[4] Ltr. Rul. 9543017 (*citing* IRC §722).
[5] Ltr. Rul. 9543017 (*citing* IRC §721(b)).
[6] Ltr. Rul. 9543017 (*citing* IRC §721).
[7] Ltr. Rul. 9543017 (*citing* Reg. §1.752-1(f)).
[8] Ltr. Rul. 9543017. *See* Chapter 20 *infra* regarding investment LLCs.
[9] Ltr. Rul. 9543017 (*citing* IRC §708(b)(1)(B)).
[10] Ltr. Rul. 9543017.

subject to tax under Section 1374, provided the S corporation did not acquire appreciated assets upon conversion from a C corporation.[11]

- Any gain or loss recognized by the S corporation as a result of its liquidation is passed through to its shareholders.[12] The shareholders then increase or decrease the basis in their stock by the amount of the gain or loss.[13]
- The shareholders recognize gain or loss upon the deemed distribution of assets from the S corporation in the liquidation. The distribution is treated as full payment in exchange for the shares in the S corporation.[14] The amount of gain or loss is equal to the difference between the fair market value of the membership interests received by the shareholders in exchange for the shares and the shareholders' adjusted basis in the shares.[15] Gain or loss is capital gain or loss, subject to the limitations of subchapter P of the Code,[16] if the corporation is not a collapsible corporation and the shares are capital assets.[17]
- The basis of the LLC membership interests received by the shareholders upon the complete liquidation of the S corporation is the fair market value of the membership interests at the time of the distribution.[18]
- If the LLC makes a Section 754 election, the LLC may adjust the basis of its assets under Sections 743 and 755.[19]
- The distribution of LLC membership interests by the S corporation to its shareholders constitutes an exchange that results in a termination of the LLC.[20] Under prior regulations, the termination resulted in a deemed distribution of the LLC's assets to the members of the LLC and a deemed immediate recontribution by the members to a new LLC.[21] Under proposed regulations, the termination is treated as a transfer by a terminated LLC of all of its assets to a new LLC in exchange for an interest in the new LLC, followed immediately thereafter by the old LLC's distribution of the new LLC membership interests to the members in liquidation of the old LLC. This results in the following tax consequences:[22]
  — There is no gain to the members under the Code provision governing gain or loss upon distribution.[23]
  — The basis in the assets of the LLC remains the same.
  — The tax year of the terminated LLC closes.
  — The elections of the terminated LLC are invalidated. New elections must be made.

---

[11] Ltr. Rul. 9543017 (*citing* IRC §1374(d)(8)).
[12] Ltr. Rul. 9543017 (*citing* IRC §1366(a)).
[13] Ltr. Rul. 9543017 (*citing* IRC §1367).
[14] Ltr. Rul. 9543017 (*citing* IRC §331(a)).
[15] Ltr. Rul. 9543017.
[16] IRC §§1201-1298.
[17] Ltr. Rul. 9543017 (*citing* IRC §§341, 1221).
[18] Ltr. Rul. 9543017 (*citing* IRC §334(a)).
[19] Ltr. Rul. 9543017.
[20] Ltr. Rul. 9543017 (*citing* IRC §708(b)(1)(B)).
[21] Ltr. Rul. 9543017 (*citing* Reg. §1.708-1(b)(1)(iv)).
[22] *See* §12.03 *infra* for a complete discussion of the tax consequences.
[23] IRC §731(a).

— The new LLC must depreciate any property as if it were newly acquired property under the same depreciation system used by the terminated LLC.

[C]   Contribution of Assets to LLC

An S corporation may convert to an LLC by forming an LLC and contributing its assets to the LLC in exchange for membership interests.[24] There are the following tax consequences:

- Neither the corporation nor the LLC will recognize gain or loss on the contribution of assets to the LLC in exchange for membership interests.[25]
- The contribution of LIFO inventory property to the LLC will not result in the recapture of the LIFO reserve.[27] However, in order to adopt the dollar-value LIFO inventory method, the transferee LLC must file IRS Form 970 and otherwise comply with the requirements of IRC Section 472 and regulations thereunder.[28]
- If any of the property contributed to the LLC has a fair market value that is different from its basis, the LLC must comply with the general requirements applicable to contributions of appreciated and depreciated property.[29]

[D]   LLC Classified as S Corporation

An S corporation may convert to an LLC that is classified as a corporation. The conversion is treated as an F reorganization.[30] However, the IRS will not issue an advance ruling on whether the transaction qualifies as an F reorganization.[31] The reorganization does not terminate the corporation's election as an S corporation. The LLC is classified as an S corporation after the conversion.[32]

§11.09   CONVERSION OF SUBSIDIARY CORPORATION TO LLC

[A]   General

A parent corporation may convert a subsidiary corporation into an LLC that is classified as a disregarded entity. The conversion is treated as a tax-free liquida-

---

[24] Ltr. Rul. 200123035.
[25] Ltr. Rul. 200123035, *citing* IRC §721(a).
[27] *Id.*
[28] Ltr. Rul. 200123035.
[29] Ltr. Rul. 200123035. These rules are discussed at §6.03 *supra*.
[30] *See* Ltr. Rul. 9636007.
[31] *Id.*
[32] *Id.*

tion of the subsidiary into the parent under IRC Section 332(a).[1] The IRS will no longer rule on the tax consequences of the conversion.[2]

The parent corporation may convert the subsidiary into an LLC through (a) a merger or conversion of a subsidiary into an LLC, (b) a transfer of assets from the subsidiary to the LLC, or (c) a liquidation of the subsidiary into the parent, and deemed transfer of the assets from the parent to the LLC.

[B] *Merger or Conversion*

A parent corporation may convert a subsidiary corporation into an LLC by forming an LLC and merging the subsidiary corporation into the LLC.[3] The parent corporation may also convert the subsidiary corporation into an LLC under any other method permitted by state law,[4] such as the filing of a certificate of conversion with the secretary of state.[5] The merger or conversion has the following tax consequences:

- The merger is treated as a transfer of assets by the subsidiary corporation to the LLC in exchange for the assumption of the subsidiary corporation's liabilities by the LLC and the subsidiary corporation's receipt of an LLC membership interest (an increased interest in the LLC's items of income, gain, deduction, or loss).[6]
- The transfer of assets is treated as followed by the subsidiary corporation's distribution of the LLC membership interest to the parent corporation in complete liquidation of the subsidiary corporation.[7]
- Neither the parent nor the subsidiary corporation recognizes gain or loss upon the subsidiary's transfer of assets to the LLC in exchange for the membership interest.[8]
- The parent corporation does not recognize gain or loss upon its receipt of the membership interest distributed in the liquidation of the subsidiary corporation pursuant to the plan of merger if the requirements of Section 332(b) are met.[9] The merger or conversion constitutes a tax-free liquidation under IRC Section 332.[10]

§11.09   [1] IRC §332(a); Ltr. Rul. 200214014. *See also* Ltr. Rul. 200305017 in which the IRS determined that the merger of a wholly owned subsidiary corporation of a foreign parent corporation into a disregarded LLC owned by the foreign parent corporation was a liquidation of the subsidiary corporation into the foreign parent corporation, subject to IRC §§331 and 336.

[2] Ltr. Rul. 200214014, *citing* Rev. Proc. 2001-3, 2001-1 I.R.B. 111, §3.01(29).

[3] Ltr. Ruls. 200305017, 200129024.

[4] *See* Ltr. Rul. 200129029.

[5] Ltr. Rul. 200252055.

[6] Ltr. Ruls. 200129029, 9409016, 9409014, 9404021.

[7] IRC §332; Ltr. Ruls. 200129029, 9409016, 9409014, 9404021 (*citing* Reg. §1.332-2(d) and Rev. Rul. 69-6, 1969-1 C.B. 104).

[8] Ltr. Ruls. 200129024, 9409016, 9409014, 9404021 (*citing* IRC §721).

[9] Ltr. Ruls. 9409016, 9409014, 9404021 (*citing* IRC §332(a)). *See also* Ltr. Ruls. 9822043 and 9822037, which determined that the merger of a subsidiary into an LLC owned by the parent corporation constituted a complete liquidation under IRC §332 and Reg. §1.331-2(d).

[10] Ltr. Ruls. 200137011, 200129029, 200129024.

- The parent corporation's basis in the membership interest is the same basis that the subsidiary corporation had in the membership interest immediately prior to its liquidation.[11]
- The subsidiary corporation does not recognize gain or loss upon distribution of the membership interest to the parent corporation in complete liquidation of the subsidiary.[12]
- The parent corporation's holding period for the membership interest includes the subsidiary corporation's holding period.[13]
- The parent corporation succeeds to and takes into account the items of the subsidiary corporation set forth in IRC Section 381(c). These items are subject to certain limitations.[14]
- The parent corporation succeeds to and takes into account the subsidiary corporation's earnings and profits, or deficit in earnings and profits, as of the date of the merger. Any deficit in earnings and profits of the parent or subsidiary may be used to offset earnings and profits accumulated only after the date of transfer.[15]
- If the parent corporation first merges a second-tier subsidiary into a first-tier subsidiary, and then converts the first-tier subsidiary into an LLC, the transaction is treated as a D reorganization with similar tax consequences.[16]

[C] Transfer of Assets by Subsidiary

A parent corporation may convert a subsidiary corporation into an LLC by forming an LLC. The subsidiary corporation transfers its assets to the LLC in exchange for membership units. The subsidiary corporation is then liquidated. The membership units in the LLC owned by the subsidiary are transferred to the parent corporation in the liquidation.[17] The tax consequences of the conversion are as follows:

- Neither the subsidiary nor the LLC recognizes gain or loss as a result of the transfer of assets to the LLC.[18]
- The liquidation of the subsidiary corporation and the transfer of the LLC membership units to the parent corporation qualify as a nontaxable liquidation under Section 332.[19]

---

[11] Ltr. Ruls. 200129029, 9409016, 9409014, 9404021 (*citing* IRC §334(b)(1)).

[12] Ltr. Ruls. 9409016, 9409014, 9404021 (*citing* IRC §§337(a), 336(d)(3)).

[13] Ltr. Ruls. 200129029, 9409016, 9409014, 9404021 (*citing* IRC §1223(2)).

[14] *See* IRC §§381-384, 1502, and the regulations thereunder; Ltr. Ruls. 200129029, 9409016, 9409014, 9404021 (*citing* IRC §381(a) and Reg. §1.381(c)(2)-1).

[15] Ltr. Ruls. 200129029, 9409016, 9409014, 9404021 (*citing* IRC §381(c)(2) and Reg. §1.381(c)(2)-1).

[16] Ltr. Rul. 200252055.

[17] *See* Ltr. Rul. 9640010.

[18] Ltr. Rul. 9640010 (*citing* IRC §721).

[19] Ltr. Rul. 9640010 (*citing* IRC §332(a) and Reg. §1.332-2(c)). *See also* Ltr. Rul. 200137011.

The transfer by a spun-off subsidiary of some or all of the assets of its active trade or business to an LLC in exchange for membership interests in the LLC will not prevent the spun-off subsidiary from being treated as engaged in a trade or business for purposes of IRC Section 355.[20]

[D] *Liquidation and Transfer of Assets by Parent*

A parent corporation may convert a subsidiary corporation into an LLC by liquidating the subsidiary and contributing the assets received upon liquidation to a newly formed LLC.[21] The tax consequences of the transaction are as follows:

- The liquidation of the subsidiary corporation qualifies as a nontaxable liquidation under IRC Section 332. If the subsidiary merges into the parent, the merger is treated as a distribution of assets in complete liquidation of the subsidiary.[22]
- The contribution to the LLC by the parent corporation of assets received from the subsidiary in exchange for membership units is nontaxable under IRC Section 721. Neither the parent corporation nor the subsidiary corporation nor the LLC recognizes gain as a result of the contribution of assets to the LLC.[23]
- The distribution of membership interests by the subsidiary corporation to the parent corporation is a distribution under IRC Section 301. If the parent and subsidiary file consolidated returns, the distribution constitutes an intercompany transaction.[24] Any gain or loss recognized under IRC Section 311(b) on the Section 301 distribution of the membership interests in not taken into account under regulations at the time of the distribution.[25]

§11.10 CONVERSION OF LLC INTO LIMITED PARTNERSHIP

The tax consequences of a conversion from an LLC into a limited partnership are similar to the tax consequences of a conversion from a limited partnership into an LLC.[1] The limited partnership is treated as the continuation of the LLC. The liquidation does not result in the termination of the LLC.[2]

The limited partnership may complete a like-kind exchange entered into by the LLC prior to its liquidation. The limited partnership is treated as both the

---

[20] Ltr. Rul. 200227016.
[21] Ltr. Rul. 9701032.
[22] Ltr. Rul. 9701032 (*citing* Reg. §1.332-2(d)).
[23] Ltr. Rul. 9701032 (*citing* IRC §721).
[24] Ltr. Rul. 9701032 (*citing* Reg. §1.1502-13(b)).
[25] Ltr. Rul. 9701032 (*citing* Reg. §1.1502-13(c), (d)).
§11.10   [1] *See* §11.02 *infra.*
[2] Ltr. Rul. 199935065.

transferor of the relinquished property previously transferred to a qualified intermediary by the LLC before its liquidation, and as the transferee of the replacement property received from the qualified intermediary.[3]

An LLC may merge into a limited partnership in which the members of the limited partnership are different than the members of the LLC. In such case, the merger is treated as an assets-over form of merger or an assets-up form of merger. The tax consequences of the merger are discussed in §11.22.

§11.11 TRANSFERS OF LLC INTERESTS BETWEEN RELATED COMPANIES

A parent corporation may change the ownership of an LLC from one subsidiary corporation to another without adverse tax consequences. The parent company may simply transfer the membership interests of one subsidiary LLC to another subsidiary LLC. The transfer is a nontaxable exchange under IRC Section 351 if both LLCs are classified as corporations.[1]

A parent corporation may also transfer the membership interests in a subsidiary LLC to another subsidiary corporation in exchange for additional stock. This is also treated as a nontaxable exchange under Section 351.[2] No gain or loss is recognized to the subsidiary corporation upon receipt of the LLC membership interests.[3] The subsidiary corporation's basis in the LLC membership interests is the same basis that the parent corporation had immediately prior to the transfer.[4]

§11.12 REINCORPORATION

The reincorporation of an LLC is treated as an F reorganization if the LLC is classified as a corporation for federal tax purposes.[1] The following tax consequences apply if one LLC transfers all of its assets and liabilities to a new LLC in order to effect the reincorporation:[2]

- No gain or loss is recognized to the old LLC upon the transfer of its assets to the new LLC in exchange for membership interests in the new LLC and the assumption of the liabilities of the old LLC by the new LLC.[3]
- The basis of the assets of the old LLC in the hands of the new LLC is the same as the basis of the assets in the hands of the old LLC immediately prior to the transfer.[4]

[3] Ltr. Rul. 199935065.
§11.11   [1] Ltr. Rul. 7821084.
[2] Ltr. Rul. 7716015.
[3] Ltr. Rul. 7716015 (*citing* IRC §1032(a)).
[4] Ltr. Rul. 7716015 (*citing* IRC §362(a)).
§11.12   [1] Ltr. Rul. 8002076.
[2] *Id.*
[3] Ltr. Rul. 8002076 (*citing* IRC §§361(a), 357(a)).
[4] Ltr. Rul. 8002076 (*citing* IRC §362(b)).

- The holding period of the assets of the old LLC in the hands of the new LLC includes the period during which those assets were held by the old LLC.[5]
- No gain or loss is recognized to the new LLC upon the receipt of the assets of the old LLC in exchange for membership interests in the new LLC.[6]
- No gain or loss is recognized by the members (same members for both LLCs) upon receipt of the membership interests in the new LLC in exchange for the membership interests in the old LLC.[7]
- The basis of the membership interests received by the members of the new LLC in exchange for the membership interests in the old LLC is the same as the members' basis in the membership interests of the old LLC.[8]
- The holding period of the membership interests received by the members of the new LLC in exchange for the membership interests in the old LLC includes the holding period of the membership interests in the old LLC.[9]
- The new LLC is treated as if there had been no reincorporation for purposes of Section 381. The tax year does not end on the date of the reincorporation. The other tax attributes of the old LLC carry over to the new LLC.[10]

§11.13 DROP-DOWN OF ASSETS INTO SUBSIDIARY LLC

[A] LLC Classified as Partnership

The drop-down of assets and liabilities by a corporation into an LLC that is classified as a partnership is a nontaxable transfer under IRC Section 721.[1] If the corporation then transfers the membership units to its parent corporation in liquidation, the transfer of membership units and the liquidation of the subsidiary qualify as a nontaxable liquidation under IRC Section 332.[2]

[B] LLC Classified as Corporation

The drop-down of assets and liabilities by a parent company into a subsidiary LLC that is classified as a corporation is a nontaxable exchange under IRC Section 351.[3] However, the transaction is treated as a nondivisive D reorganization if the

---

[5] Ltr. Rul. 8002076 (*citing* IRC §1223(a)).
[6] Ltr. Rul. 8002076 (*citing* IRC §1032(a)).
[7] Ltr. Rul. 8002076 (*citing* IRC §354(a)(1)).
[8] Ltr. Rul. 8002076 (*citing* IRC §358(a)(1)).
[9] Ltr. Rul. 8002076 (*citing* IRC §1223(1)).
[10] Ltr. Rul. 8002076 (*citing* Reg. §1.381(b)-1(a)(2)). These tax attributes are listed in IRC §381(c).
§11.13 [1] Ltr. Rul. 9640010.
[2] Ltr. Rul. 9640010 (*citing* IRC §332(a) and Reg. §1.332-2(c)).
[3] Ltr. Rul. 7203140670A.

parent company thereafter transfers the LLC membership units that it receives to its parent corporation.[4]

§11.14 CONVERSION FROM TRUST TO LLC

A trust may convert to an LLC by contributing its assets to an LLC in exchange for membership interests and then distributing the membership interests to the trust beneficiaries. No gain or loss is recognized to the trust or the LLC upon the contribution of assets to the LLC.[1] No gain or loss is recognized to the trust upon the distribution of membership interests to the beneficiaries, provided the trust does not elect to recognize gain or loss upon the distribution under IRC Section 643(e)(3)(B).

§11.15 DIVISION OF LLC

[A] General Rules

An LLC that is classified as a partnership may be divided into two or more LLCs. Any resulting LLC is treated as a continuation of the prior LLC if the members of the LLC had an interest of more than 50 percent in the capital and profits of the prior LLC. Any resulting LLC in which members did not have more than 50 percent of the capital and profits interest in the prior LLC is not considered a continuation of the prior LLC. If the members of none of the new LLCs owned more than 50 percent of the capital and profits interests of the prior LLC, none of the new LLCs will be a continuation of the prior LLC, and the prior LLC will be terminated.[1] If a member is not a member of one of the resulting LLCs after the division, the member's interest will be considered liquidated as of the date of division.[2]

The IRS regulations use four terms to describe an LLC division. The prior LLC is the LLC that existed prior to the division.[3] The resulting LLCs are the LLCs that exist after the merger.[4] The divided LLC is the LLC that transfers its assets to the new LLC.[5] The recipient LLC is the new LLC that receives the assets.[6]

There are modifications to these definitions. The divided LLC must be a continuation of the prior LLC. The divided LLC is a continuation of the prior LLC if the members of the divided LLC had an interest of more than 50 percent in the capital

---

[4] *See, e.g.,* Ltr. Rul. 7908027. An LLC dropped down assets and liabilities of one of its branches into a newly formed subsidiary LLC in exchange for all of the stock in the new LLC. The parent LLC then transferred the stock in the subsidiary LLC to its parent corporation. *See also* Ltr. Rul. 6612276340A.

§11.14 [1] Ltr. Rul. 9604014.

§11.15 [1] IRC §702(b)(2)(B); Reg. §1.708-1(d)(1).

[2] Reg. §1.708-1(d)(1).

[3] Reg. §1.708-1(d)(4)(ii).

[4] Reg. §1.708-1(d)(4)(iv).

[5] Reg. §1.708-1(d)(4)(i).

[6] Reg. §1.708-1(d)(4)(iii).

and profits of the prior LLC. If there is more than one continuing LLC, the continuing LLC with assets having the greatest fair market value net of liabilities is the divided LLC.[7]

The divided LLC is considered one continuing LLC for federal income tax purposes, even though it may actually be two different LLCs under applicable state law (i.e., the prior LLC and a different resulting LLC that is considered a continuation of the prior LLC for federal income tax purposes). For example, if one LLC transfers 80 percent of its assets to a new LLC, the new LLC is the continuing LLC and the divided LLC. The prior LLC is the recipient LLC. The new LLC is treated as transferring 20 percent of its assets to the prior LLC.

[B]   Form of Division

The tax consequences of a division depend on the form of division. There are two forms of division: the assets-over form and the assets-up form.

[1]   Assets-Over Form

In an assets-over form of division, the old LLC transfers some of its assets to a new LLC in exchange for membership interests in the new LLC. The old LLC then immediately distributes the new membership interests to some or all of the members in the old LLC in partial or complete liquidation of their membership interests. The LLC that is the continuing LLC for tax purposes is treated as contributing assets to the new LLC in exchange for membership interests.[8] If none of the LLCs are continuing LLCs for tax purposes after the division, the old LLC will be treated as contributing all of its assets and liabilities to each of the LLCs existing after the division in exchange for membership interests in those LLCs, and then immediately liquidating by distributing the membership interests to the members of the old LLC.[9]

This is the default form of division if no form of division is specified, or if the division does not qualify as an assets-up form.[10]

The final regulations on divisions do not discuss the tax consequences of the assets-over form of division in any significant detail. The tax consequences are based on other applicable provisions of the Code, regulations, and rulings.

In the normal form of assets-over division, an existing LLC transfers less than 50 percent of its assets and liabilities to a new LLC that is owned by a minority group of members. The tax consequences are relatively simple in such case. The members of the existing LLC and the new LLC retain their same capital accounts and outside basis. The new LLC receives a carryover basis in the assets received from the existing LLC. None of the parties recognizes gain or loss.

---

[7] Reg. §1.708-1(d)(4)(i).
[8] Reg. §1.708-1(d)(3)(i)(A).
[9] Reg. §1.708-1(d)(3)(i)(B).
[10] Reg. §1.708-1(d)(3)(i), (4)(i).

Under the Code and regulations, the tax consequences and mechanics of the division are as follows:

- The existing LLC is treated as transferring assets and liabilities to the new LLC in exchange for membership interests in the new LLC, if the existing LLC is the divided LLC.[11] The existing LLC is the divided LLC if the members of the existing LLC after the division owned more than 50 percent in the capital and profits of the existing LLC prior to the division.[12]
- The new LLC is treated as transferring assets and liabilities to the existing LLC in exchange for membership interests in the existing LLC, if the new LLC is the divided LLC. The new LLC is the divided LLC if the members of the new LLC after the division owned more than 50 percent in the capital and profits in the existing LLC prior to the division.[13]
- If the members of both the new LLC and existing LLC owned more than 50 percent of the capital and profits in the existing LLC after the division, then the divided LLC is the LLC with assets having the greatest fair market value net of liabilities. In such case, the divided LLC is treated as transferring assets and liabilities to the other LLC (which is the recipient LLC).[14]
- The divided LLC and its members do not recognize gain or loss on the transfer of assets and liabilities to the recipient LLC in exchange for membership interests in the recipient LLC.[15]
- The recipient LLC receives a carryover basis in the assets transferred from the divided LLC.[16]
- The divided LLC receives a basis in the membership interests in the recipient LLC equal to the money and basis of the assets transferred to the recipient LLC.[17]
- The divided LLC is treated as distributing the membership interests in the recipient LLC to certain of the members in the divided LLC (the split-off group) in liquidation of their interests in the divided LLC.
- The members of the split-off group receive a basis in their membership interests in the recipient LLC equal to the basis of their membership interests in the divided LLC, reduced by any money distributed in the same transaction.[18] Thus, any disparity between the members' outside basis in the membership interests and the recipient LLC's inside basis in the contributed assets will continue after the division.
- The recipient LLC may make an election under IRC Section 754 to adjust the basis of its assets. In such case, the recipient LLC must (a) increase the basis of its assets under Section 743(b)(1) to the extent that the members' aggregate outside basis in the recipient LLC exceeds the recipient LLC's

---

[11] Reg. §1.708-1(d)(3)(i)(A).
[12] Reg. §1.708-1(d)(4)(i).
[13] *Id.*
[14] *Id.*
[15] IRC §721(a).
[16] IRC §723.
[17] IRC §722.
[18] IRC §732(b).

inside basis for its assets, and (b) decrease the basis of its assets under Section 743(b)(2) to the extent that the members' aggregate outside basis in the recipient LLC is less than the recipient LLC's inside basis for its assets. The result is that the inside and outside basis will be the same. The recipient LLC should make the Section 754 election only if there will be a basis increase for its assets. It may increase the basis of its assets even though the divided LLC is not required to make a corresponding decrease in the basis of its assets.[19] For example, assume that a divided LLC transfers zero basis assets to the recipient LLC, and then distributes the membership interests in the recipient LLC to members with an aggregate outside basis of $10,000. The members would receive an aggregate basis of $10,000 in the membership interests in the recipient LLC under Section 732(b). The recipient LLC would have a zero carryover basis in the assets received from the divided LLC. The recipient LLC could increase the inside basis of its assets to $10,000 under Section 743(b)(1) if it makes a Section 754 election.

- The divided LLC may also make an election under Section 754 to adjust the basis of its assets. In such case, the divided LLC must (a) increase the basis of its assets under Section 734(b)(1)(B) to the extent that the members receive a lower outside basis in the membership interests of the recipient LLC than the divided LLC's basis in such membership interests immediately prior to distribution, and (b) decrease the basis of its assets under Section 734(b)(2)(B) to the extent that the members receive a higher outside basis in the membership interests of the recipient LLC than the divided LLC's basis in such membership interests immediately prior to distribution. However, the divided LLC may increase the basis of its assets only if the recipient LLC makes a Section 754 election and a corresponding decrease in the basis of its assets.[20] For example, assume that a divided LLC transfers assets with a basis of $10,000 to the recipient LLC, and then distributes the membership interests in the recipient LLC to a split-off group of members, each of whom has a zero outside basis. The split-off group would receive a zero basis in the membership interests in the recipient LLC under IRC Section 732(b). Since there is $10,000 of disappearing basis, the divided LLC that makes an election under Section 754 may increase the basis of its assets by $10,000, but only if the recipient LLC makes a corresponding $10,000 decrease in the basis of its assets. As the result, the divided LLC should not ordinarily make a Section 754 election if it has not previously done so. The basis decrease in its assets would be a disadvantage, and the basis increase in its assets would ordinarily not be available.

- A member will not recognize gain under IRC Section 752 as a result of the transfer of liabilities from the divided LLC to the recipient LLC unless there is a net decrease in the member's share of liabilities. In such case, gain is

---

[19] *See* Sloan, E.B., Lipton, R., Harrington, D., and Frediani, M., "New Prop. Regs. Provide Expanding Guidance on Partnership Mergers and Divisions—Part 2," p. 263, fn. 7 (JTAX Nov. 2000).

[20] IRC §734(b) (flush language).

recognized to the extent that the net decrease in liabilities exceeds the member's basis in the membership interest after the division.[21]

- The members may recognize gain under the disguised sales and anti-mixing bowl rules.[22] The disguised sales and anti-mixing bowl rules are discussed in Chapter 6.[23] The IRS has not yet decided if an LLC division will create new Section 704(c) property or Section 737 net precontribution gain. A division will not create new Section 704(c) property or Section 737 net precontribution gain if the division merely affects a restructuring of the form in which the members hold property, and if each member's overall interest in each LLC property does not change. However, the result may be different if the division is non-pro rata as to the members, if some property is extracted from or added to the LLCs as a result of the division, or if new members are added after the division. The IRS is continuing to study the matter.[24]

- Each LLC must continue to use the same period and method of depreciation and amortization after the division that was used prior to the division.[25]

[2] Assets-Up Form

In an assets-up form of division, the existing LLC distributes assets to some or all of its members who then contribute the assets to a new LLC in exchange for membership interests.[26]

The assets-up form of division requires that the existing LLC actually transfer ownership of its assets to the members under state law. A mere assignment of the right to receive title to the assets is not sufficient. If the split-off group does not become owners, then the division will be treated as an assets-over form of

---

[21] REG-111119-99, 2000-5 I.R.B. 455.

[22] T.D. 8925 (Jan. 4, 2001); REG-111119-99, 2000-5 I.R.B. 455. *See also* Sloan, E.B., Lipton, R., Harrington, D., and Frediani, M., "New Prop. Regs. Provide Expanding Guidance on Partnership Mergers and Divisions—Part 2," pp. 268-272 (JTAX Nov. 2000). There is an exception for certain LLC divisions. Section 737 does not apply if the transferor LLC transfers the Section 704(c) property to a second LLC in a Section 721 exchange, followed by a distribution of an interest in the transferee LLC in complete liquidation of the interest of the member that originally contributed the property to the transferor LLC. Reg. §1.737-2(b)(2). This rule may not apply to many LLC divisions because the original contributing member often remains a member in the divided LLC. No similar exception is provided under Section 704(c)(1)(B). T.D. 8925 (Jan. 4, 2001).

[23] *See* §§6.05[B], 6.05[C] *supra*, which discuss the disguised sales rules under IRC §§704(c)(1)(B) and 737, cited by the IRS in the preamble to the proposed regulations on partnership and LLC mergers.

[24] T.D. 8925 (Jan. 4, 2001).

[25] IRC §168(i)(7); Rev. Rul. 90-17,1990-1 C.B. 119; Reg. §§1.197-2(g)(2)(iv)(C), 1.197-2(g)(2)(ii)(B), 1.197-2(g)(3). *See also* Sloan, E.B., Lipton, R., Harrington, D., and Frediani, M., "New Prop. Regs. Provide Expanding Guidance on Partnership Mergers and Divisions—Part 2," pp. 263, 264, under the heading "Recovery Periods—Depreciation and Amortization" (JTAX Nov. 2000). However, the recipient LLC must treat the property as newly acquired property for depreciation purposes with respect to that portion of the basis of property that exceeds the basis of the property in the hands of the divided LLC prior to the division (e.g., as result of a Section 754 election).

[26] Reg. §§1.708-1(d)(3)(ii), 1.708-1(d)(5), Example 2.

division.[27] The members are not required to assume the liabilities of the terminated LLC. The terminated LLC may transfer the liabilities directly to the new LLC.[28]

In the normal form of division, the divided LLC distributes assets to some of its members, who contribute assets to the recipient LLC.[29] The divided LLC is the LLC that is a continuation of the prior LLC. An LLC is a continuation of the prior LLC if the members of the LLC had an interest of more than 50 percent in the capital and profits of the prior LLC. If more than one LLC is a continuation of the prior LLC, then the LLC with assets having the greatest fair market value, net of liabilities, is the continuing LLC.[30]

In some divisions, there is no continuing LLC after the division. This may occur when an LLC is divided into three or more LLCs, each with a minority group of members from the existing LLC. In this case, the division is treated partly as an asset-over form of division and partly as an assets-up form of division. In such case, the existing LLC is treated as (a) transferring the assets that it retains to a recipient LLC under the assets-over form of division, and (b) transferring the assets that it does not retain to the distributee members who then contribute those assets to a second recipient LLC under the assets-up form of division.[31]

The final regulations on divisions do not discuss the tax consequences of the assets-up form of division in any significant detail. The tax consequences are based on other applicable provisions of the Code, regulations, and rulings. The tax consequences are as follows:

- The basis of assets distributed to each member of the split-off group on liquidation of their membership interests is equal to each member's outside basis in the membership interest, reduced by any money received in the distribution.[32]
- The members of the split-off group do not recognize gain or loss on the transfer of assets and liabilities to the recipient LLC in exchange for membership interests in the recipient LLC.[33]
- The members receive a basis in the membership interests in the recipient LLC equal to their basis in the assets distributed on liquidation of the LLC.[34]
- The recipient LLC's basis in the assets received from its members is the same as the members' basis in such assets immediately prior to the transfer.[35]
- The members' holding periods for non-cash assets distributed to them includes the divided LLC's holding periods for such assets.[36]

---

[27] Reg. §1.708-1(d)(3)(ii)(A).

[28] Reg. §1.708-1(c)(3)(ii). *See also* T.D. 8925, IRS Final Regulations on Partnership Mergers and Divisions, Explanation of Revisions and Summary of Contents (Jan. 4, 2001).

[29] Reg. §1.708-1(d)(3)(ii)(A).

[30] IRC §702(b)(2)(B); Reg. §1.708-1(d)(1).

[31] Reg. §1.708-1(d)(3)(ii)(B).

[32] IRC §732(b).

[33] IRC §721(a).

[34] IRC §722.

[35] IRC §723.

[36] IRC §735(b).

- The members' holding periods for membership interests in the recipient LLC include their holding periods in the capital assets and Section 1231 assets transferred to the recipient LLC (to the extent membership interests are received in exchange for such assets).[37] The members' holding period for membership interests received in exchange for other assets begins on the date following the date of the exchange.

- The recipient LLC's holding period for the assets includes the members' holding periods for such assets.[38]

- Members of the divided LLC and recipient LLC do not recognize gain under IRC Section 752 as a result of the transfer of liabilities from the divided LLC to the members or from the divided LLC to the recipient LLC unless there is a net decrease in the member's share of liabilities.[39] In such case, gain is recognized to the extent that the net decrease in liabilities exceeds the member's basis in the membership interest.[40]

- The divided LLC that distributes assets to some of the members may make an election under Section 754. In such case, the divided LLC must (a) increase the basis of its assets by the amount of gain recognized by the member; (b) decrease the basis of its assets by the amount of loss recognized by the member; (c) increase the basis of its assets by the amount of basis decrease to the member; and (d) decrease the basis of its assets by the amount of basis increase to the member. These rules are discussed in detail in §10.06[A]. Normally, the divided LLC should make a Section 754 election only if it distributes assets that have a higher inside basis than the distributee members' outside basis in their membership interests. In such case, the divided LLC may increase the inside basis of its assets by the difference between inside and outside basis.

- Each LLC must continue to use the same period and method of depreciation and amortization after the division that was used prior to the division. However, the recipient LLC must treat the property as newly acquired property for depreciation purposes with respect to that portion of the basis of property that exceeds the basis of the property in the hands of the divided LLC prior to the division.[41]

- The members may recognize gain under the disguised sales and anti-mixing bowl rules.[42] The IRS has not yet decided whether a division will create new Section 704(c) property or Section 737 net precontribution gain. A division will not create new Section 704(c) property or Section 737 net

---

[37] IRC §1223(1).

[38] IRC §1223(2).

[39] IRC §752; Reg. §1.752-1(f).

[40] REG-111119-99, 2000-5 I.R.B. 455.

[41] IRC §168(i)(7); Rev. Rul. 90-17,1990-1 C.B. 119; Reg. §§1.197-2(g)(2)(iv)(C), 1.197-2(g)(2)(ii)(B), 1.197-2(g)(3). *See also* Sloan, E.B., Lipton, R., Harrington, D., and Frediani, M., "New Prop. Regs. Provide Expanding Guidance on Partnership Mergers and Divisions—Part 2," pp. 263, 264, under the heading "Recovery Periods—Depreciation and Amortization" (JTAX Nov. 2000).

[42] T.D. 8925 (Jan. 4, 2001); REG-111119-99, 2000-5 I.R.B. 455. *See also* Sloan, E.B., Lipton, R., Harrington, D., and Frediani, M., "New Prop. Regs. Provide Expanding Guidance on Partnership Mergers and Divisions—Part 2," pp. 268-272 (JTAX Nov. 2000).

precontribution gain if the division merely affects a restructuring of the form in which the members hold property, and if each member's overall interest in each LLC property does not change. However, the result may be different if the division is non-pro rata as to the members, if some property is extracted from or added to the LLCs as a result of the division, or if new members are added after the division. The IRS is continuing to study the matter.[43]

- The divided LLC may recognize state and local transfer taxes on the distribution.[44]
- The divided LLC, and any recipient LLC that is treated as a continuation of the prior LLC, are subject to the same elections made by the prior LLC. Subsequent elections made by the divided LLC or recipient LLC do not affect the other LLC.[45]

[C] Tax Returns

The divided LLC (the continuing LLC with assets having the greatest fair market value of assets net of liabilities) must file a tax return for the tax year in which the division occurred. It must also retain the same employer identification number of the prior LLC. The return must include the names, addresses, and employer identification numbers of all resulting LLCs that are not considered continuations of the prior LLC. The return must state that the LLC is a continuation of the prior LLC. It must set forth separately the respective distributive shares of the members for the periods prior to and including the date of the division and subsequent to the date of the division.[46]

The recipient LLC must file separate returns for the tax year beginning on the day after the division. It must apply for and use a separate employer identification number.[47]

EXAMPLE

ABCD LLC is in the real estate and insurance business. Member A owns a 40 percent interest in the capital and profits of the LLC. Each of the other members owns a 20 percent interest in the LLC. The LLC and its members report their income on a calendar year basis. They agree to separate the real estate and insurance business on November 1, 2004. The LLC transfers title to the real estate to the AB LLC owned by Members A and B. The LLC transfers the insurance business to CD LLC owned by Members C and D. AB LLC is the divided LLC and continuing LLC since its members owned

---

[43] T.D. 8925 (Jan. 4, 2001).
[44] REG-111119-99, 2000-5 I.R.B. 455.
[45] Reg. §1.708(d)(2)(ii).
[46] Id.
[47] Id.

more than 50 percent of the capital and profits interest of ABCD LLC prior to the division. The division is an assets-over form of division since the assets were transferred directly to the new LLCs. AB LLC must file a return for the entire calendar year 2004. It must indicate on the return that it was the ABCD LLC until November 1, 2004. CD LLC is considered a new LLC formed at the beginning of the day on November 2, 2004. It is required to file a return for the tax year that it adopts in compliance with the applicable regulations. Assuming that it adopts a calendar year, it must file a short return for the period from November 2, 2004 until December 31, 2004.[48]

§11.16 CONVERSION AS A RESULT OF CHANGE IN CLASSIFICATION ELECTION

An LLC may convert from one type of entity to another (i.e., corporation, partnership, or disregarded entity) by filing an elective change in classification. The Treasury Department has issued proposed regulations describing how elective changes in an entity's classification should be treated for federal income tax purposes. The proposed regulations deal with the following four elective changes in classification that are permitted under the final check-the-box regulations:[1]

1. Partnership elects to be taxed as a corporation.
2. Corporation elects to be taxed as a partnership.
3. Corporation with a single member elects to be disregarded as an entity for tax purposes.
4. Disregarded entity elects to be taxed as a corporation.

§11.17 CONVERSION FROM A SINGLE-MEMBER LLC TO A PARTNERSHIP

The status of a single-member LLC that is classified as a disregarded LLC changes when the LLC acquires more than one member. The LLC is classified as a partnership for federal tax purposes unless an election is made to classify the LLC as a corporation.[1]

A single-member LLC may convert to a partnership in several ways. First, the LLC may convert to a partnership when a new member purchases an interest in the LLC from an existing member. Second, a single-member LLC may convert to a partnership when a new member contributes cash to the LLC in exchange for a membership interest.

---

[48] Reg. §1.708-1(d)(5), Example 1.
§11.16 [1] Prop. Reg. §301.7701-3(g). *See* §5.04[F] *supra* for discussion of the tax consequences of these conversions.
§11.17 [1] Prop. Reg. §301.7701-3(f).

[A]   Conversion by Purchase

The purchase of an interest in the LLC that causes the LLC to have more than one owner is treated as the purchase of an interest in each of the LLC's assets. These assets are treated as held directly by the purchasing member for federal tax purposes. Immediately thereafter the new member and the old member are treated as contributing their respective interests in those assets to a partnership in exchange for an ownership interest in the partnership. The tax consequences are as follows:

- The old member recognizes gain or loss on the deemed sale of the interest in each asset of the LLC to the new member.[2]
- No gain or loss is recognized by either member as a result of the conversion of the disregarded LLC to a partnership.[3]
- The new member's basis in the membership interest is equal to the amount paid by the new member to the old member for the assets that the new member is deemed to have contributed to the newly created LLC. The old member's basis in the membership interest is equal to the old member's basis in his share of the assets of the LLC.[4]
- The basis of property treated as contributed to the LLC by both members is the adjusted basis of that property in the members' hands immediately after the deemed sale.[5]
- The old member's holding period for the membership interest received includes the member's holding period in the capital assets and property held by the LLC when it converted from a single-member LLC to a partnership.[6] The new member's holding period for the membership interest begins on the day following the day of purchase of the LLC interest from the old member.[7] The holding period of each purchased asset is computed by excluding the date on which the asset is acquired. The LLC's holding period for the assets deemed transferred to it includes each member's holding period for such assets.[8] This means that the LLC will have a split holding period for each asset.

[B]   Conversion by Cash Contribution

A single-member LLC may also convert to a partnership when a new member contributes cash to the LLC in exchange for a membership interest. A new member's contribution is treated as a contribution to a partnership in exchange for an

---

[2] Rev. Rul. 99-5, 1999-5 I.R.B. 8 (*citing* IRC §1001).
[3] Rev. Rul. 99-5, 1999-5 I.R.B. 8 (*citing* IRC §721(a)).
[4] Rev. Rul. 99-5, 1999-5 I.R.B. 8 (*citing* IRC §722).
[5] Rev. Rul. 99-5, 1999-5 I.R.B. 8 (*citing* IRC §723).
[6] Rev. Rul. 99-5, 1999-5 I.R.B. 8 (*citing* IRC §1223(1)).
[7] Rev. Rul. 99-5, 1999-5 I.R.B. 8 (*citing* Rev. Rul. 66-7, 1966-1 C.B. 188).
[8] Rev. Rul. 99-5, 1999-5 I.R.B. 8 (*citing* IRC §1223(2)).

ownership interest in the LLC. The old member is treated as contributing all of the assets of the LLC to the partnership in exchange for a membership interest. The tax consequences are as follows:

- No gain or loss is recognized by either member as a result of the conversion of the disregarded entity to a partnership.[9]
- The new member's basis in the membership interest is equal to the amount of cash contributed to the LLC plus the basis of any property contributed.[10] The old member's basis in the membership interest is equal to its basis in the assets of the LLC, which assets the old member is treated as contributing to a newly created partnership.
- The basis of property that the old member is deemed to have contributed to the LLC is the adjusted basis of that property in the old member's hands prior to the conversion. The basis of property contributed to the LLC by the new member is the amount of cash and the adjusted basis of property contributed to the LLC.[11]
- The old member's holding period for a membership interest received includes the old member's holding period in the capital and assets deemed contributed upon the conversion from a single-member LLC to a partnership.[12] The new member's holding period for the membership interest begins on the day following the date of the new member's contribution of money and property to the LLC.[13] The LLC's holding period for the assets transferred to it includes the old member's holding period for those assets.[14]

[C]   Employer Identification Member

An LLC that is classified as a disregarded entity must report, calculate, and pay its employment tax obligation under its own name and employer identification number. When the LLC is reclassified as a partnership after expanding to more than one member, the LLC must retain the same employer identification number that it used as a disregarded entity for employment tax and reporting purposes.[15]

§11.18   CONVERSION FROM AN LLC CLASSIFIED AS A PARTNERSHIP TO A DISREGARDED ENTITY

An LLC that is classified as a partnership for federal tax purposes may convert to a disregarded entity if one person purchases all of the membership interests

---

[9] Rev. Rul. 99-5, 1999-5 I.R.B. 8 (*citing* IRC §721(a)).
[10] Rev. Rul. 99-5, 1999-5 I.R.B. 8 (*citing* IRC §722).
[11] Rev. Rul. 99-5, 1999-5 I.R.B. 8 (*citing* IRC §723).
[12] Rev. Rul. 99-5, 1999-5 I.R.B. 8 (*citing* IRC §1223(1)).
[13] Rev. Rul. 99-5, 1999-5 I.R.B. 8 (*citing* Rev. Rul. 66-7, 1966-1 C.B. 188).
[14] Rev. Rul. 99-5, 1999-5 I.R.B. 8 (*citing* IRC §1223(2)).
[15] Rev. Rul. 2001-61, 2001-50 I.R.B. 573.

in the LLC. The LLC may also convert from a partnership to a disregarded entity as a result of a reorganization. The LLC may elect to be classified as a corporation for federal tax purposes. If no election is made, the LLC will be classified as a disregarded entity.[1] The purchase may be made in one of two ways. First, one member of an LLC may purchase all of the membership interests from the other members in the LLC. Second, a third party may purchase all of the membership interests from the members in the LLC.

[A]   *Purchase by One Member from Another*

The partnership status of the LLC will terminate if one member of an LLC purchases all of the membership interests from the other members. After the purchase, the business may be continued by the LLC, assuming that the state permits a single-member LLC. The tax consequences are as follows:

- The partnership status of the LLC terminates when the member purchases all of the membership interests from the other members.[2] The old members must treat the transaction as a sale of a partnership interest.[3] The old members must report gain or loss, if any, resulting from the sale of the membership interests.[4]
- The LLC is deemed to have made a liquidating distribution of all its assets to its members. Following this deemed distribution, the sole remaining member is treated as acquiring the assets that are deemed to have been distributed to the old members in liquidation of the old members' membership interests.[5]
- The remaining member's basis in the assets attributable to the old members' interests in the LLC is the purchase price for the membership interests.[6] The remaining member's holding period for those assets begins on the day immediately following the date of sale.[7]
- Upon termination of the partnership, the remaining member is considered to have received a distribution of assets attributable to the remaining member's former interest in the LLC. The remaining member must recognize gain or loss, if any, on the deemed distribution of those assets.[8] The remaining member would recognize gain only if the amount of money distributed

---

§11.18   [1] Prop. Reg. §301.7701-3(f); Rev. Rul. 2002-49, 2002-32 I.R.B. 288.

[2] Rev. Rul. 99-5, 1999-5 I.R.B. 8 (*citing* IRC §708(b)(1)(A)).

[3] Rev. Rul. 99-6, 1999-5 I.R.B. 6 (*citing* Reg. §1.741-1(b)).

[4] Rev. Rul. 99-6, 1999-5 I.R.B. 6 (*citing* IRC §741).

[5] Rev. Rul. 99-6, 1999-5 I.R.B. 6 (*citing* Edwin E. McCauslen v. Commissioner, 45 T.C. 588 (1966), and Rev. Rul. 67-65, 1967-1 C.B. 168). *See also* Ltr. Rul. 200222026, in which the IRS determined that 100 percent of the LLC assets were deemed distributed to the remaining member when that member, as owner of 99 percent of the membership units, purchased the membership units from a one percent member.

[6] Rev. Rul. 99-6, 1999-5 I.R.B. 6 (*citing* IRC §1012).

[7] Rev. Rul. 99-6, 1999-5 I.R.B. 6 (*citing* Rev. Rul. 66-7, 1966-1 C.B. 188).

[8] Rev. Rul. 99-6, 1999-5 I.R.B. 6 (*citing* IRC §731(a)).

exceeds his basis in his membership interest.[9] The remaining member would recognize loss only if the only property distributed is money and/or inventory and his basis in the membership interest is more than the sum of the money and his basis in the inventory. The remaining member's basis in the assets received in the deemed liquidation of the membership interest is determined under IRC Section 732(b). Under that section, the basis in the distributed assets equals the remaining member's basis in his membership interest, less any money received. The remaining member's holding period for those assets attributable to the remaining member's interest in the LLC includes the LLC's holding period for such assets.[10]

- Any debt that the LLC owes to the remaining member is treated as canceled when the LLC becomes a disregarded entity. However, there is no cancellation of indebtedness income.[11]

[B]   *Purchase of Membership Interests by Third Party*

The partnership status of an LLC will also terminate if a third party who is not a member purchases all of the membership interests in the LLC. The tax consequences are as follows:

- The old members must report gain or loss, if any, resulting from the sale of their membership interests.[12]
- For purposes of classifying the acquisition of membership interests by a new member, the LLC is deemed to have made a liquidating distribution of those assets to its members. Immediately following the distribution, the new member is deemed to have acquired by purchase all of the former LLC's assets.[13]
- The new member's basis in the assets is equal to the cash purchase price for the membership interest.[14] The basis is allocated among the assets in accordance with IRC Section 732(c).[15]
- The new member's holding period for the assets begins on the day immediately following the date of sale.[16]

[C]   *Reorganization*

An LLC that is classified as a partnership may also convert to a disregarded entity as a result of a reorganization after which a single member becomes the

---

[9] IRC §731(a).
[10] Rev. Rul. 99-6, 1999-5 I.R.B. 6 (*citing* IRC §735(b)).
[11] Ltr. Rul. 200222026.
[12] Rev. Rul. 99-6, 1999-5 I.R.B. 6 (*citing* IRC §741).
[13] Rev. Rul. 99-6, 1999-5 I.R.B. 6.
[14] Rev. Rul. 99-6, 1999-5 I.R.B. 6 (*citing* IRC §1012).
[15] Rev. Rul. 99-6, 1999-5 I.R.B. 6 (*citing* Edwin E. McCauslen v. Commissioner, 45 T.C. 588 (1966)).
[16] Rev. Rul. 99-6, 1999-5 I.R.B. 6.

sole owner of the LLC. For example, the conversion of membership interests in an LLC into shares of stock in a corporation that is the sole owner of the LLC results in a change in classification of the LLC from a partnership to a disregarded entity. The tax consequences of such reorganizations are discussed above.[17]

[D] Employer Identification Number

When an LLC that is classified as a partnership becomes a single-member LLC, it may elect to calculate, report, and pay employment taxes under its own name and employer identification number.[18] After the conversion, the LLC must retain the same employer identification number for employment tax purposes that it used as a partnership. For all federal tax purposes other than employment tax obligations and reporting, or except as otherwise provided in applicable regulations and IRS notices, the LLC must use the taxpayer identification number of its owner (assuming that it is classified as a disregarded entity).[19]

§11.19 MERGER BETWEEN TWO LLCS

[A] LLCs Classified as Partnerships

[1] General Rules

An LLC may merge into another LLC where both LLCs are classified as partnerships for federal tax purposes. The regulations refer to the surviving LLC as the resulting LLC. The resulting LLC is a continuation of the merging LLC whose members own more than 50 percent of the capital and profits interests in the resulting LLC. If the resulting LLC is a continuation of more than one of the merging LLCs, the resulting LLC is a continuation of the merging LLC that is credited with the contribution of assets having the greatest fair market value, net of liabilities. Any other merging LLC is considered terminated. If the members of none of the merging LLCs own more than a 50 percent interest in the capital and profits of the resulting LLC, all of the merging LLCs are treated as terminated, and a new LLC results.[1]

[2] Forms of Merger

The tax consequences of a merger between LLCs depend on the form of merger. There are two forms of merger: the assets-over form and the assets-up form.

---

[17] See §7.03[I] supra.
[18] Rev. Rul. 2001-61, 2001-50 I.R.B. 573, citing Notice 99-6, 1999-1 C.B. 321.
[19] Rev. Rul. 2001-61, 2001-50 I.R.B. 573, citing Reg. §301.6109-1(h)(2)(ii).
§11.19 [1] IRC §708(b)(1)(A); Reg. §1.708-1(c)(1).

[a]   *Assets-Over Form*

In an assets-over form of merger, the terminated LLC is treated as transferring its assets and liabilities to the surviving LLC (the resulting LLC) in exchange for membership interests in the surviving LLC. Immediately thereafter, the terminated LLC is treated as distributing the membership interests in the surviving LLC to the members of the terminated LLC.[2] This is the default form of merger if no form of merger is specified, or if the merger does not qualify as an assets-up form.[3]

The final regulations on mergers do not discuss the tax consequences of the assets-over form of merger in any significant detail. The tax consequences are based on other applicable provisions of the Code, regulations, and rulings. The Preamble to the proposed regulations on partnership and LLC mergers also summarizes in detail the laws applicable to assets-over form mergers.[4] The tax consequences are as follows:

- The terminated LLC and its members do not recognize gain or loss on the transfer of assets and liabilities to the surviving LLC in exchange for membership interests in the surviving LLC.[5]
- The surviving LLC's basis in assets received from the terminated LLC equals the terminated LLC's basis in the assets at the time of the merger.[6]
- The terminated LLC receives a basis in the membership interests in the surviving LLC equal to the amount of money and the adjusted basis of property contributed to the surviving LLC on the date of the merger.[7]
- Immediately after the merger, the terminated LLC is deemed to have distributed the membership interests in the surviving LLC to the members of the terminated LLC in liquidation of their interest in the terminated LLC.[8]
- The members of the terminated LLC receive a basis in the membership interests in the surviving LLC equal to the basis of their membership interests in the terminated LLC, reduced by any money distributed in the same transaction.[9] Thus, any disparity between the members' outside basis in the membership interests and the surviving LLC's inside basis in the contributed assets will continue after the merger. However, if the surviving LLC makes an election under Section 754, the members of the terminated LLC will receive a special basis adjustment under Section 743 of the Code. The

---

[2] Reg. §§1.708-1(c)(3)(i), 1.708-1(c)(5), Example 2.

[3] Reg. §1.708-1(c)(3)(i).

[4] REG-111119-99, 2000-5 I.R.B. 455.

[5] Ltr. Ruls. 9720008-013, 9719015, 9719019-029 (*citing* IRC §721.)

[6] REG-111119-99, 2000-5 I.R.B. 455 (*citing* IRC §723); Ltr. Ruls. 9720008-013, 9719015, 9719019-029 (*citing* IRC §723).

[7] Ltr. Ruls. 9720008-013, 9719015, 9719019-029 (*citing* IRC §722).

[8] Ltr. Ruls. 9720008-013, 9719015, 9719019-029.

[9] Ltr. Ruls. 9720008-013, 9719015, 9719019-029 (*citing* IRC §732(b)).

amount of the basis adjustment is the difference between the members' outside basis in their membership interests and their share of inside basis.[10]

- A member will not recognize gain under IRC Section 752 as a result of the transfer of liabilities from the terminated LLC to the surviving LLC unless there is a net decrease in the member's share of liabilities.[11] In such case, gain is recognized to the extent that the net decrease in liabilities exceeds the member's basis in the membership interest of the surviving LLC.[12]

- The members of the LLC do not recognize gain under the disguised sales and anti-mixing bowl rules since there is no distribution of assets to the members.[13] However, the transfer of encumbered property from the terminated LLC to the surviving LLC is subject to the disguised sales rules under Section 707(a)(2)(B). The terminated LLC cannot, in anticipation of the merger, encumber its assets and distribute the loan proceeds to the members. No gain or loss is recognized under the disguised sales rules if the liabilities transferred are "qualified liabilities." Liabilities are qualified liabilities if the loan proceeds were used to fund capital improvements, the loan proceeds were used to pay for ordinary and necessary expenses of operating the property, or the loans are long-standing in duration.[14] The disguised sales and anti-mixing bowl rules are discussed in Chapter 6.[15]

- The surviving LLC must continue to use the same period and method of depreciation and amortization after the merger as each merging LLC used prior to the merger.[16]

- After the merger, the surviving LLC must allocate any built-in gain to the members who contributed appreciated property to either the terminated or the surviving LLC.[17] Under Section 704(c), built-in gain must be allocated to the contributing member when the property is sold.[18]

- The tax year of the terminated LLC closes.[19]

---

[10] See Sloan, E.B., Lipton, R., Harrington, D., and Frediani, M., "New Prop. Regs. Provide Expanding Guidance on Partnership Mergers and Divisions—Part 2," pp. 261, 262 (JTAX Nov. 2000). The article also discusses the allocation of the basis adjustment to the LLC assets after a merger.

[11] Reg. §§1.752-1(f) (last sentence), 1.752-1(g), Example 2.

[12] REG-111119-99, 2000-5 I.R.B. 455 (citing IRC §752); Ltr. Ruls. 9720008-013, 9719015, 9719019-029 (citing IRC §752 and Reg. §§1.752-1(a)(2), 1.752-1(f)).

[13] REG-111119-99, 2000-5 I.R.B. 455 (citing IRC §§704(c)(1)(B), 737, and Reg. §§1.704-4(c)(4), 1.737-2(b)).

[14] Ltr. Ruls. 9720008-013, 9719015, 9719019-029 (citing IRC §707(a)(2)(B) and Reg. §§1.707-3(c)(1), 1.707-5(a)(6)(i)). The disguised sales rules are discussed in §6.05 supra.

[15] See §§6.05[B], 6.05[C] supra, which discuss the disguised sales rules under IRC §§704(c)(1)(B), 737, cited by the IRS in the preamble to the proposed regulations on partnership and LLC mergers.

[16] IRC §168(i)(7); Rev. Rul. 90-17,1990-1 C.B. 119; Reg. §§1.197-2(g)(2)(iv)(C), 1.197-2(g)(2)(ii)(B), 1.197-2(g)(3). See also Sloan, E.B., Lipton, R., Harrington, D., and Frediani, M., "New Prop. Regs. Provide Expanding Guidance on Partnership Mergers and Divisions—Part 2," pp. 263, 264, under the heading "Recovery Periods—Depreciation and Amortization" (JTAX Nov. 2000).

[17] Ltr. Ruls. 9720008-013, 9719015, 9719019-029.

[18] The built-in gain rules are discussed in §8.03 supra.

[19] Reg. §§1.708-1(c)(2), 1.708-1(c)(5), Example 1.

[b]   Assets-Up Form

In an assets-up form of merger, the LLC distributes its assets and liabilities to the members. The members then contribute the assets and liabilities to the surviving LLC in exchange for membership interests in the surviving LLC. This form of merger is less common than the assets-over form.[20]

The assets-up form of merger requires that the terminated LLC actually transfer ownership of its assets to the members under state law. A mere assignment of the right to receive title to the assets is not sufficient. If the members of the LLC do not become owners, then the merger will be treated as an assets-over form of merger.[21] The members are not required to assume the liabilities of the terminated LLC. The terminated LLC may transfer the liabilities directly to the surviving LLC.[22]

The final regulations on mergers do not discuss the tax consequences of the assets-up form of merger in any significant detail. The tax consequences are based on other applicable provisions of the Code, regulations, and rulings. The Preamble to the proposed regulations on partnership and LLC mergers also summarizes in detail the laws applicable to assets-up forms of mergers.[23] The tax consequences are as follows:[24]

- The LLC that distributed assets to members terminates on the date of distribution.[25]
- The basis of assets distributed to each member on liquidation of the membership interest is equal to the member's outside basis in the membership interest, reduced by any money received in the distribution.[26]
- The transfer of liabilities to the members has no effect on the members' basis in the assets. The decrease in their share of LLC liabilities is normally equal to their corresponding individual assumption of liabilities.[27]
- The members of the terminated LLC may recognize gain under the disguised sales and anti-mixing bowl rules if the members previously contributed appreciated assets to the LLC.[28] The disguised sales and anti-mixing bowl rules are discussed in Chapter 6.[29]

---

[20] Reg. §1.708-1(c)(3)(ii).

[21] *Id.*

[22] *Id. See also* T.D. 8925, IRS Final Regulations on Partnership Mergers and Divisions, Explanation of Revisions and Summary of Contents (Jan. 4, 2001).

[23] REG-111119-99, 2000-5 I.R.B. 455.

[24] This form of merger is similar to Rev. Rul. 84-111, 1984-2 C.B. 88, Scenario (2), in which an LLC converted into a corporation by first distributing its assets and liabilities to the members, who then contributed the assets to the corporation.

[25] Rev. Rul. 84-111, 1984-2 C.B. 88 (*citing* IRC §708(b)(1)(A)).

[26] REG-111119-99, 2000-5 I.R.B. 455 (*citing* IRC §732); Rev. Rul. 84-111, 1984-2 C.B. 88 (*citing* IRC §732(b)).

[27] Rev. Rul. 84-111, 1984-2 C.B. 88 (*citing* IRC §752).

[28] REG-111119-99, 2000-5 I.R.B. 455 (*citing* IRC §§704(c)(1)(B), 737).

[29] *See* §§6.05[B], 6.05[C] *supra*, which discuss the disguised sales rules under IRC §§704(c)(1)(B), 737, cited by the IRS in the preamble to the proposed regulations on partnership and LLC mergers.

- The members do not recognize gain or loss on the transfer to the surviving LLC of assets and liabilities in exchange for membership interests in the surviving LLC.[30]
- The members of the LLC receive a basis in the membership interests in the surviving LLC equal to their basis in the assets distributed on liquidation of the LLC.[31]
- The surviving LLC's basis in the assets received from the members of the LLC is the same as the members' basis in such assets immediately prior to the transfer.[32]
- The members' holding period for non-cash assets distributed to them includes the LLC's holding period for such assets.[33]
- The members' holding period for membership interest in the surviving LLC includes their holding periods in the capital assets and Section 1231 assets transferred to the surviving LLC (to the extent membership interests were received in exchange for such assets).[34] The members' holding period for membership interests received in exchange for other assets begins on the date following the date of the exchange.
- The surviving LLC's holding periods for the assets include the members' holding periods for such assets.[35]
- The surviving LLC must continue to use the same period and method of depreciation and amortization after the merger as each merging LLC used prior to the merger. However, it must treat the property as newly acquired property for depreciation purposes to the extent that the basis of the assets exceeds its basis prior to the merger as a result of the distribution to the members.[36]
- The members of the terminated LLC may recognize state and local transfer taxes on the distribution.[37]
- The tax year of the terminated LLC closes.[38]

[c]   Which Method to Choose

The assets-up form is preferable if the members of the LLC have an aggregate basis in their membership interests that is higher than the LLC's basis in its assets. In an assets-up form, the surviving LLC receives a basis in the assets determined

---

[30] IRC §721(a).

[31] IRC §722.

[32] REG-111119-99, 2000-5 I.R.B. 455 (*citing* IRC §723.)

[33] Rev. Rul. 84-111, 1984-2 C.B. 88 (*citing* IRC §735(b)).

[34] Rev. Rul. 84-111, 1984-2 C.B. 88 (*citing* IRC §1223(1)).

[35] Rev. Rul. 84-111, 1984-2 C.B. 88 (*citing* IRC §1223(2)).

[36] IRC §168(i)(7); Rev. Rul. 90-17,1990-1 C.B. 119; Reg. §§1.197-2(g)(2)(iv)(C), 1.197-2(g)(2)(ii)(B), 1.197-2(g)(3). *See also* Sloan, E.B., Lipton, R., Harrington, D., and Frediani, M., "New Prop. Regs. Provide Expanding Guidance on Partnership Mergers and Divisions—Part 2," pp. 263, 264, under the heading "Recovery Periods—Depreciation and Amortization" (JTAX Nov. 2000).

[37] REG-111119-99, 2000-5 I.R.B. 455.

[38] Reg. §§1.708-1(c)(2), 1.708-1(c)(5), Example 1.

by reference to the members' basis in the terminated LLC. In an asset-over form, the LLC receives a carryover basis for the assets determined by reference to the basis of the assets in the hands of the terminated LLC.[39]

The assets-over form may be preferable if the LLC transfers a substantial amount of cash to the new corporation. Under the assets-up form, the members' holding period for membership interests received in exchange for cash begins on the day after the merger. Under the assets-over form, the holding period for membership interests in the surviving LLC includes the holding period for the membership interests in the terminated LLC.[40]

The LLC may be required to recapture investment tax credits under the assets-up form. Recapture is required since the surviving LLC receives a substituted rather than a carryover basis for the assets.

The IRS determined that the assets-over form is generally preferable for both the IRS and taxpayers.[41] The reason is that the members of an LLC do not recognize gain under the disguised sales rules in an assets-over form but may recognize gain in an assets-up form. The IRS also noted that the surviving LLC in a merger receives a carryover basis for the assets, rather than a new basis determined by reference to the members' aggregate basis in the terminated LLC.

[3]   Tax Returns

The terminated LLC must file a tax return for the tax year ending on the date of the merger.

The surviving LLC must file a tax return for the entire tax year. The return must state that the surviving LLC is a continuation of the merged LLCs. The return must include the names, addresses, and employer identification numbers of the terminated LLCs. It must show as part of the return the distributive shares of the members for the periods prior to and including the date of the merger and subsequent to the date of the merger. The surviving LLC must continue to use the same employer identification number[42] and the same tax year.[43]

EXAMPLE

Member A and B are members in AB LLC. Each owns a 50 percent interest in the LLC. Members C and D are members in CD LLC. Each owns a 50 percent interest in the LLC. The LLCs merge on September 30, 2001, and form ABCD LLC. All the members have a calendar year. The LLCs also have

---

[39] REG-111119-99, 2000-5 I.R.B. 455.

[40] The holding period for membership interests received in exchange for all other assets would be the same regardless of the former merger. Under IRC §735(b), a member's holding period or property received in a distribution includes the LLC's holding period for such assets.

[41] REG-111119-99, 2000-5 I.R.B. 455.

[42] Reg. §1.708-1(c)(2).

[43] Reg. §1.708-1(c)(5), Example 1.

a calendar year. After the merger, the members have a capital and profits interest in the LLC as follows: A–30 percent; B–30 percent; C–20 percent; D–20 percent. Since Members A and B together own more than 50 percent of the capital and profits of ABCD LLC, that LLC is considered a continuation of AB LLC. It must continue to file a tax return to the calendar year basis. Since Members C and D own less than 50 percent in the capital and profits of ABCD LLC, the tax year of CD LLC closes as of September 30, 2001, the date of the merger. CD LLC is terminated as of that date. ABCD LLC must file a return for the tax year from January 1, 2001, to December 31, 2001. It must indicate on the return that it was AB LLC until September 30, 2001. CD LLC must file a return for its final tax year from January 1, 2001, until September 30, 2001.[44]

[B] LLCs Classified as Corporations

An LLC may merge into another LLC where both LLCs are classified as corporations for federal tax purposes. The tax consequences are the same as for a reorganization between two regular corporations.

A merger between related LLCs and similar reorganizations and consolidations of related LLCs are normally treated as a nondivisive D reorganization. For example, if a parent merged two subsidiary LLCs that were classified as corporations for federal tax purposes, the transaction would be characterized as follows:

- A transfer of assets of the first subsidiary to the second subsidiary in exchange for the membership interests of the second subsidiary, constituting a D reorganization.
- The distribution by the first subsidiary to the parent corporation of the membership interests in the second subsidiary, constituting a Section 354(b)(2) distribution.

The IRS determined that there was a nondivisive D reorganization in the three following cases:

1. A corporation merged into an LLC. The LLC did not issue shares in the merger, since LLCs did not issue stock under applicable laws. Both the corporation and the LLC were owned equally by two unrelated corporations (or their affiliates).[45]
2. An LLC merged into a corporation. The LLC and the corporation were both owned by the same corporation.[46]

---

[44] Prop. Reg. §1.708-1(c)(5), Example 1.

[45] Ltr. Rul. 7948066. *See also* Ltr. Rul. 7852111 (corporation merged into LLC; corporation and LLC appeared to have common shareholders).

[46] Ltr. Rul. 7947048.

3.   A parent corporation owned a German limited liability company (GmbH).
     The parent also owned a Swiss corporation that owned another German
     limited liability company. There was a series of transfers of assets, liabilities,
     and stock, after which the parent owned a single GmbH, which in turn
     owned the other GmbH (with the Swiss corporation liquidated into the
     parent).[47]

Generally, a D reorganization has the same tax consequences as an A reorganization with one exception. Gain is recognized if liabilities exceed the tax basis of
assets transferred in a D reorganization even if the transaction also meets the
requirements for an A reorganization.[48] This problem can be avoided by having
a reverse merger in which the corporation with liabilities in excess of basis is the
surviving corporation.[49]

§11.20   MERGER OF C CORPORATION INTO LLC

[A]   *LLC Classified as Partnership*

A C corporation may merge or convert[1] into an LLC that is classified as a
partnership for federal tax purposes. The merger has the following tax consequences:

* The merger is treated as a transfer of assets by the corporation to the LLC
  in exchange for the assumption of liabilities by the LLC and the corporation's
  receipt of LLC membership interests, followed by the corporation's distribution of the LLC membership interests to the corporation's shareholders in
  a complete liquidation.[2]
* The corporation and the LLC do not recognize gain or loss upon the transfer
  of assets to the LLC in exchange for the membership interests.[3]
* The corporation recognizes gain or loss upon the corporation's distribution
  of the ownership interests in the LLC to the LLC members in the complete
  liquidation of the corporation.[4] Gain or loss is recognized to the same extent
  as if the corporation sold the distributed membership interests for their fair
  market value to the members.[5]
* The shareholders of the corporation recognize capital gain or loss upon the
  deemed distribution of the LLC membership interests from the corporation
  to its shareholders. The distribution is treated as full payment in exchange

---

[47] Ltr. Rul. 7950044.
[48] IRC §357(c).
[49] *See* Rev. Rul. 75-161, 1975-1 C.B. 114.
§11.20   [1] *See, e.g.,* Wy. Stat. §17-16-1115.
[2] Ltr. Ruls. 200214016, 9701029, 9543023, 9409021, 9409016, 9404014.
[3] Ltr. Ruls. 200214016, 9701029, 9409014, 9409016, 9404024 (*citing* IRC §721(a)).
[4] Ltr. Rul. 9701029.
[5] Ltr. Ruls. 200214016, 9701029 (*citing* IRC §336).

for their stock in the corporation.[6] The amount of gain is the difference between the fair market value of the LLC membership interests and the shareholders' basis in their stock. However, if the shareholder is the parent corporation of the corporation that merges into the LLC, no gain or loss is recognized upon the distribution of the LLC membership interests from the subsidiary to the parent.[7]

- If the LLC makes a Section 754 election to adjust the basis of LLC property before the merger, the distribution of the membership interests to the shareholders constitutes a transfer under Section 743. The LLC must then adjust the basis of its assets under Sections 743 and 755.[8]

- The corporation's distribution of membership interests to the shareholders constitutes an exchange that causes the LLC to terminate.[9] The termination results in a deemed distribution of the LLC's assets to the shareholders and a deemed immediate recontribution of those assets to a new LLC by the members.[10] However, the old and new LLCs, the members and the corporation will not recognize gain or loss as a result of the deemed termination.[11]

- The merger of a corporation into an LLC classified as a partnership, or into an LLC classified as a disregarded entity that is owned by a partnership, does not qualify as a tax-free reorganization under IRC Section 368(a)(1)(A).[12]

- The consolidation by a parent corporation of two wholly owned subsidiaries through a disregarded LLC is treated as a D reorganization.[13]

[B] LLC Classified as Corporation

A corporation may merge into an LLC that is classified as a corporation for federal tax purposes. The tax consequences are the same as for a reorganization between two regular corporations.[14] For example, the merger of an LLC into a corporation is a Section 368(a)(1)(A) reorganization.[15] The reincorporation of an LLC from one state to another through merger of an LLC into a corporation (or an LLC classified as a corporation) is a Section 368(a)(1)(F) reorganization.[16] The merger of an LLC into a parent corporation is treated as a Section 332 liquidation.[17]

---

[6] Ltr. Ruls. 200214016, 9701029 (citing IRC §331(a)).

[7] Ltr. Ruls. 9543023, 9409021, 9409016, 9404014 (citing IRC §§332(a), 337). The subsidiary is treated as having liquidated into its parent as a result of the merger into the LLC.

[8] Ltr. Rul. 9701029.

[9] Ltr. Rul. 200214016; IRC §708(b)(1)(B).

[10] Ltr. Rul. 9701029 (citing Reg. §1.708(b)(1)(iv)).

[11] Ltr. Rul. 200214016.

[12] Prop. Reg. §1.368-2(b)(1)(iv), Example 4.

[13] Ltr. Rul. 200102038.

[14] Ltr. Rul. 200119016.

[15] Ltr. Rul. 200204004.

[16] Ltr. Rul. 200119016.

[17] Ltr. Rul. 200204004.

The merger of a corporation into an LLC that is classified as an S corporation will not adversely affect the LLC's status as an S corporation.[18]

A corporation may want to convert to an LLC that is classified as a corporation in order to obtain the non-tax benefits available to an LLC under state law.[19]

[C] LLC Classified as Disregarded Entity

The merger of a corporation into a single-member LLC that is a disregarded entity qualifies as a tax-free reorganization under IRC Section 368(a)(1)(A) if the following requirements are met:[20]

- The LLC is owned by a corporation.[21]
- The merger is made pursuant to state or federal law.[22] The transferor corporation, the transferee LLC, and the corporate owner of the transferee LLC are organized under the laws of the United States, a state, or the District of Columbia.[23]
- All the assets and liabilities of the transferor corporation become the assets and liabilities of the LLC.[24] The corporation may distribute assets to its shareholders before transferring its remaining assets to the LLC in the merger, even though a distribution prior to a merger would not be allowed in other types of reorganizations. The "all assets" test is met if a disregarded entity owned by the corporate transferor becomes a disregarded entity owned by the transferee LLC, or merges into the transferee LLC or another entity owned by the corporate owner of the transferee LLC.[25]
- The separate legal existence of the transferor corporation ceases after the merger.[26] The transferor or its agent may continue to act after the merger in limited circumstances, such as lawsuits related to its assets or liabilities that arose prior to the merger.
- The shareholders of the corporation that merges into the LLC receive stock in the corporation that owns the LLC,[27] or stock in a corporation that owns the corporate owner of the LLC in a triangular merger.[28] The shareholders of the transferee corporation cannot receive membership interests in the LLC[29] since that would result in a division of the transferee entity into two

---

[18] Ltr. Rul. 200248023.
[19] Ltr. Rul. 200119016.
[20] Reg. §1.368-2T(b)(1); Ltr. Rul. 200236005.
[21] Reg. §1.368-2T(b)(1)(i)(B).
[22] Reg. §1.368-2T(b)(1)(ii).
[23] Reg. §§1.368-2T(b)(1)(iii), 1.368-2T(b)(1)(iv), Example 2(ii).
[24] Reg. §1.368-2T(b)(1)(ii)(A).
[25] Reg. §1.368-2T(b)(1)(iv), Example 2(ii).
[26] Reg. §1.368-2T(b)(1)(ii)(B).
[27] Reg. §1.368-2T(b)(1)(iv), Example 2; Ltr. Rul. 200236005.
[28] Reg. §1.368-2T(b)(1)(iv), Example 4.
[29] Prop. Reg. §1.368-2T(b)(1)(iv), Example 7.

separate entities (the transferee corporation owned by its shareholders and the LLC owned by the shareholders of the transferor corporation).

- The corporation merges into the LLC. The merger of an LLC that is classified as a disregarded entity into a corporation does not qualify as a tax-free reorganization under IRC Section 368(a)(1)(A).[30]

The merger or conversion of a subsidiary corporation into a disregarded LLC owned by the parent corporation qualifies as a tax-free liquidation under IRC Section 332.[31]

§11.21   MERGER OF LLC INTO C CORPORATION

The merger of an LLC that is classified as a disregarded entity into a corporation does not qualify as a tax-free reorganization under IRC Section 368(a)(1)(A),[1] unless the corporate owner of the LLC also merges into the transferee corporation. However, the transfer of assets and liabilities from the disregarded LLC to the corporation normally qualifies as a tax-free exchange under IRC Section 351.[2]

The merger of an LLC that is classified as a corporation into a corporation may qualify as a tax-free reorganization under the regular reorganization provisions of the Code.[3]

The merger of an LLC that is classified as a partnership into a corporation is taxed in the same manner as the incorporation of an LLC.[4]

§11.22   MERGER OF LLC INTO LIMITED
PARTNERSHIP

An LLC may merge into a limited partnership, after which the members of the LLC are treated as limited partners.[1] The merger of an LLC into a limited partnership is treated in the same manner as a merger between LLCs that are classified as partnerships. The merger is either an assets-over form or an assets-up form of

---

[30] Prop. Reg. §1.368-2T(b)(1)(iv), Example 6. *See also* IRS Proposed Rules (REG-126485-01) and Hearing Notice on Definition of Statutory Merger or Consolidation, under the heading, "B. Mergers Involving Disregarded Entities" (Nov. 15, 2001).

[31] Ltr. Ruls. 200139009, 200129024; Ltr. Rul. 2003108005 (rulings with respect to the "Sub 2 Merger" and the Sub 5 Conversion"); Ltr. Rul. 200305017 (in which the IRS treated the merger of a wholly owned subsidiary corporation of a foreign parent corporation into a disregarded LLC owned by the foreign parent corporation as a liquidation of the subsidiary corporation into the foreign parent corporation, subject to IRC §§331 and 336).

§11.21 [1] Reg. §1.368-2(b)(1)(iv), Example 6. *See also* IRS Proposed Rules (REG-126485-01) and Hearing Notice on Definition of Statutory Merger or Consolidation, under the heading, "B. Mergers Involving Disregarded Entities" (Nov. 15, 2001).

[2] *See* §11.06[C] *supra.*

[3] Ltr. Rul. 200005016. *See also* §11.06[B] *supra.*

[4] *See* §11.06[A] *supra.*

§11.22 [1] Ltr. Ruls. 200129018, 200125037, 9720008-013, 9719019-029, 9719015.

merger. The tax consequences of each of these forms of merger are discussed in §11.19.

Generally, the members do not recognize gain or loss as a result of the merger. There is one important exception. A member may recognize gain if there is a net decrease in liabilities allocated to the member as a result of the merger.[2]

The members of the terminated LLC are relieved of liabilities when those liabilities are transferred to the limited partnership in a merger. The members of the terminated LLC are then allocated a share of liabilities in the surviving LLC. The IRS permits the members to net the relief of liabilities in the LLC and the assumption of liabilities in the limited partnership in determining taxable gain.[3] The net increase in the member's share of liabilities is treated as a contribution of money to the member. There is no taxable gain in such case. The net decrease in the member's share of liabilities is treated as a distribution of money to the member. The member recognizes gain to the extent that the net decrease in liabilities exceeds the member's outside basis.

The problem arises in a limited partnership merger because the nonrecourse liabilities of the LLC often become recourse liabilities after the transfer to a limited partnership. There must be one general partner in a limited partnership. Under state law, a general partner is personally liable for the debts of the limited partnership (with certain exceptions).[4] Therefore, the nonrecourse liabilities of the LLC prior to the merger (which are normally allocated to all of the members based on their profit sharing percentage in the LLC) are converted into recourse liabilities of the limited partnership after the merger. Recourse liabilities must be allocated to the general partner, or to any limited partner who is personally liable for such debts. The result is that a member of an LLC who becomes a limited partner after the merger often has a net decrease in the liabilities allocated to the member.

The transfer of recourse liabilities from the LLC to a limited partnership does not result in a deemed distribution of money or taxation to the members if the members who were personally responsible for liabilities prior to the merger continue to be personally liable after the merger.[5]

The merger of an LLC into a limited partnership should be contrasted with a merger of an LLC into another LLC. Generally, the members do not have a net decrease in liabilities as a result of merger between LLCs because nonrecourse liabilities prior to the merger continue to be nonrecourse liabilities after the merger. Each member is allocated a share of nonrecourse liabilities before and after the merger based on his or her profit sharing percentage.

---

[2] REG-111119-99, 2000-5 I.R.B. 455 (*citing* IRC §752); Ltr. Ruls., 9720008-013, 9719019-029, 9719015.

[3] Reg. §§1.752-1(f) (last sentence), 1.752-1(g), Example 2.

[4] For example, a loan secured by a deed of trust or mortgage on real property may be nonrecourse if the loan documents or state law provides that the lender has no recourse except against the property in the event of a default.

[5] Ltr. Ruls., 9720008-013, 9719019-029, 9719015 (*citing* IRC §752 and Reg. §§1.752-1(a)(2), 1.752-1(f)).

§11.23   USE OF LLC TO FACILITATE CORPORATE MERGERS AND ACQUISITIONS

[A]   Overview

Prior to 2003, there were five principal types of tax-free corporate acquisitions: statutory merger or consolidation, forward triangular merger, reverse triangular merger, B reorganization, and C reorganization. Each of these forms of acquisition had significant tax or non-tax problems.

In 2003, the IRS issued temporary regulations that permitted a corporation to use an LLC to facilitate a tax-free corporate acquisition. The regulations provided that an acquiring corporation could form an LLC classified as a disregarded entity, and then merge the target corporation into the LLC. The merger would be judged by the lenient standards of a statutory merger or consolidation, rather than the stricter standards of the four other types of tax-free acquisitions.

As a result, an acquiring corporation now has one more method of acquiring a target corporation in a tax-free reorganization without many of the problems associated with the five other types of tax-free acquisitions.

[B]   Types of Tax-Free Acquisitions

Prior to 2003, the five major types of tax-free acquisitions, and the tax and non-tax problems associated with each form of acquisition, were as follows:

- *Statutory merger or consolidation.* In a statutory merger or consolidation, the acquiring corporation merges with the target corporation pursuant to state law.[1] The acquiring corporation is normally the surviving corporation. The statutory merger or consolidation is the most flexible type of tax-free reorganization. The parties must comply with the continuity of business enterprise rules[2] and the continuity of proprietary interest rules,[3] which are not difficult to meet. Up to 50 percent or more of the consideration paid to the shareholders of the target corporation may be cash. There are two major non-tax problems with a statutory merger. The first is that the acquiring corporation must obtain the consent of its shareholders, since the acquiring corporation is a party to the reorganization under state law. This is often impractical for a large publicly-traded corporation. The second problem is that the acquiring corporation must assume all the liabilities of the target corporation, including contingent and unknown liabilities, since both the target and the acquiring corporation merge together into a single corporation.
- *Forward triangular merger.* In a forward triangular merger, the acquiring corporation forms a subsidiary. The target corporation merges into the subsidiary. The shareholders of the target corporation receive stock in the

---

§11.23   [1] IRC §368(a)(1)(A).
[2] Reg. §1.368-1(d).
[3] Reg. §1.368-1(e).

parent corporation. They may also receive up to 50 percent or more of the aggregate consideration in cash in exchange for their shares in the target corporation.[4] This type of merger is often preferable to the statutory merger. The parent corporation is not subject to any of the liabilities of the target corporation (except under the piercing the corporate veil doctrine). Only the newly formed subsidiary assumes the liabilities of the target corporation. The acquiring corporation is not required to obtain approval from its shareholders. However, there are several non-tax problems with a forward triangular merger. The target corporation is often required to obtain the consent of its lenders, landlords, and other persons with which it has contracts in order to assign or transfer the contracts to the new subsidiary corporation. The subsidiary corporation must apply for new licenses and permits in its own name from state and local agencies. Title insurance policies in the name of the old target corporation may no longer be valid.

- *Reverse triangular merger.* In a reverse triangular merger, the acquiring corporation forms a subsidiary. The subsidiary corporation merges into the target corporation (rather than vice versa as under a forward triangular merger).[5] The reverse triangular merger is similar to a forward triangular merger in several respects. The shareholders of the target corporation receive stock in the parent corporation and/or cash up to 50 percent of the aggregate consideration in exchange for their shares in the target corporation. Again, the parent corporation is not subject to any of the liabilities of the target corporation. The parent corporation is not required to obtain the consent of the shareholders. The reverse triangular merger is often preferable to the forward triangular merger in several ways. Since the target corporation is the surviving corporation, it is not required to obtain new licenses and permits from state and local agencies. It does not ordinarily need to obtain the consent of lenders, landlords, and other persons with which it has contracts (although a change in ownership of the target corporation may trigger due-on-sale clauses in the loan documents and deeds of trust, or otherwise require the consent of the other party under the terms the contract). There is one major tax problem with a reverse triangular merger. At least 80 percent of the consideration received by the target shareholders must be stock of the acquiring parent corporation.[6] This differs from a statutory merger or consolidation and a forward triangular merger in which 50 percent or more of the consideration may be cash rather than stock in the acquiring parent corporation.

- *B reorganization.* In a B reorganization, the acquiring corporation acquires stock in the target corporation solely in exchange for its voting stock (with one extremely limited exception).[7] The problem with this type of reorganization is that the shareholders of the target corporation may not receive any cash in exchange for their shares.

---

[4] IRC §§368(a)(1)(A), (D).
[5] IRC §368(a)(1)(A), (E).
[6] IRC §368(a)(1)(E).
[7] IRC §368(a)(1)(B).

- *C reorganization.* In a C reorganization, the acquiring corporation acquires substantially all the assets of the target corporation solely in exchange for its voting stock.[8] Again, the major problem is that the shareholders of the target corporation may not receive any cash in exchange for their shares.

[C] Requirements for Merger Using LLC

Under the 2003 IRS regulations, the acquiring corporation may acquire a target corporation in a tax-free merger by forming an LLC, and then merging the target corporation into an LLC, if the following requirements are met:[9]

- The acquiring corporation is the sole owner of the LLC.[10] The LLC is normally classified as a disregarded entity, although it may also be classified as a corporation.
- The acquiring corporation, the target corporation, and the LLC must be organized under the laws of the United States, a state, or the District of Columbia.[11]
- The target corporation must merge into the LLC pursuant to state or federal law.[12]
- All the assets and liabilities of the target corporation must become the assets and liabilities of the LLC.[13] However, the target corporation may distribute assets and liabilities to its shareholders prior to the merger.
- The separate legal existence of the target corporation must terminate after the merger.[14] However, the target corporation or its agents may continue to act after the merger in limited circumstances, such as lawsuits related to its assets or liabilities that arose prior to the merger.
- The shareholders of the target corporation must receive stock in the acquiring corporation[15] or stock in a corporation that owns the acquiring corporation in a triangular merger.[16] The shareholders of the target corporation cannot receive membership interests in the LLC[17] since that would result in a division of the acquiring entity into two separate entities (the acquiring corporation owned by its shareholders and the LLC owned by the shareholders of the target corporation).

The regulations achieve these results by defining two new terms: "combining entity" and "combining unit." A combining entity is a corporation.[18] A combining

---

[8] IRC §368(a)(1)(C).
[9] Reg. §1.368-2T(b)(1); Ltr. Rul. 200236005.
[10] Reg. §1.368-2T(b)(1)(i)(B).
[11] Reg. §§1.368-2T(b)(1)(iii), 1.368-2T(b)(1)(iv), Example 2(ii).
[12] Reg. §1.368-2T(b)(1)(ii).
[13] Reg. §1.368-2T(b)(1)(ii)(A).
[14] Reg. §1.368-2T(b)(1)(ii)(B).
[15] Reg. §1.368-2T(b)(1)(iv), Example 2; Ltr. Rul. 200236005.
[16] Reg. §1.368-2T(b)(1)(iv), Example 3.
[17] Reg. §1.368-2T(b)(1)(iv), Example 6.
[18] Reg. §1.368-2T(b)(1)(i)(B).

unit is a combining entity and all disregarded entities that are owned by the combining entity.[19] The assets and liabilities of one combining unit become the assets and liabilities of the other combining unit in the merger, except for the assets of the target corporation distributed to its shareholders prior to the merger. The separate legal existence of the combining entity terminates after the merger.[20]

[D]   Advantages and Disadvantages of Using LLC to Facilitate a Merger

[1]   Advantages

There are a number of advantages in using an LLC to facilitate a tax-free acquisition, including the following:

- The shareholders of the target corporation may receive up to 50 percent of the consideration in cash in a merger using an LLC. In a reverse triangular merger, the shareholders may only receive 20 percent of the consideration in cash. In a B reorganization or a C reorganization, the shareholders may not receive any cash.
- The acquiring corporation does not have to assume any other liabilities of the target corporation in a merger using an LLC. All the liabilities are assumed by the LLC that is owned by the acquiring corporation.
- The target corporation may distribute assets to its shareholders before transferring its remaining assets to the LLC in a merger using an LLC. A distribution by the target corporation prior to an acquisition is not allowed in other types of reorganizations. The acquiring corporation must acquire substantially all the assets of the target corporation in a forward triangular merger, reverse triangular merger, B reorganization, or C reorganization.[21]

As a result of the 2003 regulations, it is now possible for an acquiring corporation to acquire a target corporation using a wholly-owned limited liability company rather than a corporation as the surviving entity. This achieves the results of a forward triangular merger, with the reorganization status tested under less stringent standards of a direct statutory merger.

EXAMPLE

An acquiring corporation wants to acquire a target corporation in a tax-free reorganization. The shareholders of the target corporation want 50 percent of

---

[19] Reg. §1.368-2T(b)(1)(i)(C).

[20] Reg. §1.368-2T(b)(1)(ii).

[21] Reg. §1.368-2T(b)(1)(iv), Example 2(ii). The "all assets" test is also met if an LLC owned by the target corporation is owned by the acquiring corporation after the merger, or merges into the transferee LLC or another entity owned by the acquiring corporation.

the consideration in cash and the balance in stock of the acquiring corporation. The shareholders also want to receive a distribution of certain valuable assets of the target corporation before the merger. Prior to 2003, the only available type of tax-free reorganization was a direct statutory merger or consolidation. A forward triangular merger could not be used since the acquiring corporation was not acquiring substantially all the assets of the target corporate. A reverse triangular merger could not be used since the acquiring corporation was paying more than 20 percent of the consideration in cash and was not acquiring substantially all the assets of the target corporation. A B reorganization and a C reorganization were not available since no cash may be paid to the shareholders of the target corporation and the acquiring corporation must acquire substantially all the assets of the target corporation in such reorganizations.

Even though a direct statutory merger is permissible in this case, there are two major non-tax problems. The acquiring corporation is subject to all the contingent and unknown liabilities of the target corporation after the merger. The acquiring corporation must also obtain the consent of shareholders to the merger, which is often impractical in a large publicly-traded corporation.

After 2002, the acquiring corporation may avoid these problems by forming an LLC. The target corporation then merges into the LLC. The shareholders of the target corporation receive stock in the acquiring corporation and/or cash up to 50 percent of the aggregate consideration paid by the acquiring corporation. The shareholders of the target corporation may receive a distribution of certain assets from the target corporation prior to the merger. The acquiring corporation is not required to obtain the consent of shareholders. The acquiring corporation is not subject to the unknown and contingent liabilities of the target corporation. The shareholders of the target corporation are not taxed on receipt of stock in the acquiring corporation. They are taxed only on the cash received.

[2] Disadvantages

There are several problems with using an LLC to facilitate a tax-free acquisition, including the following:

- The target corporation must merge into the LLC owned by the acquiring corporation. The LLC may not merge into the target corporation. The merger of an LLC that is classified as a disregarded entity into a corporation does not qualify as a tax-free reorganization under IRC Section 368(a)(1)(A).[22] As a result, the LLC may be required to obtain new state licenses and permits

---

[22] Reg. §1.368-2T(b)(1)(iv), Example 5. *See also* IRS Proposed Rules (REG-126485-01) and Hearing Notice on Definition of Statutory Merger or Consolidation, under the heading, "B. Mergers Involving Disregarded Entities" (Nov. 15, 2001).

for its business after the acquisition and consents of lenders, landlords, and other persons with which it has contracts. In order to avoid this problem, the parties normally use a reverse triangular merger, a B reorganization, or a C reorganization.

- Some states do not permit a corporation to merge into an LLC.

12

Terminations

§12.01 EVENTS CAUSING TERMINATION

An LLC that is classified as a partnership for federal tax purposes terminates on one of the following events:[1]

- the members completely discontinue the business of the LLC;
- there is a sale or exchange of 50 percent or more of the total membership interests in the LLC during a 12-month period;
- there is a merger or consolidation of two or more LLCs unless the resulting LLC is considered the continuation of the merging or consolidated LLCs;
- there is a division of an LLC, unless one or more of the resulting LLCs is considered as a continuing LLC;
- the LLC files an election to be classified as a corporation;
- an existing member or a third party acquires all of the membership interests in the LLC. The partnership status of the LLC will terminate on the date that the number of members is reduced to a single member.

§12.02 CESSATION OF BUSINESS

[A] General Rules

The first event causing termination of an LLC is a complete cessation of business. The LLC will terminate if no part of the business or financial operation of the

§12.01   [1] IRC §708(b).

LLC continues to be carried on by any of the members in the LLC.[1] There is no termination until the end of the winding up period of the liquidating LLC.[2]

There is no termination if the LLC changes its primary purpose and continues to carry on an active trade or business.[3]

[B] Tax Consequences

The tax consequences of distributions to members are discussed in Chapter 10. The basic Code provisions that apply to liquidating distributions after a cessation of business are as follows:

- *IRC Section 731(b)*—The LLC does not receive a deduction for the payment to the member.[4]
- *IRC Section 731(a)(1)*—The member recognizes capital gain to the extent that a money distribution exceeds the basis of the member's interest in the LLC. The member is taxed in the year the payments are made.[5] The member recovers his or her entire basis before incurring any capital gain. However, if the total distribution amount is fixed, the retiring member may elect to recover basis and recognize capital gain on a pro rata basis. The member must attach a statement of the election to his her or return for the first year in which the payment is received.[6] There is no gain recognition as a result of a property distribution.
- *IRC Section 731(a)(2)*—The member recognizes loss if three conditions are met. First, the member must receive only cash, unrealized receivables, or inventory. Second, the member must receive a liquidating distribution of his entire membership interest. Third, the adjusted basis of LLC assets distributed to the member must be less than the member's basis in his membership interest. The loss recognized is the amount by which the basis in the membership interest exceeds the money and the LLC's basis in unrealized receivables and inventory items distributed to the member. This differs from the rule for nonliquidating distributions in which no loss is recognized.
- *IRC Sections 741 and 731(a)*— The gain or loss recognized is capital gain or loss,[7] except as provided under IRC Section 751(b).[8]
- *IRC Section 751(b)*—A portion of the member's gain is recharacterized as ordinary income to the extent of the member's share of unrealized receiv-

---

§12.02 [1] IRC §708(b)(1)(A).

[2] Reg. §1.708-1(b).

[3] Reg. §1.761-1(a)(2).

[4] Reg. §1.736-1(a)(2).

[5] Reg. §1.736-1(a)(5).

[6] Reg. §1.736-1(b)(6). If the election is made, the member recognizes capital loss if the member does not recover the full amount of basis in membership interest (e.g., because the expected payments were not received in full).

[7] IRC §§731(a) (last sentence), 741.

[8] *See* §10.05 *supra.*

ables, depreciation recapture, and substantially appreciated inventory items[9] retained by the LLC.[10] A member does not recognize ordinary income if the member receives a distribution that is exactly equal to the member's share of unrealized receivables and substantially appreciated inventory items.[11] The LLC may step up the basis of its assets by the amount of ordinary income realized by the member.[12]

- *IRC Section 732(b)*—The member receives a basis in the distributed property equal to his or her basis in the membership interest, reduced by any money distributed. The basis is first allocated to the unrealized receivables and inventory items in an amount equal to the LLC's basis in those assets. Any remaining basis in the membership interest is allocated to the other properties received in the distribution.[13] This is a substituted basis.
- *IRC Section 735(b)*—The member's holding period for the distributed property includes the LLC's holding period for the property,[14] except for the amount attributable to unrealized receivables and substantially appreciated inventory items.
- *IRC Section 736*—IRC Section 736 normally governs distributions to retiring or deceased members in exchange for their interest in LLC property (e.g., capital account, goodwill, accounts receivable, and other property). However, IRC Section 736 does not apply on termination of an LLC.[15]
- *IRC Section 1245*—There is no depreciation recapture with respect to the distributed assets.[16]

---

[9] Reg. §1.736-1(b)(4). Inventory is substantially appreciated if its fair market value exceeds the adjusted basis by more than 120 percent. IRC §751(b)(3)(A).

[10] Under IRC §751(b), a member will recognize ordinary income or loss, or capital gain or loss, if the member does not receive his proportionate share of unrealized receivables, substantially appreciated inventory items, and other property in a distribution. In that case, the member is treated as having received a proportionate distribution of all assets, and as selling back to the LLC the excess assets retained by the LLC in exchange for the excess assets retained by the member. Reg. §1.732-1(e). Gain on the deemed sale back to the LLC will be ordinary income if the member retains a disproportionate share of capital assets, and the LLC retains a disproportionate share of unrealized receivables and substantially appreciated inventory items. In that case, the member will be treated as having received his proportionate share of the unrealized receivables and inventory items, and as having sold them back to the LLC. Ordinary income is the difference between the fair market value of the capital assets being purchased from the LLC less the adjusted basis of unrealized receivables and inventory items deemed distributed to the member in excess of his proportionate share sold back to the LLC. Gain on the deemed sale back to the LLC will be treated as capital gain if a member receives a disproportionately large share of unrealized receivables and inventory items. In that case, the member will be treated as having received his proportionate share of capital assets and as having sold back to the LLC such capital assets in exchange for the unrealized receivables and inventory items retained by him in excess of his proportionate share.

[11] Reg. §§1.751-1(b)(2)(ii)-(iii), (3)(ii)-(iii).

[12] *See* §10.05[B] *supra*.

[13] IRC §732(c)(1).

[14] Ltr. Rul. 200204005.

[15] Reg. §1.736-1(a).

[16] IRC §1245(b)(3) provides that if the basis in the hands of the transferee is determined by the basis in the hands of the transferor, then there is no depreciation recapture. The distributee member receives a substituted basis, rather than a carryover basis, for Section 1245 property. However, IRC §1245(b)(6)(A) provides that the basis of Section 1245 property distributed by an LLC is deemed to

§12.03 TRANSFER OF 50 PERCENT OF LLC

[A] General Rules

The second event causing the termination of an LLC is a sale or exchange of 50 percent or more of the total interests in the LLC's capital and profits during a 12-month period.[1]

Different sales by different members are aggregated in determining whether there has been a transfer of more than 50 percent of the membership interests in an LLC during any 12-month period. However, the same membership units that are sold more than once cannot be counted more than once.[2]

Sales and exchanges include the following types of transactions for purposes of the rule:

- Tax-free exchanges.[3]
- Sale to a related party.[4]
- Sale to an existing member.[5]
- Sale by a member that is prohibited by the terms of the operating agreement.[6]
- Abandonment of a membership interest.
- Contribution of a membership interest to a corporation.[7]

There is no sale or exchange for purposes of the rule in the following cases:

- There is a transfer of the membership interest to an estate on the death of the member.[8]
- There is a gift by one member to another. A gift is not a sale or exchange.[9]
- The LLC makes a liquidating distribution to one or more of its members.[10]
- There is a prearranged transfer of more than 50 percent of the membership interests over a period of more than 12 months, provided not more than 50 percent of the membership interests are transferred in any 12-month period.[11]
- A new member is admitted to the LLC.[12]
- A member contributes property to the LLC.[13]

---

have a basis determined by reference to the basis of assets in hands of the LLC. Thus, there is no depreciation recapture.

§12.03 [1] IRC §708(b)(1)(B); Reg. §1.708-1(b)(2); Ltr. Ruls. 200209046, 9701029.

[2] Reg. §1.708-1(b)(2).

[3] Evans v. Comm'r, 54 T.C. 40 (1970).

[4] F.S.A. 200132009.

[5] Reg. §1.708-1(b)(2).

[6] Evans v. Comm'r, 54 T.C. 40 (1970).

[7] Id.

[8] Reg. §§1.708-1(b)(2), 1.736-1(a)(6).

[9] Reg. §1.708-1(b)(2).

[10] Reg. §1.708-1(b)(2); Ltr. Rul. 9751048.

[11] Ltr. Rul. 9701032.

[12] Reg. §1.708-1(b)(2).

[13] Id.

[B]   Tax Consequences

A terminated LLC is treated as transferring all of its assets and liabilities to a new LLC in exchange for an interest in the new LLC. Immediately thereafter the terminated LLC is treated as distributing membership interests in the new LLC to the purchasing member and the other remaining members in liquidation of the terminated LLC, either for continuation of the business or for its dissolution and winding-up.[14]

The deemed transfer of assets and liabilities to a new LLC has the following federal income tax consequences:[15]

- No gain or loss is recognized by the LLC or members.
- There is no change in the tax basis of property owned by the LLC.[16]
- There is no new seven-year period for purposes of the provisions for recognition of precontribution gain.[17]
- The termination does not change the capital accounts of the members.[18]
- All Section 704(c) property held by the terminated LLC (and treated as contributed to a new LLC) continues to be Section 704(c) property in the hands of the new LLC.[19] Section 704(c) property is property which has a tax basis that is different from its capital account value when it is contributed to the LLC. Income, gain, loss, and deduction with respect to that property must be allocated among the members so as to take into account the variation between the tax basis and its fair market value at the time of contribution. For example, gain from the sale of the property must first be allocated to the member who contributed the property to the extent of the built-in gain at the time of contribution.[20] The deemed contribution of assets to the new LLC does not create additional Section 704(c) property.[21] Thus, there is no capital account "book up" under Section 704(b) upon the deemed contribution of assets by the terminated LLC to the new LLC or upon the deemed distribution in liquidation of the terminated LLC.[22] The new LLC that is formed as result of the termination of the old LLC is not required to use the same method of allocations under IRC Section 704(c) as the terminated LLC.[23]

---

[14] Reg. §1.708-1(b)(4).

[15] T.D. 8717 (May 9, 1997).

[16] Reg. §1.708-1(b)(4), Example (ii). However, the LLC must adjust the basis of the assets with respect to the purchasing member if the terminated LLC has an election in effect under IRC §754. Reg. §1.708-1(b)(5).

[17] See IRC §§704(c)(1)(B), 737; Reg. §§1.704-4(a)(4)(ii), 1.737-2(a).

[18] Reg. §1.708-1(b)(4), Example (ii); Reg. §1.704-1(b)(2)(4)(l).

[19] Reg. §1.704-3(a)(9). See also Notice of Proposed Rule Making and Notice of Public Hearing on Adoption of Regulations under IRS §708(b)(1)(B), 61 Fed. Reg. 21,985 (May 13, 1996).

[20] See §8.03 supra for a detailed discussion of this subject.

[21] Reg. §1.704-3(a)(3)(i); Reg. §1.708-1(b)(4), Example (iii)

[22] Reg. §§1.704-1(1), 1.704-1(1)(5), example 13(v), 1.708-1(4), example (iii).

[23] Reg. §1.704-3(a)(2).

- The tax year of the terminated LLC closes with respect to all members.[24]
- The holding period for the new membership interests includes the holding period of the membership interests in the terminated LLC.[25]
- There is no change in the book value of the assets of the LLC.[26]
- The LLC must renew the election to adjust the basis of property under Section 754 of the Code. However, any Section 754 election made by the terminated LLC prior to the sale applies to the incoming member. Therefore, the basis of assets must be adjusted prior to their deemed contribution to the new LLC.[27] The IRS will grant an extension of time to the LLC to file a new Section 754 election for the reconstituted LLC if the LLC fails to file an election on a timely basis.[28]
- Other elections made by the terminated LLC do not carry over to the new LLC. The new LLC must elect a fiscal year accounting method and make other applicable elections.
- There is no depreciation recapture with respect to the transferred assets.[29]
- The new LLC must depreciate the remaining basis in any property as if it were newly acquired property under the same depreciation system used by the terminated LLC.[30] For example, if the LLC was depreciating property over 39 years, and had five years left on the date of termination, the LLC would be required to depreciate the remaining basis over 39 years instead of five.
- The LLC must amortize intangibles in the same manner as if there had been no termination.[31]
- Any special basis adjustment that a member had in the assets of the terminated LLC as a result of an election under Section 754 carry over to the new LLC.
- The termination is treated as a liquidation under the Section 704(b) regulations.

---

[24] Reg. §1.708-1(b)(3)(ii).

[25] IRC §§722, 1223.

[26] Reg. §1.708-1(b)(4), Example (ii); Reg. §1.704-1(b)(2)(4)(l).

[27] Reg. §1.708-1(b)(5).

[28] Ltr. Rul. 200209046.

[29] IRC §1245(b)(3) provides that if the basis in the hands of the transferee is determined by the basis in the hands of the transferor, then there is no depreciation recapture. There is a carryover basis when an LLC is terminated as a result of a sale or exchange of more than 50 percent of the membership units. There is a carryover basis for the assets on the deemed termination of the LLC. Reg. §1.708-1(b)(4), Example (ii). Prior to enactment of the current regulations, the deemed distribution of assets could result in a different basis. However, IRC §1245(b)(6)(A) provides that the basis of Section 1245 property distributed by an LLC is deemed to have a basis determined by reference to the basis of assets in hands of the LLC. Thus, there is no depreciation recapture.

[30] In Notice of Proposed Rule Making and Notice of Public Hearing on Adoption of Regulations under IRS §708(b)(1)(B), 61 Fed. Reg. 21,985 (May 13, 1996), the IRS stated that this result is mandated under current law, *citing* the anti-churning provisions of IRC §168(f)(5) and also *citing* IRC §168(i)(7) (last sentence).

[31] IRC §197(f)(2)(B).

- The deemed distribution of LLC membership interests does not trigger the application of Section 731(c).[32] That section provides that the distribution of marketable securities by an LLC is treated as a distribution of money equal to the fair market value of the securities on the date of distribution. A member recognizes gain to the extent the money distributed exceeds the member's basis in his membership interests.
- The new LLC keeps the same employer identification number as the old LLC.[33]
- The LLC that terminates must file a short-year final return for the taxable year ending with the date of its termination. The new LLC must file a return for its taxable year beginning after the date of termination of the terminated LLC.[34] Some LLCs inadvertently file a single tax return for the entire year in which there is a termination. The single return will be treated as a valid return that will start the statute of limitations running for the short years of the terminated LLC and the new LLC.[35]

§12.04   MERGERS AND CONSOLIDATIONS

The third event causing a termination of an LLC is a merger or consolidation, unless the resulting LLC is considered the continuation of the merging or consolidated LLCs.[1] The surviving LLC is treated as continuing, and the other LLC is treated as terminated. The surviving LLC is the LLC whose members own more than 50 percent of the capital and profits interest in the LLC.[2] If the resulting LLC could be considered a continuation of more than one of the merging LLCs, the LLC that is credited with the greatest dollar contribution value of assets to the resulting LLC is treated as the survivor for tax purposes.[3] If the members of none of the merging or consolidating LLCs own more than a 50-percent interest in the capital and profits of the resulting LLC, all of the merged LLCs are treated as terminated, and a new LLC results.[4]

The types of mergers and consolidations, tax consequences, elections, and filing requirements are discussed in Chapter 11.[5]

§12.05   DIVISIONS

The fourth event causing a termination of an LLC is a division, unless one or more of the resulting LLCs is treated as a continuing LLC. On the division of an

[32] Reg. §1.731-2(g)(2) (deemed distribution of partnership interests under Reg. §1.708-1(b)(1)(iv) does not trigger the application of IRC §731(c)).

[33] Reg. §1.708-1(b)(1)(iv), example (ii); Reg. §301.6109-1(d)(2)(iii); Notice 2001-5, 2001-3 I.R.B. 327.

[34] F.S.A. 200139009; Notice 2001-5, 2001-3 I.R.B. 327.

[35] F.S.A. 200139009.

§12.04   [1] See §§11.19, 11.20, 11.21 and 11.22 supra.

[2] IRC §708(b)(1)(A).

[3] Reg. §1.708-1(b)(2).

[4] Prop. Reg. §1.708-1(c)(1).

[5] See §11.15 supra.

LLC into two or more LLCs, any resulting LLC or LLCs are considered a continuation of the prior LLC if the members of the new LLC or LLCs had an interest of more than 50 percent in capital and profits of the prior LLC. Any other resulting LLC in which the members owned less than 50 percent of the prior LLC is considered a new LLC rather than a continuation of the prior LLC. If the members of none of the new LLCs owned more than 50 percent of the prior LLC, then the resulting LLCs are considered new LLCs rather than a continuation of the prior LLC. In such case, the prior LLC will be treated as terminated. The members interests in the new LLCs that are not continuations of the prior LLC are treated as liquidated as of the date of the division.[1]

The types of divisions, tax consequences, elections, and filing requirements are discussed in Chapter 11.[2]

§12.06 CHANGE IN CLASSIFICATION ELECTION

The fifth event causing the termination of an LLC as a partnership is an election to be classified as a corporation.[1]

§12.07 ACQUISITIONS RESULTING IN SINGLE-MEMBER LLC

The sixth event causing the termination of an LLC as a partnership is the acquisition of all membership interests by an existing member or a third party. A single-member LLC cannot be classified as a partnership. The classification of the LLC will change from a partnership to a disregarded entity unless the LLC makes an election to be classified as a corporation. The tax consequences of a purchase by an existing member of all membership interests,[1] and the purchase by a third party of all membership interests,[2] are discussed above.

§12.05   [1] Reg. §1.708-1(d)(1).
[2] See §11.15 supra.
§12.06   [1] See §5.04 supra.
§12.07   [1] See §11.18[A] supra.
[2] See §11.18[B] supra.

13

Loss Limitations

§13.01 GENERALLY

One of the major advantages of an LLC is that the LLC may pass through losses to investors. The losses may offset other taxable income earned by the members. Conversely, shareholders in a C corporation may not deduct corporate losses or excess deductions on their personal income tax returns. The losses may be used only to offset corporate profits, if any.

There are five main limitations on the pass-through of LLC losses to members:

1. Basis
2. At-risk limitations
3. Passive loss rules
4. Related party transactions
5. Anti-abuse rules

§13.02 BASIS

The first limitation on losses is basis. A member may deduct his distributive share of LLC losses, including capital losses, only to the extent of the member's basis in his membership interest in the LLC at the end of the LLC's tax year in which the losses occurred.[1] The three methods of determining basis are discussed in Chapter 9. Losses in excess of basis are not deductible for that year. The disallowed losses may be carried forward and deducted in subsequent years to the extent the member has basis in his membership interest at the end of those years.[2]

A proportionate share of each disallowed loss is carried forward if the total loss is comprised of different types of deductions (such as capital, ordinary income, and other losses).[3]

The disallowed losses may be carried forward indefinitely.[4] The member may absorb the loss during the first subsequent year in which there is sufficient basis. The basis in subsequent years is first determined after an annual adjustment is made for the current year's income, distributions, and contributions.

EXAMPLE 1

A member has a basis in her membership interest of $6,000. Her distributive share of LLC losses for 1999 is $10,000. The member may deduct only $6,000 of the losses in 1999. The $6,000 loss reduces the basis in her membership interest to zero. The $4,000 disallowed loss may be carried forward to the year 2000.

EXAMPLE 2

Same facts as in Example 1. The member's distributive share of LLC income during the year 2000 is $3,000. No part of the income is distributed to the member. Therefore, the member's basis at the end of the year, after making adjustments for the current year's allocations, contributions, and distributions, is increased from zero to $3,000. The member may in the year 2000 deduct $3,000 of the disallowed losses carried over from 1999. The loss deduction in the year 2000 reduces her basis in the membership interest to zero. The remaining $1,000 of disallowed losses may be carried over to 2001 or subsequent years when the member has a positive basis after adjustments for that year's allocations, contributions, and distributions.[5]

§13.02   [1] IRC §704(d).
[2] Reg. §1.704-1(d)(1).
[3] Reg. §§1.704-1(d)(2) and 1.704-1(d)(4), example (3).
[4] IRC §704(d).
[5] Reg. §1.704-1(d)(4), example (1).

The losses carried forward are personal to the member. A member loses the disallowed losses if the member terminates his interest in the LLC upon death, upon withdrawal from the LLC, or otherwise. A purchasing member may not claim disallowed losses incurred by the selling member.

A member will lose the excess loss carryover on sale of a membership interest. The reason is that a member may not deduct losses in excess of basis.[6] Gain on sale of a membership interest does not increase basis. However, a member may make a capital contribution in the year of sale and deduct the excess losses. That will increase the value of the membership interest and result in additional capital gain on sale.[7] It may be better for the member to receive additional capital gain rather than to lose the ordinary loss deduction.

A member may offset disallowed losses against gain on sale if the losses are disallowed solely because of the at-risk or passive loss limitations discussed below.

EXAMPLE

A member has a basis of $10,000 in her membership interest in an LLC. The LLC allocates $6,000 of losses to the member during the current year. Even though the member has sufficient basis to absorb the loss, the member may not deduct the losses in the current year because of the passive loss rules. The $6,000 of disallowed losses under the passive loss rules must still reduce the member's basis in her membership interest from $10,000 to $4,000. If the member sells her membership interest for $10,000, the member will have $6,000 of gain (amount realized of $10,000, less basis of $4,000). The member may offset the $6,000 of gain by the $6,000 of losses that were disallowed under the passive loss rules.

§13.03   AT-RISK RULES

[A]   In General

Members in an LLC who are individuals or closely held C corporations are subject to the same at-risk rules[1] as limited partners in a partnership. A member may not deduct losses in excess of the amount "at risk." The at-risk rules frequently apply in real estate transactions, equipment leasing transactions, and other ventures involving seller financing.

A member is at risk with respect to each separate "activity" of the LLC for the following amounts:[2]

---

[6] IRC §704(d).

[7] The member will not receive an increase in basis for the capital contribution since the capital contribution will be reduced by the excess loss carryover.

§13.03   [1] IRC §465.

[2] IRC §465(b).

1. The amount of money that member contributes to the LLC, unless borrowed from lender who has a membership interest in the LLC.[3]
2. The adjusted basis of property that the member contributes to the LLC.[4]
3. Amounts borrowed or owned by the LLC to the extent that the member is personally liable for repayment, or has pledged property as security for the repayment.[5] These rules are discussed below.[6]
4. The member's share of "qualified nonrecourse financing" if the LLC obtains financing for real estate that it acquires or holds. Qualified nonrecourse financing is nonconvertible financing for which no person is personally liable for repayment. It must be secured by real property. The financing must be obtained from a qualified person or government agency.[7] These rules are discussed below.[8]

The amount at risk is then increased by the member's share of income and decreased by the member's share of losses and distributions.[9] Losses that are disallowed under the at-risk rules are suspended and may be carried forward to subsequent years in which the member's at-risk amount is sufficient to absorb the losses.[10] The losses disallowed under the at-risk rules reduce a member's basis in the LLC.[11] However, the gain recognized on sale of membership interest increases the amount at-risk.[12] Therefore, a member may deduct losses disallowed under the at-risk rule on sale of a membership interest.

[B] Personal Liability of Member

[1] Amounts At-Risk

A member is at risk for amounts borrowed or owed by the LLC to the extent that the member is personally liable for repayment or has pledged property as security for repayment. For example, a member is at risk in the following cases:

- An LLC is liable for payment to a supplier. The supplier commences collection proceedings. The supplier agrees to withhold legal action if the LLC pays the amount due under the stipulation of settlement. One of the members of the LLC signs a stipulation on behalf of the LLC and in his individual capacity. The member is at risk because the member is liable for payment of the amount owed to the supplier.[13]

---

[3] IRC §465(b)(1)(A).
[4] *Id.*
[5] IRC §465(b)(2).
[6] *See* §13.03[B] *infra.*
[7] IRC §465(b)(6).
[8] *See* §13.03[C] *infra.*
[9] IRC §465(b)(5).
[10] IRC §465(a)(2).
[11] Prop. Reg. §1.465-1(e).
[12] Prop. Reg. §§1.465-12, 1.465-66(a).
[13] FSA 200025018.

- The LLC enters into a lease agreement under which each of the three members of the LLC is jointly and severally liable for the rent. Each member signs a personal guarantee for the rent. When the LLC defaults on the lease, the lessor commences legal action to enforce the personal guarantees. Each member of the LLC is at risk for the entire amount of the defaulted rent if the member does not have a right of reimbursement against the other members on payment of the defaulted amount. Each member of the LLC is not at risk to the extent the member has a right to reimbursement against the other members on payment of the defaulted amount.[14]

[2]   Amounts Not At-Risk

A member is not at-risk with respect to the following amounts, even though the member is personally liable:

- Amounts protected against loss through nonrecourse financing, guarantees, stop loss arrangements, or similar agreements.[15]
- Amounts borrowed from a lender who has a membership interest in the LLC.[16]
- Amounts borrowed by an LLC in excess of the fair market value of the assets pledged by the member as security for a loan. Pledged property that is used in the business of the LLC does not count as security or cause the member to be at-risk.
- Liabilities that are nonrecourse liabilities, even though the liabilities are recourse with respect to the assets contributed by the members to the LLC.
- Liabilities of the member to the LLC. The amount at-risk is not increased by the amount that the member is required to contribute to the LLC under the operating agreement until such time as the contribution is actually made.[17]
- Liabilities of the LLC guaranteed by the member.[18] The reason is that if an LLC is primarily liable to a third party, and one of the members guarantees that debt, the member is subrogated to the rights of the lender on default and has a right to recover against the LLC as the primary obligor.

[C]   Qualified Nonrecourse Financing

A member is at risk for the member's share of qualified nonrecourse financing on real property owned by the LLC, even though the member is not personally liable for repayment of the debt. One of the requirements for qualified nonrecourse

---

[14] *Id.*

[15] IRC §465(b)(4); Reg. §1.465-24(a)(2).

[16] IRC §465(b)(3)(A).

[17] Reg. §1.465-22(a).

[18] Reg. §1.465-24.

financing is that no person may be liable for repayment of the debt, except as provided in regulations.[19] This previously caused a problem when an LLC was liable for repayment, because an LLC is a person for tax purposes. Therefore, any financing for which an LLC was liable was not qualified nonrecourse financing even if no member was personally liable for the financing.[20]

The IRS determined that this result was inappropriate if the only activity of the LLC was the real property activity. It provided in the regulations that the personal liability of an LLC is disregarded in determining whether a financing is qualified nonrecourse financing if the LLC's only assets are real property used in the activity of holding real property. No other person may be liable for the financing.[21]

Financing may also be qualified nonrecourse financing if, in addition to the real property used in the activity of holding real property, the financing is secured by (a) property that is incidental to the activity of holding real property or (b) property that is neither real property used in the activity of holding real property nor incidental property if the total fair market value of such property is less than 10 percent of the total gross fair market value of all the property securing the financing.[22]

EXAMPLE

An LLC is classified as a partnership. It is engaged only in the activity of holding real property. It borrows $5,000 to use in the activity. The LLC is personally liable on the debt. No other members are liable. The debt constitutes qualified nonrecourse financing. All of the members may include their shares of the financing as at-risk amounts.[23] If the requirements for qualified nonrecourse financing are met, the at-risk limitations will not apply to the losses generated by the properties held by the LLC.[24]

---

§13.04 PASSIVE LOSSES

[A] In General

Members of an LLC who are individuals, trusts, estates, personal service corporations, and closely held C corporations may deduct passive activity losses only

---

[19] IRC §465(b)(6)(B)(iii).
[20] T.D. 8777 (1998).
[21] Reg. §1.465-27.
[22] Reg. §1.465-27(b)(2)(i).
[23] Reg. §1.465-27(b)(4), example (1).
[24] Ltr. Rul. 9738013.

against passive activity income.[1] The passive losses may not be deducted against other types of income, such as wages, interest, or dividends. Tax credits from passive activities are also limited to the member's regular tax liability allocable to passive activities.

The passive loss rules do not apply to an LLC. Instead, they apply to each member's share of loss or credit from the LLC that is a passive activity loss or credit.

A passive activity loss is the amount by which the total deductions from the passive activity exceed the total income from the activity for the tax year. The passive loss is suspended and carried forward as a deduction to the succeeding years when the taxpayer has passive income from the activity[2] or disposes of his entire interest in the activity.[3]

A passive activity is a trade or business in which the taxpayer does not materially participate and any rental activity.[4] There are two exceptions for rental real estate activities. Individuals may deduct up to $25,000 of losses from a rental real estate activity in which the individual actively participates during the year. The $25,000 amount is reduced if the taxpayer's adjusted gross income is more than $100,000. A taxpayer actively participates in a rental real estate activity if the taxpayer owns at least 10 percent of the rental property and makes management decisions in a significant and bona fide sense.

A second exception applies mainly to real estate professionals. Certain real estate professionals may treat rental real estate activities as nonpassive if they significantly participate in the real estate trade or business.[5] The taxpayer must perform more than one-half the personal services performed in the real estate trade or business in which the taxpayer materially participates. The taxpayer must also perform more than 750 hours of service during the tax year in real property trades or businesses in which the taxpayer materially participates.

Any income, gain, or loss attributable to investment and portfolio assets of the LLC are characterized as portfolio income or loss, rather than passive income or loss.[6]

[B] Member Classification as General or Limited Partner

The determination of whether income and loss from an LLC are passive depends in part on whether the member is classified as a general or limited partner. The IRS takes the position that members of an LLC are always limited partners for

---

§13.04 [1] IRC §469(a)(1)(A). Passive activity income does not include income from interest, dividends, annuities, royalties (except for royalties derived in the ordinary course of the trade or business), or certain capital gains. The passive income must be from a passive activity as defined in the Code.

[2] Reg. §1.469-1(f)(4).

[3] IRC §469(g)(1).

[4] IRC §469(c).

[5] IRC §469(c)(7).

[6] Temp. Reg. §1.469-2T(e)(3)(v).

purposes of the passive loss rules.[7] The reason is that a member is a limited partner under the regulations if the liability of the member is limited under state law to a fixed amount, such as capital contributions and amounts that the member agrees to contribute in the future.[8] The liability of LLC members is always limited under state law.

One court took the position that members of an LLC who actively participated in the management of the LLC should be treated as general partners under the passive loss rules even though the liability of the member was limited under state law.[9]

[C] Material Participation Standards for Members Classified as General Partners

A member of an LLC who is classified as a general partner is treated as materially participating in a trade or business for the tax year if the member meets one of the following tests:[10]

- The member participates in the activity for more than 500 hours during the year.
- The member's participation in the activity for the tax year constitutes substantially all of the participation in that activity for all individuals, including individuals who are not members or owners of the LLC.
- The member participates in the activity for more than 100 hours during the tax year, and the member's participation in the activity for the tax year is not less than the participation in the activity for any other individual, including individuals who are not members of the LLC.
- The activity is a significant participation activity for the tax year, and the member's aggregate participation in all significant participation activities during the tax year exceeds 500 hours.
- The member materially participated in the activity for any 5 tax years during the 10 tax years immediately preceding the current tax year.
- The activity is a personal service activity, and the member materially participated in the activity for any three tax years preceding the current tax year.
- Based on all the facts and circumstances, the individual member participates in the activity on a regular, continuous, and substantial basis during the year.

---

[7] Gregg v. United States, 87 A.F.T.R. 2d 2001-337 (D. Or. 2000). The IRS Market Segment Specialization Program's Audit Guidelines on Passive Activity Losses (Apr. 25, 1994) also states members in an LLC are analogous to limited partners for passive activity loss purposes. It further states that the material participation test for LLC members is determined under the material participation test for limited partners rather than general partners.

[8] Temp. Reg. §1.469-5T(e)(2), (e)(3)(ii).

[9] Gregg v. United States, 87 A.F.T.R . 2d 2001-337 (D. Or. 2000).

[10] Temp. Reg. §1.469-5T(a).

[D] Material Participation Standards for Members Classified as Limited Partners

A member of an LLC who is classified as a limited partner is treated as materially participating in a trade or business for the tax year if the member meets one of the following tests:

- The member participated in the activity for more than 500 hours during the year.
- The member materially participated in the activity for any 5 tax years during the 10 tax years immediately preceding the current tax year (or in any of the three preceding years for service activities).
- The activity is a personal service activity, and the member materially participated in the activity for any three tax years preceding the current tax year.[11]

EXAMPLE

Steve is the owner of a managed health care corporation. He works full-time in the business. In November 2000, he stopped working for the corporation. He transferred part of the assets to an LLC that engaged in a different line of business, alternative medicine. He worked approximately 100 hours for the LLC in the final two months in the year, and received no compensation for his services. Other members and individuals were more actively involved in the business of the LLC. The LLC incurred substantial losses during 2000. Steve has no passive income for 2000. However, Steve deducted these losses on his personal income tax return as ordinary business losses.

The IRS position is that Steve may not deduct these losses because they are passive losses. Steve should be treated as a limited partner in the LLC because all members of an LLC are treated as limited partners for passive loss purposes. As a limited partner, Steve did not materially participate in the business of the LLC because he did not work more than 500 hours for the LLC during the year and did not satisfy the other two material participation tests for limited partners.

The court's position is that Steve may treat these losses as passive losses. Steve should be a general partner for passive loss purposes because he was actively involved in the management of the LLC. Therefore, Steve should be tested under the more liberal material participation standards for general partners. Steve satisfied the first material participation test for general partners because he participated in the activity of health care for more than 500 hours during 2000. Although he worked for the LLC for only 100 hours during the year, he may aggregate those hours with the hours worked for the corporation that dissolved prior to the formation of the LLC. The reason is that the corporation was a closely held C corporation subject to the passive

---

[11] Temp. Reg. §1.469-5T(e)(2).

loss rules, and engaged in the same general type of business.[12] Therefore, Steve may deduct the losses from the LLC against other ordinary income.

§13.05 RELATED PARTY TRANSACTIONS

Losses are not allowed on transactions between an LLC and a member who owns, directly or indirectly, more than 50 percent of the capital interest or profits interest in the LLC. Losses are not allowed on transactions between two LLCs in which the same member owns, directly or indirectly, more than 50 percent of the capital interest or profits interest in the LLC.[1] The disallowed loss is a nondeductible expenditure for capital account purposes.[2] The member must also reduce his in basis in the membership interests by the amount of the disallowed loss.[3]

The loss disallowance rules are discussed in detail in Chapter 14.[4]

§13.06 ANTI-ABUSE RULES

The anti-abuse rules prevent an LLC from shifting losses in high basis, low value assets to new members.[1] The anti-abuse rules also prohibit the taxpayer from creating duplicate losses by contributing property with built-in losses to an LLC, selling the membership interest in the LLC to a third party at a loss, and then having the LLC sell the contributed property at a loss that is allocated to the buyer.[2]

EXAMPLE

A bank made loans of $1 million that are now worthless. The bank forms an LLC and contributes its worthless loans to the LLC. The bank sells its membership interest to Buyer for $50,000 since the loans have value as a tax write-off. The bank takes a deduction of $950,000. The LLC does not make an election under Section 754. Therefore, the LLC retains a carryover basis of $1 million in the loans. The LLC immediately sells the loans for $1. The LLC incurs a loss of $999,999. It allocates all of the loss to the Buyer. Since the Buyer cannot take losses in excess of its $50,000 basis, the Buyer contributes land to the LLC with a basis of $950,000, thereby increasing its basis in the LLC to $1 million. The loss allocation reduces the Buyer's basis

---

[12] Gregg v. United States, 87 A.F.T.R. 2d 2001-337 (D. Or. 2000).
§13.05 [1] IRC §707(b).
[2] Reg. §1.704-1(b)(2)(iv).
[3] IRC §705(a)(2)(B). *See also* Rev. Rul. 96-10, 1996-1 C.B. 27.
[4] *See* §14.03[C][1] *infra*.
§13.06 [1] F.S.A. 200242004 (*citing* Reg. §1.702-2).
[2] F.S.A. 200242004.

from $1 million to $1. Seven years later, the LLC distributes the land back to the Buyer. The Buyer receives a basis in the land of $1 under IRC §732(b) equal to its outside basis in the membership interest. The Buyer can defer the recognition of gain indefinitely by holding on to the land. This scheme is now prohibited under the partnership anti-abuse rules.[3]

---

[3] F.S.A. 200242004 (*citing* Reg. §1.702-2).

14

Payments and Benefits to Members

§14.01   GENERAL RULES

An LLC may make payments to members for salaries, wages, commissions, rents, royalties, interest on loans, and other amounts. The payments are characterized in one of the following six ways:

1. A guaranteed payment
2. A payment to the member other than in his capacity as a member of the LLC

3. A distributive share of LLC income
4. A disguised sale payment
5. A fringe benefit
6. A Section 736 payment (a payment to a retired member or the estate of a deceased member in a service LLC if the member is classified as a "general partner")

§14.02 GUARANTEED PAYMENTS

Guaranteed payments are payments to a member for services or capital that are determined without regard to the income of the LLC.[1] Payments for services are guaranteed payments if there is a fixed amount payable to the member unrelated to the income of the LLC.

Guaranteed payments are ordinary income to the member.[2] An LLC may deduct guaranteed payments as an expense,[3] unless the payment is made in connection with a capital expenditure under Section 263. The payment is taxable income to the member for the year that includes the last day of the tax year of the LLC in which the LLC deducted the guaranteed payments.[4] Thus, if an LLC accrues a guaranteed salary payment to a member, but does not pay the member until the following year, the member must still report the income in the year accrued by the LLC rather than in the following year received by the member.

EXAMPLE 1

An LLC uses the cash method of accounting. It has a fiscal year ending May 31. All of its members are individuals who report on a calendar year basis. During the year ended May 31, 2004, the LLC makes guaranteed payments of $120,000 to Member A. Of this amount, $70,000 was paid to Member A between June 1 and December 31, 2003, and the remaining $50,000 was paid to Member A between January 1 and May 31, 2004. The entire $120,000 is includable in Member A's taxable income for the calendar year 2004, even though $70,000 of the guaranteed payments was paid to Member A in 2003.[5]

EXAMPLE 2

The LLC promises to pay Member A $60,000 per year for services regardless of the income earned by the LLC. In 1998, the LLC accrues a $60,000

§14.02   [1] IRC §707(c).
[2] IRC §§61(a), 707(c); Reg. §1.707-1(c).
[3] IRC §707(c). The expenses deductible under IRC §162(a).
[4] Reg. §§1.706-1(a)(1), 1.707-1(c).
[5] Reg. §1.706-1(a)(2).

expense on its income tax return. However, it does not pay the member the guaranteed payment until February 1, 1999. Member A must report the guaranteed payment as compensation income on her 1998 tax return even though she does not receive the compensation until the following year.[6]

If a member is entitled to a distributive share of income, with a minimum guaranteed payment, the guaranteed payment is the amount by which the minimum guarantee exceeds the distributive share of income.[7] No amount is a guaranteed payment if the distributive share of income exceeds the guaranteed amount.[8]

EXAMPLE 3

The LLC operating agreement provides that Member A is entitled to a 25 percent distributive share of income, with a minimum guaranteed amount of $30,000. The LLC earns $200,000. Member A's distributive share of income is $50,000 (25 percent of $200,000). No amount of the payment is a guaranteed payment, since the distributive share of income exceeds the guaranteed minimum amount.

EXAMPLE 4

Same facts as in Example 3, except that the LLC earns $100,000 during the year. Member A's distributive share of income is $25,000 (25 percent of $100,000). The remaining $5,000 payment to Member A is a guaranteed payment.

The LLC may deduct the guaranteed payment only against the bottom-line income and loss of the LLC.[9] If there is a loss after a deduction of the guaranteed payment, then the member receiving the guaranteed payment is entitled to an allocable share of loss caused by the guaranteed payment.

§14.03   PAYMENTS TO A MEMBER OTHER THAN IN CAPACITY AS A MEMBER

A member may engage in transactions with the LLC other than in his capacity as a member. The LLC may deduct the payments to the same extent that it could

---

[6] IRC §706(a); Reg. §1.707-1(c).
[7] Reg. §1.707-1(c), example (2).
[8] Ltr. Rul. 200138028, *citing* Reg. §1.707-1(c).
[9] Reg. §1.707-1(c), Example (4).

have deducted the payments to a nonmember. The member must include the payments in taxable income to the same extent that the member would have included the rent, interest, compensation, or other amounts in income received from another entity.[1]

The principal types of transactions between an LLC and a member acting in a nonmember capacity are the following:[2]

[A]   Loan to the LLC

If a member loans money to an LLC, the interest payments made by the LLC to the member are deductible to the LLC and taxable to the member.

If the loan becomes worthless, any loss deduction is treated as a nonbusiness bad debt unless the member is in the business of making loans or the loan is made by the member as an employee to protect his job. The nonbusiness bad debt deduction is a short-term capital loss.

The interest income received by the member is passive income. The member's allocable share of interest expense is a passive activity deduction. Thus, the tax-payer may offset the income and expense items resulting from the interest payments.[3] Under prior regulations, the interest expense on a loan from the member to the LLC was a passive activity deduction and the interest income received by the member was portfolio income, so that the passive income deduction could not offset the portfolio interest income.

[B]   Lease of Property to LLC

If a member leases property to an LLC, the lease is treated as a transaction between an LLC and a member who is not acting in his capacity as a member.[4] The rental payments are deductible by the LLC and taxable to the member receiving the rental income.[5]

The lease of property to the LLC is subject to the self-rental rules for passive loss deductions. If the lease of property generates net losses, then the losses are passive losses that may be deducted only against passive income.[6] If the lease of property generates net income, then the net income is regular income (and not passive income) if the member materially participates in the LLC.[7] Thus, the member may not offset passive losses from one lease of property to an LLC against net income from another lease of property to the same or different LLC.[8]

---

§14.03 [1] IRC §707(a)(i).
[2] IRC §707(a); Reg. §1.707-1(a).
[3] Reg. §1.469-7(c).
[4] Ltr. Rul. 9538036, *citing* IRC §707(a) and Reg. §1.707-1(a).
[5] IRC §707(a).
[6] IRC §469(c)(2) and (4).
[7] Reg. §1.469-2(f)(6).
[8] Krukowski v. Comm'r, 279 F.3d 547 (7th Cir. 2002). There may be an exception if the taxpayer elects to treat both rental activities as a single passive activity.

[C]   Sale of Property to LLC

If a member sells property to an LLC, the payments made by the LLC to the member are nondeductible sales proceeds. The member recognizes capital gain or loss, subject to the following special rules:

[1]   Sale of Property at a Loss

No deduction is allowed for losses on sales or exchanges of property between a member and an LLC if the member owns, directly or indirectly, more than 50 percent of the capital interest or profits interest in the LLC.[9] Losses are not allowed on transactions between two LLCs in which the same members own, directly or indirectly, more than 50 percent of the capital interests or profits interests in the LLCs.[10]

In determining whether a person owns 50 percent of the LLC, the constructive ownership rules of IRC Section 267(c) apply.[11] However, if a person is not a member, the constructive ownership rules cannot apply to make that person a member. Therefore, if a person is a constructive owner of 100 percent of the membership interests by reason of his relationship to a named member, the loss disallowance rule does not apply if that person is not himself a named member.

On a subsequent sale of the property by the LLC, gain is reduced by the disallowed loss.[12] The members receive the reduced share of gain, even though they were not members at the time of the disallowed loss.

If IRC Section 707(b)(1) does not apply, then the loss may still be disallowed under IRC Section 267(e). The sale of property by a person who is not a member to an LLC is treated as a sale to each of the members separately. Loss will be disallowed to the extent of the percentage interest in the LLC held by persons related to the selling nonmember.[13]

[2]   Sale of Property at a Gain

Gain recognized on the sale of property is treated as ordinary in the case of a sale or exchange, directly or indirectly, of property that, in the hands of the transferee member or transferee LLC, is property other than a capital asset. This rule applies if there is a transaction between an LLC and a member owning, directly or indirectly, more than 50 percent of the capital interest or profits interest in the LLC. The rule also applies to a sale or exchange between two LLCs in

---

[9] IRC §707(b)(1)(A).
[10] IRC §707(b)(1)(B).
[11] IRC §707(b)(3); Reg. §1.707-1(b)(3).
[12] IRC §§707(b)(1) (last paragraph), 267(d).
[13] Reg. §§1.707-1(b)(3), 1.267(b)-1(b).

which the same members own, directly or indirectly, more than 50 percent of the capital interests or profit interests.[14]

In determining whether a person owns 50 percent of the LLC, the constructive ownership rules of Section 267(c) apply.[15] However, if a person is not a member, the constructive ownership rules cannot apply to make that person a member.

[3] Sale of Depreciable Property

Gain on the sale of property between a member and LLC in which the member owns, directly or indirectly, more than 50 percent of the capital interests or profits interests is ordinary if the property, in the hands of the transferee, is depreciable property.[16]

In determining whether a person owns 50 percent of the LLC, the constructive ownership rules of Section 267(c) apply.[17] However, if a person is not a member, the constructive ownership rules cannot apply to make that person a member.

[D] Services

Services by the member to the LLC may be treated as a nonmember transaction if the services are unrelated to the LLC's main function. The payments are deductible by the LLC and taxable to the member as an independent contractor.[18] Payments to a member for services are almost always classified as a guaranteed payment or distributive share income, rather than compensation to the member acting in a nonmember capacity.

§14.04 DISTRIBUTIVE SHARE OF INCOME

A member must report on his tax return his distributive shares of LLC income, gain, loss, and deductions.[1] The member must include in taxable income the distributive share of income, whether or not the income is actually distributed.[2]

Actual distributions from the LLC do not ordinarily result in taxation. Distributions decrease a member's basis in the LLC.[3] Undistributed income increases the member's basis in the LLC. No gain or loss is recognized on distributions except to

---

[14] IRC §707(b)(2).

[15] IRC §707(b)(3); Reg. §1.707-1(b)(3).

[16] IRC §1239.

[17] IRC §707(b)(3); Reg. §1.707-1(b)(3).

[18] Wegener v. Comm'r, 41 B.T.A. 857 (1940), *aff'd,* 119 F.2d 49 (5th Cir. 1941), *cert. denied,* 314 U.S. 643 (1941); GCM 34001 (Dec. 23, 1969).

§14.04 [1] IRC §702.

[2] IRC §702(a).

[3] IRC §733.

the extent that a money distribution exceeds the member's basis in the membership interest.[4]

The amount of income earned by the LLC, and the share of income that must be reported by each member, is determined on the last day of the LLC's fiscal year.[5] The member recognizes income for the year that includes the last day of the LLC's tax year in which the LLC reported the distributive share of income.[6]

EXAMPLE 1

An LLC has two equal members. It earns $1 million in income during 2005. It uses all of the income for expansion of the business and makes no distributions. It sends a Schedule K-1 to each member for 2005 showing the member's allocable share of income. Each member must pay taxes on $500,000 of income for 2005 even though no distributions were made.

EXAMPLE 2

An LLC uses the cash method of accounting. It has a fiscal year ending May 31. All of its members are individuals who report on a calendar year basis. For the year ended May 31, 2004, the LLC sends Member B a Schedule K-1 showing the member's share of income, gain, loss, and deductions. The member must report the items on his income tax return for the calendar year ending December 31, 2004.[7]

The LLC may not deduct the payment. However, the distribution of income is ultimately the same as a deduction, since it decreases the distributive share of income taxable to the other members of the LLC. The other members' shares of LLC income are reduced by this amount in the same year.

§14.05   DISGUISED SALE PAYMENTS

Payments to a member that are related to a contribution of property or services to the LLC may be reclassified as a payment in exchange for property or services, rather than a nontaxable distribution.

The three principal types of disguised sales are (a) a contribution of money, property or services to an LLC followed by a related distribution of money or property to the contributing member within two years after the contribution, (b)

---

[4] IRC §731. *See* Chapter 10 for various exceptions.
[5] IRC §706.
[6] Reg. §1.706-1(a)(2).
[7] *Id.*

a contribution of appreciated property to an LLC by one member followed by a distribution of that property to another member within seven years after the contribution, and (c) a contribution of appreciated property to an LLC followed by a distribution of other property to the contributing member within seven years after the contribution.

Disguised sale payments are discussed in Chapter 6.[1]

§14.06   FRINGE BENEFITS

Certain fringe benefits qualify for favorable tax treatment. Other fringe benefits are not available to members in an LLC.

[A]   Permissible Fringe Benefits

[1]   Health Plans

A member must include in gross income the value of health plan coverage provided through an LLC.[1] The member may then deduct the full amount for medical insurance for the member, spouse, and dependents.[2] There is no dollar limit on the deductible amount. This differs from the tax treatment of medical insurance for employees. The cost of medical insurance premiums paid by the employer is excluded from an employee's income.

The deduction is in lieu of the medical expense deduction.[3] The deduction is an above-the-line deduction. Thus, a member may deduct medical expenses even though the member does not itemize deductions, and even though the member's aggregate medical expenses are less than 7.5 percent of adjusted gross income.

The deduction is limited to the member's earned income from the LLC with respect to which the medical plan is established.[4] Expenses for health insurance in excess of the deductible amount may be taken into account as an itemized medical expense deduction, subject to the 7.5 percent floor on deductibility.[5] The deduction does not reduce the income base for self-employment tax purposes.[6] The member may not take a deduction for payments during any calendar month in which the member is eligible to participate in a subsidized health plan maintained by any employer of the member or spouse.[7]

---

§14.05   [1] *See* §6.05 *supra.*

§14.06   [1] The premiums paid by the LLC are treated as guaranteed payments on Form 1065, Partnership Return, and Schedule K-1. No Form 1099 or W-2 is used for such payments. Rev. Rul. 91-26, 1991-1 C.B. 184.

[2] IRC §162(l)(1)(B).

[3] IRC §162(l)(5).

[4] IRC §162(l)(2)(A).

[5] JTC Overview of Health Care Tax Provisions and Proposals to Aid Uninsured Individuals, Part 4 (JCX-4-02) (Feb. 13, 2002).

[6] IRC §162(l)(4).

[7] IRC §162(l)(2)(B).

Prior to 2003, a member could deduct only a percentage of premiums paid by the LLC for health insurance.[8] The remaining amount was deductible only if the aggregate amount of all medical expenses exceeded 7.5 percent of adjusted gross income.

[2]   Insurance

An LLC and its members may not deduct premiums paid on insurance covering the life of a member. However, insurance proceeds that are paid to an LLC on the death of an insured member are nontaxable.[9]

An LLC that acquires an insurance policy on the life of a member frequently transfers the policy to the member on retirement or withdrawal by the member from the LLC. The exclusion from income for life insurance proceeds is lost if the LLC transfers the policy for valuable consideration. However, the exclusion is not lost if the LLC transfers the policy to the insured member or any other member of the LLC.[10]

[3]   Pension and Profit-Sharing Plans

An LLC may adopt qualified pension and profit-sharing plans.[11] The LLC may establish a qualified stock bonus plan for distribution of stock of a corporate partner and its parent corporation.[12]

The LLC may not make pension or profit-sharing contributions for members who are treated as limited partners. The LLC may make contributions only for employees and self-employed persons.[13] The contributions are based on the amount of compensation earned by an employee and the amount of earned income received by a self-employed person.[14] "Earned income" means net earnings from self-employment.[15] A limited partner is not a self-employed person and does not have net earnings from self-employment.

Employees of an LLC that is owned by a member of a controlled group of corporations, and that is classified as a disregarded entity, may participate in an employee stock ownership plan or other qualified plan of the controlled group. The employees of the LLC are treated as employed by the member of the controlled group that owns the membership interests in the LLC.[16]

The transfer of stock from the corporate plan to an LLC stock bonus plan will

---

[8] IRC §162(l)(1)(B).

[9] IRC §101(a)(2).

[10] Ltr. Ruls. 9625023, 9625022, 9625013-018.

[11] *See* Ltr. Ruls. 200116051, 9343036.

[12] *Id.*

[13] If a member is classified as a limited partner, the member may fail to meet the definition of an "employee" under IRC §401(c)(1).

[14] IRC §§401(c)(1)(A), 404(a)(8).

[15] IRC §§1126, 1402(a).

[16] Ltr. Rul. 200111053.

not change the tax basis of the securities for purposes of computing net unrealized appreciation in the securities.[17] The exclusion of net unrealized appreciation[18] will apply after the transfer.[19] The transferred securities will continue to constitute "employer securities" until distributed by the LLC plan.[20]

A pension or profit-sharing plan may invest in LLCs.[21]

Contributions to a pension or profit-sharing plan are often based on a percentage of each employee's compensation. For an LLC that is classified as a partnership, the contributions are based on a percentage of the member's earnings. The earnings of the members are the members' distributive shares of net income, determined after deducting contributions for common-law employees, but before deducting contributions for each member.[22]

[4] Working Condition Fringe Benefits

Employees are not taxed on the value of working condition fringe benefits. A working condition fringe benefit is a fringe benefit that the employee would be entitled to deduct as a business expense if the employee paid the expense himself.[23] Members who perform services for an LLC are treated as employees for such purposes.[24] Thus, members are not taxed on the value of the following working condition fringe benefits:

- Business-related use of an automobile owned by the LLC if the member substantiates business use.[25]
- Job-related expenses that the LLC pays for the member.[26]
- The business-use portion of dues paid to a country club.[27] The LLC may not deduct the country club dues.
- Job placement assistance.[28]

[5] Other Permissible Fringe Benefits

A member of an LLC may exclude from income the value of the following additional fringe benefits:

---

[17] Ltr. Rul. 9343036.
[18] See IRC §402(a), (e)(4).
[19] Ltr. Rul. 9343036.
[20] Id.
[21] See L. McCarthy, "LLCs: A Flexible Alternative for Pension Plan Investments," Pension World, Aug. 1992.
[22] Ltr. Rul. 200247052.
[23] IRC §132(a)(3), (d).
[24] Reg. §1.132-1(b)(2)(ii).
[25] Reg. §1.132-5(a)(1).
[26] Reg. §1.132-1(f).
[27] Reg. §1.132-5(s).
[28] Rev. Rul. 92-69, 1992-2 C.B. 51.

- *De minimis fringe benefits.* An employee may exclude from income *de minimis* fringe benefits received from the employer. Employees include any recipient of a fringe benefit for purposes of the rule.[29] Thus, members of an LLC may exclude from income supper money and local transportation fare that the LLC provides members on an occasional basis in connection with overtime work.[30]
- *Dependent care assistance.* Members of an LLC may exclude from income dependent care assistance under IRC Section 129.[31] The dependent care assistance plan must meet various requirements. The LLC may not pay more than 25 percent of amounts under the plan to members who own more than 5 percent of the membership interests in the LLC.[32]
- *Qualified employee discounts and no-additional cost services.* An employer may provide qualified employee discounts and no-additional cost services to employees on a tax-free basis. Members of an LLC who performs services are treated as employees for such purposes.[33]
- *Athletic facilities.* An LLC may provide on-premise athletic facilities, such as a gym or swimming pool, to members, their spouses and dependents.[34]
- *Educational assistance program.* An employer may establish an educational assistance program for employees under IRC Section 127. Members of an LLC who have earned income from the LLC are treated as employees for such purposes.[35] However, the LLC may not pay more than 5 percent of the annual benefits to members who own more than 5 percent of the membership interests in the LLC.[36]

[B]   Impermissible Fringe Benefits

The following types of fringe benefits are normally taxable to members of an LLC:

- *Meals and lodging.* Members may not exclude from income the value of meals and lodging furnished for the convenience of the employer, except in limited cases.[37]

---

[29] Reg. §1.132-1(b)(4).

[30] Reg. §1.132-6(d)(2)(i).

[31] IRC §129(e)(3).

[32] IRC §129(d)(4).

[33] Reg. §1.132-1(b)(1).

[34] Reg. §1.132-1(b)(3).

[35] IRC §§127(c)(2), (c)(3), 401(c)(1).

[36] IRC §127(b)(1).

[37] One court determined that a partner is not considered an employee for purposes of the meals and lodging exclusion. Robinson v. U.S., 273 F.2d 503 (3rd Cir. 1959). However, other courts have determined that a partner may be an employee for purposes of the meals and lodging exclusion if the partner is acting in a capacity other than as a partner. Papineau, George, 16 T.C. 130 (1951), *nonacq,* Armstrong v. Phinney, 394 F.2d 661 (5th Cir. 1968).

- *Cafeteria plan.* Members may not participate in a cafeteria plan.[38]
- *VEBA.* As a practical matter, only corporations may adopt a VEBA. At least 90 percent of all participants in a VEBA must be employees.[39]
- *Incentive stock options.* Incentive stock options may be granted only to corporate employees.[40] An LLC may not grant incentive stock options to employees unless the LLC is classified as a corporation.[41]
- *Medical expense reimbursement plan.* Members may not participate in a medical expense reimbursement plan.[42] Other employees of an LLC are not taxed on medical expense reimbursements received under a nondiscriminatory plan.
- *Qualified transportation fringe benefits.* Qualified transportation fringe benefits (such as transit passes and free parking) are available only to employees.[43] They are not available to members in an LLC, except as a *de minimis* fringe benefit or working condition fringe benefit.[44]
- *Group term life insurance and other insurance.* Members may not deduct premiums for group term life insurance.[45] Employees are not taxed on group term coverage up to $50,000.[46]
- *Section 423 stock purchase plan.* Employees may purchase stock at a discount under a Section 423 employee stock purchase plan.[47] Options under the plan may be granted only to corporate employees.[48] Employees of an LLC may not participate in a Section 423 plan unless the LLC is classified as a corporation,[49] or is owned by a corporation and classified as a disregarded entity for federal tax purposes.[50]
- *Health reimbursement account.* A self-employed person may not receive medical expense reimbursements under a health reimbursement account.[51]

§14.07   SECTION 736 PAYMENT

A Section 736 payment is a payment to a retired member or the estate of a deceased member in a service LLC if the member is a "general partner." The payments are

---

[38] Prop. Reg. §1.125-1, Q&A-4; IRC §1372.

[39] Reg. §1.501(c)(9)-2(a)(1).

[40] Ltr. Rul. 9321049.

[41] Prop. Reg. §1.421-1(i)(1).

[42] *See* IRC §105(g), (h).

[43] IRC §§132(a)(5), 132(f)(5)(E). Notice 93-4, 1993-1 C.B. 295, Q&A-5, states that qualified transportation fringe benefits may not be provided to partners, 2-percent shareholders of S corporations, sole proprietors, and independent contractors.

[44] Reg. §1.132-9(b), Q&A-5, 24.

[45] This benefit is available only to corporate employees. Prop. Reg. §1.269A-1(b)(6). Congress indicated that this benefit is not available to partners or 2-percent shareholders in S corporations in H.R. Rep. No. 826, 97th Cong., 2d Sess. (1982), n.2, at 21, reprinted in 1982-2 C.B. 730, 739; S. Rep. No. 640, 97th Cong., 2d Sess. (1982), n. 2 at 22, reprinted in 1982-2 C.B. 718, 728.

[46] *See* IRC §79; Reg. §§1.79-1(a), 1.79-0.

[47] IRC §423.

[48] IRC §423(b)(1).

[49] Prop. Reg. §1.421-1(i)(1).

[50] Ltr. Rul. 200046013.

[51] Notice 2002, I.R.B. 2002-28, Part III.

classified either as Section 736(a) payments or Section 736(b) payments. These rules are discussed in Chapter 10.[1]

§14.08   DIFFERENCES BETWEEN GUARANTEED PAYMENT, DISTRIBUTIVE SHARE OF INCOME, AND OTHER PAYMENTS

In most cases, the tax results are similar whether the payment is characterized as a guaranteed payment, distributive share of income, or distribution to a member other than in his capacity as a member. The LLC reduces its income or receives a tax deduction for the payment, and the member reports taxable income. However, there are the following differences:

- *Character of income to member.* A guaranteed payment is always ordinary income.[1] A distributive share of income retains the same character as reported by the LLC on Form 1065.[2] For example, a distributive share of income may be partially trade or business income, capital gains, Section 1231 gain, or other type of income. A payment to a member acting in a nonmember capacity depends on the type of payment. For example, the payment may be a nontaxable return of principal on a loan, capital gain on the sale of property, or rental income on the lease of property.
- *Deduction by LLC.* An LLC may deduct a guaranteed payment unless the payment is made in connection with a capital expenditure.[3] An LLC may not deduct a distributive share of income. However, a distributive share income to one member reduces the taxable income that must be reported by the other members. Thus, the effect of a distributive share of income is in most cases the same as a guaranteed payment. A payment to a member acting in a nonmember capacity may or may not be deductible depending on the nature of the payment.
- *Timing difference.* There are timing differences in income recognition and deduction depending on the character of the payments. A guaranteed payment is included in the member's income in the year in which the guaranteed payment is deducted by the LLC.[4] Thus, if an LLC accrues a guaranteed salary expense in one year, but does not pay that amount to the member until the following year, the member must report the guaranteed payment in the year accrued by the LLC rather than in the following year when received by the member. A distributive share of income is included in the member's income for the tax year that includes the last day of the LLC's fiscal year.[5] Thus, the member must include LLC items in income at the end of the tax year of the LLC, rather than when distributed. A payment

§14.07   [1] *See* §10.08[E] *supra.*
14.08   [1] IRC §§61(a), 707(c); Reg. §1.707-1(c).
[2] *See* IRC §704.
[3] IRC §707(c); Reg. §1.707-1(c).
[4] Reg. §§1.706-1(a)(1), 1.707-1(c).
[5] Reg. §1.706-1(a)(1).

by the LLC to a member acting in a nonmember capacity is included in the member's income in the year of receipt, assuming that the member uses the cash method of accounting. The LLC may deduct such payment only in the year that the member recognizes income. Thus, an accrual method LLC may not deduct accrued rents, interest, compensation, or other payments to a member until it actually pays such amounts.[6]

- *Withholding taxes and self-employment income.* There are different withholding and self-employment tax rules depending on the type of payment.[7] For example, a guaranteed payment for services to a member who is classified as a limited partner is subject to self-employment taxes. A distributive share of income to a member who is classified as a limited partner is not subject to self-employment taxes.[8]

---

[6] IRC §267(a)(2), (e).
[7] *See* Chapter 16.
[8] *Id.*

15

Transfer of Membership Interests

§15.01 OVERVIEW

If an LLC is a disregarded entity for federal tax purposes (branch, division, or sole proprietorship), the sale of a membership interest in the LLC is treated as a sale of the underlying assets.[1] The member recognizes gain or loss to the same extent as if the LLC had sold the underlying assets. The member may also be liable for sales taxes under state law if the assets are tangible personal property or other assets subject to sales taxes.

If the LLC is classified as a corporation for federal tax purposes, then the member recognizes capital gain or loss upon the sale of the membership interest. The amount of gain or loss is equal to the difference between the sale price and the member's basis in the membership interest. A portion of the gain may be ordinary income if the LLC is a collapsible corporation.

Most LLCs are classified as partnerships for federal tax purposes. The tax consequences of selling or transferring a membership interest in an LLC that is classified as a partnership are discussed below.

§15.02 GAIN RECOGNIZED

A member recognizes gain or loss upon the sale or other disposition of a membership interest. The amount of gain or loss is the difference between the amount realized and the member's adjusted basis in the membership interest.[1]

The amount realized is the amount of cash and the fair market value of property received by the member, plus the amount of debt relief.[2] The debt relief includes the member's decreased share of LLC liabilities allocated to the new member.[3]

Gain or loss is capital gain or loss, subject to exceptions.[4]

EXAMPLE

An LLC has two equal members. Each member contributed $10,000 to the LLC. The LLC borrowed $20,000. The LLC then purchased property for $40,000. Each member has a basis of $20,000 in the LLC membership units, consisting of the $10,000 cash contribution plus the 1/2 share of LLC liabilities allocated to each member for basis purposes.

Member A sells her membership units to Member C for $15,000 cash plus assumption of debt. The amount realized on the sale is $25,000. This includes the $15,000 of cash received plus the $10,000 of debt relief. The amount of gain recognized is $5,000 ($25,000 amount realized less $20,000 basis).

---

§15.01   [1] *See* Ltr. Rul. 9751012 (like-kind exchange by a disregarded entity).
§15.02   [1] IRC §741; Reg. §1.741-1(a).
[2] Reg. §1.1001-2(a)(1).
[3] Reg. §§1.752-1 to 1.752-4.
[4] IRC §741. *See* §15.07 *infra*.

§15.03   BASIS

A member must determine the adjusted basis in the membership interest in order to determine the amount of gain realized upon the sale or transfer of the membership interest. There are three ways of determining basis:

- *General rule.* Under the general, a member's initial basis in a membership interest is the amount of cash and the adjusted basis of property contributed to the LLC. The initial basis for a member who purchased a membership interest is the purchase price. The initial basis is increased by additional contributions, the member's distributive share of taxable income and tax-exempt income, and the member's share of LLC liabilities. The initial basis is decreased by distributions, the member's distributive share of tax losses and nondeductible LLC expenses, and any decreases in the member's share of LLC liabilities.[1]
- *Alternative asset method.* Under the first alternative method, the member's basis is the member's share of the LLC's basis in its assets.[2] This is the basis of LLC property that would be distributed to the member on termination of the LLC. Generally, it is equal to the LLC's inside basis in its assets multiplied by the member's percentage interest in the LLC. Liabilities are ignored since they are taken into account in determining basis when an asset is purchased. A member may use this method of determining basis only if it is impractical or impossible to determine basis under the general rule.
- *Alternative capital account method.* Under the second alternative method (which is more commonly used), a member's basis is equal to the member's capital account plus share of LLC liabilities.[3] The LLC must maintain its books and records on a tax basis rather than an accounting basis. This method is normally easier to apply than the first alternative method. The member does not need access to the LLC books and records. The member can obtain the necessary information from Schedule K-1 that the member receives from the LLC each year. The member's capital account is set forth in Item J, column (e). The member's share of debt is set forth in Item F. A member may use this method of determining basis only if it is impractical or impossible to determine basis under the general rule.

These methods of determining basis are discussed in detail in Chapter 9. In practice, taxpayers frequently use a modified version of the capital account method. The taxpayer ignores liabilities and computes gain as the difference between the cash received and the capital account. If the member abandons the LLC when the member has a negative capital account, the gain recognized is equal to the negative capital account.

---

§15.03   [1] Reg. §1.705-1(a).
[2] IRC §705(b); Reg. §1.705-1(b).
[3] IRC §705(b); Reg. §1.705-1(b), Example (3).

EXAMPLE

Member A and Member B each own 500 units in an LLC and share equally in profits and losses. The LLC has assets with a fair market value of $1,800, and liabilities of $800. The tax basis of the assets is $1,000. The LLC keeps capital accounts on a tax basis. Member A has a capital account of $175, and Member B has a capital account of $25.

Member B sells her membership interest in the LLC to Member C for $500, representing her one-half share of the value of LLC assets (1/2 × $1,800 fair market value, less $800 debt). Under the short-cut method of determining gain, Member A computes her gain as the cash received upon the sale of $500, less her tax basis capital account of $25, or a total gain of $475. Under the capital account method authorized by the regulations, the amount of gain is the same, computed as follows:

Amount realized:		
Cash	$ 500	
Liabilities assumed by purchaser	400	
Total amount realized		$ 900
Less adjusted basis in membership units:		
Tax basis capital account	$ 25	
Plus 1/2 share of LLC liabilities	400	
Total adjusted basis		(425)
Gain recognized		$ 475

Normally, the member's share of income and loss is determined on the last day of the LLC's fiscal year. However, a selling member may add to his or her basis the allocable share of income for the fiscal year up to the date of sale.[4]

§15.04 ALLOCATION OF INCOME AND LOSS BETWEEN BUYER AND SELLER

[A] Methods of Allocation

The LLC must allocate profit or loss between members who buy and sell membership interests during the tax year of the LLC. The tax year of the LLC does not close upon the sale or exchange of a membership interest.[1] However, the LLC's tax year closes with respect to a member who sells all of his membership interest in the LLC.[2]

---

[4] Reg. §1.706-1(c)(2).
§15.04 [1] IRC §706(c)(1).
[2] IRC §706(c)(2)(A).

The buying and selling members' distributive shares of LLC income, gain, loss, deductions, and credit are determined by taking into account their "varying interests" in the LLC during the year of the sale or other transfer.

There are two methods for determining the buying and selling members' distributive shares: the interim closing of the books method and the proration method.[3] Under the interim closing of the books method, the LLC closes its books on the date of the sale with respect to the selling member, and allocates all income and deductions after that date to the buying member. Under the proration method, the LLC allocates income, deductions, and losses for the entire year to the buying and selling members based on a daily or monthly basis.

[B]   Allocable Cash-Basis Items

An LLC that uses the cash method of accounting must prorate certain "allocable cash-basis items" over the period to which they are attributable.[4] Cash basis items are interest, taxes, payments for services or the use of property, and any other item specified in IRS regulations.[5]

There is a two-step process for allocating cash-basis items. First, the cash-basis items are assigned to each day during the tax year in which the items accrued.[6] Second, the cash-basis items must be assigned to each member in proportion to his membership interest at the close of each day.[7]

EXAMPLE

An LLC pays $1,000 of interest on a loan during the first six months of its tax year. It repays the loan in full at the end of the six months. The LLC must allocate the interest expense only to the persons who were members in the LLC during the first six months of the year based on their percentage interest in the LLC and the number of days that they were members in the LLC during the six-month period.

[C]   Tiered LLCs

Before the Tax Reform Act of 1984, LLCs were able to make retroactive allocations to new members through use of tiered LLCs and partnerships. A multitiered structure is created when one LLC or partnership owns an interest in another LLC or partnership. The LLC would use the interim closing of the books method

---

[3] Reg. §1.706-1(c). *See* §8.04 *supra* for discussion of the two methods.
[4] IRC §706(d)(2). *See* §8.04 *supra* for discussion of the allocation of cash-basis items.
[5] IRC §706(d)(2)(B).
[6] IRC §706(d)(2)(A)(i).
[7] IRC §706(d)(2)(A)(ii).

of allocation when a new member purchased an interest in the LLC. The parent LLC claimed that it realized its share of the subsidiary LLC's income, gain, losses, and deductions on the last day of the subsidiary LLC's tax year. Therefore, the new member was entitled to a full pro rata share of losses incurred by the subsidiary that were passed through to the parent on the last day of the subsidiary's tax year.

After 1984, an LLC's share of any item of income, gain, loss, deduction, or credit of a subsidiary LLC or partnership must be apportioned over that portion of the tax year during which the parent LLC owned an interest in the subsidiary.[8] The result of the law is to prevent use of multitiered structures to effect retroactive allocation of losses.

§15.05   TERMINATION OF LLC UPON TRANSFER OF MEMBERSHIP INTERESTS

An LLC terminates if there is a sale or an exchange of 50 percent or more of the total interests in the LLC's capital and profits during a 12-month period.[1]

A terminated LLC is treated as transferring all of its assets and liabilities to a new LLC in exchange for an interest in the new LLC. Immediately thereafter the terminated LLC is treated as distributing membership interests in the new LLC to the purchasing member and the other remaining members in liquidation of the terminated LLC, either for continuation of the business or for its dissolution and winding-up.[2]

The tax consequences of a termination after a 50 percent transfer are discussed in Chapter 12.[3]

§15.06   LIKE-KIND EXCHANGES AND INVOLUNTARY CONVERSIONS

[A]   Like-Kind Exchanges

[1]   In General

No gain or loss is recognized if a taxpayer exchanges property held in a trade or business or for investment for like-kind property held in a trade or business or for investment.[1] The party transferring the property in the like-kind exchange must be the same party that receives the replacement property. Taxpayers often use an intermediary to facilitate the like-kind exchange.

The exchange of a membership interest in an LLC for a membership interest

---

[8] IRC §706(d)(3).
§15.05   [1] Ltr. Rul. 9701029 (*citing* IRC §708(b)(1)(B)).
[2] Reg. §1.708-1(b)(1)(iv). *See* §12.03 *supra* for discussion of the tax consequences of the termination.
[3] *See* §12.03[B] *supra*.
§15.06   [1] IRC §1031.

in another LLC or partnership does not qualify for nonrecognition of gain under IRC §1031.[2]

[2]   Use of Single-Member LLC to Facilitate Exchange

A taxpayer must ordinarily purchase the replacement property from the same party that acquires the taxpayer's property in a like-kind exchange. The same taxpayer who transfers the property in a like-kind exchange must receive the replacement property.

The taxpayer may use a single-member LLC to facilitate a like-kind exchange. The acquisition of the replacement property or the disposition of the exchange property by the LLC is treated as the acquisition or disposition of the property by the taxpayer, assuming that the LLC is classified as a disregarded entity for federal tax purposes.

For example, the taxpayer may transfer property in an exchange that is directly owned by the taxpayer, and then receive the replacement property through an LLC that the taxpayer forms to acquire the replacement property. The acquisition of the replacement property by the LLC is treated as an acquisition of the property by the taxpayer if the LLC is classified as a disregarded entity for federal tax purposes.[3] The taxpayer is treated as the owner of the assets under the like-kind exchange rules. The transaction does not violate the requirement that the like-kind replacement property "be held either for productive use in a trade or business or investment."[4] The investment intent or business purpose of the LLC is attributed to the owner of the LLC.[5]

An LLC with two members will be treated as owned by a single member for like-kind exchange purposes if the second member has no interest in profits and losses, does not manage the LLC, and has only limited voting rights. The LLC cannot be classified as a partnership if the members have not entered into an agreement to share profits and losses from the operation of a business. The LLC will be treated as a disregarded entity if the LLC does not elect to be classified as a corporation for federal tax purposes.[6]

This rule permits a person to own real estate and obtain some measure of protection from liabilities. The member can engage in a like-kind exchange without having to hold direct title to the property. The member can also request that the owner of the like-kind exchange property transfer the property to be acquired to an LLC prior to the exchange. The member then receives protection with respect to the new property as well as to the property transferred out in the exchange.

---

[2] IRC §1031(a)(2)(B).
[3] Ltr. Ruls. 200131014, 199911033, 9751012, 9807013.
[4] *See* IRC §1031(a)(1).
[5] Ltr. Ruls. 200131014, 9751012.
[6] Ltr. Rul. 199911033.

[3] Use of LLC as Intermediary

If a direct, simultaneous exchange of properties is not possible, the taxpayer may use a qualified intermediary to acquire the replacement property and/or exchange property.

An LLC may act as a qualified intermediary in a like-kind exchange.[7] The taxpayer may also complete a like-kind exchange by acquiring the single-member LLC that acts as the intermediary and owns the replacement property. The acquisition of the LLC is made to avoid state transfer taxes that would otherwise apply if the taxpayer directly acquired the property from the intermediary. The taxpayer's acquisition of the LLC is treated as the acquisition of the replacement property if the LLC is classified as a disregarded entity for federal tax purposes.[8]

[4] Distributions of Property from LLC

LLCs that are classified as partnerships sometimes attempt to obtain nonrecognition by first distributing the LLC property to the members. The members then make a like-kind exchange of the LLC property for other property of like kind. There are several potential problems with this tactic. The property distributed by the LLC to the members must be held by the members for investment or in the active conduct of a trade or business. The IRS may determine that the members are not holding the property distributed from the LLC for investment or in the active conduct of a trade or business, but are merely acquiring it to facilitate a like-kind exchange under Section 1031.

An LLC that has entered into a like-kind exchange may complete the exchange even though it liquidates and transfers its assets and liabilities to a newly formed limited partnership. The limited partnership is treated as the continuation of the LLC. The liquidation does not result in the termination of the LLC. The limited partnership is treated as both the transferor of the relinquished property previously transferred to a qualified intermediary by the LLC before its liquidation, and as the transferee of the replacement property received from the qualified intermediary.[9]

[B] *Involuntary Conversions and Condemnations*

An LLC may avoid gain on an involuntary conversion by purchasing replacement property that is similar or related in service or use.[10] The LLC, rather than the members, must reinvest in similar or related property.[11]

A single-member LLC that is owned by the taxpayer and that is classified as a

---

[7] Ltr. Rul. 200118023.

[8] Ltr. Rul. 200118023.

[9] Ltr. Rul. 199935065.

[10] IRC §1033.

[11] T.K. McManus v. Comm'r, 65 T.C. 197 (1975), *aff'd*, 575 F.2d 1177 (6th Cir. 1978); M. Demirjian v. Comm'r, 457 F.2d 1 (3d Cir. 1972).

disregarded entity for federal tax purposes may be used to acquire the replacement property. Receipt of the replacement property by the LLC is treated as receipt of the replacement property directly by the owner of the LLC for purposes of the nonrecognition of gain rules.[12]

§15.07   CHARACTER OF GAIN AND LOSS

Most members report all of the gain or loss on the sale of a membership interest as capital gain or loss.[1] However, the regulations require a member to divide the gain or loss into the following five categories:[2]

- Ordinary income or loss if the LLC owns hot assets (unrealized receivables and inventory items);
- 28 percent collectibles gain (but not loss) if the LLC owns collectibles held for more than one year;
- 25 percent Section 1250 capital gain (but not loss) if the LLC owns depreciable real estate held for more than one year;
- Residual short-term capital gain or loss if the member held the membership interest for less than one year;
- Residual long-term capital gain or loss if the member held the membership interest for more than one year. A member also recognizes long-term capital gain on the sale of a membership interest held for less than one year to the extent that the member contributed capital assets to the LLC that have a combined member/LLC holding period of more than one year.[3]

[A]   Category 1: Section 751 Ordinary Income or Loss—Hot Assets

The first category of gain or loss is Section 751 ordinary income or loss. A member recognizes ordinary income or loss if the LLC has unrealized receivables or inventory items (referred to as "hot assets").[4] These terms are defined to include many items other than unrealized receivables and inventory items.

Unrealized receivables include the following items:[5]

- Accounts receivable for goods delivered. These are unrealized receivables only to the extent that income was not previously included in income of the LLC.[6] An LLC will ordinarily not have any such receivables since an LLC

---

[12] Ltr. Ruls. 199909045, 199935065.
§15.07   [1] IRC §741; Reg. §1.741-1(a).
[2] Reg. §1.1(h)-1.
[3] Reg. §1.1(h)-1(f), Example 5(ii).
[4] IRC §741, referring to IRC §751.
[5] IRC §751(c).
[6] Reg. §1.751-1(c)(1).

that sells inventory must ordinarily use the accrual method of accounting or a hybrid method that accounts for inventory.[7]

- Accounts receivable for goods to be delivered in the future. These are included as unrealized receivables, even if title has not yet passed, the goods have not yet been segregated for sale to a particular customer, or the goods have not yet been made. There must be an actual contract that locks in the gain. The fair market value of the right to receive this ordinary income item may be discounted based on present value. This Section 751 item is widely ignored by taxpayers.
- Accounts receivable for services rendered or to be rendered to the extent not previously included in income of the LLC. There must be a definite right to receive the payments, rather than a mere expectancy or contract that may be terminated by the customer.
- Depreciation recapture under IRC Section 1245;
- Excess depreciation under IRC Section 1250;
- Mining exploration expense recapture;
- Stock in a DISC and certain other foreign corporations;
- Franchises, trademarks and trade names;
- Oil, gas, or geothermal property;
- Excess farm loss recapture; and
- Market-discount bonds and short-term obligations.

Inventory items include the following four main categories of assets:[8]

- Inventory and dealer property held primarily for sales to customers in the ordinary course of business.
- Any other property of an LLC that is not a capital asset or Section 1231 property. However, an asset will not be treated as a Section 1231 asset to the extent there would be depreciation recapture on sale of the asset.[9]
- Foreign investment company stock subject to IRC Section 1246(a).
- Any other property held by an LLC that would fall within one of the first three categories if held by the selling or distributee member.

The amount of ordinary income or loss realized by a member on the sale or exchange of a membership interest is equal to the ordinary income or loss that the LLC would allocate to the member if the LLC sold all of its assets in a taxable transaction for cash in an amount equal to the fair market value of such property immediately prior to the sale of the membership interest.[10]

---

[7] *See* §17.01[B] *infra.*

[8] IRC §751(d).

[9] IRC §64.

[10] Reg. §§1.751-1(a)(2), 1.1(h)-1(f), Examples 1(iii), 5(iii). If the ordinary income allocated to the member exceeds the member's overall gain from the sale of the membership interest, the member recognizes capital loss equal to the difference.

Normally, the amount of ordinary income can be determined by multiplying the member's percentage interest in the LLC by the ordinary income that the LLC would recognize on sale of the hot assets at fair market value. The formula for determining the amount of gain or loss is as follows:

Fair market value of   LLC's basis   Member's percentage
each unrealized receivable   − in such items × interest in the LLC[11]
or inventory item

The buyer and seller sometimes enter into an agreement allocating the purchase price to the LLC assets. The preamble to the final regulations states that such an agreement would be "inconsistent with the hypothetical sale approach of the regulations."[12]

A member may recognize ordinary income attributable to Section 751 property owned by the LLC in excess of the net gain from the sale of the membership interest (e.g., because of the large amount of zero basis accounts receivable owned by a cash basis LLC). In such case, the excess amount is a capital loss. The net amount of Section 751 ordinary income and capital loss must equal the gain on sale of the membership interest.[13]

EXAMPLE

There are two equal members in an LLC, Members A and B. Member B's basis in her membership interest is $10,000. Member B sells her membership interest to Member C for $50,000. LLC's balance sheet on the date of sale is as follows:

Asset	Tax Basis to LLC	Fair Market Value
Cash	$ 1,000	$ 1,000
Accounts Receivable	0	5,000
Inventory	3,000	6,000
Land held for investment	10,000	88,000
Total Assets	$14,000	$100,000

Member B first computes her net gain in the regular manner. This is $40,000 (sales price of $50,000 less basis of $10,000). Member B then determines the

---

[11] The amount realized by the selling member that is attributable to Section 751 property (unrealized receivables and inventory items) is the member's "share" of such items. Reg. §1.751-1(a)(1). A member's share depends on any special allocation provisions in the operating agreement. Thus, if the operating agreement provides that the selling member does not share in income or gain from Section 751 property, or forfeits that amount on sale of a membership interest, then the selling member does not recognize any ordinary income attributable to Section 751 property on sale of a membership interest. Francis E. Holman, 66 T.C. 809 (1976), *aff'd*, 564 F.2d 283 (9th Cir. Memo. 1977); Julian E. Jacobs, T.C. 1974-196 (1974).

[12] Preamble to Reg. §1.751-1, T.D. 8847, 1999-52 I.R.B. 701.

[13] Reg. §§1.751-1(a)(1), 1.751-1(g), Example 1(ii).

amount of gain that is Section 751 ordinary income. The amount of Section 751 ordinary income potential is $5,000 for the accounts receivable ($5,000 fair market value less LLC's basis of $0) and $3,000 for the inventory ($6,000 fair market value less LLC's basis of $3,000). Member B's share of that ordinary income potential is 50 percent of $8,000, or $4,000. Therefore, Member B recognizes $4,000 of ordinary income and $36,000 of capital gain.

EXAMPLE

Same facts as in the previous example, except that Member B's basis in her membership interest is $37,000. The net gain on sale is $3,000 (the difference between the sales price of $40,000 and the basis in the membership interest of $37,000). Member B still recognizes $4,000 of ordinary income (50 percent of the ordinary income potential in unrealized receivables and inventory items owned by the LLC). Member B also has a $1,000 capital loss. The total income, gain and loss from all categories must equal the net gain of $3,000. Since Member B recognized $4,000 of ordinary income, the residual capital loss is $1,000.[14]

EXAMPLE

Tracy has a one-quarter interest in an LLC. The adjusted basis of her membership interest at the end of the current year is $30,000. She sells her interest in the LLC to Edward for $50,000 cash. There is no agreement between the parties for any allocation of the sales price. The LLC has no liabilities. The basis and fair market value of the LLC's assets are as follows:

Asset	Basis	Fair Market Value
Cash	$40,000	$40,000
Unrealized receivables	0	$36,000
Inventory	$40,000	$92,000
Land	$40,000	$32,000
Total	$120,000	$200,000

The net gain is $20,000 ($50,000 sales price less $30,000 adjusted basis in membership interest). The ordinary income is $22,000 (1/4 × $88,000 of potential ordinary income to the LLC in the unrealized receivables and inventory). The capital loss is $2,000.[15]

---

[14] Reg. §1.751-1(g), Example 1(ii).
[15] 1999 IRS Special Enrollment Examination Questions and Official Answers, Part 2, Q&A-79.

[B]   Category 2: 28 Percent Collectibles Gain

The second category of gain is 28 percent collectibles gain. The maximum individual tax rate on capital gains from the sale of collectibles held for more than one year is 28 percent.[16] A member recognizes gain (but not loss)[17] in this category on the sale of a membership interest to the extent that:[18]

- The LLC owns collectibles;
- The member would be allocated net gain from the sale of the collectibles if the LLC sold all of its collectibles immediately prior to the member's transfer of the membership units; and
- The member held the membership interest for more than one year. A member is treated as owning a membership interest for more than one year to the extent that a member contributes assets to the LLC that have a holding period of more than one year.[19] Thus, if a member contributed long-term capital gain assets to an LLC in exchange for 50 percent of his membership interests, and sold all his membership interests less than one year thereafter, then 50 percent of the collectibles gain attributable to the member would be classified as 28 percent collectibles gain.[20] The collectibles gain attributable the selling member is treated as collectible gain even though the LLC owned the collectibles for less than one year.[21]

EXAMPLE

There are two equal members in an LLC, Members A and B. Member B's basis in her membership interest is $10,000. Member B sells her membership interest to Member C for $50,000, more than one year after her acquisition of the membership interest. The LLC's balance sheet on the date of sale is as follows:

---

[16] IRC §1(h)(5) and (6).

[17] Reg. §1.1(h)-1(f), Example 3.

[18] IRC §1(h)(6)(B); Reg. §1.1(h)-1(b)(2), (f), Examples 1(iv), 2, 3, 5(iv).

[19] Under IRC §1223(1), a member's holding period for the membership interest includes the holding period of capital assets and §1231 assets that the member contributed to the LLC in exchange for a membership interest.

[20] Reg. §1.1(h)-1(f), Example 5(iv). In such case, the 28-percent collectibles gain is determined by (a) computing the total gain that the LLC would realize if it sold all its collectibles in a taxable transaction for cash equal to the fair market value of collectibles immediately prior to the transfer of the membership interest, (b) allocating a portion of that gain to the selling member based on the member's percentage interest in the LLC (or based on a special allocation provision under the operating agreement), and (c) multiplying such amount by the percentage of long-term capital assets that the member contributed to the LLC in exchange for the membership interest.

[21] Reg. §1.1(h)-1(f), Example 5(iv). All the collectibles gain attributable to the selling member's interest in the LLC is treated as gain from the sale or exchange of a capital asset held for more than one year, whether or not the collectibles have actually been held by the LLC for more than one year. Reg. §1.1(b)-2.

Asset	Tax Basis to LLC	Fair Market Value
Cash	$ 1,000	$ 1,000
Collectible 1	0	6,000
Collectible 2	1,000	0
Land held for investment	13,000	94,000
Total Assets	$15,000	$101,000

Member B first computes her net gain in the regular manner. This is $40,000 (sales price of $50,000 less basis of $10,000). Member B then determines the amount of gain that is 28 percent collectibles gain. The LLC has two collectibles that have been held for more than one year, Collectible 1 and Collectible 2. There is $5,000 of potential gain for those collectibles ($6,000 fair market value, less $1,000 basis). Member B's share of that gain is $2,500 (1/2 × $5,000). Therefore, Member B recognizes $2,500 of collectibles capital gain that is taxed at the maximum 28 percent tax rate. The balance of the gain, $37,500, is taxed at the maximum 20 percent long-term capital gain rate. There is no ordinary income since the LLC does not have unrealized receivables or inventory items.

EXAMPLE

Same facts as in the previous example, except that Member B held her membership interest for less than one year. All of the gain is taxed as short-term capital gain. No part of the gain is taxed at the maximum 28 percent collectibles capital gain rate even though the LLC owned collectibles for more than one year.

[C]   Category 3: 25 Percent Unrecaptured Section 1250 Gain

The third category of gain is 25 percent unrecaptured Section 1250 gain.

There are two types of Section 1250 gain. The first type of gain is ordinary income recapture. Depreciable real estate placed in service prior to 1987 could be depreciated using accelerated depreciation. If such property is held more than one year, then part of the gain on the sale is subject to recapture as ordinary income. The amount of ordinary income recapture is the excess of total depreciation deductions over the amount that would have been available under straight-line depreciation (but not in excess of the total gain).[22] This first type of Section 1250 gain is taxed in category 1 as a hot asset. It is not taxed in the third category

---

[22] IRC §1250(b)(1).

as 25 percent gain. Only the gain attributable to the straight-line component of depreciation on property is 25 percent gain in this third category.

After 1986, real estate can only be depreciated under the straight-line method. Therefore, if the property is sold at a profit, none of the gain is recaptured as ordinary income under IRC Section 1250. All of the gain attributable to depreciation deductions is "unrecaptured Section 1250 gain" that is taxed at a maximum 25 percent capital gains rate. The balance of the gain, if any, is taxed at the maximum 20 percent capital gains rate.[23]

A member recognizes gain (but not loss) in this third category on the sale of a membership interest to the extent that:[24]

- The LLC owns depreciable real property.
- The LLC held the property for over one year.
- The gain is attributable to straight-line depreciation (including the straight-line component of depreciation on property placed in service prior to 1987 for which accelerated depreciation has been taken).
- The depreciation is less than the total potential gain. If the depreciation is more than the total potential gain, then only the depreciation equal to the potential gain is unrecaptured Section 1250 gain.
- The member would be allocated depreciation gain from the sale of the property if the LLC sold the property immediately prior to the transfer of the membership interest.
- The member held the membership interest for more than one year.

EXAMPLE

There are two equal members in an LLC, Members A and B. However, all of the depreciation is allocated to Member B. Member B's basis in her membership interest is $10,000. Member B sells her membership interest to Member C for $50,000, more than one year after her acquisition of the membership interest. LLC's balance sheet on the date of sale is as follows:

Asset	Tax Basis to LLC	Fair Market Value
Cash	$ 1,000	$ 1,000
Building		
(held more than one year;		
$1,000 depreciation		
previously taken)	3,000	11,000
Land held for investment	10,000	88,000
Total Assets	$14,000	$100,000

Member B first computes her net gain in the regular manner. This is $40,000 (sales price of $50,000 less her basis of $10,000). Member B then determines

---

[23] IRC §1(h)(1)(C).
[24] Reg. §1.1(h)-1(b)(3)(ii).

the amount of gain that is unrecaptured Section 1250 gain. The building is the only Section 1250 depreciable asset. There is $8,000 of potential gain, which exceeds the $1,000 of depreciation previously taken on the building. Therefore, gain equal to the depreciation is unrecaptured Section 1250 gain. Member B recognizes $1,000 of capital gain taxed at the maximum 25 percent rate. The balance of the gain, $39,000, is taxed at the maximum 20 percent long-term capital gain rate. There is no ordinary income since the LLC does not have unrealized receivables or inventory items.

[D] Category 4: Residual Short-Term Capital Gain and Loss

If the member sells a membership interest held for less than one year, then the gain or loss is determined as follows:[25]

- The member recognizes ordinary income or loss to the extent of the member's share of potential gain or loss on unrealized receivables and inventory items held by the LLC.
- The balance of the gain or loss is short-term capital gain or loss.
- There is no gain or loss in the 28 percent, 25 percent, or 15 percent categories even if the LLC owns collectibles, depreciable real estate or capital assets that it has held for more than one year.

EXAMPLE

There are two equal members in an LLC, Members A and B. Member B's basis in her membership interest is $10,000. Member B sells her membership interest to Member C for $50,000, less than one year after her acquisition of the membership interest. The LLC's balance sheet on the date of sale is as follows:

Asset	Tax Basis to LLC	Fair Market Value
Cash	$ 1,000	$ 1,000
Accounts Receivable	3,000	11,000
Land held for investment		88,000
(held more than one year)	10,000	
Total Assets	$14,000	$100,000

[25] See, for example, Reg. §1.1(h)-1(e), Example 4. In that example, the partner had a net gain of $2,500 on the sale of a partnership interest. The partner first recognized $1,500 of ordinary income equal to the partner's share of accounts receivable of the partnership. The remaining $1,000 of gain on the sale was capital gain. In the example, the partner held the partnership interests for less than one year prior to sale, but had received half of the partnership interests in exchange for long-term gain property held by the partner for over one year. Therefore, ½ of the residual capital gain on sale ($500) was short-term capital gain, and ½ of the residual capital gain was long-term capital gain.

Member B first computes her net gain in the regular manner. This is $40,000 (sales price of $50,000 less basis of $10,000). Member B then determines the amount of gain that is Section 751 ordinary income. The amount of Section 751 ordinary income potential is $8,000 ($11,000 fair market value of receivables less LLC's basis of $3,000) Member B's share of that ordinary income potential is 50 percent of $8,000, or $4,000. Therefore, Member B recognizes $4,000 of ordinary income. The balance of the gain, $36,000, is short-term capital gain.

[E]   Category 5: Residual Long-Term Capital Gain and Loss

The balance of gain or loss on the sale of a membership interest is long-term capital gain or loss.[26] This gain is normally taxed as follows:

Effective date	Maximum long-term capital gains rate for individuals, trusts, and estates for regular and alternative minimum tax purposes
After May 5, 2003 and prior to 2008	15% for individuals in the 25% rate bracket and above (replacing the prior 20% tax rate and the 18% rate for assets held more than five years)
	5% for individuals in rate brackets below the 25% bracket
2008 tax year	15% for individuals in the 25% rate bracket and above
	0% for individuals in rate brackets below the 25% bracket
2009 tax year and subsequent years	20% for individuals in the 25% rate bracket and above; 18% for such individuals for capital assets held more than five years and for which the holding period begins after December 31, 2000
	10% for individuals in rate brackets below the 25% bracket; 8% for such individuals for assets held more than five years and for which the holding period begins after December 31, 2000

---

[26] Reg. §1.1(h)-1(a), (c).

The total gain and loss in all five categories must equal the net gain or loss from sale of the membership interest.

EXAMPLE

There are two equal members in an LLC, Members A and B. Member B's basis in her membership interest is $49,000. Member B sells her membership interest to Member C for $50,000. LLC's balance sheet on the date of sale is as follows:

Asset	Tax Basis to LLC	Fair Market Value
Cash	$ 1,000	$ 1,000
Accounts Receivable	0	6,000
Collectible (held more than one year)	0	5,000
Building (held more than one year, $20,000 depreciation previously taken)	10,000	40,000
Land held for investment	10,000	48,000
Total Assets	$21,000	$100,000

Member B first computes her net gain in the regular manner. This is $1,000 (sales price of $50,000 less basis of $49,000). Member B then groups the gains and losses into the five different categories as follows:

- There is $3,000 of ordinary income. This is ½ of the total potential gain to the LLC of the unrealized receivables and inventory items (50 percent membership interest × $6,000 of potential gain for the accounts receivable).[27]
- There is $2,500 of collectibles gain taxed at the maximum 28 percent rate. This is ½ of the total $5,000 of potential gain on collectibles held by the LLC for over one year.[28]
- There is $10,000 of unrecaptured Section 1250 gain taxed at the maximum 25 percent rate. The LLC has taken $20,000 of depreciation on the building, which is less than the total potential gain of $30,000. Therefore, ½ of the $20,000 in depreciation is unrecaptured Section 1250 gain.
- There is no short-term capital gain or loss since Member B held the membership interest for more than one year.
- There is a residual long-term capital loss of $14,500. This is the amount necessary to make the total gains and losses in all categories equal

---

[27] Reg. §1.1(h)-1(f), Examples 1(v), 2.
[28] Reg. §1.1(h)-1(f), Example 1(iii).

the net gain on sale of the membership interest.[29] Member B had a net gain of $1,000 on the sale of the membership interest ($50,000 sales price, less $49,000 basis). The net gain or loss in all five categories is $1,000 ($3,000 of ordinary income, $2,500 of 28 percent collectibles gain, $10,000 of unrecaptured Section 1250 gain, and $14,500 of long-term capital loss).

[F]   Reporting and Notification

The parties must comply with the following notification and reporting requirements if the selling member recognizes any Section 751 ordinary income or loss, 28 percent collectibles gain, or 25 percent unrecaptured Section 1250 gain:

- The selling member must notify the LLC within 30 days after the sale or exchange, or by January 15 of the following year, if earlier.[30] The notification must include the names and addresses of the transferor and transferee, the taxpayer identification numbers of the transferor and the transferee, if known, and the date of the sale or exchange.
- The LLC must file an information return on Form 8308. The LLC must file the form as part of the partnership return on Form 1065. The form must identify the buying and selling members, and provide such other information as required by the IRS. The form does not require the LLC to provide information regarding the amount of ordinary income, 28-percent collectibles gain, or 25-percent unrecaptured Section 1250 gain on the sale of a membership interest.[31]
- The LLC must disclose this information to the buying and selling member before January 31 of the following calendar year.[32]
- The selling member must submit with his or her income tax return a statement setting forth the date of the sale or exchange, the amount of any gain or loss attributable to the Section 751 property, and the amount of any gain or loss attributable to capital gain or loss on the sale of the LLC interest.[33]

There is general noncompliance with these requirements because the rules are complex, and it is often difficult for the parties to obtain the necessary information to make the proper computations of gain or loss. As a result, most members usually report all the gain or loss on sale of a membership interest as short or long-term capital gain or loss.

---

[29] Reg. §1.1(h)-1(f), Example 1(iv).
[30] Reg. §§1.1(h)-1(e), 1.751-1(a)(3), 1.6050K-1(d)(1).
[31] Reg. §1.6050K-1(a), (b).
[32] Reg. §1.6050K-1(c).
[33] Reg. §1.741-1(a)(3).

§15.08   SECTION 754 ELECTION

[A]   Overview

An LLC may make an election under IRC Section 754 to adjust the basis of the LLC's assets when a member sells or exchanges a membership interest or transfers a membership interest upon death. If the election is made, the LLC will then compute depreciation and gain or loss upon the disposition of the assets with reference to the adjusted basis.

The basis adjustment may be upward or downward depending on the sale price. The amount of basis adjustment is the difference between the member's share of the LLC's inside basis in its assets and the member's outside basis in his membership interest. The basis adjustment is roughly equal to the gain recognized by the selling member upon the sale, exchange, or other transfer.

The adjustment applies only for tax purposes, and has no effect on the accounting books and records of the LLC.

[B]   Making the Election

An LLC may adjust the basis of its assets upon the sale or transfer of a membership interest only if it makes an election under IRC Section 754. The adjustment is made under Section 743(b).[1] Once the election is made, it applies to all sales, exchanges, and distributions until the election is terminated. The election is made at the LLC level rather than by the members.

The election must be made with a timely return for the tax year of the LLC[2] or an amended return.[3] The IRS may grant an extension for filing the election statement.[4]

The district director of the Internal Revenue Service must approve any revocations of the election.[5] The district director may grant a revocation based on a change in the nature of the LLC's trade or business, a substantial increase in assets, a change in the nature of its assets, increasing administrative burden, or other valid business reasons.

[C]   Election Benefits Transferee Only

The Section 743 basis adjustment is an adjustment for the transferee only.[6] No adjustment is made to the common basis of LLC property. The basis adjustment

---

§15.08   [1] Reg. §1.754-1.
[2] Reg. §1.754-1(b).
[3] Reg. §301.9100-2.
[4] Reg. §1.754-1(b)(1); Rev. Proc. 92-85, 1992-2 C.B. 69 (automatic extensions).
[5] Reg. §1.754-1(c).
[6] Reg. §1.743-1(b).

does not affect the LLC's computation of any item of income, gain, loss, credit, or deduction. It does not have any effect on the members' capital accounts.

The LLC must first compute its tax items at the LLC level without regard to the basis adjustment. The LLC then allocates all tax items to the members in accordance with the operating agreement. Finally, the LLC adjusts the transferee member's distributive share of LLC tax items to reflect the transferee's special basis in the properties that give rise to the tax items. The transferee's income, gain, or loss from the sale by the LLC of its property in which the transferee has a basis adjustment is equal to the transferee's distributive share of LLC income, gain, or loss from the sale of the property, adjusted to account for the transferee's basis adjustment for the property.

A member who receives a nonliquidating distribution from an LLC receives a carryover basis for the distributed property equal to the LLC's basis immediately prior to the distribution. The member may include the Section 754 basis adjustment in the basis of the distributed assets. If the LLC adjusts the basis of its assets for one member, and then distributes those assets to another member, then it must take the adjustment off of the distributed assets, and reallocate the basis adjustment to remaining LLC property of like kind[7] in proportion to the relative appreciation in those assets. This reallocated basis adjustment benefits only the member with respect to whom the initial basis adjustment was made.

[D] Determining Basis Adjustment

The LLC must increase the basis of its assets if the purchasing member's basis for the membership interest exceeds the member's share of the adjusted basis of LLC assets.[8] The LLC must decrease the basis of its assets if the purchasing member's basis for the membership interest is less than the member's share of the adjusted basis of LLC assets.[9] The basis adjustment is the difference between the inside and outside basis.

A member's share of the adjusted basis of LLC assets is determined by reference to a hypothetical sale of LLC's assets. The LLC is treated as having sold all of its assets for fair market value for cash in a fully taxable transaction.[10] The purchasing member's share of the adjusted basis of LLC assets is (a) the cash that the purchasing member would receive if the LLC were liquidated after the hypothetical sale, (b) plus the purchasing member's share of LLC liabilities, (c) plus the amount of

---

[7] The determination of like-kind assets for such purposes is much narrower than a Class 1 or Class 2 determination. Like-kind assets are broken down into groups such as inventory, accounts receivable, capital assets, and depreciable assets. Thus, if there had been an optional adjustment to basis for depreciable real property that was distributed to another member, then the optional adjustment that is taken off of the property may not be reallocated to other nondepreciable real property. If there is no like-kind property to which the optional adjustment to basis can be allocated, then the adjustment will be applied to subsequently acquired property of a like character when the LLC acquires additional property. IRC §755(b).

[8] Reg. §1.743-1(b)(1).

[9] *Id.*

[10] Reg. §1.743-1(d)(2).

any tax losses that would be allocated to the purchasing member in the hypothetical sale, (d) less the amount of any tax gain that would be allocated to the purchasing member in the hypothetical sale.

EXAMPLE

An LLC has three equal members, Members A, B, and C. Member C sells her membership interest to Member T for $22,000 cash. The balance sheet of the LLC shows the following:[11]

Asset	Tax Basis to LLC	Fair Market Value
Cash	$ 5,000	$ 5,000
Accounts receivable	10,000	10,000
Inventory	20,000	21,000
Depreciable asset	20,000	40,000
Total assets	$55,000	$76,000

Liabilities and Capital Accounts		
Liabilities	$10,000	$10,000
Capital accounts		
A	15,000	22,000
B	15,000	22,000
C	15,000	22,000
	$55,000	$76,000

There is a short-cut method of determining the Section 743(b) basis adjustment if the LLC determines the capital accounts of its members on a tax basis. The basis adjustment is the difference between the purchase price (ignoring liabilities and debt relief) and the selling member's tax basis capital account. In this case, the basis adjustment is the $22,000 cash purchase price, less Member B's tax basis capital account of $15,000, or $7,000. Therefore, the LLC must increase the tax basis of its assets by $7,000.

Under the regulations, the basis adjustment would be determined as follows:[12]

1. Determine the purchasing member's basis in her membership interest.

Cash	$22,000
Liabilities assumed (1/3 share of $10,000 liabilities of LLC)	3,333
Member T's adjusted basis	$25,333

2. Determine the purchasing member's share of the adjusted basis of LLC assets.

---

[11] Reg. §1.743-1(d)(3), example 1.
[12] This example is set forth in Reg. §1.743-1(d)(3), example 1.

(a) Determine the cash the LLC would receive after the transfer if it sold all of its assets at fair market value of $76,000 for cash, less $10,000 of liabilities. $66,000

(b) Determine the purchasing member's share of cash that would be received by her in liquidation after the hypothetical sale (1/3 of $66,000). $22,000

(c) Determine the gain or loss that the LLC would realize in the hypothetical sale of assets. This is equal to the $76,000 sale price/fair market value of the assets, less the LLC's $55,000 adjusted basis in its assets. $21,000

(d) Determine the gain or loss that would be allocated to the purchasing member after the hypothetical sale (1/3 of $21,000 gain). $ 7,000

(e) Decrease the purchasing member's $22,000 share of cash proceeds from the hypothetical sale by the purchasing member's $7,000 share of the gain from the hypothetical sale (or increase the cash share by the member's share of loss). $15,000

(f) Add the purchasing member's share of LLC liabilities (1/3 of $10,000). $ 3,333

(h) The purchasing member's share of adjusted basis of LLC assets. $18,333

3. Determine the Section 743 basis adjustment.

This is equal to the difference between the purchasing member's $25,333 adjusted basis in her membership interest, determined under step 1, and her $18,333 share of the adjusted basis of LLC assets, determined under step 2. $ 7,000

Therefore, the LLC must increase the basis of its assets by $7,000.

[E]   Allocation of Basis Adjustment to LLC Assets

After the Section 743(b) basis adjustment is determined, the LLC must allocate the basis adjustment to its assets. This is a three-step process. First, the LLC must determine the fair market value of each asset. Second, the LLC must allocate the basis adjustment between two classes of assets, capital gain property and ordinary income property. Third, the LLC must allocate the basis adjustment for each class to each item of property within that class.[13]

---

[13] Reg. §1.755-1(a)(1).

[1] Valuation of Assets

The first step is to determine the fair market value of each LLC asset. The LLC must value the assets on the basis of all the facts and circumstances. The fair market value of each asset cannot be less than the amount of any nonrecourse debt encumbering the asset.[14] The residual method of valuing assets no longer applies. The fair market value of each asset is determined independently of the purchase price of the membership interest.

EXAMPLE

An LLC has two assets: inventory valued at $1 million and a building valued at $2 million. John purchases a 1/3 interest in the LLC for $800,000. There is a $200,000 discount in the purchase price because John is acquiring a minority interest. The fair market value of the assets for Section 754 purposes is $1 million for the inventory and $2 million for the building.

There is a special rule if the LLC has Section 197 intangibles.[15] In such case, the LLC must determine the gross value of LLC assets. The gross value is the net proceeds that the LLC would have to receive from the sale of its assets so that the LLC could pay its liabilities in full and distribute to the purchasing member the amount that the member paid for the membership interest (ignoring the purchase price attributable to the purchasing member's assumption of LLC liabilities).[16] If the gross value of LLC assets is less than the fair market value of LLC assets other than the Section 197 intangibles, then the Section 197 intangibles are valued at zero. If the gross value of LLC assets is higher than the fair market value of LLC assets other than the Section 197 intangibles, then the Section 197 intangibles are valued at the excess amount.[17]

EXAMPLE 1

An LLC has three assets: inventory valued at $1 million, a building valued at $2 million, and a Section 197 intangible (customer list purchased from another company for $500,000). John purchases a 1/3 interest in the LLC for $800,000. The fair market value of the Section 197 intangible is zero for Section 754 purposes because the gross value of LLC assets is less than the fair market value of LLC assets other than the Section 197 intangibles. The gross value of LLC assets is $2.4 million. This is the net amount that the LLC would have to receive from the sale of its assets so that the LLC could

[14] Reg. §1.755-1(a)(3).
[15] Reg. §1.755-1(a)(2), (5).
[16] Reg. §1.755-1(a)(4).
[17] Reg. §1.755-1(a)(5).

distribute $800,000 to John (1/3 of $2.4 million). Thus, the fair market value of the assets for Section 754 purposes is $1 million for the inventory and $2 million for the building.

EXAMPLE 2

Same facts as in prior example except that John purchases a 1/3 interest in the LLC for $1,100,000. The gross value of LLC assets is $3.3 million. This is the net amount that the LLC would have to receive from the sale of its assets so that the LLC could distribute $1.1 million to John (1/3 of $3.3 million sales price). Since the gross value of LLC assets exceeds the fair market value of LLC assets other than the Section 197 intangibles by $300,000, the LLC must value the Section 197 intangible at $300,000 for Section 754 purposes. Thus, the fair market value of the assets for Section 754 purposes is $1 million for the inventory, $2 million for the building, and $300,000 for the Section 197 intangible.

[2]   Allocation Between Classes

The second step is to allocate the basis adjustment between two classes of assets, capital gain property, and ordinary income property.

The amount of basis adjustment allocated to the ordinary income property is the total amount of income, gain, or loss that would be allocated to the transferee if the LLC disposed of all of its assets in a fully taxable transaction at fair market value immediately after the transfer. The amount of basis adjustment allocated to the capital gain property is the remainder of the Section 743 basis adjustment.[18]

The amount of basis adjustment allocated to one class may be an increase even if the amount of basis adjustment allocated to the other class is a decrease. However, any decrease in basis allocated to the capital gain property class may not exceed the LLC's basis in the capital gain property class. If there is a decrease in basis in excess of the LLC's basis in the capital gain property, the excess amount is applied to reduce the basis of ordinary income property.[19]

EXAMPLE

An LLC has two equal members.[20] Member A contributes $50,000 and Asset 1 to the LLC. Asset 1 is a capital gain asset with an initial fair market value of $50,000 and a tax basis of $25,000. Member B contributes $100,000

---

[18] Reg. §1.755-1(b)(1)(ii).
[19] Reg. §1.755-1(b)(2).
[20] This example is from Reg. §1.755-1(b)(2)(ii), example 1.

to the LLC. The LLC uses cash to purchase Assets 2, 3, and 4. After one year, Member A sells her membership interest to Member T for $120,000. The LLC determines that Member T should receive an upward $45,000 basis adjustment under Section 743(b). Immediately after the sale, the adjusted bases and fair market values of the LLC's assets are as follows:

Asset	Adjusted Basis	Fair Market Value
Capital Gain Property:		
Asset 1	$ 25,000	$ 75,000
Asset 2	100,000	117,500
Ordinary Income Property:		
Asset 3	40,000	45,000
Asset 4	10,000	2,500
Total	$175,000	$240,000

The $45,000 upward basis adjustment for Member T is allocated between the classes of assets as follows:

Step 1: Divide the assets between capital gain property and ordinary income property.

Step 2: Determine the amount of gain that the LLC would recognize if it sold all of its assets in a fully taxable transaction at fair market value immediately after the transfer of the membership interest from Member A to Member T. The total gain would be $65,000, equal to the difference between the $240,000 fair market value of the assets and the $175,000 adjusted basis of the assets.

Step 3: Divide the gain between the capital gain property and the ordinary income property. There would be $67,000 of capital gain for the capital gain property and $2,500 of ordinary loss for the ordinary income property. This is based on the difference between the fair market value and the adjusted basis of assets for each class.

Step 4: Determine the amount of capital gain that would be allocated to Member T from the sale of the capital gain property. This is $46,250. This amount is equal to $25,000 of the built-in gain from Asset 1, plus 50 percent of the remaining $42,500 of appreciation in the capital gain property. Since Member A contributed appreciated property to the LLC, the member or her successor in interest is taxed on the $25,000 of built-in gain when the LLC sells the property. The remaining gain is divided equally.

Step 5: Determine the amount of ordinary income or loss that would be allocated to Member T upon the sale of the ordinary income property. This is $1,250, representing 50 percent of the $2,500 ordinary loss from the sale of ordinary income property.

Step 6: Allocate the basis adjustment to each class based on the gain or loss that the purchasing member would recognize if the LLC sold the assets. The basis increase for the capital gain property is $46,250. The basis decrease for the ordinary income property is $1,250. The net amount of increase and decrease for both classes, $45,000, is equal to the $45,000 basis increase adjustment.

[3]   Allocation Within Classes

After the basis adjustment is allocated between the two classes, the LLC must allocate the basis adjustment within each class to each asset within that class. The basis adjustment is allocated to the assets within each class based on the amount of gain or loss that the transferee member would recognize on a hypothetical sale. The basis adjustment allocated to some assets within a class may be an increase, and the basis adjustment allocated to other assets within the same class may be a decrease.[21]

The basis decrease to any item of capital gain property may not exceed the LLC's basis in that item. Any excess amount must be applied to reduce the remaining basis of other capital gain assets pro rata in proportion to the LLC's adjusted basis in such assets.[22]

EXAMPLE

Same facts as in the prior example. Of the $45,000 basis adjustment, $46,250 of gain was allocated as a basis increase to the capital gain property and $1,250 of loss was allocated as a basis decrease to the ordinary income property. The amount of basis increase or decrease is then allocated to the assets within each class based on the amount of gain or loss that the transferee member would recognize in a hypothetical sale even though the gain or loss exceeds the total amount of gain or loss allocable to that particular class. Therefore, the basis adjustment for Member T for the LLC's assets is allocated as follows:

- There is a $37,500 basis increase for Asset 1, since Member T would be allocated $37,500 of gain from the sale of that asset.
- There is an $8,750 basis increase for Asset 2, since Member T would be allocated $8,750 of capital gain from the sale of that asset. The total basis increase for class I assets (Asset 1 and Asset 2) is $46,250.
- There is a $2,500 basis increase for Asset 3 (ordinary income property), since Member T would receive an allocation of $2,500 of ordinary income from the sale of Asset 3. This is equal to 50 percent of the $5,000 of appreciation for Asset 3. There is a positive basis increase even though there is a net basis decrease of $1,250 for all of the ordinary income property.

---

[21] Reg. §1.752-1(b)(3).
[22] Reg. §1.755-1(b)(3)(iii)(B).

- There is a basis decrease of $3,750 for Asset 4, since Member T would receive an allocation of $3,750 of loss from the sale of Asset 4 in the hypothetical transaction. This is equal to 50 percent of the $7,500 of ordinary loss from the hypothetical sale of Asset 4. The total basis adjustment for the ordinary income property is a net decrease of $1,250 ($2,500 increase for Asset 3 and $3,750 decrease for Asset 4).

In certain limited cases, the amount of gain or loss that would be allocated to a member on a hypothetical sale of assets at fair market value within a class is not exactly equal to the basis adjustment that must be made for the member within that class.[23] In such case, a proportionate adjustment must be made based on the fair market value of the assets within each class.[24]

[F] Reporting and Returns

The LLC rather than the member must report the basis adjustments. The LLC must attach a statement to the LLC return when the LLC acquires knowledge of a transfer subject to Section 743.[25] In addition, the LLC must adjust specific LLC items in light of the basis adjustments. Consequently, the amounts that the LLC reports on the transferee member's Schedule K-1 must be the adjusted amounts. The transferee must notify the LLC of the transfer, information regarding the transferee and transferor (if ascertainable), and other information necessary for the LLC to compute the transferee's basis in the acquired membership interest.[26] The LLC is entitled to rely on the written representations of the transferee member concerning the amount paid for the membership interest and the transferee's basis in the membership interest, unless clearly erroneous.

The parties must comply with the following notification and reporting requirements if the LLC has made an election under Section 754:

- The buyer must notify the LLC within 30 days after the sale or exchange. The written notice must be signed under penalty of perjury. It must include the names and addresses of the buyer and the seller (if ascertainable), the taxpayer identification numbers of the buyer and the seller (if ascertainable), the relationship between the buyer and seller, if any, the date of transfer,

---

[23] This may occur when the LLC is initially allocating the basis adjustment between the two classes of assets (rather than within each class of assets). Any decrease in basis allocated to the capital gain property class may not exceed the LLC's basis in the capital gain property class. If there is a decrease in basis in excess of the LLC's basis in the capital gain property, the excess is applied to reduce the basis of ordinary income property. The resulting decreased amount of basis adjustment for the capital gain property class are increased amount of basis adjustment for the ordinary income property class are then allocated to the assets within each class based on the fair market value of the assets within that class.

[24] Reg. §1.755-1(b)(3).

[25] Reg. §1.743-1(k)(1).

[26] Reg. §1.743-1(k)(2).

the amount of any liabilities assumed or taken subject to by the buyer, the amount of cash and the fair market value of any other property paid for the LLC interest, and any other information necessary for the LLC to compute the buyer's basis.[27]
- The LLC must attach a statement to the LLC return showing the computation of the basis adjustment under Section 743(b), the LLC properties to which the adjustment is allocated, and the name and taxpayer identification number of the buyer.[28]

The parties must also comply with the regular reporting and notification requirements which apply to LLCs that have not made an election under Section 754.[29]

[G] Distribution of Section 743(b) Assets

An LLC may distribute a Section 743(b) asset to the member for whom the basis adjustment was made or to another member. In a nonliquidating distribution, each member receives a carryover basis, which cannot exceed the member's basis in his membership interest.[30] If the LLC distributes the Section 743(b) asset to the member for whom the special basis adjustment was made, the member's basis includes the Section 743(b) special basis adjustment. If the LLC distributes the Section 743(b) asset to another member, the special basis adjustment is transferred to property of like kind that is still owned by the LLC and continues to benefit only the same member.[31] The Section 743(b) basis adjustment may benefit only the member who acquires a membership interest that results in the basis adjustment.

The LLC may also distribute Section 743(b) property to a member in a liquidating distribution. The member receives a substituted basis when the LLC makes a liquidating distribution of property. The basis of LLC assets distributed to the member is the same as the member's adjusted basis in his membership interest in the LLC, reduced by any money received in the distribution. Therefore, the Section 743(b) basis adjustment has no effect on the total basis of property received by the member. The Section 743(b) basis adjustment will affect only how the basis is allocated among the distributed properties. The regulations require that the allocation be made in proportion to the relative bases of the assets to the LLC. This includes a special basis adjustment under Section 743(b).

The LLC succeeds to the entire Section 743(b) basis adjustment as part of its common basis if it makes a liquidating distribution to the member entirely in cash.[32]

---

[27] Reg. §1.743-1(k)(2).
[28] Reg. §1.743-1(k)(1).
[29] See §15.07[F] supra.
[30] IRC §732(a).
[31] Reg. §1.743-1(b)(2)(ii).
[32] Reg. §1.743-2(b)(1).

§15.09   Capital Accounts

A purchaser of a membership interest in an LLC succeeds to the capital account of the seller.[1] The capital account may affect the allocation of income or loss to the purchasing member under the LLC's operating agreement. If the LLC uses the safe-harbor rules for special allocations, the purchasing member may be required to restore a negative capital account acquired from the selling member on liquidation of the LLC.

---

§15.09[1] Reg. §1.704-1(b)(2)(iv)(l).

16

Self-Employment and Employment Taxes

§16.01 GENERAL RULE

The general rule is that members of an LLC are not subject to employment taxes. The LLC is not required to withhold income, FICA, or FUTA taxes. However, each member of the LLC must pay estimated taxes on his or her distributive share of income. The member is also subject to self-employment taxes (FICA and FUTA) on the member's share of income attributable to a trade or business if the member actively participates in the business of the LLC.

Nonmember employees of the LLC are subject to employment taxes. The LLC must withhold income, FICA, and FUTA taxes for such employees.

§16.02 MEMBERS OF THE LLC

[A] Employment Taxes

A bona fide member of an LLC is not an employee for wage-withholding purposes. The income and wages received by a member of an LLC are not subject to income, FICA, or FUTA withholding taxes.[1]

---

§16.02 [1] C.C.A. 200117003 (*citing* Rev. Rul. 69-184, 1969-1 C.B. 256); Reg. §1.707-1(C).

[B]   Self-Employment Taxes

A member's share of income from an LLC that is engaged in a trade or business is subject to self-employment taxes if the member is a general partner of the LLC.[2] A member's share of LLC income is not subject to self-employment taxes if the member is a limited partner[3] except for guaranteed payments. Guaranteed payments to limited partners for services rendered are subject to self-employment taxes.[4]

It is unclear how these rules apply to LLCs, since there are no general partners or limited partners. Members of an LLC have some of the characteristics of limited partners (e.g., limited liability) and some of the characteristics of general partners (e.g., management and voting rights).

Members of an LLC who actively engage in the business of the LLC are treated as general partners for self-employment tax purposes. Their distributive shares of trade or business income from the LLC are treated as net earnings from self-employment. For example, members of an LLC who actively engage in the practice of law are subject to self-employment taxes on their distributive shares of income from a law LLC.[5]

Members of an LLC who are passive investors and who are not managers of the LLC are probably not subject to self-employment taxes on their distributive shares of income.

[C]   IRS Regulations

[1]   General

The IRS issued proposed regulations on self-employment taxes for members of an LLC in 1997.[6] In 2003, the IRS announced that taxpayers may rely on the proposed regulations.[7]

Under the proposed regulations, LLC income is subject to self-employment taxes unless:

- The member is classified as a limited partner. Generally, a member is classified as a general partner and must pay self-employment taxes if the member works more than 500 hours, has personal liability for debts, or has authority to sign contracts on behalf of the LLC.

---

[2] IRC §§1401-1402; Regs. §§1.1402(a)-1(a)(2), 1.1402(a)-2(d), (e), (f), (g).

[3] IRC §§1402(a)(13), 707. The IRS has determined that strict compliance with state limited partnership laws is required for an inactive member of a partnership with limited management rights to qualify as a limited partner for self-employment tax purposes. Ltr. Rul. 9110003.

[4] IRC §1402(a)(13); Reg. §1.1402(a)-1(b).

[5] Ltr. Ruls. 9525058, 9432018 (both involving members of a law LLC).

[6] Prop. Reg. §1.1402(a)-2(g), (h).

[7] REG-209824-96.

- The member owns more than one class of membership interest.
- The member bifurcates his distributive share.

There are special rules for professional LLCs.

[2]   Limited Partner Classification

A member is not liable for self-employment taxes under the proposed regulations if the member is a limited partner.[8] A member is a limited partner unless any of the following apply:[9]

- The member has personal liability for the debts of or claims against the LLC by reason of being a member.
- The member has authority to contract on behalf of the LLC under the statute or law pursuant to which the LLC is organized.
- The member participates in the LLC's trade or business for more than 500 hours during the tax year.

[3]   More Than One Class of Interest

A member who is not a limited partner may nevertheless exclude from self-employment earnings a portion of his distributive share if he owns more than one class of membership interest. The member will be treated as a limited partner, and will be exempt from self-employment taxes, with respect to one of the classes of membership interests if, immediately after acquiring the interest:[10]

- Other members who are treated as limited partners own a substantial, continuing interest in the same class of membership interest. Ownership of 20 percent or more of the class is substantial;[11] and
- The member's rights and obligations with respect to that class of membership interest are identical to the rights and obligations of the same class held by members who are limited partners.

[4]   Bifurcation of Interest

A member who is not a limited partner because the member works more than 500 hours for the LLC may also exclude from self-employment earnings a portion of the member's distributive share. The member must own only one class of

---

[8] Prop. Reg. §1.1402(a)-2(g).
[9] Prop. Reg. §1.1402(a)-2(h)(2).
[10] Prop. Reg. §1.1402(a)-2(h)(3).
[11] Prop. Reg. §1.1402(a)-2(h)(6)(iv).

membership interest.[12] The member must bifurcate the membership interest by excluding from income any guaranteed payment. The member is treated as a limited partner and is exempt from self-employment taxes with respect to the remaining income if, immediately after acquiring the membership interest, both of the following apply:[13]

- Other members who are treated as limited partners own a substantial, continuing interest in the same class of membership interest; and
- The member's rights and obligations with respect to that class of membership interest are identical to the rights and obligations of the same class held by members who are limited partners.

[5]   Professional Services

A member who performs services for an LLC is not a limited partner if substantially all of the activities of the LLC involve the performance of services in the field of health, law, engineering, architecture, accounting, actuarial science, or consulting.[14] All of the income from those professional LLCs is subject to self-employment taxes.

§16.03   NONMEMBER EMPLOYEES

[A]   General Rule

Nonmember employees of an LLC are subject to the regular wage withholding and employment taxes with one exception. A member of a Section 501(d) religious organization who works under a vow of poverty, in an enterprise conducted and owned by the organization, is not subject to employment taxes if the duties are required by the religious order.[1] The member must have taken a vow of poverty and have no rights to the organization's assets when he leaves the organization. The transfer of a tax-exempt religious organization's unincorporated commercial enterprises to a limited liability company owned by the organization does not change this result.[2]

The procedures and responsibility for collection and payment of the withholding taxes depend on whether the LLC is classified as a disregarded entity, partnership, or corporation. These rules are discussed below.

---

[12] Prop. Reg. §1.1402(a)-2(h)(4).
[13] Prop. Reg. §1.1402(a)-2(h)(3).
[14] Prop. Reg. §1.1402(a)-2(h)(5).
§16.03 [1] Ltr. Ruls. 9752005, 9752004, 9752003, 9752002 (*citing* IRC §3121(b)(8)(A) and Rev. Rul. 77-290, 1977-2 C.B. 26).
[2] Ltr. Ruls. 9752005, 9752004, 9752003, 9752002.

[B]   LLC Classified as Disregarded Entity

A single-member LLC that is classified as a disregarded entity may report and pay payroll taxes for employees in one of the following two ways:[3]

- The member of the LLC may calculate, report, and pay all employment taxes for the employees of the LLC as if the employees of the LLC were employed directly by the member. The employment taxes are reported under the member's name and taxpayer identification number. If this method is chosen, the LLC should file a final employment tax return for the employment taxes previously paid by the LLC on a separate basis.
- The LLC may calculate, report, and pay all employment taxes of the LLC under its own name and taxpayer identification number. If this method is chosen, the member retains ultimate responsibility for paying employment taxes of the employees of the LLC. The Service will not proceed against the member for employment taxes for the employees of the LLC if those taxes are paid by the LLC using its own name and taxpayer identification number, even if there are differences in the timing or amount of payments or deposits as calculated under this method.

An owner of multiple LLCs may use the first method with respect to some LLCs and the second method with respect to other LLCs. The fact that the sole member of an LLC uses the second method for one LLC does not preclude the member from switching to the first method in a subsequent year. However, if the member uses the first method to pay employment taxes for an LLC for a return period that begins on or after April 20, 1999, the taxpayer must continue to use the first method until otherwise permitted by the Commissioner.[4]

Pending further study, the IRS will not rule as to who is the employer of persons employed by disregarded single-member LLCs.[5] However, the IRS has determined that the single-member owner is the taxpayer for employment tax purposes.[6] The sole member is personally responsible for employment taxes incurred by the LLC.[7] The IRS may recover the tax liability directly from the single-member owner. The IRS may not look to the LLC's assets to satisfy the tax liability of the member because the member has no direct interest in the assets of the LLC under state law. Instead, the IRS may take collection action against the member's ownership interest in the LLC.[8] For example, the IRS may collect the member's distributive share of income from the LLC.[9]

An assessment made against the LLC is a valid assessment against a single-member owner. Because of the close relationship between the LLC and the owner,

---

[3] IRS Notice 99-6, IRB 1999-3 (Jan.19, 1999).
[4] *Id.*
[5] Rev. Proc. 2002-1, Sec. 5.05.
[6] C.C.A. 200235023, Ruling 2.
[7] Ltr. Rul. 199922053.
[8] C.C.A. 200235023, Ruling 2.
[9] Ltr. Rul. 199930013.

an assessment against the LLC is the same as an assessment against the single-member owner.[10]

A Notice of Federal Tax Lien identifying the disregarded LLC as the taxpayer may be valid against a single-member owner, depending on the facts and circumstances of each case. The IRS takes the position that the Notice need not precisely identify the taxpayer. Instead, it is valid if it substantially complies with the filing requirements so that constructive notice is provided to third parties. To avoid litigating the issue, the IRS recommends that the Notice be filed in the name of the single-member owner for the tax liabilities generated by the disregarded LLC.[11]

The IRS may use a number of state law theories to collect employment tax liabilities owed by a single-member LLC that is classified as disregarded entity. These include the alter ego theory, nominee liability, and transferee liability.[12]

[C]   LLC Classified as Corporation

An LLC that is classified as a corporation is responsible for payment of employment taxes. The IRS may file a Notice of Federal Tax Lien against the LLC and file a suit to foreclose the federal tax lien or levy on the LLC assets. The collection due process requirements under Sections 6320 and 6330 must also be met.[13] The members of the LLC may be liable for the trust fund recovery penalty under Section 6672 of the Code, depending on the facts and circumstances of each case.[14]

[D]   LLC Classified as Partnership

An LLC that is classified as a partnership is responsible for payment of employment taxes. The members of an LLC are not responsible for employment taxes incurred by the LLC.[15] Unlike the typical partnership situation where the IRS asserts employment tax liability against the partners who are liable for the debts of the partnership under state law, the IRS will not assert an employment tax liability against members of the LLC because they are not liable for the debts of the LLC under state law.[16] The members of the LLC may be liable for the trust fund recovery penalty under Section 6672 of the Code, depending on the facts and circumstances of each case.[17]

---

[10] C.C.A. 200235023, Ruling 3.

[11] C.C.A. 200235023, Ruling 4.

[12] C.C.A. 200235023 (which gives an extensive summary of the rulings and arguments for each of these theories); Let. Rul. 199930013.

[13] C.C.A. 200235023.

[14] C.C.A. 200235023.

[15] Ltr. Rul. 199922053.

[16] C.C.A. 200235023.

[17] Id.

17

Accounting Methods and Procedures

§17.01   CASH METHOD OF ACCOUNTING

[A]   General Rules

An LLC may use any method of accounting that clearly reflects income and that is regularly used in keeping its books.[1] However, the LLC must use the accrual rather than cash method of accounting in the following cases (subject to exceptions noted below):

- the LLC maintains inventory, unless it is an eligible business with $10 million or less in gross receipts;[2]
- the LLC is classified as a C corporation;[3]
- the LLC has a C corporation as a member;[4] or
- the LLC is classified as a tax-shelter.[5]

[B]   Inventory Business

An LLC that sells inventory must ordinarily use the accrual method of accounting.[6] It must also account for inventory under IRC Section 471 using the uniform capitalization rules under IRC Section 263A.

However, an LLC that has $1 million or less in gross receipts may generally use the cash method of accounting.[7] An LLC that has less than $10 million in gross receipts may use the cash method of accounting and account for inventory as non-incidental materials and supplies if it meets all of the following requirements:[8]

- The LLC has $10 million or less in average gross receipts during the prior three years.[9] LLCs that have not been in existence for three years may determine average annual gross receipts for the number of years that the LLC has been an existence.[10]
- The LLC is not statutorily prohibited from using the cash method of accounting. As discussed below, certain LLCs that are classified as a C corporation, that have a C corporation as a member, or that are classified as a tax shelter

---

§17.01   [1] IRC §446(a).

[2] See §17.01[B] infra.

[3] See §17.01[C] infra.

[4] See §17.01[D] infra.

[5] See §17.01[E] infra.

[6] Reg. §1.446-1(c)(2)(i).

[7] Rev. Proc. 2001-10, 2001-2 I.R.B. 272. See also Rev. Proc. 2002-28, 2002-18 I.R.B. 815, §7.04 (last sentence). This Revenue Procedure applies to retail and wholesale businesses, and other businesses, that are not eligible to use the cash method of accounting under Rev. Proc. 2002-28.

[8] Rev. Proc. 2002-28, 2002-18 I.R.B. 815.

[9] Rev. Proc. 2002-28, 2002-18 I.R.B. 815, §5.

[10] Rev. Proc. 2002-28, 2002-18 I.R.B. 815, §5.02.

may not use the cash method of accounting even if gross receipts are under $10 million.

- The principal activity of the LLC falls within any one of the following three categories: (i) any trade or business described in the North American Industry Classification System except for mining, manufacturing, wholesale and retail businesses, and certain businesses in the information industry, (ii) a service business, including a business that provides property incident to those services, or (iii) the business of fabrication or modification of tangible personal property upon demand in accordance with customer designs or specifications.[11]
- The LLC has not previously changed, and was not previously required to change, from the cash to the accrual method of accounting as a result of becoming ineligible to use the cash method under Revenue Procedure 2002-28.[12]
- The LLC makes the election with respect to all of its trades or businesses,[13] or for any separate trade or business that meets the qualifications above and that maintains its own set of books and records.[14]
- The LLC follows the procedures for obtaining an automatic change in accounting method if the LLC is changing to the cash method of accounting and/or to the non-incidental materials and supplies method of inventory accounting.[15]

LLCs that meet these requirements have several options. They can elect to use the cash method of accounting and account for inventories under IRC Section 471. The may use the accrual method of accounting and account for inventories as non-incidental supplies. They may also use the cash method of accounting and account for inventories as non-incidental supplies.[16]

[C]   LLC Classified as Corporation

An LLC may not use the cash method of accounting if it is classified as a C corporation for federal tax purposes.[17] There is an exception if the LLC:[18]

- is a farming business;
- is a qualified personal service corporation; or
- has average gross receipts during the prior three-year period that do not exceed $5 million.

---

[11] Rev. Proc. 2002-28, 2002-18 I.R.B. 815, §4.01(1)(a)-(c).
[12] Rev. Proc. 2002-28, 2002-18 I.R.B. 815, §4.01(1).
[13] Rev. Proc. 2002-28, 2002-18 I.R.B. 815, §4.01(1).
[14] Rev. Proc. 2002-28, 2002-18 I.R.B. 815, §4.01(2).
[15] Rev. Proc. 2002-28, 2002-18 I.R.B. 815, §7.
[16] Rev. Proc. 2002-28, 2002-18 I.R.B. 815, §4.02.
[17] IRC §448(a)(1).
[18] IRC §448(b).

[D]   C Corporation Member

An LLC may not use the cash method of accounting if it has a C corporation as a member.[19] There is an exception if:[20]

- the LLC is a farming business;
- the C corporation member is a qualified personal service corporation, in which case the personal service corporation is treated as an individual; or
- the LLC has average gross receipts during the prior three-year period that do not exceed $5 million.

[E]   *Classification as Tax Shelter*

[1]   Types of Tax Shelters

An LLC may not use the cash method of accounting if it is a tax shelter. A tax shelter includes:[21]

- an "enterprise" (other than a C corporation) if there a public offering of securities required to be registered under state or federal law,
- a "syndicate," or
- a "tax shelter" as defined under IRC Section 6662(d)(2)(C)(ii).

These terms are defined below.

EXAMPLE

The Service has ruled that LLCs organized for the practice of law,[22] medicine,[23] accounting,[24] management consulting,[25] or other business[26] may continue using the cash method of accounting after conversion from a partnership, LLP, or personal service corporation. The rulings concluded that the LLCs were not tax shelters because they were not "enterprises," "syndicates," or "tax shelters under IRC §6662(d)(2)(C)(ii)."

---

[19] IRC §448(a)(2).
[20] IRC §448(b).
[21] IRC §448(d)(3), making reference to IRC §461(i)(3).
[22] Ltr. Ruls. 9602018, 9538022, 9525065, 9501033, 9432018, 9426030, 9421025, 9415005, 9407030, 9350013, 9321047.
[23] Ltr. Rul. 9452024.
[24] Ltr. Ruls. 9525065, 9525058, 9422034, 9412030 (conversion from an LLP to an LLC).
[25] Ltr. Rul. 9434027.
[26] Ltr. Rul. 9328005.

[2]   Enterprise

An LLC may not use the cash method of accounting if it is an "enterprise." An organization (other than a C corporation) is an enterprise if interests in the organization are offered for sale in an offering required to be registered with any federal or state agency that regulates the offering and sale of securities.[27] An LLC is an enterprise if any of the following apply:

- There is a public offering or sale of membership interests.[28]
- Under applicable state or federal law, failure to register the membership interests would result in a violation of the applicable federal or state securities law (regardless of whether the offering is registered).[29]
- Under applicable state or federal law, failure to file a notice of exemption from registration would result in a violation of the applicable federal or state securities law (regardless of whether the notice is filed).[30]

[3]   Syndicates

An LLC may not use the cash method of accounting if it is a "syndicate." A partnership or other entity (other than a corporation that is not an S corporation) is a syndicate if more than 35 percent of the entity's losses are allocated to limited partners or limited entrepreneurs during the year.[31] An LLC is not a syndicate if any one of the three conditions discussed in [a], [b], or [c], below, is met.

[a]   No Losses

An LLC is not a syndicate during any year in which it does not have losses.[32] Most personal service LLCs do not have losses. Companies seeking IRS rulings usually represent that they do not expect to ever incur losses.[33]

[b]   Active Participation

An LLC is not a syndicate if none of the members are limited partners or limited entrepreneurs. A limited entrepreneur is a person other than a limited partner who does not actively participate in the management of the LLC.[34] A

---

[27] IRC §461(i)(3)(A); Ltr. Rul. 9421025.
[28] Ltr. Ruls. 9602018, 9525065, 9525058, 9452024, 9434027, 9426030, 9422034, 9421025, 9415005, 9412030, 9407030, 9350013, 9328005, 9321047.
[29] Ltr. Ruls. 9421025, 9415005 (*citing* Reg. §1.448-1T(b)(2)).
[30] *Id.*
[31] IRC §1256(e)(3)(B).
[32] Ltr. Ruls. 9535036, 9415005, 9343027.
[33] *See, e.g.,* Ltr. Rul. 9350013.
[34] Ltr. Rul. 9343027 (*citing* IRC §464(e)(2)).

member of an LLC is not a limited partner or limited entrepreneur if the member is:[35]

- A person who actively participates in the management of the LLC;
- A formerly active member who actively participated in management for at least five years;
- The estate of an active member or a formerly active member;
- The spouse, child, grandchild, or parent of an active member for the period that the active member is actively participating in management of the LLC; or
- The estate of the spouse, child, grandchild, or parent of an active member for the period that the membership interest is held by the estate and the assigning active member is actively participating in the management of the LLC.

A member may be treated as an active member even if the member does not actively participate in management. Management of the LLC may be delegated to a management committee.[36] The fact that many of the management responsibilities are delegated to an executive committee does not preclude a determination that the members actively participate in management.[37] The voting rights of active members may be limited or restricted to certain major matters affecting the LLC and its management.[38]

[c]   35 Percent Allocation

An LLC is not a syndicate during any year in which not more than 35 percent of losses are allocated to members who are classified as limited partners or limited entrepreneurs.[39] For example, an LLC for attorneys is not a syndicate if less than 35 percent of losses are allocated to the nonequity members who have no vote in LLC management.[40]

[4]   Tax Shelter

An LLC may not use the cash method of accounting if it is a tax shelter.[41] An LLC is a tax shelter if a significant purpose of the LLC is tax avoidance or tax

---

[35] Ltr. Ruls. 9535036, 9525065, 9525058, 9452024, 9350013 (*citing* IRC §§1256(e)(3)(B), 1256(e)(3)(C), 464(e)(2), and Reg. §1.448-1T(b)(3)).

[36] Ltr. Ruls. 9535036, 9422034, 9421025, 9412030, 9407030.

[37] Ltr. Rul. 9407030.

[38] Ltr. Ruls. 9412030, 9407030, 9350013, 9328005, 9321047.

[39] Ltr. Ruls. 9535036, 9452023, 9434027, 9432018.

[40] Ltr. Rul. 9426030.

[41] *See* IRC §6662(d)(2)(C)(ii).

evasion. Before August 5, 1997, an LLC was a tax shelter if the principal purpose of the LLC was tax avoidance or tax evasion.[42]

The Service will not normally determine whether a significant purpose of the LLC is tax avoidance or tax evasion.[43] However, the Service may give a favorable ruling on this issue if the LLC represents that it is not organized for any federal income tax avoidance motive.[44] It will also rule that an LLC is not classified as a tax shelter solely because of its organization structure as an LLC.[45]

§17.02   ACCOUNTING METHODS AFTER CONVERSION FROM PARTNERSHIP

An LLC must continue to use the same methods of accounting after conversion from a general partnership until it receives permission to change its accounting methods or until the IRS challenges the methods on examination.[1] The rule applies regardless of whether the general partnership used proper methods of accounting prior to the conversion.[2]

§17.03   FISCAL YEAR

[A]   Choice of Fiscal Year

[1]   Generally

An LLC must normally adopt a fiscal year that is the same as one of the following:[1]

- The tax year of a majority of its members who own in the aggregate more than 50 percent of the LLC profits and capital;
- The tax year of all of the principal (5 percent or more) members if there is no tax year of a majority of the members; or
- If neither of the above tax years applies, the tax year that results in the least aggregate deferral of income to the members.[2]

---

[42] IRC §6662(d)(2)(C)(iii), prior to amendment by Pub. L. No. 105-34, §1028, 105th Cong., 1st Sess. (Aug. 5, 1997).

[43] Ltr. Ruls. 9501033, 9434027, 9432018, 9426030, 9407030; Rev. Proc. 97-3, §3.02(1), 1997-1 C.B. 507.

[44] Ltr. Ruls. 9525065, 9525058, 9452024, 9422034, 9412030.

[45] Ltr. Rul. 9415005.

§17.02   [1] Ltr. Ruls. 9637030, 9525065, 9501033, 9423040.

[2] Ltr. Ruls. 9501033, 9426030.

§17.03   [1] IRC §706(b)(1)(B); Reg. §1.706-1(b)(2).

[2] The tax year that produces the least aggregate deferral of income is determined under Reg. §1.706-1(b)(3).

An LLC may adopt a different fiscal year if the LLC (1) meets the natural business year test, (2) shows a proper business purpose based on all the facts and circumstances, (3) elects a three-month deferral, (4) elects a 52- to 53-week fiscal year, or (5) qualifies under grandfather provisions.[3] These exceptions are discussed below.

The IRS issued guidelines for obtaining automatic approval for adopting, retaining, or changing the fiscal year,[4] and procedures for adopting, retaining, or changing the fiscal year based on a proper business purpose or natural business year.[5]

The IRS may grant an LLC an extension of time to elect a taxable year other than the required year.[6]

[2] Natural Business Year

An LLC may adopt a natural business year as its fiscal year.[7] An LLC may establish that it has a natural business year under any of the following tests:[8]

- *Annual business cycle test.* If the LLC's gross receipts from sales and services over a three-year period indicate that the LLC has a peak and a non-peak period of business, the natural business year ends soon after the close of the peak period of business. A business whose income is steady from month to month throughout the year generally will not satisfy this test.
- *Seasonal business test.* If the LLC's business is operational for only part of the year (e.g., due to weather conditions), and the LLC has insignificant gross receipts during the period of business in which it is not operational, the LLC's natural business year ends soon after the operations end for the season.
- *25 percent gross receipts test.* If more than 25 percent of gross receipts of an LLC for a 12-month period are recognized in the last two months of the 12-month period, and this has occurred for three consecutive years, the LLC may adopt the 12-month period as its tax year.

---

[3] Regs. §§1.441-1(b)(2)(ii)(B), 1.706-1(b)(2)(ii).

[4] Notice 2001-35, 2001-23 I.R.B. 1314; Reg. §§1.442-1, 1.706-1(b)(8).

[5] Notice 2001-34, 2001-23, I.R.B. 1302; Reg. §§1.442-1, 1.706-1(b)(8).

[6] *See* Ltr. Rul. 9845010. The extension of time was granted after the LLC filed Form 8716 electing the change after the due date. The late filing was due to an error or misunderstanding on the part of the tax professional hired by the LLC to file the election. Form 8716 was filed within 90 days after its due date, and the late filing was not due to any lack of due diligence on the part of the LLC. The IRS acted pursuant to its authority under Reg. §301.9100-3.

[7] Reg. §1.706-1(b)(2)(ii), making reference to the business purpose test for establishing a tax year other than the required tax year. The natural business year test is one of the two tests used to establish a proper business purpose.

[8] Notice 2001-34, §5.03, 2001-23 I.R.B. 1302.

[3]   Facts and Circumstances Test

An LLC may adopt a fiscal year by showing a proper business purpose based on all the facts and circumstances.[9] The following facts and circumstances are ordinarily not sufficient to establish a business purpose:[10]

- The deferral of income to the members of the LLC, or the shifting of the members' deductions from one year to another to reduce tax liability.
- The use of a particular year for regulatory or financial accounting purposes;
- The hiring patterns of the LLC, such as the fact that the LLC typically hires staff during certain times of the year;
- The use of a particular year for administration purposes, such as the admission or retirement of members, promotion of staff, and compensation or retirement arrangements with staff and members of the LLC;
- The fact that a particular business involves the use of price lists, a model year, or other items that change on an annual basis;
- The use of a particular year by related entities;
- The use of a particular year by competitors; or
- The need to take advantage of an accountant's reduced rates, to have recordkeeping consistency, and to issue timely tax information forms to members.

[4]   Three-Month Deferral

Newly formed LLCs may elect a fiscal year having a deferral period of three months or less.[11] Other LLCs may adopt such fiscal year by obtaining prior approval of the IRS in accordance with specified procedures.[12]

In practice, this means that an LLC may have a fiscal year ending September 30 if the members of the LLC are individuals, or if a majority of the members of an LLC have a calendar year.

An electing LLC must make a "required payment" in the form of a non-interest-bearing loan to the government.[13] This is a special tax that is approximately equal to the amount of tax savings that the members realize from the deferral of income. The required payment is redetermined annually based on the income earned by the LLC. The LLC must make additional payments if income increases. The LLC receives a refund of payments if income decreases.[14] An LLC is not required to make the payment if it establishes a fiscal year under one of the two business purpose tests discussed above.

---

[9] Reg. §1.441-1(b)(2)(ii)(B); Notice 2001-34, §5.02(1)(b), 2001-23 I.R.B. 1302.

[10] Notice 2001-34, §5.02(1)(b), 2001-23 I.R.B. 1302.

[11] IRC §444(b)(1). Reg. §1.706-1(b)(7); Notice 2001-34, Notice 2001-35, §2.07.

[12] Reg. §1.706-1(b)(10).

[13] IRC §444; Temp. Reg. §§1.444-1T(b)(2), 1.444-3T(b)(1).

[14] IRC §7519(c).

An LLC must comply with the following procedures in adopting the fiscal year:

- The LLC must make the election by filing Form 8716, "Election to Have a Tax Year Other Than a Required Tax Year."[15] The election is a one-time election to use such fiscal year.
- The LLC must complete and file Form 8752, "Required Payment or Refund Under Section 7519," to compute the required payments when the election is in effect. The due date for Form 8752 is May 15 of the calendar year following the calendar year in which the applicable year begins.[16] The LLC must make a payment if the remaining amount on deposit is less than the required amount. It may obtain a refund if the amount on deposit is more than the required payment. The deposit amount is calculated by multiplying the taxable income of the LLC times the deferral ratio times the highest individual tax rate plus one percent. The deferral ratio is the number of months that elapse before the beginning of the calendar year divided by 12.
- The LLC must file an annual return on Form 720, "Quarterly Federal Excise Tax Return." The return must be filed even if no required payment is due for the year.[17]

EXAMPLE 1

An LLC is formed and elects a fiscal year ending September 30. This results in a three-month deferral of income, since the income of the LLC earned between October 1 and December 31 of the first year is taxable to the members of the LLC during the following year. Therefore, the deferral percentage is 25 percent (3 months divided by 12 months). However, there is no required payment because this is the first year of the LLC. There is no net income during the prior year.[18]

EXAMPLE 2

During the LLC's first tax year ending on September 30, it has taxable income of $1 million that is passed through to its members. Therefore, the LLC must make a required payment for its second taxable year ending on September 30. The required payment for the second tax year is $101,500 ($1 million of taxable income for the first tax year times 25 percent deferral ratio times 40.6 percent tax rate).

---

[15] Temp. Reg. §1.444-3T(b)(1).
[16] Temp. Reg. §1.7519-2T(a)(4)(ii).
[17] Temp. Reg. §1.7519-2T(a)(2)(i), (a)(4)(ii).
[18] Temp. Reg. §1.7519-1T(b)(4).

EXAMPLE 3

The LLC earns $900,000 of taxable income, which is passed through to its members during its second tax year. Therefore, the required payment for the third tax year is $91,350 ($900,000 of taxable income times 25 percent deferral ratio times 40.6 percent tax rate). The LLC is entitled to a refund of $10,150 when it files Form 8752 (deposit amount of $101,500 for the second tax year, less the required payment of $91,350 for the third tax year).

The effect of the election is that an LLC may have a tax year that ends on September 30 if all of the members are individuals with calendar years.

[5]   52- to 53-Week Fiscal Year

An LLC may adopt a 52- to 53-week fiscal year if the year ends with reference to the fiscal year that the LLC would otherwise be required to adopt.[19]

[6]   Grandfather Provisions

An LLC may continue to use a fiscal year under grandfather provisions if the LLC received permission to use a fiscal year between 1974 and 1987, and the fiscal year resulted in more than a three-month deferral.[20]

[B]   Conversion from Partnership

The tax year of a partnership does not close after conversion of the partnership to an LLC.[21] The LLC is treated as the continuation of the general partnership.[22] A change in the tax year requires the consent of the Service.[23]

---

[19] Prop. Reg. §§1.441-1(b)(2)(ii)(B), 1.441-2(e), 1.706-1(b)(3)(ii); Notice 2001-35, §§2.01(3)(b), 4.01(1), 2001-23 I.R.B. 1314.

[20] Rev. Proc. 87-32, 1987-2 C.B. 396, §5.01(2); Prop. Reg. §1.441-1(b)(2)(ii)(B), stating that a grandfathered fiscal year constitutes a business purpose for a fiscal year other than the required fiscal year.

[21] Ltr. Ruls. 9525065, 9501033.

[22] Rev. Rul. 95-55, 1995-2 C.B. 313; Rev. Rul. 95-37, 1995-1 C.B. 130; Ltr. Ruls. 9618021-23, 9602018, 9538022, 9525058, 9511033, 9501033, 9452023, 9432040, 9432037, 9432018, 9426037, 9422034, 9421025, 9420028, 9407030, 9350013, 9321047, 9226035, 9029019, 9010027 (*citing* Rev. Rul. 84-52, 1984-1 C.B. 157; IRC §708(b); and Reg. §1.708-1(b)(1)(ii) (transaction under IRC §721 is not treated as a sale or an exchange under IRC §708)).

[23] Ltr. Rul. 9525065 (*citing* Temp. Reg. §1.441-1T(b)(4)).

§17.04   CLOSING OF THE TAX YEAR

The tax year of an LLC does not ordinarily close as a result of the death of a member, the entry of a new member, the liquidation of a membership interest in an LLC, or the sale or exchange of a member's interest in the LLC.[1] There are several exceptions.

[A]   Dispositions

The tax year of an LLC closes with respect to a member who disposes of his entire interest in the LLC.[2] The tax year of an LLC does not close before the end of the LLC's tax year for a member who sells or exchanges less than his entire interest in the LLC or for a member who disposes of less than his entire interest in the LLC (whether by reason of sale, partial liquidation, gift, or otherwise).[3]

[B]   Death

The tax year of an LLC closes with respect to a member on the date of the member's death.[4] Therefore, a deceased member's entire distributive share of LLC income, gain, loss, credit, and deduction through the date of death is taxed to the deceased member. Before 1998, a member's tax year closed upon death only if the member's entire interest was sold or exchanged under an agreement existing at the time of the member's death. In the absence of such an agreement, the member's entire distributive share was taxed to the member's estate or successor in interest rather than to the deceased member.

The new law may be favorable or unfavorable depending on the deceased member's circumstances. The deceased member may have a lower tax bracket. The deceased member may also have a nonworking spouse, which will reduce the overall tax burden. However, the deceased member may have a higher tax rate than the deceased member's estate or successor in interest and may have a working spouse, subjecting the member and his spouse to the "marriage penalty."

[C]   50 Percent Change in Ownership

An LLC terminates for tax purposes if there is a sale or exchange of 50 percent or more of the LLC's capital and profits during a 12-month period.[5] The tax year of the terminated LLC closes. The terminated LLC must file a short-year final return for the tax year ending with the date of its termination. The new LLC must

---

§17.04   [1] IRC §706(c)(1).
[2] IRC §706(c)(2)(A).
[3] IRC §706(c)(2)(B).
[4] IRC §706(c).
[5] IRC §708(b); Reg. §1.708-1(b)(1).

file a return for its tax year beginning after the date of termination of the terminated partnership. The rule applies even though the new LLC uses the same employer identification number as the terminated LLC.[6]

[D]   Retiring Members

The tax year of the LLC does not close with respect to a retired member until the LLC makes the last distribution payment to the member. The retired member continues to be treated as a member until the liquidation of the member's interest in the LLC is completed.[7]

§17.05   CONSOLIDATED TAX RETURNS FOR SUBSIDIARIES

A corporation may form a subsidiary LLC and obtain the tax advantages of filing a consolidated tax return. There are planning considerations for both domestic and foreign LLCs.

An affiliated group of corporations may file a consolidated federal tax return instead of a separate return for each corporation.[1] The main advantages of filing a consolidated return are these:

- Operating losses of one corporation may offset the profits of another.
- Capital losses of one corporation may offset the capital gains of another in the affiliated group.
- There is no tax on intercompany dividends.
- Income on intercompany transactions is deferred.
- The consolidated group may use a member corporation's excess foreign tax credits.
- The parent corporation may adjust the basis in the stock in the subsidiary to reflect the subsidiary's taxable income or losses, tax-exempt income, and noncapital, nondeductible expenses. The corporate parent may use the increased stock basis to offset gain that it would otherwise recognize upon the sale of the stock in the subsidiary.

A foreign corporation may not be included in a consolidated return.[2] The parent company may obtain the same tax benefits by forming an LLC in a foreign country that has limited liability for foreign purposes and that is disregarded as an entity for U.S. tax purposes. All income and losses of the foreign subsidiary then pass

---

[6] F.S.A. 200132009; Notice 2001-5, 2001-3 I.R.B. 327. *See* §12.03 *supra,* regarding the tax consequences to the terminated and successor LLC on the sale or exchange of more than 50 percent of the membership units during any 12-month period.

[7] IRC §706(c)(2)(A); Reg. §§1.708-1(b)(1)(i)(b), 1.736-1(a)(6), 1.761-1(d).

§17.05   [1] IRC §1501.

[2] IRC §1504(b)(3).

through to the parent corporation to the same extent as those of a foreign unincorporated branch or division.

A single-member domestic LLC also provides many of the same tax benefits as a corporate subsidiary that is part of a consolidated return. The single-member LLC is disregarded as a separate entity, assuming that no election is made to classify the LLC as a corporation. Profits and losses automatically pass through to the parent corporation. Losses pass through without the limitations on net operating loss carryovers and carrybacks that apply to subsidiaries that are part of a consolidated return. Dividends paid by the LLC and gains and losses on intercompany transactions are also disregarded. The parent corporation is not required to file a consolidated return to include the single member's subsidiary LLC as part of its federal return filing. It can thus avoid the cumbersome and burdensome requirements applicable to corporations that have elected consolidated tax treatment.

One disadvantage is that the corporate parent of the single-member LLC may not increase its basis in the LLC membership units by the income that passes through from the LLC to the parent corporation. Since the LLC is disregarded as an entity, the parent corporation is treated as selling all of the underlying assets upon the sale of the LLC to a third party.

§17.06 RULING REQUESTS

An LLC must comply with Revenue Procedure 95-10[1] in order to obtain an IRS ruling on the classification of an LLC. Foreign LLCs must comply with Revenue Procedure 89-12[2] to obtain a classification ruling.[3] The IRS issued the check-the-box regulations on the classification of LLCs[4] so that ruling requests will generally not be necessary. However, it will still issue classification rulings under the check-the-box regulations.[5]

The IRS may issue a ruling granting relief from inadvertent termination of an S corporation as a result of an LLC's acquisition of stock in the S corporation if all of the following apply:[6]

1. The S corporation's election was terminated because the S corporation ceased to be a small business corporation[7] or had excessive passive investment income;[8]
2. The IRS determines that the termination was inadvertent;
3. The parties take steps to make the corporation a qualifying S corporation

---

§17.06   [1] 1995-1 C.B. 501.

[2] 1989-1 C.B. 798.

[3] Ltr. Ruls. 9216004, 9210039; Rev. Proc. 93-44, 1993-2 C.B. 545, modifying Rev. Proc. 93-7, §3.01.4, 1993-1 C.B. 465.

[4] T.D. 8697 (Dec. 18, 1996).

[5] Ltr. Rul. 200214016.

[6] See §4.03 supra.

[7] IRC §1362(d)(2).

[8] IRC §1362(d)(3).

no later than a reasonable period of time after discovery of the events resulting in the termination; and

4. The corporation, and each person who was a shareholder of the corporation at any time after termination and before corrective steps, agrees to make all adjustments required by the IRS consistent with the treatment of the corporation as an S corporation. In those cases, the corporation is treated as continuing to be an S corporation during the period specified by the IRS.

§17.07 UNIFIED AUDIT RULES

An LLC that is classified as a partnership is subject to the TEFRA unified partnership audit and litigation procedures.[1] These rules require that the tax treatment of all "partnership items" be determined at the LLC level rather than at the member level.[2] Partnership items are those items that are more appropriately determined at the LLC level, including gross income and deductions of the LLC.

LLCs with 10 or fewer members are not subject to the unified partnership audit and litigation procedures if each of the members is an individual, a C corporation, or an estate of a deceased partner.[3] The small LLC exception does not apply if any member of the LLC during the tax year is a pass-through partner.[4] A "pass-through" partner is a partnership, estate, trust, S corporation, nominee, or other similar person through whom other persons hold an interest in the LLC.[5] Thus, if an LLC that is classified as a disregarded entity owns a membership interest in a second LLC that is classified as a partnership, the second LLC does not qualify as a small partnership exempt from the unified partnership audit and litigation procedures even if the second LLC has 10 or fewer members.[6]

[A] Consistency Requirement

Members must report on their individual tax returns all LLC items in the same way that the LLC reported them on IRS Form 1065. If the treatment is inconsistent, then the IRS may assess a deficiency. This is treated as a computational adjustment that brings the member reporting into line with the LLC reporting.[7] The consistency requirement is applicable to the amount, timing, and characterization of LLC items.[8]

Members may identify inconsistent treatment of LLC items on their individual

§17.07 [1] C.C.A. 200250012; Lindsey v. Comm'r, TCM CCH Dec. 54,928(M) (2002); Rev. Proc. 99-49, 1999-2 I.R.B. Sec. 3.08(2); Rev. Proc. 97-27, Sec. 3, 1997-1 C.B. 680.
[2] IRC §6221.
[3] IRC §6231(a)(1)(B)(i).
[4] Reg. §301.6231(a)(1)-1(a)(2).
[5] IRC §6231(a)(9).
[6] C.C.A. 200250012.
[7] IRC §6222.
[8] Reg. §301.6222(a)-1.

returns by filing IRS Form 8082.[9] In that event, the IRS may not make an immediate assessment to the member with respect to those items unless the IRS conducts an LLC-level proceeding or notifies the member that all membership items arising from the LLC will be treated as nonpartnership items[10] There are special rules relating to loss of common deductions and credits arising from abusive tax shelters.

There is also an exception to the immediate assessment rules if the member makes an election within 30 days after receiving notification from the IRS that it plans to make a computational adjustment to conform the member's return to the LLC return.[11] The member may file a statement claiming that the LLC gave the member an incorrect Schedule K-1 or that the LLC issued a correct Schedule K-1, but filed an erroneous Form 1065. In that case, the member will be treated as having informed the IRS of the inconsistency on a timely basis.

[B] Tax Matters Partner

An LLC that is classified as a partnership must designate a tax matters partner (TMP) to represent the LLC in connection with tax audits. Subject to certain modifications, the rules applicable to partnerships contained in regulations[12] apply to all designations, selections, and terminations of a TMP for an LLC after December 22, 1996.[13] A TMP is designated as follows:[14]

- The general partner designated as the TMP by the LLC is the TMP.[15] Only a member-manager of an LLC is treated as a general partner for these purposes.[16] A member-manager is a member who, alone or with others, is vested with the continuing exclusive authority to make the management decisions necessary to conduct the business of the LLC.[17] Other members of an LLC are not general partners.
- Each member is treated as a general partner and may be designated as the TMP if there are no elected or designated member-managers.[18]
- The member-manager partner having the largest profits interest is the TMP, if no member-manager is designated.[19]
- The IRS selects the TMP if it is impractical to apply the largest profits interest rule.[20] Under prior law, if the general partners had no profits interest,

---

[9] Reg. §301.6222(b)-1(a).
[10] Reg. §301.6222(b)-2(a).
[11] IRC §6222(b)(2).
[12] Reg. §301.6231(a)(7)-1.
[13] Reg. §301.6231(a)(7)-2(c); T.D. 8698 (Dec. 20, 1996).
[14] IRC §6231(a)(7); Reg. §301.6231(a)(7)-2.
[15] IRC §6231(a)(7).
[16] Reg. §301.6231(a)(7)-2(a).
[17] Reg. §301.6231(a)(7)-2(b)(3).
[18] Id.
[19] Reg. §301.6231(a)(7)-1(a) to (m). These provisions apply to LLCs that are classified as partnerships.
[20] Reg. §301.6231(a)(7)-1(n) to (r). These provisions apply to LLCs that are classified as partnerships. Notice of Proposed Rulemaking, PS-34-92 (Oct. 27, 1995).

the IRS was required to select a limited partner as the TMP.[21] Under current law, the IRS may select either a general partner or a limited partner as the TMP.[22]

[C]   Audit Examination Procedures

The audit examination under the TEFRA unified audit and litigation provisions for LLCs begins on the date of notice from the IRS of the beginning of an administrative proceeding sent to the TMP. The notice is sometimes referred to as the NBAP.[23]

The audit examination ends on one of the following dates:[24]

- For a case in which the Service accepts the LLC return as filed, on the date of the "no adjustments letter" or the "no change" notice of final administrative adjustment sent to the TMP.
- For a fully agreed case, when all of the members of the LLC sign Form 870-P or 870-L.
- For an unagreed or partially agreed case, on the earliest of the date the TMP or its representative is notified by Appeals that the case has been referred to Appeals from Examination, the date that the TMP or member requests judicial review, or the date on which the period for requesting judicial review expires.

If there is no settlement as to all of the members, then the IRS will issue a notice of a final partnership administrative adjustment (FPAA).[25] The FPAA cannot be issued sooner than 120 days after the NBAP is issued. If the IRS issues the FPAA less than 120 days subsequent to the issuance of the NBAP, then the members may elect to have their membership items treated as nonmembership items.[26]

Ordinarily, the IRS will issue the FPAA first to the tax matters partner, although this is not required.[27] The IRS has 60 days thereafter to issue the FPAA to all notice members. The IRS may not issue an assessment of deficiency for a period of 150 days after the FPAA has been mailed to the tax matters partner, or until a Tax Court decision becomes final if the petitioners filed within the 150-day period.[28]

After the IRS has issued the FPAA, the tax matters partner has 90 days to file a petition in the Tax Court, the District Court, or the Claims Court.[29] If the tax matters partner does not file a petition within the 90-day period, then the notice

---

[21] Rev. Proc. 88-16, 1988-1 C.B. 691, superseded by Reg. §301.6231(a)(7)-1.
[22] Notice of Proposed Rulemaking (PS-34-92) (Oct. 27, 1995).
[23] Rev. Proc. 99-49, 1999-2 I.R.B. Sec. 3.08(2); Rev. Proc. 97-27, Sec. 3, 1997-1 C.B. 680.
[24] Id.
[25] IRC §6225.
[26] Ltr. Rul. 199938016.
[27] IRC §6225(a)(1).
[28] IRC §6225(a).
[29] IRC §6226(a).

partners and any 5 percent group[30] may file a Tax Court petition within 60 days thereafter.[31] If none of such persons filed within the applicable time periods, the members of the LLC have no recourse after that. There are no refund rights.

§17.08   Statute of Limitations for Tax Returns

An LLC must file a tax return and give a copy of Schedule K-1 to each member.[1] The statute of limitations runs three years from the date the return is filed.[2]

A six-year statute of limitations applies if there has been an omission of more than 25 percent of gross income.[3] In determining the applicability of the 25 percent rule, the member's gross income includes his distributive share of the gross income of the LLC (rather than taxable income of the LLC).[4] If a member reports only his percentage share of LLC taxable income, then he is treated as having reported that same percentage of his distributive share of LLC gross income.[5]

If the three- or six-year statute of limitations has expired for a member, the member may nevertheless be subject to assessment with respect to LLC items. The statute of limitations on LLC items does not expire before the later of three years after the date on which the LLC return was filed or the last day for filing such return (determined without extensions). Therefore, if the LLC did not file a return, the statute of limitations will run indefinitely for each member with respect to all LLC items.[6]

[30] A 5 percent group is defined in IRC §6231(a)(ii).
[31] IRC §6226(b)(1).
§17.08[1] IRC §6031.
[2] IRC §6501(a).
[3] IRC §6501(e).
[4] IRC §702(c).
[5] Reg. §1.702-1(c)(2).
[6] IRC §6229.

18

Foreign LLCs

§18.01   REASONS FOR ESTABLISHING FOREIGN LLC

[A]   Pass-Through of Losses

One reason for forming a foreign LLC is to permit the pass-through of losses from foreign operations to the U.S. parent corporation. This is a common reason for start-up foreign manufacturing operations where losses are expected during the initial years. A U.S. corporation may not include a foreign subsidiary corporation in a consolidated return.[1] Any losses are locked in the foreign corporation and cannot offset taxable income of the U.S. parent corporation.

The foreign LLC results in the immediate recognition of foreign income. The U.S. parent corporation may not defer income on foreign operations of an LLC that is classified as a partnership or disregarded entity. In contrast, a U.S. parent corporation may defer income recognition by using a foreign subsidiary corporation, subject to anti-abuse provisions such as Subpart F.

[B]   Foreign Tax Credits

A foreign LLC is attractive because of various foreign tax credit planning alternatives.

[1]   Overview of Foreign Tax Credit Rules

United States taxpayers who pay income taxes to foreign governments are entitled to deduct those taxes or credit them against U.S. tax liability, subject to certain limitations. United States tax policy is designed so that U.S. companies have the same tax burden regardless of where they conduct business. Large U.S. corporations are normally subject to a 35 percent tax rate. If the corporation conducts business in a country with a 10 percent tax rate, the corporation receives a 10 percent foreign tax credit against its U.S. tax liability. The corporation would then pay U.S. taxes at a 25 percent tax rate when it brings its foreign profits back to the United States.

There are three types of foreign tax credit—the regular tax credit under IRC Section 901, the indirect tax credit under IRC Section 902, and the deemed paid tax credit under IRC Section 960. The regular tax credit under IRC Section 901 applies when a taxpayer pays the taxes directly to the foreign government. Most individuals, corporations, and other entities are entitled to the regular tax credit.

The second type of foreign tax credit is the indirect tax credit under IRC Section 902. A U.S. corporation is entitled to the indirect tax credit under IRC Section 902 for foreign income taxes that the U.S. corporation pays indirectly through its 10 percent owned foreign subsidiaries. The indirect tax credit applies only when the U.S. corporation receives an actual dividend from the foreign subsidiary. The

---

§18.01   [1] IRC §1504(b)(3).

portion of the foreign income taxes paid by the subsidiary that are attributable to the parent corporation on receipt of the dividend are based on the percentage of the subsidiary's earnings and profits that the subsidiary pays as a dividend. The formula is as follows:

Indirect tax credit	=	actual dividend from foreign subsidiary/ earnings and profits of foreign subsidiary	×	foreign income taxes paid by subsidiary

The U.S. corporation must include in gross income the dividend received and an additional amount equal to the deemed paid credit.[2] This is referred to as the Section 78 gross up amount. Thus, the dividend amount is the actual dividend paid plus the foreign income taxes paid by the subsidiary attributable to the dividends.

EXAMPLE

A U.S. corporation owns 100 percent of the stock in a foreign corporation. The foreign corporation has $1,000 of earnings and profits. It previously paid $300 of foreign income taxes. The subsidiary distributes $100 as a dividend to the U.S. parent company. The parent company is treated as having paid 10 percent of $300 in taxes paid by the foreign subsidiary ($100 distribution/$1,000 earnings and profits). Thus, the parent corporation receives a $30 deemed paid foreign tax credit. The parent corporation's total taxable income is $130 (actual dividend of $100, plus the gross up amount of $30 equal to the deemed paid credit).

The deemed paid credit under IRC Section 960 is similar to the indirect tax credit under IRC Section 902, except that it applies to constructive dividends rather than actual dividends. For example, the deemed paid credit under IRC Section 960 applies when the U.S. corporation is currently taxed on undistributed Subpart F income earned by the foreign subsidiary.

[2]   Avoiding Excess Tiers in Corporate Structures

The use of an LLC may preserve the availability of foreign tax credits for lower tier foreign subsidiary corporations. A U.S. parent corporation may take a deemed paid tax credit for foreign taxes paid by foreign subsidiaries. The credit is available when the foreign subsidiary pays a dividend to the U.S. parent corporation. The deemed paid credit is currently available only for taxes paid by the first six

---

[2] IRC §78.

tiers of foreign subsidiaries.[3] Foreign taxes paid by lower tier subsidiaries are unavailable for the tax credit. The use of an LLC can eliminate tiers and preserve foreign tax credits in multitiered foreign tax structures. An LLC that is classified as a partnership or disregarded entity is not counted as a tier for foreign tax credit purposes.

Prior to 1998, U.S. corporations were entitled to the deemed paid tax credit only for income taxes paid by the first three levels of subsidiaries. A corporation was not entitled to the indirect credit for taxes paid by fourth and lower tier subsidiary corporations. After 1997, foreign taxes paid by fourth, fifth, and sixth tier subsidiaries qualify for the foreign tax credit if certain requirements are met. The U.S. corporation claiming the credit for taxes paid by the fourth, fifth, and sixth tier subsidiaries must own indirectly at least five percent of the voting stock of the subsidiary through a chain of other corporations connected through stock ownership of at least 10 percent of their voting stock. The first foreign corporation in the chain must be a first tier corporation. The subsidiary must be a controlled foreign corporation (more than 50 percent ownership by U.S. shareholders). The U.S. corporation taking the tax credit must be a U.S. shareholder (10 percent direct or indirect owner) in the subsidiary.[4]

[3] Pass-Through of Credits for Individuals

The use of a foreign LLC permits an individual owner to operate in a foreign country through a separate entity that affords limited liability and to receive a pass-through of foreign tax credits from that entity.

An individual cannot receive a pass-through of foreign tax credits if the individual forms a corporation in a foreign country. Individuals and less than 10 percent corporate shareholders may only claim the regular tax credit for foreign income taxes paid by them. They may not claim the indirect credit for the underlying taxes paid by a foreign corporation.

Individuals and less than 10 percent corporate shareholders can obtain a credit for the foreign taxes by operating through an unincorporated branch. However, a branch operation is often unacceptable for liability reasons or because a local entity is needed for the foreign operations.

Alternatively, individuals may form a foreign LLC that is taxed as a partnership for U.S. tax purposes. The owners of the LLC then receive the limited liability afforded by local law and the credit for foreign taxes paid by the LLC on its income. The check-the-box regulations allow U.S. taxpayers who do not qualify for the Section 902 indirect tax credit to more easily take advantage of the direct tax credit by electing partnership or "nothing" tax status for the foreign entity.[5]

---

[3] IRC §902(b).

[4] IRC §902(b).

[5] This issue as applied to limited liability companies was discussed in "Joint Committee on Taxation Staff Review of Selected Entity Classification and Partnership Tax Issues" (JCS-6-97), pp. 19-20 (Apr. 8, 1997).

[4] 10-50 Basket Limitation

An LLC is sometimes used to avoid the 10-50 percent basket limitation on foreign tax credits. The foreign tax credit is applied by first separating foreign income into separate "baskets" or types of income. The maximum credit that may be taken is then determined under the following formula:

Total taxable income within the separate basket from all foreign sources, divided by total taxable income $\times$ U.S. income tax $=$ U.S. income tax credit for that basket

One of the separate baskets is dividends received from foreign corporations in which the U.S. corporation owns between 10 percent and 50 percent of the stock.[6] If dividends fall into the 10-50 percent basket, there is a greater likelihood that the U.S. corporation will have excess foreign tax credits that it will not be able to use.

The 10-50 percent basket limitation does not apply if the foreign company is an LLC or other entity that is taxed as a partnership for U.S. tax purposes. In this case, the foreign tax credit is determined on a flow-through basis under IRC Section 901. The member's share of income from the LLC would then fall within the general limitation basket rather than the special dividend basket subject to the limitations.[7]

The Taxpayer Relief Act of 1997 phased out the 10-50 percent basket for tax years after 2002.[8] Thus, this issue will eventually disappear.

[C] Subpart F Income

U.S. companies often use a foreign holding company to manage and own foreign investments and operations and to enter into joint ventures. There is a potential subpart F income problem when the foreign operating company transfers income to the foreign parent holding company as a dividend. The dividend normally constitutes foreign personal holding company income subject to Subpart F taxation.

U.S. companies have sometimes organized their foreign operations as partnerships or LLCs so that the controlled foreign corporation's distributive share of partnership or LLC income would not constitute foreign personal holding company income. Instead, the character of the distributed share under Subpart F would be determined by looking through to the activities of the partnership

---

[6] IRC §§904(d)(1)(E), 904(d)(2)(E).

[7] This issue as applied to limited liability companies was discussed in "Joint Committee on Taxation Staff Review of Selected Entity Classification and Partnership Tax Issues" (JCS-6-97), p. 20 (Apr. 8, 1997).

[8] IRC §§904(d)(1)(E), 904(d)(2)(E).

or LLC. The distributive share would arguably not be Subpart F income if the transactions did not give rise to foreign base company income.[9]

The IRS issued final regulations to clarify the treatment of a controlled foreign corporation partner's distributive share of partnership or LLC income. Subpart F income now includes a controlled foreign corporation's distributive share of income of a partnership or LLC to the extent the income would have been Subpart F income if received directly by the controlled foreign corporation partner.[10] The determination of whether a distributive share of partnership income is Subpart F income, whether an entity is a related person, and whether an activity takes place in or outside the country under the laws of which the controlled foreign corporation is organized (e.g., for purposes of determining whether the income qualifies for the "same country" exception to Subpart F) is made with respect to the controlled foreign corporation partner, and not the partnership or LLC.[11]

Under subpart F of the Internal Revenue Code, every 10 percent U.S. shareholder in a controlled foreign corporation[12] is currently taxed on its pro rata share of subpart F income earned by the controlled foreign corporation, whether or not the corporation distributes the income to the shareholder.[13] One type of subpart F income is dividend income,[14] unless the dividends are received from certain related corporations organized in the same country[15] or unless one of the other exceptions applies.[16] Therefore, if the foreign subsidiary is classified as a corporation for U.S. tax purposes, the income transferred up to the foreign holding company will be treated as dividend income taxable as subpart F income to the U.S. shareholders of the foreign holding company.

To avoid this tax problem, multitiered foreign operations are sometimes structured to ensure that all entities in the ownership chain below the holding company have limited liability under local law and are classified for federal tax purposes as a branch of the holding company (or as a partnership in the case of joint ventures where the foreign entity has two or more owners). The foreign holding company is often formed in tax-haven jurisdictions, such as the Cayman Islands or Holland.[17]

It is now relatively easy to find a foreign entity that has limited liability under local law and that is classified as a branch or partnership for U.S. tax purposes. Under current Treasury regulations on classification of foreign corporations, it is no longer necessary to:

---

[9] *See* Brown Group Inc v. Commissioner, 77 F.3d 217 (8th Cir. 1996), *vac'g* 104 TC 105 (1995).

[10] Reg. §1.952-1(g).

[11] Reg. §1.954-1(g)(1).

[12] A controlled foreign corporation is a corporation in which more than 50 percent of the stock is owned by U.S. shareholders who own at least 10 percent of the stock in the corporation. IRC §957(a).

[13] IRC §951(a)(1).

[14] IRC §954(c)(1)(A).

[15] IRC §954(c)(3).

[16] IRC §§954(b)(3), 954(c).

[17] This issue as applied to limited liability companies was discussed in Joint Committee on Taxation Staff Review of Selected Entity Classification and Partnership Tax Issues (JCS-6-97) at 19 (Apr. 8, 1997).

- Restrict transfers of shares in the joint venture or project company;
- Expose investors to unlimited liability for the project company's debts;
- Have the project company managed by the shareholders rather than the board of directors of the company; or
- Have the company dissolve automatically upon the bankruptcy of a member/owner/shareholder.[18]

Under the Treasury regulations governing the classification of foreign companies, most foreign limited liability companies are by default classified as corporations for federal tax purposes. However, most foreign entities can elect classification as a partnership (or a branch in the case of foreign entities owned by a single holding company) by checking the box on IRS Form 8832.[19] There is an exception for certain foreign limited liability entities that are always classified as corporations.[20] Normally, the foreign LLC must file Form 8832 in order to elect branch or partnership classification and avoid the subpart F tax problem.

A second benefit of electing branch classification is that the holding company can normally sell the foreign branch and defer U.S. taxes on any gain. The sale of a foreign LLC that is classified as a "nothing" is treated as a direct sale of the underlying assets. This can result in the benefit of greater foreign source income or lower foreign source loss than would a sale of stock or partnership interests. Often it is not possible to defer taxes on the gain from the sale of shares in a corporation or units in a partnership.[21]

[D]   Other Reasons for Forming Foreign LLC

An LLC or other foreign entity taxed as a partnership for U.S. tax purposes is not subject to the foreign personal holding company rules (FPHC),[22] the controlled foreign corporation (CFC) and subpart F rules,[23] or the passive foreign income rules (PFIC).[24]

§18.02   FORMATION OF FOREIGN LLCs

The tax consequences of forming a foreign LLC and contributing property to the LLC are generally the same as for domestic LLCs, whether the LLC is

---

[18] One or more of these provisions were often required under the prior Treasury regulations on the classification of entities, which used a four-factor test.

[19] See §5.04 supra.

[20] Reg. §301.7701-2(b)(8).

[21] See Joint Committee on Taxation Staff Review of Selected Entity Classification and Partnership Tax Issues (JCS-6-97) at 20 (Apr. 8, 1997).

[22] IRC §§551-558.

[23] IRC §§951-964.

[24] IRC §956A.

classified as a partnership[1] or as a corporation.[2] However, there are several exceptions.

The IRS has authority to tax gain to the contributing member upon the transfer of appreciated assets to a U.S. or foreign LLC if the built-in gain, when recognized, would be included in the gross income of a foreign person.[3]

The Taxpayer Relief Act of 1997 repealed Section 1491 of the Internal Revenue Code, which imposed a 35 percent excise tax on the gain when appreciated property was transferred to a foreign LLC. The IRS is now authorized to issue regulations providing for gain recognition upon the transfer of appreciated property to a partnership in circumstances where the gain will ultimately be recognized by a foreign person.[4]

United States persons who contribute property to a foreign LLC must file a report with the IRS if either of the following conditions exists:

- The U.S. member owns at least a 10 percent membership interest in the foreign LLC after the transfer, or
- The aggregate fair market value of property transferred during any 12-month period exceeds $100,000[5]

There is a penalty of 10 percent of the fair market value of the transferred property for failure to provide the required information. The member must also recognize gain upon the contribution as if the contributed property had been sold for fair market value at the time of contribution. The maximum penalty is $100,000 unless the failure was due to intentional disregard. The statute of limitations does not end until three years after the member furnishes the IRS with the required information.

The reporting requirements apply after the IRS issues applicable regulations.[6] Before 1998, U.S. persons transferring property to a foreign LLC filed IRS Form 926, Return by a U.S. Transferor of Property to a Foreign Corporation, Foreign Estate or Trust, or Foreign Partnership.[7]

§18.03 CLASSIFICATION OF FOREIGN LLCs

[A] General Rules

On December 17, 1996, the IRS issued final regulations on the classification of LLCs and other entities for federal tax purposes.[1] The regulations are referred to

---

§18.02   [1] Ltr. Rul. 8106082.

[2] Ltr. Ruls. 8029031, 8011038, 7935046 (*citing* IRC §367(c)(2) and Rev. Rul. 77-449, 1977-2 C.B. 110).

[3] IRC §721(c).

[4] *Id.*

[5] IRC §6038B.

[6] IRC §6046A.

[7] *See* Notice 97-18, 1997-1 C.B. 389.

§18.03   [1] T.D. 8697 (Dec. 18, 1996), enacting final regulation under Reg. §301.7701.

as "check-the-box" regulations because they permit most unincorporated entities to select classification as a proprietorship, partnership, or corporation by checking the applicable box on an IRS form. The classification rules for foreign LLCs are different than those for domestic LLCs and are discussed below.

An LLC organized under the laws of the United States is a domestic LLC for classification purposes even if the LLC has foreign members.[2]

[B]   Special Rules Applicable to Foreign LLCs

The classification of a foreign LLC depends on the number of members and whether the members have limited liability under local law. If the foreign LLC does not make an election, it will be classified as follows:[3]

- The LLC will be classified by default as a partnership if it has two or more members and at least one member has unlimited liability.[4] A member has unlimited liability if the member has personal liability for the debts of or claims against the LLC, by reason of being a member, based solely on the statute or law under which the entity is organized.[5] A member has personal liability if creditors of the entity may seek satisfaction of debts of or claims against the LLC from the member as such.[6] If a taxpayer is uncertain whether there is limited liability in a particular case, it may file an election to secure the desired classification. A foreign LLC with two or more members may elect classification as a corporation instead of a partnership under the default rules.
- The LLC will be classified by default as a corporation if all members have limited liability.[7] The LLC may instead elect classification as a proprietorship if the LLC has a single member[8] or as a partnership if the LLC has two or more members and is otherwise eligible for partnership classification.[9]
- The LLC will by default be classified as a proprietorship or entity separate from its owners if it has a single owner with unlimited liability.[10] The LLC may instead elect classification as a corporation.[11]

For tax purposes, it is usually advisable for a foreign LLC to be classified as a partnership. It will be classified as a partnership unless:

---

[2] Ltr. Rul. 9610006.
[3] Reg. §301.7701-3(b)(2)(i).
[4] Reg. §301.7701-3(b)(2)(i)(A).
[5] Reg. §301.7701-3(b)(2)(ii).
[6] Id.
[7] Reg. §301.7701-3(b)(2)(i)(B).
[8] Reg. §301.7701-3(a); Ltr. Rul. 200207019.
[9] Reg. §301.7701-3(a).
[10] Reg. §301.7701-3(b)(2)(i)(C).
[11] Reg. §301.7701-3(a).

- The LLC is one of the foreign entities designated on a list in the regulations. This is referred to as the "(b)(8) list" or the "per se list." The IRS has designated over 80 foreign limited liability entities on this list that are always classified as corporations.[12] They may not elect to be classified as partnerships. The IRS will update the list in notices of proposed rulemaking on a prospective basis only.[13]
- The LLC elects classification as a corporation.[14] An LLC with one or more members may elect classification as a corporation.[15]
- The LLC is a single-member LLC and the member has unlimited liability.[16] The LLC is by default classified as a proprietorship, branch, or division unless it elects classification as a corporation.[17]
- The LLC has one or more members and no member has unlimited liability.[18] The LLC is by default classified as a corporation unless it elects classification as a proprietorship (LLC with a single member) or partnership (LLC with two or more members that is otherwise eligible for such election).[19]
- The LLC was classified as a corporation before January 1, 1997.[20] A foreign LLC that is classified as a corporation may nevertheless elect classification as a partnership if certain requirements are met.[21]

[C] Default Classification for Foreign LLCs Existing on January 1, 1997

A foreign LLC existing on January 1, 1997, may keep its same classification under the default rules only if it is a "foreign eligible entity" and the claimed classification affected the liability of any person for U.S. tax or information purposes at any time during the five years before January 1, 1997.[22]

Foreign LLCs on the per se list are not foreign eligible entities and may not elect partnership classification. However, under grandfather rules, LLCs that claimed classification as a partnership, branch, or division before January 1, 1997, may continue to be classified as a partnership, branch, or division after January 1, 1997, if six requirements are met.[23] The six requirements are as follows:

1. The LLC was in existence on May 8, 1996 (or formed thereafter pursuant to a written binding contract in effect on that date).

---

[12] Reg. §§301.7701-2(b)(8), 301.7701-3(a) (first sentence).

[13] T.D. 8697, Part B, Discussion of Comments on the General Approach and Scope of the Regulations (Dec. 18, 1996).

[14] Reg. §§301.7701-3(b)(2)(i), 301.7701-3(c).

[15] Reg. §301.7701-3(a).

[16] Reg. §301.7701-3(b)(2)(i)(C).

[17] Reg. §§301.7701-3(a), 301.7701-3(b)(2)(i)(C).

[18] Reg. §301.7701-3(b)(2)(i)(B).

[19] Reg. §§301.7701-3(a), 301.7701-3(b)(2)(i)(B).

[20] Reg. §301.7701-3(b)(3).

[21] Reg. §301.7701-3(b)(3)(ii).

[22] Id.

[23] Reg. §301.7701-2(d).

2. The LLC's claimed classification was relevant to any person for U.S. tax purposes on May 8, 1996.
3. Neither the LLC nor any member for whom U.S. classification was relevant treated the LLC as a corporation for purposes of filing U.S. tax returns, information returns, and withholding documents for the tax year that included May 8, 1996.
4. Any change in the LLC's claimed classification during the 60 months before May 8, 1996, occurred solely as a result of a change in the organizational documents of the LLC, and the LLC and all members of the LLC recognized the federal tax consequences of any change in the LLC's classification during the 60 months before May 8, 1996.
5. There was a reasonable basis for treating the LLC as other than a corporation.
6. The LLC was not under tax audit with respect to the classification on May 8, 1996.

Foreign LLCs on the per se list that qualify under these transition rules may instead elect to be classified as corporations. However, after such an election, they may not subsequently elect classification as a partnership or branch. Any termination under Section 708(b)(1)(B) or division under Section 708(b)(2)(B) will end the grandfather status of an entity on the per se list. The successor entity will thereafter be permanently treated as a corporation.[24]

§18.04   RULING REQUESTS

The IRS will issue rulings on the classification of foreign LLCs as partnerships or corporations if the LLC complies with the requirements of Revenue Procedure 89-12.[1] However, the IRS issued the check-the-box regulations on the classification of LLCs so that ruling requests will generally not be necessary.

§18.05   WITHHOLDING TAXES ON WAGES

An "American employer" is required to withhold FICA taxes on wages paid to citizens or residents of the United States who perform services as employees outside of the United States.[1] A U.S. or foreign LLC that is classified as a partner-

---

[24] However, the LLC's grandfather status will not end in the case of a termination caused by the sale or exchange of membership interests in an LLC described in Reg. §301.7701-2(d)(2) where the sale or exchange is to a related person within the meaning of IRC §§267(b) and 707(b) and occurs no later than 12 months after the date the LLC is formed. *See* T.D. 8697, Part B, Discussion of Comments on the General Approach and Scope of the Regulations (Dec. 18, 1996).

§18.04 [1] 1989-1 C.B. 798. *See* Rev. Proc. 93-44, 1993-2 C.B. 545, *modifying* Rev. Proc. 93-7, §3.01.4, 1993-1 C.B. 465; Ltr. Ruls. 9216004, 9210039.

§18.05 [1] Ltr. Rul. 9335062 (*citing* IRC §3121(h)(3)).

ship is an "American employer" for withholding purposes if two-thirds or more of the partners are residents of the United States.[2]

§18.06 TAX RETURNS AND REPORTING REQUIREMENTS

[A] Partnership Return

A foreign LLC must file a partnership return if it has U.S. source gross income or income that is effectively connected with the conduct of a U.S. trade or business.[1] The LLC must obtain an identifying number from its foreign members (such as a NRA Social Security number) for purposes of filing returns and other documents.[2] The LLC must obtain an identifying number from its foreign members (such as a NRA Social Security number) for purposes of filing returns and other documents.[3] The IRS has authority to make exceptions and simplify procedures.

A foreign LLC that has no gross income effectively connected with the conduct of a U.S. trade or business and that is required to file a partnership return only because it has gross income from U.S. sources is wholly or partially exempt from the partnership filing requirements if:

1. *De minimis exception.* The foreign LLC has $20,000 or less of U.S. source income, and no income connected with a U.S. trade or business. Less than 1 percent of any item of LLC gain, loss, deduction, or credit is allocable in the aggregate to direct U.S. members of the LLC.[4] The U.S. members of the LLC must directly report their shares of allocable items of LLC income, gain, loss, deduction, and credit.

2. *No U.S. partners.* The foreign LLC has no U.S. members and no income connected with a U.S. trade or business.[5] The LLC files IRS Forms 1042 and 1042-S for all items of U.S. source income payable to the foreign members, and pays the required withholding taxes.[6] The foreign LLC's obligation to file these forms is generally eliminated by IRS regulations.[7] In such case, the foreign LLC is not required to file a partnership tax return if another withholding agent actually files Forms 1042 and 1042-S and pays the associated tax.[8]

3. *Limited Schedules K-1.* The foreign LLC has U.S. source income and one or more U.S. members, but no income connected with a U.S. trade or business.[9]

---

[2] Ltr. Rul. 9335062.

§18.06   [1] IRC §6031(e).

[2] Reg. §301.6109-1(b)(2)(i); Rev. Rul. 84-158, 1984-2 C.B. 262.

[3] Reg. §301.6109-1(b)(2)(i); Revenue Ruling 84-158, 1984 C.B. 262.

[4] Reg. §1.6031(a)-1(b)(2).

[5] Reg. §1.6031(a)-1(b)(3)(ii).

[6] Reg. §1.6031(a)-1(b)(3).

[7] Reg. §1.1461-1(b)(2), (c)(4)(iv).

[8] Reg. §1.6031(a)-1(b)(3).

[9] Reg. §1.6031(a)-1(b)(3)(iii).

The foreign LLC must file a partnership return. However, it must file Schedules K-1 only for its U.S. members and for its pass-through members and partners through which U.S. members hold an interest in the foreign LLC. The LLC must also file IRS Forms 1042 and 1042-S for all items of U.S. source income payable to foreign members. It is not required to file these forms if another withholding agent actually files Forms 1042 and 1042-S and pays the associated tax.[10]

The foreign LLC is not required to file Schedules K-1 for foreign members deriving U.S. source income that is not connected with the U.S. trade or business because the foreign members are subject to information reporting on Form 1042-S. These rules generally subject foreign members, and not the foreign LLC to information reporting regime for U.S. source income that is not connected with the U.S. trade or business, and that is paid to a foreign LLC.[11] Accordingly, the foreign LLC that has no income connected with a U.S. trade or business is not required to report on Schedule K-1 the foreign member's allocable share of income, including U.S. source gains that are not subject to Form 1042-S reporting, deposit, or interest withholding.[12]

A foreign LLC that has income effectively connected with a U.S. trade or business must file a complete partnership return (with Schedules K-1 for all members) reflecting all items of LLC income, gain, loss, deduction, and credit.

The LLC must file the partnership return with the Service Center for the area in which the LLC has its principal place of business in the United States. The LLC must file the return with the Internal Revenue Service, Philadelphia, PA 19255-0011 if the LLC has no office or place of business in the United States.[13] The foreign LLC must file the return on or before the fifteenth day of the fourth month following the close of the LLC's tax year.[14]

A foreign LLC classified as a partnership that has either a foreign tax matters partner or foreign books is not allowed deductions, losses, and credits unless the LLC files the partnership return.[15]

[B]   Form 8865

U.S. members in a foreign LLC must file Form 8865, Information Return of U.S. Persons With Respect to Certain Foreign LLCs, to report the following:

- transfers of cash and other property to a foreign LLC in exchange for a membership interest;[16]

[10] Reg. §1.6031(a)-1(b)(3)(i).

[11] In contrast, income that is connected with the U.S. trade or business must be reported to a foreign LLC rather than to the foreign members directly.

[12] T.D. 8841, Explanation of IRS final regulations revising partnership filing requirements, 64 Fed. Reg. 61498 (Nov. 12, 1999).

[13] Reg. §1.6031(a)-1(e)(1)(ii).

[14] Reg. §1.6031(a)-1(e)(2).

[15] IRC §6231(f).

[16] IRC §6038B; Prop. Reg. §1.6038B.

- acquisitions or dispositions of at least a ten percent interest in a foreign LLC;[17] and
- information concerning the income and assets of the LLC, certain transactions with the LLC, the names of the members, and other specified information if the U.S. member owns at least a ten percent interest in a controlled foreign LLC.[18]

[1] Contributions to Foreign LLC

Certain U.S. persons who contribute property, including cash, to a foreign LLC in exchange for a membership interest must report the contribution on Form 8865 (page 1 and Schedules A and O). The member must report the contribution if (a) the member owns, directly or indirectly, at least a 10 percent interest in the LLC immediately after the transfer, or (b) the aggregate fair market value of property transferred during any 12 month period exceeds $100,000 (when added to the value of property transferred by such person or any related person to the LLC or a related LLC or partnership during the prior 12 months).[19]

The U.S. member must also notify the IRS when a foreign LLC disposes of appreciated property contributed by the member if the member is still a member at that time. The member must list on Form 8865 appreciated property and intangible property contributed to the foreign LLC on an item by item basis. The member may aggregate and list other items of property according to categories of inventory, other intangible or business property, cash, securities, and other property. The member who reports the transfer must identify the other members in the LLC.[20]

The member must normally file Form 8865 with the member's income tax return for the year in which the reportable contribution occurs.[21] Failure to properly report a contribution is subject to a penalty of ten percent of the fair market value of the property transferred. The maximum penalty is $100,000 unless the failure was intentional. In addition, the member must recognize gain on the contribution as if the contributed property had been sold for fair market value.[22]

[2] Acquisitions and Dispositions

U.S. members must report acquisitions and dispositions of a ten percent or more interest in a foreign LLC, and equivalent changes in proportional membership interest.[23]

U.S. members must file Form 8865 (page 1 and Schedules A and P) to report

---

[17] IRC §6046A; Prop. Reg. §1.6046A-1.
[18] IRC §6038; Prop. Reg. §1.6038-3.
[19] IRC §6038B(b)(1); Prop. Reg. §1.6038B-2(a)(1).
[20] Reg. §1.6038B-2(c).
[21] Reg. §1.6038B-2(a).
[22] Reg. §1.6038B-2(h).
[23] IRC §6046A; Reg. §1.6046A-1(b).

the acquisitions and dispositions. The form is normally filed with the member's U.S. income tax return for the tax year during which a reportable event occurs.[24]

A person who fails to report the acquisitions and dispositions is subject to a penalty of $10,000 for each reportable transaction. There is an additional penalty of up to $50,000 if the failure continues for more than 90 days after notice of failure by the IRS.[25]

[3]   Income from and Transactions with Controlled Foreign LLCs

Ten percent U.S. owners in a controlled foreign LLC must file an annual information report on Form 8865.[26] A controlled foreign LLC is an LLC in which U.S. members owning at least a ten percent interest own more than a 50 percent interest in the capital, profits, or deductions and losses of the LLC.[27] Ten percent members are not required to file an annual report if a 50 percent or more U.S. member controls the LLC, in which case only the controlling member must file the return.

Form 8865 is similar in format to a U.S. partnership return. For example, Schedule B of the form shows the business income and deductions of the LLC. Schedule K shows the member's allocable share of income, credits, and deductions. Schedule N is used to provide information on transactions between the member and the foreign LLC.

Controlling U.S. members are required to provide substantially more information on Form 8865 than ten percent members.[28] A controlling U.S. member must report information concerning the income and assets of the LLC, the names of the members in the LLC, and certain other information. A ten percent member (who is required to file a report only where there is no U.S. controlling member) must report information only with respect to that member's interest in the LLC.[29]

The information report on Form 8865 must be filed with the U.S. member's income tax return for the tax year in which the LLC's annual accounting period ends.[30] Members who are not required to file must submit a statement with their tax return identifying another member who will satisfy the filing requirements. Indirect U.S. members are not required to file if they identify a U.S. person who will fulfill the filing requirements, and if the designated filer complies.

A person who fails to file or report all of the information is subject to a penalty of $10,000 for each failure for each reportable transaction. There is an additional penalty of up to $50,000 if the failure continues for more than 90 days after notice

---

[24] Reg. §1.6046A-1(d).
[25] Reg. §1.6046A-1(i).
[26] IRC §6038(a)(5); Reg. §§1.6038-3; 1.6031(a)-1(b)(4)(ii).
[27] IRC §6038(e)(3).
[28] Reg. §1.6038-3(g)(2).
[29] Reg. §1.6038-3(g)(1).
[30] Reg. §1.6038-3(i).

of failure by the IRS. There is also a loss or reduction of the U.S. member's foreign tax credits, and criminal penalties for fraudulent returns.[31]

[C] Anti-Abuse Provisions

The IRS has regulatory authority to treat LLCs created or organized in the United States as foreign LLCs.[32] This prevents a foreign LLC from avoiding the reporting requirements and penalties by organizing the LLC in the United States.

§18.07 SECURITIES-TRADING LLCs

Foreign persons who invest in U.S. stocks and securities are not taxed on gain from the sale of the stocks and securities unless:

- The foreign person is a U.S. resident. United States residents are taxed on their worldwide income.
- The foreign person is present in the United States for more than 183 days during the year.[1]
- The gain is from the sale of stock in a U.S. real property holding company.[2] Generally, a U.S. real property holding corporation is a corporation in which more than 50 percent of the fair market value of its assets is U.S. real property interests.[3]
- The foreign person is engaged in a U.S. trade or business. Foreign persons who trade stocks and securities for their own account, including through an LLC, are not treated as engaged in a U.S. trade or business even if the trading activity is conducted directly or indirectly through an agent in United States.[4]

Capital gains from the sale of securities are not treated as FDAP income (fixed, determinable, and periodic income), and are therefore not subject to the 30 percent withholding tax on FDAP income.[5]

Before 1998, a foreign person who invested in an LLC whose principal business was trading in stocks and securities for the member's account was not treated as engaged in a U.S. trade or business if the LLC's principal office was located

---

[31] Reg. §1.6038-3(k).
[32] IRC §7701(a)(4).
§18.07 [1] IRC §871(b).
[2] IRC §897.
[3] IRC §897(c)(2).
[4] IRC §864(b)(2)(A).
[5] Reg. §§1.1441-2(b)(1)(i), 1.1441-2(b)(2)(i).

outside of the United States. The IRS regulations provided a list of 10 activities that, if conducted abroad, would result in the LLC being treated as having its principal office outside of the United States.[6] These were referred to as the "Ten Commandments." In practice, the Ten Commandments were largely a nuisance. Their main effect was to shift certain administrative jobs outside of the United States. In 1997, Congress repealed this requirement. Foreign LLCs that trade in stock and securities are no longer required to maintain their principal office outside the United States.[7]

Most securities-trading LLCs still maintain their principal offices outside of the United States. The reason is that foreign investors prefer to maintain the confidentiality of their records and membership information by keeping that information outside of the United States.

§18.08   WITHHOLDING TAXES ON PAYMENTS TO FOREIGN LLCs

[A]   Overview

A U.S. payor must withhold 30 percent on payments of FDAP income to a foreign LLC. FDAP income is fixed or determinable annual or periodic income. It includes interest, dividends, rents, royalties, and compensation not subject to the regular wage withholding. The withholding agent is not required to withhold at the 30 percent rate on the following types of payments:

- Payments to an LLC that is a withholding foreign partnership.[1] This is a foreign LLC that has entered into an agreement with the IRS to assume primary responsibility for withholding.
- Payments to a foreign LLC that the withholding agent determines are for the benefit of a U.S. member or a foreign member entitled to a reduced rate of withholding. The withholding agent must obtain a foreign withholding certificate and other documentation from the LLC to substantiate the reduced rate of withholding.
- Payments from U.S. sources that are excludable from gross income without regard to the identity of the recipient, such as interest under IRC Section 103(a).
- Payments to a foreign LLC that are effectively connected with the conduct of a U.S. trade or business and that are includable in the foreign LLC's income. The foreign LLC receiving the income must withhold on the income allocable to foreign members, whether or not distributed, at the highest graduated income tax rates.

---

[6] Reg. §1.864-2(c)(2)(iii).
[7] See Taxpayer Relief Act of 1997, Pub. L. No. 105-34, §1162, 105th Cong., 1st Sess. (Aug. 5, 1997).
§18.08   [1] Reg. §1.1441-5(c)(2).

[B] Withholding Foreign Partnership

[1] Payments to Foreign LLC

Payments to a foreign LLC that is a "withholding foreign partnership" are not subject to withholding taxes.[2] A withholding foreign partnership includes a foreign LLC that has entered into a withholding agreement[3] with the Internal Revenue Service to withhold taxes on distributions and guaranteed payments that it makes to its members. In such case, the withholding tax obligation shifts from the U.S. withholding agent (the person in the United States making the payment) to the foreign LLC.

Under the terms of the withholding agreement, the LLC may provide to each U.S. payor of amounts subject to withholding with a withholding certificate on Form W-8IMP without the attached documentation of members. The foreign LLC may then receive payments from the U.S. payors in gross without reduction for withholdings.[4]

[2] Withholding and Reporting by Foreign LLC

Although there is no withholding on payments to a foreign LLC that qualifies as a withholding foreign partnership, the foreign LLC must withhold and deposit taxes. The amount withheld is based on the Forms W-8 or W-9 that it receives from its members.

The foreign LLC must use Form 1042-S to report payments to and taxes withheld from each direct foreign member. It may report on an individual basis, or by election on a pooled basis. The foreign LLC is not required to disclose to the U.S. payor any documentation or payment information for members.[5]

An LLC that is a withholding foreign partnership must use Form W-8IMY (Part V) to represent that it has assumed primary withholding responsibility. The form must be signed by one of the members under penalty of perjury. It must contain the following information:[6]

- The name, permanent residence address, and employer identification number of the LLC, and the country under which the LLC was organized;
- A certification that the LLC is a withholding foreign partnership; and
- Any other information, certifications, or statements required by the agreement with the IRS, or by the form or accompanying instructions.

---

[2] Reg. §1.1441-5(c)(2).

[3] *See* Notice 2002-41, 2002-24 I.R.B. 1153, regarding the form of agreements for LLCs that want to qualify as withholding for partnerships.

[4] Notice 2002-41, 2002-24 I.R.B. 1153.

[5] *Id.*

[6] Reg. §1.1441-5(c)(2)(iv).

The foreign LLC is not required to attach documentation regarding the members of the LLC.[7]

[C]   Nonwithholding Foreign Partnerships

[1]   Reporting by Foreign LLC

Payments to LLCs that have not entered into a withholding agreement with the IRS are treated as payments to the members.[8] The foreign LLC must provide a withholding certificate (Form W8IMY) to the payor that identifies each of the members, whether the member is a U.S. or foreign person, the allocable share of each member, and documentation that the payor needs to provide each member with the required IRS reporting forms.[9]

The foreign LLC must use Form W-8IMP (Part VI) as the withholding certificate. The LLC must attach a statement to the form that provides sufficient information for the withholding agent to determine each member's distributive share of the amounts that the LLC is receiving from the payor. The sum of all members' distributive shares, expressed as a percentage, must equal 100 percent.

The LLC must also transmit to the withholding agent appropriate documentation regarding the status of its members.[10] The foreign members may provide the LLC with Form W-8BEN for such purpose. The LLC must keep the original copy of the forms, and transmit photocopies of the forms to the payor along with Form W-8IMP. Form W-8BEN is used to establish that the member is a foreign person, and to claim a reduced rate or exemption from withholding as a resident of a foreign country with which the United States has an income tax treaty. A U.S. citizen or resident who is a member in a foreign LLC must provide the LLC with Form W-9 instead of Form W-8BEN.[11]

The foreign member may also be required to submit Form W-8BEN to claim an exemption from domestic information reporting and backup withholding at a 31 percent rate for certain types of income that are not subject to foreign-person withholding (such as broker proceeds, short-term original issue discount, and a deposit interest).

[2]   Reporting and Withholding by U.S. Payor

The U.S. payor must report the payments allocated to U.S. members of the foreign LLC on Form 1099, and payments allocated to foreign members on Form 1042-S. The foreign LLC is not obligated to file Form 1042 and 1042-S when it

---

[7] Notice 2002-41, 2002-24 I.R.B. 1153.

[8] Reg. §1.1441-5(c)(1).

[9] Notice 2002-41, 2002-23 I.R.B. 1153; Reg. §1.1441-5(c)(3)(iii). The withholding certificate is referred to as a "nonwithholding foreign partnership withholding certificate."

[10] Reg. §1.1441-5(c)(3)(iii).

[11] Reg. §§1.1441-5(c)(1)(i)(A), 1.1441-5(c)(3)(ii).

pays the U.S. source income to its members, assuming that the U.S. withholding agent files the returns and that the foreign members' tax liability with respect to U.S. source income has been fully satisfied by withholding.[12]

The payor must withhold at a 30 percent rate on FDAP income paid to the foreign LLC unless the foreign LLC provides the payor with a withholding certificate and documentation showing that one or more of the members are U.S. persons or foreign persons entitled to a reduced rate of withholding.[13]

[D] Presumptions in the Absence of Documentation

The withholding agent may rely on the withholding certificate and documents transmitted with the certificate to determine the residency of the members of the foreign LLC, and to apply a reduced rate of withholding when applicable.

The LLC may not be able to obtain Form W-8BEN or other appropriate documentation from some of its members. In such case, the LLC must state on the form that it is lacking documentation for some of its members. It must separately identify the amounts allocated to members for whom documentation is lacking or unreliable. The LLC is not required to name such members and may aggregate the percentage interest payable to such members as a group. The payor must withhold at a 30 or 31 percent rate on payments allocable to such members.[14]

If the withholding agent does not receive a withholding certificate or any other documentation from an LLC, it must presume that the LLC is a U.S. LLC unless there are indicia of foreign status. Indicia of foreign status exist if the withholding agent notes that the payee's employer identification number begins with the two digits "98," the withholding agent's communications to the payee are mailed to an address in a foreign country, or the payment is made outside the United States. In such case, the withholding agent may presume that the LLC is a foreign LLC and withhold at the 30 or 31 percent rate for FDAP income.

[E] Trade or Business Income

Income that is effectively connected with the conduct of a U.S. trade or business is taxed at the graduated rates applicable to U.S. citizens and residents. There is no withholding on effectively connected income except for

---

[12] Reg. §§1.1461-1(b)(2), 1.1461-1(c)(4)(iv).

[13] Reg, §1.1441-5(c)(3)(ii). Reg §1.1441-5(c)(3)(i) provides that the withholding agent must apply various presumptions if it does not receive a valid withholding certificate from a foreign entity that it knows or believes to be a foreign LLC.

[14] Reg. §1.1441-5(c)(3) provides that the withholding agent must apply various presumptions if it cannot reliably associate the payment with valid documentation from the member of the foreign LLC that is attached to the withholding certificate of the foreign LLC, or if the withholding agent otherwise has insufficient information to report the payment on Form 1042-S or 1099 to the extent reporting is required.

- Personal service income;
- Income subject to withholding on dispositions of U.S. real property interests by foreign persons; and
- A foreign partner's share of effectively connected income.

Thus, there is generally no withholding on payments to a foreign LLC of effectively connected income. If the payor is planning to withhold on such payments, the foreign LLC may submit Form 8-ECI to the payor to claim that the payment is exempt from withholding as effectively connected income. The foreign LLC is not required to attach Forms W-8BEN or other documentation for the foreign members.[15]

When the foreign LLC receives the income, it will offset the income with its business expenses from conducting the trade or business. The net income from the U.S. trade or business allocable to the foreign members is then subject to withholding under IRC Section 1446, whether or not the income is actually distributed to the foreign members. The withholding tax rate is 39.6 percent for individual members of the foreign LLC and 35 percent for corporate members of the foreign LLC.

The LLC must use Form 8813, Partnership Withholding Tax Payment (Section 1446), to pay the withholding taxes on effectively connected income allocated to its foreign members. The withholding taxes are paid in four quarterly installments. The LLC must report the effectively connected income and the withholding on such income on Form 8804, Annual Return for Partnership Withholding Tax (Section 1446). The LLC must prepare Form 8805 for each foreign member who receives an allocation of effectively connected income, even if no withholding tax was paid with respect to such amount. The LLC must attach a copy of Form 8805 to Form 8804 for each member and provide each member with another copy of Form 8804. The foreign members must attach Form 8805 to their U.S. income tax returns to claim the credit for their shares of Section 1446 taxes withheld by the foreign LLC.

---

[15] Reg. §§1.1441-5(c)(3)(ii) (last sentence), 1.1441-5(c)(3)(iii).

19

Foreign-Owned Domestic LLCs

§19.01   GENERALLY

Foreign persons are subject to U.S. taxes on income from sources within the United States and on income that is effectively connected with the conduct of a U.S. trade or business.[1] If an LLC is engaged in a U.S. trade or business, all foreign members of that LLC are treated as engaged in a U.S. trade or business.[2] If an LLC has a permanent establishment in the United States, each of the LLC's members is treated as having a permanent establishment in the United States.[3] This is important, since tax treaties with foreign countries may reduce or eliminate the tax on certain income of foreign persons who do not have a permanent establishment in the United States.

An LLC organized in the United States that is owned by foreign persons is classified as a domestic partnership.[4]

---

§19.01   [1] IRC §§871-885.
[2] Ltr. Rul. 9436019; IRC §875(1).
[3] *Id.*
[4] Ltr. Rul. 9610006 (*citing* IRC §7701(a)(4)).

§19.02 TAXATION OF FOREIGN MEMBERS

[A] Tax Rate and Withholding Taxes

U.S. taxes on foreign members of an LLC are collected primarily through withholding taxes. There are generally no withholding taxes on amounts paid to domestic LLCs, even if the LLC has foreign members, if the LLC provides the payor with a Form W-9.[1] Instead, the LLC must withhold taxes on distributions or allocations of that income to foreign members.[2]

The amount of withholding taxes depends on the type of income earned by the LLC. The most common withholding taxes are as follows:

- *Portfolio income.* An LLC must withhold at a 30 percent rate on a foreign member's distributive share of interest, dividends, rents, royalties, and certain other types of fixed and determinable income (FDAP income).[3] The LLC must withhold at the time that it makes distributions to the foreign member. If the LLC does not distribute the foreign member's allocable share of income, the LLC must withhold on the member's allocable share of income when it sends the Schedule K-1 to the member (but no later than the due date for sending the form to the member).[4] The withholding tax rate may be reduced by treaty. The foreign member must file Form W-8 BEN, Certificate of Foreign Status of Beneficiary Owner for United States Tax Withholding, with the LLC in order to claim the reduced withholding tax rate and to establish foreign residency in a treaty country.[5] The LLC must file Form 1042-S, Foreign Person's U.S. Source Income Subject to Withholding, to report the withholding taxes. Capital gains from the sale of securities are not treated as FDAP income, and are therefore not subject to the 30 percent withholding tax.[6]

- *Trade or Business Income.* Foreign members are subject to withholding tax on their allocable share of trade or business income earned by the LLC, whether or not the income from the LLC is distributed.[7] The withholding tax rate is the highest tax rate applicable for individual or corporate members. The withholding tax rate applies without regard to deductions, operating losses, or other U.S. tax attributes that the foreign member may have outside of the LLC.[8] The LLC's payment of the withholding tax is treated as a distribution to the foreign member and reduces the foreign

---

§19.02 [1] Reg. §1.1441-5(b)(1)..

[2] Reg. §1.1441-5(b)(2).

[3] IRC §§1441, 1442.

[4] Reg. §1.1441-5(b)(2)(i)(A).

[5] Reg. §§1.1441-1(c)(6)(ii)(A), 1.1441-1(e)(2).

[6] Reg. §§1.1441-2(b)(1)(i), 1.1441-2(b)(2)(i).

[7] IRC §1446; Reg. §1.1441-5(b)(2)(i)(B); Rev. Proc. 89-31, 1989-1 C.B. 895.

[8] *See* Rev. Proc. 89-31, 1989-1 C.B. 895 (which provide general guidance on withholding for partnerships); Rev. Proc. 92-66, 1992-2 C.B. 428 (which provides additional guidance, and specifies the procedures to obtain a credit or refund for amounts overwithheld).

member's basis in the LLC.[9] The amount withheld is a credit against the foreign member's U.S. tax liability. The LLC must pay the withholding tax in quarterly installments on Form 8813. Additional amounts due after the close of the year are reported on Form 8804. The LLC must send each foreign member an information statement on Form 8805 showing the amount of withheld taxes. Individual members must file Form 1140-NR and corporations must file Form 1120-F to report their allocable share of the LLC's trade or business income. Foreign members must pay taxes at the graduated U.S. tax rates on such income.[10] The members receive a credit against the tax for withholding taxes paid on the income, and a refund if the withholding taxes exceed the actual graduated taxes. The return on Form 1040-NR or 1120-F must be filed even if all taxes are paid by withholding.[11] Foreign persons claim the credit for previously paid withholding taxes by attaching Form 8805 to Form 1040-NR or 1120-F. No deductions or credits are allowed unless the return is filed.[12]

- *Real estate.* There is a 35 percent withholding tax on the amount of gain realized from the LLC's disposition of U.S. real estate to the extent the gain is allocable to foreign members.[13] There is also a withholding tax on a foreign member who sells a membership interest in an LLC that owns U.S. real property. The withholding tax rate is 10 percent of the sales price, and is imposed on the purchaser.[14] This withholding tax applies if the gross assets of the LLC consist of 50 percent of U.S. real property interests, and 90 percent or more of the value of the gross assets of the LLC consist of U.S. real property interests and cash or cash equivalents.[15]

[B]   Branch Profits Tax

Foreign corporations that are members of a U.S. LLC are subject to the branch profits tax if the LLC is engaged in a trade or business.[16]

Before 1986, a foreign corporation that paid dividends or interest to foreign persons was required to withhold a portion of the payments under U.S. tax laws if more than half of its gross income for the three-year period immediately preceding the year of distribution was income effectively connected with a U.S. trade or business. Foreign corporations with branches in the United States could avoid withholding liability by keeping their U.S. income below the 50 percent threshold.

The 1986 Tax Reform Act eliminated the withholding tax on dividends paid by foreign corporations. The Act instead imposed a branch profits tax on foreign

---

[9] IRC §1446(d).
[10] IRC §871(b) for individuals; IRC §882 for corporations.
[11] Reg. §1.6012-1(b)(1)(i).
[12] IRC §774(b).
[13] IRC §1445(e)(1).
[14] IRC §1445(e)(5).
[15] IRC §1445(e)(5); Temp. Reg. §1.1445-11T(d).
[16] *See* IRC §884.

corporations. The law treats U.S. branches of foreign corporations as domestic corporations. Earnings that are transferred to the foreign owner are similar to dividends and are subject to a 30 percent branch profits tax. The law was intended to achieve tax equivalence between U.S. branches and U.S. subsidiaries of foreign corporations. Subsidiary corporations must also pay a 30 percent withholding tax on dividends paid to foreign shareholders absent treaty protection.

Individual members, however, are not subject to the branch profits tax. Corporate members are subject to a 30 percent branch profits tax on their allocable shares of after-tax U.S. trade or business earnings of the LLC that are not reinvested in a U.S. trade or business by the close of the tax year or that are disinvested in a later tax year.[17] Changes in the value of the equity of the foreign corporation's U.S. trade or business (i.e., net equity in the LLC) are used as a measure of whether earnings have been reinvested in, or disinvested from, the U.S. trade or business. An increase in the member's net equity in the LLC is generally treated as a reinvestment of earnings for the current tax year. A decrease in the member's net equity is generally treated as a disinvestment of the prior year's earnings that have not previously been subject to the branch profits tax.

Interest payments made by the U.S. branch to the foreign corporate member are also subject to the 30 percent tax with certain exceptions.[18]

The branch tax may be reduced or eliminated by treaty if the foreign corporation member is a qualified resident of the country with which the United States has an income tax treaty.[19] Foreign corporations claiming the benefits of treaties must file Form 8833 as an attachment to Form 1120-F. The branch profits tax rate under treaties is often the same as the treaty withholding tax rate for dividends paid by a wholly owned U.S. subsidiary to a foreign parent.

EXAMPLE

An Indian corporation and an Indian citizen are equal owners of a Delaware LLC. The LLC is engaged in a U.S. trade or business. All of the earnings during 1998 are distributed to the two members in 1999. The Indian citizen is subject to a 39.6 percent withholding tax and the Indian corporation is subject to a 35 percent withholding tax in 1998 on the undistributed earnings of the LLC. Both members must file U.S. tax returns and pay taxes at the graduated U.S. tax rates. Both receive credits for the withholding taxes paid. The Indian corporation is subject to the branch profits tax in 1999 when the LLC pays the Indian corporation its allocable share of 1998 earnings and

---

[17] *Id.*

[18] These exceptions include interest on bank deposits, qualified portfolio interest, and interest exempt from tax under applicable treaties.

[19] IRC §884(e)(2). There is no branch profits tax for corporations from certain treaty countries specified in IRS regulations: Aruba, Austria, Belgium, Cyprus, Denmark, Egypt, Finland, Germany, Greece, Hungary, Iceland, Ireland, Italy, Jamaica, Japan, Korea, Luxembourg, Malta, Morocco, Netherlands, Netherlands Antilles, Norway, Pakistan, People's Republic of China, Philippines, Sweden, Switzerland, and United Kingdom. Reg. §1.884-1(g)(3). Treaties that are modified or negotiated after January 1, 1987, may also reduce or eliminate the branch profits tax.

profits from the trade or business. The branch profits tax is reduced from 30 percent to 15 percent under the U.S.-Indian tax treaty if the Indian corporation files Form 8833 as an attachment to Form 1120-F. The Indian individual member is not subject to the branch profits tax.

§19.03   TERRITORIAL-BASED TAXES

A number of countries, such as the United Kingdom, have territorial-based taxes. Nonresident companies are taxed only on income derived from exercising or carrying on business within the taxing country. In those countries, corporations are normally taxed if their headquarters are located in the country. Partnerships are taxed if the business of the partnership is managed by persons residing in the country. This raises a problem for LLCs that conduct business in the United States, but are owned or managed by persons residing in the foreign country.

LLCs are managed either by designated managers or by members. If a foreign-owned LLC is managed by its members, then the foreign owners in countries with territorial-based tax systems may be taxed on income earned by the LLC in those countries. If the LLC is managed by designated managers, then the managers who reside in those countries may be taxed.

§19.04   THE UNITED STATES AS A TAX HAVEN COUNTRY

Foreigners may use the United States as a tax haven jurisdiction if they operate in the United States. Some of the leading tax-haven states are Utah, Vermont, and Wyoming. In Utah, for example, the cost of organization is less than $500. Foreigners are not required to file any state or federal tax returns for the Utah LLC or pay any U.S. taxes as long as they do not operate in the United States.

§19.05   FOREIGN TAX CREDIT

Some countries, such as Italy and Korea, do not permit taxpayers to take an indirect foreign tax credit. The taxes paid by U.S.-owned corporations may not be credited against the taxes owed in such countries on dividends and other income from the U.S. corporations. An LLC that is taxed as a partnership solves this problem. The foreign owners are treated as having directly paid the U.S. taxes and are thus entitled to a direct foreign tax credit.[1]

---

§19.05   [1] *See* §18.01[A] *supra.*

§19.06   S CORPORATIONS

Foreign corporations and nonresident aliens may not be shareholders of an S corporation.[1] Foreign persons may obtain the benefits of an S corporation (limited liability and pass-through taxation) by using an LLC. An LLC may have corporate and nonresident alien shareholders.

§19.07   SALE OF MEMBERSHIP INTERESTS

A nonresident alien or foreign corporation is generally taxed upon the sale or disposition of trade or business assets in the United States. Gain on the sale or disposition is treated as income effectively connected with the conduct of a U.S. trade or business. There is an exception if the taxpayer waits for 10 years after terminating the U.S. trade or business in which the assets were used.[1] The IRS has ruled that a foreign member's gain from the sale of a membership interest in an LLC is taxable if the LLC is engaged in a U.S. trade or business.[2] Most commentators believe that the IRS position is insupportable.[3]

§19.08   HYBRID ENTITIES

As previously mentioned, the withholding tax rates may be reduced by treaty. A foreign person claiming the benefit of a treaty must use IRS Form W-8 (which replaces Forms 1001 and 4224). The treaty benefits are not available to a nontreaty jurisdiction hybrid entity that is classified as a partnership for U.S. tax purposes, but as a corporation in the owner's treaty jurisdiction.

Before 1998, a foreign corporation could substantially reduce taxes by forming a U.S. LLC that was classified as a partnership for U.S. tax purposes and as a corporation for foreign tax purposes. The foreign corporation could repatriate cash at the reduced U.S. withholding tax rate free of tax in its home country.

The particular arrangement that concerned Congress involved Canadian corporations. A Canadian corporation would form a U.S. LLC that was classified as a partnership for U.S. tax purposes. The LLC would be classified as a corporation for Canadian tax purposes. Under that arrangement, the Canadian parent corporation would lend money to the wholly owned U.S. LLC. The U.S. LLC would in turn loan the same funds to a U.S. corporate subsidiary of the Canadian parent. The corporate subsidiary would claim a tax deduction for the interest paid to the LLC. This reduced the corporate subsidiary's taxable income in the United States. The LLC would in turn pay interest to the Canadian parent corporation, withholding at the 10 percent withholding tax rate under the U.S.-Canada tax treaty. The LLC

---

§19.06   [1] IRC §1361(b).

§19.07   [1] IRC §§871(b), 882, 864(c)(2), (3), (7).

[2] Rev. Rul. 91-32, 1991-1 C.B. 107.

[3] See, e.g., K. Blanchard, "Extrastatutory Attribution of Partnership Activities to Partners," Tax Notes, Sept. 8, 1997, at 1331.

would claim a tax deduction for the interest paid, thereby reducing its U.S. taxable income to zero. The interest paid to the Canadian parent corporation would be free of Canadian income taxes under Canada's "participation exemption." The participation exemption exempts from tax the dividends received by a Canadian corporation from a U.S. subsidiary corporation. The LLC would be treated as a U.S. subsidiary corporation, and the interest payment by the LLC to the Canadian parent corporation would be treated as a dividend under Canadian law. As a result, the only tax imposed on the interest payment would be the 10 percent U.S. withholding tax.

Congress enacted IRC Section 894(c) of the Internal Revenue Code to combat this perceived abuse. Section 894(c) denies benefits under any tax treaty between the United States and a foreign country to foreign persons that receive income through an entity that is classified as a partnership for federal income tax purposes if the three following conditions are met:

1. The item is not treated as an item of income under the tax laws of the foreign country;
2. The treaty does not contain a provision addressing the application of the treaty in the case of the item derived through a partnership or LLC; and
3. The foreign country does not impose a tax on the distribution of the income.

Final regulations establish rules under which U.S. withholding agents may reduce the withholding tax on payments of U.S. source income to hybrid entities.[1] Foreign persons who invest in an LLC or other hybrid entity may claim the benefits of reduced or exempt rates under a treaty only if the income is treated as "derived" by (and thus taxable to) the recipient under the laws of the foreign treaty country.

§19.08   [1] Reg. §1.894-1(d).

20

Investment LLCs

§20.01 USE OF LLCs AS INVESTMENT VEHICLES

An LLC may be used as an investment vehicle. For example, an LLC may be used in place of a family limited partnership to hold family investments, to facilitate gifts from parents to children, and to help protect assets from creditors. There is no personal holding company tax even if all of the passive income is retained in the LLC.[1]

An LLC may be a more appropriate vehicle for investments than a C corporation. A C corporation is subject to the accumulated earnings tax if it accumulates earnings beyond the reasonable needs of the business.[2] A C corporation that has investment and passive income exceeding 60 percent of adjusted gross income is potentially liable for the 38.6 percent penalty tax (2002 rate) on undistributed personal holding company income.[3] The penalty tax is in addition to the regular corporate income tax and the dividend tax on shareholders.

§20.02 TRANSFER OF INVESTMENT PROPERTY TO LLC

[A] General Rules

Members of an LLC may recognize gain upon the transfer of securities and other investment assets to an LLC unless proper precautions are taken.[1]

The typical case arises when a person owns a large block of stock in a single

---

§20.01 [1] Ltr. Rul. 9330009.
[2] IRC §531.
[3] IRC §§541-547.
§20.02 [1] IRC §721(b)

417

corporation that has greatly appreciated in value. The owner has most of his assets tied up in one stock and wants to diversify without selling the stock. The owner then sets up an LLC or investment partnership. Another person contributes stock in another company to the LLC. The members of the LLC or partnership then split the increases and decreases in the total portfolio value. Investment bankers commonly set up these partnership arrangements with stocks from different business sectors so that the LLC or partnership operates like a mini-mutual fund.

The tax laws provide that the transfer of investment assets to an LLC or partnership is taxable if there is diversification as a result of the transfer. There was no tax under prior law if the LLC had at least 20 percent of its assets in assets other than readily marketable stocks or securities, regulated investment companies, and real estate investment trusts. As a result, investment bankers would commonly transfer assets to the LLC consisting of some cash investments, nonpublicly traded securities, foreign currency, forward and futures contracts, precious metals, or other nonmarketable securities. The mini-mutual fund arrangement was nontaxable as long as those assets comprised over 20 percent of the portfolio value.

In 1997, Congress determined that it was too easy to avoid taxation on the transfer of investment assets to an LLC, partnership, or corporation. As a result, it expanded the list of "bad assets" to include the following:

- All stocks and securities held by an LLC, including nonpublic stocks and securities
- Cash and foreign currency (however, cash held for working capital and other non-investment purposes is not a "bad asset"[2])
- Stocks, options, forward contracts, future contracts, notional principal contracts, and derivatives
- Precious metals
- Interests in entities holding assets listed above, but only to the extent of their value. However, the transfer of the partnership interest to an LLC in exchange for membership interest in the LLC is not normally subject to the investment company rules.[3]
- Anything else set forth in regulations[4]

The new law potentially taxes many transactions other than transfers of investment assets to mini-mutual fund LLCs. For example, if an owner contributes appreciated land to a real estate LLC valued at $100,000 and the developer contributes $1,000,000 cash to develop the property, there is potential taxation on the

---

[2] The regulations exclude cash and other investment type assets from the definition of bad assets if such assets are held for non-investment purposes "pursuant to a plan in existence at the time of the transfer." Reg. §1.351-1(c)(2).

[3] Ltr. Rul. 200211017.

[4] Taxpayer Relief Act of 1997, Pub. L. No. 105-34, §1002, 105th Cong., 1st Sess. (Aug. 5, 1997), amending IRC §351(e)(1), applicable to partnerships under IRC §721(b).

appreciation under the investment company rules unless the parties can show that the LLC is not holding the cash for investment.

[B]   Statutory Provisions

The statutory provisions regarding investment LLCs can be summarized as follows:

- The general rule is that no gain or loss is recognized on the contribution of property to an LLC.[5]
- However, gain is recognized if the LLC would be treated as an investment company under IRC Section 351(e)(1) if the LLC were incorporated.[6]
- A transfer of property is a transfer to an investment company under Section 351 if both of the following requirements are met:
  — More than 80 percent of the LLC's assets by value consist of money, stocks or securities (whether or not marketable), evidences of indebtedness, currency, options, forward or future contracts, notional principal contracts or derivatives, foreign currency, interests in regulated investment companies (RICs), real estate investment trusts (REITs), common trust funds and publicly traded partnerships, certain interests in precious metals, certain interests in entities that hold those items, and other assets specified in Treasury regulations.[7]
  — The transfer results in diversification of the transferors' interests.[8] A transfer ordinarily results in diversification of the transferors' interests if two or more persons transfer nonidentical assets to an LLC in the exchange.[9]

[C]   Exceptions to Income Recognition

There are the following principal methods of avoiding income recognition on the transfer of investment assets to an LLC:

- *Contribution of diversified portfolio.* There is no income recognition on the contribution of investment assets to an LLC if each transferor contributes a diversified portfolio of stocks and securities to the LLC.[10] A stock portfolio is diversified if it satisfies the 25 percent and the 50 percent tests.[11] The portfolio satisfies the 25 percent test if no more than 25 percent of the

---

[5] IRC §721(a).
[6] IRC §721(b).
[7] IRC §351(e)(1); Reg. §1.351-1(c)(1)(ii).
[8] Reg. §1.351-1(c)(1)(i).
[9] Reg. §1.351-1(c)(5).
[10] Reg. §1.351-1(c)(6)(i).
[11] Reg. §1.351-1(c)(6).

portfolio value is in stocks or securities of any one issuer. The portfolio satisfies the 50 percent test if no more than 50 percent of the portfolio value is in stocks or securities of five or fewer issuers. Thus, there is no tax on the transfer of appreciated marketable securities to an LLC if each member transfers a diversified portfolio of marketable securities that satisfies the 25 and 50 percent tests under IRC Section 368(a)(2)(F)(ii).[12] If any one transferor does not transfer a diversified portfolio, then all other transferors recognize gain on the transfer of property to the LLC.[13]

- *Avoid 80 percent test.* There is no income recognition on the transfer of investment assets to an LLC unless at least 80 percent of the LLC's assets consist of stocks, securities, and other "bad" assets. Thus, there is no income recognition if more than 20 percent of the assets of the LLC consists of trade or business assets. The stocks and securities that the LLC owns in a subsidiary are disregarded if the LLC owns 50 percent or more of the voting stock or total value of shares of all classes of stock outstanding.[14] In such case, the LLC must look through to the assets of the subsidiary corporation. This rule permits members to transfer stock in a family business to an LLC without income recognition.

- *Transfer of identical assets.* There is no income recognition on the transfer of investment assets to an LLC if each member contributes identical assets.[15] The income recognition rules apply only if the transfers result in diversification. Thus, spouses who contribute non–community property assets to an LLC should first make nontaxable gifts or transfers of assets between themselves so that they can make identical transfers of assets to the LLC.

- *De minimis rule.* There is no income recognition on the transfer of investment assets to an LLC if the member contributes a de minimis amount of nonidentical investment assets.[16] The transfers are disregarded in determining whether diversification has occurred. One percent of the total value of assets transferred to an LLC is an insignificant portion,[17] whereas 11 percent[18] or 50 percent[19] is not. Thus, there is no diversification resulting in taxation under the investment company rules unless there are at least two significant contributors to the LLC.[20]

EXAMPLE 1

A parent corporation transfers appreciated marketable securities to an LLC. Its wholly owned subsidiary also transfers appreciated marketable securities to the LLC representing less than 1 percent of the total fair market

[12] Ltr. Ruls. 9617020, 9617018, 9617017.
[13] Reg. §1.351-1(c)(6)(i).
[14] Reg. §1.351-1(c)(4).
[15] Reg. §1.351-1(c)(5).
[16] *Id.*
[17] Reg. §1.351-1(c)(5), Examples (1)-(2).
[18] Rev. Rul. 87-9, 1987-1 C.B. 134.
[19] Reg. §1.351-1(c)(5), Examples (1)-(2).
[20] Ltr. Ruls. 9751048, 9608026.

value of the contributed assets. The subsidiary's contribution of the noniden-tical assets is disregarded in determining whether the LLC's assets are diver-sified because the contribution amount is de minimis. Thus, the transfer of the appreciated securities does not result in diversification or income recognition.[21]

EXAMPLE 2

A husband and wife and their children form an LLC for the purpose of acquiring marketable securities for investment. The husband and wife own a 1 percent interest, and the children own a 99 percent interest. The husband and wife contribute appreciated marketable securities to the LLC in exchange for a membership interest. The securities transferred consist of a diversified group of publicly owned securities. No one issue of the portfolio represents more than 25 percent of the value of all securities contributed to the LLC. Not more than 50 percent of the value of all securities contributed consist of securities of five or fewer issuers. The membership interests received by the husband and wife in exchange for the contribution of securities is based on the market value of the contributed securities relative to the value of all securities in the LLC after the contribution. There is no income recognition on the transfer of the appreciated securities to the LLC because the assets transferred constitute a diversified investment portfolio.[22]

EXAMPLE 3

A husband and wife contribute appreciated securities to an LLC in ex-change for a membership interest. The securities consist of a diversified portfolio of publicly owned securities. No one of the securities transferred represents more than 25 percent of the value of the total securities contrib-uted. Not more than 50 percent of value of the securities contributed consist of securities of five or fewer issuers. The membership interest that the hus-band and wife receive in exchange for the appreciated securities is based on the fair market value of the contributed securities relative to the value of all securities in the LLC after the contribution. After the contribution, the securities of any one issuer that the LLC holds do not represent more than 25 percent of the value of the total assets of the LLC, and not more than 50 percent of the value of all of the LLC's assets are invested in the securities of five or fewer issuers. The transfer by the husband and wife of the diversified portfolio of appreciated stocks and securities is not a transfer to an investment company. Accordingly, no gain or loss is recognized on the contribution.[23]

---

[21] Ltr. Rul. 9751048.
[22] Ltr. Rul. 200002025.
[23] Ltr. Rul. 200002025 (*citing* Reg. §1.351-1(c)(6)(i)).

EXAMPLE 4

A parent corporation transferred investment assets to an LLC. Its wholly owned subsidiary transferred an insignificant amount of nonidentical assets to the LLC, representing less than 1 percent of the total fair market value of the contributed assets. The subsidiary's contribution of the nonidentical assets was thus disregarded for purposes of determining whether the LLC's assets were diversified.[24] Since a transfer of the contributed assets did not result in diversification, there was no transfer of property to a partnership that would be treated as an investment company if it were incorporated.[25] No gain or loss was recognized on the transfer of the investment assets to the LLC, assuming the net reduction in the contributing party's liabilities as a result of their assumption by the LLC did not exceed their adjusted basis in the contributed investment assets.[26] Similarly, IRC Section 721(b), which imposes taxes on the transfer of property to an investment partnership, did not apply.[27]

§20.03 PUBLICLY TRADED LLCs

Generally, an LLC may not be publicly traded. The LLC will be taxed as a corporation if it is a publicly traded LLC.[1] A publicly traded LLC is an LLC whose interests are traded on an established securities market or are readily traded on a secondary market or the substantial equivalent of a secondary market.[2] There are the following exceptions:

- The LLC has fewer than 100 investors, and the membership units are sold in a private placement.[3]
- At least 90 percent of the income of the LLC is passive-type income.[4] Qualifying passive income includes the following:
  — Interest (other than interest from a financial or an insurance business or amounts determined on the basis of income or profits)
  — Dividends
  — Certain real property rents

---

[24] *See* Reg. §1.351-1(c)(5), (7).
[25] *See* Reg. §1.351-1(c)(1).
[26] Ltr. Rul. 9751048 (*citing* IRC §§721(a), (b)).
[27] Ltr. Rul. 9751048.
§20.03 [1] IRC §7704; Reg. §301.7701-2(b)(7).
[2] Reg. §1.7704-1(c)(1).
[3] Reg. §1.7704-1(h)(1).
[4] IRC §7704(c). See Ltr. Rul. 9751048 (LLC was not a publicly traded partnership, since its income consisted entirely of interest, dividends, and gains from the sale of stock or securities within the meaning of IRC §7704).

— Gain from the sale of real property
— Income and gains relating to minerals and natural resources
— Gains from the sale of a capital asset or certain trade or business property held for the production of the foregoing types of income
— Capital gain from the sale of stock
— Income from holding annuities
— Income from notational contracts
— "Other substantially similar income from ordinary and routine investments" to the extent determined by the IRS[5]

Under proposed regulations, qualifying passive income would include income from holding annuities, income from notional principal contracts, and "other substantially similar income from ordinary and routine investments" to the extent determined by the IRS.[6] The exception for LLCs with 90 percent passive income normally does not apply to regulated investment companies (RICs).

- The sum of capital and profits interests sold or disposed of during the year is less than 2 percent of the total capital or profits of the LLC.[7]

---

[5] IRC §7704(d); Reg. §1.704-3(a).

[6] REG-105163-97. (IRS proposed rule on application of passive activity loss rules to publicly traded partnerships, issued Dec. 18, 1997.)

[7] Reg. §1.7704-1(j)(1).

21

Estate and Gift Tax Planning

§21.01   ADVANTAGES OF LLC

LLCs have been used in estate planning since 1993, when the IRS issued a ruling permitting minority discounts for transfers of interests in an entity controlled by a single family.[1] An LLC has the following advantages for estate planning purposes:

- *Transfer of property.* An LLC may facilitate the transfer of property, especially real estate and other property that is not easily divisible. For example, a donor can make annual gifts to his children of units in an LLC that owns real estate. This is less expensive and cumbersome than preparing and recording deeds to an undivided interest in the real estate each year. The operating agreement for the LLC may permit the manager to sell or refinance the property at any time without obtaining the consent of the donees.
- *Basis step-up.* Prior to 2010, a member's death beneficiaries may step-up the basis of a membership interest on the death of the member.[2] No gain or loss is recognized on the subsequent sale or disposition of the membership interest except to the extent of appreciation or depreciation after the date of death or the six-month alternate valuation date.[3] The LLC may also step up the basis of its assets attributable to the deceased member if the LLC makes an election under IRC Section 754.[4] In contrast, the basis step-up for a corporation applies only to the stock and not to the assets owned by the corporation.
- *Valuation discounts.* A taxpayer may receive significant valuation discounts for property transferred to family members through an LLC. The valuation discounts include the minority discount, marketability discount, liquidity discount, and a number of other discounts.[5]

---

§21.01   [1] Rev. Rul. 93-12, 1993-1 C.B. 202.
[2] IRC §1014.
[3] IRC §1001.
[4] IRC §743(b).
[5] *See* §21.03 *infra.*

§21.02   GIFTS

[A]   Annual Gift Tax Exclusion

The general rule is that a gift of a membership interest in an LLC qualifies for the $11,000 (2003 amount) annual gift tax exclusion.[1] The exclusion is available if the donor relinquishes dominion and control over the membership interest,[2] and if the donee has the right to current distributions or the right to sell the membership interest.[3]

The annual gift tax exclusion is not available if the donee "lacks the tangible and immediate economic benefit" of a present interest in the property.[4] The gift of membership units in an LLC that is expected to have losses for several years in the future does not qualify for the gift tax annual exclusion if there are restrictions preventing the donee from realizing any substantial financial or economic benefits from the membership units.[5] For example, the gift of a membership interest is a gift of a future interest that does not qualify for the annual exclusion if the operating agreement (a) gives the manager complete discretion to distribute income, or to retain income in the LLC for any reason, (b) prevents the donee from transferring or assigning the gifted interests without the consent of the manager, and (c) prevents the donee from withdrawing from the LLC and receiving a return of capital contributions until a future date.[6]

The problem typically arises for LLCs that own non–income–producing assets. The donee does not receive an immediate economic benefit in such cases unless the donee is free to sell the membership interest, to withdraw the capital account, or to force a dissolution of the LLC.[7]

[B]   Gift Tax Returns and Statute of Limitations

[1]   General Rule

The taxpayer must file a gift tax return for gifts over the annual exclusion amount. The statute of limitations on assessments for gifts of membership interests in an LLC is:[8]

- Three years after the return is filed if the donor adequately discloses the gift on the return.[9]

§21.02   [1] IRC §2503(b).

[2] Ltr. Rul. 9808010.

[3] TAM 199944003.

[4] Ltr. Rul. 9751003.

[5] Hackl v. Comm'r, 118 T.C. No. 14 (2002), aff'd 92 A.F.T.R. 2d 2003-5254 (7th Cir. 2003).

[6] Ltr. Rul. 9751003; Hackl v. Comm'r, 118 T.C. No. 14 (2002).

[7] Hackl v. Comm'r, 118 T.C. No. 14 (2002), in which the annual gift tax exclusion was denied for gifts of membership units in an LLC organized to hold and operate timberland.

[8] IRS Legal Memorandum 200221010.

[9] IRC §6501(a).

- Six years after the return is filed if the taxpayer omits from the total amount of gifts made during the period for which the gift tax return is filed an amount exceeding 25 percent of the total gifts stated on the return. However, in determining which items are omitted as gifts, no item is taken into account for which there is adequate disclosure on the return.[10]
- Indefinitely, if the donor fails to make adequate disclosure of the gift on the return.[11]

[2] Adequate Disclosure

In order to start the running of the statute of limitations on gifts of membership interests in an LLC, the donor must make adequate disclosure of the gift on the gift tax return. The donor must provide the following information in order to meet the adequate disclosure requirement:[12]

- A description of the membership units transferred, the number of membership units, the percentage ownership interest represented by the units, and the nature of any class of membership units transferred.
- Any consideration received by the donor.
- The identity of, and relationship between, the donor and each donee.
- If the membership units are transferred in trust, the trust's tax identification number and a brief description of the terms of the trust. Alternatively, the donor may provide a copy of the trust.
- An appraisal meeting the requirements of Regulations Section 301.6501(c)-1(f)(3). Alternatively, the donor may provide a description of the method used to determine the fair market value of the membership interests. This should include any financial data, such as balance sheet and income statements, used in determining the value the membership interests, any restrictions on the membership interests that were considered in determining the fair market value, and a description of any discounts (such as blockage, minority, marketability, or fractional interests) claimed in valuing the property. The donor must also describe any discount claimed in valuing any property owned by the LLC. If the value of the LLC is determined based on the net value of the assets held by the LLC, the donor must provide a statement regarding the fair market value of 100 percent of the LLC without regard to any discounts, the pro rata portion of the LLC subject to the transfer, and the fair market value of the transferred membership interest as reported on the return.
- A statement describing any position that is contrary to any proposed, temporary, or final regulations or revenue rulings published at the time of the gift.

---

[10] IRC §6501(e)(2).

[11] IRC §6501(c)(9); Reg. §301.6501(c)-1(f)(2).

[12] IRS Legal Memorandum 200221010; Reg. §301.6501(c)-1(f)(2).

> **EXAMPLE**
>
> The following description of a gift of membership units on a gift tax return is not sufficient to start the running of the statute of limitations:[13]
> Class B units in ABC LLC. Units acquired on 4/6/97 for $200,000 cash. Gifts made on 4/7/97 with value on that date of $200,000 and an adjusted basis of $200,000.

[C]   Contribution to LLC

The contribution of property to an LLC is treated as a taxable gift to the other members of the LLC in proportion to their ownership interests in the LLC, unless the contribution is credited at fair market value to the capital account of the contributing member.[14]

§21.03   VALUATION DISCOUNTS

[A]   General

Property is valued for estate and gift tax purposes based upon what a willing buyer and willing seller would pay and receive for the property in an arm's-length transaction, with neither party under compulsion to buy or sell, and with both parties having reasonable knowledge of all relevant facts.[1] A taxpayer typically takes a valuation discount for estate and gift tax purposes for property held in an LLC. There are many different types of valuation discounts. The various valuation discounts include the minority discount, the marketability discount, the liquidity discount, the portfolio discount, the lack of control discount, the fractionalization discount, and the built-in gain discount.[2]

For many years, the IRS took the position that there should be no valuation discount if a single family group owned all the membership interests in an LLC.[3] It sometimes required taxpayers to value LLC membership interests using the asset valuation method. Under this method, the value of LLC membership interests is based on the valuation of each asset owned by the LLC as of the date of death.[4]

---

[13] IRS Legal Memorandum 200221010.

[14] Estate of Theodore R. Thompson v. Comm'r, 84 TCM 374 (2002); Harper v. Comm'r, T.C. Memo 2001-121 (2002); Estate of W. W. Jones, II, 116 T.C. No. 11 (2001). *See* §21.03[B][5] *infra* regarding the "gift on creation theory."

§21.03   [1] Reg. §§20.2031-1(b), 20.2031-3, 25.2512-1; United States v. Cartwright, 411 U.S. 546 (1973); Knight v. Comm'r, 115 T.C. 506 (2000).

[2] *See* §21.03[C] *infra*.

[3] Rev. Rul. 81-253, 1981-2 C.B. 187.

[4] Rev. Rul. 68-154, 1968-1 C.B. 395.

The IRS reversed its position in 1993. It determined that a 100 percent share-holder of a corporation could take a minority discount for gifts of 20 percent of the stock to each of his five children.[5] After that ruling, LLCs became widely used for estate and gift tax purposes. Taxpayers would transfer property into an LLC, and claim an immediate 30 to 50 percent discount for the property held through the LLC.

In 1994, the Service issued partnership anti-abuse regulations under IRC Section 701. The regulations prohibited minority and marketability discounts for gifts and bequests of LLC membership interests if the principal purpose of forming the LLC was to reduce estate and gift taxes. The regulations were later revised to delete such provisions.[6]

As LLCs and family limited partnerships became increasingly popular for estate planning purposes, the IRS advanced many arguments to challenge valuation discounts claimed by the taxpayers. The courts rejected most of the arguments except in egregious cases.[7] In 2001 and 2002, the IRS finally found a basis for successfully challenging valuation discounts: IRC Section 2036(a).[8]

Since April 1999, the IRS has coordinated LLC and family limited partnership valuation discount cases at the Appeals and examination level. The IRS designated a national coordinator for LLC and family limited partnership appeals. The purpose was to reach consistent results. Any Appeals officer must contact the national coordinator before offering a settlement in a valuation discount case.[9]

The IRS decided to settle LLC and family limited partnership cases by agreeing to the following discounts:[10]

Passive asset (securities, cash) LLCs and family limited partnerships	25 percent discount[11] 25 to 30 percent discount[12]
Real estate LLCs and family limited partnerships	25 to 40 percent discount[13] 35 to 40 percent discount[14]
Active business assets LLCs and family limited partnerships	35 to 40 percent discount[15]

---

[5] Rev. Rul. 93-12, 1993-1 C.B. 202.

[6] Reg. §1.701-2.

[7] See §21.03[B] infra.

[8] See §21.03[B][6] infra.

[9] BNA Daily Tax Report No. 8, p. G-1 (Jan. 13, 2003).

[10] BNA Daily Tax Report No. 213, p. G-4 (Nov. 4, 2002); BNA Daily Tax Report No. 8, p. G-1 (Jan. 13, 2003).

[11] BNA Daily Tax Report No. 213, p. G-4 (Nov. 4, 2002).

[12] BNA Daily Tax Report No. 8, p. G-1 (Jan. 13, 2003).

[13] BNA Daily Tax Report No. 213, p. G-4 (Nov. 4, 2002).

[14] BNA Daily Tax Report No. 8, p. G-1 (Jan. 13, 2003).

[15] Id.

Cases arising under Section 2036(a) regarding transfers with a retained life estate where the taxpayer is using the LLC or family limited partnership as a "pocketbook" (e.g., receiving disproportionate distributions)[16]	0 to 15 percent discount
Death-bed partnerships and LLCs created within six months of death	0 to 15 percent discount[17]
Fractional interest in real property	Reasonable cost of partition. IRS will settle cases at a higher discount based on the hazards of litigation[18]

The settlement offers are made only at the Appeals level. The same offers are not necessarily made at the audit level or after the case has been referred to the IRS District counsel.[19]

[B]   *IRS Challenges to Valuation Discounts*

[1]   Overview

The IRS will make an initial decision to accept or deny a valuation discount in estate and gift tax cases based on a number of factors. Mary Lou Edelstein, the national coordinator for family limited partnerships and LLC appeals cases, explained the factors the IRS considers important.[20] She said that if the taxpayer hopes to obtain a discount, the LLC must meet all technical formalities in its creation and operation. The decedent may not fund the LLC with an excess amount of assets or with personal assets such as automobiles and homes. The decedent must retain sufficient assets outside of the LLC to maintain a reasonable standard of living without using LLC assets.

The IRS will challenge death-bed partnerships and LLCs created within six months of death. If the LLC was created more than six months before the decedent's death, Appeals will make a determination whether the LLC held active assets such as business or real estate assets, or passive assets such as stocks and bonds. An LLC holding active assets is eligible for a 35 percent to 40 percent discount on the underlying assets. An LLC holding passive assets may receive a settlement offer of 25 percent to 30 percent.[21]

If the IRS decides to challenge a valuation discount, it will do so in one of

---

[16] *See* §21.03[B][6] *infra.*
[17] BNA Daily Tax Report No. 8, p. G-1 (Jan. 13, 2003).
[18] *Id.*
[19] *Id.*
[20] Seminar on Jan. 8, 2003, reported in BNA Daily Tax Report No. 8, p. G-1 (Jan. 13, 2003).
[21] BNA Daily Tax Report No. 8, p. G-1 (Jan. 13, 2003).

three ways. First, it may argue that there should be no valuation discount based on one or more of the following theories:

- IRC Section 2036(a). This is now the principal concern for tax practitioners who use LLCs to obtain valuation discounts.
- Sham transaction and economic substance doctrines.
- IRC Section 2703.
- IRC Section 2704(b).
- Gift on creation theory.
- IRC Section 2038.
- Cost of dissolution theory.
- IRC Section 2036(b).
- IRC Section 2701.

Second, the IRS may argue that the valuation discount claimed by the taxpayer is excessive. There are separate rules for determining the proper amount of minority discount, marketability, liquidity and lack of control discounts, built-in gains discount, assignee interest discount, portfolio discount, and other discounts.[22]

Third, the IRS may challenge the taxpayer's appraisal or the qualifications of the appraiser.[23]

If the LLC is disregarded, the IRS may still allow valuation discounts for the underlying property held by the LLC, such as a fractionalization discount for real property.[24] The IRS's official position is that the discount should be limited to the cost of partition, although it is willing to settle the cases at a higher discount based on the hazards of litigation.[25]

[2] Sham Transaction and Economic Substance Doctrines

[a] General

The IRS may challenge valuation discounts based on the sham transaction doctrine,[26] the lack of economic substance doctrine,[27] the lack of business purpose

---

[22] *See* §21.03[C] *infra.*

[23] *See* §21.03[E] *infra.*

[24] Shepherd v. Comm'r, 115 TC 376 (2000), *aff'd,* 283 F.3d 1258 (11th Cir. 2002).

[25] BNA Daily Tax Report No. 8, p. G-1 (Jan. 13, 2003). *See* Estate of Baird v. Comm'r, TC Memo 2001-58 (2001), which allowed a substantially higher discount for fractional interest in real estate.

[26] TAM 9736004.

[27] FSA 200049003, *citing* Gregory v. Helvering, 293 U.S. 465 (1935). The IRS determined that the economic substance doctrine could be used to deny valuation discounts for a membership interest in an LLC if (i) the transfers of property to the LLC and the gifts and transfers of membership interests appreciably changed the taxpayer's economic position, and (ii) the taxpayer did not have a valid business purpose or profit motive for establishing the LLC and making the gifts and transfers. *See also* Knight v. Comm'r, 115 T.C. 506 (2000).

doctrine,[28] the form over substance doctrine, and similar doctrines.[29] The theory is that the LLC should be disregarded because the formation of the LLC, the contribution of property to the LLC, the transfer of membership units in the LLC by gift or bequest, and the distribution of the property by the LLC to the transferees, constitute a single testamentary disposition. In these cases, the IRS includes the value of LLC assets in the decedent's gross estate rather than the membership interests owned by the decedent as of the date of death.

Most courts will not disregard an LLC under the sham transaction and similar doctrines, absent unusual circumstances.[30] These courts have determined that a willing buyer would take into account the form of entity in determining whether to buy the underlying assets.[31]

[b]   Circumstances Indicating Sham Transaction

The IRS is more likely to challenge minority and marketability discounts based on the sham transaction doctrine if one or more the following circumstances exist:[32]

- The taxpayer forms the LLC shortly before death.[33]
- The taxpayer is gravely ill at the time the LLC is formed.
- The heirs of the decedent orchestrate the formation of the LLC, and transfer the parent's property into the LLC, using a power of attorney.
- The taxpayer makes gifts of membership units in the LLC on the same day that the taxpayer forms the LLC, or shortly thereafter.[34]
- The principal purpose of forming the LLC is to reduce estate taxes.[35]
- The LLC owns the same assets on the date of the decedent's death that the

---

[28] Estate of Strangi v. Comm'r, 115 T.C. 478, 484 (2000).

[29] *See* Church v. United States, 85 A.F.T.R. 2d 2000-804 (W.D. Tex. 2000); Estate of Murphy v. Comm'r, 60 T.C.M. 645 (1990); Estate of Schauerhamer v. Comm'r, 73 T.C.M. 2855, T.C. Memo 1997-242 (1997); Griffin v. U.S., 89 A.F.T.R. 2d 2002-954, 42 F. Supp. 2d 700 (W.D. Tex 1998); TAMs 9842003, 9736004, 9735003, 9730004, 9725002, 9723009, 9719006.

[30] Knight v. Comm'r, 115 T.C. 506, 513-514 (2000); Church v. United States, 85 A.F.T.R. 2d 2000-804, ¶19 (W.D. Tex. 2000).

[31] Knight v. Comm'r, 115 T.C. 506, 514 (2000); Estate of Strangi v. Comm'r, 115 T.C. 478 (2000).

[32] TAM 9736004, in which the IRS disallowed minority and marketability discounts for membership interests in an LLC. *See also* Estate of Schauerhamer v. Comm'r, 73 T.C.M. 2855, T.C. Memo 1997-242 (1997); Griffin v. U.S., 89 A.F.T.R. 2d 2002-954, 42 F. Supp. 2d 700 (W.D. Tex 1998); TAMs 9842003, 9736004, 9735003, 9730004, 9725002, 9723009, 9719006.

[33] *But see* Estate of Strangi v. Comm'r, 115 T.C. 478 (2000), in which the taxpayer was allowed a valuation discount even though the taxpayer formed a limited partnership two months prior to death as part of a plan to reduce estate taxes; and Church v. United States, 85 A.F.T.R. 2d 2000-804, ¶19 (W.D. Tex. 2000), which allowed a valuation discount even though Mrs. Church died two days after the partnership was formed, and before the certificate limited partnership was filed with the Secretary of State.

[34] *See* LeFrak v. Comm'r, 66 T.C.M. 1297 (1993), in which the court ruled that the gifts were gifts of undivided interests in property and not partnership interest gifts, since the gifts were made the day before the partnership agreements were signed.

[35] TAM 9736004, FSA 200049003; Estate of Murphy v. Comm'r, 60 T.C.M. 645 (1990). The IRS lost on this issue in Church v. United States, 85 A.F.T.R. 2d 2000-804, ¶19 (W.D. Tex. 2000).

decedent transferred to the LLC. The IRS refers to the LLC in such cases as a mere "wrapper" around the assets.

- There is no legitimate business purpose for the LLC. The LLC does not transact any business other than holding property. The only purpose for organizing the LLC is to depress the value of the assets that are transferred to the LLC. Nothing of substance changes as a result of the transactions.
- The death beneficiaries receive from the LLC the same assets they would have received from the decedent if the assets had not been contributed to the LLC.
- The death beneficiaries retain control over the assets of the LLC, and their management rights do not change as a result of the transactions.
- The taxpayer fails to transfer legal title to the property to the LLC.[36]
- The taxpayer transfers to the LLC liquid assets, or assets that are not used in a trade or business, prior to the gift or testamentary transfer.[37] These assets include cash, marketable securities, undeveloped real estate, and other passive assets.
- The members fail to comply with the formalities of an LLC. For example, the LLC may be disregarded if the majority owner deposits all income from the LLC in his personal bank account.[38]

[c]   Business Purposes Claimed by Taxpayers

Taxpayers must show a proper business purpose in order to avoid application of the sham transaction doctrine. Taxpayers have used the following business purposes to justify the formation of LLC:[39]

- Consolidate family interests into a single entity.
- Provide centralized management.
- Avoid fragmentation of interests.
- Preserve the business as an ongoing enterprise for future generations.
- Protect assets from judgment creditors of the members.
- Protect assets from the family members' spouses in the event of divorce.
- Obtain better rates of return.
- Reduce administrative costs.
- Provide for competent management in case of death or disability.
- Avoid cumbersome and expensive guardianships.

---

[36] *See* Church v. United States, 85 A.F.T.R. 2d 2000-804, Conclusions of Law ¶4 (W.D. Tex. 2000).

[37] Estate of Strangi v. Comm'r, 115 T.C. 478, 486 (2000). *But see* Estate of Davis v. Comm'r, 110 T.C. 530 (1998), in which a discount was allowed for partnership that owned stock; and Estate of Winkler v. Comm'r, 57 T.C.M. 373 (1989), in which the court respected a partnership that held the proceeds of a lottery winning.

[38] Estate of Schauerhamer v. Comm'r, 73 T.C.M. 2855, T.C. Memo 1997-242 (1997). The invalidation of an LLC for failure to comply with the formalities is a separate argument from the sham transaction doctrine.

[39] Church v. United States, 85 A.F.T.R. 2d 2000-804, ¶¶4, 16 (W.D. Tex. 2000); Knight v. Comm'r, 115 T.C. 506, fn. 10 (2000); Estate of Strangi v. Comm'r, 115 T.C. 478, 485 (2000).

- Avoid or minimize probate delays and expenses.
- Minimize tax liability. This includes avoiding adverse tax consequences that may occur on dissolution of a corporation.
- Provide business flexibility, because the operating agreement may be amended.
- Eliminate ancillary probate proceedings.
- Provide a convenient mechanism for making annual gifts.
- Provide a vehicle to educate family members about assets to increase their value.
- Provide a mechanism to resolve family disputes.
- Provide more flexibility in making investments than a trust because of the fiduciary standards for a trust.

[3]   IRC Section 2703

[a]   General Rules

As an alternative to the sham-transaction doctrine, the IRS uses IRC Section 2703 to challenge minority and marketability discounts for membership units in LLCs.[40]

IRC Section 2703(a)(2) states the general rule that property must be valued for estate and gift tax purposes without regard to any option, agreement, or other right to acquire or use the property at less than fair market value, or any restriction on the right to sell or use such property. Such restrictions may be contained in the operating agreement, or may be implicit in the capital structure of the LLC.[41] The restrictions include restrictions on (i) the right to withdraw from the LLC, (ii) the right to a return of capital, (iii) buy-sell restrictions, (iv) limitations on management and voting rights, and (v) any other restrictions on the right to sell or use the LLC property, however created.[42]

IRC Section 2703(b) provides an exception to the general rule. It states that a restriction may be considered in valuing membership units if it meets each of the following requirements:[43]

- it is a bona fide business arrangement;
- it is not a device to transfer the property to members of the decedent's family for less than full and adequate consideration in money or money's worth; and
- the terms are comparable to similar arrangements entered into by persons in an arms-length transaction.

---

[40] FSA 200049003; TAM 9736004.
[41] TAM 9736004, *citing* Reg. §25.2703-1(a).
[42] TAM 9736004, *citing* Reg. §25.2703-1(a)(2).
[43] IRC §2703(b).

The IRS believes that IRC Section 2703 applies to an LLC in two different ways. First, it applies to the entity itself. The LLC should be disregarded for valuation purposes unless all the requirements of IRC Section 2703(b) are met.[44] The formation of the LLC, the transfer of property to the LLC, and the transfer of membership interests to the beneficiaries at death are treated as a single integrated transaction unless such requirements are met. Second, if IRC Section 2703 does not apply to the entity, then it applies to the restrictions in the operating agreement.[45] The restrictions in the operating agreement should be ignored for valuation purposes unless all the requirements of IRC Section 2703(b) are met. The IRS usually loses on both grounds.[46]

[b]   *Application of IRC Section 2703 to Entity*

The IRS first argues that IRC Section 2703 applies to the LLC itself. Its argument is as follows:

- The LLC should be disregarded if the LLC is not a bona fide business arrangement. The determination of whether a transfer to family members through an LLC is a bona fide transaction is based on all the facts and circumstances.[47] Intra-family transactions involving LLCs are subject to special scrutiny.[48]
- A transfer to an LLC is not a bona fide business arrangement if a member transfers property to the LLC shortly before the member's death, and the beneficiaries receive essentially the same assets that they would have received from the decedent if the assets had not been transferred to the LLC.[49] If the decedent transfers all of his property to the LLC immediately prior to death, there is merely an exchange of liquid assets for an illiquid asset.
- The LLC may also be disregarded if the decedent transferred property to the LLC for less than full and adequate consideration in money or money's worth. The transfer of property to an LLC is not for adequate consideration in money or money's worth if the property has a significantly lower value immediately after the transfer as a result of minority or marketability discounts. This is especially true for members who, because of their advanced age or health, are unlikely to ever recoup their immediate loss as a result of the transfer of property to the LLC.[50] The short life expectancy of the decedent after the transfer of property to the LLC means that there is little opportunity to recoup the diminution in value prior to death.

---

[44] FSA 200049003; TAM 9736004.

[45] *Id.*

[46] *See* Church v. United States, 85 A.F.T.R. 2d 2000-804, Conclusions of Law ¶¶8, 9 (W.D. Tex. 2000); Estate of Strangi v. Comm'r, 115 T.C. 478, 487-488 (2000).

[47] FSA 200049003.

[48] TAM 9736004.

[49] *Id.*

[50] *Id.*

The courts usually reject this theory because the estate tax is only imposed on property that the decedent owned as of the date of death. If the decedent owned a membership interest in an LLC, then the estate tax applies to the membership interest rather than the property owned by the LLC.[51]

[c]   Application to Restrictions in Operating Agreement

The IRS next argues that, if IRC Section 2703 does not apply to the LLC, then it should apply to the restrictions in the operating agreement.[52] In such case, the IRS believes that any restrictions on the right to transfer an interest in the LLC, to withdraw property from the LLC, or to liquidate an interest in the LLC, should be disregarded under IRC Section 2703 because the restrictions are a device to transfer the membership interests to the objects of the decedent's bounty for less than full and adequate consideration.

The IRS will challenge valuation discounts for membership interests in an LLC under IRC Section 2703 if (i) there is an absence of arm's-length bargaining in connection with the formation of the LLC, (ii) the member transfers personal use assets to the LLC, (iii) the member agrees to significant restrictions under the operating agreement, or (iv) the member transfers virtually all of his assets to the LLC in exchange for an interest that severely restricts his control over those assets and his right to income from the assets.[53]

The courts usually reject the IRS position because IRC Section 2703 does not apply to term restrictions, or to restrictions on sale or assignment of a membership interest that preclude membership status for a buyer.[54]

[d]   Application to Option and Buy-Sell Agreements

IRC Section 2703 does apply to option and buy-sell agreements that establish a purchase price on the death of the owner that is less than the fair market value of the membership interest. The value of the membership interest for estate and gift tax purposes must be determined without regard to such agreements unless:

- the agreement is a bona fide business arrangement;
- the agreement is not a device to transfer property to members of the decedent's family for less than full and adequate consideration in money or money's worth; and
- the terms of the agreement are comparable to similar arrangements entered into by persons in an arm's-length transaction.

---

[51] See Church v. United States, 85 A.F.T.R. 2d 2000-804, Conclusions of Law ¶8 (W.D. Tex. 2000); Estate of Strangi v. Comm'r, 115 T.C. 478, 487-488 (2000).

[52] Griffin v. United States, 89 A.F.T.R. 2d 2002-954, 42 F. Supp. 2d 700 (W.D. Tex 1998).

[53] TAM 9736004.

[54] See Church v. United States, 85 A.F.T.R. 2d 2000-804, Conclusions of Law ¶9 (W.D. Tex. 2000); Knight v. Comm'r, 115 T.C. 506, 519-520 (2000).

IRC Section 2703 only applies to option and buy-sell agreements entered into after October 9, 1990. However, the courts apply the same analysis to option and buy-sell agreements entered into prior to that date.[55] The agreements will be disregarded if they represent a testamentary device to transfer the decedent's interest in the LLC to family members for less than full and adequate consideration.[56]

[4]   IRC Section 2704(b)

As a second alternative to the sham-transaction doctrine, the IRS uses IRC Section 2704(b).[57] It argues that the restrictions on withdrawals and liquidation under the operating agreement are "applicable restrictions," and should therefore be disregarded in valuing membership interests to the extent the provisions are more restrictive than under state law. In such cases, the membership interests in the LLC should be valued based on the value of the underlying assets that would be distributed to the member on withdrawal. The IRS usually loses on this issue in the courts.[58]

IRC Section 2704(b) applies if all the following conditions are met:[59]

1. There is a lifetime or testamentary transfer of a membership interest in an LLC. An interest in an LLC as an assignee of an economic interest is treated as a membership interest for such purpose.[60]
2. The transfer is to members of the transferor's family. Family members include the member, spouse, any ancestors or legal descendants of the member or the member's spouse, brothers and sisters, and any spouse of the foregoing.[61]
3. The transferor and members of his family control the LLC immediately before the transfer. Control of an LLC means either 50 percent of the capital or profits interest in the LLC, or, in the case of a limited partnership, the holding of the interest as a general partner.[62] It is unclear whether a membership interest in an LLC should be treated as a general or limited partnership interest for such purposes.
4. There is a restriction on liquidation in the operating agreement.[63] The IRS believes that liquidation restrictions include (i) the right of a member to

---

[55] Estate of Fred O. Godley, 80 T.C.M. 158 (2000), *aff'd in part,* 89 A.F.T.R. 2d 2002-2001(e) (4th Cir. 2002).

[56] Estate of Fred O. Godley, 80 T.C.M. 158, 164 (2000), *aff'd in part,* 89 A.F.T.R. 2d 2002-2001(e) (4th Cir. 2002).

[57] Ltr. Rul. 9802004, *citing* Reg. §25.2704-1(a)(2); TAM 9736004.

[58] Church v. United States, 85 A.F.T.R. 2d 2000-804, Conclusions of Law ¶9 (W.D. Tex. 2000); Knight v. Comm'r, 115 T.C. 506, 519-520 (2000); Estate of Morton B. Harper, 79 T.C.M. 2232 (2000); Estate of W.W. Jones, II, 116 T.C. No. 11 (2001).

[59] FSA 200049003; TAM 9736004; Knight v. Comm'r, 115 T.C. 506, 519-520 (2000).

[60] FSA 200049003.

[61] Reg. §25.2702-2(a)(1).

[62] Ltr. Rul. 9802004, *citing* Reg. §25.2702-1(a)(2).

[63] TAM 9736004, *citing* Reg. §25.2704-2(b).

withdraw as a member and to receive distributions of his equity account by way of profit distributions or return of capital contributions, (ii) the right of a member to the return of all or any part of the member's capital contribution on liquidation or dissolution of the LLC, and (iii) the right to withdraw as a member from the LLC without being liable for damages. This requirement is the main problem for the IRS. Several courts have determined that restrictions on the right of a member to withdrawals, to a return of capital, or to redemption of the membership interest, are not liquidation restrictions.[64] These courts reasoned that IRC Section 2704(b) applies to restrictions on the right to liquidate the entire entity, and not to restrictions on the right to have an interest in the entity redeemed. Restrictions on withdrawals by members are not liquidation restrictions since the withdrawal by a member does not cause liquidation of the LLC.

5. The liquidation provision is more restrictive than required under state law.[65] Most states have default provisions regarding distributions, withdrawals, dissolution, buy-sell terms, voting rights and modifications of the operating agreement. The members may override the default language by including different provisions in the articles of organization or operating agreement. IRC Section 2704(b) does not apply to liquidation restrictions that are based on the default provisions under state law, or that are less restrictive than the default provisions.[66] The courts will consider default restrictions in valuing a membership interest.

6. The liquidation restriction will lapse at some later date, or the transferor or any family member, collectively or alone, may remove or reduce the liquidation restriction after the transfer. This requirement will be met if the transferor and family members own 100 percent of the membership interests.[67] Some donors avoid IRC Section 2704(b) by giving a one percent interest in the LLC to a charity.

If IRC Section 2704 applies, then a member is also treated as making a taxable gift or testamentary transfer on the date that the member's preferential liquidation or voting rights terminate. The amount of the gift or testamentary transfer is the value of the member's interest in the LLC immediately before the termination of the voting or liquidation rights (determined as if such rights would never terminate) over the value of the member's interest in the LLC immediately after the termination of rights.[68]

The Service determined that IRC Section 2704 applies to the transfer of general partnership interests to an LLC if the LLC does not become the new general partner of the partnership.[69] There is a termination of the member's voting and

---

[64] Kerr v. Comm'r, 113 T.C. 499 (1999), aff'd, 292 F.3d 490 (5th Cir. 2002); Estate of W.W. Jones, II, 116 T.C. No. 11 (2001); Estate of Morton B. Harper, 79 T.C.M. 2232 (2000).

[65] TAM 9736004, citing Reg. §25.2704-2(b).

[66] Knight v. Comm'r, 115 T.C. 506, 519-520 (2000); Kerr v. Comm'r, 113 T.C. 449 (1999), aff'd, 292 F.3d 490 (5th Cir. 2002); Estate of Morton B. Harper, 79 T.C.M. 2232 (2000).

[67] Reg. §25.2704-2(d).

[68] IRC §2704(a)(2).

[69] Ltr. Rul. 9802004.

liquidation rights in the partnership if the member cannot exercise those same rights through the LLC after transfer to the LLC. The amount of the taxable gift is the difference between the value of the general partnership interest immediately prior to the transfer and the value of the interest in the partnership held by the LLC immediately after the transfer.[70]

[5] Gift on Creation Theory

As a third alternative to the sham-transaction doctrine, the IRS uses the gift on creation theory. Under this theory, the IRS argues that a gift takes place when property is transferred to the LLC on organization of the LLC. The amount of the gift is the amount of the valuation discount for the property as a result of the transfer. Thus, if the taxpayer transfers property to an LLC, and receives back membership interests in the LLC with a lower value, the disappearing value is the amount of the gift.[71]

The problem with this theory is that there may be no donee.[72] If the transferor owns 99 percent of the membership interests after the transfer, then the transferor has presumably made a gift of 99 percent of the disappearing value back to himself.[73] The courts have rejected the IRS position where all members of the LLC receive membership interests in proportion to their contributions, and the pro rata contributions do not confer a financial benefit on or increase the wealth of any member.[74]

The gift on creation theory may apply if other members have a significant interest in the LLC at the time of the gift, and their interests are enhanced as a result of the gift. For example, the gift on creation theory may apply if the contributions by the donor are allocated to the capital accounts of other members.[75] The gift on creation theory may not be used if the contributions by the donor are allocated to the donor's own capital account.[76]

The IRS also uses a closely related theory that a gift occurs when the donor loses control of the LLC.[77]

---

[70] See Ltr. Rul. 9802004. In that case, the IRS determined that the transfer of the general partnership interest to the LLC would not constitute a lapse or termination of voting rights under IRC §2704(a)(2) because the general partner's voting rights in the LLC were created prior to October 8, 1990, the effective date of IRC §2704(a). The general partnership agreement was created prior to that date, and not amended after October 8, 1990.

[71] See Kincaid v. U.S., 682 F.2d 1220 (5th Cir. 1982); Trenchard v. Comm'r, 69 T.C.M. 2164 (1995); Estate of Strangi v. Comm'r, 115 T.C. 478, 489-491 (2000); Estate of Mario E. Bosca, T.C. Memo 1998-251 (1998); FSA 19995014.

[72] Church v. United States, 85 A.F.T.R. 2d 2000-804, Conclusions of Law ¶6 (W.D. Tex. 2000).

[73] See also Reg. §25.2511-2(a), which states that there is no need for an identifiable donee in order for the gift tax to apply.

[74] Church v. United States, 85 A.F.T.R. 2d 2000-804, ¶26, Conclusions of Law ¶5 (W.D. Tex. 2000); Estate of Strangi v. Comm'r, 115 T.C. 478, 489-490 (2000).

[75] Shepherd v. Comm'r, 115 TC 376 (2000), aff'd, 89 283 F.3d 1258 (11th Cir. 2002).

[76] Estate of Strangi v. Comm'r, 115 T.C. 478, 488-490 (2000); Estate of W. W. Jones, II, 116 T.C. No. 11 (2001).

[77] See Estate of Joseph Vac, 62 T.C.M. 942 (1991).

[6]   IRC Section 2036(a) Retained Enjoyment of Property

As a fourth alternative to the sham-transaction doctrine, the IRS argues that property transferred to an LLC should be brought back into the taxpayer's estate under Section 2036(a) of the Code.[78] Section 2036(a) applies if the taxpayer makes a transfer to an LLC and retains (a) possession or enjoyment of the property, or the right to its income, or (b) the right to determine the persons who will possess or enjoy the property or receive its income.[79]

Some courts have determined that Section 2036(a) does not apply to LLCs and family limited partnerships. The courts reasoned that membership units may not be brought back into the donor's estate if the donor does not exercise control over other members' interests in the LLC (even though the donor may exercise control over LLC property). There is also no transfer for purposes of Section 2036(a) if the donor contributes property to an LLC in exchange for membership interests and does not confer a financial benefit on or increase the wealth of any other member as a result of the contribution.[80]

Other courts have determined that Section 2036(a) should apply in egregious cases where the taxpayer donor commingles LLC assets with personal assets, does not respect the formalities of the LLC, or transfers a residence and other personal assets to an LLC which the taxpayer continues to use after the transfer.[81] The IRS refers to these cases as the "pocketbook" cases.[82]

In 2002, the IRS convinced a court that Section 2036(a) should apply even in cases in which the facts were not egregious. In *Estate of Thompson*,[83] the taxpayer transferred assets to a family limited partnership. There was no commingling of funds. There was no transfer of a personal residence to the partnership. Nevertheless, the court determined that the entire value of the property transferred to the partnership should be brought back into the decedent's estate under Section 2036(a). The main problem was that the taxpayer gave away most of his assets to the partnership prior to death. There was an implied agreement that the decedent would have access to the partnership assets to pay for living expenses.

Since 2002, other courts have determined that an LLC or family limited partnership should be disregarded, and that the entire value of LLC assets should be brought back into the estate under Section 2036(a).[84]

---

[78] Harper v. Comm'r, T.C. Memo 2001-121 (2002); Estate of Theodore R. Thompson v. Comm'r, 84 TCM 374 (2002); Estate of Strangi, T.C. Memo 2003-145 (2003); Gulig v. Comm'r, 89 AFTR 2d 2002-2977 (5th Cir. 2002); Estate of Reichardt, 114 T.C. 144 (2000); Kimbell v. U.S., 91 AFTR 2003-585 (N.D. Tex. 2003); BNA Daily Tax Report No. 213, p. G-4 (Nov. 4, 2002); BNA Daily Tax Report No. 8, p. G-1 (Jan. 13, 2003).

[79] Estate of Reichardt, 114 T.C. 144 (2000) *citing* IRC §2036(a)(1); Church v. United States, 85 A.F.T.R. 2d 2000-804, ¶¶24, 25 (W.D. Tex. 2000).

[80] Church v. United States, 85 A.F.T.R. 2d 2000-804, Conclusions of Law ¶7 (W.D. Tex. 2000).

[81] Estate of Reichardt, 114 T.C. 144 (2000); Estate of Schauerhamer v. Comm'r, 73 TCM 2855, T.C. Memo 1997-242 (1997); Estate of Strangi, T.C. Memo 2003-145 (2003).

[82] BNA Daily Tax Report No. 213, p. G-4 (Nov. 4, 2002).

[83] 84 TCM 374 (2002).

[84] *See* Kimbell v. U.S., 91 AFTR 2003-585 (N.D. Tex. 2003), in which an LLC was the general partner of a family limited partnership, and the value of all partnership assets was brought back into the estate under Section 2036(a); Estate of Strangi, T.C. Memo 2003-145 (2003).

As a result of the court cases, and informal pronouncements by the IRS,[85] tax practitioners are now concerned that many LLCs and family limited partnerships may be successfully challenged by the IRS and disregarded for estate tax purposes under IRC Section 2036(a). The IRS is more likely to assert a claim under Section 2036(a) if one or more the following facts exist:[86]

- The LLC is formed within six months of decedent's death.[87]
- The taxpayer commingles LLC funds and personal funds after the transfer.[88] The court may find commingling if there are delays in establishing a bank account for the LLC, completing LLC paperwork, or retitling ownership to stocks, bonds, and other assets transferred to the LLC.[89]
- The taxpayer transfers a home to the LLC and lives at the home after the transfer without paying fair rent to the LLC.[90]
- The taxpayer transfers other personal-use assets to the LLC, such as an automobile.[91]
- The formalities of the LLC are not respected.[92] In order to obtain a discount, the LLC must comply with all technical formalities in its creation and operation.[93]
- There is an express agreement that the taxpayer may continue to enjoy LLC property for life after transferring it to the LLC.[94] There is an express agreement if the decedent retains the right to remove or replace the managers or general partners, who in turn have the right to determine the amount and timing of distributions from the LLC.[95] For example, there would be an express agreement if the decedent owned sufficient membership units to replace the managers of the LLC.
- There is an implied agreement among the family members that the taxpayer may continue to enjoy LLC property for life after transferring it to the LLC.[96] If the decedent transferred assets to the LLC that were required for his support, then there is an implied agreement that the children or other

---

[85] BNA Daily Tax Report No. 213, p. G-4 (Nov. 4, 2002); BNA Daily Tax Report No. 8, p. G-1 (Jan. 13, 2003).

[86] Harper v. Comm'r, T.C. Memo 2001-121 (2002); Estate of Theodore R. Thompson v. Comm'r, 84 TCM 374 (2002); Estate of Strangi, T.C. Memo 2003-145 (2003).

[87] BNA Daily Tax Report No. 8, p. G-1 (Jan. 13, 2003); Estate of Strangi, T.C. Memo 2003-145 (2003).

[88] Harper v. Comm'r, T.C. Memo 2001-121 (2002); Estate of Reichardt, 114 T.C. 144 (2000).

[89] Harper v. Comm'r, T.C. Memo 2001-121 (2002).

[90] Estate of Reichardt, 114 T.C. 144 (2000); BNA Daily Tax Report No. 8, p. G-1 (Jan. 13, 2003).

[91] BNA Daily Tax Report No. 8, p. G-1 (Jan. 13, 2003).

[92] Harper v. Comm'r, T.C. Memo 2001-121 (2002); Estate of Theodore R. Thompson v. Comm'r, 84 TCM 374 (2002).

[93] BNA Daily Tax Report No. 8, p. G-1 (Jan. 13, 2003).

[94] Estate of Reichardt, 114 T.C. 144 (2000); Estate of Schauerhamer v. Comm'r, 73 TCM 2855, T.C. Memo 1997-242 (1997). *But see* Church v. United States, 85 A.F.T.R. 2d 2000-804, ¶25 (W.D. Tex. 2000), in which the court found no implied agreement.

[95] *See* Kimbell v. U.S., 91 AFTR 2003-585 (N.D. Tex. 2003).

[96] Estate of Reichardt, 114 T.C. 144 (2000); Estate of Schauerhamer v. Comm'r, 73 TCM 2855, T.C. Memo 1997-242 (1997); Estate of Strangi, T.C. Memo 2003-145 (2003). *But see* Church v. United States, 85 A.F.T.R. 2d 2000-804, ¶25 (W.D. Tex. 2000), in which the court found no implied agreement.

members of the LLC would honor the decedent's request for money from property that the decedent contributed to the LLC.[97]

- The parties do not form a business enterprise or conduct a trade or business other than the management of investment assets.[98]
- The LLC does not engage in transactions with persons other than family members.[99]
- There is a history of disproportionate distributions to the decedent or a trust for the benefit of the decedent.[100]
- The decedent retained, either directly or through a person acting under a power of attorney, sole discretion to determine the amount and timing of distributions.[101]
- The members of the LLC other than the decedent do not obtain a meaningful economic interest in the property during their lifetimes.[102]
- The decedent made all decisions regarding the creation and structure of the LLC.[103]
- The contributed property contains substantial liquid and investment assets,[104] unless those assets are reinvested in a valid functioning business enterprise.[105]
- The contributed property constitutes a majority of the decedent's assets.[106] The taxpayer should at least retain sufficient property for living expenses for the rest of his or her life based on life expectancy tables. The IRS asserts that the taxpayer should retain sufficient assets outside of the LLC to maintain a reasonable standard of living without using LLC assets.[107]
- Persons other than the decedent contribute property to the LLC and receive a special allocation of all income from such contributed property.[108]
- There is no substantial change in investment strategy or business activity after the date that the decedent contributed his assets to the LLC.[109]

There is an exception to Section 2036(a) if the taxpayer transfers property to an LLC for adequate consideration. The courts disagree on whether the transfer of property to an LLC in exchange for membership units is a transfer for adequate

[97] Estate of Theodore R. Thompson v. Comm'r, 84 TCM 374 (2002).

[98] Id.

[99] Id. See also Kimbell v. U.S., 91 AFTR 2003-585 (N.D. Tex. 2003).

[100] Harper v. Comm'r, T.C. Memo 2001-121 (2002); Estate of Theodore R. Thompson v. Comm'r, 84 TCM 374 (2002); Estate of Strangi, T.C. Memo 2003-145 (2003).

[101] Estate of Strangi, T.C. Memo 2003-145 (2003).

[102] Id.

[103] Harper v. Comm'r, T.C. Memo 2001-121 (2002); Estate of Strangi, T.C. Memo 2003-145 (2003).

[104] Estate of Theodore R. Thompson v. Comm'r, 84 TCM 374 (2002); Harper v. Comm'r, T.C. Memo 2001-121 (2002).

[105] Estate of Theodore R. Thompson v. Comm'r, 84 TCM 374 (2002); Estate the Harrison v. Comm'r, T.C. Memo 1987-8 (1987); Estate of Michelson v. Comm'r, T.C. Memo 1978-371 (1978).

[106] Estate of Theodore R. Thompson v. Comm'r, 84 TCM 374 (2002); Harper v. Comm'r, T.C. Memo 2001-121 (2002); Estate of Reichardt, 114 T.C. 144 (2000).

[107] BNA Daily Tax Report No. 8, p. G-1 (Jan. 13, 2003).

[108] Estate of Theodore R. Thompson v. Comm'r, 84 TCM 374 (2002).

[109] Id; Estate of Strangi, T.C. Memo 2003-145 (2003).

consideration. Some courts have determined that the transfer of investment assets to an LLC in exchange for a membership interest is not a transfer for full consideration in an arm's-length transaction.[110] Other courts have determined that the transfer of assets to an LLC, or the transfer of liquid and investment assets that are reinvested in a valid functioning business enterprise, is a transfer for adequate consideration.[111] It is difficult for a taxpayer to argue that the transfer is for adequate consideration, and at the same time assert a substantial minority or marketability discount for gift tax purposes.

[7]   IRC Section 2038 Retained Right to Alter, Amend, or Revoke

As a fifth alternative to the sham-transaction doctrine, the IRS argues that property transferred by a taxpayer to an LLC should be brought back into the taxpayer's estate under IRC Section 2038 if the taxpayer retained the right to alter, amend, revoke, or terminate the operating agreement of the LLC.[112]

The IRS will not win on this issue if other members of the LLC own sufficient membership interests to make an amendment, or to block an amendment proposed by the donor.[113] There is also no transfer for purposes of IRC Section 2038 if the taxpayer contributes property to an LLC in exchange for membership interests, and does not confer a financial benefit on, or increase the wealth of, any other member as a result of the contribution.[114]

[8]   Cost of Dissolution

As a sixth alternative to the sham transaction doctrine, the IRS argues that the only permissible discount for a majority owner should be the cost of dissolving the LLC. The theory is that a willing buyer would ignore the restrictions in the operating agreement for the LLC if the buyer of the majority interest could vote to dissolve the LLC. This argument has been used mainly for general partnerships. Several courts have rejected the argument.[115]

---

[110] Kimbell v. U.S., 91 AFTR 2003-585 (N.D. Tex. 2003); Estate of Theodore R. Thompson v. Comm'r, 84 TCM 374 (2002); Harper v. Comm'r, T.C. Memo 2001-121 (2002); Estate of Strangi, T.C. Memo 2003-145 (2003).

[111] Estate of Theodore R. Thompson v. Comm'r, 84 TCM 374 (2002); Estate the Harrison v. Comm'r, T.C. Memo 1987-8 (1987); Estate of Michelson v. Comm'r, T.C. Memo 1978-371 (1978).

[112] Estate of Reichardt, 114 T.C. 144 (2000); Estate of Schauerhamer v. Comm'r, 73 T.C.M. 2855, T.C. Memo 1997-242 (1997).

[113] Church v. United States, 85 A.F.T.R. 2d 2000-804, ¶¶4, 16 (W.D. Tex. 2000).

[114] Church v. United States, 85 A.F.T.R. 2d 2000-804, Conclusions of Law ¶7 (W.D. Tex. 2000).

[115] LeFrak v. Comm'r, 66 T.C.M. 1297 (1993); Estate of Cervin v. Comm'r, 68 T.C.M. 1115 (1994); McCormick v. Comm'r, 70 T.C.M. 318 (1995).

[9]   IRC Section 2036(b) Retained Voting Rights

As a seventh alternative to the sham transaction doctrine, the IRS uses IRC Section 2036(b) if a member transfers stock in a closely held corporation to an LLC. The value of closely held stock transferred by a taxpayer to an LLC may be includable in his gross estate if the taxpayer retained the right to vote the stock as a manager or member of the LLC until the date of death.[116] The IRS believes that the rule applies even though (a) the decedent was only one of the managers of the LLC, and could vote the stock only in conjunction with another unrelated manager, or (b) the decedent transferred the stock to the LLC in exchange for membership interests one or more years prior to the date of death.[117]

IRC Section 2036(b) only applies to stock in a controlled corporation. A corporation is a controlled corporation if, at any time after the transfer and during the three-year period before the date of death, the decedent owned or had the right to vote stock processing at least 20 percent of the total combined voting power of all classes of stock.[118]

IRC Section 2036(b) does not apply if the transfer is a bona fide sale for adequate and full consideration in money or money's worth.[119]

[10]   Section 2701 Estate Freezes

As an eighth alternative to the sham transaction doctrine, the IRS uses IRC Section 2701 if there are two or more classes of membership interests. IRC Section 2701 is designed to discourage "estate freezes." In a typical estate freeze prior to the enactment of IRC Section 2701, the parent would transfer an interest in an LLC or other business entity while retaining a different type of interest in the same business. The interest that was given away was structured so that it had a very low value at the time of the gift, thereby incurring little or no gift taxes. However, the interest was expected to increase in value as the business grew. The interest retained by the donor was structured so that its value would not increase. For example, the retained membership interest was often entitled to a fixed liquidation amount and a fixed annual rate of return. The size of the donor's estate was frozen for estate tax purposes.

IRC Section 2701 now contains several rules designed to prevent the member from artificially decreasing the gift tax on the member's initial gift of a partial interest in the LLC to the family member. The rules use the "subtraction method" of valuing a gift.[120] The valuation method ignores the value of certain preferential interests retained by the donor. This has the effect of increasing the value of the gift and the amount of gift taxes payable on the date of transfer.

---

[116] Ltr. Rul. 199938005 (*citing* IRC §2036(b)).
[117] Ltr. Rul. 199938005.
[118] IRC §2036(b)(2).
[119] IRC §2036(a).
[120] Reg. §25.2701-3.

A donor's retained interest in an LLC is ignored for gift tax valuation purposes if it is an equity interest that has a preference in the form of either of the following:[121]

- an extraordinary payment right, such as a put, call or conversion right, the right to compel liquidation, or a similar right, the exercise or non-exercise of which affects the value of the donated membership interest; or
- a distribution right if, immediately before the gift, the donor and family members control the LLC. A distribution right is a right to receive distributions from an LLC.

The special valuation rules do not apply if (i) the member donates membership interests in the LLC that are of the same class as the preferential retained membership interests, or (ii) the member transfers membership interests that are proportionately of the same type as the retained interests (except for any nonterminating differences with respect to management and limitations on liability).

Normally, a member's gifts of membership interests in an LLC to family members are not subject to the special valuation rules, since the member owns the same type of membership interest after the gift. The parent or other donor may retain management control of the LLC, but retained management rights do not subject the gift to the special valuation rules.[122] However, the special valuation rules may apply if the member indirectly owns a preferential payment or distribution right in a business owned by the LLC.[123]

[C] Types of Valuation Discounts

If the court respects the LLC, then the court will value the membership interests rather than the underlying value of the LLC assets. The courts usually start with the value of the underlying assets, and then discount that value based on the nature of the LLC, restrictions in the operating agreement,[124] and various other factors. The major valuation discounts are as follows:

[1] Minority Discount

The most common type of valuation discount is the minority discount. There are different rules for estate and gift tax purposes.

---

[121] Ltr. Rul. 9802004 (citing IRC §2701(b)(1)).

[122] Ltr. Rul. 9802004.

[123] Id.

[124] Estate of Fred O. Godley, 80 T.C.M. 158 (2000), aff'd in part, 89 A.F.T.R. 2d 2002-2001(e) (4th Cir. 2002).

[a]   Gift Taxes

A donor may take a minority discount for the gift of a membership interest if (a) the donor is a minority owner in the LLC, or (b) the donee is a minority owner in the LLC after receipt of the gift. For example, a majority owner is entitled to a minority discount for gifts of minority interests to family members and other persons. The rule applies even if the donor owned a majority interest in the LLC before and after the transfer.[125] The gift tax is imposed on the value of the property received by the donee rather than the value of the property owned by the donor prior to the gift.

[b]   Estate Taxes

The estate of a minority owner in an LLC may take a valuation discount for the membership interests owned by the deceased member. The estate may not take a minority discount if the deceased member owned a majority interest in the LLC, even if all of the beneficiaries receive a minority interest. All of the membership units owned by the decedent are aggregated for estate tax purposes.[126]

A 50-percent ownership interest in an LLC may or may not be entitled to a minority discount, based on all facts and circumstances.[127]

[2]   Marketability, Liquidity, and Lack of Control Discounts

The second major type of valuation discount is the marketability, liquidity, and lack of control discount. These discounts are based on the assumption that the indirect ownership of property through an LLC is worth less than the direct ownership of property outside an LLC. The court may allow a combined discount for lack of marketability, lack of liquidity, and lack of control without specifying the exact amount of each discount.[128] Other courts will specify the amount of each discount.[129]

For example, the courts may allow discounts in the following cases:

- A member may receive a lack of control discount if the member is not allowed to participate in management of the LLC.[130]
- A minority member may receive a marketability and liquidity discount because it is much more difficult for a member to sell a minority membership interest in an LLC. A minority member usually does not have the right to

---

[125] Rev. Rul. 93-12, 1993-1 C.B. 202; TAM 9449001; TAM 9436005; Estate of Bright v. United States, 658 F.2d 999 (5th Cir. 1981); Estate of Andrews v. Comm'r, 79 T.C. 938 (1982).

[126] Ahmanson Foundation v. United States, 674 F.2d 761 (9th Cir. 1981).

[127] Estate of Fred O. Godley, 80 T.C.M. 158 (2000), *aff'd in part,* 89 A.F.T.R. 2d 2002-2001(e) (4th Cir. 2002).

[128] Estate of Barudin, T.C. Memo 1996-395 (1996).

[129] Adams v. United States, 2001-2 U.S.T.C. ¶60,379 (D.C. Tex. 2000).

[130] McCormick v. Comm'r, 70 T.C.M. 318 (1995).

force a liquidation of the LLC or to receive back the member's capital contribution on withdrawal from the LLC. The IRS often challenges a marketability discount for a majority owner who has a right to liquidate an LLC.[131] Several courts have allowed marketability discounts even where the majority owner has the right to liquidate the entity.[132]

- A member may receive a small discount for an onerous right of first refusal provision in the operating agreement.[133]
- One court allowed a 20-percent marketability discount because (a) there was no ready market for the partnership interests, (b) a purchaser would be subject to the requirements of the operating agreement that made one of the family members the managing partner, and (c) there was a 60-day right of first refusal provision that forced a period of illiquidity on every selling partner.[134]

[3]   Built-In Gains Discount

A number of courts have allowed a valuation discount for estate[135] and gift tax[136] purposes for the built-in capital gains of a corporation. The theory is that a willing buyer would pay less for the company if the buyer would have to pay a capital gains tax on sale of the appreciated assets in the corporation.

The courts have not allowed a built-in capital gains discount for an LLC.[137] The reason is that a buyer can avoid the tax on the built-in gains if the LLC makes an election to adjust the basis of its assets under IRC Section 754. If this election is in effect at the time of the purchase, then the inside basis of the LLC's assets is increased to match the buyer's cost basis in the purchased membership units. The basis adjustment benefits only the purchasing member. Thus, a hypothetical willing buyer and seller would not reduce the purchase price based on a reduction for built-in capital gains because both parties could influence the manager of the LLC to make a Section 754 election, thereby eliminating any capital gains for the buyer and obtaining the highest sales price for the seller.[138]

---

[131] *See* Ltr. Rul. 7953001; Estate of Jephson v. Comm'r, 87 T.C. 297 (1986).

[132] Estate of Curry v. United States, 706 F.2d 1424 (7th Cir. 1983); Von Hagke v. United States, 79-1 U.S.T.C. ¶13,290 (D. Wis. 1979); Estate of Bennett v. Comm'r, 65 T.C.M. 1816 (1993); Estate of Ford v. Comm'r, 66 T.C.M. 1507 (1993); Estate of Folks v. Comm'r, 43 T.C.M. 427 (1982).

[133] Estate of W. W. Jones, II, 116 T.C. No. 11 (2001).

[134] Estate of Fred O. Godley, 80 T.C.M. 158 (2000), *aff'd in part*, 89 A.F.T.R. 2d 2002-2001(e) (4th Cir. 2002).

[135] Estate of Welch v. Comm'r, 85 A.F.T.R. 2d ¶2000-534 (8th Cir. 2000).

[136] Eisenberg, Irene v. Comm'r, 155 F.3d 50 (2d Cir. 1998), *acq.* 1999-4 I.R.B. 4; Estate of Davis v. Comm'r, 110 T.C. 530 (1998).

[137] Estate of W. W. Jones, II, 116 T.C. No. 11 (2001); BNA Daily Tax Report No. 8, p. G-1 (Jan. 13, 2003).

[138] Estate of W. W. Jones, II, 116 T.C. No. 11 (2001).

[4] Assignee Interest Discount

A taxpayer may claim an assignee discount for the membership interest if the donee is not admitted as a full member of the LLC. The theory is that an assignee does not have the same rights to force a liquidation of the LLC.[139] The uncertainties regarding the legal rights of the assignee under state law may further depress the price that the willing buyer would pay for the assignee interest.[140] Some courts have rejected the assignee discount.[141] No assignee discount is permitted if the donee or beneficiary automatically becomes a full member of the LLC.[142]

[5] Portfolio Discount

The taxpayer is entitled to a portfolio discount if the LLC owns two or more business operations or types of assets, the combination of which would be unattractive to a buyer. However, the taxpayer must clearly demonstrate that the LLC's mix of assets would be unattractive to a buyer. Otherwise, the court will not allow a portfolio discount.[143]

[6] Discounts for Gifts to LLC

A taxpayer may transfer membership units in an LLC to family members, and subsequently make a gift of property to the LLC. The gift of property to the LLC is an indirect gift to the other members. The value of the gift is determined by reference to the property transferred to the LLC rather than the nature of the LLC that receives the gift. The taxpayer may not receive an additional valuation discount as a result of the fact that the members of the LLC receiving the indirect gifts are minority owners.[144]

EXAMPLE

A father owns 50 percent of an LLC. His two sons each own 25 percent of the LLC. The father transfers undivided interest in real property to the

---

[139] Estate of Ethel S. Nowell, 77 T.C.M. 1239 (Issue 2) (1999); Adams v. United States, 283 F.3d 383 (5th Cir. 2000).

[140] Adams v. United States, 283 F.3d 383 (5th Cir. 2000). However, on remand, the lower court refused to apply an additional assignee interest discount because the discount already been considered as part of the other valuation discounts.

[141] Kerr v. Comm'r, 113 T.C. 499 (1999), aff'd, 292 F.3d 490 (5th Cir. 2002).

[142] Estate of Ethel S. Nowell, 77 T.C.M. 1239 (Issue 2) (1999).

[143] Knight v. Comm'r, 115 T.C. 506, 516-517 (2000). See also Adams v. United States, 2001-2 U.S.T.C. ¶60,379 (D.C. Tex. 2000), in which the court stated that the estate was entitled to determination regarding the appropriate discount for ownership by the partnership of an undesirable mix of assets.

[144] Shepherd v. Comm'r, 115 T.C. 376 (2000, aff'd, 283 F.3 1258 (11th Cir. 2002).

LLC. The transfer is treated as an indirect gift to the sons of 50 percent of the value of the property transferred. The father is entitled to a 15 percent discount for the gift because the property transferred is an undivided fractional interest in land, there is lack of complete control over the parcel, and there is the potential disagreement about disposition of the land and partition of the land. However, the father is not entitled to an additional valuation discount as a result of the transfer to a limited liability company in which the sons own a minority interest. The gift is treated as a gift of land and not gift of LLC membership units.[145]

[D]   Swing Vote Premium

In 1994, the IRS determined that a swing-vote premium was applicable to the valuation of a block of stock transferred to a family member if the block of stock enabled the donee to join with another family member to form a majority interest.[146] In that ruling, the 100 percent shareholder of a corporation transferred a 30 percent block of stock to each of his three children. The taxpayer claimed a 25 percent discount for each gift. The IRS reduced this discount to reflect the fact that each donee had the ability to combine with another donee to obtain majority control.

The court rejected this position in *Estate of Davis*.[147] In that case, the taxpayer transferred a 25.77 percent block of stock to two of his family members. The IRS attempted to reduce the valuation discount claimed by the taxpayer because the two donees could combine to obtain majority control. The court determined that the IRS gave undue weight to this argument.

[E]   Appraisals

The appraisal of the membership interest and the assets held by the LLC is one of the most important factors in determining the appropriate estate or gift tax value.[148] The IRS often attempts to discredit the taxpayer's appraisals, even without initially obtaining its own independent appraisal.[149] In almost every case, the IRS claims that the taxpayer's appraisal understates the actual value of the membership interest.

The courts will first consider the qualifications of the appraiser and the com-

---

[145] Shepherd v. Comm'r, 115 T.C. 376 (2000), *aff'd*, 283 F.3d 1258 (11th Cir. 2002).

[146] TAM 9436005.

[147] Estate of Davis v. Comm'r, 110 T.C. 530 (1998).

[148] BNA Daily Tax Report No. 8, p. G-1 (Jan. 13, 2003).

[149] Estate of Fred O. Godley, 80 T.C.M. 158, 165 (2000), *aff'd in part*, 89 A.F.T.R. 2d 2002-2001(e) (4th Cir. 2002).

pleteness of the appraisal.[150] For gift tax purposes, the taxpayer should obtain a qualified appraisal[151] by a qualified appraiser.[152]

The appraiser should base the appraisal on companies that are comparable to the LLC.[153] For LLCs and limited partnerships, the IRS prefers comparisons to closed-end mutual funds, particularly to funds that hold securities comparable to those held in the LLC or family limited partnership.[154] The appraiser must show how the various discount factors apply to the LLC. For example, if the appraiser makes a list of factors that affect the discount, the appraiser must explain how those factors account for the discount claimed for the LLC.[155]

With respect to the valuation of real estate, the IRS prefers the use of an appraiser located in the same geographic area as the property, clear maps showing comparable properties, and rental rates comparable for income producing properties. For businesses, the IRS recommends five years of income statements and balance sheets, including footnotes.[156]

§21.04   HOME OWNERSHIP

[A]   Exclusion of Gain on Sale of Property

The IRS at one time ruled that a taxpayer would be treated as the owner of a home for purposes of the exclusion from gain on sale of a home under IRC Section 121.[1] The exclusion was available if the home was not used in a trade or business, and the taxpayer continued to use the home as a principal residence (or met the ownership test for at least two of the five years ending on the date of sale). The IRS later revoked this ruling.[2] Thus, it is unclear whether the exclusion is available.

[B]   Estate Taxes

The value of the house may be included in the taxpayer's gross estate if the taxpayer continues to live in the house after the transfer to the LLC without paying fair rent to the LLC.[3] The reason is that the gross estate includes all property that the taxpayer transfers during his or her lifetime if the taxpayer retains possession or enjoyment of the property for life, and if the transfer is not a bona fide sale for adequate and full consideration.[4]

---

[150] Estate of Fred O. Godley, 80 T.C.M. 158 (2000), *aff'd in part*, 89 A.F.T.R. 2d 2002-2001(e) (4th Cir. 2002).

[151] Reg. §301.6501(c)-1(f)(3)(ii).

[152] Reg. §301.6501(c)-1(f)(3)(i).

[153] Knight v. Comm'r, 115 T.C. 506 (2000).

[154] BNA Daily Tax Report No. 8, p. G-1 (Jan. 13, 2003).

[155] Knight v. Comm'r, 115 T.C. 506 (2000).

[156] BNA Daily Tax Report No. 8, p. G-1 (Jan. 13, 2003).

§21.04   [1] Ltr. Rul. 200004022.

[2] Ltr. Rul. 200119014.

[3] Wuebker, 85 A.F.T.R. 2d ¶2000-496 (6th Cir. 2000); Estate of Reichardt, 114 T.C. 144 (2000).

[4] IRC §2036(a).

§21.05   SECTION 704(e) FAMILY PARTNERSHIPS

A taxpayer who makes a gift of a membership interest to a family member may be taxed on the donee's distributive share of income under IRC Section 704(e). IRC Section 704(e) is designed to prevent a taxpayer from assigning income attributable to personal services to a family member in a lower income tax bracket.

EXAMPLE

A lawyer in a law LLC donates 20 percent of his membership interests to his four-year old daughter. The daughter's distributive share of income from the law LLC is taxed to the father under IRC Section 704(e).

The requirements for avoiding reallocation of income from the donee to the donor under IRC Section 704(e) are discussed above.[5]

§21.06   DEFERRAL OF ESTATE TAX PAYMENTS

An estate may defer the payment of estate taxes if at least 35 percent of the estate consists of an interest in a closely held business. The sale or disposition of 50 percent or more of the ownership interests in a closely held business will terminate the extension to pay and accelerate the payment of taxes. The owners' transfer of their interest in a closely held business to an LLC in exchange for membership interests does not constitute a disposition or result in termination of the estate tax deferral.[1]

---

[5] *See* §8.05 *supra.*
§21.06   [1] Ltr. Rul. 200129019.

22

Federal and State Filing Requirements

§22.01 FEDERAL FORMS

[A] Form 1065 Partnership Return

An LLC that is classified as a partnership for federal tax purposes must file a partnership return on IRS Form 1065.[1] The form must be filed even if the LLC's principal place of business is located outside of the United States or if all of its members are nonresident aliens. However, an LLC is not required to file a return in the following cases:

- The LLC has no income, deductions, or credits for federal income tax purposes.[2]
- The LLC is a foreign LLC that does not engage in a U.S. trade or business or have income from sources within the United States.[3]
- The LLC is a foreign LLC that has income from sources within the United States, but is exempt from the filing requirements under IRS regulations.[4]

---

§22.01 [1] IRC §6031(a); Reg. §1.6031-1(a)(1).
[2] Reg. §1.6031-1(a)(3).
[3] IRC §6031(e); Reg. §1.6031-1(b).
[4] *See* §18.06, *supra,* for a discussion of the exceptions.

Form 1065 is an information return. It is used to report information about the LLC and each member's distributive share of income, deductions, gains, losses, and credits from the operation of the LLC. The LLC does not pay tax on this income.[5] Instead, all of the income, losses, and deductions pass through to the members.

A domestic LLC must file Form 1065 by the fifteenth day of the fourth month following the close of its tax year.[6] An LLC whose members are all nonresident aliens must file the return by the fifteenth day of the sixth month following the close of the tax year.[7]

One member of the LLC must sign the return.[8] The member need not be a manager or officer.

An LLC that fails to file a complete return on a timely basis is subject to a penalty unless the failure is due to reasonable cause.[9] The penalty is equal to $50 times the number of members in the LLC at any time during the tax year times the number of months and fractions of a month that the failure continues, but not to exceed five months. The period of assessment for taxes attributable to LLC items remains open indefinitely if the LLC fails to file a return.[10] The failure to file may result in a disallowance of deductions, losses, and credits flowing through to the members.[11]

[B] Schedules K and K-1

An LLC uses Schedule K-1 to report each member's share of income, credits, deductions, and losses.[12] The members then report these items on their individual tax returns. The LLC must separately state for each member on Schedule K-1 the members' distributive shares of the following items, whether or not they are actually distributed:[13]

- Ordinary income or loss from trade or business activities.
- Net income or loss from rental real estate activities.
- Net income or loss from other rental activities.
- Gains and losses from sales or exchanges of capital assets.
- Gains and losses from sales or exchanges of property described in Section 1231 of the Internal Revenue Code.
- Charitable contributions.

---

[5] IRC §701.

[6] IRC §6072(a); Reg. §1.6031(a)-1(e)(2).

[7] IRC §6072(c).

[8] See Instructions to Form 1065.

[9] IRC §6698; Reg. §1.6031-1(a)-1(a)(4).

[10] IRC §6229(a).

[11] IRC §6231(f).

[12] The rules governing LLC statements to members and nominees are set forth in IRC §6031(b) and Reg. §1.7701-3(c)(2).

[13] IRC §§702(a), 703(a)(1).

- Dividends passed through to corporate members that qualify for the dividends received deduction.
- Taxes paid to foreign countries and to possessions of the United States.[14]
- Other items of income, gain, loss, deduction, or credit to the extent provided in IRS regulations. The IRS requires separate itemization of such items as nonbusiness expenses, intangible drilling and development costs, and soil and water conservation expenditures.

Schedule K of Form 1065 is a summary schedule of all the members' shares of LLC income, credits, and deductions. Schedule K-1 shows each member's separate share. The LLC must attach a copy of each Schedule K-1 to the Form 1065 that is filed with the IRS. A copy of Schedule K-1 must be furnished to each member. If a membership interest is held by a nominee on behalf of another person, the LLC may be required to furnish Schedule K-1 to the nominee.[15]

The LLC must give a Schedule K-1 to each member who was a member in the LLC at any time during the year. It must provide the form to each member on or before the date on which the LLC must file its return, determined with regard to extensions.[16] The LLC is subject to penalties for failure to furnish Schedule K-1 to the members, failure to include all of the required information, and inclusion of incorrect information.[17] The penalty is $50 for each statement with respect to which a failure occurs, up to a maximum of $100,000 for any calendar year. The penalty is increased to the greater of $100 per statement or 10 percent of the aggregate amount of items required to be reported if the failure is due to intentional disregard. The $100,000 maximum penalty does not apply in that case.

The LLC must prepare a separate Schedule K-1 for a husband and a wife if the husband and the wife each have an interest in the LLC. If the husband and the wife hold the membership interest together, one Schedule K-1 may be prepared if the two are considered to be one member.

Generally, the members must report LLC items shown on Schedule K-1 and any attached schedules in the same way that the LLC treated the items on its return.

[C] Extension Requests

An LLC may obtain an extension of time to file the return by filing Form 8736, Application for Automatic Extension of Time to File U.S. Return for Partnership, REMIC, or for Certain Trusts. There is an automatic three-month extension if this form is filed.[18] Form 8736 must be filed by the regular due date of the LLC return. The extension does not extend the time for members to file their own income tax returns.[19]

---

[14] See IRC §901.
[15] Temp. Reg. §§1.6031(b)-1T, 1.6031(c)-1T.
[16] Temp. Reg. §1.6031(b)-1T(b).
[17] IRC §6722.
[18] Reg. §1.6081-2(a), (b)(1).
[19] Reg. §1.6081-2(e).

An LLC may obtain an additional extension of up to three months by filing Form 8800, Application for Additional Extension of Time to File U.S. Return for a Partnership, REMIC, or for Certain Trusts. The LLC must show reasonable cause to obtain this extension. Form 8800 must be filed by the extended due date of the LLC return.

[D]   Form 8832 Classification Election

The default classification rules are designed to provide most LLCs with the classification that they would likely choose without requiring them to file an election. For example, most domestic LLCs that have two or more members are automatically classified as a partnership for federal tax purposes. This is normally the desired tax classification. It permits a single tax at the member level. All items of income, gain, loss, credit, and deduction of the LLC pass through to and are taxed at the member level. Partnership classification is automatic without the need for a filing.

In certain exceptional cases, an LLC may not want to be classified under the default rules. In that event, the LLC may file Form 8832 to elect a different classification permitted by the IRS regulations.

An LLC should file the election on Form 8832 only in the following three cases:[20]

1. The LLC wants initially to be classified differently than under the default rules.
2. The LLC wants to change its previous classification.
3. There is doubt about the proper classification.

Some states require an LLC to attach a copy of Form 8832 to the state information return. In Hawaii, for example, an LLC formed after January 1, 1997, must attach a copy of that form to the LLC's first Hawaii income tax return or information return.[21]

[E]   U.S. Taxpayers in Foreign LLCs

U.S. members in a foreign LLC must file Form 8865, Information Return of U.S. Persons With Respect to Certain Foreign Partnerships, to report the following:[22]

- Transfers of cash and other property to a foreign LLC in exchange for a membership interest;[23]

---

[20] *See* §5.04 *supra* for discussion of the procedures for making the election.

[21] Tax Information Release No. 97-4, Hawaii Department of Taxation (Aug. 4, 1997).

[22] These filing requirements are discussed in §18.06.

[23] IRC §6038B; Reg. §1.6038B.

- The acquisition or disposition of at least a ten percent interest in a foreign LLC;[24] and
- Information concerning the income and assets of the LLC, certain transactions with the LLC, the names of the members, and other specified information if the U.S. member owns at least a ten percent interest in a controlled foreign LLC.[25]

[F]   Magnetic Media Filings

An LLC with more than 100 members must file its tax return with the IRS on a magnetic medium rather than paper. It must also file on a magnetic medium the Schedule K-1 sent to each member.[26] The 100 member test is made by counting the number of members over the LLC tax year. It does not matter that there were fewer than 100 members on any particular day during the tax year or that the members were not members for the full tax year. The magnetic media filing requirement applies for tax years ending on or after December 31, 2000.[27]

[G]   Single-Member LLCs

Single-member LLCs that are classified as disregarded entities and that are owned by individuals must file federal tax returns as sole proprietors.[28] The owner of the LLC must file a Schedule C to IRS Form 1040 to report income and expenses of the LLC. Single-member LLCs that are classified as corporations must file corporate tax returns.

§22.02   STATE FORMS

There are four types of state filings: (1) the tax return for the LLC; (2) the tax returns for the resident and nonresident members; (3) the composite return for the nonresident members; and (4) the annual report for the LLC.

[A]   State Tax Returns for LLC

The state tax return is often similar to the federal tax return. If the LLC is classified as a partnership, the state return is normally an information return. Some states do not require a state return if all members of the LLC are residents

---

[24] IRC §6046A; Reg. §1.6046A-1.

[25] IRC §6038; Reg. §1.6038-3.

[26] IRC §6011(e)(2); Reg. §301.6011-3(a). The IRS may waive the electronic filing requirement in the case of hardship. Reg. §301.6011-3(b). IRS Publication 1524 explains how LLCs must file returns electronically.

[27] Prop. Reg. §§301.6011-3, 301.6031-1(a)(2)(ii); T.D. 8843 (Nov. 10, 1999).

[28] IRS Publication 334, Tax Guide for Small Businesses; Reg. §301.7701-2(a).

of the state. In that event, members report on a state tax return their allocable shares of income as set forth on the federal Schedule K-1.

The LLC state tax return is used to take account of state adjustments. It is also used to apportion income of the LLC that has business or sources of income within and outside the state. Nonresident members are taxed only on income from sources within the state and from a trade or business carried on within the state. The tax filings and returns for each state are discussed in detail in Chapter 23. The following table shows the tax filings that are required in each state and the District of Columbia for LLCs that are classified as partnerships as well as the agency from which to obtain the forms.[1]

State	State Forms Required	Due Date of Return	Revenue Departments
Alabama	Form 65, Partnership/ Limited Liability Company Return of Income A copy of the federal partnership return on Form 1065 must be attached to the state return	15th day of 4th month following close of tax year	Department of Revenue Income Tax Division P.O. Box 327470 Montgomery, AL 36132-7470 Phone: (334) 242-1170 www.ador.state.al.us
Alaska	An LLC that has no corporate members is not required to file a return An LLC that has corporate members must submit a copy of the signed IRS Form 1065, pages 1-4, with "Alaska" marked on the top of page 1, and a copy of Schedule K-1 for each corporate member	30th day after federal return	Department of Revenue P.O. Box 110420 Juneau, AK 99811-0420 Phone: (907) 465-2320 www.revenue.state.ak.us
Arizona	Form 165 Form K-1, Arizona Partner's Share of Income Adjustment A single-member LLC must report its income to Arizona as a corporation on Form 120 Form 120 for LLC classified as a corporation	15th day of 4th month following close of tax year	Department of Revenue 1600 West Monroe Street Phoenix, AZ 85007-2650 (602) 255-3381 Forms: (602) 542-4260 www.revenue.state.az.us

§22.02   [1] *See* Chapter 23 *infra* for discussion of the tax filings and returns required for each state.

State	State Forms Required	Due Date of Return	Revenue Departments
Arkansas	Form AR1050, Partnership Return of Income	4 1/2 months after close of tax year	Department of Revenue P.O. Box 3628 Little Rock, AR 72203-3628 (501) 682-1100 or (800) 882-9275 www.state.ar.us/dfa
California	• Form 568, Limited Liability Company Return of Income • Schedule D (568), Capital Gain or Loss • Schedule K-1 (568), Member's Share of Income, Deductions, Credits, Etc. • Schedule K-1 NR (568), Member's Share of Income, Deductions, Credits, Etc. • FTB 3522, Limited Liability Company Tax Voucher • FTB 3537, Payment Voucher for Automatic Extension for Limited Liability Companies • FTB 3885L, Depreciation and Amortization • FTB 3832, Limited Liability Company's List of Members and Consents	15th day of 4th month following close of tax year	California Franchise Tax Board P.O. Box 942840 Sacramento, CA 94240-0040 (800) 852-5711 Forms: (800) 338-0505 www.ftb.ca.gov
Colorado	Form 106, Colorado State Partnership or S Corporation Return of Income and Composite Nonresident Income Tax Return Form 106 CR, Colorado Partnership—S Corporation Credit Form	15th day of 4th month following close of tax year	Department of Revenue 1375 Sherman Street Denver, CO 80261 (303) 866-3091 Forms: (303) 232-2414 www.state.co.us/ gov_dir/revenue_dir/ home_rev.html
Connecticut	Form CT-1065, Connecticut Partnership Income Tax Return A copy of the federal partnership return on Form 1065 must be attached to the state return	15th day of 4th month following close of tax year	Department of Revenue Services 25 Sigourney Street Hartford, CT 06106 (860) 297-5962 Forms: (860) 297-4753 www.state.ct.us/drs

State	State Forms Required	Due Date of Return	Revenue Departments
Delaware	Form 300, Delaware Partnership Return	15th day of 4th month following close of tax year	Department of Finance Division of Revenue Carvel State Office Building 820 N. French Street Wilmington, DE 19801 (302) 577-8200 Forms: (302) 577-8201 www.state.de. us/revenue
District of Columbia	• Form D-30 • Form D-65, Partnership Return of Income • Form D-2030 Must attach a copy of federal Form 1065	15th day of 3d month following close of tax year	Government of District of Columbia Office of Tax & Revenue 941 North Capitol St., N.E., 6th Floor Washington, DC 20002 (202) 442-6300 **or** (202) 727-4TAX www.dccfo.com/ Taxpayers/ taxpayers.html
Florida	Form F-1065 Must attach a copy of federal Form 1065	N/A	Department of Revenue 2410 Allen Road Tallahassee, FL 32312-2603 (850) 488-6800 Forms: (850) 922-9645 sun6.dms.state.fl.us/dor
Georgia	Form 700, State of Georgia Partnership Income Tax Return	15th day of 4th month following close of tax year	Department of Revenue 270 Washington Street Atlanta, GA 30334 (404) 656-4188 Forms: (404) 656-4293 www2.state.ga.us/ departments/dor
Hawaii	Form N-20, Partnership Return of Income An LLC that files IRS Form 8832 must attach a copy of that form to its first state return	15th day of 4th month following close of tax year	Department of Taxation P.O. Box 259 Honolulu, HI 96809-0259 (800) 222-3229 Forms: (808) 587-7572 **or** (800) 222-7572 www.state.hi.us/ tax/tax.html
Idaho	Form 65, Partnership Return of Income	15th day of 4th month following close of tax year	State Tax Commission P.O. Box 36 Boise, ID 83722 (208) 334-7660 **or** (800) 972-7660 www.state.id.us/ tax/home.htm

State	State Forms Required	Due Date of Return	Revenue Departments
Illinois	• Form IL-1065 • Form IL-2569 • Form NUC-1, Illinois Business Registration	15th day of 3d month following close of tax year	Department of Revenue Willard Ice Building 101 West Jefferson Street Springfield, IL 62702 (217) 782-3336 **or** (800) 732-8866 www.revenue.state.il.us
Indiana	• Form IT-65 • Form IN K-1 • Form WH-18, Indiana Miscellaneous Withholding Tax Statement for Nonresidents The first four pages of the federal partnership return on Form 1065 must be attached to the state return	15th day of 4th month following close of tax year	Department of Revenue Indiana Government Center North 100 N. Senate Avenue, Room N105 Indianapolis, IN 46204 (317) 232-2240 Forms: (317) 486-5103 www.state.in.us/dor
Iowa	Form IA 1065, Partnership Return of Income	15th day of 4th month following close of tax year	Department of Revenue and Finance Hoover State Office Building Des Moines, IA 50319 (515) 281-3114 Forms: (515) 281-7239 www.state.ia.us/tax
Kansas	Form K-65, Kansas Partnership Return The first four pages of the federal partnership return on Form 1065 must be attached to the state return	15th day of 4th month following close of tax year	Department of Revenue Docking State Office Building 915 S.W. Harrison Street Topeka, KS 66625 (785) 368-8222 Forms: (785) 296-4937 www.ink.org/public /kdor
Kentucky	Form 765, Kentucky Partnership Income Return Must attach a complete copy of federal Form 1065	15th day of 4th month following close of tax year	Kentucky Revenue Cabinet 200 Fair Oaks Lane Frankfort, KY 40620 (502) 564-4581 Forms by fax: (502) 564-4459 www.state.ky.us/ agencies/revenue/ revhome.htm
Louisiana	Form IT-565 if any member is a nonresident of Louisiana or is not a natural person	15th day of 4th month following close of tax year	Department of Revenue P.O. Box 201 Baton Rouge, LA 70821 (225) 925-7537 Forms: (225) 925-7532 www.rev.state.la.us

State	State Forms Required	Due Date of Return	Revenue Departments
Maine	Form 1065 ME/1120S-ME, Maine Information Return Form TR, Maine Bureau of Taxation Income Tax Division S Corporation and Partnership Transmittal Form The first four pages of the federal partnership return on Form 1065 must be attached to the state return	15th day of 3d month following close of tax year	Maine Revenue Services State Office Building 24 State House Station Augusta, ME 04333-0024 (207) 287-2076 janus.state.me.us /revenue /homepage.htm
Maryland	Form 510, Pass-Through Entity Income Tax Return	15th day of 3d month following close of tax year	Comptroller of the Treasury Revenue Administration Division Annapolis, MD 21411-0001 (410) 260-7980 **or** (800) MD TAXES www.comp.state.md.us
Massachusetts	Form 3, Partnership Return of Income A copy of the federal partnership return on Form 1065 and all schedules must be attached to the state return	15th day of 3d month following close of tax year	Department of Revenue Customer Service Bureau P.O. Box 7010 Boston, MA 02204 (617) 887-6367 **or** in MA only: (800) 392-6089 www.dor.state.ma.us
Michigan	C-8000, Single Business Tax Annual Return, or C-8030, or C-8044, Single Business Tax Simplified Return	15th day of 4th month following close of tax year	Department of Treasury Revenue Administrative Services Treasury Building 430 W. Allegan Street Lansing, MI 48922 (517) 373-3200 Forms: (800) 367-6263 www.treas.state.mi.us
Minnesota	Form M-3, Partnership Return Schedule M-KPI, Partner's Share of Income, Credits and Modifications Form M-KPC, Partner's Share of Income, Credits and Modifications (for corporate and partnership members)	15th day of 3d month following close of tax year	Minnesota Department of Revenue 600 N. Robert Street St. Paul, MN 55145 (651) 296-3781 **or** (800) 652-9094 www.taxes.state.mn.us

State	State Forms Required	Due Date of Return	Revenue Departments
	Form MW-3NR, Withholding on Nonresidents		
Mississippi	Form 86-105, Mississippi Partnership/LLP/LLC Income Tax Return Form 86-387, Withholding of Partnership Income	15th day of 3d month following close of tax year	State Tax Commission P.O. Box 1033 Jackson, MS 39215-3338 (601) 923-7000 Forms: (601) 923-7815 www.mstc.state.ms.us/ index2.htm
Missouri	Form MO-1065, Partnership Return of Income Form MO-NRP, Nonresident Partnership Form	15th day of 4th month following close of tax year	Department of Revenue P.O. Box 3022 Jefferson City, MO 65105-3022 (573) 751-5337 Forms: (800) 877-6881 www.dor.state.mo.us
Montana	Form PR-1, Partnership Return of Income	15th day of 5th month following close of tax year	Department of Revenue P.O. Box 5805 Helena, MT 59604-5805 (406) 444-6900 www.state.mt.us/ revenue/index.htm
Nebraska	Form 1065N, Nebraska Partnership Return of Income	15th day of 3d month following close of tax year	Department of Revenue Box 94818 Lincoln, NE 68509-4818 (402) 471-2971 **or** (800) 742-7474 www.nol.org/revenue
Nevada	Form TXR-04.01, Business Tax Return	No income tax	Department of Taxation 1550 E. College Parkway, Suite 100 Carson City, NV 89706 (775) 687-4892 www.state.nv.us/ taxation
New Hampshire	• Form BET, Business Enterprise Tax Return for Corporations, Combined Groups, Partnerships, Fiduciaries and Nonprofit Organizations • Form NH-1065, Partnership Business Profits Tax Return • Form DP-80, Apportionment of Income	15th day of 3d month following close of tax year	Department of Revenue Administration 45 Chenell Drive P.O. Box 457 Concord, NH 03302-0457 (603) 271-2191 Forms: (603) 271-2192 www.state.nh.us/ revenue/revenue.htm

State	State Forms Required	Due Date of Return	Revenue Departments
	• Form BT-SUMMARY, Business Tax Summary • Form NH-1065-ES, Estimated Partnership Business Tax Quarterly Payment Voucher		
New Jersey	Form NJ-1065, State of New Jersey Partnership Return	15th day of 4th month following close of tax year	Division of Taxation Taxation Building 50 Barrack Street, 1st Floor Lobby Trenton, NJ 08695 (609) 292-6400 Forms: (800) 323-4400 www.state.nj.us/treasury/taxation
New Mexico	None. Copy of federal return must be provided or requested		Taxation and Revenue Department 1100 S. St. Francis Drive P.O. Box 630 Santa Fe, NM 87504-0630 (505) 827-0700 www.state.nm.us/tax
New York City			NYC Tax Commission Municipal Building 1 Centre Street New York, NY 10007 (212)669-4410 www.ci.nyc.ny.us/html/taxcomm/home.html
New York State	• Form IT-204, Partnership Return • Form IT-204-LL, Limited Liability Company/Partnership Filing Fee Payment Form • Form IT-204 NYC, City of New York Nonresident Partner Allocation • Form IT-204-ATT, Partners' Identifying Information (corporate partners)	2 ½ months after close of tax year	Department of Taxation and Finance Taxpayer Assistance Bureau W.A. Harriman Campus Albany, NY 12227 (518) 485-6800 **or** (800) 225-5829 Forms: (800) 462-8100 www.tax.state.ny.us
North Carolina	Form D-403, Partnership Income Tax Return The LLC must attach a copy of the federal partnership return on Form 1065 and all schedules to the state return	15th day of 3d month following close of tax year	Department of Revenue P.O. Box 25000 Raleigh, NC 27640-0640 (919) 733-3991 Forms: (919) 715-0397 www.dor.state.nc.us/DOR

State	State Forms Required	Due Date of Return	Revenue Departments
North Dakota	Form 58, North Dakota Partnership Return of Income	15th day of 4th month following close of tax year	Office of State Tax Commissioner State Capitol 600 East Boulevard Avenue Bismark, ND 58505-0599 (701) 328-2770 Forms: (701) 328-3017 www.state.nd.us/taxdpt
Ohio	Form IT-4708, Nonresident Partners' Income Tax Return	15th day of 3d month following close of tax year	Department of Taxation P.O. Box 530 Columbus, OH 43216-0530 (614) 466-2166 www.state.oh.us/tax
Oklahoma	Form 514, Partnership Return of Income	15th day of 3d month following close of tax year	Oklahoma Tax Commission P.O. Box 26800 Oklahoma City, OK 73126-0800 (405) 521-3212 Forms: (405) 521-3108 www.oktax.state.ok.us
Oregon	Form 65, Oregon Partnership Return of Income	15th day of 4th month following close of tax year	Department of Revenue 955 Center Street, N.E. Salem, OR 97310 (503) 378-4988 www.dor.state.or.us
Pennsylvania	Form PA-5, S Corporation/ Partnership Information Return	30th day after due date of federal return	Department of Revenue Strawberry Square, 11th Floor Harrisburg, PA 17128-0101 (717) 783-1405 **or** (888) PA TAXES Forms by fax: (800) 362-2050 www.revenue.state.pa.us
Rhode Island	Form RI-1065, Partnership Income Information Return	15th day of 3d month following close of tax year	Division of Taxation 1 Capitol Hill Providence, RI 02908-5801 (401) 222-3934 Forms: (401) 222-1111 www.tax.state.ri.us

State	State Forms Required	Due Date of Return	Revenue Departments
South Carolina	Form SC1065, Partnership Return of Income The LLC must attach a copy of the federal partnership return on Form 1065 and all schedules to the state return	15th day of 3d month following close of tax year	Department of Revenue P.O. Box 125 Columbia, SC 29214 (803) 898-5000 Forms: (803) 898-5320 **or** (800) 768-3676 www.dor.state.sc.us
South Dakota	None	No income tax	Department of Revenue 445 E. Capitol Avenue Pierre, SD 57501 (605) 773-5141 **or** (800) 829-9188 www.state.sd.us/revenue/Revenue.html
Tennessee	None	15th day of 4th month following close of tax year	Department of Revenue Andrew Jackson State Office Building 500 Deaderick Street Nashville, TN 37242 (615) 741-2594 Forms: (615) 741-8239 www.state.tn.us/revenue
Texas	Form 05-144, Texas Corporation Franchise Tax Report	N/A	Comptroller of Public Accounts P.O. Box 13528, Capitol Station Austin, TX 78711-3528 (512) 463-4600 www.cpa.state.tx.us
Utah	Form TC-65, Utah Partnership/ Limited Liability Partnership/ Limited Liability Company Return of Income	15th day of 4th month following close of tax year	State Tax Commission 210 N. 1950 West Salt Lake City, UT 84134 (801) 297-2200 **or** (800) 662-4335 www.tax.ex.state.ut.us
Vermont	Form B1-473, Partnership/ Limited Liability Company Schedule (if LLC has nonresident members)	15th day of 3d month following close of tax year	Department of Taxes 109 State Street Montpelier, VT 05609-1401 (802) 828-2868 Forms: (802) 828-2515 www.state.vt.us/tax

State	State Forms Required	Due Date of Return	Revenue Departments
Virginia	None The state tax commissioner has the authority to issue regulations to require LLCs to furnish copies of the federal partnership return and attach schedules or any other information that the tax commissioner deems necessary	15th day of 4th month following close of tax year	Department of Taxation Office of Customer Service P.O. Box 1115 Richmond, VA 23218-1115 (804) 367-8031 Forms: (804) 236-2760 **or** (804) 236-2761 www.tax.state.va.us
Washington	Form REV40 2406A, Combined Excise Tax Return	15th day of 3d month following close of tax year	Department of Revenue P.O. Box 12900 Olympia, WA 98508-2900 (360) 753-3181 Forms by fax: (800) 647-7706 www.wa.gov/dor
West Virginia	Form IT-165, West Virginia Partnership Return of Income WV/NRN-4, West Virginia Nonresident Income Tax Agreement	15th day of 3d month following close of tax year	Department of Tax & Revenue Taxpayer Services Division P.O. Box 3784 Charleston, WV 25337-3784 (304) 558-3333 **or** (304) 558-3632 Forms: (304) 344-2068 **or** (800) 422-2075 www.state.wv.us/taxrev
Wisconsin	Form 3, Wisconsin Partnership Return	15th day of 3d month following close of tax year	Department of Revenue P.O. Box 8933 Madison, WI 53708-8933 (608) 266-1607 Forms by fax: (608) 261-6229 www.dor.state.wi.us
Wyoming	None	No income tax	Department of Revenue Herschler Bldg., 2nd Floor West 122 West 25th Street Cheyenne, WY 82002-0110 (307) 777-7961 www.revenue.state.wy.us

[B] State Tax Returns for Resident and Nonresident Members

In most states, resident members are taxed on their allocable share of LLC income, gain, loss, credits, and deductions. Corporate members are taxed on their share, subject to either allocation or apportionment.

Nonresident members are generally taxed on their share of income attributed to the state. Corporate members are taxed on their entire share of income, subject to either allocation or apportionment.

The following table shows the tax forms the resident and nonresident members must file in each state.

State	Resident Members	Nonresident Members
Alabama	Form 40 for residents and part-year residents Form 20 (corporate members)	Form 40NR and Form 40NC (credits for both nonresidents and part-year residents Form 20C (corporate members) and Form 20S (S corporation members)
Alaska	N/A for individuals Form 04-611 (corporate members)	N/A for individuals Form 04-611 (corporate members)
Arizona	Form 140 Form 120 (corporate members)	Form 140NR for nonresidents Form 140PY for part-year residents Form 120 (corporate members)
Arkansas	Form AR 1000 Form AR 1100 (corporate members)	Form AR 1000 NR for nonresidents and part-year residents Form AR 1100 (corporate members)
California	Form 540 Form 100 (corporate members)	Form 540NR for nonresidents and part-year residents Form 100 (corporate members)
Colorado	Form 104 Form DR 112 (corporate members)	Form 104 PN for nonresidents and part-year residents Form DR 112 (corporate members)
Connecticut	Form CT-1040 Form CT-1120 (corporate members)	Form CT-1040 NRPY for nonresidents and part-year residents Form CT-1120 (corporate members)
Delaware	Form 200-01 Form 1100 (corporate members)	Form 200-02 for nonresidents and part-year residents Form 1100 (corporate members)
District of Columbia	Individual income tax return Corporate income tax return	Individual income tax return Corporate income tax return
Florida	N/A for individuals Form 1120 (corporate members)	N/A for individuals Form 1120 (corporate members)

State	Resident Members	Nonresident Members
Georgia	Form 500 Form 600 (corporate members)	Form 500 and Schedule 3 for nonresidents and part-year residents Form 600 (corporate members)
Hawaii	Form N-11 Form 1100 (corporate members)	Form N-15 for nonresidents and part- year residents Form 1100 (corporate members)
Idaho	Form 40 Form 41 (corporate members)	Form 43 for nonresidents and part-year residents Form 41 (corporate members)
Illinois	Form IL 1040 Form 1120 (corporate members)	Form 43 for nonresidents and part-year residents Form 1120 (corporate members)
Indiana	Form IT-40 Form IT-20 (corporate members)	Form IT-40PNR for nonresidents and part-year residents Form IT-20 (corporate members)

Iowa	Form IA 1040
	Form IA 1120 (corporate
	  members)
		Forms IA 1040 and IA 126 (NR and PY
		  credits) for nonresidents and part-
		  year residents
		Form IA 130 (Iowa out-of-state credit
		  calculation) for part-year residents
		  only
		Form IA 1120 (corporate members)

Kansas	Form K-40 Form 120 (corporate members)	Form K-40 and Schedule 3 for nonresidents and part-year residents Form 120 (corporate members)
Kentucky	Form 740 Form 720 (corporate members)	Form 740-NP for nonresidents and part- year residents Form 720 (corporate members)
Louisiana	Form IT-540 Form 120 (corporate members)	Form IT-540B Form 120 (corporate members)

Maine	Form ME 1040
	Form ME 1120 (corporate
	  members)
		Form ME 1040NR for nonresidents and
		  part-year residents
		Form ME 1120 (corporate members)

Maryland	Form 502 Form 500 (corporate members)	Form 505 for nonresidents and part-year residents Form 500 (corporate members)

Massachusetts	Form 1
	Form 355A/B (corporate
	  members)
		Form 1-NR/PY for nonresidents and
		  part-year residents
		Form 355A/B (corporate members)

Michigan	Form MI 1040
	Form C 8000 (corporate
	  members)
		Form MI 1040 and Schedule NR for
		  nonresidents and part-year residents
		Form C 8000 (corporate members)

Minnesota	Form M-1 Form M-4 (corporate members)	Forms M-1NR and M-1 for nonresidents and part-year residents Form M-4 (corporate members)

State	Resident Members	Nonresident Members
Mississippi	Form 80-200 Form 83-105 (corporate members)	Form 80-205 for nonresidents and part-year residents Form 83-105 (corporate members)
Missouri	Form MO 1040 Form 1120 (corporate members)	Form MO 1040 for nonresidents and part-year residents Form 1120 (corporate members)
Montana	Montana Individual Income Tax Return, Form 2 Form CLT-4 (corporate members)	Montana Individual Income Tax Return, Form 2 for nonresidents and part-year residents
Nebraska	Form 1040N Form 1120N (corporate members)	Form 1040N and Schedule III for nonresidents and part-year residents Form 1120N (corporate members)
Nevada	No income tax	
New Hampshire	No tax due from owners when the entity files a return	
New Jersey	Form NJ 1040 Form CBT100 (corporate members)	Form NJ 1040NR for nonresidents and part-year residents Form CBT100 (corporate members)
New Mexico	Form PIT-1 Form CIT-1 (corporate members)	Forms PIT-110 and PIT-1 for nonresidents and part-year residents CIT-1 (corporate members)
New York	Form IT-200 Form CT3 (corporate members)	Form IT-203 for nonresidents and part-year residents Form CT3 (corporate members)
New York City	Form NYS IT-200 Form 4 (corporate members)	Form IT-203 Form 4 (corporate members)
North Carolina	Form D 400 Form CD 405 (corporate members)	Form D 400 for nonresidents and part-year residents Form CD 405 (corporate members)
North Dakota	Form 37 and Schedule 2 Form 40 (corporate members)	Form 32 and Schedule 3 for nonresidents and part-year residents
Ohio	Form IT-1040 and OH-10 Form FT 1120 (corporate members)	Forms IT-1040 and OH-10 for nonresidents and part-year residents Form FT1120 (corporate members)
Oklahoma	Form 511 Form 512 (corporate members)	Form 511NR for nonresidents and part-year residents Form 512 (corporate members)
Oregon	Form 40 Form 20 (corporate members)	Form 40N for nonresidents Form 40P for part-year residents Form 20 (corporate members)
Pennsylvania	Form PA 40 and Schedule G, credit for taxes paid by Pennsylvania residents to other states Form PA 20 (corporate members)	Form PA 40 for nonresidents and part-year residents Form PA 20 (corporate members)

State	Resident Members	Nonresident Members
Rhode Island	Form RI 1040 Form RI 1120 (corporate members)	Form RI 1040 NR for nonresidents and part-year residents Form RI 1120 (corporate members)
South Carolina	Form SC 1040 Form SC 1120 (corporate members)	Form SC 1040 for nonresidents and part-year residents Form SC 1120 (corporate members)
South Dakota	No income tax	
Tennessee	Form INC 250 (tax only on dividends and interest)	Not taxed
Texas	No individual income tax Form 05000 (corporate members)	No tax
Utah	Forms TC-40 and TC-40A Form 20 (corporate members)	Forms TC-40 and TC-40A for nonresidents and part-year residents Form 20 (corporate members)
Vermont	Form IN-111 Form CO 411 (corporate members)	Forms IN-111 and IN-113 (income adjustment schedule) for nonresidents and part-year residents Form CO 411 (corporate members)
Virginia	Form 760, Schedule 1, contributions and authorized deductions	Form 763 NR for nonresidents Form 760 PY for part-year residents Form 500 (corporate members)
Washington	No tax	
West Virginia	Form IT-140 Form WC/CNT 112 (corporate members)	Form IT-140N/PY for nonresidents and part-year residents
		Form IT-140NRS for residents of Kentucky, Virginia, Pennsylvania, Maryland, and Ohio Form WC/CNT 112 (corporate members)
Wisconsin	Form 1 Form 4 (corporate members)	Form 1 for nonresidents and part-year residents Form 4 (corporate members)
Wyoming	No income tax	No income tax

[C]   Composite Return for Nonresident Members

Many states permit an LLC to file a composite return for nonresident members. A composite return is sometimes referred to as a group or block return.

The composite return is an informational return that reports the nonresident members' respective share of income, gain, losses, credits, and deductions. The return includes other information required by the state, such as the computation of the withholding or other taxes that the LLC must pay to the state with respect to the nonresident members' share of income. The composite return is similar to a Schedule K-1.

The composite return may be filed only for eligible members of the LLC. Normally, an eligible member is a person who resided outside of the state for the entire tax year and had no income from the state other than from the LLC. Some states require the member to consent to the election to file a composite return. Other states require the LLC to obtain consent from the state taxing authority before filing a composite return. An LLC may file the composite return on behalf of some or all of the eligible nonresident members.

The following table shows the states that permit a composite return.

State	Composite Return Allowed	Statutory Provisions
Alabama	Yes. Form IT:E3, Composite Return	Al. Code §10-8A-1108
Alaska	N/A	
Arizona	Yes. Form 140NR	Ariz. Individual Income Tax Rul. 97-1 (July 22, 1997) (cannot be filed by fewer than 10 members)
Arkansas	Yes. Form AR1000, Composite Return	Reg. §6.26-51-405, issued by the Ark. Director of the Dept. of Fin. & Admin.
California	Yes. Form 540NR; FTB Publication 1067, Guidelines for Filing a Group Form 540NR	Cal. Rev. & Tax Code §18535(d)
Colorado	Yes. Form 106 — Colorado State Partnership or S Corporation Return of Income and Composite Income Tax Return	Col. Rev. Stat. Ann §39-22-601(5)(d); *but see* Col. Rev. Stat. Ann §39-22-601(4.5), which permitted composite filings by LLCs, was repealed by HB 95-1061
Connecticut	Yes. Form CT-G, Connecticut Group Income Tax Return (LLC must have 10 or more qualified nonresident members) Form CT-2NA, Connecticut Nonresident Income Tax Agreement/Election to Be Included in a Group Return	Conn. Gen. Stat. Ann. §12-719(b)
Delaware	Yes. Form 200-02 NR (Non-Resident Delaware Income Tax Return or Composite Return)	
District of Columbia	N/A	
Florida	N/A	
Georgia	Yes. Form IT-CR, Composite Return for Nonresident Partners/Shareholders (all years)	Ga. Code Ann. §48-7-129(b)

State	Composite Return Allowed	Statutory Provisions
Hawaii	Yes	Instructions to Form N-20
Idaho	Yes (on return of LLC)	Idaho Code §63-3022L
Illinois	Yes. Form IL-1023-C, Composite Income and Replacement Tax Return	35 Ill. Comp. Stat §5/502(f); Ill. Admin. Code §100.5100(a)
Indiana	Yes. Schedule IT-65Comp, Partners' Composite Indiana Adjusted Gross Income Tax Return	Ind. Info. Bulletin #72 (June 1, 1993)
Iowa	Yes. Form IA 1040C, Composite Return	Iowa Code §422.13(5); Iowa Department of Revenue in Finance Reg. §701-48.1(422)
Kansas	Yes. Schedule M-KC, Composite Income Tax Schedule	Kan. Reg. §92-12-106
Kentucky	Yes	Revenue Circular 40C010 (LLC must have 15 or more non-resident members and receive permission from Revenue Cabinet to file combined return)
Louisiana	Yes	LAC 61:1:1401
Maine	Yes	36 M.R.S.A. §5192 (5); Me. Reg. Rule No. 805
Maryland	Yes	Md. Reg. §§03.04.07.05, 03.04.02.01B(5); Md. Admin. Release No. 6 (Oct. 1, 1992)
Massachusetts	Yes	Mass. Ltr. Rul. 1998-2 (Feb. 18, 1998)
Michigan	No	
Minnesota	Yes. Schedule M-KC, Corporate Income Tax Schedule	Minn. Stat. Ann. §289A.08(7)
Mississippi	Yes	Miss. State Tax Comm Reg. §901(E)
Missouri	Yes. The LLC must pay tax at a 6 percent tax rate on the income of nonresident members reported on the composite return; alternatively, the LLC may file an individual tax return on behalf of the nonresident member and pay tax at the 6 percent tax rate or the lesser exact amount	12 Mo. Code Regs. tit. 10-2.190(1)(A); Mo. State. Ann. §143.411(4)
Montana	Yes	Mont. Code Ann. §§15-30-1112, 1113; Mont. Admin. Reg. §42.15.702

State	Composite Return Allowed	Statutory Provisions
Nebraska	No	
Nevada	No state income tax	
New Hampshire	N/A	
New Jersey	Yes. Schedule NJ-1080-C	N.J. Dept. of Treas. Reg. §18:35-1.30
New Mexico	Yes	3NMAC 3.12.14
New York	Yes	N.Y. St. Dept. of Taxn. & Fin. Reg. §158.13
New York City	No	
North Carolina	Yes	N.C. Admin. Code §17:06B.3513(c)
North Dakota	Yes	N.D. Cent. Code §57-38-31.1; Income Tax Guideline: Composite Filing Method
Ohio	Yes. Form IT-4708, Annual Composite Income Tax Return for Investors in Pass-Through Entities	Ohio Tax Commr. R. 5703-7-03
Oklahoma	Yes. An LLC must pay the tax on the nonresident owner's share of income unless the nonresident shareholder files a consent to be taxed	Okla. Stat. Ann. tit. 18, §2049; Rule 710:50-19-1
Oregon	Yes	Or. Admin. R. 150-314.760 and instructions to Schedule MNR
Pennsylvania	Yes. Form PA-40 NRC, Nonresident Consolidated Income Tax Return	Instruction to Form PA-40NCR, Nonresident Consolidated Income Tax Return, and PA-65, Commonwealth of Pennsylvania Information Booklet for Partnerships
Rhode Island	No	
South Carolina	Yes. SC1040 (one individual tax return)	S.C. Code §12-6-5030(A)
South Dakota	No state income tax	
Tennessee	N/A	
Texas	N/A	
Utah	Yes. TC-65N, Schedule N	Utah Admin. Rule R865-9I-13
Vermont	Yes. BI-471, Vermont Business Income Tax Return (check Composite Return box and obtain approval to file a composite return)	Vt. Stat. Ann. tit. 32, §5920(b)

State	Composite Return Allowed	Statutory Provisions
Virginia	Yes	Va. Rule of the Commr., Va. Dept. of Taxn., P.D. 97-335 (Aug. 27, 1997)
Washington	No state income tax	
West Virginia	Yes. Form IT-140NCR, West Virginia Nonresident Composite Income Tax Return	W. Va. Code §11-21-51a
	Form WV/NRN-4, West Virginia Nonresident Income Tax Agreement	
Wisconsin	Yes. Form ICNP	Tax Bulletin No. 53, Department of Revenue, October 1997; Instructions to Form ICNP, Combined Wisconsin Partnership Form 3
Wyoming	No state income tax	

[D]   Annual Report

The third type of state filing is the annual report. Many states require an annual report. The annual report sets forth basic information, such as the address of the LLC, the registered agent for service of process, and the names of managers. Most states require a nominal fee. Some states use the annual report to report payment of the state franchise tax or annual registration fee.

The following table shows the annual reports that are required in each state and the District of Columbia:

State	Required	Comments	To Obtain and to File Forms
Alabama	Not required	Alabama Form DLL-2, Report of Domestic Limited Liability Company, must be filed; this is not an annual report, but an initial filing report	Secretary of State Business Div. P.O. Box 5616 Montgomery, AL 36103 Phone: (334) 242-7205 Fax: (334) 242-4993
Alaska	Required	Biennial registration	Department of Commerce & Economic Development Div. of Banking Securities & Corporations Corporations Section P.O. Box 110808 Juneau, AK 99811-0808 Phone: (907) 465-3520 Fax: (907) 465-5400

State	Required	Comments	To Obtain and to File Forms
Arizona	Not required		Arizona Corporation Comm. 1300 West Washington Phoenix, AZ 85007-2929 Phone: (602) 542-3135
Arkansas	Corporation and Limited Liability Company Franchise Tax Report		Secretary of State State Capitol, Rm. 256 Little Rock, AR 72201-1094 Phone: (501) 682-1010 Fax: (501) 682-3510
California	Form LLC-E012R, Statement of Information Renewal	Biennial registration	Secretary of State Limited Liability Company Div. 1500 11th St. P.O. Box 944228 Sacramento, CA 94244-2280 Phone: (916) 653-7244 Fax: (916) 653-4620
Colorado	Required	Preprinted form generated by secretary of state for each LLC at due date of filing	Secretary of State 1560 Broadway, Ste. 200 Denver, CO 80202 Phone: (303) 894-2200 Fax: (303) 894-7732
Connecticut	Required		Secretary of State 30 Trinity St. P.O. Box 150470 Hartford, CT 06115-0470 Phone: (860) 566-2739 Fax: (860) 566-6318
Delaware	Not required		Secretary of State Townsend Bldg. P.O. Box 898 Dover, DE 19903 Phone: (302) 739-4111 Fax: (302) 739-3811 E-mail: efreel@state.de.us
D.C.	Form LLC-AR, Annual Report for Foreign and Domestic Limited Liability Companies (LLC)		Department of Consumer & Regulatory Affairs Business Regulation Admin. Corporations Div. P.O. Box 37200 Washington, DC 20013-7200 Phone: (202) 727-7283 Fax: (202) 727-3582
Florida	Form 202, L.L.C. A/R, Limited Liability Company Annual Report		Division of Corporations Florida Dept. of State P.O. Box 6327 Tallahassee, FL 32314 Phone: (850) 487-6051 Fax: (850) 487-2214 E-mail: smortham@mafl.dos.state.fl.us

State	Required	Comments	To Obtain and to File Forms
Georgia	Required		Secretary of State Corporations Div. Suite 315, West Tower #2 Martin Luther King, Jr., Dr., SE Atlanta, GA 30334-1530 Phone: (404) 656-2817 Fax: (404) 657-5804
Hawaii	Required		Department of Commerce & Consumer Affairs Business Registration Div. P.O. Box 40 Honolulu, HI 96810 Phone: (808) 586-2727 (documents processing); (808) 586-2744 (administration) Fax: (808) 586-0231
Idaho	Not required		Secretary of State State Capitol, Rm. 203 700 W. Jefferson P.O. Box 83720 Boise, ID 83720-0080 Phone: (208) 334-2300 Fax: (208) 334-2282
Illinois	• Form LLC-50.1(D), Domestic Limited Liability Company Annual Report • Form LLC-50.1(F), Foreign Limited Liability Company Annual Report		Secretary of State 213 State House Springfield, IL 62756 Phone: (217) 782-2201 Fax: (217) 785-0358
Indiana	Not required		Secretary of State State House, Rm. 201 200 W. Washington St. Indianapolis, IN 46204 Phone: (317) 232-6576 Fax: (800) 726-8000
Iowa	Not required		Secretary of State State Capitol 1007 E. Grand Ave. Des Moines, IA 50319 Phone: (515) 281-5204 Fax: (515) 242-5952

State	Required	Comments	To Obtain and to File Forms
Kansas	Form LC, State of Kansas/ Domestic and Foreign Limited Liability Company Annual Report		Secretary of State Corporations Div. State Capitol Bldg., 2d Fl. 300 S.W. 10th Ave. Topeka, KS 66612-1594 Phone: (913) 296-4575 Fax: (913) 296-4570
Kentucky	Required		Secretary of State P.O. Box 718 Frankfort, KY 40602-0718 Phone: (502) 564-3490 Fax: (502) 564-5687
Louisiana	Required		Secretary of State P.O. Box 94125 Baton Rouge, LA 70804-9125 Phone: (225) 925-4704 Fax: (225) 925-4726
Maine	Required		Bureau of Corporations, Elections & Commissions Dept. of the Secretary of State 101 State House Station Augusta, ME 04333-0101 Phone: (207) 626-8400 Fax: (207) 287-8598
Maryland	Not required		Department of Assessments & Taxation Business Services & Finance Div., Rm. 809 301 W. Preston St. Baltimore, MD 21201 Phone: (410) 767-1350; (410) 767-1330 (corporate charter information) Fax: (410) 333-7097
Massachusetts	Required		Secretary of the Commonwealth Corporations Div. One Ashburton Pl., 17th Fl. Boston, MA 02108-1512 Phone: (617) 727-2850 Fax: (617) 742-4722
Michigan	Form C&S 2700, Annual Statement– Limited Liability Company	Preprinted form generated by Department of Consumer & Industry Services for each LLC at due date of filing	Department of Consumer & Industry Services Corporation, Securities and Land Development Bureau P.O. Box 30222 Lansing, MI 48909 Phone: (517) 373-2510 Fax: (517) 373-0727

State	Required	Comments	To Obtain and to File Forms
Minnesota	Minnesota Form #68, Biennial Registration for Minnesota or Foreign Limited Liability Companies, Minnesota Statutes Chapter 322B	Biennial registration	Secretary of State 180 State Office Bldg. 100 Constitution Ave. St. Paul, MN 55155-1299 Phone: (612) 296-2079 Fax: (612) 297-5844 E-mail: secretarystate@state. mn.us
Mississippi	Not required		Secretary of State 401 Mississippi St. P.O. Box 136 Jackson, MS 39205-0136 Phone: (601) 359-1633 Fax: (601) 354-6243
Missouri	Not required		Secretary of State 208 State Capitol P.O. Box 778 Jefferson City, MO 65102 Phone: (573) 751-3318 Fax: (573) 526-4903
Montana	Annual Limited Liability Company Report		Secretary of State State Capitol Bldg., Rm. 225 P.O. Box 202801 Helena, MT 59620-2801 Phone: (406) 444-3665 Fax: (406) 444-3976
Nebraska	Not required		Secretary of State State Capitol, Ste. 2300 P.O. Box 94608 Lincoln, NE 68509-4608 Phone: (402) 471-2554 Fax: (402) 471-3237
Nevada	Annual List of Managers or Members		Secretary of State 101 N. Carson St., No. 3 Carson City, NV 89701-4786 Phone: (702) 687-5203 Fax: (702) 687-3471
New Hampshire	Form LLC-8, Annual Report		Secretary of State State House, Rm. 204 107 N. Main St. Concord, NH 03301-4989 Phone: (603) 271-3242 Fax: (603) 271-6316

State	Required	Comments	To Obtain and to File Forms
New Jersey	Not required		State of New Jersey Dept. of State P.O. Box 450 Trenton, NJ 08625 Phone: (609) 984-1900 Fax: (609) 292-9897
New Mexico	Not required		State Corporations Commission Corporation Dept. P.O. Box 1269 Santa Fe, NM 87504-1269 Phone: (505) 827-3600 Fax: (505) 827-3634
New York	Required	Biennial statement	State of New York Dept. of State Bur. of Corporations 41 State St. Albany, NY 12231-0001 Phone: (518) 473-2492 Fax: (518) 474-4765
North Carolina	Required		Secretary of State P.O. Box 29622 Raleigh, NC 27626-0622 Phone: (919) 807-2225 Fax: (919) 807-2039
North Dakota	Required	Preprinted form generated by secretary of state for each LLC at due date of filing	Secretary of State State Capitol, 1st Fl. 600 E. Blvd. Ave., Dept. 108 Bismarck, ND 58505-0500 Phone: (701) 328-2900 Fax: (701) 328-2992 E-mail: sos@pioneer.state.nd.us
Ohio	Not required		Secretary of State 30 East Broad St., 14th Fl. Columbus, OH 43266-0418 Phone: (614) 466-2655 Fax: (614) 644-0649
Oklahoma	Required		Secretary of State State Capitol Bldg., Rm. 101 2300 N. Lincoln Blvd. Oklahoma City, OK 73105-4897 Phone: (405) 521-3911 Fax: (405) 521-3771
Oregon	Required		Secretary of State Corporation Div. 255 Capitol St. NE, Ste. 151 Salem, OR 97310-1327 Phone: (503) 986-1523 Fax: (503) 986-1616

State	Required	Comments	To Obtain and to File Forms
Pennsylvania	Required		Secretary of the Commonwealth Dept. of State 302 N. Capitol Bldg. Harrisburg, PA 17120-0029 Phone: (717) 787-7630 Fax: (717) 787-1734
Rhode Island	Form LLC-19, Limited Liability Company Annual Report		Secretary of State Corporations Div. 100 North Main St. Providence, RI 02903-1335 Phone: (401) 222-3040 Fax: (401) 277-1356
South Carolina	State of South Carolina Annual Report, Limited Liability Company		Secretary of State Wade Hampton Bldg. P.O. Box 11350 Columbia, SC 29211 Phone: (803) 734-2170 Fax: (803) 734-2164
South Dakota	Required		Secretary of State State Capitol 500 E. Capitol Ave., Ste. 204 Pierre, SD 57501-5070 Phone: (605) 773-4845 Fax: (605) 773-6580
Tennessee	Required		Department of State Division of Business Services 312 Eighth Avenue North 6th Floor, William R. Snodgrass Tower Nashville, TN 37243 Phone: (615) 741-0537 and (615) 741-2286
Texas	Form 05-102, Texas Franchise Tax Public Information Report		Secretary of State Statutory Filings Div. Corporations Section P.O. Box 13697 Austin, TX 78711-3697 Phone: (512) 463-5701 Fax: (512) 475-2761
Utah	Required		Department of Commerce Division of Corporations and Commercial Code Heber M. Wells Building 160 East 300 South, Second Floor P.O. Box 146705 Salt Lake City, UT 84114-6705 Phone: (801) 530-4849 Fax: (801) 538-1557 E-mail: owalker@state.ut.us

State	Required	Comments	To Obtain and to File Forms
Vermont	Required		Secretary of State Corporations Division Heritage 1 Building 81 River Street, Drawer 09 Montpelier, VT 05609-1104 Phone: (802) 828-2386 Fax: (802) 828-2496 E-mail: jmilne@sec.state.vt.us
Virginia	Not required		Commonwealth of Virginia State Corporation Commission P.O. Box 1197 Richmond, VA 23218-1197 Phone: (804) 786-2441 Fax: (804) 371-0017
Washington	Required		Secretary of State Corporations Div. 2nd Fl., Republic Bldg. 505 E. Union Ave. P.O. Box 40234 Olympia, WA 98504-0234 Phone: (360) 753-7121 Fax: (360) 586-5629
West Virginia	Required		Secretary of State Bldg. 1, Ste. 157K 1900 Kanawha Blvd. E. Charleston, WV 25305-0770 Phone: (304) 558-6000 Fax: (304) 558-0900
Wisconsin	Not required	Foreign LLCs must file an annual report on Form 518, Annual Report; domestic LLCs are not required to file	Department of Financial Institutions Div. of Corporate & Consumer Affairs P.O. Box 7846 Madison, WI 53707-7846 Phone: (608) 261-9555
Wyoming	Required		Secretary of State State Capitol Bldg. Cheyenne, WY 82002-0020 Phone: (307) 777-5333 Fax: (307) 777-6217

23

State Tax Laws

§23.01   OVERVIEW

All 50 states and the District of Columbia have enacted laws authorizing the formation of LLCs.

In most states, the LLC is a pass-through entity for tax purposes. However, several of the states impose a franchise or entity-level tax. Other states impose a withholding tax, usually on the distributive shares of income of nonresident members. The following chart shows the states that impose an entity-level tax on LLCs classified as partnerships.

State Franchise of Entity-Level Tax

State	No franchise tax	Franchise or entity-level tax
Alabama	x	5% tax on nonresident members included in composite return
Alaska		$100 per year tax on domestic LLCs and $200 per year tax on foreign LLCs.
Arizona	x	
Arkansas		Annual $103 franchise tax. The LLC must pay taxes at a flat 7% tax rate on the net taxable income attributable to Arkansas for nonresident members who are included in a composite return or block filing.
California		• LLCs that are classified as partnerships must pay an $800 annual franchise tax. The LLC must also pay a gross receipts tax based on "total income." The tax ranges from $900 for total income between $250,000 and $500,000 to $11,790 for total income over $5 million. The LLC must payall taxes attributable to income of nonresident members unless it obtains agreements from the nonresident members to file returns and pay all taxes, which agreements must be filed with the LLC return. • LLCs that are classified as corporations must pay the California franchise tax. The tax is 8.84% for LLCs other than banks and financial LLCs. There is a minimum $800 annual franchise tax on LLCs classified as corporations.
Colorado	x	An LLC with nonresident members must either file a nonresident partners agreement for each nonresident member or pay a 4.63% tax on the nonresident member's distributive share of income.[1]
Connecticut	x	A single member LLC that is classified as a disregarded entity must pay the business entity tax of $250.
Delaware		$100 annual tax on domestic and foreign LLCs.
D.C.		9.975% tax on D.C. source income earned by unincorporated businesses.
Florida	x	Prior to July 1, 1998: Greater of 5.5% artificial entity tax or 3.3% alternative minimum tax.
Georgia	x	4% withholding tax on distributions to nonresident members, subject to exceptions.
Hawaii		$100 fee per member per year.
Idaho	x	An Idaho LLC is subject to the Idaho income tax if its income is not fully distributed to the members. LLCs are taxed at the corporate rate of 7.6 percent on undistributed income. The LLC is also taxed on nonresident income if the LLC derives income from Idaho sources and the nonresident members do not file the required returns. The tax rate is the corporate tax rate of 7.6 percent on the nonresident members' income. The permanent building excise tax also applies to such income.

§23.01   [1] Colo. Rev. Stat. Ann. §39-22-601(5)(e).

State	No franchise tax	Franchise or entity-level tax
Illinois		1.5% replacement tax.
Indiana	x	An LLC must withhold 3.4% of the distributive share of Indiana source income for nonresidents.
Iowa	x	An LLC must withhold tax on the payment of income to nonresidents.
Kansas		Franchise tax of $1 per $1,000 of net capital accounts located or used in Kansas.
Kentucky	x	
Louisiana	x	
Maine	x	LLC financial institutions are taxed at the entity level at a rate of 1% of Maine net income and $0.08 per $1,000 of Maine assets at the end of the tax year.
Maryland	x	4.8% withholding tax on nonresident members' distributive shares of Maryland income.
Massachusetts	x	
Michigan		Single business tax (SBT) of 1.8% (for tax years ending 12/31/2003) of tax base.
Minnesota		• Minimum fee from $100 to $5,000 if amount specified on Schedule A of return is over $500,000. • 8.5% withholding tax on nonresident members' distributive shares of income.
Mississippi	x	5% withholding tax on net income allocated to all members; if the LLC does not withhold, the LLC and managers are personally liable for personal income taxes that the members should have paid on their distributive shares of income.
Missouri	x	6% withholding required on distributive shares of income of nonresident members.
Montana	x	
Nebraska	x	6.68% withholding tax on share of income from Nebraska sources of each nonresident member if the member does not file Form 12N with the LLC.
Nevada	x	$25 per equivalent full-time employee working in Nevada during the quarter.
New Hampshire		5% tax on dividends and interest; 8.5% on business profits; .75% on taxable enterprise tax base if tax base is greater than $50,000 or gross business receipts exceed $100,000.
New Jersey	x	An LLC must pay the corporate business (income) taxes at the highest marginal tax rate on a foreign member's allocable share of New Jersey income if it fails to obtain the consent of the member to New Jersey taxation of that income. LLC must also pay 6.37% tax (2001 rates) on income from nonresident members who are included in a composite return.

State	No franchise tax	Franchise or entity-level tax
New Mexico	x	7.9% tax on any nonresident individual member's income allocated to New Mexico if the member elects to be included in a block return.
New York		$50 annual fee per member. The fee cannot be less than $325 or more tha $10,000.
North Carolina	x	Manager must pay taxes owed by individual nonresident members on such members' shares of LLC income. The tax rate is from 6 to 8.25% of each nonresident's share of North Carolina taxable income.
North Dakota	x	
Ohio	x	An LLC must withhold tax at a 5% rate on the distributive share of income for nonresident members and pay an 8.5% entity level tax unless the LLC files a composite return for nonresident members or complies with certain other exceptions.
Oklahoma	x	
Oregon	x	
Pennsylvania		Capital stock and franchise tax imposed on all LLCs except for restricted professional companies. $300 fee per Pennsylvania member. 2.8% withholding tax on income allocable to nonresident members. Effective, January 1, 1998, the state corporate income tax does not apply to LLCs classified as partnerships for federal tax purposes, but such LLCs remain liable for the capital stock and franchise tax.
Rhode Island		$250 minimum tax; LLC must pay tax of nonresident members who fail to file returns and pay applicable state taxes.
South Carolina	x	5% withholding tax on nonresident members' distributive shares of income.
South Dakota		$50 annual tax. The LLC must also pay additional fees of up to $16,000 based on the value of agreed contributions by members.
Tennessee		Franchise tax of .25% of net worth and excise tax of 6% on Tennessee net earnings; "Hall Income Tax" of 6% on dividends, bond interest, and similar instruments. $50 annual fee per member; minimum fee of $300; maximum fee of $3,000.
Texas		Franchise tax based on greater of .25% of net taxable capital or 4.5% of earned surplus.
Utah	x	7% tax rate on Utah income attributable to nonresident members included in composite filing.
Vermont		$250 minimum tax. An LLC must also withhold estimated taxes for each nonresident member. The estimated tax rate is 9.5 percent for 2001 on income allocated or distributed to the nonresident member as reported on the federal Schedule K-1.
Virginia		Annual registration fee of $50.

State	No franchise tax	Franchise or entity-level tax
Washington		Business and occupation tax from .011% to 3.3% of gross income, less specified deductions and exemptions.
West Virginia		Greater of $50 or .70% of capital accounts (capital accounts are the balances of members' capital accounts as set forth on IRS Form 1065). LLC must also withhold at 4% rate on each nonresident member's distributive share of income unless the member provides the LLC with Form WV/NRW-4, West Virginia Nonresident Income Tax Agreement.
Wisconsin		Temporary recycling surcharge tax in 2001 if LLC has nonfarm income of $4,000,000 or more or farm income of $1,000 or more; surcharge is the greater of $25 or 0.4345% of net business income up to a maximum of $9,800.
Wyoming		Annual tax of $100.

Most states have two types of LLC laws: the enabling legislation for the formation, operation, and dissolution of the LLC and the tax laws.[2] The following chart sets forth the citations to the applicable tax laws in each state.

State LLC Tax Laws

State	LLLC Tax Laws
Alabama	Ala. Code §§10-12-8b, 40-18-1(11), 40-18-24; Ala. Admin. Code Reg. §§810-3-24-.01 to 810-3-24-.05
Alaska	Alaska Stat. §§43.20.012, 43.20.030, 43.20.051
Arizona	Ariz. Rev. Stat. Ann. §§4-32-1313, 29-857, 43-141 to 43-1413; CTR 97-2
Arkansas	Ark. Code Ann. §§26-51-102(4), 26-51-802; Ark. Director of the Dept. of Fin. & Admin. Reg. §§6.26-51-101, -102, -405
California	Cal. Rev. & Tax. Code §§17087.6, 17220(b)(3), 17941, 17942, 17943, 18535(d), 18633.5(e), 18662, 18666, 23091, 23092, 23093
Colorado	Colo. Rev. Stat. Ann. §§39-22-103, -201, -303
Connecticut	Conn. Gen. Stat. Ann. §§12-701, 34-113
Delaware	Del. Code Ann. tit. 6, §§18-1105, -1107; tit. 30, §§1143-1145
D.C.	D.C. Code Ann. §§10-215, 29-1074, 47-1808.6
Florida	Fla. Stat. Ann. §§608.471, 220.02, 220.03(e), 608.405
Georgia	Ga. Code Ann. §§14-11-203, -212, -1104; Ga. Dept. of Rev. Reg. §560-7-3.08
Hawaii	Tax Information Release No. 97-4
Idaho	Idaho Code §§63-3006A, 63-3022L(1), (2), 63-3030(a)(9); Idaho State Tax Comm. R. 35.01.01.107

[2] See Chapter 2 supra for discussion of, and citations to, the enabling legislation in each state.

State	LLLC Tax Laws
Illinois	35 Ill. Comp. Stat. 180/5-1, 5/201, 5/501, 5/1501
Indiana	Ind. Code Ann. §§6-3-4-10, 6-3-4-11, 6-3-4-12, 23-18-6-0.5
Iowa	Iowa Code Ann. §§422.16.4, 422.32.4; Iowa Dept. of Rev. & Fin. R. 701-45.1(422) to 701-45.4(422)
Kansas	Kan. Stat. Ann. §§17-76, 138, 17-76, 139(c), 79-32,130, 79-32,131, 79-32,133
Kentucky	Ky. Rev. Stat. Ann. §§141.206, 141.208(2)
Louisiana	La. Rev. Stat. Ann. §§12:1368, 47:201 to 47:220
Maine	Me. Rev. Stat. Ann. tit. 31, §761; tit. 36, §5180
Maryland	Md. Code Ann., Corps. & Assns. §§10-102, -104, -210, -207
Massachusetts	Mass. Gen. Laws Ann. ch. 62 §17
Michigan	Mich. Comp. Laws Ann. §208.3(2)
Minnesota	Minn. Stat. Ann. §§289A.08(7), 289A.12(3), 290.01(3b), 290.06(22h), 290.92(4b), 322B.11; Minn. Dept. of Rev. Rs. 8038.3000, 8031.0100
Mississippi	Miss. Code Ann. §§79-29-112, 27-7-25; Miss. State Tax Comm. Reg. §901
Missouri	Mo. Ann. Stat. §§347.187.2, 143.411.5, 143.581, 143.401; Mo. Dept. of Rev. R. 10-2.1901
Montana	Mont. Admin. R. 42.23.701 to .703; Mont. Stat. Ann. §15-30-133
Nebraska	Neb. Rev. Stat. §§21-2633, 77-2734.01, 21-2612, 77-2727 to 2729; Neb. Admin. R. & Regs. §§25.001 to 25-07
Nevada	(no taxes)
New Hampshire	N.H. Rev. Stat. Ann. §§77:3.I(b), 77:3-a, 77:4, 77:15, 77:16, 77-A:6, 77-E; N.H. Dept. of Rev. Admin. Reg. §902.06
New Jersey	N.J. Stat. Ann. §§42:B-69, 54A:2-2, 54A:5-4, 54A:8-6; N.J. Dept. of Treas. Reg. §18:35-1
New Mexico	N.M. Admin. Code §§15.100.8, 3.11.12
New York	N.Y. Tax Law §§2.5, 2.6, 503, 601-A(f), 617, 632, 658(c)
North Carolina	N.C. Gen. Stat. §§57C-10-06, 105-114(b)(2), 105-134.1(7a), (10a), 105-163; N.C. Admin. Code Rule §17.06B.3501 to .3529
North Dakota	N.D. Cent. Code §§57-38-07, 57-38-08
Ohio	Ohio Rev. Code Ann. §§5733.01(E), 5733.04(H)
Oklahoma	Okla. Stat. Ann. tit. 68, §§202(j), 2368.D, 2363; Okla. Admin. R. 710:50-19-1
Oregon	Or. Rev. Stat. §§63.810, 63.787, 314.710 to 314.727
Pennsylvania	72 Pa. Cons. Stat. Ann. §§7301(n.0), 7306, 7401(1); Dept. of Rev. Reg. §§107.1 to 107.6
Rhode Island	R.I. Gen. Laws §§7-16-67, 7-16-73
South Carolina	S.C. Code Ann. §§12-6-600, 33-44-201, 12-2-25(A), 12-6-630

State	LLLC Tax Laws
South Dakota	S.D. Codified Laws Ann. §§47-34-5, 47-34-54, 10-43-1(1)
Tennessee	Tenn. Code Ann. §67-4-2004(16); Tenn. Code Ann. tit. 48, chs. 201-248, 211-101, 247-103
Texas	Tex. Tax Code Ann. §171.101(B), 171.002
Utah	Utah Code Ann. §§48-2c-117, 59-10-507, 59-10-801, 59-10-301 to 59-10-303
Vermont	Vt. Stat. Ann. tit. 32, §§5820, 5914, 5920, 5921
Virginia	Va. Code Ann. §§13.1-1005, 13.1-1069, 58.1-301; 23 Va. Admin. Code 10-130-10 to 10-130-265
Washington	Wash. Rev. Code Ann. §31B-2-201
West Virginia	W. Va. Code §§11-13A-2(b)(8), 11-23-3(b)(2)(C), 11-23-6(b)(3), 11-21-3(b), 11-21-71a; W. Va. State Tax Dept. Reg. §§3.2, 58.2
Wisconsin	Dept. of Rev. Pub. No. 119
Wyoming	Wyo. Stat. §§17-15-132(a)(vi), 71.04(3)

§23.02   ALABAMA

Alabama adopted the Alabama Limited Liability Company Act effective October 1, 1993.[1]

[A]   State Tax Classification

The Alabama tax classification of a limited liability company follows the federal classification.[2] An LLC is classified as a "subchapter K entity" taxable as a partnership if the LLC is classified as a partnership under federal law.[3] The LLC may elect to be classified as a corporation instead of a partnership.

Effective January 1, 1997, a single-member LLC is classified for Alabama corporate and personal tax purposes in the same manner that the LLC is classified for federal tax purposes under the check-the-box regulations.[4] Prior to 1997, a single-member LLC was classified as a partnership or corporation.[5]

§23.02   [1] S.B. 549, 1993 Ala. Acts; Ala. Code §§10-12-1 to 10-12-61.

[2] Ala. Code §10-12-8(b).

[3] Ala. Code §§10-12-8(b), §40-18-1(11). See Rev. Proc. No. 97-002, Ala. Dept. of Rev., Ala. St. Tax Rep. (CCH) ¶200-674 (July 23, 1997), which states that Alabama LLCs formed before 1996 are classified under federal check-the-box regulations for all years preceding 1997 and that Alabama will not conform to the LLC's federal classification for tax years after 1996 unless the LLC otherwise elects.

[4] Rev. Proc. No. 98-001, Ala. Dept. of Rev. (Mar. 16, 1998); Rev. Ruls. Nos. 01-003 and 01-009 (regarding an out-of-state single-member LLC that did business in Alabama). See also Rev. Rul. No. 01-007, in which the Alabama Department Revenue determined that it would follow the federal procedures regarding withholding by a single-member LLC. The LLC may separately calculate, report, and pay to the Department its withholding obligations under its own name and taxpayer identification number or under the owner's name and taxpayer identification number. The owner remains ultimately responsible to the Department for payment of the withholding taxes.

[5] See also Rev. Proc. No. 97-001, Ala. Dept. of Rev., Ala. St. Tax Rep. (CCH) ¶200-674 (Feb. 21, 1997), which states that a domestic or foreign limited liability company of two or more members is classified

[B] Taxation of LLC and Members

An LLC is not subject to the Alabama income tax. There is no franchise tax. Each member's share of the adjusted gross income or loss of the LLC is taxable to the member, whether or not distributed by the LLC.[6]

[C] Nonresident Members

Nonresident members are taxed on their distributive shares of income attributable to Alabama.[7] After 2000, each nonresident member must sign a consent form agreeing to file an Alabama tax return and pay Alabama taxes on income allocated to the member. The LLC must obtain an agreement from nonresident members to file an annual corporate or personal income tax return and pay the applicable state taxes. The LLC must pay taxes on behalf of the nonresident member if it fails to obtain the consent form.

The LLC must file a composite return on behalf of nonresident members if it has one or more nonresident members at any time during the tax year. The composite return must contain information regarding each member's share of income, deductions, and losses. The return must include the "composite payment" of tax on behalf of nonresident members or the agreements by the members to pay Alabama taxes. The composite payment on behalf of members who fail to sign an agreement is the highest marginal Alabama income tax rate for individual members or the highest marginal Alabama corporate income tax rate for corporations.

If a nonresident member signs an agreement to pay taxes, but does not pay the required taxes by the due date, the LLC must pay the taxes within 60 days after notice and demand from the Alabama Department of Revenue.

All of the income or loss of an Alabama LLC that does business solely outside of the state will be allocated back to Alabama if the LLC's activities are not taxable outside of Alabama.[8]

An LLC doing business in Alabama and at least one other state must allocate and apportion its income pursuant to the Alabama apportionment tax laws. The allocation and apportionment provisions do not apply if the LLC is not subject to income tax in any state other than Alabama or if it has income or loss from only one state. In those circumstances, assuming Alabama has nexus, the income or loss from the foreign state income is thrown back into Alabama.

---

as a partnership unless the LLC elects classification as a corporation under the federal check-the-box regulations and that the Alabama Department of Revenue will not follow the federal classification of single-member LLCs.

[6] Ala. Admin. Code Reg. §§810-3-24-01(3)(a), 810-3-24-03.

[7] Ala. Admin. Code Reg. §810-3-24-01(3)(b).

[8] Letter from Alabama Department of Revenue and Michael E. Mason to Bruce P. Ely, BNA Daily Tax Report, H-1 (Jan. 25, 1999).

[D]   Tax Returns

An Alabama LLC must file an annual tax return on Form 65, Partnership/ Limited Liability Company Return of Income. The form must be filed on or before the fifteenth day of the fourth month following the close of the LLC's fiscal year. It must be mailed to the Alabama Department of Revenue, Income Tax Division, P.O. Box 327441, Montgomery, AL 36132-7441.

The LLC must attach IRS Form 1065 to the state return. Failure to file Form 1065 constitutes improper preparation, subjecting the return to treatment as a delinquent return.

Form 65 must include the names, addresses, and Social Security numbers of the members who are entitled to shares of net income, and the distributive share for each member, whether or not distributed. The names and addresses of the individual members, including nonresidents of Alabama, and each member's share of adjusted gross income must be entered on Schedule K to Form 1065.

A foreign limited liability company maintaining a home office outside of Alabama and doing business within and without the state of Alabama must file Form 1065 and attach a rider showing the income, deductions, and net income attributable to Alabama. The allocation must be made using either the direct accounting method or the proration method corresponding to the books and accounting system maintained by the LLC. If the direct accounting method is used, the LLC must first obtain approval from the Alabama Department of Revenue. If the proration method is used, Alabama net income must be determined as provided for multistate corporations.[9]

If the LLC's books and accounts are kept on the accrual basis, the LLC must report all income accrued even though it has not actually been received or entered on the books. All income received or constructively received, such as bank interest, and all expenses actually paid must also be reported.

An Alabama LLC is not allowed a deduction for net operating losses.

One member of the LLC must sign the return. A paid preparer must also sign the return and complete the required return information.

Returns for a calendar year must be filed on or before April 15 following the close of a calendar year. Returns for a fiscal year must be filed on or before the fifteenth day of the fourth month following the close of the fiscal year. If the return cannot be filed by the due date, the LLC must file Form 4868A, Application for Extension, with the Alabama Department of Revenue. The federal extension form is not accepted. An extension will not be granted for more than six months.

The LLC must advise all members of their responsibility to file Alabama income tax returns reporting their shares of income and deductions from the LLC. Individual Alabama residents must file Form 40. Nonresident members must use Form 40NR. Corporations that are members of the LLC must file Form 20C or Form 20S.

---

[9] See Ala. Code §40-18-31.

[E] Allocations

Income, deductions, losses, and credits must be allocated among members in the manner provided in the operating agreement. If there is no provision in the operating agreement, income, deductions, losses, and credits must be allocated to members on the basis of the pro rata value of contributions made by each member to the LLC (less any contributions returned).[10]

[F] Sales Taxes

The withdrawal of inventory is subject to Alabama sales taxes. A corporation cannot avoid the sales tax by setting up a wholly owned LLC and selling the inventory to the LLC for resale. The sale for resale exception does not apply, since a wholly owned subsidiary LLC is a disregarded entity that is treated as a separate branch or division of the parent corporation.[11]

[G] Annual Report

Alabama does not require foreign or domestic LLCs to file annual reports.

[H] Filing Fees

The filing fees in Alabama are as follows:[12]

Articles of organization	$75
Foreign LLC registration application	$75
Annual fee	$ 0

[I] References

M. Sargent & W. Schwidetzky, Limited Liability Company Handbook, Law — Sample Documents — Forms, §4.02, Alabama Form of Operating Agreement (1995-1996 ed.).

---

[10] Ala. Code §10-12-28.
[11] Rev. Rul. No. 98-05, Ala. Dept. of Rev. (June 18, 1998).
[12] Ala. Code §10-12-60.

§23.03   ALASKA

Alaska adopted the Alaska Limited Liability Act effective July 1, 1995.[1]

[A]   State Tax Classification

Alaska classifies an LLC in the same manner that the LLC is classified for federal tax purposes.

[B]   Taxation of LLC and Members

Alaska does not tax LLCs that are classified as partnerships for federal tax purposes. Corporate members of an LLC must pay the regular corporate tax on their distributive shares of income from the LLC. There is no Alaska income tax on individual members or on their distributive shares of income from an LLC.[2]

[C]   Tax Returns

Alaska LLCs and foreign LLCs doing business in Alaska must file Alaska returns consistent with their federal tax status.

An LLC that is classified as a partnership, but that has no corporate members, is not required to file a return or report.[3] This rule was effective on July 1, 1995.

An LLC with one or more corporate members must follow the instructions applicable to partnerships with corporate partners. The LLC must submit the following portions of the LLC's federal tax return on Form 1065:[4]

- A copy of the signed Form 1065, pages 1-4, with "Alaska" marked on the top of page 1
- A copy of Schedule K-1 for each corporate partner only

An LLC classified as a corporation for federal income tax purposes must file an Alaska corporate tax return on Form 04-611, Corporation Net Income Tax Return. Form 04-611 is the standard Alaska corporate tax return designed to accommodate any taxpayer, including the most complex filings under the water's edge method. The standard form must be used whenever the LLC has a taxable nexus or business activity outside of Alaska or is a member of an affiliated group. The short form, Form 04-611SF, is designed for taxpayers with less complex filing

---

§23.03   [1] H.B. 420, ch. 99, 1994 Alaska Sess. Laws, Alaska Stat. §§10-50-010 to 10-50-995.

[2] Alaska Stat. §43.20.012.

[3] Instructions to Alaska Corporation Net Income Tax Return Form 04-611, p. 3 (Corporate Tax Booklet) (rev. 12/98).

[4] Alaska Stat. §§43.20.030, 43.20.051.

requirements. The short form is available to LLCs that conduct business only in Alaska and that are not members of an affiliated group.

[D]   Biennial Report

An Alaska LLC must file a biennial report on or before January 2 of the filing year.[5]

[E]   Filing Fees

The filing fees in Alaska are as follows:

Articles of organization	$350
Foreign LLC registration application	$250
Biennial registration	$100

§23.04   ARIZONA

Arizona adopted the Arizona Limited Liability Company Act effective September 30, 1992.[1] Professional LLCs are generally treated the same as other LLCs.[2]

[A]   State Tax Classification

Arizona classifies an LLC in the same manner that the LLC is classified for federal tax purposes. Arizona LLCs and foreign LLCs doing business in Arizona are classified as partnerships for Arizona income tax purposes unless classified as corporations or sole proprietorships for federal tax purposes.[3]

The Arizona Department of Revenue issued the following rulings regarding state tax classifications:

- The federal tax classification of a limited liability company or other entity under the federal check-the-box regulations determines the LLC's classification for Arizona tax purposes.[4]
- The state classification of a single-member LLC follows the federal classification. If the single-member LLC is classified as a corporation for federal

---

[5] Alaska Stat. §§10.50-750 to 10.50-765.

§23.04 [1] Ch. 113, §2, 1992 Ariz. Sess. Laws; Ariz. Rev. Stat. Ann. §§29-601 to 29-857.

[2] Ariz. Rev. Stat. Ann. §§29-841, 29-846.

[3] Ariz. Rev. Stat. Ann. §29-857.

[4] Ariz. Corp. Tax Rul., CTR 97-1, Ariz. Dept. of Rev., Ariz. St. Tax Rep. (CCH) ¶300-240 (July 22, 1997); Ariz. Partnership Tax Rul., PTR 97-1, Ariz. Dept. of Rev., Ariz. St. Tax Rep. (CCH) ¶300-242 (July 22, 1997).

income tax purposes, the LLC must report its income to Arizona as a corporation. If a single-member LLC is classified as a corporation for federal income tax purposes and makes a valid federal election to be taxed as an S corporation, the LLC must report its income to Arizona as an S corporation. If a single-member LLC is disregarded as an entity separate from its owner for federal income tax purposes, the LLC's income will be included in the Arizona tax return of its owner.[5]

- The classification of an LLC for Arizona income tax purposes applies retroactively from December 31, 1996. It also applies retroactively to LLCs that determined their federal tax classifications under the check-the-box regulations before the effective date of the Arizona Limited Liability Company Act.[6]

[B] Taxation of LLC and Members

There is no tax on an LLC that is classified as a partnership for federal tax purposes. The LLC is treated as a pass-through entity.[7] Members of the LLC are taxed on their distributive shares of income, whether or not distributed.[8]

[C] Tax Returns

An Arizona LLC that is classified as a partnership for federal tax purposes must file Arizona Form 165. The LLC's income is included in the Arizona tax returns of its members.[9]

An Arizona LLC that is classified as a corporation, including a single-member LLC, must report its income to Arizona as a corporation on Arizona Form 120.

An Arizona LLC that is classified as a corporation for federal income tax purposes and that makes a valid federal election to be taxed as an S corporation must report its income to Arizona on Arizona Form 120S.

The returns for LLCs that are classified as partnerships are due by the fifteenth day of the fourth month following the close of the tax year. This is April 15 in the case of a calendar year return. If an LLC has filed an extension, the LLC must attach a copy of the completed federal Form 1065 and supporting schedules to

---

[5] Ariz. Corp. Tax Rul., CTR 97-2, Ariz. Dept. of Rev., Ariz. St. Tax Rep. (CCH) ¶300-244 (Aug. 8, 1997); Ariz. Partnership Tax Rul., PTR 97-2, Ariz. Dept. of Rev., Ariz. St. Tax Rep. (CCH) ¶300-247 (Aug. 8, 1997).

[6] Ariz. Corp. Tax Rul., CTR 97-2, Ariz. Dept. of Rev., Ariz. St. Tax Rep. (CCH) ¶300-244 (Aug. 8, 1997); Ariz. Partnership Tax Rul., PTR 97-2, Ariz. Dept. of Rev., Ariz. St. Tax Rep. (CCH) ¶300-247 (Aug. 8, 1997).

[7] Ariz. Rev. Stat. Ann. §29-857.

[8] Ariz. Rev. Stat. Ann. §43-1412.

[9] Ariz. Corp. Tax Rul., CTR 97-2, Ariz. Dept. of Rev., Ariz. St. Tax Rep. (CCH) ¶300-244 (Aug. 8, 1997); Ariz. Partnership Tax Rul., PTR 97-2, Ariz. Dept. of Rev., Ariz. St. Tax Rep. (CCH) ¶300-247 (Aug. 8, 1997).

the Arizona return. The return must be filed with the Arizona Department of Revenue, P.O. Box 29079, Phoenix, AZ 85038-9079.

The members' shares of income from the LLC are reported on Schedule K-1NR to Arizona Form 165. The LLC is required to adjust its federal income to an Arizona basis. Line 3 of Arizona Form 165 Schedule K-1NR is the member's distributive share of that adjustment. This amount is reported on the member's Arizona tax return.

One of the members of the LLC must sign the return. When someone other than a member or employee of the LLC prepares a return, the preparer must also sign the return.

The LLC may apply for an Arizona extension by filing a completed Form 120EXT by the original due date of the return. The LLC can substitute a valid federal extension for an Arizona extension. Composite return filers must use Arizona Form 204 to obtain an extension.

The LLC must maintain books and records substantiating the information reported on the return and keep these documents for inspection. There are special procedures for maintaining books and records through computer, electronic, and imaging processes and systems.[10]

The LLC may file a composite return on Form 140NR on behalf of nonresident members. There must be at least ten participating nonresident members.[11]

[D]   Allocations

The profits and losses of an LLC are allocated among the members as provided in the operating agreement. If the operating agreement does not provide for allocations, profits are allocated among the members according to the manner in which they share distributions that exceed the repayment of their capital contributions. Losses are allocated among the members according to the relative capital contributions that they make or promise to make in the future.[12]

[E]   Annual Report

An LLC is not required to file an annual report in Arizona.

[F]   Filing Fees

The filing fees in Arizona are as follows:[13]

Articles of organization	$ 50
Foreign LLC registration application	$150

---

[10] Ariz. Gen. Tax Rul., GTR 96-1, Ariz. Dept. of Rev., Ariz. St. Tax Rep. (CCH) ¶300-223 (Mar. 6, 1996).

[11] Ariz. Ind. Inc. Tax Rul., ITR 97-1.

[12] Ariz. Rev. Stat. Ann. §29-709.

[13] Ariz. Rev. Stat. Ann. §29-851.

Notice of winding up	$ 25
Articles of merger and certificate of merger	$ 50
Furnishing written information on any LLC	$ 10
Name reservation	$ 10

[G]   References

R. Onsager, Arizona Limited Liability Company: Forms and Practice Manual (1996).

M. Sargent & W. Schwidetzky, Limited Liability Company Handbook, Law — Sample Documents — Forms §4.03, Arizona Form of Operating Agreement (1995-1996 ed.).

§23.05   ARKANSAS

Arkansas enacted the Small Business Entity Tax Pass Through Act and the Arkansas Limited Liability Company Act, which authorize LLCs, effective April 12, 1993.[1]

[A]   State Tax Classification

Arkansas classifies an LLC in the same manner in which the LLC is classified for federal tax purposes, effective January 1, 2003.[2]

[B]   Taxation of LLC and Members

Arkansas imposes an annual franchise tax of $103 on LLCs. Members of an LLC are taxed for Arkansas income tax purposes in the same manner that the members are taxed for federal income tax purposes.[3] Members of an LLC that is classified as a partnership must pay tax on their distributive shares of income from the LLC.[4]

[C]   Tax Returns

An LLC that is classified as a partnership must file a return on Form AR1050, Partnership Return of Income. Every domestic or foreign LLC that is doing busi-

---

§23.05   [1] Act 100 (H.B. 1419), 1993 Ark. Acts; Ark. Code Ann. §§4-32-10 to 4-32-1401.
[2] Ark. Code Ann. §4-32-1313.
[3] *Id.*
[4] Ark. Code Ann. §4-32-1313; Reg. §6.26-51-102, issued by the Ark. Director of the Dept. of Fin. & Admin.

ness in Arkansas or that receives income from sources within Arkansas, regardless of the amount, must file Form AR1050.

Fiscal year returns must be filed on or before the fifteenth day of the fifth month following the close of the fiscal year. Calendar year returns are filed on or before May 15. The return must be mailed to State Income Tax, P.O. Box 1000, Little Rock, AR 72203.

Each member's share of income must be reported on the same form. All income must be reported, whether or not distributed. An explanatory statement must be attached to the return if distributed income is determined on a basis other than a percentage basis.

An LLC may request an extension of time for filing a return by filing Form AR1055, Request for Extension of Time for Filing Income Tax Returns. Federal extension requests are honored as valid state extension requests.[5]

The income and expenses of an LLC having only one member must be reported on the member's individual income tax return.[6]

[D]   Nonresident Members

Nonresident members must pay tax on their distributive shares of income from the LLC.[7]

An LLC may file a composite return, also known as a block filing, on behalf of the nonresident members. The return is filed on Form AR1000, Composite Return. The LLC must agree to the following conditions before it can file the composite return:[8]

- The LLC must provide to the Revenue Division the names of the members.
- The LLC must file the composite return in the name of the LLC. The member who signs the return is responsible for any assessments or deficiencies incurred by the return. This requirement does not relieve any of the members from their personal liability for payment.
- The LLC must file a composite return on Form AR1000. The taxes are computed at a flat 7 percent tax rate on the total net income in Arkansas.
- Members who become or are residents, or would have income/losses from Arkansas sources other than the LLC, must be excluded from the block filing. Only those members who file Arkansas nonresident individual income tax returns as a result of their interest in the LLC may be included in the block filing.
- The agreement to allow composite or block filings is reviewed annually by the Revenue Division. The Revenue Division may revoke the agreement at any time. An LLC that wishes to file a composite return must contact the Revenue Division at the following address and telephone number:

[5] *Id.*
[6] Ark. Code Ann. §4-32-1313.
[7] Reg. 6-26-51-102.
[8] Reg. §6.26-51-405, issued by the Ark. Director of the Dept. of Fin. & Admin.

Manager
Individual Income Tax Management
P.O. Box 3628
Little Rock, AR 72203

Telephone: (501) 682-7225

The Revenue Division will then send the LLC an agreement to sign and return to the Revenue Division.

[E] Allocations

Allocations and distributions of income, loss, cash, and other assets must be shared among members in accordance with the operating agreement.[9] If the operating agreement is silent, each member shares equally in the profits and assets remaining after all liabilities have been satisfied.[10]

[F] Annual Report

An LLC is not required to file an annual report in Arkansas.

[G] Filing Fees

The filing fees in the state of Arkansas are as follows:[11]

Articles of organization	$ 50
Articles of merger and certificate of merger	$ 50
Articles of dissolution	$ 50
Application for certificate of authority by foreign LLC	$300
Annual registration[12]	

[H] References

L. Beard & C. Goforth, Arkansas Limited Liability Companies (1994).

§23.06 CALIFORNIA

California enacted the Beverly-Killea Limited Liability Company Act effective September 30, 1994.[1]

---

[9] Ark. Code Ann. §4-32-601.
[10] Ark. Code Ann. §4-32-503.
[11] Ark. Code Ann. §4-32-1301.
[12] Ark. Code Ann. §4-32-202.
§23.06   [1] Ch. 1200 (introduced as S.B. 469), 1994 Cal. State.; Cal. Corp. Code §§17000-17705 (West).

[A]   State Tax Classification

California follows the federal check-the-box regulations in determining the state tax classification of an LLC for income and tax years beginning after 1996.[2] An LLC is classified for state tax purposes in the same manner that it is classified for federal tax purposes. However, an LLC will continue to be taxed as a corporation until it elects otherwise if the LLC was properly classified and taxed as a corporation for California tax purposes during any income year beginning within the 60-month period before January 1, 1997.[3]

Before 1997, California classified LLCs as partnerships or corporations depending on the classification for federal tax purposes.[4]

[B]   Single-Member LLCs

A single-member LLC may be formed in California effective January 1, 2000.[5] A single-member LLC that is classified as a disregarded entity for federal purposes will also be classified as a disregarded entity for California purposes.[6]

A husband and wife who each have a separate interest in LLC will be treated as separate members. The LLC must file a partnership return and issue them a separate Schedule K-1 (FTB Form 568). A husband and wife who hold a membership interest together are treated as a single member. The LLC must file a return as a disregarded entity if they are the sole owners, and issue them a single K-1 (FTB Form 568).[7]

A single-member LLC whose entity is disregarded for federal and California tax purposes is subject to the following three tax provisions in California:[8]

1. *LLC taxes.* The LLC must pay the annual $800 California franchise tax if the LLC is doing business in California, has had its articles of organization accepted by the California Secretary of State, or has been issued a certificate of registration by the California Secretary of State.[9]

   The single-member LLC must pay the California annual gross receipts tax imposed on LLCs. This tax ranges from $900 to $11,790 depending on the "total income" of the LLC.[10]

   The LLC is required to pay tax to California on any amount due on behalf of the owner at the highest marginal tax rate. The LLC is subject to

---

[2] Cal. Rev. & Tax Code §23038(b)(2); 18 Cal. Code Reg. §§23038(b)-1(b).

[3] Cal. Rev. & Tax Code §23038(b)(2)(C).

[4] Cal. Franchise Tax Bd. Notice 92-5 (Aug. 21, 1992).

[5] 1999 Cal. Stat. ch. 490, amending Cal. Corp. Code §§17001, 17050, and 17101.

[6] Cal. Rev. & Tax. Code §23038(b)(2).

[7] Instructions to 1999 Limited Liability Company Tax Booklet, published by the California Franchise Tax Board.

[8] 18 Cal. Code Reg. §23038(b)-1(a)(4).

[9] Cal. Rev. & Tax Code §17941.

[10] Cal. Rev. & Tax Code §17942.

penalties and interest for failure to timely pay the tax unless the owner timely files and pays the amount due.

2. *LLC information returns.*[11] A single-member LLC is only required to complete Side 1 of FTB Form 568. This form is used to determine the gross receipts fee and to pay the annual LLC franchise tax and fee. The single-member LLC must also file an information return with the California Secretary of State on Form LLC-EO12R, Statement of Information Renewal. In the case of a single-member LLC whose entity is disregarded for tax purposes, the return must include the following:

   • Information sufficient to verify the LLC's liability for the LLC fees and taxes;

   • The name and tax identification number of the sole member of the LLC;

   • The consent of the member to the California tax jurisdiction and consent to be subject to California taxation; and

   • Any other information necessary for the administration of the LLC provisions.

   The LLC must file the return by the 15th day of the fourth month after the close of the tax year or income year of the owner.

3. *Tax credit limitations.* A taxpayer that directly or indirectly owns an interest in a single-member LLC that is disregarded for tax purposes may only claim credits or credit carryforwards from the LLC to the extent the member's tax liability is attributable to the LLC. Disallowed credits may be carried forward to future years.[12]

There are additional limits on the amount of credits that the LLC may claim for purposes of computing the member's alternative minimum tax. The amount of credit attributable to the LLC that is classified as a disregarded entity, including credit carryovers, that may be applied against the member's net tax is limited to the excess of the member's regular tax. This is determined by including income attributable to the LLC, less the member's regular taxes, determined by excluding the income attributable to the LLC. The LLC may carry forward to a subsequent income or tax year any excess credit that may not be claimed against the net tax during the current income or tax year.[13]

[C]   Franchise Tax

LLCs must pay an annual $800 franchise tax.[14] The tax applies whether the LLC is classified as a corporation or a partnership (or a sole proprietorship in the case of a foreign LLC). The tax is payable on the fifteenth day of the fourth month of the taxable year.[15] If the LLC is classified as a corporation, an additional $800

[11] Cal. Rev. & Tax Code §18633.5.
[12] Cal. Rev. & Tax Code §§17039, 17941, 23036.
[13] Cal. Rev. & Tax. Code §§18633.5(i)(1), 23038.
[14] Cal. Rev. & Tax. Code §§17941, 23091(a).
[15] Cal. Rev. & Tax. Code §§17941(c), 23091(c).

deposit must be paid at the time of organization. The minimum tax does not apply for any year in which the LLC is in existence for fewer than 15 days and does no business in California.[16] Therefore, an LLC with a calendar year that is formed on December 17 may be able to avoid franchise taxes for the first year.

[D] Gross Receipts Tax

LLCs that are classified as partnerships must also pay an entity-level tax based on "total income" reportable to California for the tax year.[17] "Total income" means worldwide gross income, plus the cost of goods sold paid or incurred in connection with the LLC's business.[18] The taxes for tax years beginning on or after 2001 are as follows for 2001:[19]

Income from all sources	Fee
Over $250,000, but less than $500,000	$ 900
$500,000 or more, but less than $1,000,000	$2,500
$1,000,000 or more, but less than $5,000,000	$6,000
$5,000,000 or more	$11,790

The tax rate is adjusted periodically depending on the revenue loss attributable to LLCs.[20]

The Franchise Tax Board (FTB) may aggregate the income of all commonly controlled LLCs. This determination may be made for only one LLC in a controlled group. The FTB may aggregate income only if it first determines that multiple LLCs were formed to reduce the fees payable by members of the same group.[21] Commonly controlled LLCs include all other partnerships doing business in California in which the same persons own, directly or indirectly, more than 50 percent of the capital or profits interests.

Once the total income of the group is aggregated, each group member is jointly and severally liable for the LLC fee. A commonly controlled LLC for aggregation purposes includes the LLC and any other partnership or LLC that does business in California and that is required to file a partnership return if the same persons own more than 50 percent of the capital or profits interests in the LLC.[22]

[E] Property Taxes

An LLC that is classified as a partnership is subject to property taxes in the same manner as a partnership except where a specific property tax provision otherwise provides.[23]

[16] Cal. Rev. & Tax. Code §23096.
[17] Cal. Rev. & Tax. Code §§17942, 23092.
[18] Cal. Rev. & Tax. Code §§17942(b)(1), 23092(c)(1).
[19] Cal. Franchise Tax Bd. Notice 2001-7 (Nov. 9, 2001), effective for tax years beginning in 2001.
[20] Cal. Rev. & Tax. Code §§17943, 23093.
[21] S.B. 13, ch. 2, 1995 Cal. Stat.
[22] Id.
[23] Cal. Rev. & Tax. Code §28.5.

There is no documentary transfer tax on the transfer of property to an LLC if the owners of the property retain the same proportional interests in the property after the transfer. The transfer is treated as a mere change in the form of ownership.

There is no reassessment of property under Proposition 13 upon transfer of the property to an LLC if the owners of the property retain the same proportional interests in the property after the transfer.[24] However, the State Board of Equalization (SBE) informally takes the position that there is a reassessment if the owners of the property previously transferred the property to a partnership or other legal entity in a transaction that was exempt from reassessment under the proportional interest exclusion. The transfer to the converting entity created "original co-owners." The transfer by the converting entity to the LLC is treated as a transfer representing more than 50 percent of the original co-owners' interests. The SBE has informally indicated that this problem might be avoided if the converting entity first dissolves and reconstitutes as an LLC in the same document.

A single member LLC that is classified as a disregarded entity must pay the business entity tax of $250.

There is no reassessment of property under Proposition 13 as a result of a statutory conversion or merger of a partnership into an LLC if the owners of the converting or disappearing entity maintain the same ownership interest in the surviving LLC as held in the disappearing entity.[25]

[F]   Tax Reporting Requirements for LLCs Classified as Corporations

An LLC that is classified as a corporation must file a franchise tax return and pay the $800 minimum franchise tax. The LLC pays the $800 by using Form 3522, Limited Liability Company Tax Voucher. The LLC must file Form 100, Corporation Franchise or Income Tax Return. The LLC is subject to the applicable provisions of the bank and corporation tax laws. These laws include the requirement that a corporation prepay the minimum franchise tax when it is formed or qualifies to do business in California.

[G]   Tax Reporting Requirements for LLCs Classified as Partnerships

An LLC that is classified as a partnership must file Form 568, Limited Liability Company Return of Income.[26] The return is due by the fifteenth day of the fourth month following the close of the tax year. The LLC may obtain an automatic six-month extension by filing Form 3537.[27]

Every LLC doing business in California, organized in California, or organized in another state or foreign country and registered with the California Secretary

---

[24] Cal. Rev. & Tax. Code §62(a)(2); 18 Cal. Code Regs. tit. 462, §180(b)(2).
[25] Reg. §461.180, effective April 8, 1999.
[26] Cal. Rev. & Tax Code §18633.5.
[27] Cal. Rev. & Tax. Code §18567.

of State must pay an annual tax of $800 with Form 3522, Limited Liability Company Tax Voucher. Payment is due on or before the fifteenth day of the fourth month after the beginning of the LLC's tax year.[28]

The LLC must use Form 568 to report and pay the gross receipts tax and any nonconsenting member taxes (taxes of nonresident members who do not consent to the jurisdiction of the California taxing authorities).[29] If the LLC obtains an extension of time to file return, it must pay the tax by the regular filing date by using Form 3537, Payment Voucher. The minimum $800 annual tax should not be remitted with Form 568.

The LLC may file a composite return on behalf of nonresident members.[30]

The members of an LLC are subject to California taxes in the same manner as partners in a partnership.[31] However, members are not entitled to deduct the entity-level taxes paid by the LLC.[32]

The resident and nonresident members must file California tax returns with respect to their shares of California source income.[33]

An LLC that is classified as a partnership is subject to the same penalties for failure to file a return that apply to failure to file a partnership return.[34]

The special forms applicable to California LLCs classified as partnerships are as follows:

Form	Name
568	Limited Liability Company Return of Income
Schedule D (568)	Capital Gain or Loss
Schedule K-1 (568)	Member's Share of Income, Deductions, Credits, Etc.
Schedule K-1 NR (568)	Member's Share of Income, Deductions, Credits, Etc.
FTB 3522	Limited Liability Company Tax Voucher (for payment of annual $800 tax)
FTB 3537	Payment Voucher for Automatic Extension for Limited Liability Companies
FTB 3885L	Depreciation and Amortization
FTB 3832	Limited Liability Company's List of Members and Consents
FTB 3555L	Request for Tax Clearance Certificate

The LLC must provide each member with the following tax reporting information:[35]

---

[28] Cal. Rev. & Tax. Code §17941(c).
[29] Cal. Rev. & Tax. Code §17942.
[30] Cal. Rev. & Tax Code §18535(d).
[31] Cal. Rev. & Tax. Code §17087.6.
[32] Cal. Rev. & Tax. Code §17220(b)(3).
[33] Cal. Franchise Tax Bd. Notice 92-5 (Aug. 21, 1992).
[34] S.B. 13, ch. 2, 1995 Cal. Stat.
[35] Cal. Rev. & Tax. Code §18633.5.

- A copy of the information shown on FTB Form 568;
- FTB Schedule K-1 of FTB Form 568 for resident members showing the member's distributive share of LLC income, gain, loss, deduction, credit, and other tax items; and
- FTB Schedule K-1 NR for nonresident members showing the same information.

[H]   Nonresident Members

An LLC that conducts business in California is subject to California withholding taxes if the LLC *allocates* California source income to members who are not residents of California and who are not resident aliens of the United States,[36] or if the LLC *distributes* California source income to members who are not residents of California, but who are residents or citizens of the United States.[37]

An LLC may satisfy the withholding requirements for nonresident members by obtaining a signed Form FTB 3832, "Limited Liability Company's List of Members and Consents," from such members. By signing the form, the nonresident members agree to pay California taxes on California source income from the LLC. If a nonresident member fails to sign the form, the LLC must pay tax on member's distributive share income at the highest marginal tax rate. The withholding tax rate is 7 percent for domestic nonresident members, 8.84 percent for foreign corporate members, and 9.3 percent for foreign individual members. The amount paid by the LLC is then treated as a payment made by the member.[38]

The source of a nonresident member's share of LLC income derived from sources within California is determined under the partnership provisions of the tax regulations if the LLC is classified as a partnership for federal tax purposes. The California source income allocated to a member in a single-member LLC that is classified as a disregarded entity is determined in accordance with the sole proprietorship provisions of the regulations if the LLC carries on a unitary business, trade, or profession with and without California.[39]

A nonresident member of an LLC may avoid combination under the California unitary tax rules if the member owns less than 20 percent of the LLC.[40]

[I]   Commencing and Dissolving LLCs

Commencing and dissolving LLCs are exempt from tax during the year of organization or dissolution if the tax year is 15 days or less and the LLC does no

---

[36] Cal. Rev. & Tax. Code §18666. The withholding tax rate is 8.84% for C corporation members, 1.5% for S corporation members, and 9.33% for members who are individuals, partnerships, LLCs, or fiduciaries.

[37] Cal. Rev. & Tax. Code §18662. However, withholding is not required if distributions from California sources to the nonresident member are $1,500 or less during the year, or if the Franchise Tax Board directs the payor not to withhold.

[38] Cal. Rev. & Tax. Code §18633.5.

[39] Reg. §17951-4.

[40] Reg. §17951-4.

business in California during the tax year. For example, a calendar year LLC that is formed between December 17 and December 31 is exempt from tax during the first tax year if it does no business in California during that period. A calendar year LLC that dissolves by January 15 is exempt from tax during the last tax year if it does no business in California during that period.

[J] Biennial Report

The LLC must file a biennial report on Form LLC-E012R, Statement of Information Renewal. The LLC must file the report within 90 days after it is formed.[41] The secretary of state sends the form to the LLC with the filed articles of organization. In subsequent years, the LLC must file the report during the calendar month in which the original articles of organization were filed or during any of the immediately preceding five calendar months. Foreign LLCs must file biennially in the month during which the application for qualification was filed or during any of the preceding five months.[42]

[K] Filing Fees

There are the following filing fees in California:[43]

Articles of organization	$ 70
Articles of organization if the LLC is classified as a corporation	$880
Registration of foreign LLC	$ 70
Biennial report	$ 20

[L] References

California Continuing Education of the Bar, Forming and Operating California Limited Liability Companies (1997).

G. Niesar, B. Berk, & M. Casillas, California Limited Liability Company, Forms and Practice Manual (1994).

California Continuing Education of the Bar, California Limited Liability Companies: Beyond the Basics (program handbook) (Apr.-May 1995).

M. Sargent & W. Schwidetzky, Limited Liability Company Handbook, Law — Sample Documents — Forms, §4.04[A], California Form of Operating Agreement — Member-Managed; §4.04[B], California Form of Operating Agreement — Manager-Managed (1995-1996 ed.).

---

[41] Cal. Corp. Code §17060(a).
[42] Cal. Corp. Code §17060(c).
[43] Cal. Gov. Code §12190.

R. Burt, California Continuing Education of the Bar, Forming and Operating California Limited Liability Companies (1995).

B. Clark, California's Beverly-Killea Limited Liability Company Act (1994).

§23.07   COLORADO

Colorado enacted the Colorado Limited Liability Company Act on April 12, 1990.[1]

[A]   State Tax Classification

Colorado classifies an LLC in the same manner that an LLC is classified for federal tax purposes. An LLC that is classified as a partnership under federal law is classified as a partnership for state tax purposes.[2] An LLC that is classified as a corporation for federal tax purposes is classified as a corporation for state tax purposes.[3]

Before 1995, Colorado had detailed provisions regarding taxation of limited liability companies. These sections were repealed, effective May 24, 1995.[4] Before the federal check-the-box regulations, the Colorado Department of Revenue also ruled that a Colorado LLC was generally classified as a partnership for state tax purposes. A Colorado LLC formed under the Colorado revised code did not have a preponderance of the four characteristics of corporations. It did not possess continuity of life because it dissolved upon any event terminating the membership of a member, including death and bankruptcy, absent the consent of all remaining members to continue the business. In addition, it lacked free transferability of interests because unanimous consent of the members was required before an assignee or transferree of a member's interest could acquire all attributes of membership, including the right to participate in management.[5]

[B]   Tax Returns

An LLC that is classified as a partnership is not subject to the regular taxes. Persons carrying on business as members are liable for the tax and the alternative minimum tax only in their individual capacities.[6]

An LLC that is required to file a federal partnership return must file Colorado Form 106, Colorado State Partnership or S Corporation Return of Income and

---

§23.07   [1] S.B. 90-74, 1990 Colo. Sess. Laws; Colo. Rev. Stat. Ann. §§7-80-101 to 7-80-1101.

[2] Colo. Rev. Stat. Ann. §§39-22-103(5.6), 39-22-201.5. A partnership includes limited liability companies filing as partnership for federal income tax purposes. A partner includes members of the limited liability company for state tax purposes.

[3] Colo. Rev. Stat. Ann. §39-22-103 (2.5), (10.5).

[4] Ch. 186, 1995 Colo. Sess. Laws.

[5] Rul. 93-6, Colo. Dept. of Rev. (Dec. 28, 1992).

[6] Colo. Rev. Stat. Ann. §39-22-201.

Composite Nonresident Income Tax Return. The return must be filed if any of the LLC's income is from Colorado sources.

The members' allocable shares of profits and losses and the identification of the members are set forth in Part III of Form 106. A computer printout in the same format may be attached to the return. The federal Schedules K-1 may not be used.

[C]   Nonresident Members

An LLC with nonresident members must either file a nonresident partners agreement for each nonresident member or pay a 4.63 percent tax on the nonresident member's distributive share of income.[7] The tax rate is the highest marginal tax rate for individuals.

An LLC may file a composite return as part of the regular partnership tax return and pay taxes on behalf of nonresident members.[8] Each nonresident member who is not included in a composite return must sign Form 0107, agreeing to file a Colorado income tax return, report Colorado source income, and pay the applicable Colorado taxes.

[D]   Annual Report

A Colorado LLC must file an annual report with the Colorado Secretary of State. The secretary of state issues a preprinted report form to the LLC each year.[9]

[E]   Filing Fees

The filing fees in Colorado are as follows:[10]

Articles of organization	$125
Registration as foreign LLC	$125
Annual registration	$ 85

[F]   References

R. Russo & R. Stark, Colorado Limited Liability Company Forms and Practice Manual (1996).

M. Sargent & W. Schwidetzky, Limited Liability Company Handbook, Law —

---

[7] Colo. Rev. Stat. Ann. §39-22-601(5)(e).
[8] Colo. Rev. Stat. Ann. §39-22-601(5)(d).
[9] Colo. Rev. Stat. Ann. §70-80-303.
[10] Colo. Rev. Stat. Ann. §7-80-307.

Sample Documents — Forms, §4.05, Colorado Form of Articles of Organization and Operating Agreement (1995-1996 ed.).

§23.08 CONNECTICUT

Connecticut enacted the Connecticut Limited Liability Company Act effective October 1, 1993.[1]

[A] State Tax Classification

A Connecticut LLC is classified for state tax purposes in the same manner that it is classified for federal tax purposes.[2] Foreign limited liability companies transacting business in Connecticut are also classified for state tax purposes in accordance with their federal classifications. Commencing January 1, 1997, the term "partnership" includes an LLC that is classified as a partnership for federal tax purposes.[3] A partner includes a member of an LLC that is classified as a partner for federal tax purposes.[4]

Connecticut allows single-member LLCs.[5] A foreign LLC with a single member may register to do business and operate in Connecticut.[6]

The Connecticut Department of Revenue Services issued a policy statement regarding classification of LLCs before enactment of the Connecticut Limited Liability Company Act.[7]

[B] Taxation of LLC and Members

A Connecticut LLC is a pass-through entity. There is no franchise or entity-level tax. Profits and losses pass through and are taxable to the members. Nonresident members are taxed on their distributive shares of LLC income derived from or connected with Connecticut sources.[8]

[C] Real Estate Taxes

The transfer of real property by an individual to a single-member LLC owned by the individual is not subject to the Connecticut real estate conveyance tax.

---

§23.08 [1] Pub. Act No. 93-267, 1992 Conn. Acts (Reg. Sess.); Conn. Gen. Stat. Ann. §§34-100 to 34-299.

[2] Conn. Gen. Stat. Ann. §34-113; Special Notice 98(3), Conn. Dept. of Rev. Servs. (Jan. 22, 1998).

[3] Conn. Gen. Stat. Ann. §12-701(a)(33).

[4] Conn. Gen. Stat. Ann. §12-701(a)(34).

[5] Conn. Gen. Stat. Ann. §34-101(9).

[6] Conn. Gen. Stat. Ann. §34-222.

[7] Policy Statement 92(12), Conn. Dept. of Rev. Servs.

[8] Department of Revenue Services Policy Statement 98 (1.1)(1998).

There is no change in ownership for tax purposes if the LLC is classified as a disregarded entity.[9]

The Connecticut Department of Revenue Services issued a policy statement establishing guidelines for the imposition of real estate conveyance taxes on deeds that transfer real estate pursuant to the conversion of a partnership to an LLC.[10]

[D] Sales Taxes

A contribution of property or services by an individual to a single-member LLC is subject to sales and use taxes unless expressly exempt. Services by an owner to the LLC are subject to tax if the owner is compensated other than through a distribution of LLC profits.[11]

[E] Tax Returns

A Connecticut LLC that is classified as a partnership must file a partnership tax return. The LLC must file Form CT-1065, Connecticut Partnership Income Tax Return, if it has any income, gain, loss, or deduction derived from or connected with Connecticut sources during the taxable year.[12] Income derived from or connected with Connecticut sources includes:

- Income attributable to the ownership of any interest in real property or tangible personal property located in Connecticut and in intangible personal property to the extent it is used in a business, trade, profession, or occupation carried on in Connecticut.
- Income attributable to a business, trade, profession, or occupation carried on in Connecticut. An LLC is treated as carrying on a business, trade, profession, or occupation in Connecticut if it maintains an office, shop, store, warehouse, factory, agency, or other place in Connecticut where its affairs are systematically and regularly carried on. It is also treated as carrying on a trade or business if activities in connection with the business are conducted in Connecticut with a fair degree of permanency and continuity for profit, as distinguished from isolated or incidental transactions.
- Income, gain, loss, or deduction from sources as a partner in another partnership that has income, gain, loss, or deduction derived from Connecticut sources.[13]

The LLC must complete Schedule D to Form CT-1065 for all persons who were members (other than members that are C corporations) during any part of the tax

---

[9] *Mandell*, Connecticut Superior Court, No. SC 16672 (Mar. 18, 2003).
[10] Policy Statement 93(5.1), Conn. Dept. of Rev. Servs.
[11] Special Notice 98(3), Conn. Dept. of Rev. Servs. (Jan. 22, 1998).
[12] *See* General Information to Form CT-1065.
[13] *See id.*

year if the LLC has Connecticut modifications to federal income. The LLC must complete Schedule E for all members who are nonresident individuals, nonresident trusts, or nonresident estates or who are partnerships or S corporations.

The LLC must file Form CT-1065 by the fifteenth day of the fourth month following close of its taxable year.

Nonresident members of an LLC must include their distributive shares of LLC income on Form CT-1040 NR/PY, Connecticut Nonresident or Part-Year Resident Income Tax Return.

An LLC that is classified as a corporation must file Form CT-1120, Corporation Business Tax Return.

An LLC may file a group return on Form CT-G, Connecticut Group Income Tax Return, if the LLC has 10 or more qualified electing nonresident members.

Resident individual members of the LLC must include their distributive shares of LLC income on Form CT-1040, Connecticut Resident Income Tax Return. A Connecticut resident is a person domiciled in the state or a person domiciled outside the state who maintains a permanent place of abode in Connecticut and spends more than 183 days in the state during the tax year.

An LLC that is not able to file a timely return may file for an extension on Form CT-1065EXT, Application for Extension of Time to File Connecticut Partnership Income Tax Return. The filing of this form automatically extends the due date for six months if federal Form 8736, Application for Automatic Extension of Time to File U.S. Return for a Partnership, has been filed with the Internal Revenue Service. If the federal form was not filed, the LLC may apply for a six-month extension to file if there is a reasonable basis for the request.

[F]   Annual Report

A Connecticut LLC must file an annual report on the anniversary date of the filing of the articles of organization.[14] The annual report must set forth the name of the LLC and the LLC's current principal office address. The secretary of state mails the appropriate form to each LLC at its principal office.

A foreign LLC qualified to do business in Connecticut must also file an annual report on the anniversary date of its registration or its qualification to do business in the state of Connecticut.[15]

[G]   Filing Fees

Connecticut imposes the following filing fees on limited liability companies:[16]

Articles of organization	$25
Certificate of registration for foreign LLC	$60
Annual report	$10

[14] Conn. Gen. Stat. Ann. §34-106.
[15] Conn. Gen. Stat. Ann. §34-229.
[16] Conn. Gen. Stat. Ann. §34-112.

[H]   References

M. Sargent & W. Schwidetzky, Limited Liability Company Handbook, Law —
Sample Documents — Forms, §4.06, Connecticut Form of Operating Agreement
(1995-1996 ed.).

§23.09   DELAWARE

Delaware enacted the Delaware Limited Liability Company Act effective October
1, 1992.[1]

[A]   State Tax Classification

Delaware classifies an LLC in the same manner that the LLC is classified for
federal tax purposes.[2] The same rule applies to a foreign LLC qualified to do
business in Delaware.

A member or an assignee of a member of an LLC formed in Delaware or
qualified to do business in Delaware is treated as either a resident or a nonresident
partner if the LLC is classified as a partnership for federal tax purposes. If the
LLC is not classified as a partnership, the member or assignee has the same status
as the member or assignee has for federal income tax purposes.[3] This rule applies
for purposes of any tax imposed by the state of Delaware or by any instrumentality,
agency, or political subdivision of the state of Delaware.

[B]   Taxation of LLC and Members

There is a $100 annual tax on domestic and registered foreign LLCs.[4] The tax
is payable to the secretary of state on June 1 following the close of the calendar
year or upon cancellation of a certificate of formation. LLCs that fail to pay the
fee on a timely basis are subject to interest at the rate of 1 1/2 percent per month.

The LLC is otherwise a pass-through entity for tax purposes.[5] The members
are liable for Delaware personal income taxes on their distributive shares of LLC
income. Each item of taxable income, gain, deduction, credit, and loss has the
same character for state purposes as for federal purposes,[6] subject to certain
modifications under Delaware law.[7]

---

§23.09   [1] H.B. 608, 1992 Del. Laws; Del. Code Ann. tit. 6, §§18-101 to 18-1109.
[2] Del. Code Ann. tit. 6, §18-1107(a); Tech. Information Mem. 98-1, Del. Div. of Rev. (Apr. 24, 1998).
[3] Id.
[4] Del. Code Ann. tit. 6, §18-1107(b).
[5] Del. Code Ann. tit. 30, §1143.
[6] Del. Code Ann. tit. 30, §1144.
[7] Del. Code Ann. tit. 30, §1106.

Nonresident members are taxed on their distributive shares of LLC income derived from or connected with Delaware sources.[8]

[C]   Tax Returns

A Delaware LLC that is classified as a partnership must file a partnership tax return on Delaware Form 300, Delaware Partnership Return. This is an information return. The LLC must file the return if it has one or more members who are Delaware residents or has any income or loss, regardless of the amount, derived from or connected with a Delaware source.[9]

Income from Delaware sources includes income attributable to the ownership of an interest in real property or tangible personal property located in Delaware and in intangible personal property to the extent the intangible is used in a trade, business, profession, or occupation carried on in Delaware. Income from Delaware sources also includes income attributable to a trade, business, profession, or occupation carried on in Delaware.

The return must be filed by the fifteenth day of the fourth month following the close of the taxable year. It must be mailed to the Delaware Division of Revenue, 820 North French Street, P.O. Box 2044, Wilmington, DE 19899-2044.

An LLC may request an extension to file the return by submitting a copy of the federal extension request on or before the due date of the return. A photocopy of the approved federal extension must be attached to the final return when filed. The approved federal extension extends the due date of the Delaware return to the same date as the federal extended due date.

An LLC that elects to be classified as a corporation for federal tax purposes must attach a copy of IRS Form 8832, Entity Classification Election, to its Delaware corporate income tax return.[10]

Members of an LLC, which has not elected to be classified as a corporation and that does business in Delaware, are subject to the tax filing requirements in Delaware for all years that the LLC does business in Delaware.[11]

A nonresident member of an LLC with income from Delaware sources must file Form Individual PY/NR Income Tax Return, and report his share of Delaware source LLC income or loss. A resident member must file Form 200, Delaware Resident Income Tax Return, and report his share of LLC income or loss.

[D]   Single-Member LLCs

There are special rules for single-member LLCs doing business in Delaware, which are classified as disregarded entities for federal tax purposes. An individual who is the only member of an LLC is subject to the tax filing requirements under

---

[8] Del. Code Ann. tit. 30, §1145.
[9] Del. Code Ann. tit. 30, §1174(a).
[10] Tech. Info. Mem. 98-1, Del. Div. of Rev. (Apr. 24, 1998).
[11] Id.

Title 30 of the Delaware Code for each year in which the LLC conducts business in the state.[12] A corporation that is the sole member of an LLC must file a corporate income tax return and business license and gross receipts tax return for each year in which the LLC conducts business in the state.[13]

[E] Annual Report

A Delaware LLC is not required to file an annual report.

[F] Filing Fees

Delaware imposes the following filing fees on LLCs:[14]

Certificate of formation	$ 50
Foreign LLC registration application	$ 50
Annual tax	$100

[G] References

W. Carey, Delaware Limited Liability Company: Forms and Practice Manual (1995).

M. Sargent & W. Schwidetzky, Limited Liability Company Handbook, Law — Sample Documents — Forms, §4.07, Delaware Form of Certificate of Formation, Operating Agreement and Related Documents (1995-1996 ed.).

§23.10 DISTRICT OF COLUMBIA

The District of Columbia enacted the District of Columbia Limited Liability Company Act of 1994 effective July 23, 1994.[1]

[A] Tax Classification

The District of Columbia classifies LLCs in the same manner in which they are classified for federal tax purposes.[2] Foreign LLCs qualified to do business in the

---

[12] Id.

[13] Id.

[14] Del. Code Ann. tit. 6, §§18-1105, 18-1107.

§23.10 [1] Act 10-243, 1994 D.C. Stat. (approved by the mayor on May 18, 1994; effective after a 30-day period of congressional review); D.C. Code Ann. §§29-1001 to 29-1075.

[2] D.C. Code Ann. §29-1074. Members are also classified as partners or shareholders for D.C. tax purposes based on their federal classification.

District of Columbia are classified as partnerships unless classified as corporations or proprietorships for federal tax purposes.[3]

A member or an assignee of a member of an LLC formed in the District of Columbia or qualified to do business in the District as a foreign limited liability company is treated as either a resident or a nonresident partner unless classified otherwise for federal income tax purposes. In that case, the member or assignee of a member has the same status that the member or assignee of a member has for federal income tax purposes.[4]

[B]   Taxation of LLCs and Members

The District of Columbia imposes a 9.975 percent tax on D.C. source income earned by unincorporated businesses.[5] An LLC is subject to the tax if it engages in an unincorporated business.[6] The individual members are taxed on their distributive shares of income if the unincorporated business tax does not apply.[7]

An unincorporated business is any trade or business conducted or engaged in by an individual, whether resident or nonresident, other than a trade or business conducted or engaged in by a corporation. It includes any trade or business that would be taxable if conducted by a corporation. An unincorporated business does not include the following:

- A trade or business that by law, customs, or ethics cannot be incorporated;
- A trade or business in which more than 80 percent of the gross income is derived from personal services by the individuals or members of the LLC; or
- An entity conducting or carrying on a trade or business in which capital is not a material income-producing factor.

[C]   Real Estate Taxation

There is an exemption from the deed recordation tax and the real estate transfer tax for a partnership that converts to an LLC and that signs a deed transferring partnership real estate in connection with the conversion.[8]

[D]   Tax Returns

LLCs that engage in an unincorporated business during the tax year and that have gross income from District sources exceeding $12,000 during the year must

---

[3] D.C. Code Ann. §29-1074.
[4] Id.
[5] D.C. Code Ann. §47-1808.3.
[6] D.C. Code Ann. §10-215.
[7] D.C. Code Ann. §47-1808.6.
[8] D.C. Code Ann. §29-1013(k).

file returns on Form D-30, Unincorporated Business Franchise Tax Return. LLCs that are not required to file Form D-30 and that are classified as partnerships must file information returns on Form D-65, Partnership Return of Income. If Form D-65 is used instead of Form D-30, the LLC must attach a statement to the return explaining the reasons for so doing.

The return on Form D-30 must be filed if the LLC's gross income from a trade or business within the District and other gross income from sources within the District total more than $12,000 during the year regardless of whether the LLC has net income. Gross income means gross revenues before deduction of costs of goods, expenses, and other allowable deductions in determining that income.

The return must be filed with the Department of Finance and Revenue, P.O. Box 447, Washington, DC 20044-0447, on the same basis as the individual owners are required to file for federal tax purposes.

LLCs may file a request for an extension on D.C. Form FR-128 on or before the due date of the return. Copies of the federal extension request are not acceptable. The District of Columbia law has no provision for an LLC reporting or filing as a corporation.[9]

[E] Biennial Report

A District of Columbia LLC must file a biennial report with the mayor on or before June 16 of each year.[10] The report must set forth the name and address of the LLC, the address of the registered office, and the name of the registered agent at that office. It must also set forth the names and addresses, including street numbers, of its managers, if any.

[F] Filing Fees

The filing fees in the District of Columbia are as follows:[11]

Articles of organization	$100
Foreign LLC registration application	$150
Biennial report	$100

§23.11 FLORIDA

Florida enacted the Florida Limited Liability Company Act in April 1982.[1]

---

[9] See Instructions for Form D-65.

[10] D.C. Code Ann. §29-1064.

[11] D.C. Code Ann. §§29-1036, 29-1064.

§23.11 [1] Fla. Stat. Ann. §§608.401 to 608.703. See also A. Lederman, Miami Device: The Florida Limited Liability Company, 67 Taxes 339 (June 1989).

[A]   State Tax Classification

Florida classifies an LLC in the same manner that the LLC is classified for federal tax purposes. An LLC that is classified as a partnership under federal law is classified as a partnership for state tax purposes. Prior to July 1, 1998, a Florida LLC or a foreign LLC qualified to do business in Florida was classified as a corporation regardless of its federal classification.[2]

Effective July 1, 1998, Florida permits the formation of a single-member LLC.[3] Effective January 1, 2003, single-member LLCs are treated as separate legal entities for all non-income-tax purposes.[4] Such LLCs are subject to the sales and use taxes, property taxes, excise taxes, and other miscellaneous taxes.

[B]   Taxation of LLC and Members

There is no franchise or corporate income tax on an LLC that is classified as a partnership or single-member disregarded entity for federal income tax purposes. An LLC that is classified as a partnership or single-member disregarded entity is not an "artificial entity" subject to the corporate income tax.[5]

Effective January 1, 2003, a single-member LLC that is classified as a disregarded entity is treated as a separate legal entity for all non-income tax purposes. The single-member LLC may report and account for income, employment, and other taxes under the owner's taxpayer identification number.[6]

There is no tax on any individual who engages in business in Florida as a member or manager of an LLC that is classified as a partnership.[7] A foreign LLC that is qualified to do business in the state is not subject to the corporate income tax either.[8] However, a corporation that becomes a member of an LLC cannot avoid the corporate income tax merely by becoming a member of an LLC.

Prior to July 1, 1998, Florida imposed a 5.5 percent franchise tax and a 3.3 percent alternative minimum tax on LLCs organized or doing business in Florida.[9]

A corporation is not subject to the Florida corporate income tax merely because the corporation has an ownership interest in a foreign limited liability company that does business in Florida.[10]

An LLC must pay the Florida intangible personal property tax.[11] This is an

---

[2] Fla. Stat. Ann. §§220.03(1)(e), 608.471.
[3] Fla. Stat. Ann. §608.405.
[4] Fla. Stat. Ann. §608.471(3).
[5] Fla. Stat. Ann. §608.471(1), (2).
[6] Fla. Stat. Ann. §608.503(3).
[7] Fla. Stat. Ann. §220.02.
[8] Id.
[9] Id.
[10] Technical Assistance Investment No. 98(C)1-004, Fla. Dept. of Rev. (May 4, 1998).
[11] Fla. Stat., ch. 199; Fla. Admin. Code Ann. r. 12C-2.

annual tax based on the market value as of January 1 of the intangible personal property owned by the LLC. The most common types of intangible personal property are stocks, bonds, accounts receivable or other loans not secured by real property, and shares or units of ownership in mutual and money market funds and limited liability companies. An LLC must file Form DR-601C to pay the tax.

There is a documentary transfer tax on the transfer of real property to an LLC. The tax rate is $.70 per $100 (or portion thereof) of the total consideration paid for the transfer. There is an exception in Miami-Dade County, where the rate is $.60 per $100 (or portion thereof) when the property is a single-family residence. If the Miami-Dade property is anything other than a single-family residence, the tax rate is $.60 plus $.45 surtax per $100 (or portion thereof).[12]

[C]   Apportionment of Income

LLCs doing business within and outside the state of Florida must apportion their business income to Florida based on a three-factor formula. The three factors are the value of property, payroll, and sales factors. Taxpayers may request permission from the Department of Revenue to apportion their income using a different method.

[D]   Tax Filing Requirements for LLC
Classified as Partnership

A Florida LLC that is classified as a partnership must file a tax return on Form F-1065, Partnership Information Return. The form is used to report the members' allocable shares of income.

Form F-1065 must be filed on or before the first day of the fifth month following the close of the tax year. It must be filed with the Florida Department of Revenue, 5050 West Tennessee Street, Tallahassee, FL 32399-0135.

The Florida Department of Revenue may grant an extension of time to file the form. The extension is filed on Form F-7004. If the federal Form 8736 was filed for federal income tax purposes, an extension will automatically be approved if Florida Form F-7004 is filed with the Department of Revenue on or before the original due date of the return.

A copy of the first four pages of federal Form 1065, Form 4562, Schedule K-1, and Schedule F as filed with the Internal Revenue Service must be attached to Form F-1065. Attachments may be used if the lines on Form F-1065 or on any schedules are not sufficient.

---

[12] *See* http://www.myflorida.com/dor/taxes/doc_stamp.html.

[E]   Tax Filing Requirements for LLC Classified as Corporation

All domestic and foreign LLCs that are classified as corporations must file corporate income tax returns on Form F-1120, Corporate Income/Franchise and Emergency Excise Tax Return. Form F-1120 is used to report and pay the 5.5 percent corporate income tax. There is no minimum income tax.

If the LLC is domiciled in Florida and is required to file a federal return, it must continue to file a corporate tax return in Florida even if it ceases doing business. A foreign LLC that no longer conducts business, earns income, or exists in Florida during the tax year does not have to file a return.

The return is due on or before the first day of the fourth month following the close of the tax year or the fifteenth day of the month following the due date, without extension, for filing the related federal return for the tax year, whichever is later.

An LLC may apply for an extension of time to file Form F-1120. The extension request is made on Form F-7004. Extensions are valid for six months. Only one extension is permitted. A copy of the federal extension alone does not extend the time for filing the Florida return.

[F]   Annual Report

Florida LLCs and foreign LLCs qualified to do business in Florida must file annual reports with the Department of State between January 1 and May 1 of each year.

[G]   Filing Fees

The Department of State charges the following filing fees for limited liability companies:[13]

Articles of organization	$250
Annual report	$100

§23.12   GEORGIA

Georgia enacted the Georgia Limited Liability Company Act effective March 1, 1994.[1]

---

[13] Fla. Stat. Ann. §608.452.

§23.12   [1] H.B. 264, ch. 174, 1993 Ga. Laws; Ga. Code Ann. §14-11-100 to 14-11-1109.

[A]   *State Tax Classification*

A Georgia LLC is classified for state tax purposes in the same manner that it is classified for federal tax purposes.[2] A member or assignee of a member of an LLC or a foreign LLC that is classified as a partnership is treated for Georgia tax purposes as either a resident or a nonresident partner. If the LLC is not classified as a partnership, the member or assignee of the member has the same status for Georgia tax purposes that the member or assignee of the member has for federal income tax purposes.[3]

A single-member LLC may be formed in Georgia.[4]

[B]   *Taxation of LLC and Members*

A Georgia LLC is not subject to tax. Members of the LLC are taxed on their distributive shares of income, whether or not distributed.[5] The members of the LLC must include their distributive shares of income on their individual returns.[6] There is a 4 percent withholding tax on distributions to nonresident members, subject to certain exceptions.[7]

[C]   *Real Estate Transfer Taxes*

No real estate transfer taxes are due as a result of the recordation of the election to form an LLC.[8] The election is filed with the office of the clerk of the superior court in the county in which any of the LLC's real property is located. The certified copy of the election is then recorded in the clerk's books. The LLC is indexed as the grantee.

[D]   *Conversion to LLC*

A corporation, limited partnership, or general partnership may elect to become a limited liability company by filing an election.[9] An LLC formed by election may file a copy of the election, certified by the secretary of state, in the office of the clerk of the superior court of the county where any real property owned by the

---

[2] Ga. Code Ann. §14-11-1104.
[3] *Id.*
[4] Ga. Code Ann. §14-11-203.
[5] Ga. Dept. of Rev. Reg. §560-7-3.08.
[6] Ga. Dept. of Rev. Reg. §560-7-3.08(5).
[7] Ga. Code Ann. §48-7-129.
[8] Ga. Code Ann. §14-11-212.
[9] *Id.*

LLC is located and may record the certified copy of the election in the books kept by such clerk for recordation of deeds in the county. The entity electing to become the LLC is indexed as the grantor. The LLC is indexed as a grantee. No real estate taxes are due with respect to the recordation of the election.[10]

[E]   Tax Returns

An LLC organized or qualified to do business in Georgia or deriving income from property located in Georgia must file a Georgia return on Form 700, State of Georgia Partnership Income Tax Return.[11] The return must be filed on or before the fifteenth day of the fourth month following the close of the tax year. It must be filed with the Georgia Income Tax Division, Department of Revenue, P.O. Box 740399, Atlanta, GA 30374-0399.

The Georgia return is similar to the federal return on Form 1065 in most respects. The accounting period and accounting methods for the Georgia return must be the same as those for the federal return. A copy of the federal return and all supporting schedules must be attached to the Georgia return.

Schedule 2 of IRS Form 1065 sets forth the distributable income for the members of the LLC. There is no separate schedule attached to Georgia Form 700. However, if an LLC has more than four members, the LLC must attach to Form 700 a separate schedule for the additional members in the same format as Schedule 2 of Form 1065.

If the Internal Revenue Service adjusts the net income of the LLC or has adjusted the net income of the LLC during the previous five years, the LLC must submit a detailed statement of the adjustment under separate cover to the Georgia Income Tax Division, P.O. Box 740399, Atlanta, GA 30374-0399.

[F]   Apportionment of Income

If an LLC does business within and outside the state of Georgia, there is an apportionment and allocation formula that must be used to compute Georgia net income. If business income from the LLC is derived from property owned or business done within the state and outside the state, the tax is imposed only on that portion of the business income that is reasonably attributable to the property owned and business done within the state. Where income is derived principally from the manufacture, production, or sale of tangible personal property, the portion of the net income attributable to property owned or business done within Georgia is based on the three-factor formula. The three factors are the property, payroll, and gross receipts factors.

---

[10] Ga. Code Ann. §48-6-1.
[11] Ga. Dept. of Rev. Reg. §560-7-3.08(5).

[G]   Annual Report

An LLC must file an annual report in Georgia.[12] Foreign limited liability companies qualified to do business in Georgia are also required to file annual reports. The annual report is filed with the secretary of state. It must set forth the name of the LLC, the jurisdiction under whose laws it is organized in the case of a foreign LLC, the street address and county of its registered office, the name of its registered agent at that office, the mailing address of its principal place of business, and any additional information required by the secretary of state. The annual report must be filed between January 1 and April 1 or such later date required by the secretary of state.

[H]   Filing Fees

Georgia imposes the following filing fees on LLCs:[13]

Articles of organization	$ 75
Certificate of authority to do business in Georgia	$200
Annual registration (foreign or domestic)	$ 25

[I]   References

J. Kaplan, Kaplan's Nadler Georgia Corporations, Limited Partnerships and Limited Liability Companies, With Forms (1994).

A. Pinney, Georgia Limited Liability Company Forms and Practice Manual (1995).

§23.13   HAWAII

Hawaii adopted the Uniform Limited Liability Company Act effective April 1, 1997.[1]

[A]   State Tax Classification and Applicability of General Tax Laws

The Hawaii Department of Taxation issued a tax information release regarding the classification of LLCs under the federal check-the-box regulations pending adoption by the department of its own rules on the subject.[2] The release also

---

[12] Ga. Code Ann. §14-11-1103.

[13] Ga. Code Ann. §14-11-1101.

§23.13   [1] Haw. Rev. Stat. §§428-101 to 428-1302.

[2] Tax Information Release No. 97-4, Haw. Dept. of Taxn. (Aug. 4, 1997).

discusses the applicability of the Hawaii general tax laws to LLCs. The following interim rules apply:

- The department will follow the federal check-the-box regulations for purposes of the Hawaii income tax law. Each entity, owner, or other appropriate person specified under the check-the-box regulations that is responsible for filing a return must file a Hawaii return consistent with the federal classification. The effective date of the rules is January 1, 1997. If an LLC is classified as either a partnership or a corporation for federal income tax purposes, the same classification applies for Hawaii income tax purposes regardless of whether the classification is by default or election. If a single-member LLC is disregarded as an entity separate from its owner for federal income tax purposes, the entity is also disregarded for Hawaii income tax purposes.
- An LLC that elects its classification by filing Form 8832 with the IRS must attach a copy of that form to the LLC's Hawaii income tax or information return. The form must be attached to the return covering the first tax year in which the LLC carries on business in Hawaii, derives income from sources in Hawaii, or makes distributions that are received by a pass-through entity owner who either is a resident of Hawaii or carries on a business in Hawaii.[3] If an LLC elects this classification, but is not required to file a Hawaii return for the tax year, the appropriate person specified under the check-the-box regulations must attach a copy of Form 8832 to that person's Hawaii income tax or information return for the tax year that includes the date on which the election was effective.
- The check-the-box regulations are applicable to the general excise tax law under chapter 237 of the Hawaii Revised Statutes and to other gross receipts and transaction-type Hawaii taxes. There are modifications for single-member LLCs. The entity classification under federal law controls the classification of the entity for purposes of the general excise tax,[4] transient accommodations tax,[5] public service company tax,[6] fuel tax,[7] liquor tax,[8] cigarette and tobacco tax,[9] conveyance tax,[10] rental motor vehicle and tour vehicle surcharge tax, and nursing facility tax laws.[11] All LLCs, including single-member LLCs, are taxable at the entity level for purposes of the general excise tax and the other gross receipts and transaction-type Hawaii taxes.[12] For example, if an LLC is classified as a partnership for income tax purposes, the general excise tax and the other gross receipts and transaction-

---

[3] See Haw. Admin. Rules §18-235-95.
[4] See Haw. Rev. Stat. ch. 237.
[5] See Haw. Rev. Stat. ch. 237D.
[6] See Haw. Rev. Stat. ch. 239M.
[7] See Haw. Rev. Stat. ch. 243.
[8] See Haw. Rev. Stat. ch. 244D.
[9] See Haw. Rev. Stat. ch. 245.
[10] See Haw. Rev. Stat. ch. 247.
[11] See Haw. Rev. Stat. ch. 346E.
[12] See In re Island Holidays, Ltd., 59 Haw. 307 (1978).

type taxes are imposed at the entity level. Similarly, a single-member LLC is treated as a taxable entity for purposes of these taxes even though the LLC is disregarded under the federal check-the-box regulations.

- An LLC is taxable on its business with its members, and they are taxable on their business with the LLC. A single-member LLC is taxable on its business with its member, and the member is taxable on its business with the LLC unless specifically exempted under applicable law.[13]
- Members are not subject to the general excise tax on distributive shares of income or distributions from an LLC that is classified as a partnership, provided those shares or distributions represent a return on the members' investment in and not from their business with the LLC. The same treatment applies to distributive shares of income or distributions from an LLC to its members.
- License and registration requirements are applicable at the entity level of the LLC. All LLCs, including single-member LLCs, must have a general excise tax license. They must also have, if appropriate, licenses and certificates of registration required by the transient accommodations tax, field tax, liquor tax, cigarette and tobacco tax, rental motor vehicle and tour vehicle surcharge tax, and nursing facility tax laws. A single-member LLC that is disregarded as an entity separate from the owner for income tax purposes must be licensed and registered in the LLC's name.
- The Department of Taxation will follow the IRS regulations and rulings relating to the need for a new federal employer identification number in determining whether a new general excise tax license and other new licenses or registrations are necessary. Thus, if a new federal employer identification number is required, as is the case when the business of a sole proprietorship is transferred to a partnership or to a corporation, then a new general excise tax license and other new licenses and applicable registrations are also required. However, a new federal employer identification number, a new general excise tax license, and other applicable new licenses and registrations are not required when the LLC elects, under the federal check-the-box regulations, to change its federal and Hawaii income tax classification or when a domestic partnership converts into an LLC classified as a partnership (or vice versa). When a change in name occurs, but a new license is not required, taxpayers must provide the Department of Taxation with the name change information on Form GEW-TA-RB-5.

[B]   Single-Member LLCs

One or more persons may form an LLC, which may consist of one or more members.[14]

---

[13] *See, e.g.,* Haw. Rev. Stat. §237-23.5.
[14] Haw. Rev. Stat. §428-202.

[C]   Allocations

Income, gain, loss, deductions, and credits must be allocated among the members according to the LLC operating agreement for sharing income or loss generally. If the members agree, specific items may be allocated among them in a ratio different from the ratio for sharing income or loss generally.

[D]   Tax Filing Requirements

Hawaii LLCs and LLCs qualified to do business in Hawaii must file Form N-20, Partnership Return of Income.[15] The form is an information return. It is used to report the income, deductions, credits, gains, and losses from the operation of the LLC.

The LLC must list all items of gross income and allowable deductions, as well as various additional items of information. The return must include the income, deductions, and credits attributable everywhere, together with the income, deductions, and credits attributable only to Hawaii. Hawaii follows the provisions of federal law, Subchapter K, in determining Hawaii taxable income.[16]

The return must be filed on or before the twentieth day of the fourth month following the close of the tax year of the LLC. It must be filed with the taxation district office in which the LLC has its principal place of business. If the LLC does not have a place of business in Hawaii, the return must be filed with the Department of Taxation, P.O. Box 3559, Honolulu, HI 96811-3559.

An Application for Automatic Extension of Time to File Hawaii Return for Partnership may be filed on Form N-100. There is an automatic three-month extension. The form must be filed by the due date of the LLC return.

An LLC must file an information return if it makes payments of rents, commissions, or other fixed or determinable income totaling $600 or more to any one person in the course of its trade or business during the calendar year. It must report interest payments totaling $10 or more. For example, if an LLC pays a person $600 or more in a calendar year to perform services under a subcontract-type arrangement in which no employment taxes are withheld, the LLC must file federal Form 1099-MISC, Miscellaneous Income.

LLCs must use Form N-196, Annual Summary Transmittal of Hawaii Information Returns, to summarize and send information returns to the respective taxation district office.

Although a Hawaii LLC is not subject to income tax, the members are liable for income tax on their distributive shares of LLC income, whether or not distributed. These items are included on their individual tax returns. The total amount of distributive share items is reported on Schedule K to Form N-20.

---

[15] Haw. Rev. Stat. §235-95; Haw. Admin. Rules §18-235-4-07(e).
[16] Haw. Rev. Stat. §§235-2.2, 235-2.3.

[E] Apportionment of Income

Each LLC must state specifically the income attributable to the state and the income attributable outside the state with respect to each member. Ordinary income or loss from a trade or business is attributable to the state of Hawaii by use of the apportionment of business income allocation provisions of the Uniform Division of Income for Tax Purposes Act.[17] Business income is apportioned to Hawaii by multiplying the income by a fraction, the numerator of which is a property factor, payroll factor, and sales factor, and the denominator of which is three. If the apportionment does not fairly represent the extent of the LLC's business activities in the state, the LLC may request the use of separate accounting, the exclusion of one or more of the factors, the inclusion of one or more additional factors, or the use of any other method to accurately reflect the LLC's business activities in the state. Schedules O and P of Form N-20 are used to show this computation. Income or loss of an LLC is allocated to a member only for the part of the year in which that member is a member of the LLC. The LLC must either allocate on a daily basis or divide the partnership year into segments and allocate income, loss, or special items in each segment among the persons who are members during that segment.

[F] Annual Report

An LLC must file an annual report in Hawaii.[18] The annual report must set forth the following information:

- The name of the LLC and the country of organization
- The address of its designated office and the name of its agent at that office
- The name of each manager
- The name of each member if the LLC is managed by members

[G] Filing Fees

Hawaii imposes the following filing fees on LLCs:[19]

Articles of organization	$100
Certificate of authority of foreign LLC	$100
Annual report	$ 25

---

[17] Haw. Rev. Stat. §235-29.
[18] Haw. Rev. Stat. §428-210.
[19] Haw. Rev. Stat. §428-1301.

§23.14   IDAHO

Idaho enacted the Idaho Limited Liability Company Act effective July 1, 1993.[1]

[A]   State Tax Classification

Limited liability companies are classified in Idaho in the same manner as under the federal income tax laws.[2] Effective January 1, 1998, Idaho adopted the federal check-the-box regulations for determining whether an LLC is classified as a partnership, corporation or sole proprietorship for Idaho personal income and corporate franchise tax purposes.[3]

[B]   Taxation of LLC and Members

Members of an LLC are taxed on their distributive shares of income. An individual member may elect to have the LLC pay the tax on the member's income from the LLC. The income includes a member's distributive share of income, guaranteed payments, loss, and deduction. If this election is made, the LLC must pay tax on such income at the 7.6 percent corporate rate. An individual member cannot make the election if the member meets the Idaho filing requirements and is obligated to report other income to Idaho not covered by the election. If an individual who meets the Idaho filing requirements does not make the election and does not file an Idaho individual tax return or pay the tax due, the LLC will be taxed on such income at the corporate tax rate.[4]

An LLC is taxed on a nonresident member's distributive share of income if the LLC derives income from Idaho sources and the nonresident member does not file the required Idaho returns or pay the Idaho taxes.[5] The LLC must pay tax at the 7.6 percent corporate tax rate on such member's distributive share of income. The permanent building excise tax also applies to such income.

[C]   Tax Returns

Idaho LLCs that are classified as partnerships for federal income tax purposes must file Idaho partnership tax returns on Form 65, Idaho Partnership Return of Income. The return must be filed if the LLC has one or more members residing in Idaho or if the LLC transacts business in Idaho.[6] Transacting business in Idaho is indicated by, but not limited to, the following activities:

---

§23.14   [1] H.B. 381, ch. 224, 1993 Idaho Sess. Laws; Idaho Code §§53-601 to 53-672.

[2] Idaho Code §63-3006A.

[3] Ch. 55, H.D. 485, Laws 1998.

[4] Instructions to Form 65, Idaho Partnership Return of Income.

[5] Idaho Code §63-3022L(3); Idaho State Tax Comm. R. 35.01.01.107.

[6] Idaho Code §63-3030(a)(9).

- Owning or leasing, as lessor or lessee, any property in Idaho
- Soliciting business in Idaho
- Being a member of a partnership with business in Idaho
- Engaging in any Idaho activity from which income is received, realized, or derived
- Having an agent, such as a collector, repair person, delivery person, or other person acting on behalf of the LLC in Idaho

A complete copy of the federal income tax return must be attached to the Idaho partnership income tax return. All Schedules K-1 must be attached to the return or submitted with the return on microfiche. The return must be signed by an authorized individual on behalf of the LLC.

The return and payment must be sent to Idaho State Tax Commission, P.O. Box 56, Boise, ID 83756-0201.

The due date of the return is the fifteenth day of the fourth month following the close of the tax year. For calendar year LLCs, the due date is April 15. LLCs that are classified as corporations for federal income tax purposes must file Idaho corporation income tax returns on Form 41.

Effective January 1, 1999, resident and nonresident members of an LLC may elect to pay individual income taxes on the LLC's tax return.[7] The LLC must pay taxes at the 7.6 percent corporate tax rate on such members' distributive shares of income. The LLC must also pay the $10 permanent building fund tax for each resident member making the election. Members of a publicly traded LLC may not make the election, since such entities are not classified as partnerships under Idaho law.

[D] Extensions

An LLC may obtain an extension of time to file the return by filing an extension request on Form 41E. The extension must be filed on or before the due date of the tax return. Payment of the estimated tax must accompany the extension. The extension is effective for a six-month period. No further extensions are allowed.

[E] Accounting Periods and Methods

The LLC must use the same accounting period as used for federal tax purposes. A change in the accounting period must have prior approval from the Internal Revenue Service. A copy of the federal approval on Form 1128, Application to Adopt, Change, or Retain a Tax Year, must be attached to the return.

An Idaho LLC must also use the same accounting methods as used for federal tax purposes. A change of accounting methods must have prior approval from

---

[7] Idaho Code §63-3022L(1), (2).

the Internal Revenue Service. The LLC must attach a copy of the federal approval on Form 3115, Application for Change in Accounting Method.

[F]   Amended Returns

Amended returns must be filed on Form 41X, Amended Business Income Tax Return.

If the LLC is subject to a federal audit and if the federal taxable income or tax credit is changed because of the federal audit, the LLC must send written notice to the Idaho State Tax Commission within 60 days of the final federal determination. The LLC must include copies of all schedules supplied by the Internal Revenue Service. If additional taxes are owed, the LLC is subject to a 5 percent negligence penalty if it fails to send timely notice. If the final federal determination results in an Idaho refund and the statute of limitations is closed, the LLC has one year from the date of final determination to file for a refund.

[G]   Apportionment of Income

There are special rules that apply to LLCs that operate in Idaho and in another state or country or that have at least one member that is a member of a unitary group. Business income must be apportioned. The apportionment formula consists of three factors: property, payroll, and sales. The three percentages are averaged to arrive at the Idaho apportionment factor. For most taxpayers, the sales factor is double-weighted.

Business income subject to apportionment includes income from transactions or activities in the regular course of the LLC's trade or business. Business income also includes income from tangible or intangible property if the acquisition, management, or disposition of the property is an integral part of the LLC's regular trade or business.

If the allocation and apportionment provisions do not fairly represent the LLC's business activities in Idaho, the LLC may take advantage of one of the exceptions. The exceptions include separate accounting, exclusion of a factor, and modified factors for certain industries.

An Idaho LLC is treated as part of a unitary multistate business when the operations conducted in Idaho are integrated with, depend on, or contribute to the business outside Idaho. There are two tests to determine whether the LLC is part of a unitary business. The first test is the three unities test. The three elements of a unitary business include (1) unity of ownership; (2) unity of operation as evidenced by central divisions for such functions as purchasing, advertising, accounting, and management; and (3) unity of use in the LLC's centralized executive force and centralized system of operation.

An alternative test is a contribution or dependency test. The operation of the LLC meets a contribution or dependency test if the operation of the portion of the business done in Idaho depends on or contributes to the operation of the overall business.

If unity of ownership exists, the presence of any of the following factors creates a strong presumption that the activities of the LLC constitute a unitary business:

1. All activities of the group are in the same general line or type of business.
2. The activities of the group constitute different steps in a vertically integrated enterprise.
3. The group is characterized by centralized management.

The LLC must complete Schedule 42, Supplemental Schedule for Multistate/Multinational Business, to compute the apportionment factor. Schedule 42 is also used by LLCs that have income from business activities that is taxable in Idaho or another state or country.

[H] Annual Report

An Idaho LLC is not required to file an annual report.[8]

[I] Filing Fees

There are the following filing fees in Idaho:[9]

Articles of organization	$100
Foreign LLC registration application	$100
Annual fee	$ 0

§23.15 ILLINOIS

Illinois enacted the Illinois Limited Liability Company Act in 1992, effective January 1, 1994.[1]

[A] State Tax Classification

Illinois LLCs and foreign LLCs doing business in Illinois are classified for state tax purposes in the same manner as LLCs are classified for federal tax purposes.[2] A foreign or domestic LLC that is classified under federal law as a corporation is classified as a corporation for state tax purposes.[3] A foreign or domestic LLC that is classified as a partnership for federal income tax purposes is classified as

---

[8] Idaho Code §53-613.
[9] Idaho Code §53-665.
§23.15 [1] Pub. Act No. 87-1062 (S.B. 2163), 1992 Ill. Laws; 805 Ill. Comp. Stat. 180/1-1 to 180/60-1.
[2] 35 Ill. Comp. Stat. 5/1501.
[3] 35 Ill. Comp. Stat. 5/1501(a)(4).

a partnership for Illinois tax purposes.[4] A foreign or domestic LLC that is classified as a disregarded entity for federal tax purposes is a disregarded entity for state income tax purposes.[5] Effective January 1, 1998, an LLC may have one or more members.[6]

[B]   Taxation of LLC and Members

Illinois LLCs that are classified as partnerships must pay a personal property replacement tax at a rate of 1.5 percent of net income.[7] The state also imposes the personal property replacement tax on all corporations subject to the regular income tax. A corporation includes a limited liability company that is classified as a corporation for federal tax purposes.[8]

If an LLC is classified as a partnership, income and losses of the LLC are passed through to members and taxed to them individually. Illinois has adopted the federal base as a starting point in determining income.[9]

[C]   Tax Returns

The LLC must file two forms, Form IL-1065, Partnership Replacement Tax Return, and Form IL-2569, Personal Property Replacement Tax.

The LLC reports the 1.5 percent replacement tax on Form IL-1065. If a member of the LLC is subject to the personal property replacement tax, the LLC must attach a copy of Form IL-2569 to Form IL-1065. It must also keep a copy of the form on file for each member who is subject to the Illinois personal property replacement tax. In this event, the personal property replacement tax is paid at the member level. Form IL-1065 must be filed with the Illinois Department of Revenue, P.O. Box 19031, Springfield, IL 62794-9031.

All LLCs doing business in Illinois must file Form IL-1065 except LLCs formed for the sole purpose of playing the Illinois state lottery.

Illinois LLCs that are required to file Form IL-1065 must register in Illinois by filing Form NUC-1, Illinois Business Registration. Form NUC-1 may be obtained from the Illinois Department of Revenue, P.O. Box 19010, Springfield, IL 62794-9010. The LLC must register with the Illinois Department of Revenue before filing its return.

An LLC may obtain an automatic six-month extension of time to file its tax return. It may use Form IL-505-B, Automatic Extension Payment. This form is not required.

An LLC must pay the Illinois replacement tax in full on or before the fifteenth

---

[4] 35 Ill. Comp. Stat. 5/1501(a)(16).
[5] Ill. Dept. of Revenue No. IT 01-0004-PLR (Feb. 13, 2001).
[6] 805 Ill. Comp. Stat. 180/5-1.
[7] 35 Ill. Comp. Stat. 5/201(c).
[8] 35 Ill. Comp. Stat. 5/1501(a)(4).
[9] 35 Ill. Comp. Stat. 5/203(e).

day of the fourth month following the close of the tax year. The payment date applies even though the LLC has obtained an automatic extension of time for filing the return. LLCs are not required to pay estimated taxes.

LLCs may file amended returns by filing Form IL-1065, marking the return "CORRECTED" at the top of the form and showing any applicable changes. If the LLC needs to correct or change its return after it has been filed and after the automatic extension due date has passed, the LLC must file Form IL-843, Amended Return or Notice of Change in Income.

An Illinois LLC may file a composite return for any nonresident member of the LLC.[10]

The LLC must apportion its income if any part of the income is derived outside of Illinois. The apportionment is based on a three-factor formula: the property, payroll, and sales factors.

Illinois LLCs, managers, and members are subject to the following taxes effective January 1, 1994: the Illinois retailers' occupation (sales) tax; hotel operators' occupational, service occupation, use, and service use taxes; motor fuel and cigarette taxes; real estate transfer, automobile renting, and utility taxes; and the personal liability provisions of the Uniform Penalty and Interest Act.[11]

[D] Annual Report

Illinois LLCs must file annual reports with the Illinois Secretary of State.[12] Foreign LLCs qualified to transact business in Illinois must also file annual reports. The report must set forth the following information:

- The name of the LLC
- The address, including street number, of its registered office in the state and the name of its registered agent at that address
- The address, including street number, of its principal place of business; the name and address of its managers or, if none, its members
- Any additional information required by the secretary of state

[E] Filing Fees

Illinois imposes the following filing fees on LLCs effective January 1, 1998:[13]

Articles of organization	$400
Registration of foreign LLC	$400
Annual report	$200

---

[10] 35 Ill. Comp. Stat. 5/502.
[11] Pub. Act No. 88-480 (S.B. 553), 1993 Ill. Laws.
[12] 805 Ill. Comp. Stat. 180/50-1.
[13] 805 Ill. Comp. Stat. 180/50-10.

[F] References

M. Sargent & W. Schwidetzky, Limited Liability Company Handbook, Law — Sample Documents — Forms, §4.08, Illinois Form of Articles of Organization and Operating Agreement (1995-1996 ed.).

§23.16 INDIANA

Indiana enacted the Indiana Business Flexibility Act effective July 1, 1993.[1] The act was added to the Indiana Code to provide for the formation of limited liability companies. It also amended the adjusted gross income tax definition of "partnership" to include LLCs that are treated as partnerships for federal tax purposes.

[A] State Tax Classification

Indiana LLCs are classified for state income tax purposes in the same manner that they are classified for federal tax purposes.[2]

A tax directive issued before the IRS issued the federal check-the-box regulations determined that an Indiana LLC would be classified as a partnership or corporation for tax purposes depending on whether the LLC possessed or lacked the four corporate characteristics of centralization of management, continuity of life, free transferability of interest, and limited liability.[3]

Indiana permits single-member LLCs.[4] These LLCs are classified as corporations or proprietorships depending on their classification for federal tax purposes.

[B] Taxation of LLC and Members

LLCs are not subject to an Indiana income or franchise tax.[5] However, publicly traded partnerships that are treated as limited liability companies under section 7704 of the Internal Revenue Code are classified for Indiana tax purposes in the same manner that they are classified for federal tax purposes.

Members of the LLC are taxed on their distributive shares of income, gain, loss, credit, and deductions.[6] A member's share of profit or loss from the Indiana LLC is included in the member's calculation of federal adjusted gross income and is generally subject to the same rules for arriving at Indiana adjusted gross income. Therefore, a member's distributive share, before any modifications required by Indiana statutes, is the same ratio and amount as determined under

---

§23.16 [1] S.B. 485, 1993 Ind. Acts; Ind. Code Ann. §§23-18-1-1 to 23-18-12-11.
[2] Ind. Code Ann. §6-3-1-19.
[3] Tax Policy Directive No. 2, Ind. Dept. of Rev. (May 1992).
[4] Ind. Code Ann. §23-18-6-0.5.
[5] Ind. Code Ann. §6-3-4-11(a).
[6] Id.

section 704 of the Internal Revenue Code and regulations thereunder. The members must include their shares of all LLC income, whether or not distributed, on their separate or individual Indiana income or franchise tax returns. Each member's distributive share of income is adjusted by modifications provided in the Indiana statutes.[7]

[C] Tax Returns

LLCs conducting business within Indiana must file an annual return on Form IT-65, Indiana Partnership Return. The return must be filed with the Indiana Department of Revenue.[8]

The first four pages of the LLC's partnership return on Form 1065 must be attached to the state return. The federal Schedules K-1 may not be attached to the return, but must be available for inspection upon request by the Indiana Department of Revenue.[9]

Any LLC doing business in Indiana or deriving gross income from sources within Indiana is required to file the return.[10] The following activities constitute doing business in Indiana or deriving income from Indiana sources:[11]

- Maintaining an office, warehouse, construction site, or other place of business
- Maintaining an inventory of merchandise or material for sale, distribution, or manufacture or of consigned goods
- Selling or distributing merchandise to customers directly from company-owned or -operated vehicles when the title to the merchandise is transferred from the seller or distributor to the customer at the time of sale or distribution
- Providing services to customers in Indiana or used in Indiana
- Owning, renting, or operating a business or income-producing real or personal property in Indiana
- Accepting orders in Indiana with no right of approval or rejection in another state
- Transporting interstate

The accounting period for which Form IT-65 is filed and the method of accounting adopted must be the same as used for federal tax purposes. If the LLC changes its tax year or method of accounting, it must give notice to the Department of Revenue.

The initial due date for the return is the fifteenth day of the fourth month following the close of the LLC's tax year. The Department of Revenue recognizes

---

[7] *See* Ind. Code Ann. §6-3-1-3.5(A), (B).
[8] Ind. Admin. Code, r. 45.
[9] Ind. Code Ann. §6-3-4-10(b).
[10] Ind. Code Ann. §6-3-4-10.
[11] Instructions to Form IT-65, p. 1.

the Internal Revenue Service's Application for Automatic Extension of Time on Form 8736 or Form 8800. It is not necessary to file a separate copy of the form with the department to request an Indiana extension. Instead, the federal extension form must be attached to the Indiana return of the LLC.

An LLC that files an amended federal return that affects the Indiana income or taxable income reportable by the members must file an amended Indiana return. The amended return must be filed within 120 days after the filing of the amended federal return.

The LLC must complete Schedule IN K-1, Partners' Share of Income, Deductions, Modifications, and Credits, for each member. Schedule IN K-1 shows the member's share of income, credits, and modifications. The LLC must show the federal Schedule K-1 amounts for full-year Indiana resident members. For all corporate members and nonresident individual members, the federal Schedule K-1 amounts are multiplied by the apportionment percentage calculated on the worksheet.

A limited liability company that is classified as a corporation for federal tax purposes must file Form IT-20.

[D] Withholding Taxes

An LLC is considered to be the taxpayer with respect to withholding taxes. The LLC must register with the Indiana Department of Revenue and become an Indiana withholding agent on behalf of certain specified residents and non-residents. In the case of nonresidents, the LLC must withhold Indiana state and/or county income taxes from employees who work in Indiana, but who are not residents of Indiana. The LLC must withhold state income taxes at the rate of 3.4 percent on the apportioned distributive shares of LLC income (on current year earnings) each time that it pays or credits any of its nonresident and part-year resident individual members. This rule does not apply to residents of reverse credit jurisdictions (Arizona, California, Oregon, District of Columbia) that are subject to and pay income taxes at rates of 3.4 percent or higher in their resident jurisdictions.

The withholding at the appropriate adopting county's nonresident tax rate is required for each non-Indiana resident member whose principal place of business or employment on January 1 is located in an Indiana county that has adopted a county income tax.

LLCs must withhold on income distributions to all non-Indiana-domiciled corporate partners an amount that reflects the ultimate tax liability due Indiana because of the LLC's activities.[12] A nonresident member must also file a state tax return.[13]

---

[12] Ind. Code Ann. §6-3-4-12.
[13] Ind. Code Ann. §6-3-4-12(f).

[E]   Use Tax

LLCs are subject to the use tax. The use tax is due upon the storage, use, or consumption of tangible personal property purchased in a transaction in Indiana or elsewhere unless the transaction is exempted from the sales and use tax by law or the sales tax due and paid on the transaction equals the use tax due.

[F]   Apportionment and Allocation

An Indiana LLC must file an apportionment worksheet with its return if the LLC is doing business both within and outside of Indiana and has any members who are not domiciled in Indiana.

An LLC may file a composite adjusted gross income tax return on behalf of non-Indiana-resident individual members electing to participate in the composite return.

A full-year resident member of an Indiana LLC reports the entire distributive share of LLC income or loss, as adjusted, no matter where the LLC's business is located or in which state it does business. The individual member of the LLC must complete Form IT-40, Indiana Individual Income Tax Return.

Part and full-year nonresident members must report their shares of income or loss, as adjusted, from the LLC that is derived from or attributed to sources within Indiana. Indiana source income is determined by use of the apportionment formula described in the Indiana statutes.[14] When an LLC both has nonresident members and conducts business within and outside of Indiana, the LLC must include the apportionment worksheet with Form IT-65. The nonresident members must complete Form IT-40PNR, Indiana Part-Year or Nonresident Individual Income Tax Return. The members may claim credit on their returns for amounts withheld by the LLC from the members' income. Copy C of Form WH-18 must be attached to the return to verify any such credit.

An LLC may file a composite return on behalf of nonresident members.[15] Nonresident members are exempt from the filing an Indiana individual income tax return only if they are included as members of a composite return.

A part-year nonresident member is required to file Form IT-40PNR, reporting the total amount of income or loss received while residing in Indiana and that part of Indiana's source income received while a nonresident. The member also reports apportioned Indiana income or loss, as adjusted, on Form IT-40PNR.

[G]   Corporate Members

Corporate members of the LLC must report their distributive shares of the LLC's income or loss on Form IT-20, IT-20SC, IT-20S, IT-20NP, or IT-41. The

---

[14] *See* Ind. Code Ann. §6-3-2-2(B).

[15] Ind. Code Ann. §6-3-4-12(g). The composite return is filed on Schedule IT-65COMP, Partner's Composite Adjusted Growth Income Tax Return.

distributions are fully taxable for gross, adjusted gross, and supplemental net income tax purposes.

Corporate partners doing business within and outside of Indiana must determine their taxable income from Indiana sources using the allocation and apportionment provisions set forth in the Indiana statutes.[16] These allocation and apportionment provisions generally follow the Uniform Division of Income for Tax Purposes Act. A multistate corporation that is a member of an LLC must first determine what part of its adjusted gross income (which includes all LLC income) constitutes business income and what part is nonbusiness income according to the regulations. If the corporate member's activities and the LLC's activities constitute a unitary business, the business income of the unitary business attributable to Indiana is determined by a three-factor formula. The formula consists of the property, payroll, and sales of the corporate member and its actual share of the LLC's factors for any LLC tax year ending within or with the corporate member's income year.

A corporation that is the sole owner of an LLC classified as a corporation may file a consolidated tax return with that corporation.[17]

[H]   Filing Fees

Indiana imposes the following filing fees on LLCs:[18]

Articles of organization	$ 90
Certificate of authority for foreign LLC to do business in the state	$ 90
Biennial report (in writing)	$ 30
Biennial report (filed electronically)	$ 20

[I]   References

M. Sargent & W. Schwidetzky, Limited Liability Company Handbook, Law — Sample Documents — Forms, §4.09, Indiana Form of Articles of Organization and Operating Agreement (1995-1996 ed.).

§23.17   IOWA

Iowa enacted the Iowa Limited Liability Company Act effective July 1, 1992.[1]

---

[16] See Ind. Code Ann. §6-3-2-2(B) to (H).
[17] Rev. Rul. No. 2001-12 IT, Indiana Department of Revenue (2002).
[18] Ind. Code Ann. §23-18-12-3.
§23.17   [1] H.F. 327, 1992 Iowa Acts; Iowa Code Ann. §§490A.100 to 490A.1601.

[A]   State Tax Classification

Iowa follows federal law in its classification of LLCs.[2] An LLC that is classified as a partnership for federal tax purposes is classified as a partnership for Iowa tax purposes.[3] An LLC that is classified as a corporation under federal law is treated as a corporation for state income tax purposes.[4] Iowa follows the federal tax classification for single-member LLCs.[5]

Under prior law, Iowa LLCs were generally taxed as partnerships.[6] The major attributes of a limited liability company for state tax purposes were the following:

- Limited liability of the owners
- Lack of perpetual duration
- Ability to have subsidiaries
- Formation that was possible by as few as one or two person
- Use of the words "limited company" or "LLC" in the name
- Possible limitation on the transfer or assignment of membership interests
- Formation possible by licensed professionals with restrictions similar to professional corporations[7]

[B]   Taxation of LLC and Members

Iowa LLCs that are classified as partnerships are not taxpayers under Iowa law. All items of income, gain, loss, credit, and deduction pass through to the members. The members are taxable on their distributive shares, computed on the same basis as under federal law.[8]

Nonresident members are taxed on their distributive shares of income allocable to Indiana.[9]

The Iowa corporate income tax applies to each corporation organized under Iowa law and to foreign corporations qualified to do business in Iowa. A corporation includes a limited liability company that is classified as a corporation under federal law.

[C]   Withholding Taxes

Every employer is responsible for paying withholding taxes. Employers that fail to withhold or deposit sums required to be paid are liable to the state of Iowa

---

[2] Iowa Code Ann. §422.15.2; Iowa Dept. of Rev. & Fin. R. 701-45.1(422).

[3] Tax News, Vol. 20, No. 1, Dept. of Rev. & Fin. (Aug. 1994); Rule 701-45.1(422), issued by Iowa Dept. of Rev. & Fin.

[4] Iowa Code Ann. §422.32.4; Tax News, Vol. 20, No. 1, Dept. of Rev. & Fin. (Aug. 1994); Iowa Dept. of Rev. & Fin. R. 701-45.1(422).

[5] Iowa Dept. of Rev. & Fin. R. 701-45.1(422).

[6] Tax News, Dept. of Rev. & Fin. (Aug. 1992).

[7] Id.

[8] Iowa Dept. of Rev. & Fin. R. 701-45.4(422).

[9] Iowa Dept. of Rev. & Fin. R. 701-46.4(422).

for the tax. A member or manager of an Iowa LLC is personally liable for remitting withheld taxes.[10]

The LLC must withhold taxes on payments of income to nonresidents of Iowa.[11]

[D]   Tax Returns

Every LLC deriving income from property owned in Iowa or from a trade, business, profession, or occupation carried on within Iowa and every Iowa LLC having a place of business in the state must file a partnership return on Form IA 1065, Partnership Return of Income.[12] A complete copy of IRS Form 1065, including Schedule K-1 for each member and all other supporting documents, must be attached to the Iowa return. The return must be filed regardless of the amount of income or loss and regardless of the residence of the members.

The return must be filed on the same period basis as for federal tax purposes. This rule applies even though the members may be reporting their incomes on different tax year bases.

Residents of Iowa who are members in a LLC must report on Form IA 1040 all items of income or loss shown on the federal Schedule K-1 for the LLC. These items are reported in a similar manner as on IRS Form 1040. Net modifications of the Iowa partnership return are reported on each member's IA 1040 either as "other income" if the modifications are a positive amount or as "other adjustments" if the modifications are a negative amount.

Every member of an LLC who is a nonresident and who has $1,000 or more in net income from property located in the state, or from any business, trade, profession, or occupation carried on within Iowa, and who along with his or her spouse has source income of $13,500 or more ($9,000 or more for single individuals) must file an Iowa income tax return. Nonresidents compute their tax on all source net income, less federal tax and standard or itemized deductions. Members then compute their tax on a pro rata basis based on Iowa source net income compared to all source net income.

[E]   Apportionment of Income

If an LLC is doing business wholly within Iowa, then all LLC income is taxable to Iowa. If the LLC is doing business both within and outside of Iowa, then the LLC can apportion the income received by nonresidents. Iowa taxes only the apportioned income. Iowa has its own Schedule K-1 for nonresident members. The state schedule shows how much of the federal Schedule K-1 income is taxable to Iowa. If the LLC is doing business wholly within Iowa, then 100 percent of the Schedule K-1 income will be taxed by Iowa. If the LLC is doing business within

---

[10] Iowa Code Ann. §422.16.4.
[11] Iowa Dept. of Rev. & Fin. R. 701-46.4(422).
[12] Iowa Dept. of Rev. & Fin. Rs. 701-45.1(422) to 701-45.3(422).

and outside of Iowa, then the Schedule K-1 income will be apportioned to Iowa using a single-factor business activity ratio.

[F]   Annual Report

An LLC is not required to file an annual report in Iowa.

[G]   Filing Fees

The filing fees in the state of Iowa are as follows:[13]

Articles of organization	$ 50
Certificate of authority for foreign corporation	$100
Annual registration	$ 0

[H]   References

M. Sargent & W. Schwidetzky, Limited Liability Company Handbook, Law — Sample Documents — Forms, §4.10, Iowa Form of Articles of Organization and Operating Agreement (1995-1996 ed.).

§23.18   KANSAS

Kansas enacted the Kansas Limited Liability Company Act effective July 1, 1990.[1]

[A]   State Tax Classification

A Kansas LLC is classified for state tax purposes in the same manner that it is classified for federal tax purposes.[2] Thus, a Kansas LLC and a foreign LLC qualified to do business in Kansas are taxed as partnerships unless classified as corporations for federal tax purposes.[3]

---

[13] Iowa Code Ann. §490A.124.
§23.18 [1] H.B. 3064, 1990 Kan. Sess. Laws; Kan. Stat. Ann. §§17-7601 to 17-7706.
[2] Kan. Stat. Ann. §17-76,138.
[3] Kan. Admin. Regs. 92-12-8.

[B]   Taxation of LLC and Members

An LLC must pay to the secretary of state an annual franchise tax. The amount of the tax is $1 for each $1,000 of net capital accounts located in or used in the state of Kansas as of the end of the preceding taxable year. The net capital accounts for these purposes are the net capital accounts required to be reported on the federal partnership return. However, no annual tax may be less than $20 or more than $2,500.[4] The franchise tax must be paid at the time that the annual report is filed with the secretary of state.

The same tax must be paid by a foreign LLC qualified to do business in Kansas.[5]

An LLC is not required to file its first annual report or to pay the annual franchise tax that must accompany the report unless the LLC has filed its articles of organization or application for authority at least six months before the last day of its tax period.[6]

If an LLC files with the secretary of state a notice of change in its tax period and the next annual report filed by the LLC subsequent to that notice is based on a tax period of less than 12 months, the annual tax liability is determined by multiplying the annual franchise tax for that year by a fraction. The numerator of the fraction is the number of months or any portion thereof covered by the annual report, and the denominator is 12. The tax may not be less than $20.[7]

An LLC that is classified as a partnership for federal tax purposes is not otherwise subject to tax.[8] The members are taxed on their distributive shares of income as determined under federal law, subject to state modifications.[9]

[C]   Tax Returns

A Kansas LLC must file a partnership return on Form K-65, Kansas Partnership Return. A copy of pages 1 through 4 of the federal Form 1065 must be attached to the Kansas return. Schedules K-1 to the federal return are not attached to the state return. The Department of Revenue has the right to request additional information as necessary. The return must be mailed to Kansas Income Tax, Kansas Department of Revenue, 915 S.W. Harrison Street, Topeka, KS 66699-7000.

The Kansas partnership return is an information return. It must be filed by every LLC that has income or loss derived from Kansas sources regardless of the amount of income or loss. Income or loss derived from Kansas sources includes the following:[10]

[4] Kan. Stat. Ann. §17-76,139(c).
[5] Kan. Stat. Ann. §17-76,139(b).
[6] Id.
[7] Id.
[8] Kan. Stat. Ann. §79-32,129(a).
[9] Kan. Stat. Ann. §§17-76,138; 79-32,129; 79-32,130; 79-32,131; 79-32,133.
[10] Kan. Stat. Ann. §79-3220(d); Kan. Admin. Reg. §92-12-55(e).

- Income or loss attributable to any ownership interest in real property or tangible personal property located in Kansas and in intangible property to the extent it is used in a trade, business, profession, or occupation carried on in Kansas
- Income or loss attributable to a trade, business, profession, or occupation carried on in Kansas

The Kansas partnership return must cover the same period as the corresponding federal partnership return. If the LLC files a return for the tax year that begins before January 1, the LLC must use the form for the calendar year in which the tax period begins.

The return must also be filed using the same accounting methods used for federal purposes. If the LLC changes its accounting methods for federal purposes, the change automatically applies to the Kansas partnership return.

The return is due by the fifteenth day of the fourth month following the close of the tax year. The return is due on or before April 15 for LLCs operating on a calendar year basis.

The director of taxation may grant a reasonable extension of time for an LLC to file a partnership return. LLCs that file Form 8736 with the IRS seeking an automatic extension of time automatically receive a three-month extension of time to file the Kansas partnership return. If an additional federal extension is requested, the Department of Taxation will honor that extension as well. A copy of the federal extension must be attached to the Kansas return when filed.

If there are changes in the partnership return after it has been filed, the LLC must file an amended Form K-65. The word "Amended" must be written on the face of the return. An LLC whose income has been adjusted by the IRS is required to report the adjustment to the Kansas Department of Revenue within 180 days after the federal adjustments are paid, are agreed to, or become final, whichever is earlier. The adjustments are reported by filing an amended Form K-65 for the applicable tax year and attaching a copy of the revenue agent's report detailing the adjustments.

LLCs that receive business income within and outside the state of Kansas must apportion the income. There are two different methods for apportionment based on a property factor, payroll factor, and sales factor.

LLCs may request an extension of time to file a return by filing Form E-2, Application for Extension of Time to File Tax Return and/or Prepayment of Tax for Corporate Income, Privilege Tax, and Partnership Return.

[D]   *Annual Report*

An LLC must file an annual report in Kansas. The report must be filed at the time prescribed for filing the state's income tax return.[11] If the LLC's tax year is other than the calendar year, it must give notice of the different tax year in writing

---

[11] Kan. Stat. Ann. §17-76,139.

to the secretary of state before December 31 of the year that it commences the different tax year. If the LLC applies for an extension of time for filing its annual income tax return under the Internal Revenue Code, the LLC must also apply to the secretary of state for an extension of time for filing its annual report. The extension request must be filed not more than 90 days after the due date of its annual report.

The annual report must set forth the name of the LLC, a reconciliation of the capital accounts for the preceding tax year as required to be reported on the federal partnership return, and a list of the members owning at least 5 percent of the capital of the company.

The secretary of state has authority to maintain the confidentiality of an annual report of an LLC containing the financial information required by the report. The confidentiality will be maintained upon application to the secretary of state verifying that the LLC meets the following requirements:

- Has a net worth of at least $5,000 that is equal to at least 5 percent of its total assets, determined in accordance with generally accepted accounting principles;
- Has never been the subject of a proceeding under chapter 7, 11, or 13 of the federal bankruptcy laws or any similar provisions of any state law, any amendments to the federal bankruptcy laws, or any predecessor;
- Is not subject to the reporting requirements under the Securities Exchange Act of 1934;
- Is not an applicant for or a holder of a license under the Kansas Parimutuel Racing Act; and
- Is not a vendor under the Kansas Lottery Act.

[E] Filing Fees

Kansas imposes the following filing fees on LLCs:[12]

Articles of organization	$150
Certificate of registration for foreign LLC	$150
Annual report	$ 0

[F] References

M. Sargent & W. Schwidetzky, Limited Liability Company Handbook, Law — Sample Documents — Forms, §4.11, Kansas Form of Articles of Organization and Operating Agreement (1995-1996 ed.).

[12] Kan. Stat. Ann. §17-76,136.

§23.19   KENTUCKY

Kentucky enacted laws authorizing limited liability companies in 1994.[1]

[A]   State Tax Classification

An LLC that is classified as a partnership for federal tax purposes is classified as a partnership for Kentucky income tax purposes.[2] An LLC that is classified as a corporation for federal income tax purposes is classified as a corporation for Kentucky income tax purposes.[3] Single-member LLCs are permitted effective July 19, 1998.[4]

[B]   Allocations

Profits and losses of an LLC are allocated among members as provided in the operating agreement. If the operating agreement does not provide for allocations, profits and losses are allocated on a per capita basis.[5]

[C]   Taxation of LLC and Members

There is no franchise or entity-level tax on Kentucky LLCs.
A limited liability company is not subject to the annual license tax[6] on the capital of the business of a corporation.[7] The term "corporation" is not specifically defined in the license tax provisions. The statutes assume that the entity subject to the corporate license tax is incorporated. Because an LLC is not incorporated, it is not subject to the corporate license tax.[8]

Members of an LLC carrying on business in Kentucky are liable for income taxes only in their individual capacities. The LLC must compute income under federal law, subject to certain adjustments under state law.[9] No income tax is assessed on the income of the LLC.[10]

Resident and nonresident individuals in corporations that are members in an LLC carrying on business in Kentucky are taxable on all items of income, gain, loss, deduction, or credit that are reported as their distributive shares of the LLC.[11]

---

§23.19   [1] S.B. 184, 1994 Ky. Acts; Ky. Rev. Stat. Ann. §§275.001 to 275.455.
[2] Ky. Rev. Stat. Ann. §141.208(2).
[3] Ky. Rev. Stat. Ann. §141.208(3).
[4] H.B. 666, Laws 1998.
[5] Ky. Rev. Stat. Ann. §275.205.
[6] The tax is imposed by Ky. Rev. Stat. Ann. §136.070.
[7] Kentucky Tax Alert, Rev. Cabinet (Jan. 1997).
[8] Id.
[9] Ky. Rev. Stat. Ann. §141.206(2).
[10] Ky. Rev. Stat. Ann. §141.206(3).
[11] Ky. Rev. Stat. Ann. §141.206(4).

Nonresident individuals and corporations that are members in an LLC doing business in Kentucky are taxable on their proportionate shares of the distributive income passed through to the partnership attributable to business done in Kentucky.[12] Business done in Kentucky is determined by the ratio of gross receipts from sales to purchasers or customers in Kentucky or from services performed in Kentucky compared to the total gross receipts from sales or services everywhere.[13]

[D] Tax Returns

An LLC is required to file an income tax information return. The return is filed on Form 765, Kentucky Partnership Income Tax Return. Any LLC located in Kentucky or doing business in Kentucky must file the return. The LLC must file a copy of its federal partnership return with the state return.[14]

The income and deductions of a Kentucky LLC for purposes of the form are determined under the Internal Revenue Code. The following adjustments must be made:

- Exclude interest income from U.S. government obligations
- Include interest income from obligations of other states and their political subdivisions
- Include transition income and deduction carryover amounts for depreciation differences

The LLC reports the members' distributive shares of income on Schedule K to Form 765.

Individual members who are Kentucky residents must file Form 740 and report their shares of LLC income earned within and outside of Kentucky. Nonresident members are required to file Form 740NP and report their distributive shares of income from an LLC doing business in Kentucky.

LLCs having 15 or more full-year nonresident individual members with no other Kentucky income may receive special permission from the Revenue Cabinet to file a combined return in lieu of separate returns for the qualifying members.

An LLC may obtain an extension of time to file its return by filing Form 40A102, Application for Extension of Time to File Individual, Partnership and Fiduciary Income Tax Returns for Kentucky. LLCs that receive a federal extension are not required to request a separate Kentucky extension. The requirement may be met by attaching federal Form 4868 (automatic extension) and/or Form 2688 (approved extension) to the Kentucky return.

---

[12] Ky. Rev. Stat. Ann. §141.206(5).
[13] Ky. Rev. Stat. Ann. §141.206(5)(a).
[14] Ky. Rev. Stat. Ann. §141.206(1).

[E]   Annual Report

A Kentucky LLC must file an annual report. The report must be filed between January 1 and June 30 of each year.[15] The annual report must set forth the name and address of the LLC, the state or country under whose laws it is organized, the address of its registered office, the name of its registered agent, the address of its principal office, and the names and business addresses of its managers. The first annual report is due between January 1 and June 30 of the year following the year of organization or qualification to do business in the state of Kentucky. Subsequent annual reports must be filed between January 1 and June 30 following each calendar year.

[F]   Filing Fees

Kentucky imposes the following filing fees on LLCs:[16]

Articles of organization	$40
Certificate of authority for foreign LLCs	$90
Annual report	$15

[G]   References

M. Sargent & W. Schwidetzky, Limited Liability Company Handbook, Law — Sample Documents — Forms, §4.12, Kentucky Form of Articles of Organization and Operating Agreement (1995-1996 ed.).

§23.20   LOUISIANA

Louisiana enacted the Louisiana Limited Liability Company Act on July 7, 1992.[1]

[A]   State Tax Classification

A Louisiana LLC or foreign LLC qualified to do business in Louisiana is classified for state income tax purposes in the same manner that it is classified for federal income tax purposes.[2] However, the check-the-box election by an LLC to be classified as a corporation for federal income tax purposes does not determine whether the LLC will be subject to the Louisiana franchise tax.[3]

---

[15] Ky. Rev. Stat. Ann. §275.190.
[16] Ky. Rev. Stat. Ann. §275.055.
§23.20   [1] La. Rev. Stat. Ann. §§12:1301 to 12:1369.
[2] La. Rev. Stat. Ann. §12:1368.
[3] Rev. Rul. No. 01-013.

[B]   Taxation of LLC and Members

The LLC is taxed for state income tax purposes in the same manner as for federal income tax purposes.[4] For all other taxes, including the corporate franchise tax, the LLC is taxed as a limited partnership.[5] There is no franchise or entity-level tax on Louisiana LLCs that are classified as partnerships. A Louisiana LLC is a pass-through entity. Members are taxed on their distributive shares of income from the LLC, whether or not distributed.[63] An LLC that is classified as a corporation for federal tax purposes is subject to the corporate income tax.

A corporation that is a single-member of a Louisiana LLC is subject to the Louisiana corporate franchise tax because the corporation is considered doing business in Louisiana.[7] A foreign corporation that is the sole member of the Louisiana LLC must apportion its income between Louisiana and any other state in which it does business.[8]

[C]   Tax Returns

An LLC is not required to file a partnership return if all members are natural persons who are residents of the state of Louisiana.[9] Other LLCs doing business in Louisiana or deriving any income from sources in Louisiana, regardless of the amount or the residence of the members, must file an information return on Form IT-565, Partnership Return of Income, if any member is a nonresident of Louisiana or if any member is not a natural person.

If the LLC has income that is derived from sources partly within and partly outside Louisiana, the LLC must file Form IT-565B with Form IT-565.

Each member of the LLC that is a natural person must include on the individual return the distributive share of the net income of the LLC during the LLC's accounting period (whether fiscal or calendar) that ended during this taxable year.

LLCs that have nonresident members who are not corporations must file a composite return. The return must include a schedule setting forth the name of each member in the LLC, the member's distributive share of income and other items, and whether the member has an agreement on file with the Department of Revenue to file an individual return in Louisiana. The LLC must pay the taxes on behalf of each nonresident member except for (a) members that are corporations, and (b) members who enter into an agreement with the Louisiana Department of Revenue to file an individual tax return and pay the Louisiana income tax attributable to their allocable share of Louisiana income from the LLC.

[4] Louisiana Department of Revenue, Rev. Rul. No. 02-018 (2002) (citing Louisiana Revenue Statutes Annotated §12:1368).

[5] Louisiana Department of Revenue, Rev. Rul. No. 02-018 (2002).

[6] La. Rev. Stat. Ann. §§47:201, 47:202.

[7] Louisiana Department of Revenue, Rev. Rul. No. 02-018 (2002).

[8] See Louisiana Department of Revenue, Rev. Rul. No. 02-018 (2002), which discusses the apportionment formula.

[9] La. Rev. Stat. Ann. §47:201.

Nonresident members included in the composite return do not have to file a Louisiana income tax return if they do not have any income from Louisiana sources other than the income reported on the composite return, and if the LLC makes a composite payment on behalf of the member. The composite payment is due on the earlier of the date of filing of the composite return or the due date of the composite return without regard to extensions of time to file. An extension of time to file the composite return does not extend the time to pay the composite amount.[10]

[D] Annual Report

An LLC must file an annual report in Louisiana.[11] A foreign LLC qualified to do business in Louisiana must also file an annual report.[12]

[E] Filing Fees

Louisiana imposes the following filing fees on LLCs:[13]

Articles of organization	$ 60
Certificate of authority for foreign LLCs	$100
Annual fee	$ 25

[F] References

S. Kalinka, Louisiana Limited Liability Companies and Partnerships: A Guide to Business and Tax Planning (1997).

§23.21 MAINE

Maine enacted laws authorizing LLCs effective January 1, 1995.[1]

[A] State Tax Classification

Maine classifies an LLC for state tax purposes in the same manner that the LLC is classified for federal tax purposes.[2] Thus, an LLC that is classified as a

---

[10] Louisiana Administrative Code 61:1.1401.
[11] La. Rev. Stat. Ann. §12:1308.1.
[12] La. Rev. Stat. Ann. §12:1350.1.
[13] La. Rev. Stat. Ann. §12:1364.
§23.21 [1] H.B. 1123, ch. 718, 1994 Me. Laws; Me. Rev. Stat. Ann. tit. 31, §§601 to 762.
[2] Me. Rev. Stat. Ann. tit. 31, §761.

partnership for federal purposes is classified as a partnership for state purposes. Effective June 30, 1998, the Maine statutes were amended to clarify that a single-member LLC could be formed in Maine.[3]

[B]   Taxation of LLC and Members

Maine does not impose a franchise or entity-level tax on LLCs. An LLC that is classified as a partnership is a pass-through entity. All items of income, gain, loss, deduction, and credit are passed through to and taxable to the members.[4]

Nonresident members are taxed on their distributive shares of income allocable to Maine.[5]

[C]   Real Estate Taxes

There is an exemption from the Maine real estate transfer tax for deeds between an LLC and its members for the purpose of organization, dissolution, or liquidation of the LLC. No consideration may be given in connection with the transfer other than shares, interests, or debt securities of the LLC. There is also an exemption for deeds to an LLC from a corporation, partnership, or other LLC if the grantor or grantee owns an interest in the LLC in the same proportion as in the real estate being transferred.[6]

[D]   Estimated Taxes

Until April 1, 1996, for purposes of computing and making payment of estimated taxes, a member could not deduct from a member's income any loss, or estimated loss, if any, from an LLC.[7]

[E]   Tax Returns

LLCs that are classified as partnerships and that do business in Maine or that have resident members must file Form 1065 ME/11205-ME, Maine Information Return. The form is used for submitting copies of IRS Form 1065 for the LLC. A copy of IRS Form 1065, pages 1-4, must be attached to the return. The return must indicate the number of members who are residents of Maine. An LLC with 100 or fewer members must submit a copy of all Schedules K-1 for its members. An

---

[3] Ch. 633, H.P. 1498, Laws 1998.
[4] Me. Rev. Stat. Ann. tit. 36, §5190.
[5] Me. Rev. Stat. Ann. tit. 36, §5192; Information Release from Bur. of Taxn. (June 1, 1987).
[6] H.B. 1123, ch. 718, 1994 Me. Laws.
[7] Me. Rev. Stat. Ann. tit. 31, §761.2.

LLC that has more than 100 members is not required to file Schedules K-1 or complete the Schedules of Partners/Shareholders Income.

Part 6 of the form sets forth an apportionment schedule. The schedule is for LLCs that engage in interstate commerce. Maine employs a three-factor formula to determine the percentage of business income that is apportioned to Maine. The percentage is derived by a fraction. The numerator of the fraction is a property factor, a payroll factor, and twice the sales factor. The denominator is four.

The form must be filed on or before the fifteenth day of the fourth month following the close of the tax year. The form must be filed with the Bureau of Taxation, Income Tax Division, Augusta, ME 14333. If the LLC is making a composite filing in Maine for its nonresident members, the LLC should not attach copies of the federal Schedules K-1.

[F] Composite Returns

An LLC may file a composite personal income tax return on behalf of members who are nonresidents for the entire taxable year and whose entire adjusted gross income, including the income of the spouse, comes from the LLC. The composite return may be filed only with the permission from the state tax assessor.[8] Resident members (and nonresident members with nonpartnership activity in Maine) and partners who are not natural persons cannot be included in the composite return. The LLC must obtain permission from the members on whose behalf it intends to file the composite return.

[G] Annual Report

An LLC must file an annual report in Maine. The annual report must set forth the name of the LLC, the name of its registered agent, the address of its registered office in Maine, a brief statement of the character of the business in which the LLC is actually engaged in the state, and the name and business or residence address of each manager (or each member if there are no managers).

[H] Filing Fees

Maine imposes the following filing fees on LLCs:

Articles of organization[9]	$250
Certificate of authority for foreign LLC[10]	$250
Annual report[11]	$ 60

[8] Me. Rev. Stat. Ann. tit. 31, §805; Me. Rev. Stat. Ann. tit. 36, §5192(5); Information Release from the Bur. of Taxn. (June 1, 1987); Rule 805 issued by Me. Bur. of Taxn.
[9] Me. Rev. Stat. Ann. tit. 31, §871(8).
[10] Me. Rev. Stat. Ann. tit. 31, §751.
[11] Me. Rev. Stat. Ann. tit. 31, §§751(20), 871(18).

§23.22   MARYLAND

Maryland enacted the Maryland Limited Liability Company Act effective October 1, 1992.[1]

[A]   State Tax Classification

A Maryland LLC is classified in the same manner as the LLC is classified for federal purposes. Domestic and foreign LLCs are classified as partnerships for Maryland income tax purposes unless classified as corporations or disregarded as entities for federal tax purposes.

A single-member LLC is permitted.[2]

[B]   Taxation of LLC and Members

The Maryland income tax does not apply to an LLC if the LLC is classified as a partnership for federal tax purposes.[3]

There is an exception if the LLC has any member who is a nonresident of the state of Maryland and has nonresident taxable income for the tax year.[4] The LLC must pay a 4.8 percent withholding tax on behalf of nonresident members on those members' distributive shares of income. The tax rate is the highest marginal state tax rate for individuals.[5] The tax is imposed on the individual nonresident member, although the LLC must pay the tax on behalf of the member.[6] The tax is imposed on the sum of each nonresident member's distributive share of LLC nonresident taxable income.[7] Nonresident members for these purposes do not include members that are any of the following:

- Corporations, including S corporations
- Partnerships
- Organizations that are exempt from tax under the Internal Revenue Code
- Estates
- Trusts

The tax payable for any tax year on behalf of nonresident members by the LLC may not exceed the sum of all of the nonresident members' shares of the LLC's distributable cash flow.[8] Distributable cash flow means taxable income reportable

---

§23.22   [1] Md. Code Ann., Corps. & Assns. §§4A-101 to 4A-1103.
[2] Md. Code Ann., Corps. & Assns. §§4A-101, 4A-202.
[3] Md. Code Ann., Tax-Gen. §10-104(8).
[4] Md. Code Ann., Tax-Gen. §10-102.1(b).
[5] Md. Code Ann., Tax-Gen. §10-102.1(d).
[6] Md. Code Ann., Tax-Gen. §10-102.1(c).
[7] Md. Code Ann., Tax-Gen. §10-102.1(d)(1)(iii).
[8] Md. Code Ann., Tax-Gen. §10-102.1(d)(2).

by the LLC on its federal income tax return for the year, subject to the following adjustments:

- Adjusted, in the case of an LLC using the accrual method of accounting in reporting federal taxable income, to reflect the amount of taxable income that would have been reported under the cash method of accounting.
- Increased by the sum of the following:
  — Cash receipts for the tax year that are not includible in the gross income of the LLC, including capital contributions and loan proceeds.
  — Amounts allowable to the LLC for the tax year's deductions for depreciation, amortization, and depletion.
  — The decrease, if any, in the LLC's liability reserve as of the end of the tax year.
- Decreased by the sum of the following:
  — Cash expenditures for the tax year that are not deductible in computing the taxable income of the LLC, not including distributions to members.
  — The increase, if any, in the LLC's liability reserve as of the end of the tax year.[9]

If the LLC fails to pay the tax when due, the tax may be collected from the members under Maryland law applicable to debts of a partnership, with the LLC and the members having rights of contribution against any nonresident member on whose behalf the tax is paid.[10] However, any Maryland member is liable for the tax imposed on the LLC only to the extent of distributions from the LLC to that member after the tax was due and payable by the LLC (unless it is established by the comptroller that the member participated in a pattern of distributions to one or more members with the intention of defeating the LLC liability for the tax).[11]

The Maryland income tax return is based on the federal adjusted gross income. Various amounts are subtracted from the federal adjusted gross income of residents to determine the Maryland adjusted gross income.[12] Nonresidents may make the same subtractions from federal adjusted gross income as residents. These subtractions include income derived from wages in the state if allowed by the comptroller. However, nonresidents may not subtract income derived from business that is wholly carried on in the state and in which the individual is a member of a limited liability company taxable as a partnership or proprietorship for federal tax purposes.[13]

A person is allowed a credit against the income tax for the tax year for income tax withheld and estimated tax payments made for the year. The individual may also claim a credit against the state income tax for the tax year for taxes paid by a

---

[9] Md. Code Ann., Tax-Gen. §10-102.1(a)(2).
[10] Md. Code Ann., Tax-Gen. §10-102.1(f)(1).
[11] Md. Code Ann., Tax-Gen. §10-102.1(f)(2).
[12] Md. Code Ann., Tax-Gen. §10-207(a).
[13] Md. Code Ann., Tax-Gen. §10-210.

limited liability company attributable to the individual's share of LLC nonresident taxable income.[14]

[C]   Real Estate Taxes

Effective October 1, 1997, a deed or other instrument transferring real estate from a predecessor entity or trustee of that entity to an LLC is not subject to the Maryland document recording tax.[15] The members of the LLC must be identical to the partners or individuals who owned the predecessor entity. Each member's allocation of profits and losses must remain the same. Qualifying predecessor entities include limited partnerships, limited liability partnerships, limited liability limited partnerships, joint ventures, and proprietorships with one or more persons who are principally involved in buying, selling, leasing, or managing real property.

[D]   Tax Returns

The LLC must file a partnership tax return on Maryland Form 510, Pass-Through Entity Income Tax Return, if the LLC is classified as a partnership for federal tax purposes.[16] This is an information tax return. Every Maryland LLC must file the form even if it has no income or the LLC is inactive. Every other foreign LLC that is subject to Maryland income tax laws must also file Form 510.

A multistate pass-through LLC that operates in Maryland, but that is not subject to the Maryland income tax law, is not required to file. However, a return reflecting no income allocable to Maryland may be filed for record purposes. Letters in lieu of filing are not accepted.

Form 510 must be filed by the fifteenth day of the fourth month following the close of the tax year. The return must be filed with the Comptroller of the Treasury, Revenue Administration Division, Annapolis, MD 21411-0001. A manager or other duly authorized official of the LLC must sign Form 510.

The LLC must report all items that are reported for federal purposes in the same manner as reported for federal purposes. The character of an item cannot be changed from that required or elected for federal purposes. The tax-year period used for the federal return must be used on the Maryland return.

All items of income, loss, credit, and deduction on Form 510 are passed through to the individual members and taxed at that level. Each member's distributive share is the net amount of lines 1 through 7 as reported on the federal Form 1065, Schedule K. The member must file an individual income tax return on Form 502. Nonresident individual members of the LLC must file Form 505.

---

[14] Md. Code Ann., Tax-Gen. §10-701.1.
[15] H.B. 671, ch. 683, 1997 Md. Laws.
[16] Md. Code Ann., Tax-Gen. §10-819(b)(1).

[E]   Single-Member LLCs

If the LLC has only one member and is disregarded as an entity separate from its member for federal income tax purposes, the profit or loss of the LLC must be reflected on the income tax return filed by the member of the LLC.[17] The LLC has a filing status of its member and files an appropriate return for that member.

[F]   LLCs Classified as Corporations

LLCs classified as corporations for federal tax purposes are subject to the Maryland corporate income tax.[18] Effective October 1, 1992, an LLC that is taxable as a corporation is required to file a return.[19] The state income tax rate for a corporation is 7 percent of Maryland taxable income.[20]

The LLC may be classified as a subchapter S corporation for filing purposes. The profit or loss of the LLC must be reflected on each member's return.[21] The returns must be filed on or before March 15 following the tax year.[22]

If the income tax is computed on a fiscal year, an LLC that is classified as a corporation must file a return on or before the fifteenth day of the third month after the end of the year.

[G]   Financial Institutions

Financial institutions are exempt from the Maryland income tax, but are subject to the franchise tax measured by net earnings.[23] Financial institutions include limited liability companies.[24] The financial institution franchise tax is currently imposed at the rate of 7 percent of taxable net earnings.[25]

[H]   Nonresident Members' Tax Returns

Nonresident members must report their distributive or pro rata share of income received from the LLC attributable to business conducted in Maryland. The income must be reported in the member's tax year in which the LLC's tax year ends. Credit for taxes paid by the LLC must be claimed on the same return on which the nonresident member reports the income for which taxes were paid by the LLC.

The LLC may elect to file a composite return on behalf of qualified nonresident

---

[17] Md. Code Ann., Tax-Gen. §10-819(c).
[18] Md. Code Ann., Tax-Gen. §10-104.
[19] Md. Code Ann., Tax-Gen. §10-819(b)(2).
[20] Md. Code Ann., Tax-Gen. §10-105(b).
[21] Md. Code Ann., Tax-Gen. §10-819(a), (b)(2).
[22] Md. Code Ann., Tax-Gen. §10-821.
[23] Md. Code Ann., Tax-Gen. §§8-202, 10-104.
[24] Md. Code Ann., Tax-Gen. §8-101.
[25] Md. Code Ann., Tax-Gen. §8-203.

members. All members who qualify and elect to be included on the composite return must agree that the LLC is their agent for the receipt of any refund or for the payment of any tax due.

[I] Extension Requests

An LLC may file Form 510E, Application for Extension of Time to File Pass-Through Entity Income Tax Return, to obtain an extension of time to file the return. The request for extension of time to file will automatically be granted and will not be acknowledged if the application is properly filed and submitted by the return's due date. The due date is the fifteenth day of the fourth month following the close of the tax year for the LLC or the fifteenth day of the third month for LLCs that are classified as S corporations. The application for extension of time must have been filed with the Internal Revenue Service, or an acceptable reason must be provided with the Maryland application to obtain the automatic extension.

[J] Amended Returns

An LLC may correct an error by filing an amended return. It files an amended return by submitting a revised Form 510 and checking the box for "Amended Return" on page 1. A Form 502X, Amended Maryland Tax Return, must also be submitted for each member's individual income tax return (Form 502 or 505). If the Internal Revenue Service adjusts any items on the federal return, a copy of the final IRS adjustment must be submitted within 90 days. Copies of the IRS adjustment report must be submitted for each member's individual income tax return.

[K] Withholding Taxes

LLCs that make payments to individuals for salaries, wages, or compensation for personal services must withhold income tax as required under the applicable withholding tables published by the Maryland Revenue Administration Division. The withheld taxes must be remitted with Form MW506, Employer's Return of Income Tax Withheld. This is filed on a monthly basis if the quarterly withholding is $750 or more. If the quarterly withholding is less than $750, the withheld tax may be remitted quarterly. An annual reconciliation must be filed on Form MW508, Annual Employer Withholding Reconciliation Report.

[L] Multistate LLCs

Multistate LLCs with one or more nonresident members may use separate accounting to allocate income. Multistate LLCs may elect the apportionment method of allocation. LLCs that use the distributable cash flow limitation must make an election on the return and should complete the Distributable Cash Flow Limitation Worksheet that is attached to the instructions for the return.

LLCs that conduct business in one or more states must allocate income if one or more of the members are nonresidents of Maryland. LLCs may use separate accounting or the apportionment method of allocation. All factors of the apportionment formula are expressed as fractions. The numerator of the fraction is the total of Maryland items. The denominator is the total of items everywhere during the tax year. LLCs using the apportionment method are generally required to use a three-factor formula. The three factors are property, payroll, and double-weighted receipts. The sum of the factors is divided by four to arrive at the final apportionment formula. If the apportionment formula does not fairly represent the extent of the LLC's activity within Maryland, the Maryland Revenue Administration Division may alter the formula or components.

[M] Annual Report

No annual report is required in Maryland.

[N] Filing Fees

Maryland imposes the following filing fees on LLCs:

Articles of organization	$50
Foreign LLC registration application	$50
Annual fee	$ 0

[O] References

R. Ercole, Maryland Limited Liability Company Forms and Practice Manual (1994).

M. Sargent & W. Schwidetzky, Limited Liability Company Handbook, Law — Sample Documents — Forms, §4.13[A], Maryland Form of Real Estate LLC Operating Agreement with Articles of Organization as Exhibit B; §4.12[B], Maryland Holding Company Form of Operating Agreement (1995-1996 ed.).

§23.23 MASSACHUSETTS

Massachusetts enacted the Massachusetts Limited Liability Company Act effective January 1, 1996.[1]

---

§23.23   [1] H.B. 4045, 1995 Mass. Acts; Mass. Gen. Laws Ann. ch. 156C, §§1–68.

[A] State Tax Classification

Massachusetts classifies an LLC in the same manner that the LLC is classified for federal purposes under the IRS check-the-box regulations.[2] Single-member LLCs may be formed in Massachusetts for tax years after 2002.[3] Massachusetts follows the federal tax classification of a non-U.S. business entity if the entity is a foreign LLC. There are nine non-U.S. business entities that Massachusetts classifies as foreign LLCs. A foreign LLC may request a letter ruling from the Massachusetts Department of Revenue to determine the LLC's tax treatment for Massachusetts purposes.[4]

[B] Taxation of LLC and Members

Massachusetts LLCs are not subject to the Massachusetts income tax. Instead, individuals carrying on business as members of the LLC are liable for the taxes in their individual capacities.[5]

A member of an LLC who is a resident of Massachusetts, whether or not the LLC has a usual place of business in Massachusetts, is subject to the Massachusetts income taxes on his distributive share of the income received or earned by the LLC from sources taxable under the Massachusetts income tax law. The member must separately include in his return his distributive share of the LLC income or loss from sources taxable in Massachusetts and any item of deduction or credit.[6]

A nonresident of Massachusetts who is a member of an LLC, whether or not the LLC has a usual place of business in Massachusetts, is subject to the tax on his distributive share of the income received or earned by the LLC to the same extent as if received by a resident.[7] The member must include separately in his return his distributive share of such income or loss and any item of deduction or credit.[8]

A single-member LLC that is a disregarded entity for federal purposes is not taxed as a corporation under Massachusetts law for purposes of the corporate excise tax, the minimum excise tax, or the income or property measures of corporate excise tax laws. A single-member LLC is treated as a branch or division of

---

[2] Mass. Gen. Laws Ann. ch. 62, §17; Massachusetts Department of Revenue Letter Ruling LR 00-8 (June 9, 2000); Tech. Info. Rel. No. 97-8 (June 16, 1997).

[3] S.B. 1949, Laws, 2003; Mass. Gen. Laws Ann. ch. 156C, §2; Massachusetts Department of Revenue Letter Ruling LR 00-8 (June 9, 2000).

[4] Directive No. 01-8, Massachusetts Department of Revenue (Nov. 13, 2001).

[5] Mass. Gen. Laws Ann. ch. 62, §17. See Mass. Gen. Laws Ann. ch. 62, §17 (last sentence of first paragraph), which states that a limited liability company formed under chapter 156C or a foreign limited liability company as defined in chapter 156C, §2, will be deemed to be a partnership if it is classified for the tax year as a partnership for federal income tax purposes.

[6] Mass. Gen. Laws Ann. ch. 62, §17(a).

[7] See Mass. Gen. Laws Ann. ch. 62, §5A.

[8] Mass. Gen. Laws Ann. ch. 62, §17(b).

its owner if the owner is a corporation, or as a sole proprietorship if the owner is an individual. Therefore, all tax attributes of the single-member LLC, its properties, and activities are attributed to the single member.[9]

The character of any item of income, loss, deduction, or credit included in the member's distributive share is determined as if that item were realized directly by the member from the source realized by the LLC or incurred in the same manner as incurred by the LLC. The amount of each item to be taken into account by the LLC in determining the total of its income, loss, deductions, or credits to be reported on the returns of the members must be computed in the same manner in the case of an individual.[10] However, adjustments must be made. The LLC is not allowed certain offsets, exemptions, and credits.[11]

Each nonresident member is taxable on the member's distributive share of income from any of the following categories:

- Income derived from or connected with the LLC's business carried on in Massachusetts
- Income from the ownership of any interest in real or tangible personal property located in Massachusetts
- Interest, dividends, annuities, and capital gains from property employed in the LLC's business carried on in Massachusetts

A foreign corporation that owns a single-member LLC doing business in Massachusetts is treated as doing business in and subject to tax in Massachusetts if the LLC is a disregarded entity.[12]

An LLC that is owned by a corporation, and that elects to be treated as a disregarded entity for federal tax purposes, is treated as a division of the corporate owner. All the LLC's income, losses, and other tax attributes flow through to the corporate owner. All transactions between the LLC and the corporate owner must be eliminated for apportionment purposes if the LLC is organized in the foreign jurisdiction. All the LLC's property, sales, and payroll are treated as those of the corporate owner for apportionment purposes.[13]

Beginning 2003, the manufacturing corporation includes an LLC. Therefore, an LLC is eligible for the benefits available to manufacturing corporations. These benefits include (a) an investment tax credit against the corporate tax, (b) a prop-

---

[9] S.B. 1946, Laws, 2003; Massachusetts Department of Revenue Ltr. Rul. LR 00-8 (June 9, 2000).

[10] Mass. Gen. Laws Ann. ch. 62, §17(c).

[11] *Id.*

[12] *See, e.g.*, Mass. Dept. of Revenue Ltr. Rul. LR 00-9 (June 9, 2000), which determined that a Georgia corporation was subject to Massachusetts taxation when it acquired a Massachusetts LLC that was classified as a disregarded entity. The Georgia corporation was treated as doing business in the state based on its ownership of the membership units in the LLC. The Georgia corporation was entitled to apportion its income in accordance with the provisions of Georgia law in determining the income allocable to Massachusetts for tax purposes.

[13] Mass. Dept. of Revenue Ltr. Rul. LR 00-11 (Aug. 29, 2000).

erty tax exemption for machinery, and (c) a sales and use tax exemption on certain items purchased and used in research and development.[14]

[C] Allocations

The member's distributive share of any item of income, loss, deduction, or credit is determined by the operating agreement. If the operating agreement contains no provision with respect to a member's distributive share of a particular item of income, loss, deduction, or credit, the item must be apportioned in accordance with the member's ratio of sharing income or loss of the LLC. The member's distributive share of the various classes of income, loss, deductions, and credits must be included by the member in her return for the tax year during which or with which the taxable year of the LLC ends.[15]

[D] Tax Returns

An LLC that is classified as a partnership for federal tax purposes must file Form 3, Partnership Return of Income.[16] A copy of IRS Form 1065 and all schedules, including Schedules K-1, must be attached to the return.

An LLC must file the return if the LLC has a usual place of business in Massachusetts or receives federal gross income of more than $100 during the tax year.

The LLC reports each member's distributive share of income, gain, loss, credit, and deduction on Schedule 3K-1, Partner's Massachusetts Information. Form 3 and Schedule 3K-1 are designed to isolate income and deduction items in order to produce a correct Massachusetts LLC total, as well as each member's correct Massachusetts distributive share.

There are a number of differences between the Massachusetts and U.S. personal income tax laws that are reflected on these returns. For example, for Massachusetts tax purposes, an LLC is allowed only those expense deductions that an individually owned business is allowed. Deductions that are itemized by an individual on Schedule A of Form 1040 are not allowed. The deduction for charitable contributions or for net operating loss carryover or carryback is not allowed to the LLC or the individual under Massachusetts income tax law. Massachusetts also has a net long-term capital gain deduction of 50 percent.

Each member must report his distributive share of each item of income on a tax return under state law. The type of tax return depends on the type of member of an LLC. The following table shows which returns should be filed by each member of an LLC:

---

[14] S.B. 1949, Laws, 2003.
[15] Mass. Gen. Laws Ann. ch. 62, §17(d).
[16] Mass. Gen. Laws Ann. ch. 62C, §17.

Type of Member	Form to File
Resident individual	1
Nonresident/part-year resident individual	1-NR/PY
Trust or estate	2
Domestic corporation	355A
Foreign corporation	355B
Domestic corporation (part of a Massachusetts combined group)	355C-A
Foreign corporation (part of a Massachusetts combined group)	355C-B
Corporate trust	3F
Domestic S corporation	355S-A
Foreign S corporation	355S-B

The LLC must file the partnership return on or before the fifteenth day of the fourth month after the close of the LLC's tax year. If the LLC was dissolved or reorganized during the year, it must file Form 3 to reflect LLC business activity as of the date of dissolution or reorganization. The form must be signed by one of the general partners. A manager is treated as a general partner.

The return must be mailed to the Massachusetts Department of Revenue, P.O. Box 7017, Boston, MA 02204.

LLCs may obtain an extension of time to file the state tax return by filing Form M-4868, Application for Automatic Six-Month Extension. The form must be filed on or before April 15 in the case of calendar year LLCs or on or before the original due date of the return for fiscal year filers. The return may be filed by telephone if the LLC meets certain requirements.

[E] Annual Report

Massachusetts LLCs are required to file annual reports. The annual report is due on the anniversary of the filing of the certificate of organization.[17] Foreign LLCs that are qualified to do business in Massachusetts must also file annual reports. The report is due on the anniversary of their registration.[18] The annual report must set forth the following information:

- The name of the LLC
- The address of the office required to be maintained in the state
- The name and address of the registered agent for service of process
- If the LLC has a specific date of dissolution, the date on which the LLC is to dissolve
- The name and address of each manager, if any
- The name of any other person in addition to any manager who is authorized

---

[17] Mass. Gen. Laws Ann. ch. 156A, §12.
[18] Mass. Gen. Laws Ann. ch. 156C, §48.

to sign documents to be filed with the secretary of state; at least one such person shall be named if there are no managers
- The general character of the business of the LLC
- If desired, the names of one or more persons authorized to execute, acknowledge, and record any recordable instrument purporting to affect an interest in real property
- Any other matter that the authorized person decides to include in the annual statement[19]

[F]   Filing Fees

Massachusetts imposes the following filing fees on LLCs:

Certificate of organization[20]	$500
Annual report for domestic LLCs[21]	$500
Foreign LLC registration application[22]	$500
Annual report for foreign LLC[23]	$500

§23.24   MICHIGAN

Michigan adopted the Michigan Limited Liability Company Act effective June 1, 1993.[1]

[A]   State Tax Classification

Michigan follows the federal check-the-box regulations in classifying an LLC for purposes of the single business tax (SBT) on LLCs. The federal entity classification applies to all components of the tax that are related to the federal income tax.[2]

A single-member LLC that is a disregarded entity for federal purposes is treated as a branch, division, or sole proprietor for SBT purposes. A member of an LLC that is classified as a partnership is treated as a partner for purposes of the statutory exemption and the small-business credit. A member of an LLC that is classified as a corporation is treated as a shareholder for purposes of the statutory exemption, but not a shareholder's for purposes of the small-business credit

---

[19] Mass. Gen. Laws Ann. ch. 156C, §12(c).

[20] Mass. Gen. Laws Ann. ch. 156C, §12.

[21] Mass. Gen. Laws Ann. ch. 156A, §12.

[22] Mass. Gen. Laws Ann. ch. 156A, §48.

[23] Id.

§23.24   [1] Pub. Act No. 23 (H.B. 4023), 1993 Mich. Pub. Acts; Mich. Comp. Laws Ann., §§450.4101 to 450.5200.

[2] Revenue Administration Bulletin 1999-9, Michigan Department of Treasury (Nov. 29, 1999).

(because they do not meet the statutory definition of a "shareholder" for purposes of the credit).[3]

An LLC is not required to make an entity classification election at the state level because Michigan follows the federal election.[4]

The federal entity classification determination is also effective for purposes of the Michigan personal income tax return for members of the LLC. The Michigan personal income taxes based on federal adjusted gross income. The Michigan income tax return must conform to the entity elections reported on the federal return.[5]

[B]   Taxation of LLC and Members

Michigan LLCs must pay the single-business tax (SBT).[6] The SBT is based on the value added to goods and services by the taxpayer. It is classified as a value added tax (VAT).[7] It is essentially based on gross receipts rather than income. Michigan is the only state that has adopted a value added tax. The tax rate is 1.8 percent (for tax years ending December 31, 2003) of the adjusted tax base (federal taxable income with adjustments). The first $45,000 of the tax base is exempt. LLCs with less than $250,000 in adjusted gross receipts are not required to file. The tax is imposed on every LLC with business activity in Michigan. Business activity means the sale or rental of any property and the performance of services in Michigan or outside the state to derive gain, benefit or advantage, either directly or indirectly.[8] The tax rate is scheduled to be phased out over the next 22 years at the rate of .1 percent per year in each year in which the state has a $250 million surplus.[9]

Members of an LLC must pay tax on their distributive shares of income from an LLC. For a member who is an individual, the share of business income is taxed under the Michigan Individual Income Tax Act. For a member that is a business (other than an individual) subject to the SBT, this income must be subtracted (and losses must be added) on the SBT annual return filed for the partner. However, if the member has no Michigan business activities other than its interest in the LLC, the member itself is not subject to the SBT and is not required to file a return.

[C]   Tax Returns

The LLC must file one of the following returns in Michigan to report and pay the SBT:

[3] Id.

[4] Revenue Administration Bulletin 1999-9, Michigan Department of Treasury (Nov. 29, 1999).

[5] Id.

[6] See Booklet issued by Mich. Dept. of Treas., Single Business Tax Questions and Answers, A-12 (Nov. 9, 1989).

[7] See Town & Country Dodge, Inc. v. Department of Treasury, 420 Mich. 226 (1984); Wismer & Becker Contracting Engineers v. Department of Treasury, 136 Mich. App. 690 (1985).

[8] Mich. Comp. Laws Ann. §208.3(2).

[9] Mich. Comp. Laws §208.31(5).

Form	Filing Requirement
C-8000 Single Business Tax Annual Return	The LLC is engaged in business activity in Michigan, and adjusted gross receipts are $250,000 or more.
C-8030	The adjusted gross receipts are less than $250,000, the LLC is not claiming a refund, and the LLC does not intend to use a loss carryforward from the current or previous years.
C-8044185	The adjusted gross receipts are less than $250,000, and the LLC wishes to claim a refund; or the adjusted gross receipts are $250,000 or more, the LLC meets the criteria on the form, and the LLC is using the alternate tax rate. However, Form C-8000 must be used if the LLC is apportioning gross receipts.
C-8000	The adjusted gross receipts are $250,000 or more; the adjusted gross receipts are less than $250,000, and the LLC wishes to claim a refund; the adjusted gross receipts are less than $250,000, but the LLC is reporting a business loss carryforward; or the adjusted gross receipts are less than $250,000, and the LLC is using the business loss from a preceding year.

The LLC must file quarterly estimates if the annual SBT liability is expected to be more than $600.

An LLC may obtain an extension of time to file the SBT return by filing Form C-4267, Application for Extension of Time to File Michigan Tax Returns. If no tax is owed, the LLC does not need to file the extension by the due date of the return to avoid penalty and interest. Filing the federal extension request does not automatically grant a Michigan extension. The extension of time to file is not an extension of time to pay the tax. The extension request must be accompanied with payment on or before the original due date of the annual return.

LLCs may amend their SBT annual returns by filing either Form C-8000X or Form C-8044X. Amended returns claiming a refund must be filed within four years of the due date of the original return. If the LLC makes any changes to its federal income tax return that affect the SBT tax base, the LLC must file an amended return. To avoid a penalty, the amended return must be filed within 120 days after the IRS's final determination.

The SBT returns are due on or before the last day of the fourth month after the end of the LLC's tax year. The return for a calendar year LLC is due on April 30. The LLC must mail its annual return or Form C-8030, Notice of No SBT Return Required, with payment if applicable, to the Michigan Department of Treasury, P.O. Box 30059, Lansing, MI 48909. The LLC must mail extension requests to the Michigan Department of Treasury, P.O. Box 30207, Lansing, MI 48909. The LLC must mail quarterly estimate payments to the Michigan Department of Treasury, Department 77889, Detroit, MI 48277-0889.

An LLC must file Form C-8000KP, Single Business Tax Schedule of Partners. The form is used to determine eligibility for the LLC's standard small business credit or alternate tax and to determine which members of the LLC qualify for the increased exemption. A qualified member of an LLC who may claim an increased statutory exemption is a member who:

- Spends at least 51 percent of her time working in the business;
- Owns at least 10 percent of the business; and
- Has a share of business income of at least $12,000.
- Cannot be a qualified partner or shareholder in more than one business.

[D]   *Apportionment and Nexus*

A single-member LLC that is a disregarded entity for federal purposes is subject to the apportionment factors for SBT and personal income tax based on the combined property, payroll, and sales of the combined entities. Sales between the single-member LLC and its owner are disregarded in computing the sales factor.[10]

An owner of an LLC that is classified as a disregarded entity for federal tax purposes has nexus with Michigan based on the LLC's property and activities. The owner of the LLC must file an SBT return. If the owner of a single-member LLC is a flow-through entity, its partners, members, or shareholders who are individuals must file personal income tax returns.[11]

[E]   *Personal Income Tax Withholding*

An LLC that is an employer under federal law is also an employer for state personal income tax withholding purposes. The LLC must register for income tax withholding. The Michigan withholding taxpayer may be different from the taxpayer for federal tax purposes. An LLC that is classified as a disregarded entity is not required to have a federal employer identification number. Such LLCs will be issued a Michigan Department of Treasury number for Michigan withholding tax purposes.[12]

The Michigan Department of Treasury may enter into an agreement allowing a disregarded single-member LLC to file a combined withholding tax return with its owner.[13]

---

[10] Revenue Administration Bulletin 1999-9, Michigan Department of Treasury (Nov. 29, 1999).
[11] *Id.*
[12] *Id.*
[13] *Id.*

[F]   Sales and Use Tax

An LLC is subject to the Michigan sales and use tax regardless of his classification for federal income tax purposes. A single-member LLC that is classified as a disregarded entity for federal purposes is still a legal entity for Michigan purposes, and must register for sales tax if it makes retail sales in Michigan.[14]

An LLC that purchases for use, storage, or consumption in Michigan must register for the Michigan use tax. An out-of-state LLC that is a disregarded entity and that is liable for the use tax must register as a seller.[15]

[G]   Annual Report

A Michigan LLC must file an annual report. The annual report must contain the name of the registered agent and the address of the registered office. It must be filed on or before February 15 of each year.[16]

[H]   Filing Fees

Michigan imposes the following filing fees on LLCs:[17]

Articles of organization	$50
Application for certificate of authority of foreign LLC	$50
Annual report	$ 5

[I]   References

P. Williams, How to Form Your Own Michigan LLC (Limited Liability Company) Before the Ink Dries!: A Step-by-Step Guide, With Forms (1997).

§23.25   MINNESOTA

Minnesota enacted the Minnesota Limited Liability Company Act effective January 1, 1992.[1]

[A]   State Tax Classification

Minnesota classifies an LLC in the same manner that the LLC is classified for federal tax purposes. An LLC formed in Minnesota or in a foreign state is classified

---

[14] Id.

[15] Id.

[16] Mich. Comp. Laws Ann. §450.4207.

[17] Mich. Comp. Laws Ann. §450.5101.

§23.25   [1] H.F. 1910, 1991 Minn. Laws; Minn. Stat. Ann. §§322B.01 to 322B.960.

as a partnership for state tax purposes if it is classified as a partnership for federal tax purposes.[2] Effective August 1, 1997, one member may form an LLC.[3]

The federal check-the-box regulations are followed for all elections made after January 1, 1997 except for one. The regulations are not followed for elections made by a foreign LLC with a single C corporation owner that is electing to be disregarded as a separate entity for federal tax purposes.[4]

[B] Taxation of LLC and Members

There is no income tax imposed on LLCs in Minnesota. The LLC is treated as a pass-through entity. All items of income, gain, credit, loss, and deduction pass through to and are taxed to the members. Profits and losses of the LLC are allocated among members in the same manner that applies to partnerships.

However, the LLC is subject to a minimum fee if the sum of its Minnesota source property, payroll, and sales or receipts is at least $500,000. The minimum fee is $100 if the amount specified on Schedule A of Form M-3, Partnership Return, is from $500,000 to $999,999. The fee increases to $5,000 if the amount specified on Schedule A is $20 million or more.

Minnesota treats an LLC, including a single-member LLC classified as a disregarded entity, as a separate legal entity for sales and use tax purposes. Thus, transfers of tangible personal property between a person and a single-member LLC or any other LLC are subject to the sales and use tax, subject to various exemptions.[5]

A resident member of an LLC that is classified as a partnership is entitled to a credit for taxes paid by the LLC to a foreign state. The member is treated as having paid a tax in an amount equal to the member's pro rata share of any net income tax paid by the LLC to another state. The net income tax means any tax imposed on or measured by the LLC's net income.[6]

Nonresident members are taxed on their distributive shares of income allocable to Minnesota,[7] whether or not distributed.[8]

[C] Tax Returns

Every LLC that has gross income from Minnesota sources must file a partnership return on Form M-3, Partnership Return.[9] Each member of the LLC is required to include his share of income on an individual tax return. The entire share of

[2] Minn. Stat. Ann. §290-01(3b).
[3] Minn. Stat. Ann. §322B.11.
[4] Minn. Rev. Notice 98-08 (1998).
[5] Revenue Notice No. 02-10, Minn. Dept. of Rev. (July 8, 2002).
[6] Minn. Stat. Ann. §290.06(22h).
[7] Minn. Stat. Ann. §290.92(4b).
[8] Minn. Dept. of Rev. R. 8031.0100.
[9] Minn. Stat. Ann. §289A.12(3); Minn. Dept. of Rev. R. 8038.3000.

LLC income is taxed to the member, whether or not actually distributed. However, the LLC must pay the minimum fee.

The minimum fee is determined on Schedule A of Form M-3. The LLC must complete Schedule M-15 to determine whether it owes a penalty if the minimum fee is $1,000 or more or if any individual member's share of the composite income tax is $500 or more. The LLC must compute the underpayment of estimated tax penalty separately for the minimum fee and for each nonresident member included on the composite income tax schedule who has $500 or more of tax.

LLCs that are classified as partnerships for federal income tax purposes must check the box on the top of Form M-3 specifying that the entity is a limited liability company.

LLCs must file the return by April 15 for calendar year LLCs and by the fifteenth day of the fourth month after the end of the fiscal year for other LLCs.

An LLC may obtain an extension of time to file the return by filing Form M-E, Application for Extension of the Deadline for Filing Partnership, S Corporation or Fiduciary Tax Returns. Alternatively, the LLC may use the federal extension if the LLC obtained a federal extension to file IRS Form 1065. The LLC must use Form M-73, Extension Payment, to pay the taxes due.

Form M-3 must be filed with Minnesota Partnership Tax, Mail Station 1760, St. Paul, MN 55145-1760. The LLC must attach all federal forms and schedules. LLCs with more than 200 members must submit the federal K-1 schedules and the Minnesota M-KPI and M-KPC schedules (if applicable) on diskette or microfiche.

If the IRS makes changes to the federal return, the LLC must file an amended Minnesota partnership return with the Department of Revenue or explain why no amended return is needed. The filing must be made within 180 days after notification of the change by the IRS. A copy of the IRS report must be attached to the Minnesota return.

An individual member of an LLC is required to file a Minnesota income tax return and is subject to the Minnesota income tax if the Minnesota source gross income is $6,550 or more (adjusted).

The LLC must provide the members with enough information for them to complete their Minnesota income tax returns and determine the correct Minnesota tax. The LLC must complete a separate Schedule M-KPI for each individual, estate, or trust member, showing the specific share of LLC income, credit, and modifications for each.

The LLC must use Schedule M-KPC to show each corporate and partnership member's share of LLC income, credit, and modifications. The form must be attached to the LLC's Form M-3. The LLC must also attach copies of the federal Schedules K and K-1 to its state partnership return.

[D]   Estimated Taxes

The LLC must file estimated tax deposit forms and make quarterly payments if it has estimated minimum fees of $1,000 or more or if any nonresident individual member's share of composite income tax is $500 or more. Quarterly estimated payments must be paid on Form M-71, Partnership Estimated Tax, before the fifteenth day of the fourth, sixth, and ninth months of the tax year and of the first month following the end of the tax year. Both the minimum fee and the composite income tax may be included on the same quarterly tax payment.

[E] Composite Returns

Minnesota allows LLCs to file a composite Minnesota income tax return on behalf of nonresident members who elect to be included.[10] The electing individual members may not have any Minnesota source income other than the income from the LLC and other entities electing composite filings. The individuals who have other Minnesota income may not be included on the composite schedule and must file Form M-1, Minnesota Income Tax Return.

Nonresident individual members of an LLC who are included in the composite income tax return are not subject to the nonresident partner withholding requirements.

The LLC must complete Schedule M-KC, Composite Income Tax Schedule, to file composite income tax for its nonresident individual members. The form must be attached to Form M-3. The box for composite income tax for nonresident members must be checked on the front of Form M-3.

[F] Withholding Taxes

LLCs are required to withhold Minnesota income tax for nonresident members if all of the following requirements are met:[11]

- The member is not included in the composite income tax return;
- The member has Minnesota distributive income of $1,000 or more; and
- The income was not generated by a transaction related to the termination or liquidation of the LLC in which no cash or property was distributed in the current or prior taxable year.

The withholding tax rate is 8.5 percent on the nonresident member's distributive share of income.

The LLC must file Form MW-3NR, Income Tax Withheld for Nonresidents, for the nonresident member withholding. The form must be attached to Form M-3. The LLC must check the box on the front of Form M-3 that it is withholding for nonresident members.

Minnesota LLCs are subject to personal income tax withholding requirements to the same extent as other employers.[12] LLCs are also required to collect Minnesota sales and use taxes.[13]

---

[10] Minn. Stat. Ann. §289A.08(7).
[11] Minn. Stat. Ann. §290.92(4b).
[12] S.F. 181, ch. 137, 1993 Minn. Laws.
[13] Id.

[G]   Annual Report

A Minnesota LLC must file an annual report with the secretary of state.[14] The annual report must set forth the following information:

- The name of the LLC
- The alternate name, if any, that a foreign LLC has adopted for use in the state
- The address of its registered office
- The name of its registered agent, if any
- The jurisdiction of the organization
- The name and business address of the manager or other person exercising the principal function of the chief manager of the LLC

The annual report is due two years from the date the LLC is formed or registered with the secretary of state or two years from the date of the last registration. The biennial registration is due on or before the anniversary date of formation or registration in Minnesota.

[H]   Filing Fees

Minnesota imposes the following filing fees on LLCs:

Articles of organization	$135
Certificate of registration for foreign LLC	$185
Annual report	$ 50

[I]   References

M. Sargent & W. Schwidetzky, Limited Liability Company Handbook, Law — Sample Documents — Forms, §4.14, Minnesota Form of Articles of Organization, Operating Agreement, and Member Control Agreement (1995-1996 ed.).

§23.26   MISSISSIPPI

Mississippi enacted the Mississippi Limited Liability Company Act effective July 1, 1994.[1]

---

[14] Minn. Stat. Ann. §322B.960.
§23.26 [1] S.B. 2395, ch. 402, 1994 Miss. Laws; Miss. Code Ann. §§79-29-101 to 79-29-1201.

[A]   State Tax Classification

Mississippi classifies an LLC in the same manner that the LLC is classified for federal tax purposes.[2] The same rule applies to foreign LLCs qualified to do business in Mississippi.[3]

[B]   Taxation of LLC and Members

There is no franchise or other entity-level tax on LLCs that are classified as partnerships. The LLC is a pass-through entity. All items of income, gain, deduction, credit, and loss pass through to and are taxed to the members.[4]

However, if the individual members fail to report and pay the tax, then the LLC and any member treated as a general partner are jointly and severally liable for the tax liability and subject to assessment.[5] The LLC and managers are not liable if the LLC withholds and remits 5 percent of the net gain or profit of the LLC for the tax year. The amounts are treated as payment of the estimated tax of the members. They are allocated pro rata to the members' taxpayer accounts.

Nonresident members are taxed on their distributive shares of income allocable to Mississippi, whether or not distributed.[6]

LLC net income is computed under Mississippi law in the same manner and on the same basis as for individuals. No personal exemptions are allowed for an LLC. LLC income distributed to members is subject to passive activity limitations in the same manner as under federal law. Each member must be provided with a schedule of passive activity and rental real estate activity income or loss.

[C]   Tax Returns

Each Mississippi LLC and foreign LLC with income from Mississippi must file Form 86-105, Mississippi Partnership/LLP/LLC Income Tax Return, if the LLC is classified as a partnership for federal income tax purposes.[7] The return must be filed if the LLC has income derived from a business, trade or occupation in Mississippi and/or property located within the state of Mississippi.

The returns must be filed by April 15 for calendar year LLCs and by the fifteenth day of the fourth month following the end of the fiscal year for other LLCs. The return must be mailed to the Bureau of Revenue, P.O. Box 960, Jackson, Mississippi 39205. An LLC may obtain an extension of time to file a return. An extension of time to file a federal partnership return is automatically recognized in Mississippi. The LLC must attach a copy of the federal extension to the Mississippi return.

---

[2] Miss. Code Ann. §79-29-112.
[3] Id.
[4] Miss. Code Ann. §27-7-25.
[5] Id.; Miss. State Tax Commn. Reg. §901.
[6] Miss. State Tax Commn. Reg. §901.
[7] Id.

LLCs that elect to withhold the 5 percent tax on net income of the members must file Form 62-526. The LLC must submit a separate voucher for each member in order that payment can be properly credited.

A member may claim a share of withheld taxes by the LLC as estimated taxes on the member's individual income tax return. The LLC must provide Form 62-526 to each member to show the correct amount withheld.

A resident member of an LLC must include his entire distributive share of LLC profits in his individual tax return.

If any of the members of an LLC are nonresidents of Mississippi, then the LLC must compute the income or loss from sources within Mississippi separately from the other income of the LLC. The amount of income taxable to the nonresident members and the amount of loss deductible by the nonresident members in Mississippi are limited to the income or loss from sources within Mississippi. The LLC may file a composite return for nonresident members who have no other income from Mississippi.[8]

The LLC must attach copies of the federal Schedules K and K-1 with the state partnership return. It must also distribute the federal Schedule K-1 to the individual partners.

The LLC may file an abbreviated return on Form 86-106, Partnership Income Tax Return. The form may be used only if a copy of the federal return on Form 1065 is attached.

[D]   Annual Report

No annual report is required.

[E]   Filing Fees

Mississippi imposes the following filing fees on LLCs:[9]

Certificate of formation	$ 50
Certificate of registration for foreign LLC	$250
Annual fee	$ 0

§23.27   MISSOURI

Missouri enacted laws authorizing LLCs in 1993.[1]

---

[8] Id.
[9] Miss. Code Ann. §79-29-1203.
§23.27 [1] S.B. 66, 1993 Mo. Laws; Mo. Ann. Stat. §§347.010 to 347.740.

[A] State Tax Classification

A Missouri LLC is classified in the same manner that the LLC is classified for federal tax purposes.[2]

Before May 20, 1997, an LLC that was classified as a corporation for federal income tax purposes was treated as a corporation. The persons authorized to act on behalf of the LLC were treated as officers and directors for state tax purposes. The members of the LLC were treated as shareholders for state tax purposes.[3]

[B] Taxation of LLC and Members

There is no franchise or entity-level tax on a Missouri LLC. The LLC's income passes through to the members, who are subject to personal income tax.[4]

[C] Withholding Taxes

An LLC and its authorized persons have a duty to withhold and pay taxes under the Missouri withholding tax laws on a basis consistent with the LLC's classification as a partnership or corporation under federal tax laws.[5] An LLC must withhold Missouri income tax on the distributive shares paid or credited to nonresident individual members.[6] The withholding tax rate is 6 percent (the highest individual tax rate), subject to certain exceptions and modifications.[7] No withholding is required for members of the LLC who are partnerships, corporations, trusts, or estates.[8] The LLC is not required to withhold if any of the following apply:

- The nonresident member, who is not otherwise required to file a return, elects to have the Missouri income tax paid as part of a composite return.
- The nonresident member has Missouri income from the LLC of less than $1,200.[9]
- The LLC is liquidated or terminated and income was generated by a transaction related to termination or liquidation, or no cash or other property was distributed in the current or prior taxable year.[10]

---

[2] Mo. Ann. Stat. §347.187.2.
[3] Id.
[4] Mo. Stat. Ann. §143.401.
[5] Mo. Stat. Ann. §347.187.1 (Vernon).
[6] Mo. Stat. Ann. §143.411.5; Mo. Code Regs. tit. 12, §10-2.190.
[7] Mo. Stat. Ann. §143.411.5; Mo. Dept. of Rev. R. 10-2.1901(4).
[8] Mo. Code Regs. tit. 12, §10-2.190(4)(A).
[9] Mo. Dept. of Rev. R. 10-2.1901(4).
[10] Mo. Stat. Ann. §143.411.7; Mo. Dept. of Rev. R. 10-2.1901(4).

- The member files Form MO-3NR, agreeing to file a return and pay the applicable state taxes.[11]

Withholding taxes are paid to the Department of Revenue on Form MO-1NR, Income Tax Withheld for Nonresident Individual Partners or S Corporation Shareholders. The form and payment must be filed by the due date, or an extension of the due date for filing the LLC's income tax return must be requested. An extension of time for filing the LLC's return automatically extends the time for filing Form MO-1NR. The form and Copy C of Form MO-2NR must be filed with the Department of Revenue either before or at the same time the LLC provides Copy A of Form MO-2NR to the nonresident member. Form MO-2NR, Statement of Income Tax Payments for Nonresident Individual Partners or S Corporation Shareholders, must be completed for each nonresident member to whom payments or credits subject to withholding were made.

[D]   Tax Returns

A Missouri LLC must file Form MO-1065, Partnership Return of Income. The LLC must check the box on the top of the form that it is a limited liability company that is classified as a partnership.[12] The return must cover the same period as the corresponding federal Form 1065. The form must be filed if IRS Form 1065 is required to be filed and the LLC has a member who is a Missouri resident or has any income derived from Missouri sources.[13] An LLC is treated as having income derived from Missouri sources if the items are attributable to the ownership or disposition of any interest in real or tangible property in Missouri or to a trade, business, profession, or occupation carried on in Missouri. Income from intangible personal property also constitutes income derived from sources within Missouri.

The LLC must file the partnership return by the fifteenth day of the fourth month following the close of the tax year. The LLC must file the return on or before April 15 if the LLC operates on a calendar year basis. Any member of the LLC may sign the return. The return must be mailed to the Department of Revenue, P.O. Box 2200, Jefferson City, MO 65105-2200.

The LLC may file a composite return on behalf of nonresident members.[14] The LLC must pay tax at a 6 percent tax rate on the income of nonresident members reported on the composite return. Alternatively, the LLC may file an individual tax return on behalf of the nonresident member and pay the tax at the 6 percent tax rate or the lesser exact amount.[15]

---

[11] Id.

[12] Mo. Dept. of Rev. R. 10-2.1901(2); Mont. Code Ann. §§35-8-101 to 35-8-1307.

[13] Mo. Stat. Ann. §143.581.

[14] Mo. Dept. of Rev. R. 10-2.1901(1)(A).

[15] Mo. Dept. of Rev. R. 10-2.1901(3).

[E]   Annual Report

There is no annual report in Missouri.

[F]   Filing Fees

Missouri imposes the following filing fees on LLCs:[16]

Articles of organization	$100
Foreign LLC registration application	$100
Annual fee	$ 0

§23.28   MONTANA

Montana enacted the Montana Limited Liability Company Act effective October 1, 1993.[1]

[A]   State Tax Classification

Montana classifies an LLC in the same manner that the LLC is classified for federal tax purposes.[2] A limited liability company may be formed in Montana with one member. However, to be taxed as a partnership for Montana and federal tax purposes, the LLC must have at least two members.[3] An LLC with one member is classified as a corporation.[4]

[B]   Taxation of LLC and Members

Montana does not impose a franchise or entity-level tax on an LLC.[5] Each of the members of the LLC is taxed on the distributive share of income, gain, loss, credit, and deductions.[6] All owners of LLCs that have Montana source income are subject to the Montana personal income tax. This includes nonresident individuals, foreign corporations not engaged in doing business in Montana, and the owners of pass-through entities that own an interest in the LLC.[7]

---

[16] Mo. Stat. Ann. §§347.039, 347.179.
§23.28 [1] S.B. 146, ch. 120, 1993 Mont. Laws.
[2] Mont. Admin. Rs. 42.23.702(1), 42.23.701-.702.
[3] Mont. Admin. R. 42.23.702.
[4] Mont. Admin. R. 42.23.701-.702.
[5] Mont. Code Ann. §§15-30-1102(1)(a), (c), 15-30-101(23).
[6] Mont. Code Ann. §15-30-133.
[7] Mont. Code Ann. §§15-30-1102(2), 15-30-101(23).

[C]   Allocations

Profits, losses, and surpluses of the LLC are shared equally among members unless otherwise provided in the articles of organization or operating agreement.[8]

[D]   Tax Returns

An LLC that is classified as a partnership for federal tax purposes must file a partnership return reflecting each member's share of the income and loss of the LLC.[9] The return is filed on Form PR-1, Partnership Return of Income. The LLC must file the return with the Income Tax Division, Montana Department of Revenue, P.O. Box 5805, Helena, MT 59604-5805. The LLC is not required to attach the federal return to Form PR-1. However, the Department of Revenue may request a copy of the federal return at a later date.[10]

The second page of the partnership return shows each member's distributive share of income, including nonpassive income, passive income, portfolio income, and other income. The LLC may attach federal Form K-1 rather than completing the second page of the form. However, each member's name and address, Social Security number, percentage ownership in the LLC, and Montana taxable share of ordinary income must be set forth on the first page of the form.

The members must file Montana individual income tax returns reflecting their shares of the income and loss of the LLC.

An LLC taxed as a corporation for federal tax purposes must file a Montana corporation license return (income tax return), Form CLT-4, with the Natural Resource and Corporation Tax Division of the Montana Department of Revenue.[11]

[E]   Nonresident Members

[1]   Nonresident Individuals

An LLC must comply with one of the following requirements if it has a nonresident individual member:[12]

- File a composite return and pay the composite tax on behalf of the nonresident members. The composite return is filed in lieu of the individual personal income tax return. The composite tax is paid in lieu of the personal income taxes.[13]
- File an agreement of the individual nonresident member to file an individual

---

[8] Mont. Code Ann. §35-8-503.
[9] Mont. Code Ann. §§15-30-1102(4)(a), 15-30-101(23); Mont. Admin. R. 42.23.702.
[10] Mont. Code Ann. §15-30-133.
[11] Mont. Admin. R. 42.23.702(1).
[12] Mont. Code Ann. §15-30-1113(1)(a).
[13] Mont. Code Ann. §15-30-1112.

income tax return on a timely basis, pay all taxes on income from the LLC, and be subject to the personal jurisdiction of the state of Montana for tax collection purposes.

- Remit an amount equal to the highest marginal personal income tax rate in effect multiplied by the nonresident member's share of Montana source income as reflected on the LLC's information return.

[2] Foreign Corporations

An LLC must comply with one of the following requirements if it has a foreign corporation member:[14]

- File a composite return and pay the composite tax on behalf of the foreign corporation. The composite return is filed in lieu of the corporation license (income) tax return. The composite tax is paid in lieu of the corporation license (income) tax.[15]
- File an agreement of the foreign corporation to file a corporation license (income) tax return on a timely basis, pay all taxes on income from the LLC, and be subject to the personal jurisdiction of the state of Montana for tax collection purposes.
- Remit an amount equal to the corporation license (income) tax rate in effect multiplied by the foreign corporation's share of Montana source income as reflected on the LLC's information return.

[3] Second-Tier Pass-Through Entities

An LLC must comply with one of the following requirements if it has a member that is a partnership, LLC, or other pass-through entity:[16]

- File a composite return and pay the composite tax on behalf of the pass-through entity.
- File a statement that identifies each of the pass-through entity's shareholders, members, partners, or other owners. The statement must establish that the pass-through entity's share of Montana source income will be fully accounted for on a personal income tax return or corporation license (income) tax return filed in Montana.
- Remit an amount equal to the highest marginal personal income tax rate in effect multiplied by the nonresident member's share of Montana source income as reflected on the LLC's information return.

---

[14] Mont. Code Ann. §15-30-1113(1)(b).
[15] Mont. Code Ann. §15-30-1112.
[16] Mont. Code Ann. §15-30-1113(1)(c).

[4]   Failure to File Return or Pay Taxes

An LLC is liable for payment of taxes owed by nonresident members if the nonresident members fail to file a tax return for any year that the nonresident member was not included on the LLC's composite tax return. The LLC must pay the taxes following notice from the Montana Department the Revenue that the nonresident member failed to file a return or timely pay all taxes.[17]

[5]   Multistate Tax Compact

Montana complies with the Multistate Tax Compact. That Compact allows an LLC to petition the Montana Department of Revenue for an accounting that fairly represents the LLC's or member's business activity in the state when apportionment and allocation methods fail to reflect this activity.[18]

[F]   Annual Report

An LLC must file an annual report in Montana between January 1 and April 15 of the year following the calendar year in which the LLC is organized. A foreign LLC must file the annual report between January 1 and April 15 in each year after it qualifies to do business in Montana.[19]

[G]   Filing Fees

Montana imposes the following filing fees on LLCs:[20]

Articles of organization	$70
Foreign LLC registration application	$70
Annual registration	$10

§23.29   NEBRASKA

Nebraska enacted laws authorizing limited liability companies effective September 9, 1993.[1] In 1994, Nebraska law was amended to make reference to LLCs in the tax laws applicable to motor and special fuel licensing requirements, personal property tax lists, personal income tax credits for taxes paid to another state, and

---

[17] Mont. Code Ann. §15-30-1113(6).
[18] Mont. Code Ann. §15-30-1113(7).
[19] Mont. Code Ann. §35-8-208.
[20] Mont. Code Ann. §§35-8-211, 35-8-212.
§23.29   [1] H.B. 121, 1993 Neb. Laws; Neb. Rev. Stat. §§21-2601 to 21-2653.

sales and use tax credits for investment in qualified business or employment expansion.[2]

[A] State Tax Classification

Nebraska classifies an LLC in the same manner that the LLC is classified for federal tax purposes.[3] State regulations dealing with partnership taxation specify that a partnership includes an LLC that is classified as a partnership for federal tax purposes.[4] The federal classification of an LLC as a partnership is conclusive for Nebraska purposes.[5]

[B] Taxation of LLC and Members

Nebraska does not impose a franchise or entity-level tax on an LLC.[6] Each of the members of the LLC is taxed on her distributive share of income, gain, loss, credit and deductions.[7] Residents of Nebraska who are members of an LLC must include in their Nebraska taxable income, to the extent includible in federal gross income, their proportionate shares of the LLC's federal income adjusted pursuant to the Nebraska tax laws.[8] A member of an LLC who is a Nebraska resident must include in taxable income the member's proportionate share of the net income or loss from the conduct of such business within Nebraska. The income of the LLC that is derived from or connected with Nebraska sources is determined in the normal manner, subject to adjustments.

Resident members of a Nebraska LLC are allowed a credit against Nebraska income tax for the amount of any income tax imposed by or paid to another state on income derived from sources in other jurisdictions that is also subject to the Nebraska income tax laws.[9]

Nonresident members are taxed on their distributive shares of income.[10] The nonresident member must file an agreement to file a Nebraska return and pay the applicable taxes on Form 12N.[11] The LLC must withhold Nebraska income taxes from any nonresident individual member for whom it does not receive a completed Form 12N. The withholding tax rate is determined by applying the

---

[2] L.B. 884, 1994 Neb. Laws (eff. Apr. 4, 1994).
[3] Neb. Rev. Stat. §21-2633.
[4] Neb. Admin. R. & Regs. 25.001.
[5] Id.
[6] Neb. Rev. Stat. §77-2727(1); Neb. Admin. R. & Regs. 25.002.01.
[7] Neb. Rev. Stat. §77-2727(2).
[8] Neb. Rev. Stat. §77-2734.01(1).
[9] Neb. Rev. Stat. §§77-2730, 2715.07; Neb. Admin. R. & Regs. 22-011.
[10] Neb. Rev. Stat. §77-2727(3); Neb. Admin. R. & Regs. 25.003.
[11] Neb. Rev. Stat. §77-2727(3); Neb. Admin. R. & Regs. 25.003.02.

highest personal income tax rate to the nonresident member's share of LLC income attributable to Nebraska sources.[12] That rate is currently 6.99 percent.

If the LLC is not a member of a unitary group, it must apportion its income.[13]

[C]   Member Liability for Unpaid Taxes

The members are liable for unpaid taxes of the LLC in the same manner as corporate officers are liable for unpaid taxes of a corporation if the LLC's management is reserved to the members. The managers of the LLC are liable for the unpaid taxes in the same manner as corporate officers if management of the LLC is not reserved to members.[14]

[D]   Allocations

An LLC allocates profits and losses in the manner stipulated in the operating agreement. However, the aggregate fair market value of the LLC assets must exceed liabilities after any distribution is made.[15]

[E]   Nonresident Members

Nonresidents of Nebraska who are members of an LLC must file Nebraska income tax returns. The nonresidents must include in Nebraska adjusted gross income their proportionate shares of the LLC's income. If the LLC is not a member of a unitary group, the LLC must apportion the income of the nonresident members. The apportionment is determined in the same manner as for resident members.[16]

A nonresident member must sign and forward to the LLC before the filing of the LLC's return an agreement that states that the member will file a Nebraska income tax return and pay the tax on the income derived from or connected with sources in Nebraska. The agreement must be attached to the LLC's tax return for each tax year.[17] The LLC must pay withholding taxes if the nonresident member does not sign the agreement or if the LLC fails to file the agreement with its tax return.[18] The withholding tax rate is 6.68 percent on the member's share of income from Nebraska sources. The member is entitled to a credit against the member's Nebraska income tax liability.

The tax commissioner may exempt a nonresident member from filing a Ne-

---

[12] Neb. Rev. Stat. §77-2727(4)(a); Neb. Admin. R. & Regs. 25.003.03.

[13] Neb. Rev. Stat. §77-2734.01(2). Apportionment is made under Neb. Rev. Stat. §§77-2734.05 to 77-2734.15.

[14] Neb. Rev. Stat. §21-2612.

[15] Neb. Rev. Stat. §21-2618.

[16] Neb. Rev. Stat. §77-2734.01(3).

[17] Neb. Rev. Stat. §77-2734.01(4).

[18] Neb. Rev. Stat. §77-2734.01(5).

braska income tax return if the member's only source of Nebraska income is the member's share of LLC income derived from or attributable to sources within Nebraska, the member did not file an agreement to file a Nebraska income tax return, and the LLC has paid the required withholding taxes on behalf of the member.[19] The withholding taxes paid are treated as full satisfaction of the Nebraska income tax liability of the nonresident member.

[F]   Tax Returns

A Nebraska LLC that is classified as a partnership for federal tax purposes must file Form 1065N, Nebraska Partnership Return of Income. A foreign LLC having either a resident member or income derived from sources within Nebraska must also file a return.[20] The return must be filed on or before the fifteenth day of the fourth month following the close of the tax year.[21] The return must be filed with the Nebraska Department of Revenue, P.O. Box 94818, Lincoln, NE 68509-4818.

An LLC may obtain an extension of time to file the return by filing Form 2688N.[22] The form is not used if the LLC has obtained a federal extension on or before the due date of the federal return. The Nebraska Department of Revenue accepts an approved federal extension if the copy of the approval is attached to the Nebraska return.

A nonresident member must forward the completed Form 12N, Nebraska Nonresident Income Tax Agreement, to the LLC before the original filing of the Nebraska Partnership Return of Income. The LLC must attach this agreement to its return. The nonresident member may claim the amount withheld as a credit against the member's Nebraska income tax return by attaching a copy of Form 14N to the Nebraska individual tax return that is filed on Form 1040N.

The LLC must provide all members with a schedule similar to federal Schedule K-1. The schedule must list the amounts and types of income or deductions that are included in each member's Nebraska tax return. The LLC may use federal Schedule K-1 for resident members when the amounts of income from U.S. government obligations and non-Nebraska state and local obligations are also listed. The LLC may also use federal Schedule K-1 for nonresident or corporate members when the amounts of state, local, and government obligations are also listed and all income is attributable to Nebraska.

The LLC must use the same fiscal year that the LLC uses for federal tax purposes. If the LLC changes its tax year, it must change its Nebraska tax year. A copy of an approval from the IRS to change accounting periods must accompany the first return that reflects the change.

The LLC must use the same methods of accounting for Nebraska income tax purposes that it uses for federal income tax purposes. It may not change the

[19] Neb. Rev. Stat. §77-2734.01(6).
[20] Neb. Admin. R. & Regs. 25.002.
[21] Neb. Admin. R. & Regs. 25.002.05.
[22] Neb. Admin. R. & Regs. 25.002.0513.

methods of accounting unless the change is approved by the Internal Revenue Service. A copy of the approval must accompany the first return that reflects the change in the methods of accounting.

An LLC that has reported income or deductions that are changed by the Internal Revenue Service must report the change or correction to the Nebraska Department of Revenue. The LLC must report the change within 90 days of the determination by filing a Nebraska Partnership Return of Income, Form 1065N, and checking the box "Amended Return" at the top of the return. An LLC that has reported income or allowed credits in another state that are changed or corrected by that state in a way that materially affects the tax liability in Nebraska must also report the change to Nebraska within 90 days. An LLC that files an amended return with the Internal Revenue Service or with another state that materially changes the Nebraska tax liability must file an amended return with the Nebraska Department of Revenue within 90 days of filing of the amended federal or state return. The LLC must furnish the Department with complete information regarding the amount of income and deductions reported to the Internal Revenue Service after the change or correction.[23]

An LLC filing an amended return must revise the amount of Nebraska personal income tax to be withheld from any nonresident member and must issue a revised statement of income tax withheld to the nonresident member for use in filing the member's amended Nebraska personal income tax return. The Department may assess taxes at any time if the nonresident member fails to file an amended return. The assessment period is limited to two years if a member properly reports the change in his federal tax liability.[24]

[G]   Apportionment of Income

An LLC that has income from sources within and outside of Nebraska must determine the portion of taxable income subject to Nebraska taxes for nonresident or corporate members. Each LLC must determine the portion of income subject to tax by either the apportionment formula or an approved alternative method. Corporate members must comply with Corporate Income Tax Regulation 24-056 in calculating their apportionment factors. An LLC with one or more corporate members must also provide each corporate member with a copy of Nebraska Schedule I of Form 1065N.

Any LLC that derives income from sources within and outside of Nebraska must complete Schedule I to Form 1065N if the LLC has at least one nonresident or corporate partner. The LLC must complete Schedule I without regard to the residence of its members. An LLC using an alternative method of apportionment must attach a copy of the approval of the alternative method and a computation of the apportionment factor.

Nebraska uses a single sales-factor-only formula to apportion income. The sales factor is a fraction. The numerator of the fraction is the total sales of the LLC in

---

[23] Reg. §25-007, Neb. Dept. of Rev., effective Nov. 11, 1998.
[24] Id.

Nebraska during the tax year. The denominator is the total sales of the LLC everywhere during the tax year. Total sales include gross sales of real and tangible personal property, less returns and allowances, and all other items of gross receipts. An LLC must include the following sales in the sales factor:

- Sales of property derived or shipped to a purchaser, other than the U.S. government, within Nebraska regardless of the f.o.b. point or other conditions of sale;
- Sales to the U.S. government of property shipped from an office, store, warehouse, factory, or other place of storage in Nebraska; and
- One-third of the sales of property shipped from an office, store, warehouse, factory, or other place of storage in the state if the taxpayer is not subject to tax in Nebraska when the property is delivered.

An LLC must complete Schedule III when the LLC has income derived from or attributable to sources within Nebraska and has nonresident or corporate partners.

[H]   Health Care Provider

A health care provider operated as an LLC may distribute the health care provider credits to the members in the same manner as income is distributed for use against their income tax. Health care providers were formerly entitled to a nonrefundable income tax credit equal to the amount of taxes paid under the Health Care Provider Income Tax Act.[25]

[I]   Community Betterment Programs

Each member of an LLC is entitled to report the member's share of LLC credit for contributions to certified community betterment programs as provided in the Community Development Assistance Act. The member must report the member's share of this credit in the same manner and in the same proportion as reported by the LLC.[26]

[J]   Annual Report

Nebraska does not require an LLC to file an annual report.

---

[25] Neb. Rev. Stat. §77-2715.07(4) (repealed).
[26] Neb. Rev. Stat. §77-2715.07.

[K] Filing Fees

Nebraska imposes the following filing fees on LLCs:[27]

Articles of organization	$110 plus recording fees
Foreign LLC registration application	$110
Annual fee	$ 0

[L] References

M. Sargent & W. Schwidetzky, Limited Liability Company Handbook, Law — Sample Documents — Forms, §4.15, Nebraska Form of Articles of Organization and Operating Agreement (1995-1996 ed.).

§23.30 NEVADA

Nevada enacted the Nevada Limited-Liability Companies Act effective October 1, 1991.[1]

[A] Taxation of LLC and Members

Nevada does not impose an income tax on LLCs or their members. There is no partnership income tax return.

However, all LLCs that have employees working in Nevada or that have an office or other base of operations within the state must pay a business license tax. The tax rate is $25 per equivalent full-time employee employed by the LLC in Nevada during the quarter. The total number of equivalent full-time employees employed during a quarter is determined by dividing the total number of hours worked by all employees during the quarter by 468. The total number of hours worked by all employees in a quarter is determined by adding the total number of hours worked by full-time employees in Nevada during the quarter to the total number of hours worked by part-time employees in Nevada during the quarter. The number of hours worked in Nevada by employees based outside of Nevada who perform some duties in Nevada are also counted. Full-time employees are persons employed at least 36 hours per week.

[B] Allocations

An LLC may allocate and distribute the profits to members as provided in the operating agreement. However, the assets of the LLC must be in excess of all

---

[27] Neb. Rev. Stat. §21-2634.
§23.30 [1] Nev. Rev. Stat. Ann. §§86.011 to 86.590.

liabilities of the LLC after the distribution is made except for liabilities to members on account of their contributions.[2]

[C] Tax Returns

LLCs that have employees working in Nevada or that have an office or other base of operations within the state must obtain a business license. The initial application is made on Form APP-01.00, Nevada Business Registration[3] filed with the Nevada Department of Taxation. The LLC must obtain the license before it conducts business in Nevada. The initial license fee is $25.

The LLC must file a business license return on Form TXR-04.01, Business Tax Return. The return is due quarterly on or before the last day of the quarter. The $25 per employee tax must be paid on or before the last day of the month following the close of each calendar quarter. The taxes must be paid to and the filing must be made with the Department of Taxation, 1550 East College Parkway, Carson City, NV 89706-7921.

[D] Annual Report

An LLC must file an annual list of managers or members and a designation of resident agent.[4] The LLC must file the annual report on or before the last day of the month in which the anniversary date of its formation occurs in each year. It must file a list of its managers. If there are no managers, it must file a list of its members. It must also designate the resident agent. The manager must sign the annual report. A member may sign if there are no managers.

The annual report must list the post office box or street address, either residence or business, of each manager or member.[5] The secretary of state may refuse to file the list if the LLC does not list all the addresses.

[E] Filing Fees

Nevada imposes the following filing fees on LLCs:[6]

Articles of organization	$125
Registration of a foreign LLC	$125
Annual report	$ 85

---

[2] Nev. Rev. Stat. Ann. §86.341.

[3] This form may be obtained at the Nevada Department of Taxation website, http://tax.state.nv.us/taxnew/forms.htm.

[4] Nev. Rev. Stat. Ann. §86.263.

[5] Nev. Rev. Stat. Ann. §86.269.

[6] Nev. Rev. Stat. Ann. §86.561.1.

§23.31   NEW HAMPSHIRE

New Hampshire enacted laws authorizing limited liability companies effective July 1, 1993.[1]

[A]   State Tax Classification

New Hampshire taxes an LLC as a separate legal entity regardless of its classification for federal tax purposes.[2] The members of the LLC are not taxed on their distributive shares of income.[3]

[B]   Taxation of LLC

An LLC must pay several different types of taxes in New Hampshire. These are discussed below.

[1]   Dividends and Interest

An LLC must pay a 5 percent tax on dividends and interest if gross interest and dividend income from all sources exceeds $2,400 during the tax year.[4] The following interest and dividends are taxable:[5]

- Interest from bonds, notes, and debts except interest from notes or bonds of New Hampshire and notes or bonds of any political subdivision of New Hampshire;
- Dividends, other than stock dividends paid in new stock of a company issuing the same, on shares and all corporations organized under the laws of any state;
- Dividends, other than stock dividends paid in new stock of a partnership, LLC, association, or trust issuing the same, on shares in partnerships, LLCs, associations, or trusts the beneficial interest of which is represented by transferable shares;
- Dividends, other than that portion of dividends declared by corporations to be a return of capital and considered for federal income tax purposes to be a return of capital; and
- The holder's proportionate share of income in a qualified investment trust, subject to adjustments

---

§23.31   [1] H.B. 690, ch. 313, 1993 N.H. Laws; N.H. Rev. Stat. Ann. §§304-C:1 to 304-C:85.
[2] N.H. Rev. Stat. Ann. §§77:3-a, 77:3.I(b), 77.14, 77:15 (dividend and income tax).
[3] N.H. Rev. Stat. Ann. §§77:15, 77:16 (dividend and income tax).
[4] N.H. Rev. Stat. Ann. §77:3-I(b).
[5] N.H. Rev. Stat. Ann. §77:4.

The tax is assessed only on the LLC. The members of the LLC are not taxed on the interest and dividend income received by them from the LLC.[6] There is one exception. A resident of New Hampshire is taxed on his or her distributive share of dividends and interest income from an LLC located in a foreign state to the extent that the income would be taxable if the LLC were organized or doing business in New Hampshire.[7]

There is an apportionment formula if the LLC has members who reside in a foreign state.[8]

[2]   Business Profits Tax

An LLC must pay an 8.5 percent tax on business profits.[9] Every business organization having gross income from all sources, before expenses, in excess of $50,000 is subject to the business profits tax.[10] LLCs are subject to the business profits tax in the same manner as partnerships.[11]

Partnerships and LLCs having a place of business in the state are subject to the tax if any member of the LLC is a resident of the state. If any member of an LLC is not an inhabitant of New Hampshire, then the LLC is subject to the business profits tax only on so much of the income that is proportionate to the aggregate interest of the members who are inhabitants of the state in the profits of the LLC.[12]

[3]   Business Enterprise Tax

An LLC must pay a business enterprise tax. The tax is imposed at the rate of .75 percent on the compensation, interest, and dividends paid by an LLC engaged in business activities in New Hampshire for periods after July 1, 1993.[13]

For purposes of the tax, taxable compensation includes all wages, salaries, fees, bonuses, commissions, and other payments to employees, officers, and directors of the LLC. It also includes the amount of deduction allowed under the business profits tax for certain personal service income and net earnings from self-employment income.[14]

Taxable dividends include any distribution of money or property paid to owners of an LLC or other business enterprise from the accumulated revenues and profits of the business.

---

[6] N.H. Rev. Stat. Ann. §§77-14, 77-15; N.H. Dept. of Rev. Admin. Reg. §902.06.
[7] N.H. Rev. Stat. Ann. §77:16.
[8] N.H. Rev. Stat. Ann. §77:14.
[9] N.H. Rev. Stat. Ann. §77-A:2.
[10] N.H. Rev. Stat. Ann. §77-A:6.I.
[11] N.H. Rev. Stat. Ann. §77-A:1.I.
[12] *Id.*
[13] N.H. Rev. Stat. Ann. §77-E:2.
[14] N.H. Rev. Stat. Ann. §77-E:1.

Interest subject to the business enterprise tax includes interest paid or accrued on business debt.

All LLCs carrying on business in New Hampshire are required to pay the tax if the gross business receipts exceed $150,000 during the year or the enterprise value tax base is greater than $75,000.[15] A business enterprise subject to the tax includes limited liability companies.[16]

[C]   *Tax Returns*

An LLC must file the following tax returns in New Hampshire:

- Form BET, Business Enterprise Tax Return for Corporations, Combined Groups, Partnerships, Fiduciaries and Non-Profit Organizations. The LLC must file the return only if the gross receipts are greater than $150,000 or the enterprise value tax base is greater than $75,000.
- Form NH-1065, Partnership Business Profits Tax Return. The LLC must file this return only if gross business income is greater than $50,000.
- Form DP-80, Apportionment of Income. An LLC that has business activities both within and outside the state of New Hampshire and that is subject to income taxes or a franchise tax measured on net income in another state, whether or not actually imposed by the other state, must apportion its gross business profits to New Hampshire by using this form.
- Form BT-SUMMARY, Business Tax Summary. This form is used to summarize the payments of the business enterprise tax, the business profits tax, estimated taxes, penalties, and additions to tax. The LLC must attach a complete copy of the applicable federal forms and schedules with this return.
- Form NH-1065-ES, Estimated Partnership Business Tax Quarterly Payment Voucher. Every LLC required to file a business profits tax return and/or a business enterprise tax return must also make estimated tax payments unless the annual estimated tax payment for each individual tax is less than $200. Estimated tax payments must be sent to Document Processing Division, P.O. Box 637, Concord, NH 03302-0637. Quarterly payments are due on April 15, June 15, September 15, and December 15 of each year for calendar year LLCs.
- Form DP-10, Interest and Dividend Tax Return. If the taxpayer files its own New Hampshire interest and dividends tax return, the LLC is not required to pay taxes on the interest and dividends received. There is differing tax treatment depending on whether payments are received from entities with transferable shares. Income from entities without transferable shares is taxable to the LLC as if it came from its original source. Income from entities with transferable shares is taxable to the LLC. The entire amount received or constructively received is subject to tax and must be listed on the form.

[15]N.H. Rev. Stat. Ann. §77.E:5.
[16]N.H. Rev. Stat. Ann. §77-E:1.III.

Transferable shares mean that a person can freely transfer the shares without causing a dissolution of the organization or without obtaining prior member approval. An LLC must file its own interest and dividends tax return when all the following apply:[17]
— The LLC has over $2,400 of gross interest and dividends income;
— The LLC has a usual place of business in New Hampshire;
— The LLC has at least one New Hampshire member; and
— The LLC has nontransferable shares.
Nonresident members of an LLC are not subject to the tax. LLC interest and dividend income is subject to the tax only to the extent that the members are residents of the state or are unascertained.[18]
- Form DP-80, Business Profits Tax Apportionment. An LLC must apportion its income if its business activities are conducted both within and outside the state of New Hampshire and the business and the LLC are subject to a net income tax, a franchise tax based on net income, or a capital stock tax, whether or not actually imposed by the other state.

[D] Annual Report

An LLC must file an annual report between January 1 and April 1 of each year.[19]

[E] Filing Fees

New Hampshire imposes the following filing fees on LLCs:[20]

Certificate of formation	$ 35
Foreign LLC registration application	$200
Annual report	$100

[F] References

M. Sargent & W. Schwidetzky, Limited Liability Company Handbook, Law — Sample Documents — Forms, §4.16, New Hampshire Form of Operating Agreement (1995-1996 ed.).

---

[17] N.H. Rev. Stat. Ann. §77:18.
[18] N.H. Rev. Stat. Ann. §77:14.
[19] N.H. Rev. Stat. Ann. §304-C:80.
[20] N.H. Rev. Stat. Ann. §304-C:81.

§23.32   NEW JERSEY

New Jersey enacted the New Jersey Limited Liability Company Act effective January 26, 1994.[1]

[A]   State Tax Classification

A New Jersey LLC is classified for state tax purposes in the same manner that it is classified for federal tax purposes. Members of an LLC that is classified as a partnership are liable for the New Jersey gross income tax only in their individual capacities.[2] A member or an assignee of a member of an LLC is treated as a partner in a partnership for all purposes of taxation under New Jersey law unless the LLC is otherwise classified for federal income tax purposes.[3]

A single-member LLC may be formed in New Jersey effective August 14, 1998. A single-member LLC is classified as a sole proprietorship unless the LLC elects to be classified as a corporation under federal law.[4]

[B]   Taxation of LLC and Members

[1]   General

There is no entity-level or franchise tax on New Jersey LLCs that are classified as partnerships.[5] The members of the LLC are liable for the tax only in their individual capacities. Members are taxed on their distributive shares of income, whether or not distributed.[6]

An LLC that is classified as a corporation for federal tax purposes is subject to the New Jersey entity-level corporate income tax.

A foreign corporation that is the sole member of a single-member LLC is subject to the New Jersey corporation business (income) tax unless the LLC is classified as a corporation for federal income tax purposes. In that case, the corporation is not disregarded as an entity for federal tax purposes and is required to pay tax. If the LLC is disregarded as an entity for federal tax purposes, the corporate member is subject to the New Jersey corporation business tax.[7]

---

§23.32   [1] S.B. 890, ch. 210, 1993 N.J. Laws; N.J. Stat. Ann. §§42:2B-1 to 42:2B-70.
[2] N.J. Stat. Ann. §§42:2B-69, 54:A:2-2.
[3] N.J. Stat. Ann. §42:2B-69.
[4] S.B. 378, ch. 79, 1998 N.J. Laws; N.J. Stat. Ann. §42:2B-69.b; N.J. Dept. of Treas. Reg. §18:35-1.1.
[5] N.J. Stat. Ann. §54A:2-2; Dept. of Treas. Reg. §18:35-1.3.
[6] N.J. Stat. Ann. §54A:5-4; N.J. Dept. of Treas. Reg. §18:35-1.3(b), (c).
[7] State Tax News, N.J. Dept. of Treas., Winter 1998.

[2]   Consent Requirements

An LLC that is classified as a partnership for federal tax purposes should obtain the consent of each of its members that the State of New Jersey has the right and jurisdiction to tax the member's allocable share of income derived by the LLC from activities in New Jersey. No consent is required for a member that is (a) a corporation exempt from the New Jersey corporation business (income) tax, or (b) an individual, trust, or estate subject to the New Jersey gross (personal) income tax.

[3]   Nonconsenting Members

An LLC that fails to obtain the consent of such members must pay corporation business (income) taxes on such members' share of New Jersey income. The tax is due on or before the 15th day of the fourth month following the close of each tax year. The LLC must also make estimated tax payments for the nonconsenting members on or before the 15th day the fourth month of the tax year, based on the income of the LLC during the prior year.

The tax is imposed on the entire net income allocable to the nonconsenting member for the year multiplied by an allocation factor. The allocation factor is determined according to the Jersey corporation business (income) tax provision relating to taxpayers who maintain a regular place of business outside the State of New Jersey. The LLC must multiply the allocation fraction for the year by the maximum corporation business (income) tax rate for the year.

[4]   Consenting Members

The New Jersey tax is imposed on the entire New Jersey net income allocated to a consenting member. There are allocation factors to determine the portion of the member's entire net income allocated to New Jersey. One allocation factor is used if the relationship between the member and the LLC is unitary. Another allocation factor is used for all other members.

[C]   Tax Returns

An LLC that is classified as a partnership for federal tax purposes must file Form NJ-1065, State of New Jersey Partnership Return. Form NJ-1065 is an information return. Every LLC that has income from sources in New Jersey or that has a New Jersey resident member must file Form NJ-1065.[8] An LLC must file even if its principal place of business is outside of the state of New Jersey. The LLC must file a copy of the federal return with its state return.[9]

---

[8] N.J. Stat. Ann. §54A:8-6(b).
[9] N.J. Dept. of Treas. Reg. §18:35-1.3(f).

The New Jersey Gross Income Tax Act does not follow all federal income tax provisions for partnerships. All income, expense, gain, or loss that results from the ordinary course of business of the LLC must be included in the amount reported on the partnership return as "adjusted net ordinary income." Form NJ-1065 then makes adjustments to certain items of federal income to conform to the New Jersey Gross Income Tax Act. The form is also used to separate income derived from New Jersey sources from amounts derived from sources outside of New Jersey. These adjustments and allocations provide the basis for the reporting of LLC income by both New Jersey resident members and nonresident members.

The return for a calendar year LLC must be filed by April 15. Fiscal year returns on due by the fifteenth day of the fourth month after the end of the tax year. The LLC may obtain an extension of time for filing the form. It may use the federal automatic extension by attaching a copy of the application on the New Jersey return. Federal Form 8736 or 8800 may be used.

The form must be filed with State of New Jersey, Division of Taxation, CN 194, Trenton, NJ 08647-0194. An LLC may obtain the applicable forms by calling 800-323-4400 or requesting the forms from the New Jersey Division of Taxation, 50 Barrack Street, CN 269, Trenton, NJ 08646-0269, Attn: Forms Distribution Center.

The LLC must use the same method of accounting for state tax purposes that it uses for federal tax purposes.

An LLC must file an amended partnership return if it filed an amended federal return or if the IRS changes or corrects any item of income, gain, or loss previously reported. The New Jersey return must be filed within 90 days of the date of the amended federal return or, in the case of a federal audit, within 90 days after the final determination of the change. The LLC files the amended return by using a blank Form NJ-1065 and checking the "Amended" box. The LLC must then complete the form, entering the corrected information and attaching an explanation of the changes.

The LLC must file the following returns along with the partnership return:

- Schedule NJK-1 for each resident member. This form records the members' distributive shares of income. The members are taxed on this income, whether or not the income is actually distributed. Members who are residents of New Jersey are subject to the gross income tax on the various categories of their LLC income regardless of the sources from which the income was derived. Members who are nonresidents of New Jersey are subject to the gross income tax on their distributive shares of the various categories of LLC income, but only to the extent the income is allocated to New Jersey. Schedule NJK-1 must be attached to Form NJ-1065. The LLC must furnish each member with a copy of the schedule on or before the date on which the state partnership return must be filed. A Schedule NJK-1 must be given to every member who was a member in the LLC at any time during the year.
- Schedule NJ-NR-A. This form must be filed if any of the following apply:
  — The LLC is doing business both within and outside of New Jersey.
  — One hundred percent of the business is carried on outside of New Jersey.
  — There are nonresident members.

This form is used to apportion allocated income to New Jersey and to sources outside of New Jersey.

The LLC may also request an extension of time to file the New Jersey gross income tax return by filing Form NJ-630.

Schedule NJK-1 must also be filed for every nonresident member, but only if the LLC has income from New Jersey sources.

The Division of Taxation may also require that the LLC file the federal Form 1065, including all schedules and supporting attachments, during the course of an audit.

[D] Composite Returns

An LLC doing business or conducting activities in New Jersey or having income derived from sources within New Jersey may file a composite return on behalf of qualified nonresident individual members.[10] The composite return is filed on Schedule NJ-1080-C.[11] The composite return is treated as a group of separate returns for the members. It also meets the individual filing requirements of each qualified individual included on the composite return.[12] An LLC may include a nonresident member on the composite return if all of the following apply:

1. The member was a nonresident for the entire tax year.
2. The member did not maintain a permanent place of abode in New Jersey at any time during the tax year.
3. The member was not a fiscal year filer.
4. The member did not have income derived from or connected with New Jersey sources other than income reported on a composite return.
5. The member waives the right to claim any New Jersey personal exemption, credit, or deduction and agrees to have the tax calculated directly on such income at the highest tax rate in effect for single taxpayers for the tax year.
6. The member elects to be included in a composite return. The election is made by completing and delivering to the LLC Form NJ-1080-B (Election to Be Included in a Composite Return) or a form substantially similar to that form. The form must be filed prior to the filing of the composite return by the LLC.[13]

The member must make the composite return election annually. The election is binding on the member and the member's heirs, successors, and assigns. The member must also consent to personal jurisdiction in New Jersey for New Jersey personal income tax purposes.

The nonresident member may not revoke the election to be included in the

---

[10] N.J. Dept. of Treas. Reg. §18:35-1.30(a).
[11] N.J. Dept. of Treas. Reg. §18:35-5-2.
[12] N.J. Dept. of Treas. Reg. §18:35-1.30(i).
[13] N.J. Dept. of Treas. Reg. §18:35-1.30(b).

composite return or make an election to be included in a composite return after April 15 following the close of the tax year.

The LLC must file the composite return on or before the fifteenth day of the fourth month following the close of the tax year of the qualified electing nonresident members. The LLC may obtain an extension of time to file by filing Form NJ-630.[14]

[E]   Annual Report

New Jersey does not require LLCs to file an annual report.

[F]   Filing Fees

New Jersey imposes the following filing fees on LLCs:[15]

Certificate of formation	$100
Registration as foreign LLC	$100
Annual report	$ 50

[G]   References

M. Sargent & W. Schwidetzky, Limited Liability Company Handbook, Law — Sample Documents — Forms, §4.17, New Jersey Form of Operating Agreement (1995-1996 ed.).

§23.33   NEW MEXICO

New Mexico enacted the New Mexico Limited Liability Company Act effective June 12, 1993.[1]

[A]   State Tax Classification

New Mexico classifies an LLC in the same manner that the LLC is classified for federal purposes.[2]

---

[14] N.J. Dept. of Treas. Reg. §18:35-1.30(f).
[15] N.J. Stat. Ann. §42:2B-65.
§23.33 [1] H.B. 448, ch. 280, 1993 N.M. Laws; N.M. Stat. Ann. §§53-19-1 to 53-19-74.
[2] 3 N.M. Admin. Code §15.100.8.

[B]   Taxation of LLC and Members

There is no franchise or entity-level tax on New Mexico LLCs that are classified as partnerships for federal tax purposes.

An LLC that is not required to file a return as a corporation for federal income tax purposes is not a corporation and is therefore not subject to the New Mexico franchise tax.[3]

An LLC that is required to file a return as a corporation for federal income tax purposes and that does business in New Mexico is considered a corporation subject to the New Mexico franchise tax.[4]

Members of an LLC that is classified as a partnership for federal income tax purposes are taxed on their distributive shares of income.[5] The members of an LLC must report their distributive shares on their individual tax returns.

[C]   Nonresident Members

The New Mexico income tax is imposed on the net income of nonresident members to the extent that the income is derived from employment, business activities, or property within New Mexico. The income of the nonresident member that is in the form of distributions from an LLC that either engages in business in New Mexico or derives income from property in New Mexico is subject to the New Mexico income tax. A nonresident member may elect to allocate and apportion his distributive share of LLC income if the LLC is taxable in another state and if the LLC is a taxable entity.[6]

A member's distributive share of nonbusiness and business income must be allocated and apportioned in accordance with state regulations. The apportionment and allocation are used to determine the portion of the distributive share taxable under the New Mexico Income Tax Act.[7] Alternatively, a nonresident member whose only income from New Mexico sources is royalty income of less than $5,000 may elect to report the income in accordance with regulations.[8]

The LLC may allocate the members' distributive shares of the unincorporated business income to the members' places of residence in accordance with state regulations. However, if the LLC fails to provide a member with information distinguishing nonbusiness income from business income, the entire distribution from the LLC is considered business income and not subject to the allocation.[9]

The LLC must apportion the members' distributive shares of the unincorporated business income to New Mexico by multiplying each member's distributive share times the New Mexico apportionment percentage determined by application of

[3] 3 N.M. Admin. Code §15.100.8.1.
[4] 3 N.M. Admin. Code §15.100.8.2.
[5] 3 N.M. Admin. Code §3.11.12.1.
[6] N.M. Tax. & Rev. Dept. Rul. 70-400-6 (Oct. 22, 1970); 3 N.M. Admin. Code §3.11.12.
[7] 3 N.M. Admin. Code §3.11.12.2.
[8] *See* 3 N.M. Admin. Code §3.11.8.
[9] 3 N.M. Admin. Code §3.11.12.3.

the Uniform Division of Income for Tax Purposes Act to the entire business income. If the LLC fails to provide a member with the necessary New Mexico apportionment percentage or information sufficient to enable the member to calculate the percentage, the LLC must apportion the member's entire distributive share of business income as if the LLC's activities, property, payroll, and sales were all in New Mexico.[10]

[D]   Block Returns for Members of LLCs

An LLC may file a block return for members of the LLC if the LLC is classified as a partnership for federal tax purposes.[11] The return may be filed for any "qualified owner." A qualified owner includes a member who is not a resident of New Mexico and who has no income from New Mexico sources (including spouses' income on a joint return) other than the member's share of LLC income from New Mexico.

Qualifying members may elect to have the LLC file a block income tax return on behalf of the individual members after obtaining prior approval of the Department of Taxation and Revenue. The filing of the block return is in lieu of the filing of an individual personal income tax return by the qualified members.[12]

An LLC may file a block return on behalf of qualified individual nonresident members if the following conditions are met:

- The LLC assumes responsibility for payment of any tax liability of each nonresident member included in the block return for income taxes due to New Mexico for the tax year for which the return is filed.
- All members included in the block return report, for federal income tax purposes, on the same fiscal year basis as the fiscal year for which the block return is being reported.

The block return may not be used for any owner who is a resident of New Mexico or who is a nonresident of New Mexico having income from other sources within New Mexico, including income of a spouse.[13] An LLC that is classified as a corporation for federal income tax purposes may not file a block return.[14]

Each member included in the block return must provide the authorized representative of the LLC with a power of attorney authorizing the filing of the New Mexico income tax return on her behalf. The block return must be accompanied by the following information for each member, whether included or excluded from the block return:

---

[10] 3 N.M. Admin. Code §3.11.12.4.
[11] 3 N.M. Admin. Code §3.11.12.14.1(1).
[12] 3 N.M. Admin. Code §3.12.14.2.
[13] 3 N.M. Admin. Code §3.12.14.4.
[14] 3 N.M. Admin. Code §3.12.14.5(1).

- The name of each member
- The member's address
- The member's Social Security number
- The distribution of income to the member
- The percentage of ownership interest of the member in the LLC
- A statement as to whether the member is included or excluded from the block return[15]

The tax is imposed at the rate of 7.9 percent of the distribution of the LLC's income to the member without allowance for exemptions, deductions, or rebates of any kind other than the deduction for interest from investments and obligations of New Mexico, the United States, or other jurisdictions that which states are prohibited from taxing under U.S. laws. The resulting tax is multiplied by the New Mexico ratio. The amount due on the block return is the aggregate amount due for all owners included on the return.[16]

The 7.9 percent tax is imposed only on the portion of the income allocated and apportioned to New Mexico in accordance with the provisions of the Uniform Division of Income and Tax Purposes Act and the regulations and instructions of the department under the Income Tax Act and the Uniform Division of Income for Tax Purposes Act.[17]

[E] Annual Report

New Mexico does not require LLCs to file an annual report.

[F] Filing Fees

New Mexico imposes the following filing fees on LLCs:[18]

Articles of organization	$ 50
Registration as foreign LLC	$100
Annual fee	$ 0

[G] References

M. Sargent & W. Schwidetzky, Limited Liability Company Handbook, Law — Sample Documents — Forms, §4.18, New Mexico Form of Articles of Organization and Operating Agreement (1995-1996 ed.).

---

[15] 3 N.M. Admin. Code §3.12.14.6(3).
[16] 3 N.M. Admin. Code §3.12.14.6(6).
[17] 3 N.M. Admin. Code §3.12.14.6(5).
[18] N.M. Stat. Ann. §53-10-63.

§23.34 NEW YORK

New York enacted laws authorizing limited liability companies effective October 24, 1994.[1]

[A] State Tax Classification

New York classifies an LLC in the same manner that the LLC is classified for federal tax purposes.[2] A member of an LLC is classified as a partner for state tax purposes if the LLC is classified as a partnership for federal tax purposes.[3]

An LLC that is classified as a partnership for federal tax purposes is also considered a partnership for New York tax purposes.[4]

An LLC that is owned by a single partnership is treated as a branch of the partnership unless the LLC elects to be classified as a corporation under federal law.[5] The partners of the partnership are not considered members of the LLC. The partnership must include the income, gain, loss, and deduction items of the LLC on its New York partnership return. The LLC is not required to file a separate partnership return. Neither the partners nor the partnership are liable for the LLC's annual member filing fee.

An LLC that meets the required gross income threshold and that is not a dealer in stocks and securities is considered a portfolio investment partnership. If the LLC meets the portfolio investment partnership criteria, the preferred members of the LLC are treated as limited partners.[6]

A New York corporation that forms a foreign state LLC that is classified as a partnership for federal and New York State tax purposes is itself treated as a corporate member of a partnership for New York State tax purposes. The New York corporation may exclude from the receipts factor of the business allocation percentage a portion of its receipts from the sales to the LLC.[7]

[B] Taxation of LLC and Members

LLCs that are classified as partnerships for federal income tax purposes must pay a filing fee equal to $50 multiplied by the number of members in the LLC

---

§23.34 [1] S.B. 7511-A, ch. 576, 1994 N.Y. Laws; N.Y. L.L.C. Law §§101 to 1403.

[2] N.Y. Tax Law §§2.5, 2.6.

[3] N.Y. Tax Law §2.6; Advisory Opinion TSB-A-02(14)C, New York Commissioner of Taxation and Finance (July 9, 2002).

[4] FGIC CMRC Corp. (Advisory Opinion), N.Y. Commr. of Taxn. & Fin., TSB-A-96(11)C (Apr. 1, 1996); N.Y. St. Dept. of Taxn. & Fin. Mem. TSB-M-94(6)I, (8)C (Oct. 25, 1994).

[5] Hirth Real Estate Entities (Advisory Opinion), N.Y. Commr. of Taxn. & Fin., TSB-A-97(7)I (Aug. 6, 1997).

[6] FGIC CMRC Corp. (Advisory Opinion), N.Y. Commr. of Taxn. & Fin., TSB-A-96(11)C (Apr. 1, 1996).

[7] New Venture Gear, Inc. (Advisory Opinion), N.Y. Commr. of Taxn. & Fin., TSB-A-97(13)C (June 26, 1997).

as of the last day of the LLC's tax year.[8] The minimum fee is $325. The maximum fee is $10,000.

A domestic or foreign LLC that does not have any income, gain, loss, or deduction from New York sources is required to file a New York State Partnership Return if it has a member who is a New York State resident. However, it is not subject to the minimum filing fee.[9] Domestic and foreign LLCs with no New York source income are not subject to the filing fee solely because they were formed under the laws of New York. Dormant LLCs with no income, gain, or loss are also not subject to the fee.

The fee must be paid on or before the due date of the partnership return. In the case of a calendar year LLC, the fee must be paid by April 15. The fee is paid at the time the partnership return is filed if the LLC is not requesting an extension of time to file the partnership return. An LLC that does not timely pay the fee is subject to an interest and late payment fee of 1/2 percent per month, subject to a maximum of 25 percent on the amount of the fee not timely paid.

An LLC that is classified as a partnership for federal tax purposes is not subject to New York income taxes.[10] Members are taxed on their distributive shares of income as determined under federal law, subject to certain modifications under state law.[11] Nonresident members are taxed on their distributive shares of income derived from or connected with New York sources.[12]

An LLC that is classified as a partnership is not subject to the corporate franchise (income) tax, even if the members are corporations. However, the corporate members of an LLC that conducts business in New York are subject to the corporate franchise (income) tax.[13]

An LLC that provides telecommunications services in New York is subject to the excise (telecommunications) tax even if the LLC is classified as a partnership.[14]

The transfer of real estate from a general partnership to an LLC is exempt from the New York real estate transfer tax if there is no change in beneficial ownership of the real property as a result of the transfer.[15]

An LLC is treated as carrying on a business in New York if it maintains or operates an office, shop, store, warehouse, factory, agency, or other place where its affairs are systematically and regularly carried on. It is also treated as carrying on a business in New York if it performs any series of acts or transactions with regularity and continuity for profit, as distinguished from isolated or incidental transactions.

[8] N.Y. Tax Law §658(c)(3).

[9] N.Y. St. Dept. of Taxn. & Fin. Mem. TSB-M-94(6)I, (6)C, (7)S.

[10] N.Y. Tax Law §601-A(f). The statute provides that a partnership includes a "subchapter K LLC," which is an LLC that is classified as a partnership for federal tax purposes. *See also* Advisory Opinion TSB-8-02(14), New York Comm'r of Taxation and Finance (July 9, 2002).

[11] N.Y. Tax Law §617.

[12] N.Y. Tax Law §632.

[13] Advisory Opinion TSB-8-02(14) to Grant McCarthy Gagnon, New York Comm'r of Taxation and Finance (July 9, 2002).

[14] *Id.*

[15] 149 Realty Associates et al. (Advisory Opinion), New York Comm'r of Taxation and Finance, TBS-A-99(5)R.

[C]   Allocations

An LLC allocates profits and losses among members as provided in the operating agreement. If the operating agreement is silent, profits and losses are allocated on the basis of the value of each member's contribution, as provided in the business records of the LLC.[16]

[D]   Passive Income Earned by Nonresidents

Nonresidents investing in an LLC are not subject to the New York income tax on passive income earned from the LLC if the LLC limits its in-state activities to trading for its own account. The investment income is passive income if the members are nonmanaging members. The New York tax does not apply to such income, since passive investment income does not fall within the federal definition of net earnings from self-employment.[17]

[E]   Sales Taxes

The transfer of property between a single-member LLC and its member is a taxable retail sale unless an exemption applies.[18]

[F]   Tax Returns

An LLC that is classified as a partnership must file Form IT-204, Partnership Return.[19] Any domestic or foreign LLC that is required to file a New York State Partnership Return must also complete and file Form IT-204-LL, Limited Liability Company/Partnership Filing Fee Payment Form. Limited liability investment companies that are required to file New York State tax returns must also complete and file Form IT-204-LL.

Form IT-204 is used to report income, deductions, gains, losses, and credits from operations of the LLC during the calendar year or fiscal year. The form is an information return. No tax is paid except for the annual filing fee of $50 per member. Every LLC must file the return if the LLC has a partner who is a resident of New York or has any income from New York State sources regardless of the amount of income. A partner that is a corporation or a partnership is not treated as a resident of New York State even though the entity may have been formed under the laws of New York.

An LLC that is filing a return because it has a New York resident partner, but that does not conduct business in New York, does not have to submit Schedules

---

[16] N.Y. L.L.C. Law §503.
[17] N.Y. St. Dept. of Taxn. & Fin., TSB-A-98(8) (1998).
[18] N.Y. St. Dept. of Taxn. & Fin., TBS-A-99(7)S (Jan. 28, 1999).
[19] N.Y. Tax Law §658(c).

K-1 for the nonresident members. In addition, Schedule A does not have to be filed. Schedule B must be filed only for the resident members.

An LLC must complete Schedule B, Part 4 of the form if it has nonresident members of the LLC. This schedule is used to show the allocation to New York State of the nonresident members' shares of income and deductions. The LLC must file the return by April 15 for calendar year LLCs or by the fifteenth day of the fourth month after the end of the tax year for fiscal year LLCs. The tax return must be filed with the State Processing Center, P.O. Box 61000, Albany, NY 12261-0001.

The LLC must use the same accounting period and methods for state tax purposes as it uses for federal tax purposes. If the LLC changes its partnership tax year or accounting methods for federal purposes, it must do the same for state tax purposes.

An LLC may obtain an extension of time to file the partnership return by filing Form IT-370-PF, Application for Automatic Extension of Time to File for Partnerships of Fiduciaries. The extension request must be filed by the due date of the partnership return. Federal Form 8736 may be used in lieu of the state form. Federal Forms 2758 and 4868 are not acceptable.

An LLC must file an amended return if it files an amended federal partnership return or if a federal audit of the partnership return changes any item of income, deduction, or tax preference previously reported to the Internal Revenue Service. The amended return must be filed within 90 days of the date of the federal amended partnership return. In the case of a federal audit, the amended return must be filed within 90 days after the final determination of the change. The LLC must attach a copy of the federal report of examination changes.

An LLC must file Form IT-204-LL to report the $50 per member annual filing fee. The form must be filed by every LLC, limited liability investment company, or other entity that is required to file the New York Partnership Tax Return.

A single-member LLC that is not classified as a partnership for federal tax purposes is not subject to the $50 filing fee and is not required to file Form IT-204, Partnership Return, or Form IT-204-LL.[20]

There is no proration of the filing fee if the LLC has a short taxable year for federal tax purposes.

The LLC must attach Form IT-204-LL to the front of IT-204 when it is filed. The LLC must fully pay the filing fee and attach a check for the filing fee to the form.

An LLC may file a group New York nonresident income tax return in lieu of the nonresident members filing individual income tax returns.[21] An LLC may obtain approval from the Commissioner of Taxation to file a group New York State nonresident personal income tax return on behalf of 10 or more qualified members who elected to have the LLC file a return on their behalf.[22] In such case, the distributive share of income allocable to New York is taxed at the highest individual tax rate.

---

[20] See Instructions to Form IT-204-LL.

[21] N.Y. St. Dept. of Taxn. & Fin. Regs. §151.17(a) (1997).

[22] Id.

[G]   New York City Taxes

New York City imposes a 4 percent unincorporated business tax on LLCs.

Every LLC doing business in New York City and having a member who is a nonresident of New York City must complete Form IT-204-NYC, City of New York Partnership Allocation. This form must be attached to the LLC's New York State Partnership Return. An LLC is treated as doing business in New York City if either of the following applies:

- It maintains or operates in New York City an office, shop, store, warehouse, factory, agency or other place where its business is systematically and regularly carried on; or
- It performs a series of acts or transactions in New York City with regularity for profit, as distinguished from isolated or incidental transactions.

An LLC that carries on or liquidates any trade, business, profession, or occupation wholly or partly within New York City and that has gross income from all businesses, regardless of where carried on, of more than $10,000 must file Form NYC-204, Unincorporated Business Tax Return. In addition, every LLC that has unincorporated business gross income of $10,000 or less, but that has any amount of unincorporated business taxable income, must file a return for each tax year for which it carries on business in New York.

The LLC may also be required to file one of the following additional forms:

- Form NYC-5UB, Partnership Declaration of Estimated Unincorporated Business Tax. This form must be filed if the estimated tax can reasonably be expected to exceed $1,000 for the calendar or fiscal year.
- Form NYC-64, Application for Automatic Extension. This is an application for a six-month extension that must be filed before the due date of the return.
- Form NYC-113, Unincorporated Business Tax Amended Return and/or Claim for Refund. This form is used to amend Form NYC-204 as originally filed or as later adjusted.
- Form NYC-115, Unincorporated Business Tax Report of Change in Taxable Income. This form reports changes made by the Internal Revenue Service and/or the New York State Department of Taxation and Finance.
- Form NYC-221, Underpayment of Estimated Unincorporated Business Tax.
- Form NYC-CR-A, Commercial Rent Tax Annual Return. This must be filed by every LLC that rents premises for business purposes in Manhattan in certain districts.
- Form NYC-RPT, Real Property Transfer Tax Return. This must be filed when the LLC acquires or disposes of an interest in real property located in New York City, including a leasehold interest.

The LLC must make an equitable allocation if business is carried on both inside and outside New York City.

In most cases, items of business income, gain, loss, or deduction are entered on the return as reported for federal tax purposes. The New York State Department of Taxation and Finance may make appropriate revisions.

[H] City of Yonkers Taxes

Every LLC doing business in the city of Yonkers and having a partner who is a nonresident of Yonkers must complete Form Y-204, City of Yonkers Nonresident Partner Allocation. The LLC must attach this form to the New York State Partnership Return.

[I] Annual Report

New York does not require an LLC to file an annual report or to have annual meetings of members.

[J] Filing Fees

New York imposes the following filing fees on limited liability companies:[23]

Articles of organization	$200
Application for authority of foreign LLC	$250

The New York Secretary of State also imposes the following filing fees on professional service LLCs:[24]

Application of authority for professional LLC	$200
Certificate of authority for professional LLC	
(issued by New York State Department of Education)	$ 50

[K] References

S. Gold, New York's Limited Liability Company Law (1994).
M. Sargent & W. Schwidetzky, Limited Liability Company Handbook, Law — Sample Documents — Forms, §4.19, New York Form of Articles of Organization and Operating Agreement (1995-1996 ed.).

---

[23] N.Y. L.L.C. Law §1101.
[24] N.Y. L.L.C. Law §1306.

§23.35 NORTH CAROLINA

North Carolina enacted the North Carolina Limited Liability Company Act effective October 1, 1993.[1]

[A] State Tax Classification

North Carolina classifies an LLC in the same manner that the LLC is classified for federal tax purposes.[2] Accordingly, if the LLC is classified as a corporation, the LLC is subject to the North Carolina corporate tax.[3] If the LLC is classified as a partnership, the LLC and its members are subject to tax in the same manner as partnerships and partners.[4] If the LLC is classified as a disregarded entity (proprietorship, division, or branch), the LLC and its members are subject to tax in a manner consistent with that classification.[5] The classification does not require the foreign or domestic LLC to obtain an administrative ruling from the IRS on its classification under the Internal Revenue Code.[6]

An LLC is defined for North Carolina personal income tax purposes to include domestic LLCs and foreign LLCs that are classified as partnerships for federal income tax purposes.[7]

[B] Taxation of LLC and Members

LLCs are not subject to the North Carolina franchise tax, since the definition of corporation specifically excludes LLCs.[8]

Members of the LLC are taxed on their distributive shares of income.[9] The taxable income of the LLC is determined under federal law, subject to certain adjustments.[10]

There are special rules if an LLC that is classified as a partnership or disregarded entity passes through income to a corporate member. The LLC's income, assets, and activites flow through to the corporate member for purposes of determining the corporate member's income tax and the corporate member's capital stock, surplus, and undivided profits franchise tax base under the North Carolina tax laws. If an LLC is classified as a corporation, the income, assets, and other tax attributes do not flow through to the corporate member for purposes of determin-

---

§23.35   [1]N.C. Gen. Stat. §§57C-1-01 to 57C-10-7.
[2]N.C. Gen. Stat §57C-10-06.
[3]N.C. Gen. Stat §105-130.2(5).
[4]N.C. Gen. Stat §105-134.1(7a), (10a).
[5]Id.
[6]Id.
[7]N.C. Gen. Stat. §105-134.1(7a), (10a).
[8]Id.
[9]N.C. Gen. Stat. §105-134.5(d).
[10]N.C. Admin. Code §17.06B.3501.

ing the corporate member's franchise tax base. Instead, the LLC must report the income and franchise tax as a corporate entity.[11]

[C] Investment Credit

LLCs qualify for the North Carolina investment credit.[12] An individual member of an LLC is allowed a credit equal to the allocated share of the tax credit for which the LLC is eligible.[13] The aggregate amount of the credit allowed for individual members for one or more investments in a single tax year may not exceed $5,000. The rule applies whether paid directly to the owner or indirectly as a member of the LLC or other pass-through entity. An LLC must file an application for the credit.

[D] Tax Returns

LLCs doing business in North Carolina that are required to file partnership returns must file Form D-403, Partnership Income Tax Return. The LLC must attach a copy of the federal partnership return on Form 1065 and all schedules to the federal return.[14] The return must include the names of the individual members of the LLC and should be signed by a managing member and the person preparing the return. The LLC must attach a copy of the federal return and all schedules, including each federal Schedule K-1.

The return must be filed on or before the fifteenth day of the fourth month following the close of the fiscal year. The return must be filed by April 15 for calendar year LLCs.

An LLC may obtain an extension of time to file the return. There is an automatic six-month extension. To receive the extension, the LLC must file Form D-410, Application for Automatic Extension of Time to File State Income Tax Return. The LLC must pay the full amount of tax that the partnership expects to owe for its nonresident partners by the original due date of the return. The LLC may use federal Form 8736 in lieu of the state form.

The LLC must furnish to each member a completed Schedule NC K-1, Partner's Share of North Carolina Income, Adjustments, Tax Credit, Etc. The form must be sent to each member on or before the due date for filing the partnership return. The Schedule NC K-1 is used to report each member's share of LLC income, adjustments, credits, and taxes paid by the manager of the LLC.[15] The LLC must provide each member with a list of the amounts and sources of dividends. It must

---

[11] Directive CD-02-2, North Carolina Department of Revenue (May 31, 2002).
[12] N.C. Gen. Stat. §§105-163.011(b1), 105-163.010(7).
[13] N.C. Gen. Stat. §105-163.011(b1).
[14] N.C. Admin. Code §17:06B.3503.
[15] Id.

also provide each member with the amounts and types of tax credits that are set forth as the member's distributive share of tax credits.

[E]   Nonresident Members

An LLC that has one or more nonresident members must report the distributive share of income of each nonresident member. It must also include with the return the tax due on the nonresident member's share of that income.[16] The tax rate ranges from 6 to 8.25 percent of each nonresident's share of North Carolina taxable income. The managing member is responsible for making the report and is required to compute and pay the tax due for each nonresident member. If the nonresident member is a corporation, partnership, trust, or estate, the managing member is not required to pay the tax on that member's share of LLC income if the member signs an affirmation that the member will pay the tax with its corporate, partnership, trust, or estate income tax return. In those cases, a copy of the affirmation must be attached to the LLC return when it is filed. The tax rate is the same as the tax rate for single individuals.

The manager of the LLC may withhold taxes from the distributions to nonresident members and use the withheld amounts to pay the taxes due. In such case, the nonresident member is not required to file a return.[17]

A nonresident member, other than a corporation, is not required to file a North Carolina individual income tax return if the only income from North Carolina sources is the nonresident member's share of income from the LLC and the manager of the LLC has reported the income and paid the tax due. A nonresident member may file an individual income tax return and claim credit for the tax paid by the manager of the LLC if the payment is properly identified on the individual income tax return.[18]

In determining the tax owed by nonresident members, an LLC must apportion to North Carolina the income derived from activities carried on within and outside of North Carolina. Income derived by the LLC from activities outside of North Carolina that are segregated from its other business activities are not included in determining the tax due for nonresident members. The allocation does not affect the income of the resident member. The resident member is taxed on his share of the net income of the LLC, whether or not attributable to North Carolina.

[F]   Estimated Income Taxes

An LLC is not required to estimate its taxes. Resident individual members who meet certain statutory requirements must pay estimated income taxes on Form

---

[16] N.C. Gen. Stat. §105-154(d); 1995-1996 Individual Income Tax Bulletin, N.C. Dept. of Rev.
[17] N.C. Admin. Code §17.06B.3513(c).
[18] 1995-1996 Individual Income Tax Bulletin, N.C. Dept. of Rev.

NC-40. Nonresident individual members are not required to pay the estimated tax on their distributive shares of LLC income.

[G] Annual Report

An LLC must file an annual report in North Carolina. The report must be filed within 60 days following the last day of the month in which the LLC was organized. Effective January 1, 1998, the due date is the fifteenth day of the fourth month following the close of the LLC's fiscal year.[19] The annual report must set forth the following information:

- The name of the LLC and the state or country under whose laws it was organized.
- The street address and mailing address, if different, of the registered office, the county in which the office is located, and the name of the registered agent at that office.
- The address and telephone number of its principal office.
- The names and business addresses of its managers.
- A brief description of the nature of the business.

[H] Filing Fees

North Carolina imposes the following filing fees on LLCs:

Articles of organization	$125
Application for certificate of authority of foreign LLC	$250
Annual report	$200

[I] References

H.B. Ives III, North Carolina Limited Liability Companies (1994).

M. Sargent & W. Schwidetzky, Limited Liability Company Handbook, Law — Sample Documents — Forms, §4.20, North Carolina Form of Operating Agreement (1995-1996 ed.).

§23.36 NORTH DAKOTA

North Dakota enacted the North Dakota Limited Liability Company Act effective July 1, 1993.[1]

---

[19] N.C. Gen. Stat. §57C-2-23.
§23.36 [1] S.B. 2222, 1993 N.D. Laws; N.D. Cent. Code §§10-32-01 to 10-32-156.

[A]   State Tax Classification

North Dakota classifies an LLC in the same manner that the LLC is classified for federal tax purposes. An LLC having two or more members that is formed in North Dakota or in another state is classified as a partnership if the LLC is classified as a partnership for federal tax purposes.[2] The members are treated as partners of the partnership.

An LLC that has two or more members that is classified as a corporation for federal tax purposes is also classified as a corporation for state tax purposes.[3] An LLC having a single member that is classified as a corporation for federal tax purposes is classified as a corporation for state tax purposes. An LLC having a single member that is disregarded for federal tax purposes is also disregarded as an entity separate from its owner for state tax purposes.[4]

[B]   Taxation of LLC and Members

An LLC is not subject to tax. There is no entity-level or franchise tax on LLCs. Members of the LLC are taxed on their distributive shares of profits of the LLC, whether or not distributed. The members are also entitled to deduct their shares of any net losses of the LLC.[5]

[C]   Tax Returns

An LLC doing business in North Dakota or having sources of income in North Dakota must file a North Dakota partnership return if it is required to file a federal partnership return. The return is filed on Form 58, North Dakota Partnership Return of Income. A copy of the federal return must be attached to the North Dakota Partnership Return.

The LLC must use the same tax year for state purposes as it uses for federal purposes.

Form 58 must be filed on or before the fifteenth day of the fourth month following the close of the tax year. The return must be filed with the Office of the State Tax Commissioner, State Capitol, 600 East Boulevard, Bismarck, ND 58505-0599. At least one member of the LLC must sign the return.

An LLC doing business in North Dakota that is required to file federal Form 1099 must also file the form with the Office of the State Tax Commissioner. A Form 1099 reporting interest, dividends, pensions, or annuities does not have to be filed unless the LLC withholds income taxes from the payment.

---

[2] N.D. Cent. Code §57-38-07.1.
[3] Id.
[4] N.D. Cent. Code §57-38-07.2.
[5] N.D. Cent. Code §57-38-08.

An LLC may file an application for an extension of time to file the return on Form F-101, Application of Extension of Time for Filing Return.

[D] Apportionment and Allocation

An LLC that carries on its business entirely within North Dakota must report all of its income or loss in North Dakota.

An LLC that carries on its business partly within and partly outside of North Dakota must allocate and apportion its income under North Dakota law, which follows the Uniform Division of Income Tax Act. An LLC must complete Schedule B to apportion the income. However, if a multistate LLC consists entirely of resident members (limited to individuals, states, and trusts), the LLC is not required to complete Schedule B.

The LLC must report the distributive shares of income or loss of nonresident members on Schedule A of Form 58. This income or loss is limited to the income or loss from North Dakota sources. An LLC must use Form 37-S or Form 37 if the member is an individual. The LLC must use Form 38 if the member is an estate or a trust. The LLC must use Form 40 for a subchapter C corporation and Form 60 for a subchapter S corporation.

An LLC may file a composite return as an alternative method of filing for nonresident individuals who are members of an LLC operating in North Dakota. Under this method, the LLC files one individual tax return, referred to as a composite return, for two or more of the members.

[E] Annual Report

North Dakota requires that an LLC file an annual report.[6] The annual report must be filed on or before November 15 of each year. The annual report must set forth the following information:

- The name of the LLC and the state of organization
- The address of the registered office of the LLC, the name of the registered agent in the state, and the address of its principal office
- A brief statement of the character of the business of the LLC
- The names and respective addresses of the managers of the LLCs or the names and respective addresses of the managing member or members of the LLC

The first annual report of the LLC must be filed with the secretary of state by December 16 of the year following the calendar year in which the certificate of organization or certificate of authority was issued by the secretary of state.

---

[6] N.D. Cent. Code §10-32-149.

[F] Filing Fees

North Dakota imposes the following filing fees on LLCs:[7]

Certificate of organization	$125
Certificate of authority for foreign LLC	$125
Annual report	$ 50

§23.37 OHIO

Ohio enacted laws authorizing LLCs effective July 1, 1994.[1]

[A] State Tax Classification

Ohio classifies an LLC in the same manner as the LLC is classified for federal tax purposes. An LLC that is classified as a corporation for federal tax purposes is classified as a corporation for state tax purposes.[2] Single-member LLCs may be formed in Ohio effective November 21, 1997.[3]

Ohio issued an information release in response to the federal check-the-box regulations. For Ohio corporate income tax purposes, an LLC that does business in Ohio and that defaults or makes the federal election to be treated as a partnership will generally not be taxed as a corporation.[4] If an LLC chooses to be taxed as a corporation for federal income tax purposes, the LLC will be subject to the Ohio franchise tax for taxable years ending after September 28, 1997.[5]

[B] Taxation of LLC and Members

Income, gains, losses, deductions, and credits pass through to the members and are taxed to them individually.

There is an 8.5 percent entity level tax on the LLC[6] and a 5 percent withholding tax[7] if the LLC has nonresident members. The taxes do not apply in the following cases[8]:

---

[7] N.D. Cent. Code §10-32-150.

§23.37 [1] H.B. 170, 1994 Ohio Laws; Ohio Rev. Code Ann. §§1705.01 to 1705.58.

[2] Ohio Rev. Code Ann. §5733.01(E).

[3] H.B. 170, 1997 Ohio Laws; Ohio Rev. Code Ann. §§1705.01 to 1705.58.

[4] Ohio Information Release, Income Tax Audit Div., Ohio Dept. of Taxn. (Aug. 19, 1997).

[5] *Id.* (*citing* Ohio Rev. Code Ann. §5733.01(E), (F), which states that if a for-profit entity is taxed as a corporation for federal income tax purposes, then the entity is taxed as a corporation for Ohio franchise tax purposes).

[6] Ohio Rev. Code Ann. §5733.41.

[7] Ohio Rev. Code Ann. §5747.41.

[8] Instructions to Form IT-4708, Pass-Through Entity Composite Income Tax Return.

- The LLC is classified as a partnership for federal tax purposes, and the members are limited to full-year Ohio resident individuals, Ohio estates, and/or corporations that timely pay the Ohio corporation franchise tax.
- The LLC is classified as a partnership for federal tax purposes, and the LLC files Ohio Form IT-4708, Pass-Through Entity Composite Income Tax Return, for all members who are not full-year Ohio resident individuals or Ohio resident estates. The LLC may file a composite return for both resident and nonresident individuals.[9] C corporation members cannot be included on the composite return. The 8.5 percent entity level tax and the 5 percent withholding tax do not apply to the distributed share of income for any member included on the composite return.
- The LLC is classified as a disregarded entity for federal tax purposes.
- The nonresident members submit a written statement to the LLC agreeing that the member has a nexus with Ohio and is subject to and liable for the corporation franchise tax with respect to that member's distributive share of income. The member must make a good faith and reasonable effort to comply with the tax requirements.
- There are a number of other exceptions.[10]

[C] Tax Returns

An LLC that is classified as a partnership for federal tax purposes must file Form IT-4708, Nonresident Partners' Income Tax Return, if it has any members who are nonresidents of the state. The form is used to apportion and allocate income to sources within and outside the state of Ohio. Schedule A of the form sets forth the items of income, gain, loss, deduction, and credit from the federal IRS Form 1065. Schedule B sets forth the allocation amounts for nonbusiness income of the LLC. Schedule C apportions the business income to sources within and outside the state of Ohio. Schedule D sets forth the tax computation schedule. The LLC must attach a copy of the federal Schedule K-1 for each nonresident member for whom the return is filed.

An LLC is not required to file an Ohio partnership return if it has only resident partners. The resident members of an LLC are taxed on their distributive shares of income, gain, loss, credit, and deduction based on the amounts reported on the federal Form 1065.

Ohio uses the federal tax base as the starting point in determining income of an LLC.[11]

An LLC may file a single return for two or more nonresident members who have no other Ohio taxable income.[12] The composite return is filed on Form IT-4708, Annual Composite Income Tax Return for Investors in Pass-Through Entities.

---

[9] Ohio Rev. Code Ann. §5747.08(D); Instructions to Form IT-4708, Pass-Through Entity Composite Income Tax Return.

[10] *See* Instructions to Form IT-4708, Pass-Through Entity Composite Income Tax Return.

[11] Ohio Rev. Code Ann. §5733.04(H).

[12] Ohio Tax Commr. R. 5703-7-03.

[D]   Annual Report

Ohio does not require that an LLC file an annual report or hold annual meetings of members.

[E]   Filing Fees

Ohio imposes the following filing fees on LLCs:[13]

Articles of organization	$85
Certificate of registration of foreign LLC	$85
Annual fees	$ 0

[F]   References

M. Sargent & W. Schwidetzky, Limited Liability Company Handbook, Law — Sample Documents — Forms, §4.21, Ohio Form of Operating Agreement (1995-1996 ed.).

§23.38   OKLAHOMA

Oklahoma enacted the Oklahoma Limited Liability Company Act effective September 1, 1992.[1]

[A]   State Tax Classification

Oklahoma classifies an LLC in the same manner that the LLC is classified for federal tax purposes. A domestic LLC and a foreign LLC are taxed for all purposes as domestic partnerships and foreign partnerships under title 68 of the Oklahoma Statutes.[2] Single-member LLCs are disregarded as separate entities under Oklahoma law.

[B]   Taxation of LLC and Members

Members are taxed on their distributive shares of income.[3] A member's distributive share of income is the same as under federal law.[4] Nonresident members are

---

[13] Ohio Rev. Code Ann. §111.16(F).
§23.38 [1] Okla. Stat. Ann. tit. 18, §§2000-2060.
[2] Okla. Stat. Ann. tit. 68, §202(j).
[3] Okla. Stat. Ann. tit. 68, §2363.
[4] *Id.*

subject to tax if gross income from Oklahoma sources is more than $1,000. Resident and nonresident members are not allowed credits for income taxes paid to other jurisdictions on LLC income.[5]

[C]   Tax Returns

LLCs that are classified as partnerships for federal tax purposes must file returns each year on Form 514, Partnership Return of Income.[6] An LLC that has elected not to file a partnership income tax return under section 761 of the Internal Revenue Code is not required to file an Oklahoma return.[7] The partnership return sets forth the taxable income and the adjustments to arrive at Oklahoma income. The return includes a schedule showing the distributions to members of the various items of income as set forth on the federal return and the adjustments required by applicable Oklahoma tax laws. The return must be signed by one of the members.[8]

The Oklahoma distributive share of LLC income is the same portion as that reported for federal income tax purposes. OTC Form 514 is used to report that income.[9]

An LLC must file an amended return if it later becomes aware of any changes made to income, deductions, credits, or loss or if the federal return is corrected due to an Internal Revenue Service audit. In such case, the LLC must file OTC Form 514, labeled "Amended" at the top of page 1. The LLC must attach to the Oklahoma amended return a copy of the federal amended Form 1065 or a copy of the federal audit changes. The LLC must then give a corrected Schedule K-1 to each member, reflecting Oklahoma distributable income as adjusted.[10]

An LLC that registers with the Oklahoma Secretary of State must file an income tax return in the same manner as required under the Internal Revenue Code. All rulings issued by the Internal Revenue Service are binding in regard to the filing of tax returns and the reporting of income.[11] A domestic LLC is treated in the same manner as a domestic partnership, and a foreign LLC is treated and taxed in the same manner as a foreign partnership if the LLC is classified as a partnership for federal tax purposes.[12]

The LLC must report the income to Oklahoma on the same form as prescribed under federal regulations and in the manner provided in the Oklahome Statutes.[13] An LLC's operations carried on within and outside the state of Oklahoma must be the same as for corporations, subchapter S corporations, partnerships, and other organizations that are covered under Public Law 86-272. The activities

---

[5] Okla. Admin. R. 710:50-19-1(3).
[6] Okla. Stat. Ann. tit. 68, §2368.D.
[7] Id.
[8] Id.
[9] Okla. Admin. R. 710:50-19-1.
[10] Okla. Admin. R. 710:50-19-2.
[11] Okla. Admin. R. 710:50-20-1(a).
[12] Id.
[13] Okla. Admin. R. 710:50-20-1(b); see Okla. Stat. Ann. tit. 68, §2385.

described in title 18, section 2049 of the Oklahoma Statutes are not considered in determining the transaction of business by an LLC for Oklahoma income tax purposes.[14]

The LLC must attach a copy of federal Form 1065 and all Schedules K-1 to Form 514.

All LLCs having Oklahoma source income must file their returns on Form 514. Each member having Oklahoma source income sufficient to make the return must also make a return reporting the distributive share.

The LLC must file the partnership return with the Oklahoma Tax Commission, P.O. Box 26800, Oklahoma City, OK 73126-0800. The return must be filed on or before the fifteenth day of the fourth month following the close of the tax year. The LLC may obtain an extension of time to file the return for a period of up to six months. The LLC may use the federal extension of time and attach it to the Oklahoma tax return.

The LLC must use the same taxable year and methods of accounting for state tax purposes as used for federal income tax purposes.

Every LLC making payments of salaries, wages, premiums, annuities, or other periodic gains, profits, or income of $750 or more during the tax year to any taxpayer must complete a report. The report must be made on Forms 500 and 501 on or before February 15 of the following calendar year. The LLC may file Form 504, Application for Extension of Time to File Oklahoma Income Tax Return.

A foreign LLC must file a partnership return in Oklahoma if it has income from sources in Oklahoma or carries on a business in Oklahoma. The Oklahoma statute sets forth the activities of a foreign LLC that do not constitute transacting business within Oklahoma for purposes of the state tax laws.[15]

All resident members must file individual income tax returns in Oklahoma if they are required to file federal individual income tax returns. All nonresident members who have gross income of $1,000 or more must file Oklahoma returns even though their net income may actually be a loss.[16]

[D]   Apportionment of Income

The LLC must apportion income to sources within and outside the state of Oklahoma using a three-factor formula unless its income is from real and tangible personal property, such as rents, oil and mining production, and gains or losses from the sale of such property. In that case, the income or loss must be allocated in accordance with the situs of such property. The member's distributive share of Oklahoma income or loss must be in the same proportion as the member's distributive share of income or loss shown on the federal partnership return.[17]

---

[14] Okla. Stat. Ann. tit. 68, §2049(c); Okla. Admin. R. 710:50-20-1(c).
[15] Okla. Stat. Ann. tit. 18, §2049.
[16] Okla. Admin. R. 710:50-19-1(2).
[17] Id.

[E] Nonresident Members

An Oklahoma LLC may file a composite return for nonresident members if the following requirements are met:[18]

- The LLC computes each member's share of Oklahoma income.
- The LLC deducts a standard deduction of 15 percent for individuals from the Oklahoma income, limited to $2,000, with no minimum amount or proration. When the filing status for federal purposes is known, the maximum allowable standard deduction may not exceed $1,000 for any member using the married, filing separate status. The LLC may use the deduction only for individuals.
- No allowance is provided for personal exemptions, federal income tax, or deductions for dependents.
- The LLC reports and makes payment on a fiduciary return, OTC Form 513.
- The tax is computed using the proper schedule for filing status, such as single, married, corporate, and so on. If the status is not known, the LLC must use the rates on the fiduciary return.
- All members having Oklahoma income from other sources must file their individual returns. Members may elect to file their own returns with the state of Oklahoma.
- The LLC must provide a schedule showing the name, Social Security number, Oklahoma income tax deduction, and taxable income of each member. It is not acceptable to file the listing of nonresident individual members on microfiche.[19]

[F] Sales and Use Taxes, Other Taxes

LLCs are subject to sales and use taxes; to gasoline, cigarette, and tobacco products taxes; and to severance, tourism promotion, motor vehicle, aircraft excise, real estate mortgage, and documentary stamp taxes effective September 1, 1993.[20] LLCs are exempt from franchise taxes.

[G] Filing Fees

Oklahoma imposes the following filing fees on LLCs:[21]

Articles of organization	$100
Foreign LLC registration application	$300

---

[18] Okla. Admin. R. 710:50-19-1(4).
[19] Id.
[20] S.B. 527, 1993 Okla. Sess. Laws.
[21] Okla. Stat. Ann. tit. 18, §2055.

[H] Annual Report

An LLC must file an annual report in Oklahoma.[22]

[I] References

M. Allen, Limited Liability Companies: The Entity of Choice in Oklahoma (1994).

M. Sargent & W. Schwidetzky, Limited Liability Company Handbook, Law — Sample Documents — Forms, §4.22, Oklahoma Form of Articles of Organization and Operating Agreement (1995-1996 ed.).

§23.39 OREGON

Oregon enacted the Oregon Limited Liability Company Act effective January 1, 1994.[1]

[A] State Tax Classification

Oregon classifies an LLC in the same manner that the LLC is classified for federal tax purposes.[2] The same rule applies to foreign LLCs qualified to do business in Oregon. A member of a foreign or domestic LLC is treated for Oregon tax purposes in the same manner as the member is treated for federal income tax purposes.[3] Single-member LLCs are allowed effective October 4, 1997.[4]

Before 1997, Oregon classified LLCs as partnerships unless otherwise classified under federal law. Single-member LLCs were not permitted.

[B] Taxation of LLC and Members

Oregon law is linked to federal partnership law effective April 15, 1995. An LLC that is classified as a partnership for federal tax purposes is not subject to tax.[5]

Members of the LLC are taxed on their distributive shares of income.[6] The income of the LLC is determined under federal law, subject to certain modifications.[7] Each item of income, gain, loss, credit, and deduction has the same character

---

[22] Okla. Stat. Ann. tit. 18, §2055.2.

§23.39 [1] S.B. 285, ch. 173, 1993 Or. Laws; Or. Rev. Stat. §§63.001 to 63.990.

[2] Or. Rev. Stat. §63.810.

[3] *Id.*

[4] Or. Rev. Stat. §63.001(13).

[5] Or. Rev. Stat. §314.712.

[6] *Id.*

[7] *Id.*

as under federal law.[8] The members' distributive shares are the same as on the federal return.[9]

[C]   Tax Returns

An LLC that is classified as a partnership for federal tax purposes must file Form 65, Oregon Partnership Return of Income. All LLCs having income from sources in Oregon or having one or more Oregon resident members must file the partnership return.[10]

The LLC must attach the following information to the return in the following order:

- A list of members if the LLC has more than 10 members at any time during the year.
- An apportionment schedule if the LLC has business activities both within and outside the state of Oregon or has members who are not Oregon residents during the year.
- An Oregon depreciation schedule on Form 150-101-025 if Oregon depreciation is different from federal depreciation.
- A schedule showing to whom all assets and liabilities were distributed if the return is the final return for the LLC.
- A copy of federal Form 1065, pages 1 through 4, and all supporting schedules.
- The federal Schedules K-1 if the LLC has fewer than 11 members during the year.

The LLC must file the return by the fifteenth day of the fourth month after the end of the LLC's tax year. The due date is April 15 for calendar year LLCs. The partnership tax return must be sent to the Oregon Department of Revenue, P.O. Box 14260, Salem, OR 97309-5060.

Members report their shares of modifications to federal LLC income on Form 40, 40N, or 40P. The Oregon individual income tax booklet lists the filing requirements for members' individual income tax returns. There are separate instructions for full-year resident members and part-year nonresident members. Nonresident members of an LLC may file individual nonresident returns or join together to file a multiple nonresident tax return.

The Oregon tax forms may be obtained from the Oregon Department of Revenue, P.O. Box 14999, Salem, OR 97309-0990.

---

[8] Or. Rev. Stat. §314.714(1).
[9] Or. Rev. Stat. §314.714(2).
[10] Or. Rev. Stat. §314.724.

[D]   Annual Report

Oregon requires domestic and foreign LLCs to file annual reports.[11] The annual report must set forth the following information:

- The name of the LLC and the state or country in which it is organized.
- The street address of its registered office and the name of its registered agent at that office.
- The address, including street number and mailing address, of its principal office.
- The names and addresses of the managers; if the LLC is managed by its members, the name and address of at least one member.
- The category of the classification code established by the secretary of state that most closely designates the primary business activity of the LLC.
- The federal employer identification number of the LLC.
- Additional identifying information required by the secretary of state from time to time.

[E]   Filing Fees

Oregon imposes the following filing fees on LLCs:[12]

Articles of organization	$ 40
Foreign LLC registration application	$440
Domestic annual report	$ 30
Foreign LLC annual report	$220

[F]   References

M. Sargent & W. Schwidetzky, Limited Liability Company Handbook, Law — Sample Documents — Forms, §4.23, Oregon Form of Articles of Organization and Operating Agreement (with Abstract) (1995-1996 ed.).

§23.40   PENNSYLVANIA

Pennsylvania enacted laws authorizing formation of LLCs effective February 5, 1995.[1]

---

[11] Or. Rev. Stat. §63.787.
[12] Or. Rev. Stat. §63.007.
§23.40   [1] Act 106 (S.B. 1059), 1994 Pa. Laws; 15 Pa. Cons. Stat. Ann. §§8901-8998.

[A]   State Tax Classification

Effective January 1, 1998, Pennsylvania classifies an LLC as follows:[2]

- All LLCs are classified as corporations for purposes of the capital stock franchise tax.[3] Therefore, a single-member LLC that is classified as a disregarded entity or federal tax purposes is subject to the capital stock franchise tax.[4]
- The LLC is classified in the same manner that the LLC is classified for federal tax purposes for purposes of the corporate net income tax.[5] Therefore, an LLC that is classified as a partnership for federal tax purposes is not subject to the corporate net income tax for tax years after 1997.[6] The same rule applies to single-member disregarded entities.
- An LLC is classified under Pennsylvania law in the same manner that the LLC is classified under federal law for purposes of the Pennsylvania personal income tax.[7] Therefore, an LLC that is classified as a partnership for federal tax purposes is also classified as a partnership for state tax purposes. Each member is taxed on his or her distributed share of income of the LLC.[8]

[B]   Taxation of LLC and Members

An LLC is not subject to Pennsylvania income taxes.[9] Members of the LLC are taxed on their distributive shares of income,[10] whether or not distributed.[11] Nonresident members are taxed on their distributive shares of income attributable to Pennsylvania sources.[12] The LLC must withhold Pennsylvania personal income taxes on its income from sources within Pennsylvania that is allocable to nonresident members.[13] The withholding tax rate is 2.8 percent on the Pennsylvania income allocable to nonresident members.[14] Members must file a PA-40 to report

---

[2] Corp. Tax Opinion: Subjectivity of Limited Liability Companies, Pennsylvania Department of Revenue (Feb. 2, 2000).

[3] 72 Pa. Cons. Stat. Ann. §7601(a) (definition of corporation).

[4] Corp. Tax Opinion: Subjectivity of Limited Liability Companies, Pennsylvania Department of Revenue (Feb. 2, 2000).

[5] 72 Pa. Cons. Stat. Ann. §7401 (definition of corporation).

[6] Corp. Tax Opinion: Subjectivity of Limited Liability Companies, Pennsylvania Department of Revenue (Feb. 2, 2000).

[7] 72 Pa. Cons. Stat. Ann. §7301(d.1) and (n.0).

[8] Corp. Tax Opinion: Subjectivity of Limited Liability Companies, Pennsylvania Department of Revenue (Feb. 2, 2000).

[9] 72 Pa. Cons. Stat. Ann. §7306.

[10] *Id.;* Pa. Dept. of Rev. Reg. §107.2.

[11] 72 Pa. Cons. Stat. Ann. §7306.

[12] Pa. Dept. of Rev. Reg. §107.2(c).

[13] Corp. Tax Opinion: Subjectivity of Limited Liability Companies, Pennsylvania Department of Revenue (Feb. 2, 2000) (*citing* 72 Pa. Cons. Stat. Ann. §7324).

[14] 72 Pa. Cons. Stat. Ann. §7324.1.

their share of income that flows through to them from the LLC, whether the LLC is classified as a partnership or disregarded entity.[15]

Pennsylvania imposes a capital stock and franchise tax on all domestic entities and foreign entities. Effective January 1, 1998, a "domestic entity" is defined to include every limited liability company other than a restricted professional service company.[16] A "foreign entity" is also defined to include every limited liability company other than restricted professional service companies.

The capital stock tax is a property tax imposed on domestic LLCs and other companies. The franchise tax is imposed on foreign LLCs and companies on the basis of capital stock value. It is assessed for the privilege of doing business in Pennsylvania.

The capital stock and franchise taxes are imposed on the basis of capital stock value. There is a statutory formula for determining capital stock value. Certain assets are excluded in arriving at the taxable value. The capital stock and franchise taxes are calculated as if the LLC had filed a federal corporate return. The members of an LLC are treated as shareholders of the LLC for purposes of the capital stock and franchise taxes.

[C] Corporate Income Tax

Pennsylvania exempts LLCs from the state's corporate income tax. Effective for tax years beginning on or after January 1, 1998, an LLC that is classified as a partnership for federal tax purposes or that is disregarded as an entity is not subject to the corporate net income taxes. An LLC is subject to the corporate net income taxes only if it is classified as a corporation for federal tax purposes.[17] LLCs that are classified as partnerships for federal income tax purposes are still subject to the capital stock and franchise taxes, and its members are still subject to the personal income tax on distributions.

[D] Local Taxes

A political subdivision of Pennsylvania may impose any applicable taxes or license fees on LLCs to the extent authorized pursuant to the Local Tax Enabling Act.[18]

---

[15] Corp. Tax Opinion: Subjectivity of Limited Liability Companies, Pennsylvania Department of Revenue (Feb. 2, 2000).

[16] 72 Pa. Cons. Stat. Ann. §7601.

[17] *See* Act of June 7, 1997, No. 1997-7 (H.B. 134), 1997 Pa. Laws, amending Act of Mar. 4, 1971, Pub. L. 6, No. 2, 1971 Pa. Laws.

[18] Act of Dec. 31, 1965, Pub. L. 1257, 1965 Pa. Laws.

[E]   Reorganizations

Domestic and foreign LLCs are treated as corporations in applying the reorganization provisions of Pennsylvania law.[19]

[F]   Taxation of Members

Pennsylvania taxes the members' allocable shares of income, whether or not the income is distributed. The LLC must place all items of LLC income, gains, losses, expenses, costs, and liabilities for the taxable year in one of the following seven classes:

1.   Net income or loss from operations of a business, profession, or farm
2.   Pennsylvania taxable interest derived from obligations that are not statutorily free from taxation in Pennsylvania
3.   Pennsylvania taxable dividends
4.   Net gain or loss from the sale, exchange, or disposition of property
5.   Net income or loss from rents, royalties, patents, and copyrights
6.   Estate and trust income received from an estate or trust
7.   Gambling and lottery winnings

[G]   Tax Returns

An LLC that is classified as a partnership for federal tax purposes and that has a resident member or income derived from Pennsylvania sources must file an information return on Form PA-65, Commonwealth of Pennsylvania Partnership Information Return. The return sets forth items of income, loss, deduction, and other information required by the Department of Revenue.[20]

Form PA-65 must be filed if the LLC earned or received any income or incurred any loss allocable to Pennsylvania and if the LLC had one or more members who are Pennsylvania resident individuals, estates, or trusts.

An LLC with nonresident members must use Form PA-V, Payment Voucher, to make the final remittance of the 2.8 percent withholding tax due on the nonresident members' distributive shares of Pennsylvania taxable income.

An LLC must attach to Form PA-65 all appropriate schedules. However, the federal supporting schedules, in lieu of the Pennsylvania schedules, are acceptable.

The LLC must provide Form PA Schedule RK-1 to each resident partner and Form PA Schedule NRK-1 to each nonresident member. The LLC must apportion allocated income in accordance with the instructions set forth on the forms. Qualifying nonresident members may file a consolidated or group return to apportion

---

[19] Tax Reform Code of 1971, §303(a).

[20] Pa. Dept. of Rev. Reg. §107.6. Corp. Tax Opinion: Subjectivity of Limited Liability Companies, Pennsylvania Department of Revenue (Feb. 2, 2000).

and allocate their Pennsylvania taxable income. The LLC must use Form PA-40NRC for the consolidated group return.

The LLC must file Form PA-65 with the Pennsylvania Department of Revenue, Bureau of Individual Taxes, Department 280509, Harrisburg, PA 17128-0509. The partnership return on federal Form 1065 must be attached to Form PA-65.

An LLC that needs additional time to file the return may obtain an extension by using the federal extension or submitting Form REV-276, Application for Extension of Time to File.

Form PA Schedule NRH (Form PA-65) must be used to apportion income from an LLC business that is derived from sources both within and outside of Pennsylvania.

[H]   Annual Report

Pennsylvania requires domestic and foreign restricted professional services companies to file a certificate of annual registration each year with the Department of State.[21]

[I]   Filing Fees

Pennsylvania imposes the following filing fees on domestic and foreign LLCs:[22]

Certificate of organization	$100
Foreign LLC registration application	$180
Annual report	$ 0

[J]   References

M. Sargent & W. Schwidetzky, Limited Liability Company Handbook, Law — Sample Documents — Forms, §4.24, Pennsylvania Form of Operating Agreement (1995-1996 ed.).

§23.41   RHODE ISLAND

Rhode Island enacted the Rhode Island Limited Liability Company Act on September 19, 1992.[1]

---

[21] 15 Pa. Cons. Stat. Ann. §8998.
[22] 15 Pa. Cons. Stat. Ann. §153.
§23.41   [1] S.B. 2413, 1992 R.I. Pub. Laws; R.I. Gen. Laws §§7-16-1 to 7-16-75.

[A]   State Tax Classification

Rhode Island classifies an LLC in the same manner that the LLC is classified for federal tax purposes.[2]

[B]   Taxation of LLC and Members

An LLC is not subject to the Rhode Island personal income tax.[3] An LLC that is classified as a partnership or sole proprietorship for federal tax purposes must pay an annual fee minimum tax of $250.[4] An LLC that is classified as a corporation for federal tax purposes must pay the regular corporate taxes.[5]

Members in a domestic or foreign LLC that is classified as a partnership for federal tax purposes are subject to state income taxes on their distributive shares. The following rules apply to resident and nonresident members:[6]

- Any member of the LLC during any part of the tax year must file a Rhode Island income tax return. The member must include in Rhode Island gross income that portion of the LLC's Rhode Island income allocable to the member.
- Any member of the LLC who is a nonresident must sign and forward to the LLC before the original due date of the Rhode Island LLC return an agreement. The agreement must state that the member will file a Rhode Island income tax return and pay income tax on the nonresident member's share of the LLC income that was derived from or attributable to sources within Rhode Island. The agreement must be attached to the LLC's Rhode Island return for the tax year.
- The LLC must send to the tax administrator the tax on the nonresident member's share of LLC income derived from or attributable to sources within the state if the nonresident member's signed agreement is not attached to the LLC's return. The LLC must also file the return for the nonresident member if the agreement is attached to the return, but the nonresident member thereafter fails to file a timely return. The return in that case must be filed within 30 days after the date of notice by the Rhode Island Tax Administrator to the LLC. The tax is computed at the statutory rate applicable to corporations.
- A nonresident member must file a Rhode Island income tax return even though the member's only source of Rhode Island income was the member's share of LLC income derived from or attributable to sources within the state of Rhode Island. The amount of payment by the LLC on behalf of the

---

[2] R.I. Gen. Laws §7-16-73(b).
[3] R.I. Gen. Laws §44-30-1(b).
[4] R.I. Gen. Laws §7-16-67(b)(ii); Reg. §CT 98-14, R.I. Div. of Taxn., effective May 1, 1998.
[5] R.I. Gen. Laws §7-16-67(b)(i); Reg. §CT 98-14, R.I. Div. of Taxn., effective May 1, 1998.
[6] R.I. Gen. Laws §7-16-73(c); Reg. §CT 98-14, R.I. Div. of Taxn.

nonresident member is allowed as a credit against the member's Rhode Island income tax liability.

[C]   Tax Returns

Every LLC having income derived from sources within Rhode Island must file Form RI-1065, Partnership Income Information Return.[7] Each member must include on the member's individual tax return the member's distributive share of LLC net income for the tax year, whether or not distributed. The return must be filed on or before the fifteenth day of the third month following the close of the tax year. The return must be mailed to the Division of Taxation, One Capital Hill, Providence, RI 02908-5801. A copy of the federal return for the fiscal year must be attached to the annual return.[8]

Any member of a domestic or foreign LLC that is classified as a partnership or sole proprietorship must include in Rhode Island gross income that portion of the member's share of the LLC's Rhode Island gross income.[9]

The tax year for the LLC must be the same as the federal tax year.

The LLC must report to the Rhode Island Division of Taxation any changes or corrections in the federal taxable income within 90 days after a final determination is made. An LLC filing an amended federal income tax return must also file an amended Rhode Island return within 90 days thereafter.

A nonresident member must provide to the LLC a statement that the member will file a Rhode Island income tax return and pay income tax on the member's share of Rhode Island source income. The LLC has 30 days from the date of notice by the Tax Administrator to pay the nonresident member's tax at the corporate tax rates on the member's share of Rhode Island source income from the LLC if the LLC does not attach the statement to its return, or if it is attached but the member fails to timely pay the Rhode Island taxes. The nonresident member must still file a Rhode Island income tax return. However, the amount of payment by the LLC on the member's behalf is a credit against the member's Rhode Island income tax liability.[10]

An LLC may obtain an extension of time to file the tax return by filing Form RI-8736, Application for Automatic Extension of Time to File R.I. Partnership or R.I. Fiduciary Income Tax Return. The LLC must file Form RI-8800, Application for Additional Extension of Time to File R.I. Partnership or R.I. Fiduciary Income Tax Return, in order to obtain an additional extension of time.

An LLC that elects to be classified as a corporation for federal income tax purposes must file a return on or before the fifteenth day of the third month following the close of the fiscal year. An LLC that is classified as a partnership for federal income tax purposes must file a return on or before the fifteenth day

---

[7] R.I. Gen. Laws §7-16-67.
[8] Reg. §CT 98-14, R.I. Div. of Taxn., effective May 1, 1998.
[9] Id.
[10] Id.

of the fourth month following the close of its fiscal year. A copy of the federal return for the fiscal year must be attached to the annual return.[11]

[D] Annual Report

A Rhode Island LLC must file an annual report.[12] The annual report must disclose the following information:

- The name and address of the principal office of the LLC.
- The state or other jurisdiction under which the LLC was formed.
- The name and address of the registered agent.
- The current mailing address of the LLC and the name or title of the person to whom communications may be directed.
- A brief statement of the character of the business of the LLC.
- Any additional information required by the secretary of state.
- If the LLC has managers, the name and address of each manager.

[E] Filing Fees

Rhode Island imposes the following filing fees on LLCs:[13]

Articles of organization	$150
Foreign LLC registration application	$150
Annual report	$ 50

[F] References

M. Sargent & W. Schwidetzky, Limited Liability Company Handbook, Law — Sample Documents — Forms, §4.25, Rhode Island Form of Articles of Organization and Operating Agreement (1995-1996 ed.).

§23.42 SOUTH CAROLINA

South Carolina enacted the Limited Liability Company Act effective June 16, 1994.[1] The law was replaced by the Uniform Limited Liability Company Act effective June 1, 1996.[2] The 1996 law incorporated several pro-taxpayer provisions consistent with IRS pronouncements since original enactment.

---

[11] Id.
[12] R.I. Gen. Laws §7-16-66.
[13] R.I. Gen. Laws §7-16-65.
§23.42 [1] H.B. 4283, 1994 S.C. Acts; S.C. Code Ann. §§33-44-101 to 33-44-1207.
[2] H.B. 4830, Rat. 396, 1996 S.C. Acts.

[A]   State Tax Classification

South Carolina classifies an LLC in the same manner that the LLC is classified for federal tax purposes.[3] An LLC is included in the definition of a partnership or corporation for state tax purposes depending on its federal classification.[4]

Effective June 10, 1997, single-member LLCs that are disregarded for federal tax purposes (not classified as corporations) are disregarded for all South Carolina tax purposes.[5] If the LLC is owned by an individual, it will be treated as a sole proprietorship. The income from the LLC is reported on the individual's tax return. If the LLC is owned by a corporation (a 100 percent owned subsidiary), it will be treated as a division of the corporation. The income of the LLC is reported on the parent corporation's income tax return.[6] A single-member LLC that is classified as a corporation for federal tax purposes is classified as a corporation for South Carolina tax purposes.[7]

After the IRS issued the check-the-box regulations, the South Carolina Department of Revenue reaffirmed that it would follow the federal entity classification rules. The effective date of the federal rules for South Carolina was also January 1, 1997.[8]

LLCs are also exempt from classification as distinct legal entities and from choice of law issues, subject to certain exceptions.[9]

[B]   Taxation of LLC and Members

An LLC that is classified as a partnership for federal income tax purposes is not subject to South Carolina taxes.[10]

Each member of an LLC that is classified as a partnership must include the member's share of South Carolina LLC income on the member's individual income tax return.[11] All of the provisions of the Internal Revenue Code apply in determining the gross income, adjusted gross income, and taxable income of an LLC and its members, subject to modification provided by South Carolina and to allocation and apportionment for nonresident members.[12] The amount included must be based on the LLC income of the year ending within the member's tax year if the tax year of the LLC and the member are different.

Single-member LLCs that are classified as corporations for federal tax purposes are required to file federal corporate returns and pay corporate license fees.[13] The

---

[3] S.C. Code Ann. §12-6-630.
[4] S.C. Code Ann. §12-2-25(A).
[5] S.C. Code Ann. §12-2-25(B).
[6] Rev. Rul. No. 98-11, S.C. Dept. of Rev. (May 6, 1998).
[7] Id.
[8] Information Letter No. 96-25, S.C. Dept. of Rev. (Dec. 19, 1996).
[9] S.C. Code Ann. §§33-44-201, 33-44-1001(a).
[10] S.C. Code Ann. §12-6-600.
[11] Id.
[12] Id.
[13] Information Letter No. 94-23, S.C. Dept. of Rev. (Sept. 12, 1994).

law changed in 1994 as a result of the change in the definition of "corporation."[14] A corporation was defined to include an LLC that is classified as a corporation. The change was effective June 16, 1994. An LLC formed after June 16, 1994, is required to complete the initial annual report of corporations and pay the initial license fee with the Department of Revenue upon formation if the LLC is classified as a corporation.[15]

The statute exempting a single-member limited liability company from income tax if the LLC is classified as a disregarded entity does not exempt the LLC from other South Carolina taxes. Thus, a single-member LLC must pay sales taxes. However, contributions of substantially all the assets and liabilities of a corporation into a new single-member LLC that elects to be classified as a division of the corporate owner for federal and South Carolina tax purposes are not subject to South Carolina sales taxes.[16]

[C] Tax Returns

Every foreign and domestic LLC doing business or owning property in South Carolina must file an information return on Form SC1065, Partnership Return of Income.[17] The LLC must file the partnership return with the South Carolina Department of Revenue, Partnership Return, Columbia, SC 29214-0008. The LLC must attach a copy of federal Form 1065 and copies of all schedules to the return. The income or loss of the LLC is computed in the same manner and on the same basis as for individuals.

The LLC must attach a copy of each federal Schedule K-1 to Form SC1065. Members who have income or loss must file tax returns regardless of their tax liability. The LLC must furnish Schedule SC-K to each individual member. This schedule shows the amount of each item apportioned or allocated to South Carolina. The LLC must furnish to South Carolina members information concerning the total amounts of their proportionate shares of South Carolina adjustments and the amounts allocated or apportioned to states other than South Carolina.

An LLC may obtain an extension of time to file the return by filing Form SC4868.

[D] Apportionment of Income

If the LLC carries on a trade or business entirely within the state, all of the net income must be apportioned to South Carolina. Multistate LLCs whose principal profits are derived from manufacturing, producing, collecting, buying, assembling, processing, selling, distributing, or dealing in tangible personal property must compute the portion of business income attributable to South Carolina by

---

[14] The definition is contained in S.C. Code Ann. §12-2-25-3.
[15] Information Letter No. 94-23, S.C. Dept. of Rev. (Sept. 12, 1994).
[16] Private Revenue Opinion No. 00-4, S.C. Dept. of Rev. (July 10, 2000).
[17] S.C. Code Ann. §12-6-4910.

applying a four-factor apportionment formula. LLCs whose principal profits are derived from other sources must compute the income attributable to South Carolina based on a ratio of gross receipts within the state to total gross receipts.

[E] Withholding Tax

LLCs must withhold annually 5 percent of the South Carolina taxable income of members who are nonresidents of South Carolina. The LLC must complete Schedule W-H to compute the withholding. Any South Carolina real estate gain subject to buyer withholding is not subject to this withholding. The income tax must be paid to the South Carolina Department of Revenue along with Form 1065. The return must be filed by the fifteenth day of the fourth month following the end of the tax year of the LLC. The LLC must provide each nonresident member with Form 1099-MISC by that date, showing the respective amounts of income and tax withheld. The nonresident member claiming credit for the withholding must attach a copy of Form 1099-MISC to the member's tax return as verification. The LLC must attach a schedule disclosing the name, address, tax identification number, South Carolina taxable income, and tax withheld for each nonresident member.

LLCs that request an extension of time to file Form SC1065 must estimate the South Carolina taxable income of nonresidents and pay a 5 percent withholding tax on this amount along with the filing of the extension request. The extension request must be filed by the fifteenth day of the fourth month following the end of the tax year.

Nonresident members may provide the LLC with affidavits agreeing to be subject to the jurisdiction of the South Carolina Department of Revenue and the courts of South Carolina for purposes of determining and collecting the South Carolina tax, interest, and penalties. The LLC must attach the affidavits to Form SC1065. The LLC is not required to withhold income tax on behalf of those members. An affidavit does not need to be filed again once it is first submitted. The LLC is not required to withhold income taxes if it has no South Carolina taxable income for the year.

[F] Composite Return

An LLC may report the income of nonresident members on a composite return. The LLC is not required to withhold taxes or file affidavits for such members.[18] A composite return is a nonresident individual tax return on Form SC1040NR filed by the LLC. The composite return computes and reports the income and taxes of the nonresident members. The LLC must file the return on or before April 15 following the members' tax year. The LLC must pay any taxes along with filing the return. Each participating nonresident member's separate income is computed

---

[18] S.C. Code Ann. §12-6-5030.

in the same manner as if the member were separately reporting income on a Form SC1040NR.

[G]   LLCs Classified as Corporations

LLCs that are classified as corporations for federal tax purposes may use federal Form 1099 for reporting dividends and other distributions to members.[19]

[H]   Conversion to LLC

When a partnership converts to an LLC, the LLC is considered to be the same entity as the partnership. The partnership will not terminate. There will be no change in the adjusted bases of the owners' interests if there is no change in the owners' shares of liabilities. There is a carryover in the owners' holding period for their ownership interests. The tax year of the partnership does not close. The new LLC does not need to obtain a new taxpayer identification number. No documentary transfer tax is due. The LLC is not required to obtain a new retail license for sales tax purposes. However, the LLC should obtain a new retail license for each retail location. If the license is transferred to the name of the LLC, the Department of Revenue will assume that the managing members are personally liable for any sales or use tax that the LLC fails to pay.[20]

[I]   Annual Report

An LLC must file an annual report in South Carolina.[21]

[J]   Filing Fees

South Carolina imposes the following filing fees on LLCs:[22]

Articles of organization	$110
Certificate of authority for foreign LLC	$110
Annual registration or renewal of foreign LLC name	$ 10

---

[19] Act 101, uncodified §12, 1995 S.C. Acts.
[20] Rev. Rul. 95-9, S.C. Dept. of Rev. (June 27, 1995).
[21] S.C. Code Ann. §33-44-211.
[22] S.C. Code Ann. §§33-43-1401, 33-44-1204.

§23.43   SOUTH DAKOTA

South Dakota enacted the South Dakota Limited Liability Company Act on July 1, 1993.[1] South Dakota adopted the Uniform Limited Liability Company Act, effective July 1, 1998.[2]

[A]   Taxation of LLC and Members

There is no state income tax in South Dakota. LLCs are not subject to the South Dakota bank franchise (income) tax. Banks and financial institutions are required to pay a bank franchise (income) tax. A limited liability company is classified as a corporation for purposes of the bank franchise tax, effective July 1, 2003.[3]

However, LLCs must pay an annual reporting fee of $50.[4] The tax is due and payable on January 2 of each year. The tax is delinquent if not paid by February 1. There is a penalty of $50 for late filings.

[B]   Tax Returns

An LLC must file an annual report with the Secretary of State. The LLC must deliver the first annual report to the Secretary of State with the filing of the articles of organization. The LLC must deliver an annual report thereafter on or before the first day of the second month following the anniversary month of the filing date.[5]

The LLC must pay a fee in conjunction with the annual report. The maximum aggregate fees paid with all annual reports are $16,000. The fees are based on the total agreed contributions to the LLC as follows:[6]

Agreed Contribution	Fee
Not in excess of $50,000	$90
$50,001 to $100,000	$150
In excess of $100,000	150 for the first $100,000, plus $.50 for each additional $1,000

The LLC must set forth in each annual report the dollar amount of the total agreed contributions to the LLC.[7] It must pay additional fees with the annual report in accordance with the above schedule if the members agreed to make additional contributions during the prior year.

---

§23.43   [1] S.B. 139, 1993 S.D. Laws; S.D. Codified Laws Ann. §§47-34-1 to 47-34-59.
[2] S.D. Codified Laws Ann. §§47-34A-101 to 47-34A-1207.
[3] S.D. Codified Laws Ann. §§10-43-1(1), (10).
[4] S.D. Codified Laws Ann. §47-34A-212(c).
[5] S.D. Codified Laws Ann. §47-34A-211.
[6] S.D. Codified Laws Ann. §47-34A-212.
[7] S.D. Codified Laws Ann. §47-34A-211(a)(5).

[C]   Filing Fees

Articles of organization[8] $10
Annual report[9] $50 plus a fee based on the agreed
                                          contributions of members[10]

§23.44   TENNESSEE

Tennessee enacted the Tennessee Limited Liability Company Act effective June 1, 1994.[1]

[A]   State Tax Classification

Tennessee classifies an LLC in the same manner that the LLC is classified for federal tax purposes. An LLC that is classified as a partnership for federal tax purposes is classified as a partnership for state tax purposes. An LLC that is classified as a corporation for federal tax purposes is classified as a corporation for purposes of all state and local Tennessee taxes.[2]

The Tennessee laws governing classification of LLCs were enacted before the federal check-the-box regulations were issued by the Treasury Department. The state statute does not specifically address the classification of LLCs in light of the revisions made by the check-the-box provisions. However, the intent of the state statute is to classify LLCs for state and local tax purposes in the same way they are classified for federal tax purposes. Therefore, the Tennessee Department of Revenue follows the federal check-the-box regulations in classifying LLCs for purpose of Tennessee franchise, corporate excise (income), and stocks and bonds income taxes.[3]

[B]   Taxation of LLC and Members

For tax years beginning on or after July 1, 1999,[4] LLCs are subject to a franchise tax of .25 percent of net worth[5] and an excise tax of 6 percent on Tennessee net earnings.[6]

---

[8] S.D. Codified Laws Ann. §47-34A-1206.

[9] S.D. Codified Laws Ann. §47-34A-212(c).

[10] S.D. Codified Laws Ann. §47-34A-212(a), (b).

§23.44   [1] H.B. 952, ch. 868, 1994 Tenn. Pub. Acts; Tenn. Code Ann. §§48-201-101 to 48-248-606.

[2] Tenn. Code Ann. §48-211-101. See also Rev. Rul. No. 01-23, Tennessee Department of Revenue (Oct. 29, 2001) regarding the taxation of LLCs that elect to be classified as a corporation.

[3] Rev. Rul. 97-41, Tenn. Dept. of Rev. (Oct. 14, 1997).

[4] See Important Notice, Tennessee Department of Revenue (June 16, 1999), regarding the application of the franchise tax in the excise tax to LLCs.

[5] Tenn. Code Ann. §§67-4-2004(16), 67-4-2106.

[6] Tenn. Code Ann. §§67-4-2004(16), 67-4-2007.

LLCs must pay a "Hall Income Tax" of 6 percent on dividends, bond interest, and similar instruments.[7]

Tennessee imposes an annual fee on LLCs equal to $50 per member of the domestic or foreign LLC. The fee is imposed on the date of the initial filing with the secretary of state and on the date that the annual report is filed each year thereafter.[8] There is a minimum fee of $300 and a maximum fee of $3,000. If the LLC is prohibited by its articles from doing business in Tennessee and represents that it has not and is not doing business in Tennessee, the filing fee is $300 regardless of the number of members.[9]

An LLC organized outside the state of Tennessee that is commercially domiciled in Tennessee and that is classified as a corporation for federal income tax purposes is taxed as a financial institution for Tennessee franchise tax and corporate excise (income) tax purposes if the LLC derives more than 50 percent of its income from making, acquiring, selling, or servicing loans or extensions of credit. If the LLC receives all applications for loans in Tennessee and the LLC is unable to determine where the loan proceeds were applied, then the LLC must source all of the income from the loans in question to Tennessee. The LLC may apportion its net worth and net income for tax purposes if it files a corporate income tax return in at least one other state, even though it maintains an office only in Tennessee. If the LLC maintains two offices, one in Tennessee and one in another state, it has the right to apportion its income.[10]

The members of a foreign LLC that is classified as a partnership for federal tax purposes are subject to all state and local Tennessee taxes in the same manner and to the same extent as partners in a foreign partnership.[11]

The members of a domestic LLC that is classified as a partnership for federal tax purposes are subject to all state and local Tennessee taxes in the same manner and to the same extent as partners in a domestic partnership.[12]

[C]   Sales Taxes

The transfer of inventory and other assets by a parent corporation to a newly formed LLC in exchange for 100 percent of the membership interests in the LLC is not subject to the Tennessee sales and use tax. The transfer of assets is exempt as an occasional sale.[13]

[D]   Real Estate Taxes

An LLC may file various documents with the office of the register of deeds in the county where the LLC has its principal office in Tennessee. In the case of a

[7] Tenn. Code Ann. §67-2-102.
[8] Tenn. Code Ann. tit. 48, ch. 247-103(d).
[9] Id.
[10] Rev. Rul. No. 98-43, Tenn. Dept. of Rev. (Oct. 21, 1998).
[11] Tenn. Code Ann. tit. 48, ch. 211-101.
[12] Id.
[13] Ltr. Rul. No. 00-47, TN, Tenn. Dept. of Rev. (Nov. 29, 2000).

merger, the documents must be filed in the county in which the newer surviving LLC has its principal office in Tennessee. The register of deeds may charge $5 plus $.50 per page in excess of five pages as the filing fee.[14]

[E] Annual Report

Domestic and foreign LLCs qualified to do business in Tennessee must file annual reports.[15] The annual report must be filed with the secretary of state on or before the first day of the fourth month following the close of the LLC's fiscal year. The annual report must set forth the following information:

- The name of the LLC and the jurisdiction in which it was formed.
- The street address of its registered office and the name of its registered agent at that office in the state of Tennessee.
- The street address of its principal executive office.
- If the LLC is managed by a board or its equivalent, the names and business addresses of the members of the board or its equivalent.
- The names and business addresses of its managers or their equivalent.
- The federal employer identification number of the LLC or representation that it has been applied for if the LLC has not yet obtained a federal employer identification number.
- The number of members of the LLC at the date of filing.

A professional limited liability company must make a special annual filing if required by a rule promulgated by the licensing authority having jurisdiction over professional services rendered by the employees of the professional limited liability company.[16]

[F] Financial Statements

A board-managed LLC must also prepare financial statements at least annually. If the financial statements for the LLC are prepared on the basis of generally accepted accounting principles, the financial statements for the members must also be prepared on that basis.[17] Any report of an accountant accompanying the financial statements for the LLC must also accompany the financial statements for the member. Otherwise, the chief manager or person responsible for the LLC's accounting records must state such person's reasonable belief as to whether the financial statements were prepared on the basis of generally accepted accounting principles and, if not, describe the basis of preparation. The person responsible for the accounting records must also describe the respects in which the financial

---

[14] Tenn. Code Ann. tit. 48, ch. 247-103(e).
[15] Tenn. Code Ann. tit. 48, ch. 228-203.
[16] Tenn. Code Ann. tit. 48, ch. 248-602.
[17] Tenn. Code Ann. tit. 48, ch. 228-201.

statements were not prepared on a basis consistent with generally accepted accounting principles. The financial statements must be sent to each requesting member within one month after a request is made. The financial statements for the most recently completed fiscal year must be mailed to the member within four months after the close of the fiscal year.[18]

A member of a member-managed LLC has the right to true and full information regarding the status of the business and financial condition of the LLC.[19]

[G]   Filing Fees

Tennessee imposes the following filing fees on LLCs:[20]

Certificate of formation	$10
Annual report	$300-$3,000
Filing with the office of the register of deeds	$5
Application for certificate of authority of foreign LLC	$50-$3,000

[H]   References

M. Sargent & W. Schwidetzky, Limited Liability Company Handbook, Law — Sample Documents — Forms, §4.26, Tennessee Form of Articles of Organization and Operating Agreement (1995-1996 ed.).

A. Blumstein, "Key Tax Aspects of the Tennessee Limited Liability Company Act," 30 Tenn. B.J. 14 (No. 4, 1994).

§23.45   TEXAS

Texas adopted the Texas Limited Liability Company Act effective September 1, 1991.[1]

[A]   State Tax Classification

Texas classifies an LLC as a corporation for Texas franchise tax purposes. The franchise tax is imposed on every LLC doing business in Texas, including foreign LLCs qualified to do business in Texas.[2] The tax applies even if the LLC is classified as a partnership for federal income tax purposes or as a partnership by another

---

[18] Tenn. Code Ann. tit. 48, ch. 228-201(c).
[19] Tenn. Code Ann. tit. 48, ch. 228-202.
[20] Tenn. Code Ann. tit. 48, ch. 247-103(a).
§23.45   [1] H.B. 278, 1991 Tex. Gen. Laws; Tex. Rev. Civ. Stat. Ann. art. 1528n, 1.01 to 11.07.
[2] Tex. Tax Code Ann. §171.001(A)(2).

state in which the LLC is organized. The franchise tax also applies to a single-member LLC that is classified as a disregarded entity under federal law.[3]

[B]   Taxation of LLC

The Texas franchise tax is imposed on the LLC at the greater of the following:[4]

- .25 percent of net taxable capital. An LLC's net taxable capital is computed using three steps. First, the LLC's stated capital is added to its surplus to determine the taxable capital. The LLC's total taxable capital for these purposes is the sum of the members' contributions to the LLC and the LLC's surplus.[5] The members' contributions are the sum of any cash contributions and the agreed value of other noncash contributions, plus the amount of cash and other contributions that any member has agreed to make in the future if the member's promise is in writing and signed by the member.[6] The surplus is the LLC's net assets minus its members' contributions.[7] The taxable capital of an LLC is computed in the same way as for a corporation except that the members' contributions are added to the LLC's surplus to determine taxable capital.[8] Second, the taxable capital as so determined is apportioned to the state of Texas. Third, there is subtracted from that amount any other allowable deductions.[9]

- 4.5 percent of net taxable earned surplus. Net taxable earned surplus is an amount calculated on the basis of reportable federal taxable income. The net taxable earned surplus of an LLC is calculated in three steps.[10] First, the taxable earned surplus of the LLC is calculated. Second, that amount is apportioned to determine the amount attributable to Texas. Third, there is subtracted from that amount any allowable deductions in business losses carried forward to the tax reporting period. Withdrawals and distributions from the LLC are not included in earned surplus. They are not considered gross receipts for apportionment purposes unless there is a gain recognized by the corporate member for federal income tax purposes. The distributions and withdrawals are allocated based on the LLC's state of incorporation.[11]

---

[3] Texas Comptroller of Public Accounts, Ltr. Rul. 200106899L (2001); Ltr. Rul. 200301789L (Mar. 6, 2003).

[4] The application of the franchise tax to LLCs is discussed in detail in regulations. Tex. Admin. Code tit. 34, §3.562.

[5] Tex. Tax Code Ann. §171.101(B).

[6] Tex. Admin. Code tit. 34, §3.562(c).

[7] Tex. Tax Code Ann. §171.109(A)(1).

[8] Tex. Tax Code Ann. §171.101.

[9] Id.

[10] Tex. Tax Code Ann. §171.110.

[11] Tex. Admin. Code tit. 34, §3.562; 23 Tex. Treas. Reg. 4236 (May 1, 1998).

The reportable federal taxable income of an LLC that is classified as a corporation for federal income tax purposes is computed as if the LLC were a corporation.[12]

[C]   Foreign LLCs

An LLC qualified to do business in Texas may not withdraw from qualification until it pays all franchise taxes, penalties, and interest owed through the end of the period in which it is dissolved.[13] A foreign LLC that is dissolved, merged out of existence, or otherwise terminated under the laws of its state of incorporation or organization must also pay all taxes, penalties, and interest through the date of dissolution.[14]

[D]   Single-Member LLCs

Single-member LLCs may be formed in Texas. The reportable federal taxable income of an LLC that is classified as a sole proprietor for federal tax purposes is the taxable income and deductions reported on the member's individual income tax return. This includes any schedules and attachments to the member's income tax return that relate to the LLC.[15] Compensation to a member who is treated as the sole proprietor for federal income tax purposes is not deductible in computing income.

The reportable federal taxable income of a single-member LLC that is treated as a division or branch of a corporation for federal income tax purposes is computed as if the LLC were a separate corporation for federal income tax purposes. A single-member LLC may not deduct officer and director compensation from earned surplus.[16]

[E]   LLC Classified as Corporation

The reportable federal taxable income of an LLC that is classified as a corporation for federal income tax purposes is computed as if the LLC were a corporation.[17]

[F]   Corporate Members of an LLC

A corporate member of an LLC must use the cost method of accounting for its investment in the LLC. A corporate member's distributive share of the LLC's

---

[12] Id.

[13] Tex. Admin. Code Ann. tit. 34, §3.568.

[14] Id.

[15] Tex. Admin. Code Ann. tit. 34, §3.562; 23 Tex. Treas. Reg. 4236 (May 1, 1998).

[16] Tex. Admin. Code tit. 34, §3.562(g); 23 Tex. Treas. Reg. 4236 (May 1, 1998).

[17] Tex. Comp. Pub. Accts., Reg. §3.562, 23 Tex. Reg. 4236 (May 1, 1998).

income or loss is not included in the member's earned surplus or gross receipts to the extent the items were reflected on the LLC's report.[18]

[G] Withdrawals and Distributions

Withdrawals and distributions from the LLC are not included in earned surplus. They are not considered gross receipts for apportionment purposes unless the corporate member recognized a gain for federal income tax purposes. The distributions and withdrawals are allocated based on the LLC's state of incorporation.[19]

[H] Tax Returns

A Texas LLC must file a Texas corporation franchise tax report on Form 05-144, Texas Corporation Franchise Tax Report. The initial return and payment are due within 90 days after the date the initial privilege period ends. The annual return and payment must be postmarked on or before May 15 of the reporting year.

An LLC may file Annual Franchise No Tax Due Information Report — Short Form if all of the following conditions are satisfied:

1. The LLC is not the survivor of a merger;
2. All of the income of the LLC is unitary; and
3. For the accounting period on which the report is based, the LLC has no gross receipts in Texas, or the LLC's total taxable capital is less than $40,000 and its earned surplus (including officer and director compensation if applicable) is less than $2,222.

The report is filed on Form 05-141; the regular long-form report is the Comptroller of Public Accounts Form 05-146, Texas Corporation Franchise Tax Report.

Foreign LLCs must satisfy all tax liabilities and obtain a Certificate of Account Status from the comptroller of public accounts before filing articles of dissolution or applications for withdrawal.

[I] Annual Report

Texas does not require an LLC to file an annual report except for the tax reports. Form 05-102, Texas Franchise Tax Public Information Report, is the equivalent of an annual report. It is filed along with Form 05-144 at the time that the regular tax return is filed. The information report must list the following information:

---

[18] Id.
[19] Id.

- Whether there are officers and directors of the LLC.
- The principal office of the LLC.
- The principal place of business in Texas.
- The name, title, mailing address, and Social Security number of each officer and director, if any, of the LLC.
- The name of each corporation in which the LLC owns 10 percent or more.
- The name of each corporation that owns 10 percent or more of the LLC.
- The registered agent and registered office in the state of Texas.

[J] Filing Fees

Texas imposes the following filing fees on LLCs:[20]

Articles of organization	$200
Application by foreign LLC for certificate of authority	$500
Annual fee	$ 0

[K] References

Texas Secretary of State, Filing Guide for Corporation, Limited Liability Company, Limited Partnership, Assumed Name, Registered Limited Liability Partnership & Trademark Documents (1994).

M. Sargent & W. Schwidetzky, Limited Liability Company Handbook, Law — Sample Documents — Forms, §4.27, Texas Form of Articles of Organization and Operating Agreement (1995-1996 ed.).

§23.46 UTAH

Utah enacted the Utah Limited Liability Company Act and began accepting filings for LLCs on July 1, 1991.[1] Utah adopted the Revised Limited Liability Co. Act, effective July 1, 2001.[2]

[A] State Tax Classification

Utah classifies an LLC in the same manner that the LLC is classified for federal tax purposes.[3] Before January 1, 1994, the Utah State Tax Commission treated Utah LLCs as partnerships for state tax purposes.

---

[20] Tex. Rev. Civ. Stat. Ann. art. 1528n, 9.01.

§23.46 [1] H.B. 221, 1991 Utah Laws; Utah Code Ann. §§48-2b-101 to 48-2b-158.

[2] Utah Code Ann. §§48-2c-101 to 48-2c-1902.

[3] Utah Code Ann. §§48-2c-117, 59-10-801.

[B] Taxation of LLC and Members

There is no franchise or entity-level tax imposed on Utah LLCs. An LLC is a pass-through entity.[4]

The members of the LLC are taxed in Utah on their distributive shares of income.[5] Each item of LLC income, gain, loss, or deduction has the same character for a member as it has for federal income tax purposes.[6] When an item is not characterized for federal income tax purposes, it has the same character for a member as if the member realized the income from the same source or incurred the expense in the same manner as did the LLC.

Nonresident members are taxed on their distributive shares of income derived from or connected with Utah sources.[7]

[C] Composite Returns

An LLC may file a composite income tax return on behalf of individual nonresident members if all of the following three conditions are met:

1. Individual nonresident members with no other income from Utah sources may be included on the return. Nonresident members listed on the return may not file a Utah individual income tax return.
2. Schedule N must be included with the return. The schedule must list the information for all individual nonresident members included in the composite filing.
3. If the nonresident members have other sources of Utah income or are entitled to credit, the members must file individual Forms TC-40. They cannot be included in the composite return. Refunds will not be issued or allowed on the composite return filed.

The tax is computed using the 7 percent maximum tax rate applied to Utah taxable income attributable to Utah sources after allowing certain deductions. There is a deduction equal to 15 percent of Utah taxable income attributable to nonresident members included in the composite return. No deductions are allowed for standard deductions or itemized deductions, personal exemptions, federal tax determined for the same period, or any other deductions.

[D] Allocations and Distributive Shares

A special allocation must have substantial economic effect in accordance with federal law if a member's distributive share of an item of LLC income, gain, loss,

---

[4] Utah Code Ann. §59-10-301.
[5] *Id.*
[6] Utah Code Ann. §59-10-302.
[7] Utah Code Ann. §59-10-303.

or deduction is determined for federal purposes by a special provision in the LLC operating agreement. In determining the state taxable income of a resident member, any modifications, such as U.S. government bond interest, that relate to an item of LLC income, gain, loss, or deduction must be made in accordance with the member's distributive share for federal income tax purposes of the items to which the modification relates. If a member's share of any such item is not required to be taken into account separately for federal income tax purposes, the member's distributive share of such item must be determined in accordance with her distributive share of LLC income or loss for federal income tax purposes.

The items of income, gain, loss, and deduction allocated to nonresident or part-year residents are adjusted and apportioned. In determining the adjusted gross income, there is included only that part derived from or connected with sources in the state of Utah. The Utah portion may be set forth beside the total for each item amount as an attachment to the return.

In determining the sources of a nonresident member's income, no consideration will be given to provisions in the LLC operating agreement that do either of the following:

- Characterize as payments to the member for services or for the use of capital or allocate to the member, as income or gain from sources outside of the state, a greater portion of the member's distributive share of LLC income or gain than the ratio of LLC income or gain from sources outside the state to LLC income or gain from all sources; or
- Allocate to the member a greater portion of LLC income, loss, or deduction connected with sources in the state than the member's proportionate share, for federal income tax purposes, of LLC loss or deduction generally.

The Utah State Tax Commission may, on application, authorize the use of other methods of determining a nonresident member's portion of LLC income derived from or connected with sources in the state that are appropriate and equitable. The commission may impose such terms and conditions that it believes necessary in connection with such other methods.

[E]   Tax Returns

A Utah LLC must file a tax return on Form TC-65, Utah Partnership/Limited Liability Partnership/Limited Liability Company Return of Income.[8] The return must be filed by every LLC having a resident member in the state of Utah or any income derived from sources in Utah for the taxable year. The LLC must attach a copy of the federal partnership tax return on Form 1065 to the state tax return, with Schedules K-1.[9] It must also attach a schedule of modifications to the federal tax return. It must file a complete copy of federal Schedule K-1 for each nonresident member whose Utah reportable income is over $1,000.

---

[8] Utah Admin. R. R865-9I-21; Utah Code Ann. §59-10-507.
[9] Utah Code Ann. §59-10-507.

The return must be filed with the Utah State Tax Commission, 210 North 1950 West, Salt Lake City, UT 84134-0270. The return must be filed on or before the fifteenth day of the fourth month after the close of the fiscal year or by April 15 for calendar year LLCs.

An LLC may automatically obtain an extension of time for up to six months to file the return.

[F] Annual Report

Utah requires an LLC to file an annual report.[10] The annual report must be filed during the month of the LLC's anniversary date of formation or its anniversary date of obtaining a certificate of authority to transact business in Utah. The annual report must set forth the following information:

- The name of the LLC and the state or county in which the LLC was formed.
- The street address of the registered office and the name of the registered agent for service of process at that office.
- Any change of the registered agent.
- The new street address or legal name of any manager or member with management authority if the manager or member named in the articles of organization or application for registration of a foreign LLC has changed.
- Any change in the persons constituting the managers or members with management authority of a foreign LLC.

[G] Filing Fees

Utah imposes the following filing fees on LLCs:[11]

Articles of organization	$75
Foreign LLC registration application	$75
Annual registration	$15

[H] References

M. Sargent & W. Schwidetzky, Limited Liability Company Handbook, Law — Sample Documents — Forms, §4.28, Utah Form of Operating Agreement (1995-1996 ed.).

---

[10] Utah Code Ann. §48-2c-203.
[11] Utah Code Ann. §48-2c-214.

§23.47   VERMONT

Vermont enacted laws authorizing the formation of limited liability companies effective July 1, 1996.[1]

[A]   State Tax Classification

Vermont classifies an LLC in the same manner that the LLC is classified for federal tax purposes.[2] Single-member LLCs are permitted.

[B]   Taxation of LLC and Members

An LLC that is classified as a partnership for federal tax purposes must pay an annual tax of $250 for tax years beginning on or after January 1, 1998.[3] The LLC is not otherwise subject to tax.

If the LLC elects classification as a corporation for federal tax purposes under the check-the-box regulations, the LLC is subject to the corporate income tax and must file a corporate income tax return.[4]

The members of the LLC are subject to tax on their distributive shares of Vermont LLC income. Vermont conformed its state laws to the Internal Revenue Code.[5] Therefore, the federal provisions applicable to taxation of LLC members apply for state tax purposes.

[C]   Tax Returns

An LLC that is classified as a partnership for federal tax purposes and that has any nonresident members must file Form B1-473, Vermont Partnership/Limited Liability Company Schedule.[6] Every LLC having any income derived from Vermont sources must file the partnership return. The return must be filed by the due date of IRS Form 1065. The commissioner of taxes may extend the due date if the LLC files a copy of the federal extension request or similar request in writing before the due date. The return must be filed with a copy of the completed IRS Form 1065 and Schedule K. The LLC must attach IRS Form 1065 and Schedule K-1s for all members. The return must be sent to Vermont Department of Taxes, 109 State Street, Montpelier, VT 05609-1401.

Each member's distributive share of income from the LLC is set forth in part

---

§23.47   [1] H.B. 112, ch. 179, 1996 Vt. Laws; Vt. Stat. Ann. tit. 11, §§3001-3162.
[2] Vt. Stat. Ann. tit. 32, §5921.
[3] Id.
[4] Vt. Rul. of Commr., P.D. 98-152 (Oct. 14, 1998); Vt. Stat. Ann. tit. 32, §5921.
[5] Vt. Stat. Ann. tit. 32, §5820(a).
[6] Vt. Stat. Ann. tit. 32, §5861a.

2 of the form. The LLC must attach a separate schedule if it has more than seven members.

An LLC that is classified as a corporation must file a tax return with the commissioner of taxes if it engages in activities in Vermont that would subject a C corporation to the requirement of filing an annual return in Vermont.

[D] Nonresident Members

A nonresident member is taxed in Vermont on income derived from LLC operations in Vermont. The LLC must withhold and pay estimated taxes with respect to nonresident members. The amount of withholding is equal to the highest federal marginal tax rate in effect for individuals multiplied by the state tax rate multiplied by the nonresident member's pro rata share of income attributable to Vermont.[7] The tax rate is 9.26 percent for 2003.[8] The amount of withholding from each nonresident member is a credit against the member's individual tax liability. The nonresident member is considered to have paid all income taxes based on the withholding.[9]

An LLC may enter into an agreement with the Vermont Department of Taxes to file a composite individual income tax return on Form BI-471 on behalf of nonresident members. In order to qualify for block filing, the members of the LLC included in the filing may not have been a residents of Vermont at any time during the year. In addition, a member and his or her spouse must not have had any income from sources within Vermont other than from the LLC.

[E] Affordable Housing Projects

An LLC that engages solely in the business of operating affordable housing projects in Vermont is not liable for income taxes imposed on members with respect to income of the LLC if all of the following apply:

1. The LLC notifies its nonresident members of their obligation to file Vermont personal income tax returns and to pay taxes on the income earned from the investment;
2. The LLC instructs each nonresident member to pay the tax; and
3. The LLC files copies of all Schedules K-1 with its limited liability company return, with segregated duplicate copies of all nonresident members' Schedules K-1.

---

[7] Vt. Stat. Ann. tit. 32, §§5920(c); Form WH-435, Estimated Income Tax Payments for Nonresident Shareholders or Partners.

[8] *See* Instructions to Form WH-435, Estimated Income Tax Payments for Nonresident Shareholders or Partners.

[9] Vt. Stat. Ann. tit. 31, §5920(e).

[F]   Apportionment of Income

An LLC must apportion its income using part 3 of Form PS-421 and Form BA-402, Vermont Apportionment & Allocation Schedule, if the LLC has income or loss from Vermont sources and at least one other state and if one or more members are nonresidents or part-year residents of Vermont. Vermont employs a three-factor formula for the allocation based on sales and receipts, salaries and wages, and property. The LLC may use other factors if these factors do not fairly and reasonably reflect the Vermont portion of the income.[10]

[G]   Annual Report

An LLC must file an annual report in Vermont. The annual report must be filed within 2 1/2 months after the close of the LLC's fiscal year.[11] The annual report must include the following information:

- The name of the LLC and the state in which it was organized
- The address of its designated office and the name of its designated agent at that office in the state of Vermont
- The address of its principal office
- The names and business addresses of any managers

[H]   Filing Fees

There are the following filing fees in Vermont:[12]

Articles of organization	$ 75
Application for certificate of authority of foreign LLC	$100
Annual report	$ 15

§23.48   VIRGINIA

Virginia enacted the Virginia Limited Liability Company Act effective July 1, 1991.[1]

[A]   State Tax Classification

Virginia classifies an LLC in the same manner as the LLC is classified for federal tax purposes.[2]

---

[10] Reg. §1.5833-1.

[11] Vt. Stat. Ann. tit. 11, §3161.

[12] Vt. Stat. Ann. tit. 11, §3013.

§23.48   [1] Va. Code Ann. §§13.1-1000 to 13.1-1123. See also S.B. Farmer & L. Mezzullo, *The Virginia Limited Liability Company Act*, 25 U. Rich. L. Rev. 789 (Summer 1991).

[2] Va. Code Ann. §58.1-301.

[B] Taxation of LLC

An LLC that is classified as a partnership is not subject to Virginia income taxes.[3]

An LLC is required to pay a $50 annual registration fee. All domestic and foreign LLCs registered to transact business in Virginia must pay the fee. The payment must be made on or before September 1 of each year after the calendar year in which the LLC was formed or registered to do business in Virginia. There is a $25 late payment penalty fee.[4] The Tax Commission sends a statement of assessment to the comptroller and to each LLC on or before August 15 of each year. If the LLC fails to pay the tax on or before October 1 of the year assessed, the commission will mail a notice to the LLC of impending cancellation of its certificate of organization or certificate of registration. The certificate is automatically canceled if the annual fee is not paid by December 31 of that year. A domestic LLC is dissolved upon cancellation.

No member, manager, or agent of the LLC has personal obligations for liabilities of the LLC, whether in tort, contract, or otherwise, as a result of the failure of the LLC to pay the annual registration fee or by reason of the cancellation and dissolution of the LLC for failure to pay.

An LLC is subject to the Virginia local business, professional, and occupational license (BPOL) taxes even if the LLC is classified as a disregarded entity under federal law. LLCs that maintain a definite place of business within the taxing jurisdiction are subject to adopt BPOL tax. The tax is based on the gross receipts of the LLC attributable to the definite place of business. If both a parent LLC and an operating LLC have a definite place of business in Virginia, both entities are subject to the BPOL tax.[5]

[C] Taxation of Members

A Virginia LLC is a pass-through entity. Profits and losses are passed through to the members.[6] The members of an LLC that is classified as a partnership are subject to Virginia income taxes in their individual capacities.[7] Each item of LLC income, gain, loss, or deduction has the same character for state tax purposes as for federal tax purposes.[8] Each member's share of LLC income is the same as that reported on the federal return, subject to certain state modifications.[9]

An LLC that is owned by two other limited liability companies may not pass through the property, payroll, and sales factors to the members of the member

---

[3] 23 Va. Admin. Code 10-130-10.
[4] Va. Code Ann. §§13.1-1061 to 13.1-1066.
[5] Rul. of the Commr., Va. Dept. of Taxn., P.D. 99-9 (Jan. 11, 1999).
[6] 23 Va. Admin. Code 10-130-10.
[7] Va. Code Ann. §13.1-1069.
[8] 23 Va. Admin. Code 10-130-20.A.4.
[9] 23 Va. Admin. Code 10-130-20.A.1.

LLC. Instead, the LLC must pass through these factors to the intervening LLC entities.[10]

[D]   Tax Returns

An LLC is not required to file a report or tax return with the Department of Taxation. However, the tax commissioner has the authority to issue regulations to require LLCs to furnish copies of the federal partnership return and attach schedules or any other information that the tax commissioner deems necessary.[11]

[E]   Single-Member LLCs

A single-member LLC is required to file a Virginia corporate income tax return only if it makes an election to be classified as a corporation for federal tax purposes. If no election is made, the single-member LLC is taxed as a pass-through entity, and the LLC's income is reported on the member's personal income tax return.[12]

The single member of the LLC is required to file and pay estimated personal income taxes on the income of the LLC.[13]

The LLC is not subject to the Virginia personal income tax withholding requirements if it has no employees, and if the LLC does not pay wages or salary to its sole member. There are no withholding requirements until the LLC pays wages or salary.[14]

A single-member LLC is not required to register and collect sales taxes if it provides only nontaxable services. It is required to register and submit to the use tax on any purchases that it makes for which the sales tax was not collected.[15]

Receipts from business conducted between a single-member LLC and an affiliated group are subject to the Virginia business, professional, and occupational licenses tax. A single-member LLC may not benefit from the exclusion from the tax that is available for transactions between members of an unaffiliated group. An individual owner of an LLC is not an incorporated entity, and therefore cannot be a common parent corporation for purposes of the exclusion.[16]

If the LLC conducts business within and outside of the State of Virginia, the LLC's income, property, payroll, and sales are included in the member's return to determine the income apportioned to Virginia.[17]

---

[10] Rul. of the Commr., Va. Dept. of Taxn., P.D. 97-59 (Feb. 12, 1997).
[11] Va. Code Ann. §58.1-392.
[12] Rul. of the Commr., Va. Dept. of Taxn., P.D. 99-57 (Apr. 20, 1999).
[13] Id.
[14] Id.
[15] Id.
[16] Rul. of the Commr., Va. Dept. of Taxn., P.D. 99-176 (June 30, 1999).
[17] Rul. of the Commr., Va. Dept. of Taxn., P.D. 97-343 (Aug. 28, 1997).

[F]   Nonresident Members

Nonresident members are taxed on their distributive shares of income of the LLC based on the corporate statutory formula[18] or on alternative allocation and apportionment methods approved by the Tax Commissioner.[19] The LLC may file a combined return for nonresident members with the consent of the Tax Commissioner.[20]

Nonresident members of an LLC are not subject to income taxes if the activities of the LLC do not rise to the level of a trade or business. For example, an LLC is not treated as a trade or business in Virginia if it derives all of its income from investments in stocks and bonds.[21]

A Delaware LLC doing business in Virginia was permitted to file a Virginia unified nonresident individual income tax return on behalf of all nonresident members who have no other Virginia income sources. The LLC's filing was required to include the following:[22]

- The LLC's total income and the amount attributable to Virginia;
- The LLC income or loss of nonresident members having no other Virginia income sources;
- A statement of the nonresident members' election by unanimous written consent to file a unified return;
- The name, address, Social Security number, and Virginia taxable income of each nonresident member;
- Computation of the LLC's Virginia taxable income attributable to nonresident members, without deductions, exemptions, or credits for income taxes paid to any other state;
- Signed statements from nonresident members affirming responsibility for their respective shares of total Virginia taxes;
- The filing of unified returns and payments made for declaration of estimated taxes; and
- The commissioner's letter authorizing the filing of a unified return.[23]

An Illinois LLC doing business in Virginia was permitted to file a Virginia unified nonresident individual tax return on behalf of all nonresident members under similar circumstances. Nonresident members who did not have other Virginia source income were not entitled to claim credits on their individual nonresident income tax returns for taxes paid on their behalf by the LLC.[24]

---

[18] 23 Va. Admin. Code 10-130-20.C.

[19] 23 Va. Admin. Code 10-110-180.

[20] 23 Va. Admin. Code 10-130-20.C.2.

[21] Rul. of the Commr., Va. Dept. of Taxn., P.D. 95-280 (Nov. 3, 1995), in which the LLC had no tangible personal property and no payroll and the expenses were all nonbusiness expenses.

[22] Rul. of the Commr., Va. Dept. of Taxn., P.D. 97-334 (Aug. 27, 1997).

[23] Id.

[24] Rul. of the Commr., Va. Dept. of Taxn., P.D. 97-335 (Aug. 27, 1997).

[G]   Annual Report

Virginia does not require an LLC to file an annual report.

[H]   Filing Fees

Virginia imposes the following filing fees on LLCs:[25]

Articles of organization	$100
Certificate of registration for foreign LLC	$100
Annual registration fee[26]	$ 50

[I]   References

M. Sargent & W. Schwidetzky, Limited Liability Company Handbook, Law —
Sample Documents — Forms, §4.29, Virginia Form of Operating Agreement (with
Organization Checklist) (1995-1996 ed.).

§23.49   WASHINGTON

Washington enacted laws authorizing LLCs effective October 1, 1994.[1]

[A]   State Tax Classification

An LLC is a business entity distinct from its members.[2] The classification of
an LLC for state income tax purposes is not applicable, since LLCs are taxed in
the same manner as other businesses for purposes of the Washington business
and occupations tax.

[B]   Taxation of LLC and Members

LLCs that do business in Washington are subject to various taxes, including
the state business and occupations tax; sales and use taxes; local, city, and county
sales and use taxes; lodging taxes; convention and trade center taxes; special
hotel/motel taxes; state public utility taxes; and other miscellaneous excise taxes.
The main tax is the state business and occupations tax, which is imposed on any
entity doing business in the state of Washington. The rate of tax ranges from .011

---

[25] Va. Code Ann. §13.1-1005.
[26] Va. Code Ann. §13.1-1062.
§23.49 [1] H.B. 1235, 1994 Wash. Laws; Wash. Rev. Code Ann. §§25.15.005 to 25.15.902.
[2] Wash. Rev. Code Ann. §25.15.060.

to 3.3 percent depending on the business or occupation in which the LLC engages. Different businesses are subject to varying types of exemptions and deductions. The tax is not an income tax. It is a tax imposed on the privilege of engaging in business activities in Washington.

Washington does not impose state personal income taxes on individuals.

[C] Tax Returns

An LLC doing business in Washington must file monthly, quarterly, and annual tax returns, reporting the state business and occupations tax, the sales tax, and other excise taxes. The return must be filed on Form REV40 2406A, Combined Excise Tax Return. The due date is printed on each monthly, quarterly, and annual return mailed to the taxpayer. The monthly returns are due on the twenty-fifth day of the month following the close of the month. The quarterly returns are due on the last day of the month following the close of the quarter. The annual return is due by January 31.

[D] Annual Report

Washington requires an LLC to file an annual report.[3] The annual report must set forth the following information:

- The name of the LLC and the state or country of organization.
- The street address of its registered office and the name of its registered agent at that office.
- In the case of a foreign LLC, the address of its principal office in he foreign state or country in which it was organized.
- The address of its principal place of business in the state of Washington.
- The names and addresses of the LLC members, or if the management of the LLC is vested in a manager or managers, then the name and address of manager or managers.
- A brief description of the nature of its business.

The annual report must be filed with the secretary of state within 120 days after the date on which the LLC filed its certificate of formation or on which a foreign LLC filed its application for registration. Subsequent annual reports must be filed with the secretary of state on such dates determined by the secretary of state.

---

[3] Wash. Rev. Code Ann. §25.15.105.

[E]   Filing Fees

There are the following filing fees in the state of Washington.[4]

Articles of organization	$175
Foreign LLC registration application	$175
Initial registration fee	$ 10
Annual registration fee after initial registration	$ 50

[F]   References

Washington State Bar Association, Continuing Legal Education, Limited Liability Companies in Washington (1994).

M. Sargent & W. Schwidetzky, Limited Liability Company Handbook, Law — Sample Documents — Forms, §4.30, Washington Form of Operating Agreement (1995-1996 ed.).

§23.50   WEST VIRGINIA

West Virginia enacted the West Virginia Limited Liability Company Act on March 6, 1992.[1]

[A]   State Tax Classification

An LLC that is classified as a partnership for federal tax purposes is also classified as a partnership for West Virginia income tax purposes.[2] If it is not classified as a partnership for federal tax purposes, then it is classified as a C corporation for West Virginia tax purposes.

[B]   Taxation of LLC and Members

An LLC that is classified as a partnership is not subject to the West Virginia personal income tax.[3] Members are taxed on their distributive shares of income.[4]

LLCs must pay severance and business franchise taxes.[5] The business franchise

---

[4] Wash. Rev. Code Ann. §25.15.805.

§23.50   [1] W. Va. Code §§31B-1-101 to 31B-13-1306.

[2] TSE-391, pt. B.8 (last sentence), W. Va. Dept. of Tax & Rev. (Jan. 19, 1993).

[3] W. Va. Code §11-21-3(b); W. Va. State Tax Dept. Reg. §3.2.

[4] Id.

[5] W. Va. Code §§11-13A-1 to 11-13A-25. See also W. Va. Code §11-13A-2(b)(8), which provides that a partnership that is subject to the tax includes a limited liability company that is classified as a partnership for federal tax purposes. The severance tax is imposed on every person engaged in severing, extracting, and producing for sale, profit, or commercial use any natural resource product.

tax is imposed on the privilege of doing business in the state. It is imposed on every LLC owning or leasing real or tangible personal property located in the state. For tax years after June 30, 1997, the tax is the greater of $50 or .70 percent of the tax base. Before June 30, 1997, the tax was the greater of $50 or .75 percent of the capital accounts.[6]

[C] Tax Returns

An LLC must file an annual tax return on Form IT-165, West Virginia Partnership Return of Income. The return must be mailed to the Department of Tax and Revenue, Internal Auditing Division, P.O. Box 1071, Charleston, WV 25324-1071. The LLC must file the return on or before the fifteenth day of the fourth month following the close of the tax year. The tax year for West Virginia purposes is the same as that for federal purposes. An LLC may obtain an extension of time to file return.

An LLC is required to file the return if any of the following apply:[7]

- It is organized in West Virginia.
- It is organized in another state and has a member who is a resident of West Virginia.
- It has any income from sources connected with Virginia. Income is treated as connected with West Virginia if it is attributable to ownership of any interest in real or tangible personal property in West Virginia or a business, trade, profession, or occupation carried on in West Virginia.

The LLC may obtain an extension of time to file its return by filing Form WV/NRW-2 or a substitute form. There is an automatic extension if the LLC obtains a federal extension.

All items of income and deduction reported on the West Virginia partnership return are the same as for federal tax purposes.

West Virginia requires certain items of income and deductions to be added to or subtracted from the LLC's federal partnership income. These modifications are set forth on Schedule A to Form IT-165.

The LLC must apportion income if it does business within and outside the state. The apportionment is based on a three-factor formula, including property, payroll, and sales. The apportionment schedule is set forth on Schedule B to Form IT-165.

An LLC must file Form WV/BFT-120, Business Franchise Tax Return, to report its annual business franchise tax. The report is used to determine the capital base subject to the West Virginia business franchise tax. The capital base is the average of the dollar amounts of the beginning and ending balances of certain entries from the balance sheet of IRS Form 1065 or as the form would have been filed with the IRS for the tax year. Capital accounts are the balance of the members'

---

[6] W. Va. Code §11-23-6(b)(3).
[7] W. Va. State Tax Dept. Reg. §58.2.

capital accounts as set forth on IRS Form 1065. LLCs not required by federal law to complete and file balance sheets are required to complete a pro forma balance sheet in order to calculate the tax liability. The pro forma balance sheet is a balance sheet that the LLC would have filed with the IRS if it had been required to do so.

[D] Withholding Taxes

An LLC doing business in West Virginia or deriving income from real or tangible property in West Virginia must withhold West Virginia income taxes from distributions for members who are not residents of West Virginia.[8] The nonresident member may avoid the withholding tax by providing the LLC with a West Virginia Nonresident Income Tax Agreement on Form WV/NRW-4.[9] The amount of withholding is 4 percent of the nonresident member's share of the LLC's federal taxable income or the portion of that income that is derived from or attributable to West Virginia sources, whether or not distributed.[10] The entire amount withheld must be remitted with the West Virginia partnership tax return.

The LLC is statutorily liable for payment of the amount of tax required to be withheld.[11] The tax is treated as a tax on the LLC. No member of the LLC has a right of action against the LLC with respect to any money withheld from members' distributive shares of income that is paid over to the tax commissioner.[12]

The LLC must furnish each nonresident member with a written information statement setting forth the following information:

- The amount of West Virginia effectively connected taxable income, whether distributed or not, for federal income tax purposes
- The amount deducted and withheld under West Virginia law
- Any other information that the tax commissioner may require

The LLC may satisfy this requirement by setting forth this information on any of the following:

- Form WV/NRW-2, Statement of West Virginia Income Tax Withheld for Nonresident Individual or Organization
- The supplemental information area of the nonresident member's copy of IRS Schedule K-1
- An attachment to the federal Schedule K-1 listing the same information

The LLC must file the information statements with its West Virginia return on Form IT-165. The information statements must be furnished to nonresident mem-

---

[8] TSD-391, W. Va. Dept. of Tax & Rev. (Jan. 19, 1993); W. Va. Code §11-21-71a.
[9] W. Va. Code §11-21-71a(k).
[10] The withholding taxes are computed under W. Va. Code §11-21-71a(b).
[11] W. Va. Code §11-21-71a(j), (k).
[12] W. Va. Code §11-21-71a.

bers on or before the due date of the LLC's tax return. A nonresident member must attach the statement to the West Virginia individual income tax return to claim a credit for the tax withheld.

Each nonresident member is allowed a credit for the member's share of the tax withheld by the LLC.[13] The nonresident member's share of the withholding taxes is treated as distributed by the LLC to the member.[14] The nonresident member may claim the amount withheld as a credit against the West Virginia income tax liability by attaching a copy of the information statement provided by the LLC.

[E] Composite Returns

Instead of withholding taxes on distributions of West Virginia source income to nonresident members, the LLC may satisfy the withholding requirements by filing Form IT-140NRC, West Virginia Nonresident Composite Income Tax Return.[15] The composite return may be filed for one or more of the nonresident members. The composite return is filed on a group basis as though there was only one taxpayer. The LLC must maintain a list setting forth the name, address, taxpayer identification number, and percentage of ownership of each nonresident member included in the return. This list may not be submitted with the composite return. Instead, it must be available to the department upon request. The return does not have to be signed by each nonresident member if it is signed by a member of the LLC. The LLC is responsible for collecting and remitting all income tax due at the time the return is filed. The return must be filed by the fifteenth day of the fourth month following the close of the tax year. There is a $50 processing fee that must accompany the composite return.

Any nonresident member included in the composite return who has income from any other West Virginia sources must file a separate nonresident personal income tax return for the tax year to report and pay personal income tax on the other West Virginia source income. The nonresident may claim a credit for the share of West Virginia income taxes remitted with the composite return.

[F] Annual Report

An LLC is required to file an annual report in West Virginia.[16] The annual report must list the following information:

- The name of the LLC and the state or country under whose laws it is organized.
- The address of its designated office and the name and address of its agent for service of process in West Virginia.

---

[13] Id.
[14] Id.
[15] W. Va. Code §11-21-51a.
[16] W. Va. Code §31B-2-211.

- The address of its principal office.
- The names and addresses of any managers.

The LLC must file the first annual report to the secretary of state between January 1 and April 1 of the year following the calendar year in which the LLC was organized or authorized to do business in the state. Subsequent annual filings must be sent to the secretary of state between January 1 and April 1 following each calendar year.

[G]   Filing Fees

There are the following filing fees in West Virginia:

Articles of organization	$ 10
Registration as foreign LLC	$150
Annual fee[17]	$ 25

§23.51   WISCONSIN

Wisconsin enacted the Wisconsin Limited Liability Company Act effective January 1, 1994.[1]

[A]   Department of Revenue Publication No. 119

The Wisconsin Department of Revenue issued Publication No. 119 in November 1996, setting forth its interpretation of the Wisconsin laws applicable to limited liability companies as of November 1, 1996. This publication has been modified in part by subsequent laws and regulations. The Department of Revenue interpretations of LLC state tax laws, as modified by subsequent legislation and regulations, are set forth below.

[B]   State Tax Classification

Wisconsin classifies an LLC in the same manner that the LLC is classified for federal tax purposes. A "corporation" subject to Wisconsin taxation includes a limited liability company that is classified as a corporation for federal tax purposes.[2] A single-member LLC that is disregarded as a separate entity for federal tax purposes is disregarded as a separate entity under the Wisconsin income and

---

[17] W. Va. Code §31B-1-108(c).

§23.51   [1] Act 112 (A.B. 820), 1993 Wis. Laws; Wis. Stat. Ann. §§183.0102 to 183.1305.

[2] Wis. Stat. Ann. §71.22(1).

franchise tax laws, and its owner is subject to the tax on or measured by the LLC's income.[3] Wisconsin recognized single-member LLCs commencing on July 1, 1996.[4]

[C] Contributions to LLC

Wisconsin follows the Internal Revenue Code with respect to the tax consequences of forming an LLC. To the extent allowed under the Code, contributions to an LLC are tax-free to both the LLC and the member. The member's basis in the LLC is equal to the basis in the property contributed.

[D] Recycling Surcharge

An LLC that is classified as a partnership is subject to the temporary recycling surcharge in the same manner as a partnership. The surcharge is reported on Wisconsin Form 3S, Partnership Temporary Recycling Surcharge.[5] The members of an LLC are jointly and severally liable for the temporary recycling surcharge if the LLC is delinquent in the payment of the tax and the LLC is classified as a partnership.[6]

An LLC that is classified as a corporation is subject to the temporary recycling surcharge in the same manner as a corporation. The surcharge is calculated on Wisconsin Form 4 or 5, as appropriate.[7]

The LLC is exempt from the temporary recycling surcharge if it meets any of the following conditions:

- It is not engaged in farming and has less than $4,000 of gross receipts from all trade and business activities for federal income tax purposes.
- It is engaged solely in farming and has less than $1,000 in net farm profit for federal income tax purposes.
- It is engaged in both farming and other trade or business activities and has less than $4,000,000 of gross receipts from all nonfarm trade or business activities for federal income tax purposes and less than $1,000 of net farm profits for federal income tax purposes.

An LLC uses its gross receipts to determine whether the temporary recycling surcharge applies. Gross receipts are the total receipts or sales from all trade and business activities, except farming, that are reportable for federal income tax purposes, before deducting returns and allowances or any other business expenses. An LLC that is subject to the surcharge then uses its "net business income" to

---

[3] Id.
[4] Wis. Stat. §1803.0201.
[5] Wis. Stat. Ann. §§77.92(4), 77.93(3m), 77.93(5).
[6] Wis. Stat. Ann. §§77.93(3m), 77.93(5).
[7] Wis. Stat. Ann. §§71.22(1), 77.93(1).

determine the amount of surcharge owed. The net business income is computed by combining the following items:

1. Ordinary income from trade or business activities from federal Form 1065, Schedule K, line 1;
2. Separately stated items of income, loss, and deduction from federal Form 1065, subject to certain exceptions;
3. Payments made to members not acting in their capacities as members under section 707(a) of the Internal Revenue Code; and
4. Development and enterprise zone credits computed and passed through to the members.

[E]   Withholding Taxes

LLCs are treated in the same manner as other business entities for withholding tax purposes. If the LLC is an employer, the LLC must withhold, deposit, and furnish reports of Wisconsin income taxes withheld in the same manner as other employers.[8]

If a member of an LLC performs services for the LLC and the IRS does not treat the member as an employee, the LLC is not required to withhold income taxes from payments made to the member for services performed.

A member, employee, or other responsible person who has a duty to withhold and deposit taxes for an LLC may be held personally liable for the LLC's Wisconsin income taxes withheld or required to be withheld.[9]

[F]   Sales and Use Taxes

For sales and use tax purposes, LLCs are treated in the same manner as other business entities. The LLC, as a retailer or consumer, must register, report, and pay Wisconsin sales and use taxes in the same manner as other retailers or consumers.[10]

A member, employee, or other responsible person who is under a duty to collect and remit sales and use taxes for an LLC may be personally liable for the LLC's Wisconsin sales and use taxes.[11]

[G]   Excise Taxes (Beverage, Fuel, Cigarette, and Tobacco)

For excise tax purposes, LLCs are treated in the same manner as other business entities. The LLC is required to register, pay, and furnish reports of Wisconsin excise taxes in the same manner as other business entities.

[8] Wis. Stat. Ann. §§71.63(3), 71.65(1)(a), 71.77.
[9] Wis. Stat. Ann. §71.83(1)(b)(2).
[10] Wis. Stat. Ann. §§77.52(7), 77.53(9), 77.53(9m).
[11] Wis. Stat. Ann. §77.60(9).

A member, employee, or other responsible person who is under a duty to pay motor vehicle fuel, alternate fuel, or aviation fuel taxes for the LLC may be held personally liable for the LLC's Wisconsin excise taxes that the LLC is required to pay.[12]

[H] Taxation of LLC Members Who Are Full-Year Wisconsin Resident Individuals, Estates, and Trusts

All LLC income or loss of full-year Wisconsin residents is includible in the computation of Wisconsin taxable income regardless of the situs of the LLC or the nature of income from the LLC. This includes business income, service income, and professional income unless otherwise exempt. Exempt income includes U.S. government interests.[13]

EXAMPLE

An LLC is engaged in business in and outside of Wisconsin. Member A is a full-year Wisconsin resident and has a 10 percent interest in the LLC. The LLC has ordinary income of $100,000, of which $60,000 is attributable to business conducted in Wisconsin. Member A is subject to Wisconsin income tax on $10,000 of the income.

The gain or loss from the disposition of an LLC interest is includible in Wisconsin net income for a full-year Wisconsin resident.[14]

[I] Taxation of LLC Members Who Are Nonresident Individuals, Estates, and Trusts

A nonresident member's share of LLC income or loss attributable to a business located in Wisconsin, services performed in Wisconsin, or real or tangible personal property located in Wisconsin is includible in the computation of Wisconsin taxable income. Business income is taxable whether or not the individual member conducts business in Wisconsin. However, LLC income derived from personal services, including professional services, is taxed to nonresident members if those nonresident members personally perform services in Wisconsin. The amount of personal service income attributable to a nonresident member's services performed in Wisconsin is taxable.[15]

---

[12] Wis. Stat. Ann. §78.70(6).
[13] Wis. Stat. Ann. §§71.02(1), 71.04(1)(a).
[14] Wis. Stat. Ann. §71.04(1)(a).
[15] *Id.*

EXAMPLE 1

A nonresident member of an LLC has a 30 percent interest in the LLC. The LLC is engaged in business within and outside of Wisconsin. The LLC has ordinary income of $150,000, of which $60,000 is attributable to its business activities in Wisconsin. The nonresident member is subject to Wisconsin income taxes on $18,000 of that income.

EXAMPLE 2

A nonresident member of an LLC has a 5 percent interest in an engineering firm that is organized as an LLC and operates within and outside of Wisconsin. The LLC receives income solely from the performance of engineering services. The nonresident member does not personally perform engineering services in Wisconsin. The nonresident's share of LLC income is not taxed in Wisconsin.

An interest in an LLC is intangible personal property. Any gain or loss realized on the disposition of an LLC interest is not includible in Wisconsin taxable interest. Gain or loss from the sale of intangible personal property follows the residence of a nonresident member.[16]

An LLC with two or more nonresident members whose only Wisconsin taxable income is their shares of LLC income or loss may file a combined Wisconsin individual fiduciary return on behalf of those qualified members. The LLC files its return on Form 1CNP.

[J] Taxation of LLC Members Who Are Part-Year Wisconsin Resident Individuals

Members of an LLC who are part-year residents must compute income taxes on their shares of LLC income or loss for the part of the year during which they were residents.[17] The computation is made as follows:[18]

Step 1. Assign an equal portion of each item of income, loss, or deduction to each day of the LLC's tax year.

Step 2. Multiply each daily portion of those items of income, loss, or deduction by a fraction that represents the member's portion, on that day, of the total LLC interest.

---

[16] *Id.*
[17] Wis. Stat. Ann. §71.04(3)(a).
[18] *Id.*

Step 3.   Net the items of income, loss, or deduction against the prior calculation for all of the days during which the member was a resident of the state.

During the time that the member is a nonresident, all LLC income or loss attributable to a business located in Wisconsin, to services the individual personally performs in Wisconsin, or to real and tangible personal property located in Wisconsin is taxable to the nonresident. The disposition of a membership interest in an LLC while a member is a nonresident is treated in the same manner as for nonresident partners. Since a member's interest in an LLC is classified as intangible personal property, any gain or loss realized on the disposition of an LLC interest for a nonresident is not includible in Wisconsin taxable income. Gain or loss from the sale of intangible personal property follows the residence of a nonresident member.[19]

EXAMPLE

A member has a 25 percent interest in an LLC that is engaged in business within and outside of Wisconsin. The LLC has ordinary income of $50,000, of which $40,000 is attributable to business activities in Wisconsin. The member is a Wisconsin resident for 90 days during the LLC's tax year. The member is subject to Wisconsin income taxes on $10,616 of LLC income, calculated as follows:

For the period of residence: 25% × 90/365 × $50,000 =	$ 3,082
For the period of nonresidence: 25% × 275/365 × $40,000 =	7,534
Total:	$10,616

[K]   Taxation of Corporate Members in LLC Classified as Partnership

Corporations engaged in business in Wisconsin are subject to the Wisconsin franchise or income tax. A corporation that is a member of an LLC is taxed depending on the location of the corporation's activities and the LLC's activities and on whether or not the LLC is an extension of the corporation's business.

---

[19] Wis. Stat. Ann. §§71.02(1), 71.04(2) and (3).

[1] Corporate Member Engaged in Business Wholly Within Wisconsin

A corporation that is engaged in business only in Wisconsin and that is a member of an LLC is taxed on the corporation's share of LLC net income or loss. A corporation engaged in business solely within Wisconsin is subject to tax on all income under the Wisconsin franchise or income tax laws.[20]

EXAMPLE 1

A corporation that is a member of an LLC is engaged in business only in Wisconsin. It owns a 40 percent membership interest in the LLC that is engaged in business only in Wisconsin. The LLC has $250,000 of net income. The corporation must include its $100,000 share of LLC net income in its Wisconsin net income.

EXAMPLE 2

A corporation is engaged in business only in Wisconsin. It acquires a 2 percent interest in an LLC that is engaged in business within and outside of Wisconsin. Its membership interest in the LLC is not an extension of the corporation's business. The corporation is not engaged in business in the states where the LLC is engaged in business. The LLC has $200,000 of net income, of which $80,000 is attributable to the Wisconsin operations. The corporation must report 100 percent of its net income to Wisconsin, including its $4,000 share of LLC net income, since the corporation is engaged in business only in Wisconsin.

[2] Corporate Member Engaged in Business Within and Outside of Wisconsin

A corporation that is engaged in business within and outside of Wisconsin and that is a member of an LLC is taxable on the corporation's share of LLC income or loss based on an apportionment formula.[21] The apportionment formula and factors depend on whether the LLC membership interest is an extension of the corporation's business. If the LLC is an extension of the corporation's business, the corporation must combine its share of the LLC's apportionment data with its own apportionment data to determine the income allocable to Wisconsin. If the ownership interest is not an extension of the corporation's business, no part of

---

[20] Wis. Stat. Ann. §71.25(4).
[21] Wis. Stat. Ann. §71.25(5)(a)14.

the LLC's property, payroll, or sales is included in either the numerator or the denominator of the corporation's property, payroll, and sales factors, respectively.[22]

EXAMPLE 1

A corporation is engaged in business within and outside of Wisconsin. It acquires a 60 percent interest in an LLC that is engaged in business in Wisconsin. The LLC is an extension of the corporation's business. The corporation must determine its Wisconsin net income under the apportionment method. The LLC has $300,000 of business income. The corporation must include $180,000, or 60 percent of the $300,000 of business income, in the corporation's apportionable income or loss. Sixty percent of the LLC's Wisconsin property, payroll, and sales are included in the numerator of the corporation's property, payroll, and sales factors, respectively, and 60 percent of the LLC's total property, payroll, and sales are included in the denominator of the corporation's property, payroll, and sales factors, respectively.

EXAMPLE 2

A corporation is engaged in business within and outside of Wisconsin. It acquires a 5 percent interest in an LLC that is engaged in business within and outside of Wisconsin. Its interest in the LLC is not an extension of the corporation's business. The corporation must determine its Wisconsin net income under the apportionment method. The LLC must include 5 percent of the LLC's business income or loss in the corporation's apportionable income or loss. No part of the LLC's property, payroll, or sales is included in either the numerator or the denominator of the corporation's property, payroll, and sales factors, respectively.

EXAMPLE 3

A corporation is engaged in business only in Wisconsin. It acquires a 55 percent interest in an LLC that is engaged in business within and outside of Wisconsin. The LLC is an extension of the corporation's business. Therefore, the corporation is engaged in business in the states where the LLC is engaged in business. The corporation must determine its Wisconsin net income under the apportionment method. It must include 55 percent of the LLC's business income or loss in its apportionable income or loss. Fifty-five percent of the LLC's Wisconsin property, payroll, and sales are included in the numerator of the corporation's property, payroll, and sales factors, respectively. Fifty-five percent of the LLC's total property, payroll, and sales

---

[22] Wis. Stat. Ann. §71.25(9)(e)8; Wis. Admin. Code §Tax 2.39(7).

are included in the denominator of the corporation's property, payroll, and sales factors, respectively.

[3]   Corporate Member Not Engaged in Business in Wisconsin

A corporation is subject to the Wisconsin franchise or income tax if it is not engaged in business in Wisconsin, but acquires an interest in an LLC that is engaged in business in Wisconsin where the LLC is an extension of the corporation's business. The corporate member is treated as engaged in business in Wisconsin as a result of holding an interest in the LLC. The corporation's share of LLC income or loss is includible in its apportionable income.[23] The corporation must combine its share of the LLC's apportionable data with its own apportionable data to determine the income allocable to Wisconsin.[24]

EXAMPLE

A corporation is not engaged in business in Wisconsin. It acquires a 50 percent interest in an LLC that is engaged in business in Wisconsin. The LLC is an extension of the corporation's business. Therefore, the corporation is engaged in business in Wisconsin and is subject to the Wisconsin franchise or income tax. The corporation must determine its Wisconsin net income under the apportionment method. It must include 50 percent of the LLC's business income or loss in its apportionable income or loss. Fifty percent of the LLC's Wisconsin property, payroll, and sales are included in the numerator of the corporation's property, payroll, and sales factors, respectively. Fifty percent of the LLC's total property, payroll, and sales are included in the denominator of the corporation's property, payroll, and sales factors, respectively. In addition, any Wisconsin destination sales made by the corporation are included in the numerator of its sales factor.

A corporation that is not engaged in business in Wisconsin and that acquires an interest in an LLC that is engaged in business in Wisconsin is not subject to Wisconsin franchise or income taxation if the LLC membership interest is not an extension of the corporation's business. The corporate member is not treated as engaged in business in Wisconsin based on an investment in an LLC.

EXAMPLE

A Delaware LLC that is a corporation is not engaged in business in Wisconsin. It acquires a 3 percent interest in an LLC that is engaged in

---

[23] Wis. Stat. Ann. §71.25(5)(a)14.
[24] Wis. Stat. Ann. §71.25(9)(e)8; Wis. Admin. Code §Tax 2.39(7).

business in Wisconsin. Its interest in the LLC is not an extension of the corporation's business. The corporation is not engaged in business in Wisconsin and is not subject to Wisconsin franchise or income tax on a share of the LLC's Wisconsin income.

[L] Taxation of LLC Members That Are Partnerships

An LLC or a partnership that is a member in another LLC doing business in Wisconsin must file a Wisconsin partnership return. The LLC member is considered to have income from business transacted in Wisconsin.

Partners in a partnership that is a member of an LLC are treated in the same manner as partners in other partnerships doing business in Wisconsin. Therefore, full-year Wisconsin resident individual partners must pay Wisconsin income taxes on their distributive shares of partnership income, including their shares of LLC income earned by the partnership. Nonresident individual partners are subject to Wisconsin income taxes on their distributive shares of partnership income, including their shares of LLC income derived by the LLC from business transacted in Wisconsin.

[M] Taxation of LLCs Classified as Corporations

A membership interest in an LLC that is classified as a corporation is treated in the same manner as stock in a regular corporation. The members in the LLC are taxed as follows.

[1] Full-Year Wisconsin Resident Members

Full-year resident individuals, estates, and trusts that are members of an LLC are subject to Wisconsin income tax on distributions of income received from an LLC regardless of where it is located. A Wisconsin resident must include any gain or loss in taxable income from the disposition of an LLC membership interest.[25]

[2] Nonresident Members

Nonresident members are not subject to Wisconsin income tax on distributions of LLC income if the LLC is classified as a corporation. Nonresident members do not include in their taxable income gain or loss realized on the sale or other disposition of a membership interest.[26]

---

[25] Wis. Stat. Ann. §§71.02(1), 71.04(1)(a).
[26] Id.

[3]   Part-Year Wisconsin Resident Members

Part-year resident members of an LLC that is classified as a corporation are taxed on distributions of LLC income received while residents of Wisconsin. Part-year residents must include in Wisconsin taxable income gain or loss realized on the disposition of LLC interests while Wisconsin residents.[27] Part-year residents are not taxed on distributions of LLC income received while nonresidents of Wisconsin. Part-year residents do not include in Wisconsin taxable income gain or loss realized on the disposition of LLC membership interests while nonresidents.

[4]   Corporate Members

A corporation that is a member of an LLC that is also classified as a corporation is subject to Wisconsin franchise or income tax on income distributions from the LLC, regardless of where the LLC is located, if the corporation's entire business income is attributable to Wisconsin. The corporation must include in Wisconsin net income gain or loss on the sale or other disposition of a membership interest.[28]

A multistate corporation that is a member of an LLC classified as a corporation must include income distributions and gain or loss upon disposition of an LLC membership interest in apportionable income if there is a unitary relationship between the corporation and the LLC or if the LLC is not an affiliate or a subsidiary and the LLC membership interest is part of the corporation's unitary investment activity and serves an operational function.[29]

[5]   Members Classified as Partnerships

An LLC that is classified as a corporation may have members who are partnerships or LLCs classified as partnerships. Distributions from the corporate LLC to the partnership LLC are treated in the same manner as dividend income. The partnership LLC member of the corporate LLC must include in Wisconsin taxable income gain or loss from the disposition of the LLC income. Gain or loss from the disposition is treated as income or loss from intangibles.

[N]   Gross Income

In determining gross income, an LLC must add back all state taxes and taxes of the District of Columbia that are value-added taxes, single-business taxes, or taxes measured by net income, gross income, gross receipts, or capital stock. These

---

[27] Wis. Stat. Ann. §§71.02, 71.04(2), (3).
[28] Wis. Stat. Ann. §§71.25(4), 71.26(2).
[29] Wis. Stat. Ann. §§71.25(5)(a), 71.26(2).

taxes are not deductible for Wisconsin tax purposes.[30] The taxes are added back on the state return to the extent they were deducted on the federal return.

[O] Disregarding Provisions in Operating Agreement

The provisions of an LLC operating agreement are disregarded in computing taxes, a member's distributive share of income, and the situs of LLC income if the provisions of the operating agreement do any of the following:[31]

- Characterize the consideration for payments to the member as services for the use of capital;
- Allocate to the member as income or gain from sources outside the state a greater proportion of the member's distributive share of LLC income or gain than the ratio of LLC income or gain from sources outside the state to LLC income or gain from all sources;
- Allocate to a member a greater proportion of LLC items of loss or deduction from sources in Wisconsin than the member's proportionate share of total LLC loss or deduction; or
- Determine a member's distributive share of an item of LLC income, gain, loss, or deduction for federal income tax purposes if the principal purpose of that determination is to avoid or evade Wisconsin taxes.

[P] Allocations

Profits and losses of a Wisconsin LLC are allocated among members on the basis of their contributions unless otherwise provided in the operating agreement. Distributions of cash or the assets of an LLC are made to members in the same manner that profits are allocated unless a distribution is varied by an operating agreement.[32]

[Q] Credit for Taxes Paid to Another State

Wisconsin residents who are members of an LLC that is classified as a partnership may claim credits for income or franchise taxes paid by the LLC to another state.[33] The income taxed by the other state is also considered income for Wisconsin tax purposes.

---

[30] Wis. Stat. Ann. §71.21(5).
[31] Wis. Stat. Ann. §71.04(3)(c).
[32] Wis. Stat. Ann. §§183.0503, 183.0602.
[33] Wis. Stat. Ann. §71.07(7).

[R]   Other Credits

Members of an LLC may also claim the following credits that pass through from the LLC:

- Development zones day care credit[34]
- Development zones environmental remediation[35]
- Development zones investment credit[36]
- Development zones jobs credit[37]
- Development zones location credit[38]
- Development zones sales tax credit[39]
- Federal historic structure credit[40]
- Farmland preservation credit[41]
- Farmland tax relief credit[42]

The LLC may not claim any of the credits listed above with respect to its members. Members of an LLC may not claim the research credit, research facilities credit, or development zone additional research credit. The development zone credits that the LLC passes through to its members are added to the LLC's income.[43]

[S]   Tax Returns

Wisconsin requires an LLC that is classified as a partnership to file the following tax returns:

- Form 3, Wisconsin Partnership Return.[44] A copy of federal Form 1065 and any other required schedules and statements must be attached to the return. A copy of any extension must be attached to the return. This form is used to report the income, deductions, gains, and losses from the operations of the LLC. Every LLC that is classified as a partnership and that has income from Wisconsin sources, regardless of the amount, must file Form 3. The return must be filed with the Wisconsin Department of Revenue, P.O. Box 59, Madison, WI 53785-0001. The return must be filed by the fifteenth day of the fourth month following the close of the LLC's tax year. The LLC may obtain an extension of time to file the return by obtaining a federal extension

---

[34] Wis. Stat. Ann. §71.07(2dd).
[35] Wis. Stat. Ann. §71.07(2de).
[36] Wis. Stat. Ann. §71.07(2di).
[37] Wis. Stat. Ann. §71.07(2dj).
[38] Wis. Stat. Ann. §71.07(2dl).
[39] Wis. Stat. Ann. §71.07(2ds).
[40] Wis. Stat. Ann. §71.07(9m).
[41] Wis. Stat. Ann. §§71.58(1), 71.58(8), 71.59(1).
[42] Wis. Stat. Ann. §71.07(3m).
[43] Wis. Stat. Ann. §71.21(4).
[44] Wis. Stat. Ann. §71.20(1).

request and attaching the copy of the federal extension to the Wisconsin return.

- Schedule 3K-1, Partner's Share of Income, Deductions, Etc. This form sets forth each member's distribu tive share of the LLC's income, gain, loss, deductions, and credit.
- Form 3S, Wisconsin Partnership Temporary Recycling Surcharge. This form is used to report the temporary recycling surcharge of up to $9,800. The temporary recycling surcharge applies to LLCs doing business in Wisconsin for tax years ending after April 1, 1991, and ending before April 1, 1999. Every LLC that is classified as a partnership and that does business in Wisconsin must file the form and pay the tax unless it meets one of the applicable exemptions.

An LLC that is classified as a corporation must file Wisconsin Form 4 or 5, Corporation Franchise or Income Tax Return.[45]

[T] *Conversion from Partnership to LLC*

If an existing partnership becomes an LLC and the IRS does not treat it as a termination of the existing partnership, the same treatment applies for Wisconsin tax purposes. If the members' interests in the LLC's profits, losses, and capital remain the same after the conversion from a partnership to an LLC, no gain or loss is recognized upon the conversion. If the conversion is not treated as a partnership termination, no existing accounting periods or methods are affected. The partnership and the LLC do not have to file short-period returns for the year of the conversion.

If an existing partnership becomes an LLC and the IRS does not require the LLC to obtain a new federal employer identification number, the LLC is not required to obtain a new Wisconsin employer identification number.

If a partnership becomes an LLC and the IRS does not require the LLC to obtain a new federal employer identification number, the LLC is not required to obtain a new Wisconsin seller's permit or a new use tax or consumer's use tax number. An existing partnership that becomes an LLC is not subject to sales or use tax on the transfer of its assets to the LLC if there is no change in the ownership interest of its members.

[U] *Conversion of Corporation to LLC*

The conversion of a corporation into an LLC is generally treated as a taxable reorganization. The corporation must dissolve and reorganize as an LLC. An existing corporation that dissolves and becomes an LLC must obtain a new Wisconsin employer identification number. An existing corporation that dissolves and

---

[45] Wis. Stat. Ann. §§71.22(1), 71.24(1).

becomes an LLC must obtain a new Wisconsin seller's permit and a new use tax or consumer's use tax number. An existing corporation that becomes an LLC is not subject to sales or use tax on the transfer of its assets to the LLC if there is no change in the ownership interest of its members.

[V]   Real Estate Transfer Fees

The conveyance of real estate from a partnership to an LLC pursuant to the reorganization of a partnership as an LLC is subject to the Wisconsin real estate transfer fee.[46]

[W]   Annual Report

A domestic LLC is not required to file an annual report in Wisconsin. A foreign LLC that is qualified to do business in Wisconsin must file an annual report.[47]

[X]   Filing Fees

There are the following filing fees in Wisconsin:[48]

Articles of organization	$ 90
Foreign LLC registration certificate	$100
Annual registration fee	$ 0

[Y]   References

M. Sargent & W. Schwidetzky, Limited Liability Company Handbook, Law — Sample Documents — Forms, §4.31, Wisconsin Form of Articles of Organization (and Related Documents) and Operating Agreement (1995-1996 ed.).

§23.52   WYOMING

Wyoming was the first state to authorize LLCs. It enacted the Wyoming Limited Liability Company Act in 1977.[1]

---

[46] Wolter, Wis. Tax Appeals Commn., No. 96-T-941 (May 6, 1998).
[47] Wis. Stat. §183.0120.
[48] Wis. Stat. Ann. §183.0114.
§23.52   [1] Wyo. Stat. §§17-15-101 to 17-15-147.

[A]   Taxation of LLC and Members

There is an annual tax of $100 on each LLC. The tax is due and payable on January 2 of each year. The tax is delinquent if not paid by February 1.[2] There is a penalty of $100 if the tax is not timely paid.[3]

Wyoming has no other individual or corporate income taxes. Members are not taxed on their distributive shares of LLC income.

[B]   Allocations

Unless otherwise provided in the operating agreement, an LLC's profits and losses are allocated on the basis of the value of the contributions made by each member, less the contributions returned by the LLC to the member.[4]

[C]   Annual Report

An LLC is not required to file an annual report in Wyoming.

[D]   Filing Fees

Wyoming imposes the following filing fees on LLCs:[5]

Articles of organization	$100 or more depending on total capitalization
Registration of foreign LLC	$100 or more depending on capitalization
Annual tax	$100

If the capital of the LLC is between $50,001 and $100,000, the fees for filing the articles of organization and for issuing a certificate of authority for a foreign LLC are increased to $200. If the capital of the LLC is over $100,000, the filing fee is $200 for the first $100,000 of capital, plus $1 for each additional $1,000 of capital, with a maximum fee of $25,000. Members of an LLC who are part-year residents must compute income taxes on their shares of LLC income or loss for the part of the year during which they were residents.[6] The computation is made as follows:[7]

1.   Assign an equal portion of each item of income, loss, or deduction to each day of the LLC's tax year.

---

[2] Wyo. Stat. §17-15-132(a)(iv).
[3] Wyo. Stat. §17-15-132(a)(vi).
[4] Wyo. Stat. §17-15-119.
[5] Wyo. Stat. §17-15-132.
[6] Wyo. Stat. §71.04(3)(a).
[7] *Id.*

2. Multiply each daily portion of those items of income, loss, or deduction by a fraction that represents the member's portion, on that day, of the total LLC interest.

3. Net the items of income, loss, or deduction against the prior calculations for all of the days during which the member was a resident of the state.[8]

---

[8] Wyo. Stat. §17-15-132(a)(i).

24

Asset Protection, Charging Orders, and Creditors' Rights

§24.01   RIGHTS OF CREDITORS OF MEMBER

[A]   Overview

LLCs are sometimes used to protect a person's assets from creditors. A parent typically transfers assets into an LLC, and then transfers some or all the membership interests to family members. The intended result is that creditors who obtain a judgment against any member of the LLC will not be able to attach the LLC assets.

State laws provide one or more the following remedies for creditors who obtain a judgment against a member of an LLC:

- Charging order against the membership interest;
- Foreclosure of the membership interest; and
- Other remedies as approved by the court.

State	Charging Order	Foreclosure	Other Remedies	Statutory Authority
Alabama	x			Ala. Code §10-12-35
Alaska	x			Alaska Stat. §10.50.380
Arizona	x			Ariz. Rev. Stat. Ann. §29-655

State	Charging Order	Foreclosure	Other Remedies	Statutory Authority
Arkansas	x			Ark. Code Ann. §4-32-705
California	x	x	x	Cal. Corp. Code §17302; Cal. Code of Civ. Proc. §§708.310, 708.320
Colorado	x	x	x	Colo. Rev. Stat. Ann. §7-80-703
Connecticut	x			Conn. Gen. Stat. Ann. §34-171
D.C.	x			D.C. Code Ann. §29-1038
Delaware	x			Del. Code Ann. tit. 6, §18-703
Florida	x			Fla. Stat. Ann. §608.433(4)
Georgia	x	x	x	Ga. Code Ann. §14-11-504
Hawaii	x	x		Haw. Rev. Stat. Ann. §428-504
Idaho	x			Idaho Code §53-637
Illinois	x	x	x	805 ILCS §180/30-20
Indiana	x			Ind. Code Ann. §23-18-6-7
Iowa	x			Iowa Code §490A.904
Kansas	x			Kan. Stat. Ann. §17-76,113
Kentucky	x			Ky. Rev. Stat. §275.260
Louisiana	x			La. Rev. Stat. Ann. §12:1331
Maine	x			Me. Rev. Stat. Ann. tit. 31, §686
Maryland	x			Md. Corps. & Ass'ns Code Ann. §4A-607
Massachusetts	x			M.G.L.A. ch. 156C, §40
Michigan	x			Mich. Comp. Laws Ann. §450.4507
Minnesota	x			Minn. Stat. §322B.32
Mississippi	x			Miss. Code Ann. §79-29-703
Missouri	x			Mo. Rev. Stat. §347.119
Montana	x	x	x	Mont. Code Ann. §35-8-705

State	Charging Order	Foreclosure	Other Remedies	Statutory Authority
Nebraska				No statutory provision
Nevada	x	x	x	Nev. Rev. Stat. Ann. §86.401
New Hampshire	x			N.H. Rev. Stat. Ann. §304-C:47
New Jersey	x			N.J. Stat. Ann. §42:2B-45
New Mexico	x			N.M. Stat. Ann. §53-19-35
New York	x			N.Y. LLC §607
North Carolina	x			N.C. Gen. Stat. §57C-5-03
North Dakota	x			N.D. Cent. Code §10-32-34
Ohio	x			Ohio Rev. Code Ann. §1705.19
Oklahoma	x			Okla. Stat. Ann. tit. 18, §2034
Oregon	x			Or. Rev. Stat. §63.259
Pennsylvania	x	x	x	15 Pa. Cons. Stat. §§8904(a), 8345
Rhode Island	x			R.I. Gen. Laws §7-16-37
South Carolina	x	x	x	S.C. Code Ann. §33-44-504
South Dakota	x	x	x	S.D. Codified Laws Ann. §47-34A-504
Tennessee	x			Tenn. Code Ann. §48-218-104
Texas	x		x (case law)	Tex. Rev. Civ. Stat. Ann. art. 1528n, 4.06A
Utah	x	x	x	Utah Code Ann. §48-2c-1103
Vermont	x	x	x	Vt. Stat. Ann. tit. 11, §3074
Virginia	x			Va. Code Ann. §13.1-1041
Washington	x			Wash. Rev. Code §25.15.255
West Virginia	x	x	x	W. Va. Code §31B-5-504
Wisconsin	x			Wis. Stat. §183.0705
Wyoming	x	x		Wyo. Stat. §17-15-145

[B] Charging Order

All of the states permit a creditor to obtain a charging order against the membership interest of the judgment debtor. A judgment creditor must apply to the court of competent jurisdiction for the charging order. The charging order charges the member's interest in the LLC with payment of the judgment, plus interest. To the extent charged, the judgment creditor is treated as an assignee of the member's economic interest.

The creditor has no voting rights. The debtor and other members of the LLC retain voting rights and therefore have the power to decide if and when distributions will be made. The creditor cannot compel the LLC to make distributions to satisfy the member's debt. The creditor's only right is to receive distributions by the LLC to that particular member.

There is an exception to this rule in some states if the LLC is a single-member LLC. The LLC is treated as a disregarded entity. The creditor may attach the assets of the single-member LLC in satisfaction of the judgment.

[C] Foreclosure

A number of states provide for foreclosure in addition to the charging order.[1] On request of the judgment creditor, the court may order foreclosure of the membership interest subject to the charging order. The purchaser at the foreclosure sale has the rights of a transferee. The judgment debtor has no rights in the LLC after the foreclosure sale.

To protect the rights of the judgment debtor and the other members of the LLC, the statutes normally provide that the foreclosed membership interest may be redeemed (a) by the judgment debtor, (b) with property other than LLC property, by one or more of the other members of the LLC, and (c) with LLC property, by one or more of the other members with the consent of all the members whose interests are not so charged.[2]

Some states, such as Texas, permit foreclosure by case law rather than statute. Alaska[3] and Oklahoma prohibit foreclosure sales.

[D] Other Remedies

Several state statutes provide that the court may appoint a receiver of the share of distributions payable to the judgment debtor from the LLC and may make all

---

§24.01   [1] *See, e.g.,* Ariz. Rev. Stat. Ann. §29-1044.B; Ga. Code Ann. §14-11-504; Mont. Code Ann. §35-8-705; Nev. Rev. Stat. Ann. §86.401.3, 4; 15 Pa. Cons. Stat. §8345; S.C. Code Ann. §33-44-504(c); S.D. Codified Laws Ann. §47-34A-504(b), (c); Utah Code Ann. §48-2c-1103(3); Vt. Stat. Ann. tit. 11, §3074(b), (c); W. Va. Code §31B-5-504(b), (c).

[2] *See, e.g.,* Ariz. Rev. Stat. Ann. §29-1044.C; Cal. Corp. Code §17302(c); 805 ILCS §180/30-20(c); Mont. Code Ann. §35-8-705; Nev. Rev. Stat. Ann. §86.401.3, 4; N.H. Rev. Stat. Ann. §§304-A:28.II; 15 Pa. Cons. Stat. §8345; S.C. Code Ann. §33-44-504(c); S.D. Codified Laws Ann. §47-34A-504(b), (c); Utah Code Ann. §48-2c-1103(3); Vt. Stat. Ann. tit. 11, §3074(b), (c); W. Va. Code §31B-5-504(b), (c).

[3] Alaska Stat. §10.50.380(c).

other orders, directions, accounts, and inquiries that the judgment debtor could have made or that the circumstances of the case may require.[4] Georgia permits a judgment creditor to pursue any remedies in addition to the charging order and foreclosure, including process of garnishment served on the LLC.[5]

Some state statutes provide that the charging order, foreclosure, and/or other remedies specified in the statute are the sole and exclusive remedies of the judgment creditor against the debtor with respect to the member's interest in the LLC.[6]

The charging order, foreclosure, and other remedies specified in the statutes do not deprive a member of rights under applicable exemption laws with respect to the member's interest in the LLC.[7]

§24.02   RIGHTS OF CREDITORS OF LLC

Persons who obtain a judgment against the LLC may under certain circumstances attach the assets of the member. Several states provide that a member may be liable to judgment creditors of the LLC to the same extent that shareholders of a corporation are liable under the "piercing the corporate veil" doctrine. Other states provide that a member is liable for his own misconduct, such as malpractice in a professional LLC. There are other circumstances under which a member may be liable to a judgment creditor of the LLC, or sued directly by the third party. These are discussed in detail in Chapter 2.[1]

§24.03   TAX CONSEQUENCES OF CHARGING ORDER

There is a split of authority on the tax consequences of a charging order. Some commentators believe that the creditor who obtains the charging order is liable for taxes on the debtor's allocable share of LLC income.[1] In such case, the LLC must send the creditor a Schedule K-1 reflecting the taxable income allocated to the charging order. The creditor must pay taxes on the income whether or not

---

[4] See, e.g., Ariz. Rev. Stat. Ann. §29-1044.A; 805 ILCS §180/30-20(a); Mont. Code Ann. §35-8-705; Nev. Rev. Stat. Ann. §86.401; N.H. Rev. Stat. Ann. §§304-A:28.I; 15 Pa. Cons. Stat. §8345; S.C. Code Ann. §33-44-504(a); S.D. Codified Laws Ann. §47-34A-504(a); Utah Code Ann. §48-2c-1103(1); Vt. Stat. Ann. tit. 11, §3074(a); W. Va. Code §31B-5-504(a).

[5] Ga. Code Ann. §14-11-504(b).

[6] See, e.g., Ala. Code §10-12-35(a); Alaska Stat. §10.50.380(c); Ariz. Rev. Stat. Ann. §29-1044.E; Cal. Corp. Code §17302(e); 805 ILCS §180/30-20(e); Kan. Stat. Ann. §17-76,113; Minn. Stat. §322B.32; Nev. Rev. Stat. Ann. §86.401.5; N.J. Stat. Ann. §42:2B-45; N.D. Cent. Code §10-32-34.3; Okla. Stat. Ann. tit. 18, §2034; S.C. Code Ann. §33-44-504(e); S.D. Codified Laws Ann. §47-34A-504(e); Utah Code Ann. §48-2c-1103(5), (6); Vt. Stat. Ann. tit. 11, §3074(e); W. Va. Code §31B-5-504(e); Wyo. Stat. §17-15-145.

[7] See, e.g., Ala. Code §10-12-35(b); Alaska Stat. §10.50.380(d); Ariz. Rev. Stat. Ann. §29-1044.D; Cal. Corp. Code §17302(d); Del. Code Ann. tit. 6, §18-703; 805 ILCS §180/30-20(d); N.H. Rev. Stat. Ann. §§304-A:28.III; Wyo. Stat. §17-15-145.

§24.02   [1] See §2.03 supra.

§24.03   [1] See, e.g., Arthur A. DiPadova & Kevin A. Kilroy, "How Family With the Partnerships Help Protect Assets," 137 N.J.L.J. 11, 44 (1994); Lewis D. Solomon and Lewis J. Saret, Asset Protection Strategies: Tax and Legal Aspects, §3.23, at p. 62 (1999).

distributed. The creditor will be reluctant to seek a charging order since the creditor will be "KO'd by the K-1."

Other commentators believe that the creditor who obtains a charging order is not liable on the undistributed income allocable to the judgment debtor. Instead, the creditor is only liable for actual distributions of income to the creditor.[2]

One commentator suggested that if a judgment creditor is somehow taxable on the charging order proceeds, then the debtor should have cancellation of indebtedness income to the extent that the judgment creditor actually receives distributions (thereby relieving the debtor of the obligation to pay the creditor).[3]

In Revenue Ruling 77-137, the IRS determined that the assignee of a limited partnership interest was the beneficial owner of such interest. As assignee, the creditor was required to "report the distributive share of partnership items of income, gain or loss, deduction, and credit attributable to the assignee interest . . . in the same manner and the same amounts that would be required if [the assignee] was a substitute limited partner." The most important factor was that the assignee acquired substantially all dominion and control over the limited partnership interest, even though the general partner did not consent to the transfer. Under the terms of the assignment, the assignee irrevocably assigned profits and losses of the partnership and all distributions, including liquidating distributions, to the assignee. The assigning partner agreed to exercise any residual powers in favor of and in the interests of the assignee partner. The assignor was the nominal limited partner under local law after the assignment.

In *Evans v. Commissioner*,[4] the court concluded that the assignee of a general partner, and not the assigning general partner himself, was the "partner" for purposes of reporting partnership distributive shares.

In GCM 36960, the IRS determined that an assignee of a limited partnership interest is required to report distributive shares of partnership income or loss attributable to the assigned interest, even though he or she does not become a substituted limited partner, when the assignee acquires dominion and control over the partnership interest. However, to the extent that the assignor retains substantial rights with respect to the interest that are not exercisable solely on behalf of the assignees, the assignee does not have the requisite dominion and control.

These rulings deal with a partner who voluntarily assigns his partnership interest to a third party. They do not deal with a judgment creditor and a debtor partner or member of an LLC. A judgment creditor who obtains a charging order arguably does not have the requisite dominion and control. The assignee does not participate in the management and affairs of the LLC without the consent of the manager or members of the LLC. The assignee is not a party to any action affecting the assignor's retained economic rights as a member of the LLC. The managers and members of the LLC do not have any fiduciary obligations to the assignee. The assignee may not become a member of the LLC without compliance with the terms of the LLC operating agreement. The judgment creditor receives

[2] Christopher M. Riser, Tax Consequences of Charging Orders, Asset Protection J. (Winter 1999).
[3] *Id.*
[4] Evans v. Commissioner, 447 F.2d 547 (7th Cir. 1971).

only a right to future distributions allocable to the judgment debtor, if and when such distributions are made. The debtor retains all other rights.[5]

§24.04   TAX CONSEQUENCES OF FORECLOSURE

The tax consequences of a foreclosure are clearer than the tax consequences of a charging order. The reason is that the debtor often retains significant rights in a membership interest subject to a charging order but does not retain any rights with respect to a membership interest after a foreclosure.

The person acquiring a membership interest through a foreclosure sale is taxable on his or her distributable share of income, gain, loss, or deductions. The judgment debtor is taxable on the distributable share through the date of foreclosure. The judgment debtor is not taxable on the distributable share allocable to the foreclosed membership interest after the date of the foreclosure unless the judgment debtor redeems the membership interest.

---

[5] Christopher M. Riser, Tax Consequences of Charging Orders, Asset Protection J. (Winter 1999).

APPENDIX A

FORMS

FORM 1-1   IRS Form 8832, Election Classification

Form **8832** (Rev. September 2002) Department of the Treasury Internal Revenue Service	**Entity Classification Election**	OMB No. 1545-1516

Type or Print	Name of entity	EIN ▶
	Number, street, and room or suite no. If a P.O. box, see instructions.	
	City or town, state, and ZIP code. If a foreign address, enter city, province or state, postal code and country.	

1   Type of election (see instructions):

a ☐ Initial classification by a newly-formed entity.

b ☐ Change in current classification.

2   Form of entity (see instructions):

a ☐ A domestic eligible entity electing to be classified as an association taxable as a corporation.

b ☐ A domestic eligible entity electing to be classified as a partnership.

c ☐ A domestic eligible entity with a single owner electing to be disregarded as a separate entity.

d ☐ A foreign eligible entity electing to be classified as an association taxable as a corporation.

e ☐ A foreign eligible entity electing to be classified as a partnership.

f ☐ A foreign eligible entity with a single owner electing to be disregarded as a separate entity.

3   Disregarded entity information (see instructions):
a   Name of owner ▶ ....
b   Identifying number of owner ▶ ....
c   Country of organization of entity electing to be disregarded (if foreign) ▶ ....

4   Election is to be effective beginning (month, day, year) (see instructions) . . . . ▶ ___/___/___

5   Name and title of person whom the IRS may call for more information | **6   That person's telephone number** ( )

Consent Statement and Signature(s) (see instructions)

Under penalties of perjury, I (we) declare that I (we) consent to the election of the above-named entity to be classified as indicated above, and that I (we) have examined this consent statement, and to the best of my (our) knowledge and belief, it is true, correct, and complete. If I am an officer, manager, or member signing for all members of the entity, I further declare that I am authorized to execute this consent statement on their behalf.

Signature(s)	Date	Title

For Paperwork Reduction Act Notice, see page 4.   Cat. No. 22598R   Form **8832** (Rev. 9-2002)

General Instructions

Section references are to the Internal Revenue Code unless otherwise noted.

Purpose of Form

For Federal tax purposes, certain business entities automatically are classified as corporations. See items **1** and **3** through **8** under the definition of **corporation** on this page. Other business entities may choose how they are classified for Federal tax purposes. Except for a business entity automatically classified as a corporation, a business entity with at least two members can choose to be classified as either an association taxable as a corporation or a partnership, and a business entity with a single member can choose to be classified as either an association taxable as a corporation or disregarded as an entity separate from its owner.

Generally, an eligible entity that does not file this form will be classified under the default rules described below. An eligible entity that chooses not to be classified under the default rules or that wishes to change its current classification must file Form 8832 to elect a classification. The IRS will use the information entered on this form to establish the entity's filing and reporting requirements for Federal tax purposes.

60-month limitation rule. Once an eligible entity makes an election to change its classification, the entity generally cannot change its classification by election again during the 60 months after the effective date of the election. However, the IRS may (**by private letter ruling**) permit the entity to change its classification by election within the 60-month period if more than 50% of the ownership interests in the entity as of the effective date of the election are owned by persons that did not own any interests in the entity on the effective date of the entity's prior election. See Regulations section 301.7701-3(c)(1)(iv) for more details.

Note: *The 60-month limitation does not apply if the previous election was made by a newly formed eligible entity and was effective on the date of formation.*

Default Rules

Existing entity default rule. Certain domestic and foreign entities that were in existence before January 1, 1997, and have an established Federal tax classification generally do not need to make an election to continue that classification. If an existing entity decides to change its classification, it may do so subject to the 60-month limitation rule. See Regulations sections 301.7701-3(b)(3) and 301.7701-3(h)(2) for more details.

Domestic default rule. Unless an election is made on Form 8832, a domestic eligible entity is:

1. A partnership if it has two or more members.

2. Disregarded as an entity separate from its owner if it has a single owner.

A change in the number of members of an eligible entity classified as an association does not affect the entity's classification. However, an eligible entity classified as a partnership will become a disregarded entity when the entity's membership is reduced to one member and a disregarded entity will be classified as a partnership when the entity has more than one member.

Foreign default rule. Unless an election is made on Form 8832, a foreign eligible entity is:

1. A partnership if it has two or more members and **at least** one member does not have limited liability.

2. An association taxable as a corporation if all members have limited liability.

3. Disregarded as an entity separate from its owner if it has a single owner that does not have limited liability.

Definitions

Association. For purposes of this form, an association is an eligible entity that is taxable as a corporation by election or, for foreign eligible entities, under the default rules (see Regulations section 301.7701-3).

Business entity. A business entity is any entity recognized for Federal tax purposes that is not properly classified as a trust under Regulations section 301.7701-4 or otherwise subject to special

treatment under the Code. See Regulations section 301.7701-2(a).

Corporation. For Federal tax purposes, a corporation is any of the following:

1. A business entity organized under a Federal or state statute, or under a statute of a federally recognized Indian tribe, if the statute describes or refers to the entity as incorporated or as a corporation, body corporate, or body politic.

2. An association (as determined under Regulations section 301.7701-3).

3. A business entity organized under a state statute, if the statute describes or refers to the entity as a joint-stock company or joint-stock association.

4. An insurance company.

5. A state-chartered business entity conducting banking activities, if any of its deposits are insured under the Federal Deposit Insurance Act, as amended, 12 U.S.C. 1811 et seq., or a similar Federal statute.

6. A business entity wholly owned by a state or any political subdivision thereof, or a business entity wholly owned by a foreign government or any other entity described in Regulations section 1.892-2T.

7. A business entity that is taxable as a corporation under a provision of the Code other than section 7701(a)(3).

8. A foreign business entity listed on page 5. See Regulations section 301.7701-2(b)(8) for any exceptions and inclusions to items on this list and for any revisions made to this list since these instructions were printed.

Disregarded entity. A disregarded entity is an eligible entity that is treated as an entity that is not separate from its single owner. Its separate existence will be ignored for Federal tax purposes unless it elects corporate tax treatment.

Eligible entity. An eligible entity is a business entity that is not included in items **1** or **3** through **8** under the definition of corporation above.

Limited liability. A member of a foreign eligible entity has limited liability if the member has no personal liability for any debts of or claims against the entity by reason of being a member. This determination is based solely on the statute or law under which the entity is organized (and, if relevant, the entity's organizational documents). A member has personal liability if the creditors of the entity may seek satisfaction of all or any part of the debts or claims against the entity from the member as such. A member has personal liability even if the member makes an agreement under which another person (whether or not a member of the entity) assumes that liability or agrees to indemnify that member for that liability.

Partnership. A partnership is a business entity that has **at least** two members and is not a corporation as defined on page 2.

Who Must File

File this form for an **eligible entity** that is one of the following:

• A domestic entity electing to be classified as an association taxable as a corporation.

• A domestic entity electing to change its current classification (even if it is currently classified under the default rule).

• A foreign entity that has more than one owner, all owners having limited liability, electing to be classified as a partnership.

• A foreign entity that has at least one owner that does not have limited liability, electing to be classified as an association taxable as a corporation.

• A foreign entity with a single owner having limited liability, electing to be an entity disregarded as an entity separate from its owner.

• A foreign entity electing to change its current classification (even if it is currently classified under the default rule).

Do not file this form for an eligible entity that is:

• Tax-exempt under section 501(a) or

• A real estate investment trust (REIT), as defined in section 856.

Effect of Election

The Federal tax treatment of elective changes in classification as described in Regulations section 301.7701-3(g)(1) is summarized as follows:

• If an eligible entity classified as a partnership elects to be classified as an association, it is deemed that the

partnership contributes all of its assets and liabilities to the association in exchange for stock in the association, and immediately thereafter, the partnership liquidates by distributing the stock of the association to its partners.

• If an eligible entity classified as an association elects to be classified as a partnership, it is deemed that the association distributes all of its assets and liabilities to its shareholders in liquidation of the association, and immediately thereafter, the shareholders contribute all of the distributed assets and liabilities to a newly formed partnership.

• If an eligible entity classified as an association elects to be disregarded as an entity separate from its owner, it is deemed that the association distributes all of its assets and liabilities to its single owner in liquidation of the association.

• If an eligible entity that is disregarded as an entity separate from its owner elects to be classified as an association, the owner of the eligible entity is deemed to have contributed all of the assets and liabilities of the entity to the association in exchange for the stock of the association.

Note: *For information on the Federal tax treatment of elective changes in classification, see Regulations section 301.7701-3(g).*

When To File

See the instructions for line 4.

A newly formed entity may be eligible for late election relief under Rev. Proc. 2002-59, 2002-39 I.R.B. 615 if:

• The entity failed to obtain its desired classified election solely because Form 8832 was not timely filed,

• The due date for the entity's desired classification tax return (excluding extension) for the tax year beginning with the entity's formation date has not passed, and

• The entity has reasonable cause for its failure to make a timely election.

To obtain relief, a newly formed entity must file Form 8832 on or before the due date of the first Federal tax return (excluding extensions) of the entity's desired classification. The entity must also

write "FILED PURSUANT TO REV. PROC. 2002-59" at the top of the form. The entity must attach a statement to the form explaining why it failed to file a timely election. If Rev. Proc. 2002-59 does not apply, an entity may seek relief for a late entity election by requesting a private letter ruling and paying a user fee in accordance with Rev. Proc. 2002-1, 2002-1 I.R.B. 1 (or its successor).

Where To File

File Form 8832 with the Internal Revenue Service Center, Philadelphia, PA 19255. Also attach a copy of Form 8832 to the entity's Federal income tax or information return for the tax year of the election. If the entity is not required to file a return for that year, a copy of its Form 8832 **must** be attached to the Federal income tax or information returns of **all** direct or indirect owners of the entity for the tax year of the owner that includes the date on which the election took effect. Although failure to attach a copy will not invalidate an otherwise valid election, each member of the entity is required to file returns that are consistent with the entity's election. In addition, penalties may be assessed against persons who are required to, but who do not, attach Form 8832 to their returns. Other penalties may apply for filing Federal income tax or information returns inconsistent with the entity's election.

Specific Instructions

Name. Enter the name of the eligible entity electing to be classified using Form 8832.

Employer identification number (EIN). Show the correct EIN of the eligible entity electing to be classified. Any entity that has an EIN will retain that EIN even if its Federal tax classification changes under Regulations section 301.7701-3.

If a disregarded entity's classification changes so that it is recognized as a partnership or association for Federal tax purposes, and that entity had an EIN, then the entity must use that EIN and not the identifying number of the single owner. If the entity did not already have its own EIN, then the entity must apply for an EIN and not use the identifying number of the single owner.

A foreign person that makes an election under Regulations section 301.7701-3(c) must also use its own taxpayer identifying number. See sections 6721 through 6724 for penalties that may apply for failure to supply taxpayer identifying numbers.

If the entity electing to be classified using Form 8832 does not have an EIN, it must apply for one on **Form SS-4,** Application for Employer Identification Number. If the filing of Form 8832 is the only reason the entity is applying for an EIN, check the "Other" box on line 9 of Form SS-4 and write "Form 8832" to the right of that box. If the entity has not received an EIN by the time Form 8832 is due, write "Applied for" in the space for the EIN. **Do not** apply for a new EIN for an existing entity that is changing its classification if the entity already has an EIN.

Address. Enter the address of the entity electing a classification. Include the suite, room, or other unit number after the street address. If the Post Office does not deliver mail to the street address and the entity has a P.O. box, show the box number instead of the street address.

Line 1. Check box 1a if the entity is choosing a classification for the first time **and** the entity does not want to be classified under the applicable default classification. **Do not** file this form if the entity wants to be classified under the default rules.

Check box 1b if the entity is changing its current classification.

Line 2. Check the appropriate box if you are changing a current classification (no matter how achieved), or are electing out of a default classification. **Do not** file this form if you fall within a default classification that is the desired classification for the new entity.

Line 3. If an eligible entity has checked box 2c or box 2f and is electing to be disregarded as an entity separate from its owner, it must enter the name of its owner on line 3a and the owner's identifying number (social security number, or individual taxpayer identification number, or EIN) on line 3b. If the owner is a foreign person or entity and does not have a U.S. identifying number, enter "none" on line 3b. If the entity making the election is foreign, enter the name of the country in which it was formed on line 3c.

Line 4. Generally, the election will take effect on the date you enter on line 4 of this form or on the date filed if no date is entered on line 4. However, an election specifying an entity's classification for Federal tax purposes can take effect no more than 75 days prior to the date the election is filed, nor can it take effect later than 12 months after the date on which the election is filed. If line 4 shows a date more than 75 days prior to the date on which the election is filed, the election will take effect 75 days before the date it is filed. If line 4 shows an effective date more than 12 months from the filing date, the election will take effect 12 months after the date the election was filed.

Consent statement and signatures. Form 8832 must be signed by:

1. Each member of the electing entity who is an owner at the time the election is filed; or

2. Any officer, manager, or member of the electing entity who is authorized (under local law or the organizational documents) to make the election and who represents to having such authorization under penalties of perjury.

If an election is to be effective for any period prior to the time it is filed, each person who was an owner between the date the election is to be effective and the date the election is filed, and who is not an owner at the time the election is filed, must also sign.

If you need a continuation sheet or use a separate consent statement, attach it to Form 8832. The separate consent statement must contain the same information as shown on Form 8832.

Paperwork Reduction Act Notice

We ask for the information on this form to carry out the Internal Revenue laws of the United States. You are required to give us the information. We need it to ensure that you are complying with these laws and to allow us to figure and collect the right amount of tax.

You are not required to provide the information requested on a form that is subject to the Paperwork Reduction Act unless the form displays a valid OMB control number. Books or records relating to a form or its instructions must be retained as long as their contents may become material in the administration of any Internal Revenue law. Generally, tax returns and return information are confidential, as required by section 6103.

The time needed to complete and file this form will vary depending on individual circumstances. The estimated average time is:

Recordkeeping . . 1 hr., 49 min.

Learning about the law or the form . . 2 hr., 7 min.

Preparing and sending the form to the IRS . . . 23 min.

If you have comments concerning the accuracy of these time estimates or suggestions for making this form simpler, we would be happy to hear from you. You can write to the Tax Forms Committee, Western Area Distribution Center, Rancho Cordova, CA 95743-0001. **Do not** send the form to this address. Instead, see **Where To File** on page 3.

Foreign Entities Classified as Corporations for Federal Tax Purposes:

American Samoa—Corporation
Argentina—Sociedad Anonima
Australia—Public Limited Company
Austria—Aktiengesellschaft
Barbados—Limited Company
Belgium—Societe Anonyme
Belize—Public Limited Company
Bolivia—Sociedad Anonima
Brazil—Sociedade Anonima
Canada—Corporation and Company
Chile—Sociedad Anonima
People's Republic of China—Gufen Youxian Gongsi
Republic of China (Taiwan)—Ku-fen Yu-hsien Kung-szu
Colombia—Sociedad Anonima
Costa Rica—Sociedad Anonima
Cyprus—Public Limited Company
Czech Republic—Akciova Spolecnost
Denmark—Aktieselskab
Ecuador—Sociedad Anonima or Compania Anonima
Egypt—Sharikat Al-Mossahamah
El Salvador—Sociedad Anonima
Finland—Julkinen Osakeyhtio/ Publikt Aktiebolag
France—Societe Anonyme
Germany—Aktiengesellschaft
Greece—Anonymos Etairia
Guam—Corporation
Guatemala—Sociedad Anonima
Guyana—Public Limited Company
Honduras—Sociedad Anonima
Hong Kong—Public Limited Company
Hungary—Reszvenytarsasag

Iceland—Hlutafelag
India—Public Limited Company
Indonesia—Perseroan Terbuka
Ireland—Public Limited Company
Israel—Public Limited Company
Italy—Societa per Azioni
Jamaica—Public Limited Company
Japan—Kabushiki Kaisha
Kazakstan—Ashyk Aktsionerlik Kogham
Republic of Korea—Chusik Hoesa
Liberia—Corporation
Luxembourg—Societe Anonyme
Malaysia—Berhad
Malta—Public Limited Company
Mexico—Sociedad Anonima
Morocco—Societe Anonyme
Netherlands—Naamloze Vennootschap
New Zealand—Limited Company
Nicaragua—Compania Anonima
Nigeria—Public Limited Company
Northern Mariana Islands— Corporation
Norway—Allment Aksjeselskap
Pakistan—Public Limited Company
Panama—Sociedad Anonima
Paraguay—Sociedad Anonima
Peru—Sociedad Anonima
Philippines—Stock Corporation
Poland—Spolka Akcyjna
Portugal—Sociedade Anonima
Puerto Rico—Corporation
Romania—Societe pe Actiuni
Russia—Otkrytoye Aktsionernoy Obshchestvo

Saudi Arabia—Sharikat Al-Mossahamah
Singapore—Public Limited Company
Slovak Republic—Akciova Spolocnost
South Africa—Public Limited Company
Spain—Sociedad Anonima
Surinam—Naamloze Vennootschap
Sweden—Publika Aktiebolag
Switzerland—Aktiengesellschaft
Thailand—Borisat Chamkad (Mahachon)
Trinidad and Tobago—Limited Company
Tunisia—Societe Anonyme
Turkey—Anonim Sirket
Ukraine—Aktsionerne Tovaristvo Vidkritogo Tipu
United Kingdom—Public Limited Company
United States Virgin Islands— Corporation
Uruguay—Sociedad Anonima
Venezuela—Sociedad Anonima or Compania Anonima

See Regulations section 301.7701-2(b)(8) for any exceptions and inclusions to items on this list and for any revisions made to this list since these instructions were printed.

FORM 1-2   Organization Questionnaire

1. Name of limited liability company. The name of the LLC must end with "LLC" or "Limited Liability Company," or certain designated abbreviations.

2. Address of limited liability company:

3. Telephone number and fax number of limited liability company:

4. Purpose of the limited liability company:

5. Name and address of initial agent for service of process (*e.g.*, President of LLC):

6. Names, addresses and tax identification numbers of Members of the limited liability company. There must be at least two Members. The Members are the owners of the limited liability company (similar to shareholders in a corporation). The Members may be individuals, general partnerships, limited partnerships, trusts, estates, corporations, or other entities, domestic or foreign:

    Names and Addresses of   *Social Security Number or*
    Members   *Federal Tax I.D. Number*

7. Capital contributions and ownership interests (ownership interests will be evidenced by Membership Units at $1 per Unit unless otherwise provided):

Member   *Amount of capital contribution*   *Percentage ownership*
            (describe property contributed if   *interest in the LLC*
            other than cash)

8. Names of managers. These are the persons who make all major decisions concerning the limited liability company (similar to directors in a corporation):

9. Names and title of officers.

Title   *Name*

President

Vice President

Secretary

Treasurer

Other (please specify)

10. Fiscal year of the limited liability company (*e.g.,* January 1 to December 31). The limited liability company must ordinarily have a fiscal year from January 1 to December 31 unless more than 50 percent of the Members have a different fiscal year.

11. Membership Units may be transferred only if the transferor obtains the following consent of Members (check one box):

☐ Unanimous consent of all Members

☐ Majority vote

☐ Other (describe):

12.   The business of the limited liability company may be continued on the death, withdrawal, bankruptcy or expulsion of a Member only if the following consent is obtained (check one box):

☐   Unanimous consent of all Members

☐   Majority vote

☐   Other (describe):

13.   Contact person for business:

Name: _____

Address: _____

_____

Phone Number: (   )

14.   Number of employees on the date of organization:

15.   Accounting methods used (cash or accrual):

16.   Approximate date that the corporation expects to pay wages to employees in excess of $100:

17.   Name, address and telephone number of accountant:

FORM 1-3   Operating Agreement

_____, LLC

This Operating Agreement is made by and among _____
_____, LLC
(LLC) and the persons signing this Agreement as members (Members) and managers (Managers) of the LLC. The parties agree as follows:

ARTICLE 1.   FORMATION

Section 1.01.   Organization of LLC

The Members have formed an LLC pursuant to the California Limited Liability Company Act, Title 2.5 (Sections 17000-17705) of the California Corporations Code. Articles of Organization have been filed with the California Secretary of State.

Section 1.02.   Name of LLC

The name of the LLC is _____, LLC. The business of the LLC shall be operated under that name or any other name for which the LLC has filed a fictitious business name statement.

Section 1.03.   Purpose of LLC

The principal purpose of the LLC shall be to engage in the business of _____ and such other activities that are related or incidental thereto. The LLC may engage in any other lawful activities.

Section 1.04.   Principal Place of Business

The principal place of business of the LLC shall be _____
_____. The Managers may change the principal place of business of the LLC by giving notice of the change of address to each Member.

Section 1.05.   Term of LLC

The term of the LLC shall be perpetual unless terminated or dissolved as provided in this Agreement.

ARTICLE 2.   MEMBERS

Section 2.01.   Initial Members

The names and addresses of the initial Members of the LLC are set forth on Schedule A attached to this Agreement.

Section 2.02.   Liability of Members

The liability of the Members is restricted and limited to the amount of capital contributions that each Member makes or agrees to make to the LLC. Except as provided in Sections 17101 and 17254 of the California Corporations Code, no Member shall be personally liable for the debts, obligations, liabilities or judgments of the LLC, whether arising in contract, tort or otherwise, solely by reason of being a Member of the LLC.

Section 2.03.   Voting Rights of Members

(a)   Majority Vote Required.   The following actions shall be taken by a vote of the holders of a majority of Membership Units:
 (i)   election and removal of Managers under Sections 3.01 and 3.02 of this Agreement;
 (ii)   determining salaries and other compensation of Managers and Members under Sections 8.01 and 8.02 of this Agreement;
 (iii)   approving the admission to membership of a transferee or an assignee of an economic interest under Article 14 of this Agreement;
 (iv)   dissolution of the LLC under Section 16.01(b) of this Agreement;
 (v)   continuing the business of the LLC after all of the Managers cease to be Managers for any reason under Section 16.01(c) of this Agreement;
 (vi)   amending the Articles of Organization or the Operating Agreement under Sections 17.01 and 17.02 of this Agreement;
 (vii)   a merger of the LLC under Section 17551 of the California Corporations Code.

(b)   Unanimous Vote Required.   The unanimous vote of all Members shall be required before the LLC may enter into agreements, commitments or obligations that increase the personal liability of Members who have not consented to assuming such personal liability.

(c)   Other Actions.   Except as otherwise provided in this Agreement, all other actions may be taken by the Managers by majority vote without approval of the Members, including the issuance of additional Membership Units.

Section 2.04.   Signing Documents

No Member, acting solely in his capacity as a Member, may bind the LLC or sign any document on behalf of the LLC.

ARTICLE 3. MANAGERS

Section 3.01. Election of Managers

The Members shall elect _____ Managers to manage the business and affairs of the LLC. The Managers shall serve until their successors are duly elected and qualified. The Managers need not be Members. In voting for Managers, each Member shall have a number of votes equal to the number of Membership Units owned by that Member. The initial Managers of the LLC, who have been elected by the holders of a majority of Membership Units, are the following persons:

_____

_____

Section 3.02. Removal and Resignation

The Members may remove a Manager at any time, with or without cause, by vote of the holders of a majority of Membership Units. A Manager may resign at any time by giving written notice to the Members or to the other Managers. The Members may fill a vacancy caused by resignation or removal of a Manager by a vote of the holders of a majority of Membership Units.

Section 3.03. Powers of Managers

The Managers shall have the sole and exclusive right to manage the business and affairs of the LLC except as otherwise provided in this Agreement. The Managers shall have the power and authority to take such action that they deem necessary, appropriate or convenient in connection with the management and conduct of the business and affairs of the LLC, including without limitation the power to:

(a) acquire real or personal property for the LLC;

(b) dispose of property, either in the ordinary course of the business or when the Managers determine that such disposition is in the best interests of the LLC;

(c) finance the LLC's activities by borrowing money from third parties on such terms and conditions that the Managers deem appropriate. When the LLC borrows money, the Managers are authorized to pledge, mortgage, encumber or grant a security interest in LLC properties as security for the repayment of the loan;

(d) employ, retain or otherwise secure the services of professionals or other persons; or

(e) take any and all other action permitted by law and which is customary or reasonably related to the conduct of the business of the LLC, including the powers set forth in Section 17003 of the California Corporations Code.

Section 3.04.   Standard of Care of Managers

The Managers shall exercise ordinary business judgment in managing the affairs of the LLC. The Managers shall not be liable or obligated to the Members for any mistake of fact or judgment made by the Managers in operating the business of the LLC that results in any loss to the LLC or its Members unless fraud, deceit or a wrongful taking is involved. The Managers do not in any way guarantee the return of the Members' capital or a profit from the operations of the LLC. The Managers shall not be responsible to any Member because of a loss of that Member's investment or a loss in operations, unless it is caused by fraud, deceit or a wrongful taking by the Managers.

Section 3.05.   Devotion of Time by Managers

The Managers shall devote such care, time and attention to the affairs of the LLC that is reasonably necessary. In this connection, the Members acknowledge that the Managers may be managers of other LLCs and general partners of other partnerships. The Managers may engage in other business of the type conducted by the LLC, whether or not competitive with the business of the LLC.

Section 3.06.   Voting Rights of Managers

When there is more than one Manager, decisions of the Managers shall be made by a majority vote of the Managers at a meeting, or by unanimous written consent.

Section 3.07.   Restrictions on Managers

Except as otherwise provided in this Agreement, the Managers shall be subject to all the restrictions imposed on managers by the California Limited Liability Company Act, and shall have all the rights and powers granted to managers under that Act.

Section 3.08.   Liability of Managers

No Manager shall be personally liable for the debts, obligations, liabilities or judgments of the LLC, whether arising in contract, tort or otherwise, solely by reason of being a Manager or officer of the LLC.

ARTICLE 4.   OFFICERS

Section 4.01.   Officers

The Managers may appoint officers for the purpose of signing documents and taking other actions on behalf of the LLC. The officers shall hold office until the Managers remove such persons or elect new officers. The Managers may remove an officer at any time, with or without cause. The officers shall have only the powers delegated to them by the Managers. The officers may resign at any time after notice to the Managers.

Section 4.02. Officers

The following persons shall be the initial officers of the LLC:

_____ President

_____ Vice President

_____ Secretary

_____ Treasurer

Section 4.03. President

The President shall be the general manager and chief executive officer of the LLC. The President shall have general supervision, direction and control of the business of the LLC, subject to the control of the Managers. The President shall preside at all meetings of Members and Managers. The President shall have the general powers and duties of management usually vested in the president and general manager of an LLC and such other powers and duties prescribed by the Managers from time to time.

Section 4.04. Vice President

In the absence or disability of the President, the Vice President shall perform all the duties of the President. The Vice President shall have such other powers and duties as from time to time determined by the Managers.

Section 4.05. Secretary

The Secretary shall keep minutes of all meetings of Members and Managers at the principal office of the LLC. The Secretary shall work with the Managers in maintaining the other books and records of the LLC that the Managers are required to maintain under Article 11 of this Agreement.

Section 4.06. Treasurer

The Treasurer is the chief financial officer of the LLC. The Treasurer shall maintain adequate books and records of the financial transactions of the LLC. The Treasurer shall also send to Members financial statements and other financial reports that the LLC is required to send to Members. The Treasurer shall have such other powers and perform such other duties prescribed by the Managers from time to time.

ARTICLE 5.   CONTRIBUTIONS AND CAPITAL ACCOUNTS

Section 5.01.   Initial Capital Contributions

Each Member shall contribute to the capital of the LLC cash and/or property in the amount set forth on Schedule A attached to this Agreement. A Member's interest in the LLC shall be evidenced by Units. The number of Units owned by each Member is set forth on Schedule A attached to this Agreement.

Section 5.02.   Additional Capital Contributions

The Managers may issue additional Units to existing Members and new Members. The Managers shall determine the consideration to be issued for such Units. The Units need not be issued for the same type or amount of consideration.

The Members shall not be required to make additional capital contributions, but may make additional capital contributions with the consent of the Managers.

Alternative provision: The Managers of the LLC may raise additional capital by making capital calls on existing Members. The additional capital contribution shall be made by the Members in proportion to the Units owned by each Member compared to the total Membership Units issued to all Members. No Member shall be required to advance additional capital except on 30 days' prior written notice. If any Member fails to make his or her capital contribution, then the following provisions shall apply:

(a) Such capital contribution shall be made by the other Members who elect to advance the funds. The capital contribution shall be treated as a loan or advance to the Member who failed to make the capital contribution, and shall bear interest at the lesser of 12 percent or the maximum lawful rate. The loan shall be secured by a lien on the defaulting Member's Membership Units. All future distributions, whether of profit or capital attributable to the defaulting Member's Units, shall be paid to contributing Members and applied first to interest and then to principal.

(b) The defaulting Member shall have no right to participate in the management of the LLC or to exercise voting rights under this Agreement until the default is cured. The defaulting Member shall be entitled to cure the default at any time by payment of the principal amount of the obligation and all unpaid interest thereon as provided above. Thereafter, all rights of the defaulting Member under this Agreement shall be restored. The contributing Members who make additional loans as provided above shall have the right to exercise the defaulting Member's rights under this Agreement until the default is cured.

(c) If the Managers are not able to obtain substantially all the additional capital subject to the capital call provisions set forth above, the Managers may raise the additional capital by issuance of additional Units or by borrowing the funds from a bank or other lender.

Section 5.03.   Interest on Contributions

No interest shall be paid on contributions to the capital of the LLC.

Section 5.04.   Withdrawal and Return of Capital

A Member may withdraw from the LLC at any time. No Member shall have the right on withdrawal from the LLC for any reason to withdraw any portion of the capital of the LLC or to a return of that Member's capital contribution, except upon dissolution of the LLC under Section 16.03 of this Agreement.

If there is a withdrawal of a Member that does not cause a dissolution of the LLC, the LLC shall not be required to buy back the Membership Units of the withdrawing Member or to return that Member's capital account balance.

Section 5.05.   Capital Accounts

The LLC shall establish a capital account for each Member (and for each transferee who has not become a Member).

The capital account for each Member shall be increased by (a) the cash contributed by the Member to the LLC, (b) the fair market value of property contributed by the Member to the LLC, as determined by the Member and the LLC at the time of contribution, net of liabilities encumbering the property or assumed by the LLC, and (c) the amount of income and gain allocated by the LLC to the Member, including income and gain exempt from tax.

The capital account for each Member shall be decreased by (a) cash distributions from the LLC to the Member, (b) the fair market value of property distributed to the Member, as determined by the LLC and the Member at the time of distribution, net of any liabilities encumbering the property or assumed by the Member, and (c) the amount of losses and deductions allocated by the LLC to the Member.

If a Member transfers Units in accordance with Article 14, the capital account attributable to the transferred Units shall carry over to the new owner of the Units.

ARTICLE 6.   ALLOCATIONS

Section 6.01.   Allocation of Profits and Losses

The net profits and net losses of the LLC, and other items of income, gain, loss, deductions and credits, shall be allocated to the Members in proportion to the number of Membership Units owned by each Member compared to the number of Membership Units owned by all Members.

The LLC's net profits and losses, and all other items of income, gain, loss, deductions and credits, shall be determined by the accountant regularly engaged by the LLC to audit the books and records of the LLC. The determination shall be made as soon as practical after the close of the calendar year.

Section 6.02.   Allocations for Contributed Property

If a Member contributes property to the LLC that has a tax basis different from its capital account value, then the LLC shall make the special allocations required by Section 704(c) of the Internal Revenue Code. These special allocations apply solely for tax purposes. They shall not affect or be taken into account in computing a Member's capital account, or share of profits, losses or distributions pursuant to any provision of this Agreement. Section 704(c) requires the following two special allocations with respect to contributed property:

(a) If the LLC sells the property, the built-in gain or loss shall be allocated to the Member who contributed the property. Built-in gain is the amount by which the value assigned to the property for capital account purposes exceeds the tax basis of the property on the date of contribution. Built-in loss is the amount by which the tax basis of the property exceeds the capital account value of the property on the date of contribution. Built-in gains and losses shall be reduced each year by the difference between book depreciation and tax depreciation.

(b) Tax depreciation on the property shall be allocated to the non-contributing Members in an amount that is at least equal to the book depreciation allocable to such Members (up to the maximum allowable depreciation). This allocation shall, to the extent that tax depreciation is available, give the non-contributing Members the same tax depreciation deductions that they would have received if the property had been contributed with a tax basis equal to the assigned capital account value.

In making allocations, the LLC shall use the "traditional method" described in Section 1.704-3(b) of the Income Tax Regulations. However, the contributing Member and the Manager may agree to use any other method allowed under applicable regulations.

Section 6.03.   Special Allocations

(a) **General.** There are no special allocations as of the date of this Agreement. During any year in which special allocations are made, the LLC shall comply with the safe-harbor guidelines for special allocations under Section 1.704-1 of the Treasury Regulations. The LLC shall use the alternative safe-harbor test under Section 1.704-1(b)(2)(ii) of the Treasury Regulations (including the qualified income offset provision referred to below) so that the Members will not be required to restore deficit account balances on dissolution of the LLC. The accountant for the LLC shall comply with the safe-harbor guidelines below in making these allocations:

(b) **Capital Accounts.** The LLC shall maintain capital accounts for each Member in accordance with Section 5.05 of this Agreement, with any adjustments required under Section 1.704-1(b)(2)(iv) of the Treasury Regulations. Under those regulations, the following adjustments to capital accounts shall be made:

(i) The capital accounts shall reflect the fair market value of the property on the date of contribution to the LLC, rather than the tax basis of the property.

(ii) Distributed assets shall be revalued for book purposes to fair market value whenever there is a distribution. The LLC shall treat the distribution as if it sold the asset for fair market value. The gain or loss shall be allocated to the members' capital accounts. There will be no gain or loss for tax purposes since the distribution of property to a member is not a taxable event.

(iii) If a member contributes encumbered property to the LLC, the LLC shall credit the member's capital account with the fair market value of the property less liabilities encumbering the property that the LLC assumes or takes subject to.

(iv) The amount of depreciation taken for book purposes shall be based on tax depreciation multiplied by a fraction, the numerator of which is the book value of the assets on the date of contribution and the denominator of which is the tax basis.

(v) If the LLC distributes encumbered property to a member, the LLC shall reduce the member's capital account by the fair market value of the property less the debt encumbering the property that the member assumes or takes subject to. The LLC shall also treat the distribution as a sale resulting in book gain or loss that is allocated to all of the members.

(vi) The Managers of the LLC may elect to revalue all of its other property on the date of contribution or distribution. The revaluation of noncontributed or nondistributed property must be for substantial non-tax business purposes. There shall be a corresponding revaluation of all of the members' capital accounts.

(c) Liquidating Distributions. Liquidating distributions shall be made in accordance with the Members' positive capital account balances. Liquidating distributions in excess of positive capital account balances shall be made based on the number of Membership Units owned by each Member pursuant to Section 7.02 of this Agreement.

(d) Restrictions on Loss Allocations. The LLC may not allocate losses to a Member to the extent such losses create a deficit capital account balance for that Member[2] in excess of the Member's share of LLC minimum gain that would be recognized on a foreclosure of the LLC's property.[3] The LLC minimum gain for such purposes is the amount by which nonrecourse liabilities encumbering LLC property exceed the book value of the property. Any loss not allocated to a Member because of the foregoing provision shall be allocated to the other Members (to the extent such other Members are not also limited with respect to the allocation of losses under this paragraph).

Any loss reallocated hereunder shall be taken into account in computing subsequent allocations of income and losses so that the net amount of any item so allocated, and the income and losses allocated to each Member under this Article

[2] *See* Reg. §1.704-1(b)(2)(ii)(d)(3).
[3] *See* Reg. §1.704-1(b)(2)(ii)(d)(6).

6, shall to the extent possible be equal to the amount that would have been allocated to each Member under this Article 6 if no reallocation of losses had occurred hereunder.

In determining whether an allocation creates a negative capital account balance, the LLC shall first reduce each Member's capital account by (i) all reasonably expected future depletion adjustments for oil and gas depletion; (ii) all reasonably expected future allocations of loss or deduction mandated by certain Code provisions that may override 704(b) of the Internal Revenue Code; and (iii) all reasonably expected future distributions that, as of the end of the year, exceed reasonably expected increases in the member's capital account.[4] Therefore, the LLC shall reduce a Member's capital account balance for purposes of this rule by any scheduled year-end distributions that the Member delays receiving until the beginning of the following year.

(e) Qualified Income Offset. The special allocation rules above restrict the LLC from making loss allocations to a Member that create a deficit capital account balance, but shall not restrict the LLC from making distributions to a Member that cause or increase a deficit account balance. However, if a Member unexpectedly receives any adjustment, allocation or distribution described in Section 1.704-1(b)(2)(ii)(d)(4), (5) or (6) of the Treasury Regulations that causes a deficit capital account balance, the LLC shall allocate to that Member items of income and gain (consisting of a pro rata portion of each item of LLC income and gain for the year) in an amount sufficient to eliminate such deficit balance as quickly as possible.[5]

Any special items of income and gain hereunder shall be taken into account in computing subsequent allocations of income and losses so that the net amount of any item so allocated, and income and losses allocated to each Member under this Article 6, shall, to the extent possible, be equal to the amount that would have been allocated to each Member under Article 6 if no special allocation had occurred hereunder.

Section 6.04.   Special Allocations for Nonrecourse Property

If the LLC purchases property with a nonrecourse loan, then the LLC shall comply with the safe-harbor guidelines for nonrecourse allocations under Section 1.704-2 of the Income Tax Regulations. Under these regulations, the following rules shall apply:

(a) General Rules. All of the safe-harbor requirements for special allocations under Section 6.03 of this Agreement shall apply. The LLC shall maintain capital accounts, liquidating distributions shall be made in accordance with positive capital account balances, loss allocations may not increase a deficit capital account balance, and there shall be a qualified income offset.

(b) Reasonably Consistent Requirement. Nonrecourse deductions shall be allocated in a manner that is reasonably consistent with allocations that have substantial economic effect on some other significant LLC item attributable to the

---

[4] Reg. §1.704-1(b)(2)(iv)(k).
[5] *See* Reg. §1.704-1(b)(2)(ii)(d) (last flush paragraph).

property securing the nonrecourse liabilities. The accountant for the LLC shall make this determination after consultation with the Managers.

(c) LLC Minimum Gain Chargeback. If the LLC purchases property with a loan that is nonrecourse as to the LLC, but with respect to which one or more Members bear the economic risk of loss, then the LLC shall comply with the Member minimum gain chargeback rules under Section 1.704-2 of the Income Tax Regulations. The Member minimum gain chargeback rules shall apply if a Member makes a nonrecourse loan to the LLC to purchase property, or if the Member guarantees a nonrecourse loan to the LLC. The following rules shall apply in such case:

(i) LLC losses and deductions attributable to the nonrecourse liability shall be allocated to the Members who bear the economic risk of loss.[6] All of the Members shall be treated as bearing the economic risk of loss to the extent that the book value of the property exceeds the outstanding loan balance encumbering the property. The LLC may allocate the depreciation and other deductions to all the Members in accordance with the normal provisions of this Agreement if the book value of the property exceeds the outstanding loan balance.

(ii) The Member against whom the liability is recourse shall be treated as bearing the economic risk of loss when the book value of the property is less than the liabilities encumbering the property. The LLC shall allocate all of the deductions attributable to the property to that Member to the extent that the deductions reduce the book value of the property below the outstanding loan balance. For example, if a Member makes a nonrecourse loan to an LLC that is used to purchase a building, the lending Member bears the economic risk of loss if the LLC fails to repay the loan. The LLC shall allocate all of the depreciation to the lending Member when the book value of the property is less than the outstanding loan balance.

(iii) The LLC shall keep track of increases in Member minimum gain. Member minimum gain is the book gain that the LLC would recognize if the LLC abandoned the property or gave the property back to the lender for no consideration.[7] This is the amount by which the outstanding liabilities encumbering the property exceed the book value the property.[8] Member minimum gain normally arises when the LLC takes deductions that cause the book value of the property to decline below the liabilities encumbering the property. As provided above, the LLC shall make a special allocation of these deduction items to the Member who bears the risk of loss. During any year in which there is a net increase in Member minimum gain, the LLC shall note in its records that the Member minimum gain arose as a result of deductions allocated to a particular Member.

(iv) During any year in which there is a net decrease in Member minimum gain, there shall be a Member minimum gain chargeback. Under the member

---

[6] Reg. §1.704-2(i)(1).

[7] Reg. §1.704-2(k)(3).

[8] The book gain in such case would be the amount realized (the debt canceled by the lender) less the book value of the property.

minimum gain chargeback rules, the LLC shall make a special allocation of income or gain to the Member who received the deductions in prior years that gave rise to the Member minimum gain. The amount of the special allocation shall be equal to the net decrease in Member minimum gain during the year.[9]

Section 6.05. Allocations in Respect of Transferred Units and New Units Issued

If Membership Units are transferred, or if a Member's percentage interest in the LLC is increased or decreased as a result of the issuance of additional Units or otherwise, each item of income, gain, loss, deduction and credit of the LLC during such fiscal year shall be assigned pro rata to each day in the year to which such items are attributable (*i.e.*, the day on or during which it is accrued or otherwise incurred). The amount of each such item so assigned shall be allocated to the Members based on the Membership Units owned by each Member at the close of the day.

However, for the purpose of accounting convenience and simplicity, the LLC shall treat the transfer of a Unit, or increase or decrease in a Member's percentage interest, which occurs at any time during a semi-monthly period as having taken place on the last day of the semi-monthly period. Sales, dispositions and issuances of Units that take place during the first 15 days of a month shall be treated as having been made on the 15th day of the month. All other sales, dispositions and issuances of Units shall be treated as having been made on the last day of the month.

Notwithstanding the foregoing, gain or loss realized by the LLC on the sale or other disposition of assets of the LLC shall be allocated solely to the Members owning Units as of that date.

The Managers may elect to use any reasonable proration method of accounting instead of the interim closing of the books method of accounting.

ARTICLE 7.   DISTRIBUTIONS

Section 7.01. Amount and Time of Distributions

The Managers shall distribute cash available for distribution to the Members at such time that the Managers deem advisable. In determining the amount of cash available for distribution, the Managers shall set aside a reasonable allowance for anticipated expenses, contingencies, capital needs and other reserves and costs incident to the business of the LLC. The Managers shall normally distribute to Members each year an amount that is at least equal to the income taxes that the Members are required to pay on their distributive share of income and gain.

---

[9] Reg. §1.704-2(i)(4).

Section 7.02.   Allocation of Distributions

Distributions shall be made to Members in proportion to the number of Membership Units owned by each Member compared to the number of Units owned by all Members.

Section 7.03.   Distributions Other Than Cash

No Member shall have the right to receive property other than money upon the distribution of profits or cash available for distribution. No Member may be compelled to accept a distribution of any asset in kind in lieu of a proportionate distribution of money made to the other Members. Except on dissolution and winding up of the LLC, no Member may be compelled to accept a distribution of any asset in kind.

Section 7.04.   Priorities Among Members

No Member shall be entitled to any priority or preference over any other Member as to the distribution of cash available for distribution or as to the return of capital on dissolution of the LLC.

Section 7.05.   Restrictions on Distributions

No distribution shall be made if, after giving effect to the distribution:

(a) the LLC would not be able to pay its debts as they become due in the usual course of business; or
(b) the LLC's total assets would be less than the sum of its total liabilities.

ARTICLE 8.   COMPENSATION OF MANAGERS AND MEMBERS

Section 8.01.   Salaries of Managers

The Managers shall be entitled to salaries, wages or other compensation only if approved in advance by the holders of a majority of Membership Units.

Section 8.02.   Salaries of Members

The Members shall be entitled to salaries, wages or other compensation only if approved in advance by the holders of a majority of Membership Units.

ARTICLE 9.   MEETINGS OF MEMBERS

Section 9.01.   Place of Meetings

Meetings of Members shall be held at the principal executive office of the LLC, or at such other place within California selected by the persons calling the meeting.

Section 9.02.   Call of Meetings

Meetings may be called pursuant to the written request of the Managers or of Members holding more than ten percent of the Membership Units. Meetings may be called for consideration of any of the matters as to which Members are entitled to vote under this Agreement or under the California Limited Liability Company Act. The call of the meeting shall specify the time of the meeting, which shall not be less than 10 nor more than 60 days after delivery of the written request for the meeting to one or more Managers.

Section 9.03.   Notice of Meeting

Whenever Members are required or permitted to take action at a meeting, the Managers shall give written notice of the meeting not less than 10 nor more than 60 days before the date of the meeting to each Member entitled to vote at the meeting. The notice shall state the place, date and hour of the meeting and the general nature of the business to be transacted. No other business may be transacted at the meeting, unless approved by all Members.

Whenever the Managers receive a request for a meeting in accordance with Section 9.02 of this Agreement, the Managers shall immediately give notice of the meeting to Members. The notice shall specify that the meeting will be held at the time specified by the person calling the meeting. If the Managers do not give notice within 20 days after receipt of the request, the person calling the meeting may give notice.

Notice of the meeting shall be given personally, by mail or by other means of written communication. The notice shall be addressed to each Member at the address appearing on the books of the LLC for the Member or the address given by the Member to the LLC for the purpose of notice. The notice shall be deemed to have been given at the time when delivered personally, deposited in the mail, or sent by other means of written communication.

Section 9.04.   Quorum

The holders of a majority of Membership Units represented in person or by proxy shall constitute a quorum at any duly held or called meeting of Members. The Members present at any such meeting may continue to transact business until adjournment, notwithstanding the withdrawal of enough Members to leave less than a quorum, if any action taken other than adjournment is approved by the requisite vote of Members.

Section 9.05.   Adjournment of Meetings

A meeting of Members may be adjourned to another time or place. Any business that might have been transacted at the original meeting may be transacted at the adjourned meeting. If a quorum is not present at an original meeting, that meeting may be adjourned by the vote of the holders of a majority of Units represented either in person or by proxy. Notice of the adjourned meeting need not be given to Members entitled to notice if the time and place of the adjourned meeting are announced at the meeting at which the adjournment is taken. However, notice of the adjourned meeting shall be given to each Member if the adjournment is for more than 45 days or if, after the adjournment, a new record date is fixed for the adjourned meeting.

Section 9.06.   Meetings Not Duly Called, Noticed or Held

The transactions of any meeting of Members, however called and noticed, and wherever held, shall be as valid as though taken at a meeting duly held after regular call and notice, if a quorum is present at that meeting, either in person or by proxy, and if, either before or after the meeting, each of the persons entitled to vote, not present in person or by proxy, signs a written waiver of notice, a consent to the holding of the meeting, or an approval of the minutes of the meeting. Attendance by a Member at a meeting shall constitute waiver of notice, except when that Member objects at the beginning of the meeting to the transaction of any business on the ground that the meeting was not lawfully called or convened. Attendance at a meeting is not a waiver of any right to object to the consideration of matters required to be described in the notice of the meeting and not so included, if the objection is expressly made at the meeting.

Section 9.07.   Conference Telephone

Members may participate in a meeting through the use of conference telephones or similar communications equipment if all Members participating in the meeting can hear each other.

Section 9.08.   Statement of Proposal

Any action approved at a meeting, other than by unanimous approval, shall be valid only if the general nature of the proposal so approved was stated in the notice of meeting or in any waiver of notice.

Section 9.09.   Consent to Action Without Meeting

Any action that may be taken at any meeting of the Members may be taken without a meeting if a consent in writing, setting forth the action so taken, is signed and delivered to the Managers of the LLC within 60 days of the record date for that action by Members having not less than the minimum number of votes that would be necessary to authorize or take that action at a meeting at which all Members entitled to vote thereon were present and voted.

Section 9.10.   Proxies

(a) Every Member entitled to vote may authorize another person or persons to act by proxy for that Member.

(b) No proxy shall be valid after the expiration of 11 months from the date of the proxy unless otherwise provided in the proxy.

(c) A Member may revoke a proxy by a writing stating that the proxy is revoked, by a subsequent proxy signed by the Member, or by attendance and voting at a meeting by the Member who signed the proxy.

(d) The Managers may, in advance of any meetings of Members, prescribe additional regulations concerning the manner of signing and filing of proxies and their validation, consistent with the requirements of Sections 17001(ah) of the California Corporations Code.

ARTICLE 10.   MEETINGS OF MANAGERS

Section 10.01.   General

When there is more than one Manager, the provisions set forth in this Article shall govern meetings of Managers.

Section 10.02.   Time of Meetings

Meetings of Managers shall be held when meetings are called pursuant to Section 10.03 of this Agreement.

Section 10.03.   Call of Meetings

Meetings may be called pursuant to the written request of one or more Managers. Meeting may be held for consideration of any of the matters as to which Managers are entitled to vote under this Agreement or under the California Limited Liability Company Act.

Section 10.04.   Notice, Time, and Place of Meeting

The Manager or Managers calling a meeting shall give notice of the meeting to all Managers at least 48 hours prior to the meeting. The notice shall state the time and place of the meeting. The notice shall be given by facsimile, personal delivery, telephone or mail. If the notice is given by mail, the notice shall be sent at least four days prior to the meeting.

Meetings of the Members shall be held at the principal office of the LLC or at any place designated by the Managers calling the meeting.

Section 10.05.   Quorum

A majority of the Managers present in person or by conference telephone shall constitute a quorum at a meeting of Managers.

Section 10.06.   Meetings Not Duly Called, Noticed or Held

The transactions of any meeting of Managers, however called and noticed, shall be as valid as though taken at a meeting duly held after regular call and notice, if (a) all Managers are present at the meeting and sign a written consent to the holding of the meeting, (b) all Managers are present at the meeting and do not protest before the meeting that the meeting was not properly called or noticed, or (c) a majority of the Managers are present at the meeting, either in person or by conference telephone, and those not present sign a waiver of notice and consent to the meeting either before or after the meeting.

Section 10.07. Consent to Action Without Meeting

Any action that may be taken at any meeting of the Managers may be taken without a meeting if all of the Managers sign a consent in writing, setting forth the action so taken.

ARTICLE 11. BOOKS, RECORDS AND BANK ACCOUNTS

Section 11.01. Accounting Practices

The LLC shall use the _____ method of accounting. The fiscal year of the LLC is the year ending _____.

Section 11.02. Financial Statements

The Managers shall maintain true and proper books, records, reports and accounts in which all transactions of the LLC shall be accurately entered. The Managers shall issue an annual report to Members containing a balance sheet as of the end of each fiscal year and an income statement for each fiscal year. The Managers shall send a copy of that annual report to each Member not later than 120 days after the close of each fiscal year.

Section 11.03. Maintenance of Records

The Managers shall maintain at the principal office of the LLC within California all of the following records:

(a) a current list of the full name and last known business or residence address of each Member and each transferee who has not yet become a Member, set forth in alphabetical order, together with the contribution and the share in profits and losses of each Member and transferee;

(b) a current list of the full name and business or residence address of each Manager;

(c) a copy of the Articles of Organization and all amendments thereto, together with any powers of attorney pursuant to which the Articles of Organization or amendments were signed;

(d) copies of the LLC's federal, state and local income tax or information returns and reports for the six most recent taxable years;

(e) a copy of the Operating Agreement and all amendments thereto, together with any powers of attorney pursuant to which the Operating Agreement or amendments thereto were signed;

(f) copies of the financial statements of the LLC for the six most recent fiscal years; and

(g) the books and records of the LLC for the current and past four fiscal years.

Section 11.04.   Access to Records and Inspection Rights

(a) **Request for Documents.**   Each Member and transferee (and their representatives) may, upon reasonable request to the Managers and for purposes reasonably related to that person's interest in the LLC, obtain copies of the following documents at the expense of the LLC:

(i) a current list of the full name and last known business or residence address of each Member and each transferee who has not yet become a Member, set forth in alphabetical order, together with the contribution and the share in profits and losses of each Member and transferee;

(ii) a current list of the full name and business or residence address of each Manager;

(iii) the LLC's federal, state and local income tax or information returns and reports for the six most recent taxable years; and

(iv) the Articles of Organization, Operating Agreement and all amendments thereto.

(b) **Other Inspection Rights.**   Each Member, Manager and transferee shall have the right, for purposes reasonably related to that person's interest in the LLC, to each of the following:

(i) inspect and copy, during normal business hours, any records the LLC is required to maintain under Section 11.03 of this Agreement; and

(ii) obtain from the Managers, promptly after becoming available, a copy of the LLC's federal, state and local income tax or information returns for each year.

(c) **Over 35 Members.**   If the LLC ever has more than 35 Members, the following additional reporting and inspection rights shall apply:

(i) The Managers shall send an annual report to each of the Members not later than 120 days after the end of the fiscal year. The annual report shall contain a balance sheet and an income statement and statement of changes in financial position for the fiscal year.

(ii) Members representing at least five percent of the voting interests of Members, or three or more Members may make a written request to a Manager for an income statement of the LLC for the initial three-month, six-month or nine-month period of the current fiscal year ended more than 30 days prior to the date of the request, and a balance sheet of the LLC as of the end of that period. The statement shall be delivered or mailed to the Members within 30 days thereafter.

(iii) The financial statements referred to in subparagraphs (c)(i) and (ii) shall be accompanied by the report, if any, of the independent accountants engaged by the LLC. If there is no report or independent account, the financial statements shall be accompanied by a certificate of a Manager of the LLC that the financial statements were prepared without audit from the books and records of the LLC.

(d) Tax Information.   The Managers shall send to each Member and transferee within 90 days after the end of each fiscal year that information that is necessary to complete federal and state income tax or information returns. If the LLC has 35 or fewer Members, the Managers shall send a copy of the LLC's federal, state and local income tax or information returns for the year.

Section 11.05.   Banking

The Managers Member shall open and maintain one or more bank accounts in the name of the LLC. All of the funds of the LLC shall be deposited in the bank accounts. No other funds shall be deposited in the accounts. The funds in the LLC bank accounts shall be used solely for the business of the LLC. All withdrawals from the bank account shall be made only on checks signed by the Managers or such other persons as the Managers may from time to time designate.

ARTICLE 12.   LLC CERTIFICATES

Section 12.01.   LLC Certificates

The Managers may in their discretion issue certificates evidencing the Units owned by each Member. The certificates shall be signed by one or more Managers or officers, whose signature may be a facsimile.

Section 12.02.   Restrictive Legend

Each LLC certificate shall bear the following restrictive legend, in addition to any other legend that may be required by state and federal securities laws:

THE UNITS REPRESENTED BY THIS CERTIFICATE ARE SUBJECT TO CERTAIN RESTRICTIONS ON TRANSFER PURSUANT TO THE TERMS OF AN OPERATING AGREEMENT ENTERED INTO BY THIS LLC AND THE HOLDER HEREOF, A COPY OF WHICH MAY BE OBTAINED AT THE PRINCIPAL OFFICE OF THE LLC.

ARTICLE 13.   TAXES

Section 13.01.   Tax Matters Partner

The Managers shall designate one of the Managers to be the "tax matters partner" pursuant to Section 6231(a)(7) of the Internal Revenue Code. If there is only one Manager, that person shall be the tax matters partner. The tax matters partner shall take any action that is necessary to make each Member a "notice partner" under Section 6223 of the Internal Revenue Code. The tax matters partner may not take any action authorized under Sections 6222 through 6232 of the Internal Revenue Code without the consent of the Managers.

Section 13.02. Tax Elections

The Managers may make any tax elections under the Internal Revenue Code or the tax laws of any applicable state or local jurisdiction, including the following:

(a) amortization of the organizational and startup expenses of the LLC under Section 195 of the Internal Revenue Code ratably over a period of 60 months as permitted by Section 709(b) of the Internal Revenue Code;

(b) election under Section 754 of the Internal Revenue Code to adjust of the basis of LLC property if the LLC distributes property under Section 734 of the Internal Revenue Code or if a Member transfers a Membership Unit under Section 743 of the Internal Revenue Code. The Managers may in their sole discretion decide not to make such an election; and

(c) any other election that the Managers deem appropriate and in the best interests of the LLC.

ARTICLE 14. TRANSFER OF MEMBERSHIP INTERESTS INTERESTS; ADMISSION OF NEW MEMBERS

Section 14.01. Conditions for Transfer

A Member may not sell, assign, transfer, encumber or otherwise dispose of Membership Units except under the provisions of this Article 14. Transfers without compliance with this Agreement shall be treated as void.

Section 14.02. Transfers to Family Members

A Member may transfer Units by inter vivos gift, testamentary disposition or sale to a Family Member, or to a trust for the benefit of Family Members, if (a) the Managers consent to the transfer, which consent shall not be unreasonably withheld, and (b) the transferee complies with Section 14.07 of this Agreement. A Family Member shall mean a Member's spouse, parents, siblings, in-laws, children or grandchildren.

Section 14.03. Transfers to Existing Members

A Member may sell or transfer Units to another Member if the transferee complies with Section 14.07 of this Agreement.

Section 14.04. Sales to Third Parties

A Member may sell or transfer Units to a person other than a Family Member (as defined in Section 14.02) or existing Member upon compliance with the following conditions:

(a) Offer to Purchase.   If a Member decides to sell Membership Units and receives a bona fide offer for the purchase of all or a part of those Units, the Member shall either refuse the offer or give the Managers written notice setting forth full details of the offer. The notice shall specify the name of the offeror, the number of Units covered by the offer, the terms of payment, and all other material terms and conditions of the offer.

(b) Right of First Refusal.   Upon receipt of the notice of sale, the Managers shall send a copy of the notice to all Members. The Members shall have the exclusive right and option, exercisable at any time during a period of 30 days from the date of the notice, to purchase the Units covered by the offer at the same price and on the same terms and conditions set forth in the notice. If there is more than one purchasing Member, each purchasing Member shall be entitled to purchase the offered Units based on the number of Units owned by that Member compared to the number of Units owned by all purchasing Members. If the purchasing Members do not purchase all of the offered Units, the selling Member may sell the remaining Units on the terms and conditions set forth in the notice of sale.

(c) Rights of Transferee.   A transfer to anyone who is not already a Member or a Family Member (as defined in Section 14.02) shall give the transferee an economic interest in the LLC (the right to receive distributions and allocations of income, gains, losses, deductions, credits or similar items to which the Member would have been entitled to receive prior the sale or other transfer). The transferee shall not become a Member after the sale unless (i) the holders of a majority of Membership Units consent to the transferee becoming a Member; and (ii) the transferee complies with Section 14.07 of this Agreement.

Section 14.05.   Death, Bankruptcy or Incompetency

(a) Option to Purchase.   If a Member dies, or is adjudged incompetent or a bankrupt by a court of competent jurisdiction, the remaining Members shall have a right of first refusal to purchase the Membership Units of any successor in interest in accordance with Section 14.04 of this Agreement when that successor in interest sells or transfers the Membership Units.

(b) Interest of Successor in Interest.   The successor in interest shall receive only an economic interest in the LLC (the right to receive distributions and allocations of income, gains, losses, deductions, credits or similar items to which the Member would have been entitled to receive prior to death, bankruptcy or incompetency). The successor in interest shall not become a Member unless (i) the holders of a majority of Membership Units consent to the successor in interest becoming a Member; and (ii) the successor in interest complies with Section 14.07 of this Agreement.

(c) Exercise of Rights by Legal Representative.   If a Member who is an individual dies or is adjudged by a court of competent jurisdiction to be incompetent to manage the Member's person or property, the Member's executor, administrator, guardian, conservator or other legal representative may exercise all of the Member's rights for the purpose of settling the Member's estate or administering the

Member's property, including any power the Member had under the Articles of Organization or this Agreement.

Section 14.06.   Assignment of Economic Interest

(a) Right to Assign.   A Member may not assign an economic interest in a Membership Unit without transferring the entire Membership Unit unless the Member obtains the consent of the Managers.

(b) Rights of Assignee.   An assignment of an economic interest does not dissolve the LLC, entitle the assignee to vote or participate in the management and affairs of the LLC, entitle the assignee to vote or participate in the management and affairs of the LLC, or allow the assignee to become or exercise any rights of a Member. An assignment of an economic interest only gives the assignee an economic interest in the LLC (the right to receive, to the extent assigned, the distributions and the allocations of income, gains, losses, deductions, credits or similar items to which the assignor would have been entitled to receive). The assignee may become a Member if (i) the holders of a majority of Membership Units consent to the assignee becoming a Member; and (ii) the assignee complies with Section 14.07 of this Agreement.

(c) Effect of Assignment.   Upon the assignment of all or part of an economic interest, the assignor shall provide the Managers with the name and address of the assignee and the details of the interest assigned. Upon receipt of that notice, the Managers shall amend the list required by Section 17058(a)(1) of the California Corporations Code. Until the assignee becomes a Member, the assigning Member shall continue to be a Member and to have the power to exercise any rights and powers of a Member, including the right to vote.

(d) Liabilities.   Except to the extent assumed by agreement, the assignee shall have no liability to the LLC prior to becoming a Member solely as a result of the assignment.

(e) Encumbrances.   The pledge of or granting of a security interest, lien or other encumbrance in or against a Membership Unit shall not cause the Member to cease to be a Member or give to anyone else the power to exercise any rights or powers of a Member.

Section 14.07.   Restrictions on All Transfers

No transfer may be made to any person unless all of the following requirements have been met:

(a) The transferee agrees to be bound by all of the restrictions and provisions of this Agreement.

(b) The transfer does not violate any state or federal securities laws. The Managers may require the Member or transferee to obtain an opinion of counsel that the transfer is being made in compliance with the applicable state and federal securities laws.

(c) The transferee pays any reasonable expenses in connection with the transfer.

(d) The transfer, when added to the total of all other Units sold, assigned or transferred during the preceding 12 month period, does not result in a termination of the LLC under Section 708 of the Internal Revenue Code. An LLC is terminated under Section 708 if there is a sale or exchange of 50 percent or more of the Membership Units during any 12 month period. The Managers may waive compliance with this requirement.

(e) The transferee is a bona fide resident of the State of California.

Section 14.08. Liabilities of Transferee Member

A transferee who becomes a Member shall not be obligated for liabilities unknown to the transferee at the time the transferee became a Member and that could not have been ascertained from the Articles of Organization or this Agreement.

ARTICLE 15. INDEMNIFICATION

Section 15.01. Indemnification in Actions by Third Parties

The LLC shall have power to indemnify any person who was or is a party or is threatened to be made a party to any proceeding, by reason of the fact that such person is or was a Manager, Member, employee, officer or agent of the LLC, against expenses, judgments, fines, settlements and other amounts actually and reasonably incurred in connection with that proceeding. The indemnification shall be made only if the Managers determine that the person acted in good faith and in a manner that the person reasonably believed to be in the best interests of the LLC. The termination of any proceeding by judgment, order, settlement, conviction or plea of nolo contendere shall not by itself create a presumption that the person did not act in good faith and in a manner that the person reasonably believed to be in the best interests of the LLC.

Section 15.02. Advance of Expenses

The LLC shall have the power to advance expenses incurred in defending any proceeding prior to the final disposition of that proceeding.

Section 15.03. Liability of Members

The amount of indemnification shall be limited to the assets of the LLC. No Member shall be personally liable as a result of an agreement by the LLC to indemnify any person.

ARTICLE 16. TERMINATION AND DISSOLUTION

Section 16.01. Dissolution Events

The LLC shall be dissolved, and its affairs shall be wound up, upon any of the following events:

(a) the expiration of the term provided for the existence of the LLC in Section 1.05 of this Agreement;

(b) the consent to dissolve by the holders of a majority of Membership Units;

(c) the death, withdrawal, resignation, expulsion or bankruptcy of all of the Managers, or of Members resulting in one remaining Member, unless the holders of a majority of Membership Units agree in writing within 90 days thereafter to continue the LLC and to elect a new Manager (if there are no Managers) or to designate a new Member (if there is only one remaining Member).

(d) a decree of judicial dissolution under Section 17351 of the California Corporations Code.

Section 16.02. Responsibility for Winding Up

Upon dissolution of the LLC, the business of the LLC shall be wound up by the Managers. If there is no remaining Manager, the business of the LLC shall be wound up by the Members.

Section 16.03. Liquidation and Distribution

The persons responsible for winding up the affairs of the LLC shall liquidate the assets of the LLC as promptly as possible, consistent with obtaining a reasonable value for the assets. The liquidation proceeds shall be distributed in the following order:

(a) to creditors of the LLC other than Members;

(b) to Members who are creditors for unpaid loans and advances to the LLC;

(c) to any reserve that the Managers deem reasonably necessary for contingent or unforeseen liabilities or obligations of the LLC;

(d) to the Members in accordance with their positive capital account balances;

(e) to the Members in proportion to the Membership Units owned by each Member compared to the Membership Units owned by all Members.

To the extent possible, a Member shall receive as his or her distributive share the same property that the Member contributed to the LLC.

Section 16.04. Filing Dissolution Documents

Upon dissolution of the LLC, the Managers or person winding up the business of the LLC shall sign and file in the office of the California Secretary of State of the State the following:

(a) FTB 3555L, Assumption of Tax Liability to be forwarded by the California Secretary of State to the California Franchise Tax Board.

(b) Certificate of Dissolution on Form LLC-3.

(c) Certificate of Cancellation on Form LLC-4/7.

ARTICLE 17.   AMENDMENT

Section 17.01.   Amendment of Articles of Association

The Articles of Association may be amended by the vote of the holders of a majority of Membership Units.

Section 17.02.   Amendment of Operating Agreement

This Operating Agreement may be amended by the vote of the holders of a majority of Membership Units.

ARTICLE 18.   SECURITIES LAWS

Section 18.01.   California Securities Laws

Pursuant to Section 25102(f) of the California Corporations Code, the Members who are acquiring Units by original issuance (rather than by transfer) certify that:

(a) They have (i) a preexisting personal or business relationship with the LLC or one or more of its officers, Managers or control persons, or (ii) the capacity to protect their own interests in connection with the LLC and the acquisition of Units by reason of their business or financial experience or the business or financial experience of their professional advisors who are unaffiliated with and who are not compensated by the LLC or any affiliate or selling agent of the LLC, directly or indirectly,

(b) They are acquiring the Units for their own account (or for a trust account if the Member is a trust) and not with a view to or for sale in connection with any distribution of the Units.

Section 18.02.   Other Investment Representations

Each Member also represents, acknowledges or understands that:

(a) The Member is a bona fide resident of the State of California.

(b) The Member is financially able to bear the economic risk of an investment in the LLC, including a total loss of the investment.

(c) The Membership Units are restricted under the Securities Act of 1933 and may not be resold without registration under that Act or pursuant to an exemption from registration.

(d) The LLC is newly organized and has no financial or operating history. The Membership Units are a highly speculative investment and involve a high degree of risk of loss.

(e) The Member has received and reviewed all information that the Member considers necessary or appropriate in deciding whether to acquire the Membership Units. The Member has had an opportunity to ask question and receive answers from the LLC and its officers and Managers regarding the terms and conditions of purchase of the Membership Units and the business, financial affairs and other aspects of the LLC. The Member has also had the opportunity to obtain all information (to the extent the LLC possesses such information or can acquire it without unreasonable effort or expense) that the Member deems necessary or advisable to evaluate the investment and to verify the accuracy of information provided to the Member.

(f) Neither the officers, Managers, employees, agents nor any other person associated with the LLC has made any representations that (i) the Member may freely transfer the Units, (ii) a specified profit or other amount will be realized as a result of the investment in the LLC, (iii) past performance by officers, Managers or other persons in any way indicates a predictable investment return or overall business results for the LLC, (iv) the LLC will be able to make cash distributions from operations or otherwise by a specified date, or that such distributions will be made at all, or (v) the investment in Units will result in any specific tax benefits.

(g) The Member has been advised to consult with his or her own attorney and accountant regarding all legal and tax matters concerning an investment in the LLC, and the Member has done so to the extent the Member considers necessary. The Member has and will in the future look solely to and rely upon his or her own advisers regarding the tax consequences of this investment.

ARTICLE 19.   MISCELLANEOUS PROVISIONS

Section 19.01.   Severability

If any provision of this Agreement is declared by a court of competent jurisdiction to be invalid, void or unenforceable, the remaining provisions shall continue in full force and effect.

Section 19.02.   Counterparts

This Agreement may be signed in several counterparts, and all counterparts so executed shall constitute one agreement, which shall be binding on all of the parties. It shall not be necessary for all Members to sign the same copy of this Agreement.

Section 19.03.   Arbitration

If there is a dispute that cannot be resolved by or among the Members and/or Managers arising out of or related to this Agreement or the LLC, or to the interpretation, application, enforceability or validity of this Agreement, the dispute shall be resolved by binding arbitration in Los Angeles, California in accordance with the Rules of the American Arbitration Association. Judgment on the award may be entered in any court having jurisdiction thereof. The arbitration proceedings shall be limited to one day of oral hearings in order to reduce costs and expenses.

Section 19.04.   Successors

Subject to the restrictions against assignment of interests contained herein, this Agreement shall inure to the benefit of and shall be binding upon the heirs, successors in interest, assigns, personal representatives, estates and legatees of each of the Members.

Section 19.05.   Entire Agreement

This Agreement and the Articles of Organization for the LLC contain the entire understanding among the Members and supersede any prior written or oral agreements respecting the subject matter contained herein. There are no representations, agreements, arrangements or understandings, oral or written, between or among the Members relating to the subject matter of this Agreement that are not set forth herein.

Section 19.06.   Third Party Beneficiaries

There are no third party beneficiaries to this Agreement.

Section 19.07.   Waiver of Conflict of Interest

Each of the Members and other parties to this Agreement understand and acknowledge that (a) _____ has retained the law firm of Barton, Klugman & Oetting to prepare this Agreement and the other organization documents for the LLC, and to represent him and the LLC after its formation; (b) Barton, Klugman & Oetting does not represent any Member other than _____ and has no duty to advise or consult with any Member in the absence of a written agreement explicitly providing for such representation; (c) each Member has been and is hereby advised to seek and consult with independent legal and investment counsel regarding the legal and investment consequences to him or her arising from or in connection with this Agreement; (d) if there is a dispute between or among the LLC, Members, Managers, officers, employees or other persons, then Barton, Klugman & Oetting may represent the LLC and/or any Member or Manager to the extent permitted by the California Rules of Professional Conduct; (e) there is an inherent conflict of interest among the parties to this Agreement because the LLC, Members, Managers, officers and employees have conflicting rights, interests, responsibilities and liabilities in the formation, operation and dissolution of the LLC; and (f) each Member waives any and all objections to those conflicts of interest.

DATED: _____, 20___

_____, LLC

By _____

, Manager

By _____

, Manager

MEMBERS: [List]

SCHEDULE A

Name and Address of Each Member	Capital Contribution	Membership Units

APPENDIX B

SUMMARY OF REVENUE RULINGS, REVENUE PROCEDURES, AND ANNOUNCEMENTS

PART 1. REVENUE RULINGS

99-6 Conversion from Partnership Status to Disregarded Entity[1]

An LLC that is classified as a partnership for federal tax purposes may convert to a disregarded entity if one person purchases all of the membership interests in the LLC. The LLC may elect to be classified as a corporation for federal tax purposes. If no election is made, the LLC will be classified as a disregarded entity.

The tax consequences are as follows if one member of an LLC purchases all of the membership interests from the other members:

- The partnership status of the LLC terminates when the member purchases all the membership interests from the other members. The old members must treat the transaction as a sale of a partnership interest. The old members must report gain or loss, if any, resulting from the sale of the membership interests.
- The LLC is deemed to have made a liquidating distribution of all its assets to its members. Following this deemed distribution, the sole remaining member is treated as acquiring the assets that are deemed to have been distributed to the old members in liquidation of the old members' membership interests.
- The remaining member's basis in the assets attributable to the old members' interests in the LLC is the purchase price for the membership interests. The remaining member's holding period for those assets begins on the day immediately following the date of sale.
- Upon termination of the partnership, the remaining member is considered to have received a distribution of assets attributable to the remaining member's former interest in the LLC. The remaining member must recognize gain or loss, if any, on the deemed distribution of those assets. The remaining member's basis in the assets received in the deemed liquidation of the

[1] 1999-5 I.R.B. 6.

membership interest is determined under IRC Section 732(b). The remaining member's holding period for those assets attributable to the member's interest in the LLC includes the LLC's holding period for such assets.

The tax consequences are as follows if a third party who is not a member purchases all of the membership interests in the LLC:

- The old members must report gain or loss, if any, resulting from the sale of their membership interests.
- For purposes of classifying the acquisition of membership interests by a new member, the LLC is deemed to have made a liquidating distribution of those assets to its members. Immediately following the distribution, the new member is deemed to have acquired by purchase all of the former LLC's assets.
- The new member's basis in the assets is equal to the basis of the membership interest allocated among the assets in accordance with IRC Section 732(c).
- The new member's basis in the assets is equal to the cash purchase price for the membership interest.
- The new member's holding period for the assets begins on the day immediately following the date of sale.

99-5 Conversion from Partnership Status to Disregarded Entity[2]

An LLC that is classified as a partnership for federal tax purposes may convert to a disregarded entity if one person purchases all of the membership interests in the LLC. The LLC may elect to be classified as a corporation for federal tax purposes. If no election is made, the LLC will be classified as a disregarded entity.

The tax consequences are as follows if one member of an LLC purchases all of the membership interests from the other members:

- The partnership status of the LLC terminates when the member purchases all the membership interests from the other members. The old members must treat the transaction as a sale of a partnership interest. The old members must report gain or loss, if any, resulting from the sale of the membership interests.
- The LLC is deemed to have made a liquidating distribution of all its assets to its members. Following this deemed distribution, the sole remaining member is treated as acquiring the assets that are deemed to have been distributed to the old member in liquidation of the old members' membership interests.
- The remaining member's basis in the assets attributable to the old members' interests in the LLC is the purchase price for the membership interests. The remaining member's holding period for those assets begins on the day immediately following the date of sale.

[2] 1999-5 I.R.B. 8.

- Upon termination of the partnership, the remaining member is considered to have received a distribution of assets attributable to the remaining member's former interest in the LLC. The remaining member must recognize gain or loss, if any, on the deemed distribution of those assets. The remaining member's basis in the assets received in the deemed liquidation of the membership interest is determined under IRC Section 732(b). The remaining member's holding period for those assets attributable to the member's interest in the LLC includes the LLC's holding period for such assets.

The tax consequences are as follows if a third party who is not a member purchases all of the membership interests in the LLC:

- The old members must report gain or loss, if any, resulting from the sale of their membership interests.
- For purposes of classifying the acquisition of membership interests by a new member, the LLC is deemed to have made a liquidating distribution of those assets to its members. Immediately following the distribution, the new member is deemed to have acquired by purchase all of the former LLC's assets.
- The new member's basis in the assets is equal to the basis of the membership interest allocated among the assets in accordance with IRC Section 732(c).
- The new member's basis in the assets is equal to the cash purchase price for the membership interest.
- The new member's holding period for the assets begins on the day immediately following the date of sale.

98-37   Entity Classification[3]

The IRS determined that 37 revenue rulings and one revenue procedure, a majority of which dealt with the entity classification of LLCs, were now obsolete.

98-15   Tax-Exempt Organizations[4]

A tax-exempt hospital may form an LLC with a for-profit corporation and contribute its hospital and other operating assets to the LLC. The tax-exempt organization will continue to maintain its tax-exempt status if (a) the governing instruments of the LLC require that the LLC give charitable purposes priority over maximizing profits for the owners of the LLC, (b) the tax-exempt organization appoints a majority of the board of directors of the LLC, (c) the LLC designates an independent management company to run the hospital, (d) the terms of the management contract are reasonable, and (e) distributions by the LLC to the tax-exempt organization are used for charitable purposes.[5] The tax-exempt organiza-

---

[3] 1998-2 C.B. 133.
[4] 1998-12 I.R.B. 6.
[5] *Id.*

tion will not be a private foundation and will not have unrelated business income even though its only source of revenue is distributions from the LLC.[6]

However, the hospital may lose its tax-exempt status if (a) the LLC can deny services to certain segments of the community such as indigents, (b) the for-profit owner of the LLC can appoint one-half or more of the directors of the LLC, (c) the governing documents for the LLC do not require the LLC to give priority to charitable purposes instead of profits, or (d) the for-profit owner controls the management company.

95-55 Conversion of General Partnership to LLC[7]; Classification of New York LLC

There is no termination of a general partnership on conversion of the partnership to an LLC. The LLC must continue to use the same method of accounting after the conversion.

New York LLCs are classified as partnerships or corporations depending upon the provisions of the articles of organization and the operating agreement.

95-37 Conversion of Partnership into an LLC[8]

The conversion of a partnership into an LLC is treated the same as a partnership to partnership conversion. No gain or loss is recognized if the partners' shares of liabilities remain the same. There is no termination of the partnership. The tax year of the partnership does not end. The LLC is not required to obtain a new employer identification number.

95-9 Classification of South Dakota LLC[9]

A South Dakota LLC is classified as a partnership for federal tax purposes.

94-79 Classification of Connecticut LLC[10]

Connecticut LLCs are classified as partnerships or corporations depending upon the provisions of the articles of organization and the operating agreement.

94-51 Classification of New Jersey LLC[11]

New Jersey LLCs are classified as partnerships or corporations depending upon the provisions of the articles of organization and the operating agreement.

---

[6] *Id.*
[7] 1995-2 C.B. 313.
[8] 1995-1 C.B. 130.
[9] 1995-1 C.B. 222.
[10] 1994-2 C.B. 407.
[11] 1994-2 C.B. 407.

Appendix B   Summary of Revenue Rulings

94-30   Classification of Kansas LLC[12]

Kansas LLCs are classified as partnerships or corporations depending upon the provisions of the articles of organization and the operating agreement.

94-6   Classification of Alabama LLC[13]

Alabama LLCs are classified as partnerships or corporations depending upon the provisions of the articles of organization and the operating agreement.

94-5   Classification of Louisiana LLC[14]

Louisiana LLCs are classified as partnerships or corporations depending upon the provisions of the articles of organization and the operating agreement.

93-93   Classification of Arizona LLC[15]

Arizona LLCs are classified as partnerships or corporations depending upon the provisions of the articles of organization and the operating agreement.

93-92   Classification of Oklahoma LLC[16]

Oklahoma LLCs are classified as partnerships or corporations depending upon the provisions of the articles of organization and the operating agreement.

93-91   Classification of Utah LLC[17]

Utah LLCs are classified as partnerships or corporations depending upon the provisions of the articles of organization and the operating agreement.

93-81   Classification of Rhode Island LLC[18]

Rhode Island LLCs are classified as partnerships or corporations depending upon the provisions of the articles of organization and the operating agreement.

93-53   Classification of Florida LLC[19]

Florida LLCs are classified as partnerships or corporations depending upon the provisions of the articles of organization and the operating agreement.

[12] 1994-1 C.B. 316.
[13] 1994-1 C.B. 314.
[14] 1994-1 C.B. 312.
[15] 1993-2 C.B. 321.
[16] 1993-2 C.B. 318.
[17] 1993-2 C.B. 316.
[18] 1993-2 C.B. 314.
[19] 1993-2 C.B. 312.

93-50   Classification of West Virginia LLC[20]

West Virginia LLCs are classified as partnerships.

93-49   Classification of Illinois LLC[21]

Illinois LLCs are classified as partnerships or corporations depending upon the provisions of the articles of organization and the operating agreement.

93-38   Classification of Delaware LLC[22]

Delaware LLCs are classified as partnerships or corporations depending upon the provisions of the articles of organization and the operating agreement.

93-30   Classification of Nevada LLC[23]

Nevada LLCs are classified as partnerships for federal tax purposes.

93-6   Classification of Colorado LLC[24]

Colorado LLCs are classified as partnerships for federal tax purposes.

93-5   Classification of Virginia LLC[25]

Virginia LLCs are classified as partnerships for federal tax purposes.

93-4   Classification of German GmbH[26]

A German GmbH is classified as a corporation for U.S. tax purposes.

88-76   Classification of Wyoming LLC[27]

Wyoming LLCs are classified as partnerships for federal tax purposes.

88-8   Classification of Foreign LLC[28]

An entity organized under foreign law is classified for federal tax purposes solely on the basis of the characteristics set forth in Reg. §301.7701-2(b)(1). The

[20] 1993-2 C.B. 310.
[21] 1993-2 C.B. 308.
[22] 1993-2 C.B. 233.
[23] 1993-1 C.B. 231.
[24] 1993-1 C.B. 229.
[25] 1993-1 C.B. 227.
[26] 1993-1 C.B. 255.
[27] 1988-2 C.B. 360.
[28] 1988-1 C.B. 403.

IRS determined that this ruling was applicable to determining the classification of foreign LLCs.[29]

84-52   Conversion of General Partnership into LLC[30]

A conversion of a general partnership into a limited partnership is a nontaxable exchange if the partners retain the same percentage interest in the limited partnership. There is no termination of the partnership. The IRS determined that this ruling governs the conversion of a general partnership into an LLC,[31] the conversion of a limited partnership into an LLC,[32] and a merger of a limited partnership into an LLC.[33]

77-214   Classification of German GmbH[34]

A German GmbH that is owned by two domestic subsidiaries of a U.S. parent corporation is classified as a partnership for federal tax purposes.

PART 2.   REVENUE PROCEDURES

2002-69   Community Property LLCs

An LLC that is owned by a husband and wife may elect to be classified either as a partnership or disregarded entity if (a) the LLC is wholly owned by a husband and wife as community property under the laws of a state, a foreign country, or a U.S. possession, (b) no person other than one or both of the spouses are owners for tax purposes, and (c) the LLC is not classified as a corporation for federal tax purposes.

2002-59   Late Election Classification

An LLC may request relief from the IRS for a late initial classification election. The LLC must apply to the IRS prior to the unextended due date for the first tax return. It must file an application on Form 8832. The form must state at the top of the document that it is "FILED PURSUANT TO REV. PROC. 2002-59." The LLC must attach a statement to the form explaining the reason for failure to file a classification election on a timely basis. The LLC is eligible to apply for relief if (a) the LLC failed to obtain the desired classification solely because of failure to file Form 8832 on a timely basis, (b) the due date for the LLC's tax return for the tax year beginning with the date of formation has not yet passed, and (c) the

---

[29] Ltr. Ruls. 9216004, 9210039, 9152009.
[30] 1984-1 C.B. 157.
[31] Rev. Rul. 95-37; Ltr. Rul. 9321047.
[32] Rev. Rul. 95-37; Ltr. Rul. 9119029.
[33] Ltr. Rul. 9210019.
[34] 1977-1 C.B. 408.

LLC has reasonable cause for failure to make the classification election on a timely basis.[35] There is no filing fee for requesting the late classification.

2002-15   Late Election Classification

An LLC that fails to file a timely classification election on Form 8832 may request the IRS to approve the late election classification. The LLC may request relief from the IRS for a late initial classification election by complying with Revenue Procedure 2002-15. The LLC must apply to the IRS within six months and 75 days after the formation of the LLC. It must file an application on Form 8832. The form must state at the top of the document that it is "FILED PURSUANT TO REV. PROC. 2002-15." The LLC must attach a statement to the form explaining the reason for failure to file a classification election on a timely basis. The LLC is eligible to apply for relief under this Revenue Procedure if (a) the LLC failed to obtain the desired classification because of failure to file Form 8832 on a timely basis, (b) the due date for the LLC's tax return for the tax year beginning with the date of formation has not yet passed, and (c) the LLC has reasonable cause for failure to make the classification election on a timely basis. Revenue Procedure 2002-59 superseded this Revenue Procedure.

99-49   Audit Examination Procedures[36]

The audit examination under the TEFRA unified audit and litigation provisions for LLCs begins on the date of notice from the IRS of the beginning of an administrative proceeding sent to the Tax Matters Partner. The notice is sometimes referred to as the NBAP.

The audit examination ends on one of the following dates:

- In a case in which the Service accepts the LLC return as filed, on the date of the "no adjustments letter" or the "no change" notice of final administrative adjustment sent to the tax matters partner.
- In a fully agreed case, when all of the members of the LLC sign Form 870-P or 870-L.
- In an unagreed or partially agreed case, on the earliest of the date the tax matters partner or its representative is notified by Appeals that the case has been referred to Appeals from Examination, the date that the tax matters partner or member requests judicial review, or the date on which the period for requesting judicial review expires.

96-1   Rulings on Classification[37]

The IRS will issue rulings on whether a domestic or foreign limited liability company is classified as a partnership for federal tax purposes.

[35] Rev. Proc. 2002-15, §4.
[36] 1999-52 I.R.B., Sec. 3.08(2).
[37] 1996-1 C.B. 385.

Appendix B   Summary of Revenue Rulings

95-10   Ruling Requests on Classification[38]

An LLC must meet certain requirements in order to obtain a ruling that it is classified as a partnership for federal tax purposes.

93-45   Ruling Requests for Foreign LLCs[39]

Rev. Proc. 93-3 was modified with respect to ruling requests for foreign LLCs.

93-44   Ruling Requests for Foreign LLCs[40]

The Service will rule on the classification of foreign LLCs. Section 3.01.04 of Rev. Rul. 93-7 which restricted such rulings in specified cases was deleted.

93-7   Ruling Requests for Foreign LLCs[41]

The Service will not issue rulings on the classification of a foreign LLC if a taxpayer who holds an interest in the LLC (a) is a corporation and independent parties hold less than 20 percent of the interests in the LLC, or (b) is not a corporation and independent parties hold only a nominal interest in the LLC. [Sec. 3.01.04 of Ruling].

89-12   Ruling Requests[42]

In order to obtain an IRS ruling on the classification of an LLC, the LLC or it members must make all of the applicable representations and supply all of the relevant information required by Rev. Proc. 89-12. However, Section 4 of Rev. Proc. 89-12 is not applicable to LLCs,[43] if managers are not members,[44] or if all members continue to share management authority equally.[45] Otherwise, the LLC must continue to comply with Section 4 of Rev. Proc 89-12 at all times after issuance of the ruling, and in particular Sections 4.01 and 4.03 of the ruling.[46] Those sections require the managers to maintain a minimum interest in LLC income, gain, loss, deduction and credit and a minimum capital account balance.

---

[38] 1995-1 C.B. 501.
[39] 1993-2 C.B. 545.
[40] 1993-2 C.B. 545.
[41] 1993-1 C.B. 465.
[42] 1989-1 C.B. 798.
[43] Ltr. Rul. 9321070.
[44] Ltr. Rul. 9227033.
[45] Ltr. Rul. 9030013.
[46] Ltr. Rul. 9218078.

PART 3.   NOTICES

2002-15   Late Election Classification

An LLC that fails to file a timely classification election on Form 8832 may request the IRS to approve the late election classification. The LLC may request relief from the IRS for a late initial classification election by complying with Revenue Procedure 2002-15. The LLC must apply to the IRS within six months and 75 days after the formation of the LLC. It must file an application on Form 8832. The form must state at the top of the document that it is "FILED PURSUANT TO REV. PROC. 2002-15." The LLC must attach a statement to the form explaining the reason for failure to file a classification election on a timely basis. The LLC is eligible to apply for relief under this Revenue Procedure if (a) the LLC failed to obtain the desired classification because of failure to file Form 8832 on a timely basis, (b) the due date for the LLC's tax return for the tax year beginning with the date of formation has not yet passed, and (c) the LLC has reasonable cause for failure to make the classification election on a timely basis.

Notice 97-1, TD 8697[47]

On December 17, 1996, the IRS issued final regulations on the classification of LLCs and other entities for federal tax purposes. The regulations are referred to as "check the box" rules because they permit most unincorporated entities to select classification as a proprietorship, partnership or corporation by checking the applicable box on an IRS form.

Notice of Proposed Rulemaking PS-34-92 (Oct. 27, 1995) Tax Matters Partner

The Service issued proposed regulations regarding the designation of a tax matters partner (TMP) for an LLC.

Notice 95-14   Classification of LLCs[48]

The IRS stated that it was considering a proposal to treat all domestic unincorporated business organizations as partnerships unless all members elect to be treated as a corporation.

---

[47] 1997-2, I.R.B. 22.
[48] 1995-1 C.B. 297.

Appendix B   Summary of Revenue Rulings

PART 4.   ANNOUNCEMENTS

Announcement 97-5   Entity Election Classification[49]

IRS Form 8832, Entity Classification Election, may be used by entities that elect classification under the IRC §7701 regulations. This form is used by LLCs that do not want the default classification or wish to change their previous classification.

Announcement 95-34   Self-Employment Taxes of Members[50]

The IRS will hold public hearings on the proposed regulations concerning the treatment of members of LLCs.

Announcement 88-118   Classification of Various Entities[51]

The IRS reported that it had completed its six-year investigation on the classification of various entities, with a special emphasis on limited liability. An entity could be classified as a partnership for federal tax purposes even though no person was personally liable.

Announcement 83-4   Classification of LLC

The IRS withdrew proposed regulations on the classification of LLCs. The proposed regulations would have provided that an entity may not be classified as a partnership unless some member is personally liable for the debts and liabilities of the entity.

Announcement 82-140   Classification of LLC

The IRS announced a delay in the effective date of regulations on the classification of LLCs. The proposed regulations provide that an entity may not be classified as a partnership unless some member is personally liable for the debts and liabilities of the entity.

Announcement 82-60   Classification of LLC

The IRS announced a delay in the effective date of regulations on the classification of LLCs. The proposed regulations provide that an entity may not be classified as a partnership unless some member is personally liable for the debts and liabilities of the entity.

---

[49] 1997-3, I.R.B. 15.
[50] 1995-18, I.R.B. 19.
[51] I.R.B. 1998-38.

Announcement 81-166   Classification of LLC

The IRS announced a delay in the effective date of regulations on the classification of LLCs. The proposed regulations provide that an entity may not be classified as a partnership unless some member is personally liable for the debts and liabilities of the entity.

APPENDIX C

SUMMARY OF PRIVATE LETTER RULINGS AND GENERAL COUNSEL MEMORANDA

PART 1. PRIVATE LETTER RULINGS

200321006   Deferred Payment of Estate Taxes

The change in business operations of a farm from a sole proprietorship to cash leases of the farm to disregarded LLCs owned and operated by the beneficiaries of the residuary trust do not materially alter the decedent's closely held business. Thus, the leases of the farmland do not constitute a distribution, sale, exchange, or other disposition of an interest in a closely held business and thus does not result in acceleration of estate taxes that have been deferred on an installment basis.

200316003   Synthetic Fuel Credit

The indirect owner of a single-member LLC is entitled to the synthetic fuel credit under IRC Section 29 attributable to the single-member LLC. The two lower-tier LLCs are disregarded entities. The topmost LLC is therefore regarded as owning their assets and is entitled to the credit.

2003108005   Conversion of Subsidiary and Merger of Subsidiary into Disregarded LLC

The merger of a subsidiary corporation into a disregarded LLC owned by the parent corporation and the conversion of a subsidiary corporation into a disregarded LLC owned by the parent corporation qualified as a tax-free liquidation under Section 332 (rulings with respect to the "Sub 2 Merger" and the Sub 5 Conversion").

200305017   Merger of Subsidiary into Disregarded LLC

The merger of a wholly owned subsidiary corporation of a foreign parent corporation into a disregarded LLC owned by the foreign parent corporation was treated as a liquidation of the subsidiary corporation into the foreign parent corporation, subject to IRC Sections 331 and 336. The merger did not trigger recognition of gain under gain recognition agreement entered into by the parties under IRC Section 367.

200257007-008   Ownership by LLC of Stock in S Corporation

An LLC that is classified as a partnership for federal tax purposes may not own stock in an LLC. The IRS granted an S corporation relief from inadvertent termination of its status as an S corporation as a result of the transfer of stock in the corporation to an LLC.

200252055   Conversion of Subsidiary into LLC

A parent corporation merged a second-tier subsidiary into a first-tier subsidiary, and then converted the first-tier subsidiary into an LLC. The transaction was treated as a D reorganization. No gain or loss was recognized by the parent corporation as a result of the conversion.

20025012   Unified Partnership Audit and Litigation Procedures

LLCs with 10 or fewer members are not subject to the unified partnership audit and litigation procedures if each of the members is an individual, a C corporation, or an estate of a deceased partner. The small LLC exception does not apply if any member of the LLC during the tax year is a pass-through partner. A "pass-through" partner is a partnership, estate, trust, S corporation, nominee, or other similar person through whom other persons hold an interest in the LLC. Thus, if an LLC that is classified as a disregarded entity owns a membership interest in a second LLC that is classified as a partnership, the second LLC does not qualify as a small partnership exempt from unified partnership audit and litigation procedures even if the second LLC has 10 or fewer members.

200248023   Merger of Corporation into LLC Classified as an S Corporation

The merger of a corporation into an LLC that was classified as an S corporation pursuant to a Section 368(a)(1)(F) reorganization did not adversely affect the LLC's status as an S corporation.

200243023   LLC Formed by State Agency

A state or other governmental organization may form an investment LLC. Membership must be limited to a state, a political subdivision of a state, or another entity that may exclude its income under IRC Section 115(1). The gross income from the LLC allocable to the members qualifies for the exclusion under IRC Section 115(1).

Appendix C   Summary of Private Letter Rulings

200242004   Anti-Abuse Rules and Shifting of Losses to Third Parties

The anti-abuse rules prevent an LLC from shifting losses in high basis, low value assets to new members. The anti-abuse rules also prohibit the taxpayer from creating duplicate losses by contributing property with built-in losses to an LLC, selling its membership interest in the LLC to a third party at a loss, and then having the LLC sell the contributed property at a loss that is allocated to the buyer. The taxpayer may not receive any basis in a membership interest issued in exchange for the contribution of worthless property.

200240048   LLC as Subchapter S Corporation

An LLC may elect to be classified as an S corporation by filing Form 2553 and by filing Form 8832. The LLC was granted an extension of time to file Form 8832.

200236005   Merger of Corporation into LLC

The merger of a target corporation into an LLC that is a disregarded entity owned by the acquiring corporation is a tax-free merger under Section 368(a)(1)(A).

200235023   Employment Tax Liability and IRS Collection Procedures

If a multi-member LLC elects to be taxed as a corporation, then the LLC is liable for the employment tax. The members of the LLC may be liable for the trust fund recovery penalty under Section 6672, depending on the facts and circumstances of each case. If the LLC is classified as a partnership, the partnership will be liable for the employment tax. The Service will not assert an employment tax liability against the members of the LLC because they are not liable for the debts of the LLC under state law. These members, however, may be liable for the trust fund recovery penalty, depending on the facts and circumstances of each case.

If a single-member LLC elects to be taxed as a corporation, then the LLC is liable for the employment taxes. The single-member owner of the LLC and others may be liable for the trust fund recovery penalty under Section 6672, depending on the facts and circumstances of each case. If there has been no corporate election, then the LLC is disregarded for federal tax purposes and the single-member owner is the taxpayer. When the single-member owner is the taxpayer, the Service may recover the tax liability from the property and rights to property of the single-member owner, but the single-member owner under state law has no interest in the assets of the LLC. In short, the Service may not look to the LLC's assets to satisfy the tax liability of the single-member owner. The Service, however, may take collection action against the single-member owner's ownership interest in the LLC.

An assessment made against a disregarded LLC is a valid assessment against the single-member owner. Because of the close relationship of the disregarded LLC to the single-member owner, an assessment against the disregarded LLC is tantamount to an assessment against the single-member owner.

A Notice of Federal Tax Lien ("NFTL") identifying the disregarded LLC as the taxpayer may be a valid notice against the single-member owner, depending on the facts of each case. The IRS's position is that a NFTL need not precisely identify the taxpayer. Instead, the NFTL is valid if it substantially complies with the filing requirement so that constructive notice is provided to third parties. To avoid litigating this issue, the IRS recommends that the NFTL be filed in the name of the single-member owner for the tax liabilities generated by the disregarded LLC.

There are a variety of state law theories that the Service could use to collect a single-member owner's tax liability from the disregarded LLC: asserting alter ego liability and asserting nominee or transferee liability.

200227016 Transfer of Assets to LLC Following Section 355 Spin-Off

The transfer by a spun-off subsidiary off some or all of the assets of its active trade or business to an LLC in exchange for membership interests in the LLC will not prevent the spun-off subsidiary from being treated as engaged in the trade or business for purposes of IRC Section 355.

200223036-045 Division of an LLC Owning Marketable Securities

If an LLC owns marketable securities, and then divides into two or more LLCs in an asset-over form, then the members of each LLC must compute the amount of gain from a marketable securities distribution based only on the marketable securities held by the divided LLC in which they are a member.[1]

200222026 Conversion from Partnership Classification to Cap Disregarded Entity; Cancellation of Indebtedness Income

All of the assets of an LLC were deemed distributed to the remaining member when that member, as owner of 99 percent of the membership units, purchased the membership units from a related one percent member. The debt from the LLC to the remaining member was treated as canceled. However, there was no cancellation of indebtedness income.

200214016 Merger of Corporation into an LLC

The merger of a corporation into an LLC is treated as a nontaxable contribution of assets by the corporation to the LLC in exchange for membership interests, followed by a taxable distribution of the membership interests to the shareholders of the corporation in redemption of their stock. The corporation recognizes gain to the same extent as if it sold the membership interests to the shareholders for fair market value. The shareholders of the corporation also recognize capital gain

---

[1] Ltr. Ruls. 200223036-045.

or loss on distribution of the membership interests. The gain is equal to the difference between the fair market value of the membership interests less their basis in the stock. There is a technical termination of the LLC as a result of the merger. However, no gain or loss is recognized as result of the deemed termination.

200211015   Transfer to Investment LLC

The transfer of a partnership interest to an LLC in exchange for a membership interest in the LLC does not constitute a transfer of property to an investment company under IRC Section 721(b).

200209027   Section 754 Basis Adjustment

An LLC was granted an extension of time to make an election to adjust the basis of its assets under Section 754.

200205025   Section 754 Basis Adjustment

An LLC was granted an extension of time to make an election to adjust the basis of its assets under Section 754.

200205005   Extension of Time to Elect Classification

An LLC was granted an extension of time to elect classification as a corporation.

200204004   Extension of Time to Elect Classification

An LLC was granted an extension of time to elect classification as a corporation.

200204005   Capital Call Provisions

The amendment of an LLC's operating agreement that imposed below-market call provisions on capital accounts in order to facilitate a public offering did not constitute a taxable transfer of property under IRC Section 83 because the member's right to the capital accounts was substantially vested prior to the amendment to the operating agreement.

200202077   Charitable Organization Ownership of LLC

A private foundation formed an LLC to own, build, operate and lease a racetrack and campground that was related to the exempt functions of the private foundation. The LLC's ownership and operation of the functionally related business did not constitute a business enterprise or result in the excess business holdings excise tax to the charitable organization that owned the LLC.

200201024 Multiple Member LLC Classified as Disregarded Entity

An LLC with two members was classified as a single-member disregarded entity since the second member had no interest in the profits or losses of the LLC, and had limited participation in the LLC.

200150027 Charitable Organization's Ownership of LLC

A tax-exempt organization formed a single-member LLC to receive a charitable contribution of real estate. The LLC was used to protect the charitable organization from liabilities. The IRS would not rule on the deductibility of a charitable contribution of real property to the LLC.

The assets owned or transferred to the LLC are treated as owned or transferred to the charitable organization. The LLC is treated as part of the charitable organization unless it elects classification as a separate corporation. Thus, the charitable organization is not required to file separate returns or make separate public disclosures for the LLC. The single-member LLC is not required to file an application for exemption on Form 1023. The acceptance of the charitable contribution by the LLC will not adversely affect the tax-exempt status of the charitable organization that owns the LLC.

200151046 Unrelated Business Income from Timber Contracts

A charity's share of income from an LLC's disposition of timber contracts is not subject to the tax on unrelated business income.

200151039 Extension of Time to Elect Classification

An LLC was granted an extension of time to elect classification as a corporation.

200147018-020 Extension of Time to Elect Classification

A foreign LLC was granted an extension of time to elect classification as a corporation.

200143012 S Corporation Ownership of LLC

An S corporation owned all of the stock in another S corporation that was a qualified Subchapter S subsidiary. The qualified Subchapter S subsidiary was the sole owner of an LLC that was classified as a disregarded entity. The LLC owned a general partnership interest in a limited partnership. The parent S corporation was treated as the general partner in the limited partnership since both the qualified Subchapter S subsidiary and the LLC were disregarded entities.[2]

---

[2] Ltr. Rul. 200143012.

Appendix C   Summary of Private Letter Rulings

200139020   Cooperative LLC

An LLC that is formed under the state's cooperative LLC act may elect to be classified as either a corporation or partnership if it has at least two members.

200139016   Extension of Time for Classification Election

The IRS granted a foreign LLC an extension of time to elect classification as a partnership.

200139002   Conversion of LLC into Corporation

An LLC converted to a corporation by forming a new corporation. The conversion was completed by a merger of the corporate member into the new corporation, and by a transfer of membership units in the LLC to the corporation by the other member. After the conversion, the LLC was a wholly-owned subsidiary of the new corporation. The transfer of property and/or membership units to the corporation in exchange for shares is treated as a tax-free incorporation under IRC Section 351. The LLC is treated as liquidating into the corporation because the classification of the LLC changes from a partnership to a disregarded entity when it becomes wholly-owned by the new corporation. The LLC does not recognize gain or loss on the deemed distribution of its assets in liquidation.

200137038   Foreign Sales Corporation (FSC)

A U.S. parent corporation is entitled to a 100 percent dividends received exclusion for dividends received from a foreign sales corporation. The foreign sales corporation was owned indirectly through a single-member LLC that was classified as a disregarded entity.

200135015   Transfer of Patent to LLC

The holder of a patent may transfer patent rights to an LLC that is classified as a partnership. The LLC is treated as any other partnership for purposes IRC Section 1235 and regulations thereunder. After the transfer, the holder of the patent rights retains his status as a "holder" for purposes of IRC Section 1235. Thus, assuming the other requirements of IRC Section 1235 are met, the member's share of gain recognized by the LLC on disposition of an interest in the patents qualifies as long-term capital gain.

200134025   Charitable Contribution to Single Member LLC Owned by Tax-Exempt Organization

A tax-exempt organization may form single-member LLCs to receive and hold separate contributions of real estate and other high-liability assets. The LLC is used to protect the tax-exempt parent organization from liability. The contribution of property to the LLC is deductible as a charitable contribution under IRC Section

170(a), subject to the same percentage limitations and other restrictions that apply to deductible contributions made directly to the exempt entity. The single-member LLC is not required to file an application for exemption on Form 1023.

200133038   Extension of Time to Elect Classification

An LLC was granted an extension of time to elect classification as a disregarded entity. The LLC had previously made an election to be classified as a corporation.

200133018   Extension of Time to Elect Classification

A foreign LLC was granted an extension of time to elect classification as a disregarded entity.

200133030   Ordinary Income on Sale of Depreciable Property to Related LLC

The sale by a corporation of assets to an LLC will not result in the recognition of ordinary income if the LLC is not a related party under IRC Section 1239. The same rule applies whether the LLC is classified as a partnership or as a corporation.

200132014   Prepaid Subscription Income on Transfer to LLC

A publisher will not recognize prepaid subscription income under IRC Section 455(b) on the transfer of his assets and liabilities to an LLC that is classified as a disregarded entity.

200132009   Tax Returns for Terminated LLC

An LLC terminates if the members sell more than 50 percent of the membership interests to a related party. The LLC that terminates must file a short-year final return for the taxable year ending with the date of its termination. The new LLC must file a return for its taxable year beginning after the date of termination of the terminated partnership. A full-year return starts the running of the statute of limitations for the new and old LLC if the members fail to file the short-year returns.

200131016   Extension of Time to Elect Classification

A foreign LLC was granted an extension of time to elect classification as a disregarded entity.

200131014   Like-Kind Exchange

The taxpayer may complete a like-kind exchange by transferring the replacement property to a single-member LLC that is classified as a disregarded entity.

Appendix C   Summary of Private Letter Rulings

200130025   Section 754 Election

The IRS granted an extension of time for an LLC to make an election under IRC Section 754 to adjust the basis of its assets.

200129029   Conversion of Subsidiary Corporation into LLC

The conversion of a subsidiary corporation into an LLC that is classified as a disregarded entity is treated as the liquidation of the subsidiary corporation into the parent corporation. The conversion constitutes a liquidation under IRC Section 332. No gain or loss is recognized by the parent corporation on the deemed receipt of assets and liabilities from the subsidiary corporation pursuant to IRC Section 332(a). Capital gain or loss is recognized by the subsidiary on its deemed distribution of assets to, or the assumption of liabilities by, the parent corporation pursuant to IRC Sections 336(d)(3) and 337(a). The basis of each asset in the hands of the parent corporation is equal to the basis of the assets in the hands of the subsidiary corporation immediately before his conversion into a single-member LLC pursuant to IRC Section 334(b)(1). The holding period of each asset of the subsidiary corporation in the hands of the parent corporation includes the period during which the assets were held by the subsidiary corporation pursuant to IRC Section 1223(2). The parent corporation will succeed to and take into account the items of the subsidiary described in IRC Section 381(c), subject to the conditions and limitations specified in IRC Sections 381-384 and regulations thereunder pursuant to IRC Section 381(a) and Regulations Section 1.381(a)-1. Except to the extent that the subsidiary's earnings in profits are already reflected in the parent corporation earnings and profits, the parent corporation must take into account the earnings and profits, or deficit in earnings and profits, of the subsidiary as of the date of the subsidiary's conversion into a single-member LLC pursuant to IRC Section 381(c)(2)(A), and Regulations Sections 1.381(c)(2)-1, 1.1502-33(a)(2).

200129024   Merger of Subsidiary Corporation into LLC Owned by Parent

The merger of a subsidiary corporation into an LLC owned by the parent corporation qualifies as a tax-free liquidation under IRC Section 332 if the LLC is classified as a disregarded entity for federal tax purposes. The merger was tax-free even though the parent corporation, the subsidiary and the LLC made a number of purchases and sales of stock prior to the transaction.

200129019   Deferral of Estate Taxes

The owners' transfer of their interest in a closely held business to an LLC in exchange for membership interests does not constitute a disposition or result in the termination of the estate tax deferral under IRC Section 6166.

200129018   Extension of Time to Pay Estate Taxes

The transfer of real estate assets from a trust to an LLC does not materially alter the business, and is a mere change in form. Thus, the transfer of real estate from two trusts to an LLC does not constitute disposition of property of a closely held business under IRC Section 6166(g)(1)(A), or result in the acceleration of estate taxes.

200125037   Transfer of Real Estate to Trust; Generation-Skipping Tax

The transfer of commercial real estate from a trust to an LLC will not affect the trust's generation-skipping transfer tax exemption.

200125013   Cooperative Housing Corporation

A cooperative housing corporation may issue stock allocable to nonresidential space leased to a bank to its tenant stockholders without affecting its status and without the recognition of gain or loss by the co-op or its stockholders. The contribution by the tenant-stockholders of the shares of stock allocated to the commercial space to an LLC in exchange for membership interests is not taxable to the tenant-stockholders or to the LLC pursuant to IRC Section 721(a). The basis in the membership interests received by each tenant-stockholder is the same as the basis the tenant-stockholder had in the corporation shares allocated to the commercial space contributed to the LLC pursuant to IRC Section 722. The basis in the corporation shares received by the LLC from the tenant-stockholders is the cumulative bases that the tenant-stockholders had in the shares prior to their contribution to the LLC pursuant to IRC Section 723.

200124029   Charitable Lead Annuity Trust

A charitable lead annuity trust may form an LLC and sell an interest in the LLC to the remainder beneficiaries in exchange for a promissory note. The sale does not constitute an act of self-dealing under Section 4941 of the Code.

200123035   Conversion of S Corporation to LLC; Contribution of LIFO Inventory to LLC

An S corporation may convert to an LLC by forming an LLC and contributing its assets to the LLC in exchange for membership interests. Neither the corporation nor the LLC recognize gain or loss on the contribution of assets to the LLC in exchange for membership interests. The contribution of LIFO inventory property to the LLC will not result in the recapture of the LIFO reserve. However, in order to adopt the dollar-value LIFO inventory method, the transferee LLC must file IRS Form 970 and otherwise comply with the requirements of IRC Section 472 and regulations thereunder. The LIFO inventory contributed to the LLC constitutes Section 704(c) property, and any built-in gain or loss attributable to the inventory contributed by a member must be allocated back to the member when the LLC recognizes that gain or loss on the sale of the inventory.

200124029   Charitable Lead Trust

The creation and funding of an LLC by a charitable lead trust and the remainder beneficiaries' purchase of an interest in the LLC in exchange for a secured promissory note, is not an act of self-dealing under IRC Section 4941.

200114006   Employment Tax Assessments

Employment tax assessments erroneously made under the name and employment identification number of a single member LLC still serve as valid assessments against the sole owner of the LLC.

200105045   Employment Tax Assessments

Employment tax assessments erroneously made under the name and employment identification number of a single member LLC still serve as valid assessments against the sole owner of the LLC.

200102024   S Corporation's Receipt of LLC's Gross Receipts Not Passive

An S corporation's distributive share of LLC gross receipts attributable to an active trade or business (commercial contracting) is not passive income under IRC Section 1375.

200049003   Denial of Estate Tax Valuation Discounts

The economic substance doctrine may be used to deny valuation discounts for a membership interest in an LLC if (i) the transfers of property to the LLC and the gifts and transfers of membership interests appreciably changes the taxpayer's economic position, and (ii) the taxpayer does not have a valid business purpose or profit motive for establishing the LLC and making the gifts and transfers.

200124030   Contribution of LIFO Inventory to LLC

The contribution of LIFO inventory by LLC members to an LLC that is classified as a partnership does not trigger recapture of the LIFO reserve. However, the LLC must file IRS Form 970 and comply with IRC Section 472 in order to adopt the dollar-value LIFO inventory method. Any LIFO inventory contributed to the LLC is IRC Section 704(c) property. Thus, any built-in gain or loss attributable to the inventory must be allocated to the contributing member for tax purposes when the inventory is sold. On approval by the IRS, the LLC may treat the items included in its opening inventory as having been acquired at the same time, and determine their cost by the average cost method as provided under IRC Section 472(b)(3).

200124022   Disregarded LLC Owned by Charitable Organization

A tax-exempt charitable organization may form a wholly owned LLC to purchase, renovate, and operate a parking lot. The LLC was a disregarded entity. The operation of the parking lot constituted charitable activites related to be exempt functions of the parent organization. There was no unrelated business income or debt-financed property. The LLC's charitable activities were attributable to the parent organization but did not jeopardize the tax-exempt status of the parent organization.

200122035   Extension of Time to Elect Partnership Classification

A foreign LLC was granted an extension of time to elect classification as a partnership.

200119016   Conversion of Cooperative from Corporation to LLC

A corporation that was taxed as a cooperative converted from a corporation to an LLC that was classified as a corporation under federal law. After the reorganization, the LLC continued to be treated as a cooperative under subchapter T of the Code.

200118054   Nonprofit Organization Participation in an LLC

A tax-exempt organization may participate in an ambulatory surgery center organized as an LLC. The participation in the LLC will not result in unrelated business income, or jeopardize the tax-exempt status of the LLC.

200118023   LLC as Qualified Intermediary in Like-Kind Exchange

An LLC may act as a qualified intermediary in a like-kind exchange.[3] The taxpayer may also complete a like-kind exchange by acquiring the single-member LLC that acted as the intermediary and owned the replacement property. The acquisition of the LLC is made to avoid state transfer taxes that would otherwise apply if the taxpayer directly acquired the property from the intermediary. The taxpayer's acquisition of the LLC is treated as the acquisition of the replacement property if the LLC is classified as a disregarded entity for federal tax purposes.[4]

---

[3] Ltr. Rul. 200118023.
[4] Ltr. Rul. 200118023.

Appendix C Summary of Private Letter Rulings

200116051 Employee Stock Ownership Plan

The employees of an LLC may participate in a Section 423 employee stock purchase plan of the corporate owner of the LLC. If the corporate owner of the LLC is a subsidiary of a parent corporation, the employees of the LLC may receive stock of the parent corporation under a Section 423 stock purchase plan or an incentive stock option plan.

200114017 Extension of Time to Elect Taxation as Corporation

The IRS granted an extension of time for an LLC to file an election on Form 8832 to be classified as a corporation. The extension was requested after the deadline for filing the classification election.

200114004 Gift Taxes

An LLC's prepayment of annual distributions on preferred membership interests constitutes a qualified payment under IRC Section 2701(c)(3) and Regulation §25.2701-2(b)(6)(i)(B).

200112021 Stock Option Plans for Corporate Owned LLCs

If the corporate owner of the LLC is a subsidiary of a parent corporation, the employees of the LLC may receive stock of the parent corporation under a Section 423 stock purchase plan or an incentive stock option plan.

200112004 Extension of Time to Elect Classification

A foreign LLC owned by a limited partnership was granted an extension of time to elect classification as a disregarded entity. The deadline for filing an election had already passed.

200111053 Participation in ESOP by Disregarded LLC

Employees of an LLC that is owned by a member of a controlled group of corporations, and that is classified as a disregarded entity, may participate in an employee stock ownership plan or other qualified plan of the controlled group. The employees of the LLC are treated as employed by the member of the controlled group that owns the membership interests in the LLC.

200110016 Extension to File a Classification Election

The IRS granted an extension of time for an LLC to file an election on Form 8832 to be classified as a corporation. The extension was requested after the deadline for filing the classification election.

200109032-033   Extension of Time to Elect Classification

A foreign LLC owned by a qualified S corporation subsidiary was granted an extension of time to elect classification as a disregarded entity. The deadline for filing an election had already passed.

200109019   Conversion of Corporation to LLC Classified as Corporation

A corporation may convert to an LLC that is classified as a corporation without adverse tax consequences by filing an election to be classified as a corporation effective as of the date of the conversion.

200107018   S Corporation Ownership of S Corporation Subsidiary through LLC

An S corporation may own stock in another S corporation only if it owns 100 percent of the stock in the S corporation subsidiary and files an election with the IRS.[5] The parent S corporation may transfer some or all of the stock in the S corporation subsidiary to an LLC if the parent corporation owns the LLC, and if the LLC is classified as a disregarded entity for federal tax purposes. The transfer of the stock to the subsidiary will not cause the termination of the parent corporation's qualified Subchapter S subsidiary election.

200103023   LLC Owned by Trust

An LLC owned by a trust is a disregarded entity and treated as a branch of the trust.

200102038   D Reorganization

The consolidation by a parent corporation of two wholly owned subsidiaries through a disregarded LLC is treated as a D reorganization.

200102037   Rental Income Received by Disregarded Entity; LLC Owned by Grantor Trust

The owner of the LLC that is a disregarded entity may not deduct rent paid to the LLC to lease real property owned by the LLC, and the LLC is not taxed on the rental income received.

The LLC may be treated as a disregarded entity even though it is owned by an individual and by a grantor trust owned by the individual.

---

[5] IRC §1361(b)(3).

Appendix C   Summary of Private Letter Rulings

200052005   Extension of Time to Elect Classification

A foreign LLC was granted an extension of time to elect classification as a disregarded entity. The deadline for filing an election had already passed.

200046031   Extension to File a Classification Election

The IRS granted an extension of time for an LLC to file an election on Form 8832 to be classified as a corporation. The extension was requested after the deadline for filing the classification election.

200045024   Extension of Time to Elect Partnership Classification

A foreign entity that was acquired by two foreign LLCs was granted an extension of time to elect classification as a partnership.

200045022   Extension of Time to Elect Partnership Classification

A foreign LLC was granted an extension of time to elect classification as a partnership.

200045015   Extension of Time to Elect Partnership Classification

A foreign LLC was granted an extension of time to elect classification as a partnership.

200025018   At-Risk Amounts

A member of an LLC is at risk for amounts that the LLC owes to a supplier if the member signs a stipulation of judgment for delinquent payments on behalf of the LLC in his individual capacity. The member is at risk because the member is liable for payment of the amount owed to the supplier. A member is also at risk for amounts that the LLC owes to the lessor for delinquent rent if the member signed a personal guarantee. Each member of the LLC is at risk for the entire amount of the defaulted rent if the member does not have a right of reimbursement against the other members on payment of the defaulted amount. Each member of the LLC is not at risk to the extent the member has a right to reimbursement against the other members on payment of the defaulted amount.

200024024   Extension to File a Classification Election

The IRS granted an extension of time for an LLC to file an election on Form 8832 to be classified as a corporation. The extension was requested after the deadline for filing the classification election.

200022016   Conversion of General Partnership in the LLC

There is no tax to the general partnership, the LLC or its members get a general partnership converged into an LLC, or the liabilities of the members remain the same. There is no termination of the general partnership. The LLC is not required to obtain a new employer identification number after the conversion. The LLC's basis in the assets is the same as the partnership's basis in its assets immediately prior to conversion. The members' holding period includes their holding period in their general partnership interest. The members retain their same capital accounts.

200019042   Residency of Single Member LLC

The Philadelphia Service Center will not certify that a single-member LLC is a resident of United States for purposes of reduced withholding taxes payable in foreign countries with respect to the income received by the LLC from foreign sources. However, the Service may certify that the single owner of the LLC is a resident of the United States. This should establish that the income derived by the LLC in the treaty country is derived by a U.S. resident and entitled to treaty benefits.

200009025   Corporate Member of LLC; Dividends Received
Deduction; Allocation of FSC Income; Multi-Tiered LLC

A corporate member of an LLC is entitled to a dividends received deduction for the member's allocable share of dividends received by the LLC, including a 100 percent deduction for dividends received by the LLC from a foreign sales corporation. The dividends received deduction applies to a corporation that is a shareholder and LLC that in turn owns a membership interest in another LLC that owns the foreign sales corporation.

200008015   Single Member LLC Ownership in an S Corporation

A single member LLC may own stock in an S corporation if the LLC is classified as a disregarded entity for federal tax purposes, and the LLC is owned by an individual.

200005016   C Reorganization

The acquisition of membership units in an LLC that has elected to be classified as a corporation qualifies as a tax-free C reorganization.

200002025   Valuation of Family LLC for Estate and Gift Tax Purposes

The IRS may ignore restrictions in an LLC operating agreement, and deny any minority, marketability, or liquidity discounts for estate and gift tax purposes, if the LLC has no economic substance other than to reduce taxes. The valuation

Appendix C Summary of Private Letter Rulings

discounts may be denied based on the economic substance doctrine, IRC Section 2703, or IRC Section 2704.

200001016 Classification Election Extension

The IRS granted a foreign LLC an extension of time to elect classification as a partnership for federal tax purposes. The LLC failed to file a timely election.

20001004 Investment Interest Limitations

Investment interest paid by an LLC may be deducted only to the extent of investment income. Investment income includes interest income earned by the LLC on bank accounts, but does not include interest income earned on deferred payments of accounts receivable.

199952071 Charitable Remainder Unitrust

An LLC may be the grantor of a charitable remainder unitrust. An LLC that is classified as a partnership for federal tax purposes is a permissible recipient of the unitrust amount.

199952068 Classification Election Extension

The IRS granted a foreign LLC an extension of time to elect classification as a partnership for federal tax purposes. The LLC failed to file a timely election.

199947034 Special Valuation Rules

The reorganization of a C corporation as an LLC that is classified as a corporation does not constitute a transfer of an interest subject to the Section 2701 special valuation if (a) the membership units have identical rights, preferences, and restrictions as the corporate stocks surrendered in the exchange, or (b) the exchanging family member holds substantially the same interest before and after the transaction.

199945038 Condemnations

A taxpayer whose property has been taken in a condemnation may avoid nonrecognition on the gain by acquiring replacement property. The taxpayer must purchase the replacement property in order to qualify for nonrecognition. The taxpayer may use a single-member LLC that is classified as a disregarded entity to acquire the replacement property.

199938016 Tax Audit Procedures

The IRS commences audit proceedings for an LLC by filing a notice of beginning of administrative proceeding (NBAP). If there is no settlement as to all of the members, then the IRS will issue a notice of a final partnership administrative adjustment (FPAA) (IRC Section 6225). The FPAA cannot be issued sooner than 120 days after the NBAP is issued. If the IRS issues the FPAA less than 120 days subsequent to the issuance of the NBAP, then the members may elect to have their membership items treated as nonmembership items. It is not appropriate for the IRS to intentionally fail to issue timely notices so as to allow the LLC and members to elect out of the regular audit procedures for LLCs.

199936011 Disguised Sales

An LLC is treated as having made a disguised sale under IRC Section 707 if it makes a cash distribution to a member who contributed property to the LLC within two years after the date of the contribution, where the purpose of the cash distribution was to make an adjusting payment to the members in order to change the relative percentage interests in the LLC. The LLC receives a cost basis in the assets that it is treated as having purchased from the member. The antiabuse regulations under IRC Section 701 do not apply to the transaction because the principal purpose of the transaction was not to reduce the member's aggregate tax liability in a manner inconsistent with Subchapter K.

199935065 Like-Kind Exchanges

A limited partnership is treated as the continuation of an LLC where the LLC liquidates and transfers its assets and liabilities to its members, after which the members immediately retransfer the assets and liabilities to a newly formed limited partnership. The liquidation does not result in the termination of the LLC. The limited partnership may complete a like-kind exchange entered into by the LLC prior to its liquidation. The limited partnership is treated as both the transferor of the relinquished property previously transferred to a qualified intermediary by the LLC before its liquidation, and as the transferee of the replacement property received from the qualified intermediary.

199930013 Levy Against Owner of Single-Member LLC

A single-member disregarded entity is treated as a separate entity for IRS tax collection and tax lien purposes. The IRS may only collect from the property of a taxpayer to satisfy the taxpayer's liability. It may not proceed against the taxpayer's limited liability company even though the LLC is disregarded for federal tax purposes. The IRS has various other collection options, including (1) collecting from the taxpayer's distributive share of income, and (2) collecting from the assets of the LLC on the ground that it is the alter ego of the taxpayer. Whether any of these options is available must be determined on a case-by-case basis.

199922053 Self-Employment Taxes

The members of an LLC with more than one member are not responsible for employment taxes incurred by the LLC. The sole member of a single-member LLC bears personal responsibility for employment taxes incurred by the LLC.

199920023   Extension to File a Classification Election

The IRS granted an extension of time for an LLC to file an election on Form 8832 to be classified as a corporation. The extension was requested after the deadline for filing the classification election.

199917049-051   LLC as an Investment Company

There is no tax on the transfer to an LLC of partnership interests containing a diversified portfolio of investment assets. The LLC is not treated as an investment company. There is no tax on the distribution of membership units in the LLC in exchange for the contribution of partnership interests.

199916010   Withholding Taxes after Conversion from General Partnership to LLC

The LLC remains the same employer for withholding tax purposes after the conversion from a general partnership. The LLC is not required to begin withholding FICA and FUTA taxes with a new contribution base after the conversion. The same rule applies even if the LLC obtains a new employer identification number after the conversion.

199915040   Contribution of Leasehold Interest to LLC

The contribution of a long-term leasehold interest to an LLC in exchange for a membership interest is a nontaxable contribution of property to the LLC.

199914006   Two-Member LLC Treated as Single-Member LLC; Reimbursement by LLC of Capital Expenditures

The reimbursement of capital expenditures by an LLC to a member in excess of 20 percent of the fair market value at the time of the contribution did not cause the contribution of property to the LLC to be treated as a sale under Section 707 of the Internal Revenue Code. Even though the LLC had two members, it was treated as owned by a single member, since the second member had no interest in profits and losses, did not manage the LLC, and had only limited voting rights. The LLC was not classified as a partnership, since the members did not enter into an agreement to share profits and losses from the operation of a business.

199913051   Reorganization of Group Health Care Organizations

Two groups of health care organizations may combine their operations by forming a limited liability company and contributing their assets to the limited liability company. Placing the charitable activities under the control of the LLC will not change the exempt status of the charities or the nonprivate foundation status of the exempt entities involved in the reorganization. There will be no unrelated business taxable income as a result of the reorganization. The public charities may remain in control of the LLC after the reorganization, with the LLC serving the interests only of the charities.

199913035   Reorganization of Group Health Care Organizations

Two groups of health care organizations may combine their operations by forming a limited liability company and contributing their assets to the limited liability company. Placing the charitable activities under the control of the LLC will not change the exempt status of the charities or the nonprivate foundation status of the exempt entities involved in the reorganization. There will be no unrelated business taxable income as a result of the reorganization. The public charities may remain in control of the LLC after the reorganization, with the LLC serving the interests only of the charities.

199912030   Sale of Membership Units

The sale of membership units by a majority member to a third party does not result in the termination of the LLC, provided that no membership units in the LLC are transferred within a 12-month period before or after the sale to the third party.

199911033   Like-Kind Exchanges

An LLC with two members will be treated as owned by a single member for like-kind exchange purposes if the second member has no interest in profits and losses, does not manage the LLC, and has only limited voting rights. The LLC cannot be classified as a partnership, since the members have not entered into an agreement to share profits and losses from the operation of a business. The LLC will be treated as a disregarded entity if the LLC does not elect to be classified as a corporation for federal tax purposes.

199909056   Formation of LLC by Public Charity; Unrelated Business Income

A public charity formed an LLC to obtain loans and financing for minority and disadvantaged businesses in the community. The tax-exempt status of the public charity was not adversely affected even though the public charity acted as the manager of the LLC, received interest and loan fees, issued membership interests in the LLC to for-profit investors, and paid a profit participation interest to the investors. The public charity must own a controlling interest in the LLC and operate the LLC primarily for charitable purposes. Income earned by the public charity from the LLC is not considered income from an unrelated business under Section 513 of the Internal Revenue Code.

Appendix C Summary of Private Letter Rulings

199909045 Involuntary Conversion

A taxpayer may avoid gain on an involuntary conversion by purchasing replacement property that is similar or related in service or use.[6] The same taxpayer whose property was taken in the involuntary conversion must acquire the replacement property. However, a single-member LLC that is owned by the taxpayer, and that is classified as a disregarded entity for federal tax purposes, may be used to acquire the replacement property. Receipt of the replacement property by the LLC is treated as receipt of the replacement property directly by the owner of the LLC for purposes of the nonrecognition of gain rules.

199909025 Aggregation of Built-In Gains and Losses

A securities LLC may make Section 704(c) allocations for built-in gains and losses and reverse Section 704(c) allocations by aggregating gains and losses from qualified financial assets using any reasonable approach that is consistent with Section 704(c). Once the LLC adopts the aggregate approach, the LLC must apply the same aggregate approach to all of its qualified financial assets for all taxable years in which the LLC qualifies as a securities LLC.

199908057 Extension to File a Classification Election

The IRS granted an extension of time for an LLC to file an election on Form 8832 to be classified as a corporation. The extension was requested after the deadline for filing the classification election.

199908043 Division of LLC

An LLC classified as a partnership was divided into two LLCs. Each LLC was considered as a continuation of the original LLC where the members of the original LLC were also members of the newly formed LLCs, holding the same proportionate interests.

199906028 Allocation of Tax Credits

The allocation of tax credits and tax credit recapture are not reflected by adjustments to the capital accounts of members of an LLC. Therefore, any allocations of tax credits or tax credit recapture cannot have economic effect under the safe-harbor regulations for special allocations. Accordingly, the tax credits must be allocated in accordance with the members' interest in the LLC at the time the tax credit or tax credit recapture arises. If the expenditure that gives rise to tax credit in a tax year also gives rise to a valid allocation of LLC loss or deduction, or other downward adjustment in capital accounts, for such year, then the members' interest in the LLC for such credit must be in the same proportion as the members'

---

[6] IRC §1033.

respective distributive shares of such loss or deduction (and adjustments). The same principles apply in determining the members' interest in an LLC for tax credits that arise from receipts by the LLC. The fuel tax credit under IRC Section 29 is based on receipts from the sale of qualified fuels. Therefore, the LLC may allocate the credit in proportion to the allocation of receipts from the sale of qualified fuel if the allocation of the receipts complies with the safe-harbor regulations on allocations.

199904027   Allocation of Tax Credits under IRC Section 29

The fuel tax credit under IRC Section 9 is based on receipts from the sale of qualified fuels. Therefore, the LLC may allocate the credit in proportion to the allocation of receipts from the sale of qualified fuel if the allocation of the receipts complies with the safe-harbor regulations on allocations.

199904020-199904022   Extension to File a Classification Election

The IRS granted an extension of time for an LLC to file an election on Form 8832 to be classified as a corporation.

199904018   Extension to File a Classification Election

The IRS granted an extension of time for an LLC to file an election on Form 8832 to be classified as a corporation.

199904008   Inadvertent Termination of S Corporation

The transfer of stock in an S corporation to an LLC that is classified as a partnership will disqualify the corporation as an S corporation. An LLC that is classified as a partnership is not an eligible shareholder of an S corporation. The IRS may grant relief from inadvertent termination in such cases.

9853045   Extension of Time to Elect Classification as Corporation

The IRS may grant an extension of time for an LLC to elect classification as a corporation. The LLC wanted to be classified as a corporation so that it could elect to be classified as an S corporation.

9846027   Patronage Dividends of Cooperatives

A cooperative's distributive share of operational income from an LLC that is attributable to sales to persons to whom the cooperative has a preexisting obligation to pay patronage dividends with respect to such income constitutes patronage source income eligible for the patronage dividend deduction. For purposes of Section 1388(a) of the Internal Revenue Code, it was appropriate to look through the LLC to its cooperative owners. Thus, the patrons were continuing to do business with the cooperative on a cooperative basis. The LLC was treated as a pass-through entity wholly owned by the cooperative, which was in turn wholly owned by its members.

9846022   Patronage Dividends of Cooperatives

A cooperative's distributive share of operational income from an LLC that is attributable to sales to persons to whom the cooperative has a preexisting obligation to pay patronage dividends with respect to such income constitutes patronage source income eligible for the patronage dividend deduction. For purposes of Section 1388(a) of the Internal Revenue Code, it was appropriate to look through the LLC to its cooperative owners. Thus, the patrons were continuing to do business with the cooperative on a cooperative basis. The LLC was treated as a pass-through entity wholly owned by the cooperative, which was in turn wholly owned by its members.

9845010   Extension of Time to Elect a Tax Year

The IRS granted a limited liability company an extension of time to elect a taxable year other than the required year. The extension of time was granted after the LLC filed Form 8716 electing the change after the due date. The late filing was due to an error or misunderstanding on the part of the tax professional hired by the LLC to file the election. Form 8716 was filed within 90 days after its due date, and the late filing was not due to any lack of due diligence on the part of the LLC. The IRS acted pursuant to its authority under Regulation Section 301.9100-3.

9845009   Extension to File Election Classification

The IRS granted an extension for an LLC to file a classification election on Form 8832. The foreign LLC wanted to elect classification as a partnership, but had failed to file the form on a timely basis.

9845008   Extension to File Election Classification

The IRS granted an extension for an LLC to file a classification election on Form 8832. The foreign LLC wanted to elect classification as a disregarded entity, but had failed to file the form on a timely basis.

9841030   Conversion from General Partnership to LLC; Employer Identification Number

There is no tax to the general partnership, the LLC, or the members if a general partnership converts into an LLC, except as provided under Section 752 of the Internal Revenue Code. There is no termination of the general partnership. The LLC is treated as the continuation of the partnership. The taxable year of the partnership does not close.

A member's basis in the LLC membership interest is equal to the member's adjusted basis in the general partnership interest if the member's share of liabilities does not change after the conversion.

An LLC is not required to obtain a new employer identification number after the conversion from a general partnership.

9841013   Allocation of Tax Credits under IRC Section 29

The fuel tax credit under IRC Section 29 is based on receipts from the sale of qualified fuels. Therefore, the LLC may allocate the credit in proportion to the allocation of receipts from the sale of qualified fuel if the allocation of the receipts complies with the safe-harbor regulations on allocations.

9840054   LLC as Title Holding Company

An organization may use an LLC for an exempt title-holding company under IRC Section 501(c)(25). The merger of the title-holding company into an LLC will not adversely affect the status of the company as a title-holding company or result in the imposition of the unrelated business income tax on either of the merged parties.

9850001   Like-Kind Exchange

A taxpayer may use an LLC to acquire replacement property in a like-kind exchange if the LLC is a single-member LLC that is classified as a disregarded entity for federal tax purposes. The taxpayer may also merge an LLC that has acquired the replacement property into another LLC owned by the taxpayer without adversely affecting the like-kind exchange.

9839016-017   LLC as Nonprofit Organization

Nonprofit organizations formed an LLC to coordinate mutually beneficial activities and promote a regional network of hospitals and other health care entities that agreed to common supervision and oversight by the LLC.

9834040   Conversion from General Partnership to LLC; Employer Identification Number; Tiered Partnership Rules

There is no tax to the general partnership, the LLC, or the members if a general partnership converts into an LLC, except as provided under Section 752 of the Internal Revenue Code. There is no termination of the general partnership. The LLC is treated as the continuation of the partnership. The taxable year of the partnership will not close for any of the partners.

An LLC is not required to obtain a new employer identification number after the conversion from a general partnership. The tiered partnership rules do not apply.

The transfer of appreciated assets to the LLC will not result in a contribution or distribution of partnership property with respect to the partnership or the LLC under Sections 704(c)(1)(B) and 737 of the Internal Revenue Code.

9834039   Conversion from General Partnership to LLC; Employer Identification Number; Tiered Partnership Rules

There is no tax to the general partnership, the LLC, or the members if a general partnership converts into an LLC, except as provided under Section 752 of the Internal Revenue Code. There is no termination of the general partnership. The LLC is treated as the continuation of the partnership. The taxable year of the partnership will not close for any of the partners.

An LLC is not required to obtain a new employer identification number after the conversion from a general partnership. The tiered partnership rules do not apply.

The transfer of appreciated assets to the LLC will not result in a contribution or distribution of partnership property with respect to the partnership or the LLC under Sections 704(c)(1)(B) and 737 of the Internal Revenue Code.

9822043   Merger of Subsidiary into LLC

The merger of a subsidiary into an LLC owned by the parent corporation constitutes a complete liquidation under Section 332 of the Internal Revenue Code and Regulation Section 1.331-2(d).

9822037   Merger of Subsidiary into LLC

The merger of a subsidiary into an LLC owned by the parent corporation constitutes a complete liquidation under Section 332 of the Internal Revenue Code and Regulation Section 1.331-2(d).

9814006   Low-Income Housing Credits

An LLC may be formed to invest in low-income housing buildings eligible for the low-income housing credit under IRC Section 42.

9811027   Special Valuation Rules

A partnership is not subject to the special valuation rules of Section 2703 of the Internal Revenue Code if it was entered into prior to October 9, 1980, provided the partnership agreement was not substantially modified after that date. A general partner's transfer of a partnership interest to an LLC in order to limit liability does not constitute a substantial modification of the partnership agreement for such purposes.

9811026   Special Valuation Rules

A partnership is not subject to the special valuation rules of Section 2703 of the Internal Revenue Code if it was entered into prior to October 9, 1980, provided the partnership agreement was not substantially modified after that date. A general partner's transfer of a partnership interest to an LLC in order to limit liability does not constitute a substantial modification of the partnership agreement for such purposes.

9809003 Conversion from General Partnership to LLC; Employer Identification Number; Tiered Partnership Rules

There is no tax to the general partnership, the LLC, or the members if a general partnership converts into an LLC, except as provided under Section 752 of the Internal Revenue Code. There is no termination of the general partnership. The LLC is treated as the continuation of the partnership. The taxable year of the partnership will not close for any of the partners.

An LLC is not required to obtain a new employer identification number after the conversion from a general partnership. The tiered partnership rules do not apply.

The transfer of appreciated assets to the LLC will not result in a contribution or distribution of partnership property with respect to the partnership or the LLC under Sections 704(c)(1)(B) and 737 of the Internal Revenue Code.

9807013 Like-Kind Exchanges

A taxpayer may transfer replacement property directly to the taxpayer's wholly owned, single-member LLC in a Section 1031 exchange. The transfer of the property to the LLC will not disqualify the like-kind exchange.

9802047 Cooperative Housing Corporation

Tenant-shareholders may contribute some of their shares in a cooperative housing corporation to an LLC. The income that the cooperative housing corporation receives from the LLC in its capacity as a tenant-shareholder qualifies as income derived from the tenant-shareholders for purposes of the 80% rule under Section 216(b)(1)(D) of the Internal Revenue Code. The LLC must be classified as a partnership for federal income tax purposes. All of the stock in the LLC must be freely transferable and not stapled to any stock in the cooperative housing corporation.

9802004 Estate Freezes and Special Valuation Rules

Section 2704 of the Internal Revenue Code applies to the transfer of general partnership interests in a partnership to an LLC if the LLC does not become the new general partner of the partnership. There is a termination of the member's voting and liquidation rights in the partnership if the member cannot exercise those same rights through the LLC after transfer to the LLC. The amount of the taxable gift is the difference between the value of the general partnership interest immediately prior to the transfer, and the value of the interest in the partnership held by the LLC immediately after the transfer.

The transfer of the general partnership interest to the LLC did not constitute a lapse or termination of voting rights under Section 2704(a)(2) because the general partner's voting rights in the LLC were created prior to October 8, 1990, the effective date of Section 2704(a). The general partnership agreement was created before that date, and not amended after October 8, 1990.

9752002-9752005   FICA Taxes for Religious LLC

A member of a Section 501(d) religious organization who works under a vow of poverty, in an enterprise conducted and owned by the organization, is not subject to employment taxes if the duties are required by the religious order. The member must have taken a vow of poverty and have no rights to the organization's assets when he leaves the organization. The transfer of a tax-exempt religious organization's unincorporated commercial enterprises to a limited liability company owned by the organization does not change this result.

9751048   Publicly Traded LLCs; Investment LLCs; Distribution of Units by Corporation to Shareholders

A parent corporation and its subsidiary transferred investment assets to an LLC. The LLC was not a publicly traded partnership within the meaning of Section 7704 of the Internal Revenue Code since its income consisted entirely of interest, dividends and gains from the sale of stock or securities.

The transfer of the investment assets to the LLC did not result in taxation under Section 721(b) as a contribution to an investment company since the LLC was not an investment company for purposes of the rule. The subsidiary corporation contributed no more than one percent of the total fair market value of the contributed assets to the LLC. Therefore, the subsidiary's contribution was considered insignificant and the nonidentical assets were disregarded in determining whether the LLC's assets were diversified. Since the transfer did not result in diversification, there was no transfer of property to a partnership that would be treated as an investment company if it were incorporated.

The transfer of the investment assets to the LLC was non-taxable under Section 721(a) if the net reduction in the member's liabilities as a result of the LLC's assumption of those liabilities did not exceed the member's adjusted basis in the contributed assets.

The corporation recognized gain on the distribution on membership interest in the LLC to its shareholders. The distribution was treated as if the LLC sold the membership units to its shareholders at fair market value.

The corporation's distribution of the membership units to its shareholders constituted a transfer under Section 743. Therefore, the LLC was required to adjust the basis of its assets under Sections 742 and 755.

The corporation's distribution of the membership units to its shareholders constituted an exchange causing the LLC to terminate under Section 708(b)(1)(D).

9751012   Like-Kind Exchanges

A parent corporation may transfer property in a like-kind exchange to an intermediary (accommodation party) and then have the intermediary transfer the replacement property to an LLC formed by the parent corporation. The LLC is treated as the same entity as the parent corporation assuming the LLC has not filed an election to be classified as a corporation.

9750004-9750008   LLC Ownership of Stock in S Corporation

An LLC that is classified as a partnership for federal tax purposes may not own stock in an S corporation. An LLC's acquisition of stock in an S corporation will terminate the S corporation election.

The IRS may grant relief from inadvertent termination as a result of the LLC's acquisition of stock in the S corporation if all of the following apply:

- The S corporation's election was terminated under Section 1362(d)(2) or (3) of the Internal Revenue Code.
- The IRS determines that the termination was inadvertent.
- The parties take steps to make the corporation a qualifying S corporation no later than a reasonable period of time after discovery of the events resulting in the termination.
- The corporation, and each person who was a shareholder of the corporation at any time after termination and prior to corrective steps, agree to make such adjustments consistent with the treatment of the corporation as an S corporation that the IRS requires. In such cases, the corporation is treated as continuing to be an S corporation during the period specified by the IRS.

9745017   LLC Ownership of Stock in S Corporation

An LLC may own the stock in an S corporation if all of the following apply:

- The LLC is a single member LLC
- The LLC is disregarded as an entity separate from its owner (rather that classified as a corporation) under the federal check-the-box classification rules
- The owner of the LLC is a permitted S corporation shareholder

An LLC owned by an individual or qualified trust may own the stock in an S corporation.

9741037   Applicability of Section 1491 of the Internal Revenue Code in Merger of Two LLCs

The merger of two Delaware LLCs did not result in a transfer to a foreign partnership subject to former Section 1491. Under Section 1491, there was a 35 percent excise tax on transfers of property by U.S. persons to an LLC that was classified as a corporation or partnership.

9741021   Merger of General and Limited Partnerships into LLC; At-Risk Limitations

If a general partnership and limited partnership with identical ownership interests convert or merge into an LLC, the LLC is treated as the continuation of the largest partnership. The LLC retains the employer identification number of the largest partnership. None of the partners, partnerships or LLC recognizes gain or loss on the exchanges of their partnership interests for interests in the LLC or on the merger of the partnerships into the LLC.

If the requirements for qualified nonrecourse financing are met, the at-risk limitations will not apply to the losses generated by the properties held by the LLC.

9741018   Merger of General and Limited Partnerships into LLC; At-Risk Limitations

If a general partnership and limited partnership with identical ownership interests convert or merge into an LLC, the LLC is treated as the continuation of the largest partnership. The LLC retains the employer identification number of the largest partnership. None of the partners, partnerships or LLC recognizes gain or loss on the exchanges of their partnership interests for interests in the LLC or on the merger of the partnerships into the LLC.

If the requirements for qualified nonrecourse financing are met, the at-risk limitations will not apply to the losses generated by the properties held by the LLC.

9740001   Relief from Unforeseen Consequences of an LLC Election

In appropriate cases, the IRS may grant relief from unforeseen consequences of a LLC election. The parent corporation merged a first and second-tier subsidiary into itself. The parent corporation received a favorable ruling from the IRS that the merger of the subsidiaries into the parent constituted a tax-free liquidation. In order to obtain the favorable ruling, the parent corporation was required to represent that the liquidation of the two subsidiaries would not be preceded by or followed by a reincorporation of any of the businesses or assets of either of the subsidiaries.

Subsequently, the parent corporation transferred certain assets acquired in the merger to a limited liability company that was classified as a partnership for federal tax purposes and as a corporation for state tax purposes. The IRS issued a favorable ruling that the LLC would be classified as a partnership for federal tax purposes and that the prior favorable ruling on the merger would not be adversely affected. The parent corporation was required to reaffirm its prior representations, including the representation that it had no intention to reincorporate any of the businesses or assets that it acquired in the subsidiary corporation.

Later, the state amended its laws so that the LLC would be classified as a partnership rather than as a corporation for state tax purposes. This created a problem for the LLC, which would have lost its prior exemption from the state's personal property tax. The IRS permitted the LLC to restore its prior favorable tax treatment by electing to be taxed as a corporation for federal income tax purposes. The election by the LLC to be classified as a corporation was a reincorporation of the business and assets acquired in the prior merger and a potential violation of the representations made in connection with the prior letter rulings. However, the IRS granted relief because there were no plans or intentions, at the time of the merger, to reincorporate any of the business or assets acquired by the parent in the merger of the subsidiaries. The IRS ruled that the LLC's election to be taxed as a corporation would not adversely affect the prior favorable rulings that the mergers were tax free distributions and complete liquidation.

9739036-039   Tax-Exempt Hospitals

A tax-exempt hospital may form an LLC with two for-profit subsidiaries of two other tax-exempt hospitals for the purpose of providing diagnostic laboratory services for the patients of each of the hospitals, and expanding diagnostic laboratory services available to the general public. The contribution of cash and diagnostic laboratory equipment to the LLC in exchange for membership units, and the LLC's provision of diagnostic laboratory services to patients of each of the three hospitals and the general public, will not adversely affect the tax-exempt status of any of the three hospitals. The transaction will not adversely affect the non-private-foundation status of any of the three hospitals. The income received will not be treated as unrelated business income.

9739014   LLC Ownership of Stock in S Corporation

The owner of a single-member LLC may own stock in an S corporation if the LLC is classified as a disregarded entity for federal tax purposes and the member of the LLC otherwise qualifies as an S corporation shareholder. The transfer of S corporation shares to a single-member LLC does not terminate the S corporations election.

9738013   Merger of Limited Partnerships into LLC; At-Risk Limitations

If two limited partnerships with identical ownership interests convert or merge into an LLC, the LLC is treated as the continuation of the largest limited partnership. The LLC retains the employer identification number of the largest limited partnership. None of the limited partners, limit partnerships or LLC recognizes gain or loss on the exchanges of their partnership interests for interests in the LLC or on the transfer of assets from the limited partnerships to the LLC.

If the requirements for qualified nonrecourse financing are met, the at-risk limitations will not apply to the losses generated by the properties held by the

LLC. The debt may be qualified nonrecourse financing even though the LLC is liable for repayment.

9736043   Unrelated Business Income

An exempt organization that provided prepaid group dental services to subscribers did not have unrelated business income on its allocable share of income from an LLC that provided financing to subscribers for the prepaid group general services.

9736004   Minority and Marketability Valuation Discounts

The IRS disallowed minority and marketability discounts for membership interests donated to family members under the sham transaction doctrine and Sections 2703 and 2704 of the Internal Revenue Code. The Service noted the following:

- The member's transfer of property to the LLC and the gifts of membership interests occurred shortly before the member's death.
- The death beneficiaries received from the LLC the same assets that they would have received from the decedent if the assets had not been funneled through the LLC.
- The only ascertainable purpose for organizing the LLC was to depress the value of the assets that were transferred to the LLC. Nothing of substance was intended to change as a result of the transactions. The death beneficiaries retained control over the assets, and their management rights did not change as a result of the transactions.
- All of the transactions, including the transfer of assets from the decedent to the LLC and the subsequent gifts of membership interests to the family members should be viewed as a single testamentary transaction occurring at the decedent member's death.

9720008–9720013   Formation of LLC; Merger of LLCs into Limited Partnership

A member's basis in the LLC membership interest equals the amount of money and the adjusted basis in property contributed to the LLC.

The LLC's basis in the contributed assets equals the members' adjusted basis in the assets immediately before the contribution.

LLCs may merge into a limited partnership, after which the members of the LLC are limited partners. The tax consequences are as follows:

- If the members of one of the merging LLCs own more than 50 percent of the limited partnership after the merger (the majority LLC), the limited partnership will be treated as the continuation of the majority LLC.
- The other merging LLCs (the minority LLCs) are treated as contributing their assets and liabilities to the limited partnership in exchange for limited

partnership interests. The minority LLCs are then deemed to terminate, and their taxable years close.

- No gain or loss is recognized by the LLCs or members on the contribution of assets by the minority LLCs and the members of the majority LLC to the limited partnership in exchange for limited partnership interests.
- The limited partnership's basis in the contributed assets equals the contributors' basis in the assets at the time of contribution.
- The minority LLCs and the members of the majority LLC have a basis in their limited partnership interests equal to the amount of money and adjusted basis of other property contributed to the limited partnership at the time of contribution.
- Immediately after the merger, the minority LLCs are deemed to have distributed the limited partnership interests received in the merger to the members of the LLC in liquidation of each member's interest in the minority LLCs. The basis of a limited partnership interest received by a member in liquidation of the LLC is the adjusted basis of the member's interest in the LLC, reduced by any money distributed in the same transaction.
- If no member of the minority LLCs receives money, unrealized receivable or inventory as a result of the liquidating distributions, no gain or loss is recognized by the minority LLCs or any of their members on the distributions of partnership interests to the members in the liquidations of the minority LLCs.
- The limited partners and general partners may recognize gain if the transfer of liabilities from the LLC to the partnership results in a net decrease in an LLC member's share of liabilities. The transfer of nonrecourse liabilities from the LLC to the partnership may result in a net decrease in a member's share of liabilities. A liability is nonrecourse as to the members of an LLC if no member currently bears the economic risk of loss for the liability. These liabilities are allocated to all the members in the LLC based on their share of profits. Thus, a member's basis is increased by the amount of nonrecourse liabilities multiplied by the member's percentage interest in profits. The nonrecourse liabilities normally become recourse liabilities when they are transferred to a limited partnership in a merger because a general partner is personally liable for all partnership liabilities. Recourse liabilities are allocated to the partners who are personally liable. All of the recourse liabilities are allocated to the general partner if no limited partner is currently liable for such debts after the merger. A member/limited partner is treated as receiving a distribution of money from the limited partnership to the extent of the decrease in his allocable share of liabilities. The deemed distribution of money reduces the limited partner's basis in the partnership interest. The limited partner recognizes gain to the extent the deemed distribution of money exceeds the limited partner's basis in the partnership.
- The transfer of recourse liabilities from the LLC to the partnership does not result in a deemed distribution of money or taxation to members if the members who were personally responsible for the liabilities prior to the merger continue to be personally liable after the merger.
- The transfer of encumbered property from the LLC to the partnership is

subject to the disguised sale rules of Section 707(a)(2)(B) of the Internal Revenue Code. However, no gain or loss is recognized to the merging LLCs or its members under the disguised sale rules if the liabilities transferred are "qualified liabilities." The liabilities are qualified liabilities if the loan proceeds have been utilized to fund capital improvements or for the ordinary and necessary expenses of operating the properties and if the debts are longstanding in duration.

- Section 704(c) applies to the transfer of appreciated property by the LLC to the partnership.

9719019-9719029   Formation of LLC; Merger of LLCs into Limited Partnership

A member's basis in the LLC membership interest equals the amount of money and the adjusted basis in property contributed to the LLC.

The LLC's basis in the contributed assets equals the members' adjusted basis in the assets immediately before the contribution.

LLCs may merge into a limited partnership, after which the members of the LLC are limited partners. The tax consequences are as follows:

- If the members of one of the merging LLCs own more than 50 percent of the limited partnership after the merger (the majority LLC), the limited partnership will be treated as the continuation of the majority LLC.
- The other merging LLCs (the minority LLCs) are treated as contributing their assets and liabilities to the limited partnership in exchange for limited partnership interests. The minority LLCs are then deemed to terminate, and their taxable years close.
- No gain or loss is recognized by the LLCs or members on the contribution of assets by the minority LLCs and the members of the majority LLC to the limited partnership in exchange for limited partnership interests.
- The limited partnership's basis in the contributed assets equals the contributors' basis in the assets at the time of contribution.
- The minority LLCs and the members of the majority LLC have a basis in their limited partnership interests equal to the amount of money and adjusted basis of other property contributed to the limited partnership at the time of contribution.
- Immediately after the merger, the minority LLCs are deemed to have distributed the limited partnership interests received in the merger to the members of the LLC in liquidation of each member's interest in the minority LLCs. The basis of a limited partnership interest received by a member in liquidation of the LLC is the adjusted basis of the member's interest in the LLC, reduced by any money distributed in the same transaction.
- If no member of the minority LLCs receives money, unrealized receivable or inventory as a result of the liquidating distributions, no gain or loss is recognized by the minority LLCs or any of their members on the distributions of partnership interests to the members in the liquidations of the minority LLCs.

- The limited partners and general partners may recognize gain if the transfer of liabilities from the LLC to the partnership results in a net decrease in an LLC member's share of liabilities. The transfer of nonrecourse liabilities from the LLC to the partnership may result in a net decrease in a member's share of liabilities. A liability is nonrecourse as to the members of an LLC if no member currently bears the economic risk of loss for the liability. These liabilities are allocated to all the members in the LLC based on their share of profits. Thus, a member's basis is increased by the amount of nonrecourse liabilities multiplied by the member's percentage interest in profits. The nonrecourse liabilities normally become recourse liabilities when they are transferred to a limited partnership in a merger because a general partner is personally liable for all partnership liabilities. Recourse liabilities are allocated to the partners who are personally liable. All of the recourse liabilities are allocated to the general partner if no limited partner is currently liable for such debts after the merger. A member/limited partner is treated as receiving a distribution of money from the limited partnership to the extent of the decrease in his allocable share of liabilities. The deemed distribution of money reduces the limited partner's basis in the partnership interest. The limited partner recognizes gain to the extent the deemed distribution of money exceeds the limited partner's basis in the partnership.
- The transfer of recourse liabilities from the LLC to the partnership does not result in a deemed distribution of money or taxation to members if the members who were personally responsible for the liabilities prior to the merger continue to be personally liable after the merger.
- The transfer of encumbered property from the LLC to the partnership is subject to the disguised sale rules of Section 707(a)(2)(B) of the Internal Revenue Code. However, no gain or loss is recognized to the merging LLCs or its members under the disguised sale rules if the liabilities transferred are "qualified liabilities." The liabilities are qualified liabilities if the loan proceeds have been utilized to fund capital improvements or for the ordinary and necessary expenses of operating the properties and if the debts are long standing in duration.
- Section 704(c) applies to the transfer of appreciated property by the LLC to the partnership.

9719015   Formation of LLC; Merger of LLCs into Limited Partnership

A member's basis in the LLC membership interest equals the amount of money and the adjusted basis in property contributed to the LLC.

The LLC's basis in the contributed assets equals the members' adjusted basis in the assets immediately before the contribution.

LLCs may merge into a limited partnership, after which the members of the LLC are limited partners. The tax consequences are as follows:

- If the members of one of the merging LLCs own more than 50 percent of the limited partnership after the merger (the majority LLC), the limited partnership will be treated as the continuation of the majority LLC.

- The other merging LLCs (the minority LLCs) are treated as contributing their assets and liabilities to the limited partnership in exchange for limited partnership interests. The minority LLCs are then deemed to terminate, and their taxable years close.
- No gain or loss is recognized by the LLCs or members on the contribution of assets by the minority LLCs and the members of the majority LLC to the limited partnership in exchange for limited partnership interests.
- The limited partnership's basis in the contributed assets equals the contributors' basis in the assets at the time of contribution.
- The minority LLCs and the members of the majority LLC have a basis in their limited partnership interests equal to the amount of money and adjusted basis of other property contributed to the limited partnership at the time of contribution.
- Immediately after the merger, the minority LLCs are deemed to have distributed the limited partnership interests received in the merger to the members of the LLC in liquidation of each member's interest in the minority LLCs. The basis of a limited partnership interest received by a member in liquidation of the LLC is the adjusted basis of the member's interest in the LLC, reduced by any money distributed in the same transaction.
- If no member of the minority LLCs receives money, unrealized receivable or inventory as a result of the liquidating distributions, no gain or loss is recognized by the minority LLCs or any of their members on the distributions of partnership interests to the members in the liquidations of the minority LLCs.
- The limited partners and general partners may recognize gain if the transfer of liabilities from the LLC to the partnership results in a net decrease in an LLC member's share of liabilities. The transfer of nonrecourse liabilities from the LLC to the partnership may result in a net decrease in a member's share of liabilities. A liability is nonrecourse as to the members of an LLC if no member currently bears the economic risk of loss for the liability. These liabilities are allocated to all the members in the LLC based on their share of profits. Thus, a member's basis is increased by the amount of nonrecourse liabilities multiplied by the member's percentage interest in profits. The nonrecourse liabilities normally become recourse liabilities when they are transferred to a limited partnership in a merger because a general partner is personally liable for all partnership liabilities. Recourse liabilities are allocated to the partners who are personally liable. All of the recourse liabilities are allocated to the general partner if no limited partner is currently liable for such debts after the merger. A member/limited partner is treated as receiving a distribution of money from the limited partnership to the extent of the decrease in his allocable share of liabilities. The deemed distribution of money reduces the limited partner's basis in the partnership interest. The limited partner recognizes gain to the extent the deemed distribution of money exceeds the limited partner's basis in the partnership.
- The transfer of recourse liabilities from the LLC to the partnership does not result in a deemed distribution of money or taxation to members if the

members who were personally responsible for the liabilities prior to the merger continue to be personally liable after the merger.

- The transfer of encumbered property from the LLC to the partnership is subject to the disguised sale rules of Section 707(a)(2)(B) of the Internal Revenue Code. However, no gain or loss is recognized to the merging LLCs or its members under the disguised sale rules if the liabilities transferred are "qualified liabilities." The liabilities are qualified liabilities if the loan proceeds have been utilized to fund capital improvements or for the ordinary and necessary expenses of operating the properties and if the debts are long standing in duration.
- Section 704(c) applies to the transfer of appreciated property by the LLC to the partnership.

9716007   S Corporation Ownership of LLC

An S corporation could own membership interests in an LLC classified as a partnership for federal tax purposes. The LLC could in turn own stock in another corporation. Before 1997, an S corporation was also prohibited from directly owning 80 percent of the stock in another corporation. However, it could own the stock indirectly through an LLC that was classified as a partnership for federal tax purposes.

An S corporation may not own stock in a foreign corporation.

9713007   Transfer of Business from Limited Partnership to LLC

A partnership may transfer some of its lines of business to an LLC to limit the liability of the partners with respect to that business. Generally, no gain or loss is recognized to the LLC or the members on the transfer of business or contribution of assets to the LLC under Section 721 of the Internal Revenue Code.

9701032   Conversion of Subsidiary into LLC

A parent corporation may convert a subsidiary corporation into a LLC by liquidating the subsidiary and contributing the assets received on liquidation to a newly formed LLC. The merger the subsidiary corporation into the parent corporation qualifies as a nontaxable liquidation under Section 332 of the Internal Revenue Code. The contribution to the LLC by the parent corporation of assets received from the subsidiary in exchange form membership units is nontaxable under Section 721. Neither the parent corporation, subsidiary corporation nor LLC recognizes gain as a result of the contribution of assets to the LLC.

9701029   Merger of C Corporation into LLC

The merger of a C corporation into an LLC is treated as a transfer of assets by the corporation to the LLC in exchange for the assumption of liabilities by the LLC and the corporation's receipt of LLC membership interests, followed by the corporation's distribution of the membership interests in the LLC to the shareholders of the corporation in complete liquidation.

The corporation and the LLC will not recognize gain or loss on the transfer of assets to the LLC in exchange for the membership interests.

The corporation recognizes gain or loss on the corporation's distribution of the ownership interests in the LLC to the LLC members in the complete liquidation of the corporation. Gain or loss is recognized to the same extent as if the corporation were to sell the distributed membership interests for their fair market value to the members.

The corporation's shareholders recognize capital gain or loss on the deemed distribution of the LLC membership interests from the corporation to its shareholders. The distribution is treated as full payment in exchange for their stock in the corporation.

If the LLC made an election under Section 754 of the Internal Revenue Code before the merger, the distribution of the membership interests to the shareholders will constitute a transfer under Section 743. The LLC must then adjust the basis of its assets under Sections 743 and 755.

The corporation's distribution of membership interests to the shareholders constitutes an exchange which causes the LLC to terminate under Section 708(b)(1)(B). The termination results in a deemed distribution of the LLC's assets to the shareholders, and a deemed immediate recontribution of those assets to a new LLC by the members.

9647028-032   Classification of Indiana LLC

An LLC organized under the laws of Indiana is classified as a partnership for federal income tax purposes.

9644059   Classification of Iowa LLC

An LLC organized under the laws of Iowa is classified as a partnership for federal income tax purposes.

9640010   Conversion of Subsidiary Corporation to LLC; Ownership by S Corporation of Subsidiary Indirectly Through LLC

A parent corporation may convert a subsidiary corporation into an LLC by forming an LLC and transferring the assets of the subsidiary corporation to the LLC in exchange for membership units. The subsidiary corporation is then liquidated. The membership units in the LLC owned by the subsidiary are transferred to the parent corporation in the liquidation. Neither the subsidiary nor the LLC recognize gain or loss as a result of the transfer of assets to the LLC. The liquidation of the subsidiary corporation and the transfer of the LLC membership units to the parent corporation qualify as a complete liquidation under Section 332 of the Internal Revenue Code.

Before 1997, an S corporation was also prohibited from directly owning 80 percent of the stock in another corporation. However, it could own the stock indirectly through an LLC that was classified as a partnership for federal tax purposes.

9639055 Classification of LLC

An LLC organized under the laws of State B is classified as a partnership for federal income tax purposes.

9637033 Classification of LLC; S Corporation Ownership

An LLC formed under the laws of Country N is classified as a partnership for federal tax purposes.

An S corporation may own a foreign LLC that is classified as a partnership for federal tax purposes.

9637030 Conversion from General Partnership to LLC; Cash Method of Accounting

There is no tax to the general partnership, LLC or the members if a general partnership converts into an LLC, except as provided under Section 752. There is no termination of the general partnership. The LLC is treated as the continuation of the partnership. The taxable year of the partnership will not close for any of the partners.

An LLC organized for the landscaping and nursery business must continue to use the cash method of accounting after conversion from a general partnership unless it seeks permission from the IRS to change its accounting method.

9636007 Conversion of S Corporation to LLC Taxed as S Corporation

An S corporation may convert to an LLC that is classified as a corporation. The conversion is treated as an F reorganization. The IRS will not issue an advance ruling on whether the transaction qualifies as an F reorganization. The reorganization does not terminate the corporation's election as an S corporation. The LLC is classified as an S corporation after the conversion.

9633021 Conversion from Limited Partnership to LLC; Employer Identification Number

There is no tax to the partners if a limited partnership converts into an LLC. There is no termination of the limited partnership. The partnership does not need to close its tax year. The LLC is treated as a continuation of the partnership.

An LLC is not required to obtain a new employer identification number after the conversion from a limited partnership.

9633014 Classification of LLC

An LLC formed under the laws of State B is classified as a partnership for federal tax purposes.

Appendix C   Summary of Private Letter Rulings

9626031   S Corporation Ownership of Stock Through an LLC

An S corporation may not own 80 percent or more of the stock in any other corporation, such as a domestic or foreign corporation. An S corporation may own more than 80 percent of the stock in any U.S. or foreign corporation if it owns the stock indirectly through an LLC. The Code only prohibits an S corporation from directly owning more than 80 percent of the stock in another corporation.

9625022-023   Life Insurance Transferred to LLC; Classification of Kansas LLC

Gross income does not include amounts paid under a life insurance contract that are paid by reason of the death of the insured. The exclusion is limited if the policy is transferred for valuable consideration. However, there is no limitation on the exclusion if the policy is transferred to the insured, a partner of the insured, a partnership in which the insured is a partner, or to a corporation in which the insured is a shareholder or officer. An LLC that is classified as a partnership for federal tax purposes is treated as a partnership for purposes of this rule. A Kansas LLC is classified as a partnership for federal tax purposes.

9625013-018   Life Insurance Transferred to LLC; Classification of Kansas LLC

Gross income does not include amounts paid under a life insurance contract that are paid by reason of the death of the insured. The exclusion is limited if the policy is transferred for valuable consideration. However, there is no limitation on the exclusion if the policy is transferred to the insured, a partner of the insured, a partnership in which the insured is a partner, or to a corporation in which the insured is a shareholder or officer. An LLC that is classified as a partnership for federal tax purposes is treated as a partnership for purposes of this rule.

A Kansas LLC is classified as a partnership for federal tax purposes.

9623016   Classification of LLC; Conversion from General Partnership to LLC

An LLC organized under the laws of State B for the practice of law is classified as a partnership for federal tax purposes.

There is no tax to the general partnership, LLC or the members if a general partnership converts into an LLC, except as provided in Section 752 of the Internal Revenue Code. There is no termination of the general partnership. The LLC is treated as a continuation of the general partnership.

9622007   Classification of Louisiana LLC

An LLC organized under the laws of Louisiana is classified as a partnership for federal income tax purposes.

9618023 Conversion from General Partnership to LLC; Basis in LLC; Employer Identification Number

There is no tax to the general partnership, LLC or the members if a general partnership converts into an LLC except as provided by Section 752 of the Internal Revenue Code. There is no termination of the general partnership. The LLC is treated as a continuation of the general partnership.

The basis of each member's interest in the LLC immediately after the conversion is the same as the basis of that member's interest in the general partnership immediately prior to the conversion except as provided by Section 752.

An LLC is not required to obtain a new employer identification number after the conversion from a general partnership. The tiered partnership rules do not apply.

9618022 Conversion from General Partnership to LLC; Basis in LLC; Employer Identification Number

There is no tax to the general partnership, LLC or the members if a general partnership converts into an LLC except as provided by Section 752 of the Internal Revenue Code. There is no termination of the general partnership. The LLC is treated as a continuation of the general partnership.

The basis of each member's interest in the LLC immediately after the conversion is the same as the basis of that member's interest in the general partnership immediately prior to the conversion except as provided by Section 752.

An LLC is not required to obtain a new employer identification number after the conversion from a general partnership. The tiered partnership rules do not apply.

9618021 Conversion from General Partnership to LLC; Basis in LLC; Employer Identification Number

There is no tax to the general partnership, LLC or the members if a general partnership converts into an LLC except as provided by Section 752 of the Internal Revenue Code. There is no termination of the general partnership. The LLC is treated as a continuation of the general partnership.

The basis of each member's interest in the LLC immediately after the conversion is the same as the basis of that member's interest in the general partnership immediately prior to the conversion except as provided by Section 752.

An LLC is not required to obtain a new employer identification number after the conversion from a general partnership. The tiered partnership rules do not apply.

9617020 Investment LLC

There is no tax on the transfer of appreciated marketable securities to an LLC if each member transfers a diversified portfolio of marketable securities that satisfies the 25 and 50 percent tests under Section 368(a)(2)(F)(ii) of the Internal Revenue Code.

Appendix C   Summary of Private Letter Rulings

9617018   Investment LLC

There is no tax on the transfer of appreciated marketable securities to an LLC if each member transfers a diversified portfolio of marketable securities that satisfies the 25 and 50 percent tests under Section 368(a)(2)(F)(ii) of the Internal Revenue Code.

9617017   Investment LLC

There is no tax on the transfer of appreciated marketable securities to an LLC if each member transfers a diversified portfolio of marketable securities that satisfies the 25 and 50 percent tests under Section 368(a)(2)(F)(ii) of the Internal Revenue Code.

9615025   S Corporations and Passive Rental Income

A corporation's election as an S corporation is terminated if the corporation has Subchapter C earnings and profits at the close of each of three consecutive taxable years, and has gross receipts for each of such years that are more than 25 percent of which are passive investment income. The receipt by an S corporation of a distributive share of rental income from an LLC is not passive income for such purposes if the corporation provides significant services or incurs substantial costs in the rental business.

9611041   Classification of Connecticut LLC

An LLC organized under the laws of Connecticut is classified as a partnership for federal income tax purposes.

9611008   Classification of LLC

An LLC organized under the laws of State X is classified as a partnership for federal income tax purposes.

9610006   Classification of Foreign-Owned LLC

An LLC organized in the United States that is owned by foreign persons is classified as a domestic partnership.

9609029   Classification of Delaware LLC

A Delaware LLC is classified as a partnership for federal tax purposes.

9607006   Classification of LLC; Conversion from Limited Partnership to LLC

An LLC organized under the laws of State B is classified as a partnership for federal tax purposes.

There is no tax if a limited partnership converts to an LLC. There is no termination of the partnership. The basis of each member's interest in the LLC is the same as that member's interest in the partnership before the conversion. The LLC is treated as a continuation of the partnership.

9606006   Classification of Louisiana LLC

. A Louisiana LLC is classified as a partnership for federal tax purposes.

9604014   Formation of LLC; Contribution to LLC by Trust; Distribution of Membership Interests by Trust

No gain or loss is recognized on contribution of property to an LLC assuming the LLC is not an investment company.

A trust may contribute its assets to an LLC in exchange for membership interests and then distribute the membership interests to the trust beneficiaries. No gain or loss is recognized to the trust or the LLC on contribution of assets to the LLC. No gain or loss is recognized to the trusts on distribution of membership interests to the beneficiaries if the trusts do not elect to recognize gain or loss on the distributions under Section 643(e)(3)(B) of the Internal Revenue Code.

9602018   Conversion from General Partnership to LLC; Cash Method of Accounting

There is no tax to the general partnership, LLC or the members if a general partnership converts into an LLC. There is no termination of the general partnership.

An LLC organized for the practice of law may continue to use the cash method of accounting after conversion from a general partnership.

9602012   Classification of Delaware LLC

A Delaware LLC is classified as a partnership for federal tax purposes.

9552015   Classification of LLC

An LLC organized under the laws of State B is classified as a partnership for federal tax purposes.

9551032   Classification of Texas Limited Banking Association

A Texas Limited Banking Association is not a limited liability company, and is therefore classified as a corporation for federal tax purposes.

9547020   Classification of LLC

An LLC organized under the laws of State B is classified as a partnership for federal tax purposes.

Appendix C Summary of Private Letter Rulings

9543023 Merger of C Corporation into LLC

The merger of a C corporation into an LLC is treated as an asset transfer in exchange for LLC membership interests, followed by the liquidation of the corporation. No gain or loss is recognized in the merger.

9543017 Merger of S Corporation into LLC

The merger of an S corporation into an LLC is treated as an asset transfer in exchange for LLC membership interests, followed by the liquidation of the S corporation. No gain or loss is recognized in the merger.

9538036 Classification of LLC

An LLC organized for a medical practice is classified as a partnership for federal income tax purposes.

9538022 Conversion from General Partnership to LLC; ; Cash Method of Accounting; Basis of Assets and Membership Interests

There is no tax to the general partnership, LLC or the members if a general partnership converts into an LLC. There is no termination of the general partnership.

An LLC organized for the practice of law must continue to use the cash method of accounting after conversion from a general partnership.

The LLC will take a carryover basis in the assets, and the members will take a carryover basis in their membership interests.

9536008 S Corporations and Rental Income

An S corporation's share of rental income from an LLC is not passive income under Section 1362(d)(3)(D)(i) of the Internal Revenue Code, but is passive income under Section 469. The LLC rented property subject to franchise agreements. As a limited partner in the franchises, the LLC provided significant services and incurred substantial costs in the rental business.

9536007 S Corporations and Rental Income

An S corporation's share of rental income from an LLC is not passive income under Section 1362(d)(3)(D)(i) of the Internal Revenue Code, but is passive income under Section 469. The LLC rented property subject to franchise agreements. As a limited partner in the franchises, the LLC provided significant services and incurred substantial costs in the rental business.

9535036 Conversion of General Partnership Interests in Limited Partnership to LLC; Cash Method of Accounting; Classification of LLC

The general partners of a limited partnership may convert into an LLC without taxation.

A limited partnership may continue to use the cash method of accounting after the general partners of the limited partnership convert their general partnership interests to membership interests in an LLC.

An LLC organized under the laws of State N is classified as a partnership for federal income tax purposes.

9533011 Classification of LLC

An LLC organized under the laws of State X is classified as a partnership for federal income tax purposes.

9532008 LLC Owned by S Corporation

An S corporation may own an LLC during the period of time that the LLC is classified as a partnership for federal tax purposes.

9529015 Classification of LLC

An LLC organized under the laws of State B is classified as a partnership for federal income tax purposes.

9526029 Classification of Brazilian LLC

A Brazilian *limitada (Sociedade por Quotas de Responsabilidade Limitada)* is classified as a partnership for federal tax purposes.

9525065 Conversion from General Partnership to LLC; Cash Method of Accounting; Employer Identification Number

There is no tax to the general partnership, LLC or the members if a general partnership converts into an LLC. There is no termination of the general partnership. The LLC is treated as a continuation of the general partnership. There is no close of the partnership's taxable year.

An LLC organized for the practice of accounting may continue to use the cash method of accounting after conversion from a general partnership.

An LLC is not required to obtain a new employer identification number after the conversion from a general partnership.

9525058 Conversion from General Partnership to LLC; Cash Method of Accounting; Self-Employment Taxes

There is no tax to the general partnership, LLC or the members if a general partnership converts into an LLC. There is no termination of the general partnership.

Appendix C   Summary of Private Letter Rulings

An LLC organized for the practice of law may continue to use the cash method of accounting after conversion from a general partnership.

The members are subject to self-employment taxes after the conversion.

9524022   Classification of French SAS

A *Societe par actions simplifiee* (SAS) is classified as a partnership for federal tax purposes if the SNC does not possess more corporate characteristics than noncorporate characteristics.

9520046   Classification of Texas LLC

A Texas LLC is classified as a partnership for federal income tax purposes.

9520036   Classification of Texas LLC; LLC Owned by Two
Subsidiaries of Common Parent

A Texas LLC that is owned by two foreign subsidiaries of a foreign parent corporation is classified as a partnership for federal tax purposes.

9511033   Classification of LLC; Conversion from General
Partnership to LLC

An LLC organized under the laws of State S is classified as a partnership for federal tax purposes.

There is no tax to the general partnership, LLC or the members if a general partnership converts into an LLC, except as provided in Sections 731 and 752 of the Internal Revenue Code. There is no termination of the general partnership. The LLC is treated as a continuation of the general partnership.

9511023   Classification of Foreign LLC

A foreign LLC is classified as a partnership for federal income tax purposes.

9510037   Classification of Texas LLC

A Texas LLC is classified as a partnership for federal income tax purposes even though the LLC was owned by two wholly-owned subsidiaries of a common parent.

9507004   Classification of Delaware LLC

A Delaware LLC is classified as a partnership for federal income tax purposes even though the LLC was owned by a parent and a subsidiary.

9501033   Classification of Maryland LLC; Conversion from General Partnership to LLC; Cash Method of Accounting

A Maryland LLC is classified as a partnership for federal tax purposes.

There is no tax to the general partnership, LLC or the members if a general partnership converts into an LLC. There is no termination of the general partnership. The LLC is treated as a continuation of the general partnership. There is no close of the partnership's taxable year.

An LLC organized for the practice of law may continue to use the cash method of accounting after conversion from a general partnership.

9510037   Classification of Texas LLC

A Texas LLC is classified as a partnership for federal tax purposes.

9452024   Conversion from General Partnership to LLC; Cash Method of Accounting

There is no tax to the general partnership, LLC or the members if a general partnership converts into an LLC. There is no termination of the general partnership. The LLC is treated as a continuation of the general partnership.

An LLC organized for the practice of medicine may continue to use the cash method of accounting after conversion from a general partnership.

9443024   Classification of Utah LLC; Conversion of Limited Partnership to LLC

A Utah LLC is classified as a partnership for federal tax purposes.

There is no tax if a limited partnership converts to an LLC. There is no termination of the partnership. The LLC is treated as a continuation of the partnership.

9443018   Classification of Florida LLC

A Florida LLC is classified as a partnership for federal tax purposes.

9436019   Classification of LLC; Taxes on Foreign Members of LLC

An LLC organized under the laws of State B is classified as a partnership for federal tax purposes.

If an LLC is engaged in a U.S. trade or business, all foreign members of that LLC will be treated as engaged in a U.S. trade or business. If an LLC has a permanent establishment in the United States, each of the LLC's members will be treated as having a permanent establishment in the United States.

Appendix C   Summary of Private Letter Rulings

9434027   Classification of LLC; Conversion from General Partnership to LLC; Cash Method of Accounting

An LLC is classified as a partnership for federal tax purposes.

There is no tax to the general partnership, LLC or the members if a general partnership converts into an LLC. There is no termination of the general partnership. The LLC is treated as a continuation of the general partnership.

An LLC organized for the practice of management consulting may continue to use the cash method of accounting after conversion from a general partnership.

9433088   Classification of LLC; Related Members; Free Transferability of Interests; Continuity of Life

An LLC will have the corporate characteristics of free transferability, even if there are restrictions on transfer, if the LLC is owned by related members. In such cases, the restrictions on transfer are not meaningful.

An LLC will not have the corporate characteristic of continuity of life, even if all members are related, if the operating agreement provides for dissolution on the death, bankruptcy, dissolution or withdrawal of a member unless the remaining members agree to continue the LLC.

9433023   Classification of LLC

An LLC organized under the laws of State B is classified as a partnership for federal tax purposes.

9433008   Classification of LLC; LLC Owned by S Corporation

An LLC organized under the laws of State A is classified as a corporation for federal tax purposes.

If an LLC owned by an S corporation is reclassified by the IRS as a corporation, the S corporation's election as an S corporation will be terminated unless the S corporation obtains a ruling from the IRS that the termination was inadvertent.

9432018   Classification of LLC; Conversion from General Partnership to LLC; Cash Method of Accounting; Self-Employment Taxes

An LLC is classified as a partnership for federal tax purposes.

There is no tax to the general partnership, LLC or the members if a general partnership converts into an LLC. There is no termination of the general partnership. The LLC is treated as a continuation of the general partnership.

An LLC organized for the practice of law may continue to use the cash method of accounting after conversion from a general partnership.

The members of an LLC are liable for self-employment taxes on their distributive shares of LLC income attributable to a trade or business carried on by the LLC.

9426037 Conversion from General Partnership to LLC

There is no termination of the partnership if a New York general partnership reorganizes as a Delaware LLC.

9426030 Conversion from General Partnership; Cash Method of Accounting

An LLC organized for the practice of law must continue to use the cash method of accounting after conversion from a general partnership.

9425013 Classification of North Dakota LLC

A North Dakota LLC is classified as a partnership for federal tax purposes.

9423040 Conversion from General Partnership to LLC; Accounting Methods After Conversion

There is no termination of the partnership if a general partnership reorganizes as a Delaware LLC.

The LLC must continue to use the same method of accounting as the general partnership until it receives permission to change its accounting methods or until the IRS challenges the method on examination

9423037 Conversion from General Partnership to LLC

There is no termination of the partnership if a general partnership reorganizes as a Delaware LLC.

9422034 Classification of Indiana LLC; Conversion from General Partnership to LLC; Cash Method of Accounting; Tax Shelter Classification; Professional LLC

An LLC organized under the laws of Indiana is classified as a partnership for federal tax purposes.

There is no tax to the general partnership, LLC or the members if a general partnership converts into an LLC. There is no termination of the general partnership. The LLC is treated as a continuation of the general partnership. The LLC must continue to use the same taxable year as the LLP.

An LLC organized for the practice of accounting may continue to use the cash method of accounting after conversion from a general partnership.

Appendix C Summary of Private Letter Rulings

9421025 Classification of LLC; Conversion from General Partnership to LLC; Depreciation Recapture; Cash Method of Accounting

An LLC is classified as a partnership for federal tax purposes.

There is no tax to the general partnership, LLC or the members if a general partnership converts into an LLC. There is no depreciation recapture under Section 1245 of the Internal Revenue Code. There is no termination of the general partnership. The LLC is treated as a continuation of the general partnership.

An LLC organized for the practice of law may continue to use the cash method of accounting after conversion from a general partnership.

9420028 Conversion from General Partnership to LLC

There is no termination of the partnership if a general partnership reorganizes as a Delaware LLC.

9417009 Conversion from Limited Partnership to LLC

There is no tax if a limited partnership converts to an LLC. There is no termination of the partnership. The LLC is treated as a continuation of the partnership. There is a carryover of basis in the partnership interests and partnership assets. The holding period of the membership interests includes the holding period of the partnership interests. The LLC's basis in the assets is the same as the basis of those assets in the partnership immediately prior to the conversion.

9416029 Classification of LLC; Conversion from Limited Partnership to LLC

An LLC organized under the laws of State B is classified as a partnership for federal tax purposes.

There is no tax if a limited partnership converts to an LLC. There is no termination of the partnership. The LLC is treated as a continuation of the partnership.

There is a carryover of basis in the partnership interests and partnership assets. The holding period of the membership interests includes the holding period of the partnership interests. The LLC's basis in the assets is the same as the basis of those assets in the partnership immediately before the conversion.

9416028 Classification of LLC; Conversion from Limited Partnership to LLC

An LLC organized under the laws of State B is classified as a partnership for federal tax purposes.

There is no tax if a limited partnership converts to an LLC. There is no termination of the partnership. The LLC is treated as a continuation of the partnership.

There is a carryover of basis in the partnership interests and partnership assets. The holding period of the membership interests includes the holding period of the partnership interests. The LLC's basis in the assets is the same as the basis of those assets in the partnership immediately prior to the conversion.

9416026   Classification of Delaware LLC

A Delaware LLC is classified as a partnership for federal tax purposes.

9416025   Classification of Delaware LLC

A Delaware LLC is classified as a partnership for federal tax purposes.

9415005   Classification of LLC; Conversion from General Partnership to LLC; Cash Method of Accounting

A Delaware LLC is classified as a partnership for federal tax purposes.

An LLC organized for the practice of law may continue to use the cash method of accounting after conversion from a general partnership.

9412030   Classification of LLC; Conversion from LLP to LLC; Cash Method of Accounting; Tax Shelter Classification; Professional LLC

An LLC organized under the laws of State J is classified as a partnership for federal tax purposes.

There is no tax to the LLP, LLC or the members if an LLP merges into an LLC. There is no termination of the LLP. The LLC is treated as a continuation of the LLP. The LLC must continue to use the same taxable year as the LLP.

An LLC organized for the practice of accounting may continue to use the cash method of accounting after conversion from an LLP.

9409016   Classification of Louisiana LLC; Merger of Corporation into LLC

A Louisiana LLC is classified as a partnership for federal tax purposes.

The merger of a subsidiary corporation into a related LLC is non-taxable. It is treated as a transfer of corporate assets to the LLC and the liquidation of the subsidiary.

9409014   Classification of Louisiana LLC; Merger of Corporation into LLC

A Louisiana LLC is classified as a partnership for federal tax purposes.

The merger of a subsidiary corporation into a related LLC is non-taxable. It is treated as a transfer of corporate assets to the LLC and the liquidation of the subsidiary.

Appendix C   Summary of Private Letter Rulings

9407030   Classification of LLC; Conversion from General Partnership; Cash Method of Accounting; Tax Shelter Classification; Professional LLC

An LLC organized under the laws of State B is classified as a partnership for federal tax purposes.

There is no tax if a general partnership converts to an LLC. There is no termination of the partnership. The LLC is treated as a continuation of the partnership.

An LLC organized for the practice of law may continue to use the cash method of accounting after conversion from a general partnership.

9404021   Classification of Louisiana LLC; Merger of Corporation into LLC

A Louisiana LLC is classified as a partnership for federal tax purposes.

The merger of a subsidiary corporation into a related LLC is non-taxable. It is treated as a transfer of corporate assets to the LLC and the liquidation of the subsidiary.

9350003   Classification of LLC; Conversion from General Partnership; Cash Method of Accounting; Tax Shelter Classification; Professional LLC

An LLC organized under the laws of State Z is classified as a partnership for federal tax purposes.

There is no tax if a general partnership converts to an LLC. There is no termination of the partnership. The LLC is treated as a continuation of the partnership.

An LLC organized for the practice of law may continue to use the cash method of accounting after conversion from a general partnership.

9343036   Stock Bonus Plan Established by LLC

An LLC may establish a qualified stock bonus plan for distribution of stock of a corporate partner and its parent corporation. A corporate employer may transfer plan assets consisting of employer securities to a plan maintained by an LLC. The stock of the corporate employer will continue to constitute "employer securities" until distributed by the LLC's plan to the plan participants.

9341018   Classification of German GmbH; Free Transferability of Interests

A German GmbH is classified as a partnership for federal tax purposes.

The GmbH lacked the corporate characteristic of free transferability of interests and modified free transferability where the governing documents provided that the owner must first offer the shares to the company and then to the existing shareholders and no transfers could be made to third parties without the consent of the other members.

**9335063 FICA Taxes on Work Outside the United States;
Classification of Foreign LLC**

An "American employer" is required to withhold FICA taxes on wages paid to citizens or residents of the United States who perform services as an employee outside of the United States. A U.S. or foreign LLC that is classified as a partnership is an "American employer" for withholding purposes if two-thirds or more of the partners are residents of the United States.

An LLC organized under the laws of Country Y is classified as a partnership for U.S. tax purposes.

**9335062 FICA Taxes on Work Outside the United States;
Classification of Foreign LLC**

An "American employer" is required to withhold FICA taxes on wages paid to citizens or residents of the United States who perform services as an employee outside of the United States. A U.S. or foreign LLC that is classified as a partnership is an "American employer" for withholding purposes if two-thirds or more of the partners are residents of the United States.

An LLC organized under the laws of Country Y is classified as a partnership for U.S. tax purposes.

9335032 Classification of Delaware LLC

A Delaware LLC is classified as a partnership for federal tax purposes.

9333032 Classification of Illinois LLC

An Illinois LLC is classified as a partnership for federal tax purposes.

9331049 S Corporations; China LLC

An S corporation election will be terminated if it organizes a limited liability company in China. The China LLC was apparently classified as corporation for U.S. tax purposes. The Service granted relief from termination under Section 1362(f) of the Internal Revenue Code.

9330009 S Corporations; Investment LLCs

An S corporation may organize an LLC without creating a second class of stock that would disqualify S corporation election.

An LLC may be used as an investment vehicle. There is no personal holding company tax even if all of the passive income is retained in the LLC.

9331010 Classification of LLC; Formation of LLC

An LLC formed under the laws of State Z is classified as a partnership for federal tax purposes.

Appendix C   Summary of Private Letter Rulings

No gain or loss is recognized on contribution of property to an LLC assuming the LLC is not an investment company. There is a carryover basis in the assets. The LLC members have a basis in their membership interests equal to the amount of money and adjusted basis of assets contributed to the LLC.

9328005   Cash Method of Accounting

A Utah LLC, previously classified as a partnership, may use the cash method of accounting.

9326035   Classification of LLC; Majority Consent for Continuation of LLC

An LLC will lack the corporate characteristic of continuity of life if it may by continued on loss of a member by the unanimous consent of all managers and the majority consent of members.

9325048   Classification of LLC

An LLC owning working interests in oil and gas wells is classified as a partnership for federal tax purposes.

9325039   Classification of Illinois LLC; Majority Consent for Continuation of LLC

An Illinois LLC is classified as a partnership for federal tax purposes. The ruling was withdrawn for reconsideration because a majority in number rather than a majority in interest was required to vote for continuing the LLC after withdrawal of a member.

9321070   Conversion from General Partnership; Classification of Utah LLC; Centralized Management

If a general partnership transfers selected assets directly to an LLC owned by the partners, the assets will be treated as distributed to the partners and then contributed to the LLC.

An LLC formed under the laws of Utah (referred to as State C) is classified as a partnership for federal tax purposes.

An LLC formed by an individual and a corporation of which she was the sole director lacked centralized management.

9321047   Classification of Arizona LLC; Conversion from General Partnership; Cash Method of Accounting; Tax Shelter Classification; Professional LLC

An LLC formed under the laws of Arizona (referred to as State O) is classified as a partnership for federal tax purposes. An Arizona LLC lacks the corporate characteristic of continuity of life even if only a majority of the remaining members must agree to continue the business after withdrawal of a member.

There is no tax if a general partnership converts to an LLC. There is no termination of the partnership. The LLC is treated as a continuation of the partnership.

An LLC organized for the practice of law may use the cash method of accounting.

9320045   Classification of Utah LLC; Centralization of Management

An LLC formed under the laws of Utah (referred to as State B) and that owned working interests in oil and gas wells is classified as a partnership for federal tax purposes.

There is no centralization of management if the LLC reserves management to members.

9320019   Classification of Utah LLC

An LLC formed under the laws of Utah (referred to as State B) and that owned working interests in oil and gas wells is classified as a partnership for federal tax purposes.

9318011   Classification of LLC

An LLC formed under the LLC laws of an unspecified state is classified as a partnership for federal tax purposes.

9313009   Classification of Utah LLC; Formation of LLC

An LLC formed under laws of Utah (unspecified state in the ruling) is classified as a partnership for federal tax purposes.

There is no tax on the contribution of oil and gas working interest to the LLC in exchange for membership interest.

9308039   Classification of West Virginia LLC

A West Virginia LLC is classified as a partnership for federal tax purposes.

9308027   Classification of Delaware LLC

An LLC formed under the laws of Delaware (referred to as State A) is classified as a partnership for federal tax purposes.

9306008   Classification of United Kingdom LLC

A United Kingdom LLC is classified as a partnership for federal tax purposes. It lacks free transferability of interests if there are restrictions on at least 20 percent of all LLC interests.

Appendix C Summary of Private Letter Rulings

9242025 Classification of Texas LLC

A Texas LLC is classified as a partnership for federal tax purposes if it lacks at least two corporate characteristics.

9227033 Classification of Nevada LLC

A Nevada LLC is classified as a partnership for federal tax purposes.

9226035 Conversion from General Partnership to LLC

There is no tax if a general partnership converts to an LLC. There is no termination of the partnership. The LLC is treated as a continuation of the partnership.

9219022 Classification of Utah LLC

An LLC formed under the laws of Utah (referred to as State Z) is classified as a partnership for federal tax purposes.

9218078 Classification of Texas LLC

A Texas LLC is classified as a partnership for federal tax purposes if it lacks at least two corporate characteristics.

9216004 Classification of Foreign LLC

A foreign LLC organized under the laws of Country A is classified as a partnership for federal tax purposes.

9210039 Classification of Foreign LLC

A foreign LLC organized under the laws of Country A is classified as a partnership for federal tax purposes.

9210019 Classification of Texas LLC; Merger of Limited Partnership into LLC

A Texas LLC is classified as a partnership for federal tax purposes if it lacks at least two corporate characteristics. The LLC lacked the corporate characteristic of free transferability where only the consent of the manager was required for transfers of interests.

There is no tax if a limited partnership merges into an LLC. There is no termination of the partnership. The LLC is treated as a continuation of the partnership.

9215009 Classification of Foreign LLC

A foreign LLC organized under the laws of City X in Country Y is classified as a corporation.

9152009   Classification of United Kingdom LLC; Continuity of Life

A United Kingdom LLC is classified as a partnership for federal tax purposes.

A United Kingdom LLC lacks the corporate characteristic of continuity of life even though dissolution is not automatic and requires further shareholder action. This ruling was distinguished from Letter Ruling 9002056 because the organizational documents for the LLC in this ruling required the shareholders to meet and to vote for dissolution on bankruptcy of the LLC.

9147017   Classification of LLC

An LLC formed under the laws of State Y is classified as a partnership for federal tax purposes.

9119029   Classification of Florida LLC; Conversion from Limited Partnership to LLC

A Florida LLC is classified as a partnership for federal tax purposes.

There is no tax if a limited partnership converts to an LLC. There is no termination of the partnership. The LLC is treated as a continuation of the partnership.

9052039   Classification of LLC

An LLC formed under the laws of State Z is classified as a partnership for federal tax purposes.

9030013   Classification of Florida LLC

A Florida LLC is classified as a partnership for federal tax purposes.

9029019   Classification of Florida LLC; Conversion from General Partnership to LLC

An LLC formed under the laws of Florida (referred to as State Z) is classified as a partnership for federal tax purposes.

There is no tax if a general partnership converts to an LLC. There is no termination of the partnership. The LLC is treated as a continuation of the partnership.

9010028   Classification of German GmbH

A German GmbH lacked the corporate characteristic of free transferability of interests where the articles prohibited transfers without the consent of the other partners, which consent could not be unreasonably withheld. In addition, the owner was required to first offer the shares to the other owners before selling to a third party. The IRS later withdrew Letter Ruling 9035041.

Appendix C   Summary of Private Letter Rulings

9010027   Conversion from General Partnership to LLC; Centralization of Management

There is no tax if a general partnership converts to an LLC. There is no termination of the partnership. The LLC is treated as a continuation of the partnership.

There is no centralized management if a Florida LLC reserves management to members in proportion to membership interests.

9002056   Classification of United Kingdom LLC; Continuity of Life

A United Kingdom LLC is classified as a partnership for federal tax purposes.

A United Kingdom LLC lacks the corporate characteristic of continuity of life if the memorandum and articles of association require the shareholders to meet and vote in favor of dissolution after a dissolution event.

8937010   Classification of Florida LLC

A Florida LLC is classified as a partnership for federal tax purposes.

8908035   Conversion from LLC to Unlimited Liability Company

There is no tax on the conversion from an LLC organized under the laws of a foreign country into an unlimited liability company.

8828022   Classification of Foreign LLC

An LLC organized under the laws of a foreign country is classified as a corporation.

8809073   Conversion from LLC to Unlimited Liability Company

There is no tax on the conversion from an LLC organized under the laws of a foreign country into an unlimited liability company.

8436030   Classification of German GmbH

The IRS declined to rule on the classification of a German GmbH.

8401001   Classification of Brazilian LLC

A Brazilian *limitada* is classified as a corporation for federal tax purposes.

8309062   Classification of German GmbH

A German GmbH is classified as a partnership for federal tax purposes.

8304138   Classification of Foreign LLC

A foreign LLC organized under the laws of Country Z is classified as a corporation.

8304138   Classification of Foreign LLC

A foreign LLC organized under the laws of Country X is classified as a partnership for federal tax purposes.

8221136   Classification of German GmbH

A German GmbH is classified as a partnership for federal tax purposes.

8114095   Classification of German GmbH

A German GmbH is classified as a corporation for federal tax purposes.

8106082   Classification of Spanish Limitada; Liquidating
Distributions; Formation of LLC

A Spanish *limitada* is classified as a partnership for federal tax purposes.
No gain is recognized on a liquidating distribution except to the extent that the money received exceeds a member's basis in his LLC interest.

8104129   Classification of Foreign LLC

A foreign LLC organized under the laws of Country X is classified as a partnership for federal tax purposes.

8029031   Contribution of Property to Foreign LLC

LLC shareholders do not recognize gain or loss on the contribution of property to a foreign LLC under Section 351 of the Internal Revenue Code, whether or not additional shares are issued. There is a carryover basis in assets.

8023109   Merger of LLCs

The merger of a subsidiary LLC into a parent LLC is treated as a Section 332 liquidation if the LLCs are classified as corporations for federal tax purposes.

8019112   Classification of Brazilian LLC

One Brazilian *limitada* was classified as a partnership for federal tax purposes and the other *limitada* was classified as a corporation.

Appendix C   Summary of Private Letter Rulings

8012080   Classification of Foreign LLC

A foreign LLC organized under the laws of Country X is classified as a partnership for federal tax purposes.

8007029   Classification of Saudi Arabian LLC

A Saudi Arabian LLC is classified as a partnership for federal tax purposes.

8006068   Classification of Saudi Arabian LLC

A Saudi Arabian LLC is classified as a corporation for federal tax purposes.

8004010   Classification of LLC

An LLC organized under the laws of State X is classified as a partnership for federal tax purposes. There is no centralization of management if all of the major management and policy decisions of the LLC are made by its partners.

8003072   Classification of Brazilian LLC

A Brazilian *limitada* is classified as a partnership for federal tax purposes.

8002076   Reincorporation of LLC

The reincorporation of an LLC is a nontaxable F reorganization.

7952027   Classification of German GmbH

A German GmbH is classified as a corporation for federal tax purposes.

7950044   Non-divisive D Reorganization

The transfer of assets, liabilities and stock between related German LLCs is a non-divisive D reorganization.

7948066   Non-divisive D Reorganization

There was a non-divisive D reorganization where a corporation merged into an LLC. The LLC did not issue shares in the merger since LLCs did not issue stock under applicable laws. The corporation and the LLC were owned equally by two unrelated corporations (or their affiliates).

7947048   Non-divisive D Reorganization

There was a non-divisive D reorganization where an LLC merged into a corporation. The LLC and the corporation were both owned by the same corporation.

7941054 Classification of Brazilian LLC

A Brazilian *limitada* is classified as a corporation for federal tax purposes.

7937054 Classification of German GmbH; ; Formation of LLC

A German GmbH is classified as a corporation for federal tax purposes.
No gain or loss is recognized on the contribution of assets and liabilities to an LLC on formation of the LLC.

7936050 Classification of Chilean Limitada

A Chilean *limitada* is classified as a corporation for federal tax purposes if it possesses more corporate characteristics than noncorporate characteristics.

7935046 Classification of Hong Kong LLC; Formation of LLC

No opinion was expressed on whether a Hong Kong LLC is classified as a corporation for federal tax purposes.
No gain or loss is recognized on the contribution of assets and liabilities to an LLC on formation of the LLC except to the extent of boot received.

7928063 Classification of Brazilian LLC

A Brazilian *limitada* is classified as a corporation for federal tax purposes.

7926034 Classification of Saudi Arabian LLC

A Saudi Arabian LLC is classified as a corporation for federal tax purposes.

7921079 Classification of Saudi Arabian LLC

A Saudi Arabian LLC is classified as a partnership for federal tax purposes.

7911065 Conversion of Corporation into LLC

The conversion of a corporation into an LLC is a nontaxable exchange under Section 1036 of the Internal Revenue Code.

7908027 Drop-Down of Assets from Parent to Subsidiary LLC

The drop-down of assets and liabilities by a parent LLC into a newly formed subsidiary LLC followed by the transfer of stock in the subsidiary LLC from the parent LLC to its parent corporation is a non-divisive D reorganization.

Appendix C   Summary of Private Letter Rulings

7908004   Classification of German GmbH

A German GmbH is classified as a corporation for federal tax purposes.

7907066   Conversion of LLC to Corporation

The conversion of an LLC to a corporation by charter amendment is a nontaxable exchange under Section 351 of the Internal Revenue Code.

7852111   Non-divisive D Reorganization

There was a non-divisive D reorganization where a corporation merged into an LLC. The LLC and the corporation apparently had common shareholders.

7843099   Transfer of Property to LLC

The transfer of property to an LLC that is classified as a corporation is a nontaxable transaction under Section 351 of the Internal Revenue Code.

7843006   Classification of Greek LLC

A Greek LLC is classified as a corporation for federal tax purposes if it has more corporate characteristics than noncorporate characteristics.

7841008   Classification of Italian SRL

A *societa a responsabilit limitata* (SRL) is classified as a corporation for federal tax purposes if it possesses more corporate characteristics than noncorporate characteristics.

7836019   Conversion of Corporation into LLC

The conversion of a corporation into an LLC is a nontaxable exchange under Section 1036 of the Internal Revenue Code.

7833112   Formation of LLC

No gain or loss is recognized on the contribution of assets and liabilities to a foreign LLC on formation of the LLC except for gain on the transfer of inventory.

7831021   Classification of Brazilian LLC; Conversion from Corporation to LLC

A Brazilian *limitada* is classified as a corporation for federal tax purposes.
The conversion of a Brazilian corporation to an LLC is a nontaxable exchange under Section 1036 of the Internal Revenue Code.

7826023   Classification of Portuguese LLC

A Portuguese LLC is classified as a corporation for federal tax purposes.

7821084   Transfer of LLC Interest to Subsidiary LLC

The transfer by a parent company of LLC shares from one subsidiary LLC to another subsidiary LLC (where both LLCs are classified as corporations) is a nontaxable exchange under Section 351 of the Internal Revenue Code.

7817129   Classification of Brazilian LLC

A Brazilian *limitada* is classified as a partnership for federal tax purposes.

7814012   Classification of Brazilian LLC

A Brazilian *limitada* is classified as a corporation for federal tax purposes.

7810072   Conversion from Corporation to LLC

The conversion of a corporation to an LLC is a nontaxable F reorganization.

7747089   Classification of One-Person GmbH

A one-person GmbH is classified as a sole-proprietorship for federal tax purposes.

7741040   Conversion from LLC to Corporation

There is no tax on the conversion from an LLC organized under the laws of Greece into a corporation.

7729058   Conversion from Corporation to LLC

The conversion of a corporation to an LLC is a nontaxable F reorganization.

7716015   Change in LLC Ownership to Related Subsidiary

A parent corporation's transfer of LLC stock to a subsidiary is a nontaxable contribution under Section 351 of the Internal Revenue Code.

7203140670A   Drop-Down of Assets into Subsidiary LLC

The drop-down of assets and liabilities into a subsidiary LLC is a nontaxable exchange under Section 351 of the Internal Revenue Code.

Appendix C   Summary of Private Letter Rulings

7111100730A   Conversion from Corporation to LLC

The conversion of a corporation to an LLC is a nontaxable F reorganization.

7108110470A   Classification of Mexican Limitada

A Mexican *sociedade de responsabilidad limitada* is classified as a partnership for federal tax purposes if it does not possess more corporate characteristics than noncorporate characteristics. The IRS determined that the *limitada* lacked the corporate characteristics of free transferability and continuity of life, and was thus classified as a partnership for federal tax purposes.

6707214880A   Classification of Foreign LLC

An LLC formed under the laws of a foreign country is classified as a partnership for federal tax purposes.

PART 2.   GENERAL COUNSEL MEMORANDUM

39798   Classification of LLC

The lack of personal liability of members of an LLC will not preclude the IRS from classifying an LLC as a partnership.

35294   Classification of Columbian SRL

A Columbian *Sociedad de Responsabilidad Limitada* (SRL) is classified as a corporation for federal tax purposes if it possesses more corporate characteristics than noncorporate characteristics. The SRL was treated as a separate jurisdictional entity taxed as a corporation.

TABLE OF INTERNAL REVENUE CODE SECTIONS

References are to sections.

Table of Internal Revenue Code Sections

Table of Internal Revenue Code Sections

TABLE OF TREASURY REGULATIONS

References are to sections.

Table of Treasury Regulations

TABLE OF INTERNAL REVENUE SERVICE RELEASES

References are to sections.

9834040	11.01[B]	200109032	5.04[H]
9840054	2.03[B]	200109033	5.04[H]
9841030	11.01[B]	200110016	5.04[H]
9845008	5.04[H]	200111053	14.06[A][3]
9845010	17.03[A][1]	200111530	5.02[B]
9849008	5.04[I]	200112004	5.04[H]
9851054	2.03[B]	200112021	5.02[E][1]
9853045	4.06, 5.01[D]	200114017	5.04[H]
9859009	5.04[H]	200115023	5.04[H]
199901051	5.04[H]	200115024	5.04[H]
199904008	4.03[B]	200116051	5.02[E][1], 14.06[A][3]
199904018	5.04[H]	200118023	15.06[A][3]
199904020-022	5.04[H]	200118054	2.03[B]
199908057	5.04[H]	200119014	21.04[A], 21.09
199909045	6.03, 8.03[B][1], 15.06[B]	200119016	5.01, 5.01[D], 11.20[B]
199909056	2.03[B]	200122035	5.04[H], 6.01[A][1],
199911033	5.01, 5.02[D], 15.06[A][2],		8.03[B][1], 11.08[C]
	15.06 [A][2]	200124022	2.03[B], 2.03[B][5]
199913035	2.03[B]	200124029	2.03[B][5]
199913051	2.03[B]	200124030	8.03[B][1], 7.06[A]
199914006	5.01, 5.02[D], 6.05[A]	200125013	2.03[C], 6.01[A][1], 6.01[A][4]
199915010	6.05[A][3]	200125037	11.22
199915040	6.01[A][1]	200129018	11.22
199916010	11.01[A][1]	200129019	21.06
199917049-051	20.02[B]	200129024	5.02[E][1], 11.09[B],
199917049	20.02[B], 20.02[C]		11.15[D][1], 11.20[C]
199920023	5.04[H]	200129029	11.09[B], 11.15[D][1]
199922053	16.03[B], 16.03[D]	200131016	5.04[H]
199930013	5.02[E][2], 16.03[B]	200132014	5.02[E][1]
199935065	11.10, 15.06[A][4], 15.06[B]	200133018	5.04[H]
199936011	6.05[A]	200133038	5.04[H]
199938005	21.03[B][9]	200134025	2.03[B][4], 2.03[C][4],
199938016	17.08[C]		5.02[E][1]
199947034	11.07[B][2], 21.08	200135015	6.03[A][10]
199952068	5.04[H]	200137011	11.09[D], 11.15[D][1]
199952071	2.03[B]	200137038	7.03[E]
200001016	5.04[H]	200139002	11.06[A][1], 11.06[A][4],
200002025	20.02[C]		11.06[A][5], 11.06[B]
200004022	21.04[A], 21.09	200139009	11.20[C]
200005016	3.05[K], 11.21	200139016	5.04[H]
200008015	4.03	200143012	4.02
200009025	7.03[F]	200147018-020	5.04[H]
200022016	11.01[B]	200150027	2.03[B][4]
200024024	5.04[H]	200151039	5.01, 5.04[H]
200044040	2.03[B]	200151046	2.03[B][2]
200045015	5.04[H]	200201024	5.01
200045022	5.04[H]	200202003-020	5.04[H]
200045024	5.04[H]	200202052	5.04[H]
200046013	5.02[E][1], 14.06[B]	200202077	2.03[C][4]
200046031	5.04[H]	200204004	5.01, 11.20[B]
200052005	5.04[H]	200204005	10.03[C], 10.08[C], 11.06[C],
200102024	4.01[A]		12.02[B]
200102037	5.02[C], 5.02[E][1]	200205005	5.04[H]
200102038	5.02[E][1], 11.20[A]	200207019	5.04[H], 18.03[B]
200107018	4.03[A]	200209009	5.04[H]
200109011	11.07[B]	200209040	5.04[H]

Table of Internal Revenue Service Releases

85-32	6.06[B]	89-37	6.01[A][1]
87-9	20.02[C]	93-4	14.06[B]
88-76	1.01	97-18	18.02
90-16	7.03[I]	99-6	16.03[B]
90-17	11.15[B][1], 11.15[B][2],	1999-1 C.B. 321	11.18[D], 20.02[D]
	11.19[A][2][a], 11.19[A][2][b]	99-6, 1999-3 I.R.B. 1	5.04[G]
91-26	14.06[A][1]	2001-5	12.03, 12.03[B], 17.04[C]
91-31	7.03[I]	2001-34	17.03[A][4]
91-32	19.07	2001-34, §5.02	17.03[A][2]
92-69	14.06[A][4]	2001-34, §5.02(1)(b)	17.03[A][3]
92-97	7.03[I], 8.03[B][1]	2001-35, §2.01(3)(b)	17.03[A][5]
93-12	21.01, 21.03[A], 21.03[C][a],	2001-35, §2.07	17.03[A][4]
	21.04[A]	2001-35, §4.01(1)	17.03[A][5]
93-38	5.10	2002-41	18.08[B][1], 18.08[B][2]
93-53		2002-28	14.06[B]
94-4	7.03[I], 8.03[B][1]		
95-37	11.01[B], 11.02, 17.03[B]		
95-41	9.03[C]	**Technical Advice Memoranda**	
95-55	11.01[B], 17.03[B]		
98-15	2.03[B]		
98-37	5.10	9436005	21.03[C][a], 21.03[D]
99-5	11.17[A], 11.17[B], 11.18[A]	9449001	21.03[C][a]
99-6	11.18[A], 11.18[B]	9719006	21.03[B][2][a], 21.03[B][2][b]
99-43	7.03[I]	9723009	1.03[B][2][a], 21.03[B][2][b]
2001-61	11.18[C], 11.18[D], 20.02[D]	9725002	21.03[B][2][a], 21.03[B][2][b]
2002-49	11.18	9730004	21.03[B][2][a], 21.03[B][2][b]
		9735003	21.03[B][2][a], 21.03[B][2][b]
		9736004	21.03[B][2][a], 21.03[B][2][b],
GENERAL COUNSEL MEMORANDA			21.03[B][3][a], 21.03[B][3][b],
			03[B][3][c], 21.03[B][4]
34,001	14.03[D]	9739002	7.03[I]
		9842003	21.03[B][2][a], 21.03[B][2][b]
IRS ANNOUNCEMENTS		199944003	21.02[A]
Ann. 99-102	2.03[B][4]	**Field Service Advice**	
		199936011	6.05[A][2]
IRS NEW RELEASES		19995014	21.03[B][5]
		200025018	13.03[B]
IR-82-145	1.01, 5.10	200049003	21.03[B][2][a], 21.03[B][2][b],
			21.03[B][3][a], 21.03[B][3][b]
			21.03[B][4]
IRS NOTICES		200132009	12.03[A], 17.05
		200139009	12.03[B]
88-75	5.05	200242004	13.06

TABLE OF CASES

INDEX

Index

Index

Index

Index

Index

Index

Index

Recapture
contribution of property to LLC, 6.01[A][6], [7]
depreciation recapture, 6.01[A][6], 10.03[C]
general business credit recapture, 6.01[A][7]
investment tax credit recapture, 6.01[A][7]
Recognition of gain
contribution to LLC, 6.01[A][1]
transfers to foreign LLC, 18.02[A]
Recomputed basis
depreciation recapture, 10.03[D],10.03[E][2]
distributed property, 10.03[D], 10.03[E][1]
gain on Section 1245 property distributed by LLC, 10.03[D]
general rules, 10.03[D],10.03[E][2]
types of tax-free reorganizations, 11.23[B]
Recourse debt
allocation to members, 9.03[B]
definition, 9.03[B]
zero asset value test, 9.03[B]
Refinancing proceeds
disguised sales rules, 6.05[A][6]
distributions of, 3.03[F]
Regulations
definition, 1.02
Reimbursements to members
disguised sales rules, 6.05[A]
Reincorporation
general, 11.12
basis of assets, 11.12
fiscal year, 11.12
gain or loss recognition, 11.12
holding period, 11.12
Related LLCs
transfers of LLC interests between, 11.11, 14.03[C][1]
Related parties
depreciable property sales between related parties, 14.03[C][3]
loss disallowance on transactions between, 14.03[C][1], 21.05
sale of property at a gain, 14.03[C][1]
sale of property at a loss, 14.03[C][1]
transactions between related LLCs, 14.03[C][1]
Religious organizations
wage withholding for nonmembers, 16.01
Remedial allocation method
contributed property, 8.03[D]

depreciation, 8.03[D]
Rental income
see also *Leases* above
passive income, 4.01, 13.04[A], 14.03[B]
payments to members, 14.03[B]
received by or from disregarded entity, 5.02[E][1]
received from LLC by S corporation, 4.01
Reorganizations
A reorganization, 11.23[B]
B reorganization, 11.23[B]
C reorganization, 11.23[B]
conversion from partnership classification to disregarded entity, 11.18
conversion from single-member LLC to partnership, 11.17
division of LLC, 11.15
forward triangular merger, 11.23[B]
general, 11.01-11.16
D reorganization, 11.19[A]
F reorganizations, 11.06[B], 11.07[B][2]
merger of corporation into LLC, 11.23[B]
mergers between LLCs, 11.19
merger of C corporation into LLC, 11.20
parent-subsidiary mergers, 11.09, 12.02[B]
reincorporations, 11.12
reverse triangular merger, 11.23[B]
Reporting requirements
annual reports, 22.02[A], 22.02[B]
extension request, 22.01[C]
federal forms, 22.01
foreign LLCs, 18.02[B], 18.06, 22.01[E]
magnetic media filings, 22.01[F]
partnership return, 22.01[A]
Schedule K-1, 22.01[B]
Section 754 election, 15.08[F]
state returns, 22.01
state tax returns, 22.02[A]
transfers to foreign LLC, 18.02[B]
transfer of membership interest, 15.07[F]
Restoration of capital account deficit
capital adjustment provision, 8.02[D][1]
qualified income offset, 8.02[D][2]
reasonably expected future distributions, 8.02[D][1]
restrictions on allocations, 8.02[D][1]
safe-harbor regulations, 8.02[D]
time for making, 8.02[D]
Restrictions on transfer
general, 3.05[B]
Retiring members
accounts receivable, 10.08[E][1]
capital account distribution, 10.08[E][2]

Index

Index

Index